ActionScript
The Definitive Guide

ActionScript
The Definitive Guide

Colin Moock

O'REILLY®

Beijing · Cambridge · Farnham · Köln · Paris · Sebastopol · Taipei · Tokyo

ActionScript: The Definitive Guide
by Colin Moock

Copyright © 2001 O'Reilly & Associates, Inc. All rights reserved.
Printed in the United States of America.

Published by O'Reilly & Associates, Inc., 101 Morris Street, Sebastopol, CA 95472.

Editor: Bruce Epstein

Production Editor: Darren Kelly

Cover Designer: Ellie Volckhausen

Printing History:

    May 2001:   First Edition.

ISBN: 1-56592-852-0

[7/01]

[M]

Table of Contents

Foreword

When I arrived at Macromedia in the summer of 1998 to join the Flash team, a small and dynamic group had already produced an amazing product. Flash 3 had near-universal acceptance as the standard for vector animation on the Web. Its devoted, energetic user base of talented artists produced stunning visual content that appeared on more sites every day.

ActionScript's beginnings can be traced to a bullet point titled "Enhanced Interactivity" on a Flash 4 feature planning list. Flash 3 offered a basic suite of actions to control Flash's movie clips and buttons and provide interactivity. However, I recall being impressed by a tic-tac-toe game, which, although a straightforward task in most programming languages, was difficult and time-consuming to implement using Flash 3 actions.

That was before ActionScript came into being. Today, one doesn't blink when encountering dynamic web sites created solely in Flash 4. And now, sites are appearing that exploit the even more sophisticated ActionScript capabilities of Flash 5.

A key goal of ActionScript was approachability; it was vital that ActionScript be easy to use for non-programmers. Rather than present a blank script-editing window, we created a visual, easily understandable interface in Flash 4 for adding interactivity to Flash movies. The simplicity of Flash 4 ActionScript made it easy to learn and kept the Flash Player small, a vital consideration.

The Flash Player is crafted to download quickly even over low-bandwidth connections. The Flash team repeats the mantra, "How much code will this add to the Player?" before adding any feature to it. ActionScript was no exception to this rule. The goal with ActionScript, as with every new Player feature, is maximum bang (feature richness) for minimum bucks (Player size increase).

We knew that users would put ActionScript to unforeseen uses, but all the same, it was a joyous shock to see what users were able to achieve with it. Within a month of the release of Flash 4, amazing sites employing ActionScript were appearing on the Web—e-commerce sites, chat rooms, message boards, arcade games, board games, and even Flash sites to create Flash sites. The floodgates had been opened, bringing forth a new breed of animated, interactive, highly graphical web content.

When the time came to design Flash 5, above all else I wanted ActionScript to evolve into a full-blown scripting language with features programmers are accustomed to in languages such as JavaScript—functions, objects, sophisticated control flow statements, and multiple datatypes. These are "power tools" that have helped programmers be more productive in other languages, and I wanted ActionScript to support them as well. Rather than design the language from scratch, I chose to model ActionScript closely after JavaScript, the de facto standard for client-side scripting on the Internet. More specifically, ActionScript was modeled after the ECMAScript standard (ECMA-262). As a result, JavaScript programmers transitioning to Flash will find ActionScript immediately familiar. In addition, ActionScript programmers can leverage their knowledge of ActionScript into JavaScript programming and share existing code easily between the two languages.

The requirements of approachability and minimizing Player size remained tantamount. JavaScript is a subtle and complex language, and we sought to expose its full power to advanced users while retaining the ease of use of Flash 4 ActionScript. To this end, the new Flash 5 Actions panel has two modes: Normal Mode, a streamlined version of the Flash 4 ActionScript editor, and Expert Mode, a straight-ahead text editor for power users. To minimize Player size, sacrifices had to be made in the ECMAScript-compatibility of ActionScript. For example, ActionScript does not support compiling code at runtime using *eval()*; this feature would have required the incorporation of the entire ActionScript compiler into the Player, resulting in an unacceptable size increase. For the same reason, regular expression matching is not supported. Both of these features are very useful and demonstrate the difficult decisions the Flash team was forced to make to balance the competing needs of Player size and features.

To these two requirements, we added a third: compatibility. We designed Flash 5 ActionScript to smoothly upgrade Flash 4 scripts to Flash 5 syntax. In addition, Flash 5 supports Flash 4 ActionScript as a subset, so Flash 5 is actually an excellent way to author Flash 4 movies. Colin has outlined backward-compatibility issues as well as the major differences between ActionScript and JavaScript (often due to compatibility reasons) in Appendix C, *Backward Compatibility*, and Appendix D, *Differences from ECMA-262 and JavaScript.*

Throughout the development process, the Flash team received invaluable input from the Flash user community, a vocal and tightly knit group with formidable talents and passions. The Flash community's guidance has played a large role in shaping the features that go into the product. Macromedia's goal is to produce software that fulfills the needs of its customers; it does this by listening to customers and learning from the way they work.

Finally, Flash is an ongoing story, a living work that we will constantly endeavor to improve to meet your needs. Flash developers are artists of the Information Age, and the Flash team's job is to produce the best paintbrushes and chisels possible. This book is the first comprehensive tutorial and reference devoted entirely to the ActionScript language. As such, it marks a key point in ActionScript's evolution: ActionScript is now a subject sophisticated enough to merit this excellent book, packed with up-to-date material and leaving no feature unexplored.

Enjoy the book and enjoy Flash 5 ActionScript. We all look forward to seeing what you come up with!

—Gary Grossman
Principal Engineer, Macromedia Flash Team
March 2001

Preface

This book teaches both ActionScript's fundamentals and its advanced usage. Over the next 675 meaty pages, we'll be exploring every detail of the ActionScript language—from the basics of variables and movie clip control to advanced topics such as objects and classes, server communication, and XML. By the end, we'll have covered everything there is to know about Flash programming.

This book is not just for programmers. The text moves pretty quickly, but a prior knowledge of programming is not required to read it. All you need is experience with the non-ActionScript aspects of Flash and an eagerness to learn. Of course, if you are already a programmer, so much the better; you'll be applying your code-junkie skills to ActionScript in no time.

This book fully documents the material that may be undocumented or underdocumented by Macromedia or by other third-party books. Flash is notorious for word-of-mouth techniques and esoteric features. How are layers, movie clips, and loaded movies stacked in the Player? (See Chapter 13, *Movie Clips.*) What governs the execution order of code on any given frame? (See Chapter 13.) Do event handlers have a local scope? (See Chapter 10, *Events and Event Handlers.*) Why does the number 90 sometimes show up as 89.9999999997? (See Chapter 4, *Primitive Datatypes.*) It has been my particular goal to chart these unknown waters. Of course, I also cover the basic programming techniques required in any language, such as how to make a segment of code execute repeatedly. (See Chapter 8, *Loop Statements.*)

This book is designed to be kept on your desk, not to wallow away its life on your shelf. Part III, *Language Reference*, exhaustively covers every object, class, property, method, and event handler in ActionScript. You'll use it regularly to learn new things and remind yourself of the things you always forget.

Above all, this book is a Definitive Guide. It's the product of years of research, thousands of emails to Macromedia employees, and feedback from users of all levels. I hope that it is self-evident that I've suffused the book with both my intense passion for the subject and the painfully won real-world experience from which you can benefit immediately. It covers ActionScript with exhaustive authority and—thanks to a technical review by Gary Grossman, the creator of ActionScript—with unparalleled accuracy.

What Can ActionScript Do?

Frankly, there's no practical limit to what a full-fledged language like Flash 5 ActionScript can achieve. Let's take a look at some of ActionScript's specific capabilities to offer a taste of the topics we'll cover throughout the book. Begin thinking about how you can combine these techniques to accomplish your particular goals.

Timeline Control

Flash movies are composed of frames residing in a linear sequence called the *timeline*. Using ActionScript, we can control the playback of a movie's timeline, play segments of a movie, display a particular frame, halt a movie's playback, loop animations, and synchronize animated content.

Interactivity

Flash movies can accept and respond to user input. Using ActionScript, we can create interactive elements such as:

- Buttons that react to mouseclicks (e.g., a classic navigation button)
- Content that animates based on mouse movements (e.g., a mouse trailer)
- Objects that can be moved via the mouse or keyboard (e.g., a car in a driving game)
- Text fields that allow users to supply input to a movie (e.g., a fill-in form)

Visual and Audio Content Control

ActionScript can be used to examine or modify the properties of the audio and visual content in a movie. We may, for example, change an object's color and location, reduce a sound's volume, or set the font face of a text block. We may also modify these properties repeatedly over time to produce unique behaviors such as physics-based motion and collision detection.

Programmatic Content Generation

Using ActionScript, we can generate visual and audio content directly from a movie's Library or by duplicating existing content on the Stage. Programmatically generated content may serve as a strictly static element, such as a random visual pattern, or as an interactive element, such as an enemy spaceship in a video game or an option in a pull-down menu.

Server Communication

ActionScript provides a wide variety of tools for sending information to and receiving information from a server. The following applications all involve server communication:

- Link to a web page
- Guest book
- Chat application
- Multiplayer networked game
- E-commerce transaction
- Personalized site involving user registration and login

These examples, of course, offer only a limited account of potential ActionScript applications. The goal of this book is to give you the fundamental skills to explore the myriad other possibilities on your own. This is not a recipe book—it's a lesson in cooking code from scratch. What's on the menu is up to you.

The Code Depot

We'll encounter dozens of code samples over the upcoming chapters. To obtain relevant source files and many other tutorial files not included in the book, visit the online Code Depot, posted at:

> *http://www.moock.org/asdg*

The Code Depot is an evolving resource containing real-world ActionScript applications and code bases. Here's a selected list of samples you'll find in the Code Depot (you can download them individually or as a single *.zip* file):

- A multiple-choice quiz
- An XML-based chat application
- A guest book application
- A custom mouse pointer and button

- An asteroids game code base

- Programmatic motion effects

- Demos of HTML text fields

- Preloaders

- String manipulation

- Interface widgets, such as slider bars and text scrollers

- Mouse trailers and other visual effects

- Volume and sound control

Additionally, any book news, updates, tech notes, and errata will be posted at the preceding URL as well as on the book's web site.

Showcase

Practically every Flash site in existence has at least a little ActionScript in it. But some sites have, shall we say, more than a little. Table P-1 presents a series of destinations that should provide inspiration for your own work. See also the sites listed in Appendix A, *Resources.*

Table P-1. ActionScript Showcase

Topic	URL
Experiments in design, interactivity, and scripting	*http://www.yugop.com* *http://www.praystation.com** *http://www.presstube.com* *http://www.pitaru.com* *http://www.flight404.com* *http://www.bzort-12.com* *http://kaluzhny.nm.ru/3D.html** *http://www.protocol7.com** *http://www.uncontrol.com** *http://www.digitalnotions.com/dev/flash5** *http://flash.onego.ru** *http://www.figleaf.com/development/flash5**
Games	*http://www.gigablast.com* *http://www.sadisticboxing.com* *http://www.flashkit.com/arcade** *http://www.huihui.de*
Interface and dynamic content	*http://www.mnh.si.edu/africanvoices* *http://www.curiousmedia.com*

* Downloadable *.fla* files provided. Otherwise only *.swf* files available.

Typographical Conventions

In order to indicate the various syntactic components of ActionScript, this book uses the following conventions:

- `Constant width` for code samples, clip instance names, frame labels, property names, and variable names.

- *Italic* for function names, method names, class names, layer names, filenames, and file suffixes such as *.swf.*

- **`Constant width bold`** for code that you must type when following a step-by-step procedure.

- *`Constant width italic`* for code that you must replace with an appropriate value (e.g., *`your name here`*) or for variable and property names referenced in a code comment.

- Method and function names are followed by parentheses.

Pay special attention to notes set apart from the text with the following icons:

This is a tip. It contains useful supplementary information about the topic at hand.

This is a warning. It helps you solve and avoid annoying problems.

We'd Like to Hear from You

We have tested and verified the information in this book to the best of our ability, but you may find that features have changed (or even that we have made mistakes!). Please let us know about any errors you find, as well as your suggestions for future editions, by writing to:

O'Reilly & Associates, Inc.
101 Morris Street
Sebastopol, CA 95472
(800) 998-9938 (in the U.S. or Canada)
(707) 829-0515 (international/local)
(707) 829-0104 (fax)

We have a web page for the book, where we list errata, examples, or any additional information. You can access this page at:

  http://www.oreilly.com/catalog/actscript

To comment or ask technical questions about this book, send email to:

  bookquestions@oreilly.com

For more information about our books, conferences, software, Resource Centers, and the O'Reilly Network, see our web site at:

  http://www.oreilly.com

Acknowledgments

I am honored to know, privileged to work with, and deeply indebted to the following people:

- The tremendously talented Flash team at Macromedia, who through constant innovation have shaped a medium, and who recognize the people behind the terminals that constitute the Web. Macromedia's combination of professionalism, exploration, and personal passion is rare within the construct of a corporation.

- The consummate professionals at O'Reilly: Tim O'Reilly, Troy Mott, Mike Sierra, Rob Romano, Edie Freedman, and the many copyeditors, indexers, proofreaders, and sales and marketing folks who helped bring this book to the shelves.

- Derek Clayton, my personal programming mentor and friend. In addition to providing almost-daily code advice, Derek contributed the Perl code in Chapter 17, *Flash Forms*, and schooled me in Quake far too many times. He also wrote an *XMLSocket* server in Java and a generic flat file database system in Perl, both available from the online Code Depot.

- Wendy Schaffer, who, in addition to proofreading the first draft of the manuscript, bore the task of supporting me with love and life during the all-consuming task of writing this book.

- Bruce Epstein, who served as the developmental editor, helping to refine nearly every sentence in the manuscript, often contributing content to round out topics. Bruce's insightful editorial work and guidance were invaluable.

- Gary Grossman, the creator of ActionScript at Macromedia, who somehow always found time to answer questions, explain subtleties, and even entertain debates during ActionScript's development. Gary acted as lead technical editor for the book, helping to clarify important concepts and details. Much of the accuracy of this text is the direct result of his participation.

- Slavik Lozben, Macromedia Flash Engineer, whom I cannot thank enough for creating movie clip events and *swapDepths*! Without Slavik's intelligence and willingness to engage in discourse, I'd still be writing the chapter on events and event handlers. Slavik also contributed greatly as a technical editor.

- Erica Norton, Macromedia ActionScript QA Engineer, who answered and researched question after question with alacrity. In addition to entertaining regular discussions, Erica took time out of her demanding schedule to be a technical editor.

- Jeremy Clark, Macromedia's Flash Product Manager, who enthusiastically supported the book with ideas, advice, friendship, and answers to my endless stream of questions. Eric Wittman, Macromedia's Director of Flash Product Management, whose sagacious direction has shaped Flash for years. Janice Pearce, of Macromedia's Flash QA team, who clarified various Flash production issues and graciously supplied early builds of Flash 5. Matt Wobensmith, Macromedia's Flash Community Manager, and a regular and valuable source of knowledge. Troy Evans, Macromedia's Flash Player Product Manager, who guides and champions the Flash Player. Bentley Wolfe, from Macromedia's technical support team, who seems to never leave his keyboard.

- Richard Koman of O'Reilly & Associates, who provided editorial guidance during the proposal and early draft stages.

- David Fugate, my literary agent from Waterside Productions, whose diligence and confidence made business affairs practically invisible.

- D. Joe Duong, who knows too much for his age, in a kind of defiance of the amount of time he spends teaching others. I am lucky enough to be one of those others. Mike Linkovich, the code philosopher, who is as inspiring as he is edifying. James Porter and Andrew Murphy for reading and testing, and reading and testing, and reading and testing. And, of course, Graham Barton, the deserter.

- Doug Keeley, Terry Maguire, and Jon Nicholls, who created ICE, a company where occupation and passion are allowed to coexist.

- Professor Paul Beam, who saw the connection between literature, communication, and computers in the unlikely setting of an English graduate program at the University of Waterloo.

- Professor Jack Gray, for his wisdom and friendship.

- Andrew Harris, David Luxton, Michael Kavanagh, Stephen Burke, Cheryl Gula, Christine Nishino, Stephen Mumby, Karin Trgovac, and Judith Zissman, whom I hold in esteem for their art, ideas, and friendship.

- The Flash community, from whom I draw inspiration and understanding, including James Patterson, Yugo Nakamura, Naoki Mitsuse, Joshua Davis, James Baker, Marcell Mars, Phillip Torrone, Robert Reinhardt, Mark Fennell, Branden Hall, Josh Ulm, Darrel Plant, Todd Purgason, John Nack, Jason Krogh, Hillman Curtis, Glenn Thomas, and whomever I've inevitably omitted.

- The Moocks (Margaret, Michael, Jane, and Biz) for teaching me to think, dream, explore, and love.

- The Schaffers, for years of family and friendship.

And lastly I'd like to thank you the reader for taking the time to read this book. I hope it helps to make my passion your own.

—Colin Moock
Toronto, Canada
April 2001

I

ActionScript Fundamentals

This part covers the core syntax and grammar of the ActionScript language: variables, data, statements, functions, event handlers, arrays, objects, and movie clips. By the end of Part I, you'll know everything there is to know about writing ActionScript programs.

- Chapter 1, *A Gentle Introduction for Non-Programmers*
- Chapter 2, *Variables*
- Chapter 3, *Data and Datatypes*
- Chapter 4, *Primitive Datatypes*
- Chapter 5, *Operators*
- Chapter 6, *Statements*
- Chapter 7, *Conditionals*
- Chapter 8, *Loop Statements*
- Chapter 9, *Functions*
- Chapter 10, *Events and Event Handlers*
- Chapter 11, *Arrays*
- Chapter 12, *Objects and Classes*
- Chapter 13, *Movie Clips*
- Chapter 14, *Lexical Structure*
- Chapter 15, *Advanced Topics*

1

A Gentle Introduction for Non-Programmers

I'm going to teach you to talk to Flash.

Not just to program in Flash but to say things to it and to listen to what it has to say in return. This is not a metaphor or simply a rhetorical device. It's a philosophical approach to programming.

Programming languages are used to send information to and receive information from computers. They are collections of vocabulary and grammar used to communicate, just like human languages. Using a programming language, we tell a computer what to do or ask it for information. It listens, tries to perform the requested actions, and gives responses. So while you may think you are reading this book in order to "learn to program," you are actually learning to communicate with Flash. But, of course, Flash doesn't speak English, French, German, or Cantonese. Flash's native language is ActionScript, and you're going to learn to speak it.

Learning to speak a computer language is sometimes considered synonymous with learning to program. But there is more to programming than learning a language's syntax. What would it be like if Flash could speak English—if we didn't need to learn ActionScript in order to communicate with it?

What would happen if we were to say, "Flash, make a ball bounce around the screen?"

Flash couldn't fulfill our request because it doesn't understand the word "ball." Okay, okay, that's just a matter of semantics. What Flash expects us to describe is the objects in the world it knows: movie clips, buttons, frames, and so on. So, let's rephrase our request in terms that Flash recognizes and see what happens: "Flash, make the movie clip named `ball_one` bounce around the screen."

Flash still can't fulfill our request without more information. How big should the ball be? Where should it be placed? In which direction should it begin traveling? How fast should it go? Around which part of the screen should it bounce? For how long? In two dimensions or three? Hmm . . . we weren't expecting all these questions. In reality, Flash doesn't ask us these questions. Instead, when Flash can't understand us, it just doesn't do what we want it to, or it yields an error message. For now, we'll pretend Flash asked us for more explicit instructions, and reformulate our request as a series of steps:

1. A ball is a circular movie clip symbol named `ball`.

2. A square is a four-sided movie clip symbol named `square`.

3. Make a new green ball 50 pixels in diameter.

4. Call the new ball `ball_one`.

5. Make a new black square 300 pixels wide and place it in the middle of the Stage.

6. Place `ball_one` somewhere on top of the square.

7. Move `ball_one` in a random direction at 75 pixels per second.

8. If `ball_one` hits one of the sides of the square, make it bounce (reverse course).

9. Continue until I tell you to stop.

Even though we gave our instructions in English, we still had to work through all the logic that governs our bouncing ball in order for Flash to understand us. Obviously, there's more to programming than merely the syntax of programming languages. Just as in English, knowing lots of words doesn't necessarily mean you're a great communicator.

Our hypothetical English-speaking-Flash example exposes four important aspects of programming:

- No matter what the language, the art of programming lies in the formulation of logical steps.

- Before you try to say something in a computer language, it usually helps to say it in English.

- A conversation in one language translated into a different language is still made up of the same basic statements.

- Computers aren't very good at making assumptions. They also have a very limited vocabulary.

Most programming has nothing to do with writing code. Before you write even a single line of ActionScript, think through exactly what you want to do and write out your system's functionality as a flowchart or a blueprint. Once your program has been described sufficiently at the conceptual level, you can translate it into ActionScript.

In programming—as in love, politics, and business—effective communication is the key to success. For Flash to understand your ActionScript, you have to get your syntax absolutely correct down to the last quote, equal sign, and semicolon. And to assure that Flash knows what you're talking about, you must refer only to the world it knows using terms it recognizes. What may be obvious to you is not obvious to a computer. Think of programming a computer like talking to a child: take nothing for granted, be explicit in every detail, and list every step that's necessary to complete a task. But remember that, unlike children, Flash will do precisely what you tell it to do and nothing that you don't tell it to do.

Some Basic Phrases

On the first day of any language school you'd expect to learn a few basic phrases ("Good day," "How are you," etc.). Even if you're just memorizing a phrase and don't know what each word means, you can learn the effect of the phrase and can repeat it to produce that effect. Once you've learned the rules of grammar, expanded your vocabulary, and used the words from your memorized phrases in multiple contexts, you can understand your early phrases in a richer way. The rest of this chapter will be much like that first day of language school—you'll see bits and pieces of code, and you'll be introduced to some fundamental programming grammar. The rest of the book will build on that foundation. You may want to come back to this chapter when you've finished the book to see just how far you've traveled.

Creating Code

For our first exercise, we'll learn how to add four simple lines of code to a Flash movie. Nearly all ActionScript programming takes place in the Actions panel. Any instructions we add to the Actions panel are carried out by Flash when our movie plays. Open the Actions panel now by following these steps:

1. Launch Flash with a new blank document.
2. On the main timeline, select frame 1 of layer 1.
3. Select Window → Actions.

The Actions panel is divided into two sections: the Script pane (on the right) and the Toolbox pane (on the left). The Script pane houses all our code. The Toolbox pane provides us with quick access to the Actions, Operators, Functions, Properties, and

Objects of ActionScript. You'll likely recognize the Basic Actions, shown in Figure 1-1, from prior Flash versions.

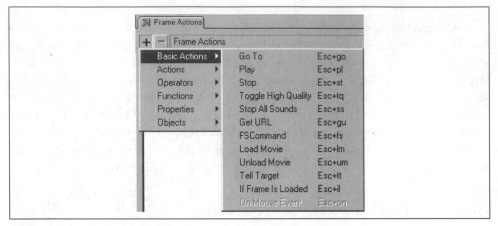

Figure 1-1. Flash 5 Basic Actions

But there's lots more to discover in the Toolbox pane: Figure 1-2 shows all available Actions, including some old friends from Flash 2, 3, and 4. If you continue exploring the Toolbox pane, you'll even find things like Sound, Array, and XML. By the end of this book, we'll have covered them all.

The Toolbox pane's menus may be used to create ActionScript code. However, in order to learn the syntax, principles, and structural makeup of ActionScript, we'll be typing all our code.

 So-called *Actions* are more than just Actions—they include various fundamental programming-language tools: variables, conditionals, loops, comments, function calls, and so forth. Although these are lumped together in one menu, the generic name *Action* obscures the programming structures' significance.

We'll be breaking Actions down to give you a programmer's perspective on those structures. Throughout the book, I use the appropriate programming term to describe the Action at hand. For example, instead of writing, "Add a *while* Action," I'll write, "Create a *while* loop." Instead of writing, "Add an *if* Action," I'll write, "Make a new conditional." Instead of writing, "Add a *play* Action," I'll write, "Invoke the *play()* function (or method)." These distinctions are an important part of learning to speak ActionScript.

Ready to get your hands dirty? Let's say hello to Flash!

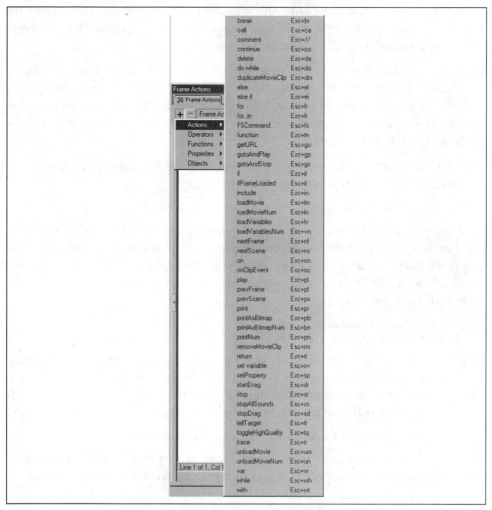

Figure 1-2. Expanded Actions

Say Hi to Flash

Before you can type code into the Actions panel, you must disengage the Action-Script autopilot as follows:

1. Select Edit → Preferences.

2. On the General tab, select Actions Panel → Mode → Expert Mode.

3. Expert Mode is also selectable from the pop-up menu accessible via the arrow at the far right of the Actions panel, though this only sets the current frame's mode. See Chapter 16, *ActionScript Authoring Environment.*

Howdya like that? You're already an expert. When you enter Expert Mode, the Parameters pane at the bottom of the Actions Panel disappears. Don't worry— we're not programming with menus so we won't be needing it.

Next, select frame 1 of layer 1. Your ActionScript (a.k.a., *code*) must always be attached to a frame, movie clip, or button; selecting frame 1 causes subsequently created code to be attached to that frame. In Expert Mode, you can type directly into the Script pane on the right side of the Actions panel, which is where we'll be doing all our programming.

And now, the exciting moment—your first line of code. It's time to introduce your-self to Flash! Type the following into the Script pane:

```
var message = "Hi there, Flash!";
```

That line of code constitutes a complete instruction, known as a *statement*. On the line below it, type your second and third lines of code, shown following this para-graph. Replace *your name here* with your first name (whenever you see *italicized code* in this book it means you have to replace that portion of the code with your own content):

```
var firstName = "your name here";
trace (message);
```

Hmmm. Nothing has happened yet. That's because our code doesn't do anything until we export a *.swf* file and play our movie. Before we do that, let's ask Flash to say hi back to us. Type your fourth line of code under the lines you've already typed (man, we're really on a roll now . . .):

```
trace ("Hi there, " + firstName + ", nice to meet you.");
```

Okay, Flash is ready to meet you. Select Control → Test Movie and see what hap-pens. Some text should appear in the Output window as shown in Figure 1-3.

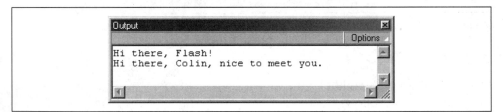

Figure 1-3. Flash gets friendly

Pretty neat, eh?! Let's find out how it all happened.

Keeping Track of Things (Variables)

Remember how I said programming was really just communicating with a computer? Well it is, but perhaps with a little less personality than I've been portraying so far. In your first line of code:

```
var message = "Hi there, Flash!";
```

you didn't really say hi to Flash. You said something more like this:

> Flash, please remember a piece of information for me—specifically, the phrase "Hi there, Flash!" I may need that information in the future, so please give it a label called message. If I ask you for message later, give me back the text "Hi there, Flash!"

Perhaps not as friendly as saying hi, but it illustrates one of the true foundations of programming: Flash can remember something for you, provided that you label it so that it can be found later. For example, in your second line of code, we had Flash remember your first name, and we named the reference to it firstName. Flash remembered your name and displayed it in the Output window when you tested your movie.

The fact that Flash can remember things for us is crucial in programming. Flash can remember any type of data, including text (such as your name), numbers (such as 3.14159), and more complex datatypes that we'll discuss later.

Official variable nomenclature

Time for a few formal terms to describe how Flash remembers things. So far you know that Flash remembers data. An individual piece of data is known as a *datum*. A datum (e.g., "Hi there, Flash!") and the label that identifies it (e.g., message) are together known as a *variable*. A variable's label is called its *name*, and a variable's datum is called its *value*. We say that the variable *stores* or *contains* its value. Note that "Hi there, Flash!" is surrounded by double quotation marks (quotes) to indicate that it is a *string* of text, not a number or some other *datatype*.

In your first line of code, you specified the value of the variable message. The act of specifying the value of a variable is known as *assigning the variable's value*, or generally, *assignment*. But before you can assign a value to a variable, you must first create it. We formally bring variables into existence by *declaring* them using the special keyword *var*, which you used earlier.

So, in practice, here's how I might use more formal terms to instruct you to create the first line of code you created earlier: Declare a new variable named message, and assign it the initial value "Hi there, Flash!" Then you should write:

```
var message = "Hi there, Flash!";
```

The Wizard Behind the Curtain (the Interpreter)

Recall your first two lines of code:

```
var message = "Hi there, Flash!";
var firstName = "your name here";
```

In each of those statements, you created a variable and assigned a value to it. Your third and fourth lines, however, are a little different:

```
trace (message);
trace ("Hi there, " + firstName + ", nice to meet you.");
```

These statements use the *trace()* command. You've already seen the effect of that command—it caused Flash to display your text in the Output window. In the third line, Flash displayed the value of the variable **message**. In the last line, Flash also converted the variable **firstName** to its value (whatever you typed) and stuck that into the sentence after the words "Hi there." The *trace()* command, then, causes any specified data to appear in the Output window (which makes it handy for determining what's going on when a program is running).

The question is, what made the *trace()* command place your text in the Output window? When you create a variable or issue a command, you're actually addressing the *ActionScript interpreter*, which runs your programs, manages your code, listens for instructions, performs any ActionScript commands, executes your statements, stores your data, sends you information, calculates values, and even starts up the basic programming environment when a movie is loaded into the Flash Player.

The interpreter translates your ActionScript into a language that the computer understands and uses to carry out your code. During movie playback, the interpreter is always active, dutifully attempting to understand commands you give it. If the interpreter can understand your commands, it sends them to the computer's processor for execution. If a command generates a result, the interpreter provides that response to you. If the interpreter can't understand the command, it sends you an error message. The interpreter, hence, acts like ActionScript's switchboard operator—it's the audience you're addressing in your code and the ambassador that reports back to you from Flash.

Let's take a closer look at how the interpreter works by examining how it handles a simple *trace()* action.

Consider this command as the interpreter would:

```
trace ("Nice night to learn ActionScript.");
```

The interpreter immediately recognizes the keyword *trace* from its special list of legal command names. The interpreter also knows that *trace()* is used to display text in the Output window, so it also expects to be told which text to display. It finds "Nice night to learn ActionScript." between parentheses following the word *trace* and thinks "Aha! That's just what I need. I'll have that sent to the Output window right away!"

Note that the command is terminated by a semicolon (;). The semicolon acts like the period at the end of a sentence; with few exceptions, every ActionScript statement should end with a semicolon. With the statement successfully understood and all the required information in hand, the interpreter translates the command for the processor to execute, causing our text to appear in the Output window.

That's a gross oversimplification of the internal details of how a computer processor and an interpreter work, but it illustrates these points:

- The interpreter is always listening for your instructions.

- The interpreter has to read your code, letter by letter, and try to understand it. This is the same as you trying to read and understand a sentence in a book.

- The interpreter reads your ActionScript using strict rules—if the parentheses in our *trace()* statement were missing, for example, the interpreter wouldn't be able to understand what's going on, so the command would fail.

You've only just been introduced to the interpreter, but you'll be as intimate with it as you are with a lover before too long: lots of fights, lots of yelling—"Why aren't you listening to me?!"—and lots of beautiful moments when you understand each other perfectly. Strangely enough, my dad always told me the best way to learn a new language is to find a lover that speaks it. May I, therefore, be the first to wish you all the best in your new relationship with the ActionScript interpreter. From now on I'll regularly refer to "the interpreter" instead of "Flash" when describing how ActionScript instructions are carried out.

Extra Info Required (Arguments)

You've already seen one case in which we provided the interpreter with the text to display when issuing a *trace()* command. This approach is common; we'll often issue a command and then provide the interpreter with ancillary data used to execute that command. There's a special name for a datum sent to a command: an *argument*, or synonymously, a *parameter*. To supply an argument to a command, enclose the argument in parentheses, like this:

```
command(argument);
```

When supplying multiple arguments to a command, separate them with commas, like this:

```
command(argument1, argument2, argument3);
```

Supplying an argument to a command is known as *passing* the argument. For example, in the code `gotoAndPlay(5)`, *gotoAndPlay* is the name of the command, and 5 is the argument being passed (in this case the frame number). Some commands, such as *stop()*, require parentheses but do not accept arguments. We'll learn why in Chapter 9, *Functions*.

ActionScript's Glue (Operators)

Let's take another look at your fourth line of code, which contains this *trace()* statement:

```
trace ("Hi there, " + firstName + ", nice to meet you.");
```

See the + (plus) signs? They're used to join (*concatenate*) our text together and are but one of many available *operators*. The operators of a programming language are akin to conjunctions ("and," "or," "but," etc.) in human languages. They're devices used to combine and manipulate phrases of code. In the *trace()* example, the plus operator joins the quoted text "Hi there, " to the text contained in the variable `firstName`.

All operators link phrases of code together, manipulating those phrases in the process. Whether the phrases are text, numbers, or some other datatype, an operator nearly always performs some kind of transformation. Very commonly, operators combine two things together, as the plus operator does. But other operators compare values, assign values, facilitate logical decisions, determine datatypes, create new objects, and provide various other handy services.

When used with two numeric operands, the plus sign (+) and the minus sign (−), perform basic arithmetic. The following displays "3" in the Output window:

```
trace(5 - 2);
```

The *less-than* operator checks which of two numbers is smaller or determines which of two letters is alphabetically first:

```
if (3 < 300) {
   // Do something...
}

if ("a" < "z") {
   // Do something else...
}
```

The combinations, comparisons, assignments, or other manipulations performed by operators are known as *operations*. Arithmetic operations are the easiest operations to understand because they follow basic mathematics: addition (+), subtraction (−), multiplication (*), and division (/). But some operators will be less recognizable to you because they perform specialized programming tasks. Take the *typeof* operator, for example. It tells us what kind of data is stored in a variable. So, if we create a variable x, and give it the value 4, we can then ask the interpreter what datatype x contains, like this:

```
var x = 4;
trace (typeof x);
```

When that line of code is executed in Flash, we get the word "number" in the Output window. Notice that we provide the *typeof* operator with a value upon which to operate, but without using parentheses: typeof x. You might therefore wonder whether or not x is an *argument* of *typeof*. In fact, x plays the same role as an argument (it's an ancillary piece of data needed in the computation of the phrase of code), but in the context of an operator, the argument-like x is officially called an *operand*. An operand is an item upon which an operator operates. For example, in the expression 4 + 9, the numbers 4 and 9 are operands of the + operator.

Chapter 5, *Operators*, covers all of the ActionScript operators in detail. For now just remember that operators link phrases of code in some kind of transformation.

Putting It All Together

Let's review what you've learned. Here, again, is line one:

```
var message = "Hi there, Flash!";
```

The keyword *var* tells the interpreter that we're declaring (creating) a new variable. The word message is the name of our variable. The equals sign is an operator that assigns the text string ("Hi there, Flash!") to the variable message. The text "Hi there, Flash!" hence, becomes the value of message. Finally, the semicolon (;) tells the interpreter that we're finished with our first statement.

Line two is pretty much the same as line one:

```
var firstName = "your name here";
```

Here we're assigning the text string you typed in place of *your name here* to the variable firstName. A semicolon ends our second statement.

We then use the variables message and firstName in lines three and four:

```
trace (message);
trace ("Hi there, " + firstName + ", nice to meet you.");
```

The keyword *trace* signals the interpreter that we'd like some text displayed in the Output window. We pass the text we want displayed as an argument. The opening parenthesis marks the beginning of our argument. In line four, the argument itself includes two *operations*, both of which use the plus *operator*. The first operation joins its first *operand*, "Hi there, " to the value of its second operand, firstName. The second operation joins ", nice to meet you." to the result of the first operation. The closing parenthesis marks the end of our argument, and the semicolon once again indicates the end of our statement.

Blam! Your first ActionScript program. That has a nice ring to it, and it's an important landmark.

Further ActionScript Concepts

You've already been introduced to many of the fundamental elements that make up ActionScript: data, variables, operators, statements, functions, and arguments. Before we delve deeper into those topics, let's sketch out the rest of ActionScript's core features.

Flash Programs

To most computer users, *a program* is synonymous with *an application*, such as Adobe Photoshop or Macromedia Dreamweaver. Obviously, that's not what we're building when we program in Flash. Programmers, on the other hand, define a program as a collection of code (a "series of statements"), but that's only part of what we're building.

A Flash movie is more than a series of lines of code. Code in Flash is intermingled with Flash movie elements, like frames and buttons. We attach our code to those elements so that it can interact with them.

In the end, there really isn't such a thing as a Flash "program" in the classic sense of the term. Instead of complete programs written in ActionScript, we have *scripts*: code segments that give programmatic behavior to our movie, just as JavaScript scripts give programmatic behavior to HTML documents. The real product we're building is not a program but a complete movie (including its code, timelines, visuals, sound, and other assets).

Our scripts include most of what you'd see in traditional programs without the operating-system-level stuff you would write in languages like C++ or Java to place graphics on the screen or cue sounds. We're spared the need to manage the nuts 'n' bolts of graphics and sound programming, which allows us to focus most of our effort on designing the behavior of our movies.

Expressions

The statements of a script, as we've learned, contain the script's instructions. But most instructions are pretty useless without data. When we set a variable, for example, we assign some data as its value. When we use the *trace()* command, we pass data as an argument for display in the Output window. Data is the content we manipulate in our ActionScript code. Throughout your scripts, you'll retrieve, give, store, and generally sling around a lot of data.

In a program, any phrase of code that yields a single datum when a program runs is referred to as an *expression*. The number 7 and the string, "Welcome to my web site," are both very simple expressions. They represent simple data that will be used as-is when the program runs. As such, those expressions are called *literal expressions*, or *literals* for short.

Literals are only one kind of expression. A variable may also be an expression (variables stand in for data, so they count as expressions). Expressions get even more interesting when they are combined with operators. The expression 4 + 5, for example, is an expression with two operands, 4 and 5, but the plus operator makes the entire expression yield the single value 9. Complex expressions may contain other, shorter expressions, provided that the entire phrase of code can still be converted into a single value.

Here we see the variable **message**:

```
var message = "Hi there, Flash!";
```

If we like, we can combine the variable expression **message** with the literal expression " How are you?" as follows:

```
message + " How are you?"
```

which becomes "Hi there, Flash! How are you?" when the program runs. You'll frequently see long expressions include shorter expressions when working with arithmetic, such as:

```
(2 + 3) * (4 / 2.5) - 1
```

It's important to be exposed to expressions early in your programming career because the term "expression" is often used in descriptions of programming concepts. For example, I might write, "To assign a value to a variable, type the name of the variable, then an equal sign followed by any expression."

Two Vital Statement Types: Conditionals and Loops

In nearly all programs, we'll use *conditionals* to add logic to our programs and *loops* to perform repetitive tasks.

Making choices using conditionals

One of the really rewarding aspects of Flash programming is making your movies smart. Here's what I mean by smart: Suppose a girl named Wendy doesn't like getting her clothes wet. Before Wendy leaves her house every morning, she looks out the window to check the weather, and if it's raining, she brings an umbrella.

Wendy's smart. She uses basic logic—the ability to look at a series of options and make a decision about what to do based on the circumstances. We use the same basic logic when creating interactive Flash movies.

Here are a few examples of logic in a Flash movie:

- Suppose we have three sections in a movie. When a user goes to each section, we use logic to decide whether to show her the introduction to that section. If she has been to the section before, we skip the introduction. Otherwise, we show the introduction.

- Suppose we have a section of a movie that is restricted. To enter the restricted zone, the user must enter a password. If the user enters the right password, we show her the restricted content. Otherwise, we don't.

- Suppose we're moving a ball across the screen and we want it to bounce off a wall. If the ball crosses a certain point, we reverse the ball's direction. Otherwise, we let the ball continue traveling in the direction it was going.

These examples of movie logic require the use of a special type of statement called a *conditional*. Conditionals let us specify the terms under which a section of code should—or should not—be executed. Here's an example of a conditional statement:

```
if (userName == "James Bond") {
  trace ("Welcome to my web site, 007.");
}
```

The generic structure of a conditional is:

```
if (this condition is met) {
  then execute these lines of code
}
```

You'll learn more about the detailed syntax in Chapter 7, *Conditionals*. For now, remember that a conditional allows Flash to make logical decisions.

Repeating tasks using loops

Not only do we want our movies to make decisions, we want them to do tedious, repetitive tasks for us. That is, until they take over the world and enslave us and grow us in little energy pods as . . . wait . . . forget I told you that . . . ahem. Suppose you want to display a sequence of five numbers in the Output window, and you want the sequence to start at a certain number. If the starting number were 10, you could display the sequence like this:

```
trace (10);
trace (11);
trace (12);
trace (13);
trace (14);
```

But if you want to start the sequence at 513, you'd have to retype all the numbers as follows:

```
trace (513);
trace (514);
trace (515);
trace (516);
trace (517);
```

We can avoid that retyping by making our *trace()* statements depend on a variable, like this:

```
var x = 1;
trace (x);
x = x + 1;
trace (x);
x = x + 1;
trace (x);
x = x + 1;
trace (x);
x = x + 1;
trace (x);
```

On line 1, we set the value of the variable **x** to 1. Then at line 2, we send that value to the Output window. On line 3, we say, "Take the current value of **x**, add 1 to it, and stick the result back into our variable **x**," so **x** becomes 2. Then we send the value of **x** to the Output window again. We repeat this process three more times. By the time we're done, we've displayed a sequence of five numbers in the Output window. The beauty being that if we now want to change the starting number of our sequence, we just change the initial value of **x**. Because the rest of our code is based on **x**, the entire sequence changes when the program runs.

That's an improvement over our first approach, and it works pretty well when we're displaying only five numbers, but it becomes impractical if we want to count to 500. To perform highly repetitive tasks, we use a *loop*—a statement that causes a block of code to be repeated an arbitrary number of times. There are several types of loops, each with its own syntax. One of the most common loop types is the *while* loop. Here's what our counting example would look like as a *while* loop instead of as a series of repeated statements:

```
var x = 1;
while (x <= 5) {
  trace (x);
  x = x + 1;
}
```

The keyword *while* indicates that we want to start a loop. The expression *(x <= 5)* governs how many times the loop should execute (as long as **x** is less than or equal to 5), and the statements *trace (x);* and *x = x + 1;* are executed with each repetition (or *iteration*) of the loop. As it is, our loop saves us only 5 lines of code, but it could potentially save us hundreds of lines if we were counting to higher numbers. And our loop is flexible. To make our loop count to 500, we simply change the expression *(x <=5)* to *(x <=500)*:

```
var x = 1;
while (x <= 500) {
  trace (x);
  x = x + 1;
}
```

Like conditionals, loops are one of the most frequently used and important types of statements in programming.

Modular Code (Functions)

So far your longest script has consisted of four lines of code. But it won't be long before that 4 lines becomes 400 or maybe even 4,000. Sooner or later you're going to end up looking for ways to manage your code, reduce your work, and make your code easier to apply to multiple scenarios. Which is when you'll first really start to love *functions*. A function is a packaged series of statements. In practice, functions mostly serve as reusable blocks of code.

Suppose you want to write a quick script that calculates the area of a 4-sided figure. Without functions, your script might look like this:

```
var height = 10;
var width = 15;
var area = height * width;
```

Now suppose you want to calculate the area of five 4-sided figures. Your code quintuples in size:

```
var height1 = 10;
var width1 = 15;
var area1 = height1 * width1;
var height2 = 11;
var width2 = 16;
var area2 = height2 * width2;
var height3 = 12;
var width3 = 17;
var area3 = height3 * width3;
var height4 = 13;
var width4 = 18;
var area4 = height4 * width4;
var height5 = 20;
var width5 = 5;
var area5 = height5 * width5;
```

Because we're repeating the area calculation over and over, we are better off putting it in a function once and executing that function multiple times:

```
function area(height, width){
  return height * width;
}
area1 = area(10, 15);
area2 = area(11, 16);
area3 = area(12, 17);
area4 = area(13, 18);
area5 = area(20, 5);
```

We first created the area-calculating function using the *function* statement, which defines (declares) a function just as *var* declares a variable. Then we gave our function a name, **area**, just as we give variables names. Between the parentheses, we listed the arguments that our function receives every time it's used: **height** and **width**. And between the curly braces ({ }), we included the statement(s) we want our function to execute:

```
return height * width;
```

After we create a function, we may run the code it contains from anywhere in our movie by using its name. In our example we called the *area()* function five times, passing it the **height** and **width** values it expects each time: *area(10, 15)*, *area(11, 16)*, and so on. The result of each calculation is returned to us and we store those results in the variables **area1** through **area5**. Nice and neat, and much less work than the non-function version of our code.

Don't fret if you have questions about this function example, as we'll learn more about functions in Chapter 9. For now, just remember that functions give us an extremely powerful way to create complex systems. Functions help us reuse our code and package its functionality, extending the limits of what is practical to build.

Built-in functions

Notice that functions take arguments just as the *trace()* Action does. Invoking the function *area(4, 5);* looks very much the same as issuing the *trace()* command such as *trace (x);*. The similarity is not a coincidence. As we pointed out earlier, many Actions, including the *trace()* Action, are actually functions. But they are a special type of function that is built into ActionScript (as opposed to user-defined, like our *area()* function). It is, therefore, legitimate—and technically more accurate—to say, "Call the *gotoAndStop()* function," than to say, "Execute a *gotoAndStop* Action." A built-in function is simply a reusable block of code that comes with ActionScript for our convenience. Built-in functions let us do everything from performing mathematical calculations to controlling movie clips. All the built-in functions are listed in Part III, *Language Reference*. We'll also encounter many of them as we learn ActionScript's fundamentals.

Movie Clip Instances

With all this talk about programming fundamentals, I hope you haven't forgotten about the basics of Flash. One of the keys to visual programming in Flash is movie clip *instances*. As a Flash designer or developer, you should already be familiar with movie clips, but you may not think of movie clips as programming devices.

Every movie clip has a symbol definition that resides in the Library of a Flash movie. We can add many copies, or *instances*, of a single movie clip symbol to a Flash movie by dragging the clip from the Library onto the Stage. A great deal of advanced Flash programming is simply a matter of movie clip instance control. A bouncing ball, for example, is nothing more than a movie clip instance being repositioned on the Stage repetitively. We can alter an instance's location, size, current frame, rotation, and so forth, through ActionScript during the playback of our movie.

If you're unfamiliar with movie clips and instances, consult Flash's documentation or Help files before continuing with the rest of this book.

The Event-Based Execution Model

One final topic we should consider in our overview of ActionScript fundamentals is the *execution model*, which dictates when the code in your movie runs (is executed). You may have code attached to various frames, buttons, and movie clips throughout your movie. But when does it all actually run? To answer that question, let's take a short stroll down computing history's memory lane.

In the early days of computing, a program's instructions were executed sequentially in the order that they appeared, starting with the first line and ending with the last line. The program was meant to perform some action and then stop. That kind of program, called a *batch* program, doesn't handle the interactivity required of an *event-based* programming environment like Flash.

Event-based programs don't run in a linear fashion as batch programs do. They run continuously (in an *event loop*), waiting for things (*events*) to happen and executing code segments in response to those events. In a language designed for use with a visual interactive environment (such as ActionScript or JavaScript), the events are typically user actions such as mouseclicks or keystrokes.

When an event such as a mouseclick occurs, the interpreter sounds an alarm. A program can then react to that alarm by asking the interpreter to execute an appropriate segment of code. For example, if a user clicks a button in a movie, we could execute some code that displays a different section of the movie (classic navigation) or submits variables to a database (classic form submission).

But programs don't react to events unless we create *event handlers*. Here's some pseudo-code that shows generally how event handlers are set up:

```
when (this event happens) {
   execute these lines of code
}
```

This is typically written in the general form:

```
on (event) {
   statements
}
```

In practice, an event handler for a button that moves the playhead to frame 200 would read:

```
on (press) {
   gotoAndStop(200);
}
```

Because event-based programs are always running an event loop, ready to react to the next event, they are like living systems. Events are a crucial part of Flash movies. Without events, our scripts wouldn't do anything—with one exception: Flash executes any code on a frame when the playhead enters that frame. The implied event is simply the playhead entering the particular frame, which is so intrinsic to Flash that no explicit event handler is required.

Events literally make things happen, which is why they come at the end of your first day of ActionScript language school. You've learned what's involved in writing scripts and what governs when those scripts will actually be executed (i.e., events). I'd say you're ready to try your first real conversation.

Building a Multiple-Choice Quiz

Now that we've explored the basic principles of ActionScript, let's apply those principles in the context of a real Flash movie. We'll start our applied study of Flash programming by creating a multiple-choice quiz using very simple programming techniques, most of which you've already learned. We'll revisit our quiz in later chapters to see how it can be improved after learning more advanced programming concepts. We'll eventually make the code more elegant so that it's easier to extend and maintain, and we'll add more features to our quiz so that it can easily handle any number of questions.

The finished *.fla* file for this quiz may be found in the online Code Depot. This is a lesson in Flash programming, not Flash production. It is assumed that you are already comfortable creating and using buttons, layers, frames, keyframes, and the

Text tool. The quiz shows real-world applications of the following aspects of ActionScript programming:

- Variables
- Controlling the playhead of a movie with functions
- Button event handlers
- Simple conditionals
- Text field variables for on-screen display of information

Quiz Overview

Our quiz, part of which is shown in Figure 1-4, will have only two questions. Each question comes with three multiple-choice answers. Users submit their answers by clicking the button that corresponds to their desired selections. The selections are recorded in a variable so that they may be used to grade the user's score. When all the questions have been answered, the number of correct answers is tallied and the user's score is displayed.

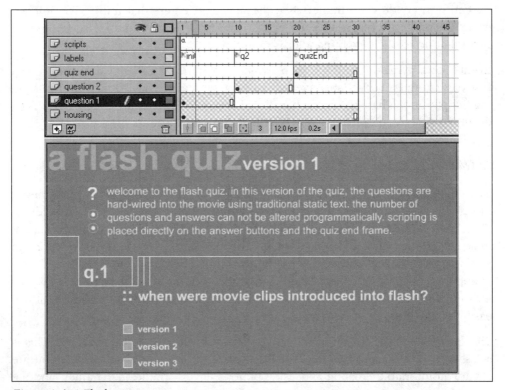

Figure 1-4. A Flash quiz

Building the Layer Structure

When building Flash movies, it's important to organize your content into manageable divisions by keeping different content elements on individual layers. Layering content is a good production technique in general, but it is essential in Flash programming. In our quiz, and in the vast majority of our scripted movies, we'll keep all our timeline scripts on a single isolated layer, called *scripts*. I keep the *scripts* layer as the first one in my layer stack so that it's easy to find.

We'll also keep all our frame labels on a separate layer, called (surprise, surprise) *labels*. The *labels* layer should live beneath the *scripts* layer on all your timelines. In addition to these two standard layers (*scripts* and *labels*), our quiz movie has a series of content layers on which we'll isolate our various content assets.

Start building your quiz by creating and naming the following layers and arranging them in the order that they appear here:

> *scripts*
> *labels*
> *quiz end*
> *question 2*
> *question 1*
> *housing*

Now add 30 frames to each of your layers. Your timeline should look like the one in Figure 1-5.

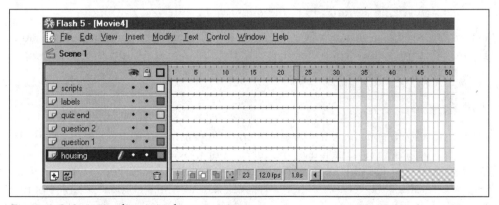

Figure 1-5. Quiz timeline initial setup

Creating the Interface and Questions

Before we get into the scripts that run the quiz, we need to set up the questions and the interface that will let the user proceed through the quiz.

Here are the steps you should follow:

1. With frame 1 of the *housing* layer selected, use the Text tool to type your quiz title directly on the Stage.

2. At frame 1 of the *question 1* layer, add the question number "1" and the text for Question 1, "When were movie clips introduced into Flash?" Leave room for the answer text and buttons below your question.

3. Create a simple button that looks like a checkbox or radio button and measures no higher than a line of text (see Figure 1-6).

4. Below your question text (still on the *question 1* layer), add the text of your three multiple-choice answers: "Version 1," "Version 2," and "Version 3," each on its own line.

5. Next to each of your three answers, place an instance of your checkbox button.

6. We'll use Question 1 as a template for Question 2. Select the first frame of the *question 1* layer and choose Edit → Copy Frames.

7. Select frame 10 of the *question 2* layer and choose Edit → Paste Frames. A duplicate of your first question appears on the *question 2* layer at frame 10.

8. While still in frame 10 of the *question 2* layer, change the question number from "1" to "2" and change the text of the question to, "When was MP3 audio support added to Flash?" Change the multiple-choice answers to "Version 3," "Version 4," and "Version 5."

9. Finally, to prevent Question 1 from appearing underneath Question 2, add a blank keyframe at frame 10 of the *question 1* layer.

Figure 1-6 shows the Flash movie after you've added the first question to the quiz. Figure 1-7 shows how your timeline will look after you've added the two questions to the quiz.

Initializing the Quiz

Our first order of business in our quiz script (and in most scripts) is to create the main timeline variables we'll use throughout our movie. In our quiz we do this on the first frame of the movie, but in other movies we'll normally do it after preloading part or all of the movie. Either way, we want to initialize our variables before any other scripting occurs. Once our variables are defined, we invoke the *stop()* function to keep the user paused on the first frame (where the quiz starts).

For more complex movies, we may also set the initial conditions by calling functions and assigning variable values in preparation for the rest of the movie. This step is known as *initialization*. Functions that start processes in motion or define the initial conditions under which a system operates are frequently named *init*.

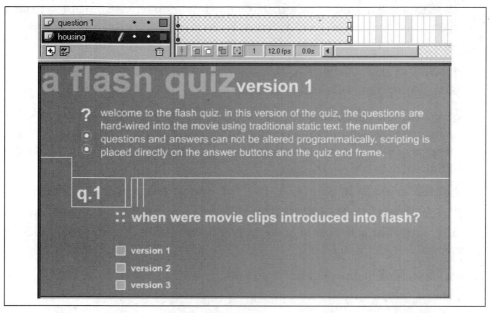

Figure 1-6. Quiz title and Question 1

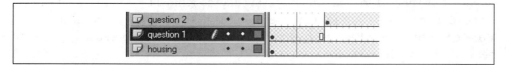

Figure 1-7. Quiz timeline with two questions

Our quiz *init* code, shown in Example 1-1, is attached to frame 1 of the *scripts* layer of our movie.

Example 1-1. Init Code for Quiz

```
// Init main timeline variables
var q1answer;          // User's answer for question 1
var q2answer;          // User's answer for question 2
var totalCorrect = 0;  // Counts number of correct answers
var displayTotal;      // Text field for displaying user's score

// Stop the movie at the first question
stop();
```

Line 1 of our *init* sequence is a *code comment*. Code comments are notes that you add in your code to explain what's going on. A single-line comment starts with two forward slashes and a space, which is then followed by a line of text:

```
// This is a comment
```

Notice that comments can be placed on the same line as your code, like this:

```
x = 5; // This is also a comment
```

Line 2 of Example 1-1 creates a variable named `q1answer`. Recall that to create a variable we use the *var* keyword followed by a variable name, as in:

```
var favoriteColor;
```

So, the second through fifth lines of our code declare the variables we'll need, complete with comments explaining their purpose:

- `q1answer` and `q2answer` will contain the value of the user's answer (1, 2, or 3, indicating which of the three multiple-choice options was selected for each question). We'll use these values to check whether the user answered the questions correctly.

- `totalCorrect` will be used at the end of the quiz to tally the number of questions that the user answered correctly.

- `displayTotal` is the name of the text field that we'll use to show the value of `totalCorrect` on screen.

Take a closer look at Line 4 of Example 1-1:

```
var totalCorrect = 0;   // Counts number of correct answers
```

Line 4 performs double duty; it first declares the variable `totalCorrect` and then assigns the value 0 to that variable using the assignment operator, =. We want `totalCorrect` to default to 0 in case the user hasn't answered any of the questions correctly. The other variables don't need default values because they are all set explicitly during the quiz.

After our variables have been defined, we call the *stop()* function, which halts the playback of the movie on frame 1, where the quiz begins:

```
// Stop the movie at the first question
stop();
```

The *stop()* function has the exact same effect as any *stop* Action you may have used in Flash 4 or earlier (it pauses the playhead in the current frame).

 Observe, again, the use of the comment before the *stop()* function call. That comment explains the intended effect of the code that follows. Comments are optional, but they help clarify our code if we leave it for a while and need a refresher when we return or if we pass our code to another developer. Comments also make code easy to scan, which is important during debugging.

Now that you know what our *init* code does, let's add it to our quiz movie:

1. Select Frame 1 of the *scripts* layer.

2. Choose Window → Actions. The Frame Actions panel appears.

3. Make sure you're using Expert Mode, which can be set as a permanent preference under Edit → Preferences.

4. Into the right side of the Frame Actions panel, type the *init* code as shown earlier in Example 1-1.

Variable Naming Styles

By now you've seen quite a few variable names, and you may be wondering about the capitalization. If you've never programmed before, a capital letter in the middle of a word, as in `firstName`, or `totalCorrect`, may seem odd. Capitalizing the second word (and any following words) of a variable name visually demarcates the words within that name. We use this technique because spaces and dashes aren't allowed in a variable name. But don't capitalize the first letter of a variable name—an initial capital letter is conventionally used to name object classes, not variables.

If you use underscores instead of capital letters to separate words in variables, as in `first_name` and `total_correct`, be consistent. Don't use `firstName` for some variables and `second_name` for others. Use one of these styles so that other programmers will find your code understandable. Variable names in some languages are case-sensitive, meaning that `firstName` and `firstname` would be considered two different variables. ActionScript, however, treats them as the same thing. But it's bad form to use two different cases to refer to the same variable; if you call a variable `xPOS`, don't refer to it elsewhere as `xpos`.

Always give your variables and functions meaningful names that help you remember what they are for. Avoid useless names like "foo," and use single-letter variables, such as "x" or "i" only for simple things like the index (i.e., counting variable) in a loop.

Adding Frame Labels

We've got our quiz's *init* script done and our questions built. We should now add some frame labels so that we can control the playback of our quiz.

In order to step the user through our quiz one question at a time, we've separated the content for Question 1 and Question 2 into frames 1 and 10. By moving the playhead to those keyframes, we'll create a slide show effect, where each slide contains a question. We know that Question 2 is on frame 10, so when we want to display Question 2, we can call the *gotoAndStop()* function like this:

```
gotoAndStop(10);
```

which would cause the playhead to advance to frame 10, the location of Question 2. A sensible piece of code, right? Wrong! Whereas using the specific number 10 with our *gotoAndStop()* function works, it isn't flexible. If, for example, we added five frames to the timeline before frame 10, Question 2 would suddenly reside at frame 15, and our *gotoAndStop(10)* command would not bring the user to the correct frame. To allow our code to work even if the frames in our timeline shift, we use *frame labels* instead of frame numbers. Frame labels are expressive names, such as q2 or quizEnd, by which we can refer to specific points on the timeline. Once a point is labeled, we can use the label to refer to the frame by name instead of by number.

The flexibility of frame labels is indispensable. I hardly ever use frame numbers with playback-control functions like *gotoAndStop()*. Let's add all the labels we'll need for our quiz now, so that we can use them later to walk the user through the quiz questions:

1. On the *labels* layer, click frame 1.
2. Select Modify → Frame. The Frame panel appears.
3. In the Label text field, type **init**.
4. At frame 10 of the *labels* layer, add a blank keyframe.
5. In the Frame panel, in the Label text field, type **q2**.
6. At frame 20 of the *labels* layer, add a blank keyframe.
7. In the Frame panel, in the Label text field, type **quizEnd**.

Scripting the Answer Buttons

Our questions are in place, our variables have been initialized, and our frames have been labeled. If we were to test our movie now, we'd see Question 1 appear with three answer buttons that do nothing when clicked and no way for the user to get to Question 2. We need to add some code to the answer buttons so that they will advance the user through the quiz and keep track of his answers along the way.

For convenience, we'll refer to the multiple-choice buttons as button 1, button 2, and button 3, as shown in Figure 1-8.

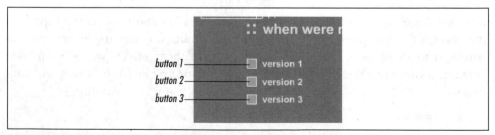

Figure 1-8. The answer buttons

Our three buttons get very similar scripts. Example 1-2 through Example 1-4 show the code for each button.

Example 1-2. Code for Question 1, Button 1

```
on (release) {
  q1answer = 1;
  gotoAndStop ("q2");
}
```

Example 1-3. Code for Question 1, Button 2

```
on (release) {
  q1answer = 2;
  gotoAndStop ("q2");
}
```

Example 1-4. Code for Question 1, Button 3

```
on (release) {
  q1answer = 3;
  gotoAndStop ("q2");
}
```

The button code consists of two statements (lines 2 and 3) that are executed only when a mouseclick is detected. In natural language, the code for each button says, "When the user clicks this button, make a note that he chose answer 1, 2, or 3, then proceed to Question 2." Here's how it works.

Line 1 is the beginning of an *event handler*:

```
on (release) {
```

The event handler waits patiently for the user to click button 1. Recall that an event handler listens for things (such as mouseclicks) that happen while the movie is running. When an event occurs, the code contained in the appropriate handler is executed.

Let's dissect the event handler that begins on line 1. The keyword *on* signals the start of the event handler. (If the word *on* seems a little awkward to you, think of it as *when* until you're comfortable with it.) The keyword *release*, enclosed in parentheses, indicates the *type of event* that the event handler is listening for; in this case, we're listening for a *release* event, which occurs when the user clicks and releases the mouse over the button. The opening curly brace ({) marks the beginning of the block of statements that should be executed when the *release* event occurs. The end of the code block is marked by a closing curly brace (}) on line 4, which is the end of the event handler.

Line 2 is the first of the statements that will be executed when the *release* event occurs. The code in line 2 should be getting quite familiar to you:

```
q1answer = 1;
```

It sets the variable `q1answer` to 1 (the other answer buttons set it to 2 or 3). The `q1answer` variable stores the user's answer for the first question. Once we have recorded the user's answer for Question 1, we advance to Question 2 via line 3 of our button code:

```
gotoAndStop ("q2");
```

Line 3 calls the *gotoAndStop()* function, passing it the frame label "q2" as an argument, which advances the playhead to the frame q2 where Question 2 appears.

Now that you know how the button code works, let's add it to the Question 1 buttons:

1. With the Actions panel open, select button 1 on the Stage. The Frame Actions title changes to Object Actions. Any code you add now will be attached to button 1 (the selected object on the Stage).

2. Into the right side of the Actions panel, type the code from Example 1-2.

3. Repeat steps 1 and 2 to add button code to buttons 2 and 3. On button 2, set `q1answer` to 2; on button 3, set `q1answer` to 3, as shown in Example 1-3 and Example 1-4.

The code for the Question 2 buttons is structurally identical to that of the Question 1 buttons (we change only the name of the answer variable and the destination of the *gotoAndStop()* call). Example 1-5 shows the code for button 1 of Question 2.

Example 1-5. Code for Question 2, Button 1

```
on (release) {
  q2answer = 1;
  gotoAndStop ("quizEnd");
}
```

We use the variable `q2answer` instead of `q1answer` because we want the buttons to keep track of the user's selection for Question 2. We use "quizEnd" as the argument for our *gotoAndStop()* function call to advance the playhead to the end of the quiz (i.e., the frame labeled `quizEnd`) after the user answers Question 2.

Let's add the button code for the Question 2 buttons:

1. Click on frame 10 of the *question 2* layer.

2. Click on button 1.

3. Into the Actions panel, type the code from Example 1-5.

4. Repeat steps 2 and 3 to add button code to buttons 2 and 3. On button 2, set `q2answer` to 2. On button 3, set `q2answer` to 3.

Having just added button code to six buttons, you will no doubt have noticed how repetitive the code is. The code on each button differs from the code on the others by only a few text characters. That's not exactly efficient programming. Our button code cries out for some kind of centralized entity that records the answer and advances to the next screen in the quiz. In Chapter 9 we'll see how to centralize our code with *functions*.

Building the Quiz End

Our quiz is nearly complete. We now have two questions working with an answer-tracking script that lets the user answer the questions and progress through the quiz. We still need a quiz-ending screen where we tell the user how well he fared.

To build our quiz-end screen, we need to do some basic Flash production and some scripting. Let's do the production first:

1. At frame 20 of the *question 2* layer, add a blank keyframe. This prevents Question 2 from appearing underneath the contents of our quiz-end screen.

2. At frame 20 of the *quiz end* layer, add a blank keyframe.

3. While you're still on that frame, put the following text on the Stage: "Thank you for taking the quiz. Your final score is: /2." Make sure to leave a decent amount of blank space between "is:" and "/2." We'll put the user's score there.

4. At frame 20 of the *scripts* layer, add a blank keyframe.

That takes care of the production work for our quiz-end screen. Your end screen should look something like the one shown in Figure 1-9.

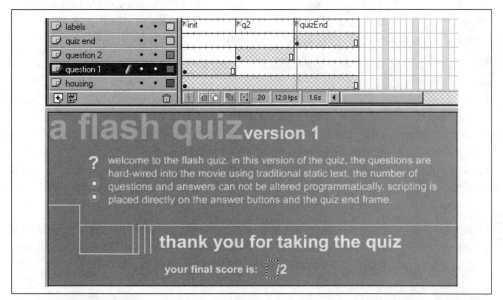

Figure 1-9. Judgment day

Now let's work on the quiz-end script. When the playhead lands on our `quizEnd` frame, we want to calculate the user's score. We need a calculation script to execute when the playhead reaches frame 20. Because any script placed on a keyframe in the timeline is automatically executed when the playhead enters that frame, we can simply attach our calculation script to the keyframe we added at frame 20 of the *scripts* layer.

In the calculation script, we first determine the user's score, and then we display that score on the screen:

```
// Tally up the user's correct answers
if (q1answer == 3){
  totalCorrect = totalCorrect + 1;
}
if (q2answer == 2){
  totalCorrect++;
}
// Show the user's score in an on-screen text field
displayTotal = totalCorrect;
```

Lines 1 and 8 are code comments that summarize the functionality of the two sections of the script. On line 2, the first of two conditionals in our calculation script begins. In it, we see our **q1answer** variable put to use:

```
if (q1answer == 3){
```

The keyword *if* tells the interpreter we're about to provide a list of statements that should be executed only if a certain condition is met. The terms of that condition are described in the parentheses that follow the *if* keyword: *(q1answer == 3)*, and the opening curly brace begins the list of statements to be conditionally executed. Therefore, line 2 translates into, "If the value of **q1answer** is equal to 3, then execute the statements contained in the following curly braces."

But how exactly does the condition *q1answer == 3* work? Well, let's break the phrase down. We recognize **q1answer** as the variable in which we've stored the user's answer to Question 1. The number 3 indicates the correct answer to Question 1, because movie clips first appeared in Flash 3. The double equal sign (==) between our variable and the number 3 is the *equality* comparison operator, which compares two expressions. If the expression on its left (**q1answer**) equals the one on its right (3), our condition is met, and the statements within the curly braces are executed. If not, our condition is not met, and the statements within the curly braces are skipped.

Flash has no way of knowing the right answers to our quiz questions. Checking if **q1answer** is equal to 3 is our way of telling Flash to check if the user got Question 1 right. If he did, we tell Flash to add one to his total score as follows:

```
totalCorrect = totalCorrect + 1;
```

Line 3 says, "Make the new value of `totalCorrect` equal to the old value of `totalCorrect` plus one," (i.e., *increment* `totalCorrect`). Incrementing a variable is so common that it has its own special operator, ++.

So instead of using this code:

```
totalCorrect = totalCorrect + 1;
```

We normally write:

```
totalCorrect++;
```

which does exactly the same thing, but more succinctly.

At line 4, we end the block of statements to execute if our first condition is met:

```
}
```

Lines 5 through 7 are another condition:

```
if (q2answer == 2){
   totalCorrect++;
}
```

Here we're checking whether the user answered Question 2 correctly (MP3 audio support first appeared in Flash 4). If the user chose the second answer, we add one to `totalCorrect` using the increment operator ++.

Because there are only two questions in our quiz, we're done tallying the user's score. For each question that the user answered correctly, we added one to `totalCorrect`, so `totalCorrect` now contains the user's final score. The only thing left is to show the user his score, via line 9, the last line of our quiz-end script:

```
displayTotal = totalCorrect;
```

You already know enough about variables to guess that the statement on line 9 assigns the value of `totalCorrect` to the variable `displayTotal`. But how does that make the score appear on screen? So far, it doesn't. In order to make the score appear on screen, we need to create a special kind of variable called a *text field* variable that has a physical representation on the screen. Let's make one now so you can see how it works:

1. Select the Text tool.

2. On the *quiz end* layer, click frame 20.

3. Place your pointer just before the text "/2" that you created earlier, then click the Stage.

4. Drag out a text box big enough to hold a single number.

5. Choose Text → Options.

6. In the Text Options panel, change Static Text to Dynamic Text.

7. In the Variable text field, type **displayTotal**.

The variable `displayTotal` now has a screen representation. If we change `displayTotal` in our script, the corresponding text field variable will be updated on the screen.

Testing Our Quiz

Well, that's it. Our quiz is finished. You can now check whether the quiz works using Control → Test Movie. Click on the answers in different combinations to see if your quiz is keeping score correctly. You can even create a restart button by attaching the following code to a new button:

```
on (release) {
  gotoAndStop("init");
}
```

Because `totalCorrect` is set to 0 in the code on the `init` frame, the score will reset itself each time you send the playhead to `init`.

If you find that your quiz isn't working, try comparing it with the sample quiz provided at the online Code Depot. You may also want to investigate the troubleshooting techniques described in Chapter 19, *Debugging*.

Onward!

So how does it feel? You've learned a bunch of phrases, some grammar, some vocabulary, and even had a drawn-out conversation with Flash (the multiple-choice quiz). Quite a rich first day of language school, I'd say.

As you can see, there's a lot to learn about ActionScript, but you can also do quite a bit with just a little knowledge. Even the amount you know now will give you plenty to play around with. Over the rest of this book, we'll reinforce the fundamentals you've learned by exploring them in more depth and showing them in concert with real examples. Of course, we'll also cover some topics that haven't even been introduced yet.

Remember: think communication, think cooperation, and speak clearly. And if you find yourself doing any fantastically engaging work or art that you'd like to share with others, send it over to me at *http://ww.moock.org/webdesign/flash/contact.html*.

Now that you have a practical frame of reference, you'll be better able to appreciate and retain the foundational knowledge detailed over the next few chapters. It will give you a deeper understanding of ActionScript, enabling you to create more complex movies.

2

Variables

In a typical scripted movie, we have to track and manipulate everything from frame numbers to a user's password to the velocity of a photon torpedo fired from a spaceship. In order to manage and retrieve all that information, we need to store it in *variables*, the primary information-storage containers of ActionScript.

A variable is a like a bank account that, instead of holding money, holds information (*data*). Creating a new variable is like setting up a new account; we establish a place to store something we'll need in the future. And just as every bank account has an account number, every variable has a name associated with it that is used to access the data in the variable.

Once a variable is created, we can put new data into it as often as we want—much like depositing money into an account. Or we can find out what's in a variable using the variable's name—much like checking an account balance. If we no longer need our variable, we can "close the account" by deleting the variable.

The key feature to note is that variables let us refer to data that either changes or is calculated when a movie plays. Just as a bank account's number remains the same even though the account balance varies, a variable's name remains fixed even though the data it contains may change. Using that fixed reference to access changing content, we can perform complex calculations, keep track of cards in a card game, save guest book entries, or send the playhead to different locations based on changing conditions.

Is that a gleam of excitement I see in your eye? Good, I thought I might have lost you with all that talk about banks. Let's start our exploration of variables by seeing how to create them.

Creating Variables (Declaration)

Creating a variable is called *declaration*. Declaration is the "open an account" step of our bank metaphor, where we formally bring the variable into existence. When a variable is first declared, it is empty—a blank page waiting to be written upon. In this state, a variable contains a special value called `undefined` (indicating the absence of data).

To declare a new variable, we use the *var* statement. For example:

```
var speed;
var bookTitle;
var x;
```

The word *var* tells the interpreter that we're declaring a variable, and the text that follows, such as `speed`, `bookTitle`, or `x`, becomes our new variable's name. We can create variables anywhere we can attach code: on a keyframe, a button, or a movie clip.

We can also declare several variables with one *var* statement, like this:

```
var x, y, z;
```

However, doing so impairs our ability to add comments next to each variable.

Once a variable has been created, we may assign it a value, but before we learn how to do that, let's consider some of the subtler details of variable declaration.

Automatic Variable Creation

Many programming languages require variables to be declared before data may be deposited into them; failure to do so would cause an error. ActionScript is not that strict. If we assign a value to a variable that does not exist, the interpreter will create a new variable for us. The bank, to continue that analogy, automatically opens an account when you try to make your first deposit.

This convenience comes at a cost, though. If we don't declare our variables ourselves, we have no central inventory to consult when examining our code. Furthermore, explicitly declaring a variable with a *var* statement can sometimes yield different results than allowing a variable to be declared *implicitly* (i.e., automatically). It's safest to declare first and use later (i.e., *explicit declaration*), as shown throughout this book.

Legal Variable Names

Before running off to make any variables, be aware that variable names:

- Must be composed exclusively of letters, numbers, and underscores. (No spaces, hyphens, or punctuation allowed.)

- Must start with a letter or an underscore.

- Must not exceed 255 characters. (Okay, okay, that's a lie, but reevaluate your naming scheme if your variable names exceed 255 characters.)

- Are case-insensitive (upper- and lowercase are treated identically but you should be consistent nonetheless).

These are legal variable names:

```
var first_name;
var counter;
var reallyLongVariableName;
```

These are illegal variable names that would cause errors:

```
var 1first_name;              // Starts with a number
var variable name with spaces; // Contains spaces
var another-illegal-name;     // Contains a hyphen
```

Creating dynamically named variables

Although you'll rarely, if ever, use dynamically created variable names, it's possible to generate the name of a variable programmatically. To create a variable name from any expression, use the *set* statement. For example, here we assign the value "bruce" to **player1name**:

```
var i = 1;
set ("player" + i + "name", "bruce");
```

Arrays and objects, discussed in later chapters, provide us with a much more powerful means of tracking dynamically named data and should be used instead of dynamic variable names.

Declare Variables at the Outset

It's good practice to declare your variables at the beginning of every movie's main script space, which is usually the first keyframe that comes after a movie's preloader. Be sure to add a comment explaining each variable's purpose for easy identification later. The beginning of a well-organized script might look like this:

```
// ^^^^^^^^^^^^^^^^^^^^^^
// Initialize variables
// ^^^^^^^^^^^^^^^^^^^^^^
var ballSpeed;    // Velocity of ball, max 10
var score;        // Player's current score
var hiScore;      // High score (not saved between sessions)
var player1;      // Name of player 1, supplied by user
```

We can give variables an initial value at the same time we create them, as follows:

```
var ballSpeed = 5;    // Velocity of ball, max 10
var score = 0;        // Player's current score
var hiScore = 0;      // High score (not saved between sessions)
```

Assigning Variables

Now comes the fun part—putting some data into our variables. If you're still playing along with the bank analogy, this is the "deposit money into our account" step. To assign a variable a value, we use:

```
variableName = value;
```

where *variableName* is the name of a variable, and *value* is the data we're assigning to that variable. Here's an applied example:

```
bookTitle = "ActionScript: The Definitive Guide";
```

On the left side of the equal sign, the word **bookTitle** is the variable's *name* (its *identifier*). On the right side of the equal sign, the phrase "ActionScript: The Definitive Guide" is the variable's *value*—the datum you're depositing. The equal sign itself is called the *assignment* operator. It tells Flash that you want to assign (i.e., deposit) whatever is on the right of the equal sign to the variable shown on the left. If the variable on the left doesn't exist yet, Flash creates it (though relying on the interpreter to implicitly create variables isn't recommended).

Here are two more variable assignment examples:

```
speed = 25;
output = "thank you";
```

The first example assigns the integer 25 to the variable **speed**, showing that variables can contain numbers as well as text. We'll see shortly that they can contain other kinds of data as well. The second example assigns the text "thank you" to the variable **output**. Notice that we use straight double quotation marks (" ") to delimit a text string in ActionScript.

Now let's look at a slightly more complicated example that assigns **y** the value of the expression 1 + 5:

```
y = 1 + 5;
```

When the statement **y = 1 + 5;** is executed, 1 is first added to 5, yielding 6, and then 6 is assigned to **y**. The expression on the right side of the equal sign is *evaluated* (calculated or resolved) before setting the variable on the left side equal to that result. Here we assign an expression that contains the variable **y** to another variable, **z**:

```
z = y + 4;
```

Once again, the expression on the right of the equal sign is evaluated and the result is then assigned to z. The interpreter retrieves the current value of y (it checks its account balance, so to speak) and adds 4 to it. Because the value of y is 6, z will be set to 10.

The syntax to assign any data—whether numbers, text, or any other type—to a variable is similar regardless of the datatype. For example, we haven't studied arrays yet, but you should already recognize the following as a variable assignment statement:

```
myList = ["John", "Joyce", "Sharon", "Rick", "Megan"];
```

As before, we put the variable name on the left, the assignment operator (the equal sign) in the middle, and our desired value on the right.

To assign the same value to multiple variables in a hurry, we may piggyback assignments alongside one another, like this:

```
x = y = z = 10;
```

Variable assignment always works from right to left. The preceding statement assigns 10 to z, then assigns the value of z to y, then assigns the value of y to x.

Changing and Retrieving Variable Values

After we've created a variable, we may assign and reassign its value as often as we like, as shown in Example 2-1.

Example 2-1. Changing Variable Values

```
var firstName;                     // Declare the variable firstName
firstName = "Graham";              // Set the value of firstName
firstName = "Gillian";             // Change the value of firstName
firstName = "Jessica";             // Change firstName again
firstName = "James";               // Change firstName again
var x = 10;                        // Declare x and assign a numeric value
x = "loading...please wait...";    // Assign x a text value
```

Notice that we changed the variable x's *datatype* from numeric to text data by simply assigning it a value of the desired type. Some programming languages don't allow the datatype of a variable to change but ActionScript does.

Of course, creating variables and assigning values to them is useless if you can't retrieve the values later. To retrieve a variable's value, simply use the variable's name wherever you want its value to be used. Anytime a variable's name appears (except in a declaration or on the left side of an assignment statement), the name is converted to the variable's value. Here are some examples:

```
newX = oldX + 5;  // Set newX to the value of oldX plus 5
ball._x = newX;   // Set the horizontal position of the
                  // ball movie clip to the value of newX
trace(firstName); // Display the value of firstName in the Output window
```

Note that in the expression `ball._x`, `ball` is a movie clip's name, and the `._x` indicates its x-coordinate property (i.e., horizontal position on stage). We'll learn more about properties later. The last line, `trace(firstName)`, displays a variable's value while a script is running, which is handy for debugging your code.

Checking Whether a Variable Has a Value

Occasionally we may wish to verify that a variable has been assigned a value before we make reference to it. As we learned earlier, a variable that has been declared but never assigned a value contains the special "non-value," `undefined`. To determine whether a variable has been assigned a value, we compare that variable's value to the `undefined` keyword. For example:

```
if (someVariable != undefined) {
   // Any code placed here is executed only if someVariable has a value
}
```

Note the use of the *inequality operator*, `!=`, which determines whether two values are *not* equal.

Types of Values

The data we use in ActionScript programming comes in a variety of types. So far we've seen numbers and text, but other types include Booleans, arrays, functions, and objects. Before we cover each datatype in detail, let's examine some datatype issues that specifically relate to variable usage.

Automatic Typing

Any ActionScript variable can contain any type of data, which may seem unremarkable, but the ability to store *any* kind of data in *any* variable is actually a bit unusual. Languages like C++ and Java use *typed* variables; each variable can accept only one type of data, which must be specified when the variable is declared. ActionScript variables are *automatically* typed—when we assign data to a variable, the interpreter sets the variable's datatype for us.

Not only can ActionScript variables contain any datatype, they can also dynamically *change* datatypes. If we assign a variable a new value that has a different type than the variable's previous value, the variable is automatically retyped. So the following code is legal in ActionScript:

```
x = 1;                    // x is a number
x = "Michael";            // x is now a string
x = [4, 6, "hello"];      // x is now an array
x = 2;                    // x is a number again
```

In languages like C++ or Java that do not support automatic retyping, data of the wrong type would be converted to the variable's existing datatype (or would cause an error if conversion could not be performed). Automatic and dynamic typing have some important ramifications that we'll consider in the following sections.

Automatic Value Conversion

In some contexts, ActionScript expects a specific type of data. If we use a variable whose value does not match the expected type, the interpreter attempts to convert the data. For example, if we use a text variable where a number is needed, the interpreter will try to convert the variable's text value to a numeric value for the sake of the current operation. In Example 2-2, z is set to 2. Why? Because the subtraction operator expects a number, so the value of y is converted from the string "4" to the number 4, which is subtracted from 6 (the value of x), yielding the result 2.

Example 2-2. Automatic String-to-Number Conversion

```
x = 6;      // x is a number, 6
y = "4";    // y is a string, "4"
z = x - y;  // This sets z to the number 2
```

Conversely, if we use a numeric variable where a string is expected, the interpreter attempts to convert the number to a string. In Example 2-3, z is set to the string "64", not the number 10. Why? Because the second operand in the expression x + y is a string. Therefore, the (+) performs string concatenation instead of mathematical addition. The value of x (6) is converted to the string "6" and then concatenated with the string "4" (the value of y), yielding the result "64".

Example 2-3. Automatic Number-to-String Conversion

```
x = 6;      // x is a number, 6
y = "4";    // y is a string, "4"
z = x + y;  // This sets z to the string "64"
```

The automatic type conversion that occurs when evaluating a variable as part of an expression is performed on a *copy* of the variable's data—it does not affect the original variable's type. A variable's type changes only when the variable is assigned a data value that does not match its previous value's type. So at the conclusion of Example 2-2 and Example 2-3, y remains a string, and x remains a number.

Notice that the operator on line 3 (– in Example 2-2, + in Example 2-3), has a profound impact on the value assigned to z. In Example 2-2 the string "4" becomes the number 4, whereas in Example 2-3 the opposite occurs (the number 6 becomes the string "6"), because the rules for datatype conversion are different for the + operator than for the – operator. We'll cover data conversion rules in Chapter 3, *Data and Datatypes*, and operators in Chapter 5, *Operators*.

Determining the Type Manually

Automatic datatyping and conversion can be convenient, but as Example 2-2 and Example 2-3 illustrate, may also produce unexpected results. Before performing commands that operate on mixed datatypes, you may wish to determine a variable's datatype using the *typeof* operator:

```
productName = "Macromedia Flash";  // String value
trace(typeof productName);         // Displays: "string"
```

Once we know a variable's type, we can proceed conditionally. Here, for example, we check whether a variable is a number before proceeding:

```
if (typeof age == "number"){
  // okay to carry on
} else {
    trace ("Age isn't a number");  // Display an error message
}
```

For full details on the *typeof* operator, see Chapter 5.

Variable Scope

Earlier we learned how to create variables and retrieve their values using variables attached to a single frame of the main timeline of a Flash document. When a document contains multiple frames and multiple movie clip timelines, variable creation and value retrieval becomes a little more complicated.

To illustrate why, let's consider several scenarios.

Scenario 1

Suppose we were to create a variable, **x**, in frame 1 of the main timeline. After creating **x**, we set its value to 10:

```
var x;
x = 10;
```

Then, in the next frame (frame 2), we attach the following code:

```
trace(x);
```

When we play our movie, does anything appear in the Output window? We created our variable in frame 1, but we're attempting to retrieve its value in frame 2; does our variable still exist? Yes.

When you define a variable on a timeline, that variable is accessible from all the other frames of that timeline.

Scenario 2

Suppose we create and set **x** as we did in Scenario 1, but instead of placing the variable-setting code on frame 1 directly, we place it on a button in frame 1. Then, on frame 2, we attach the same code as before:

```
trace(x);
```

Does Scenario 2 also work? Yes. Because **x** is attached to our button, and our button is attached to the main timeline, our variable is indirectly attached to the main timeline. We may, therefore, access the variable from frame 2 as we did before.

Scenario 3

Suppose we create a variable named **secretPassword** on frame 1 of the main timeline. When the movie plays, the user must guess the password in order to gain access to a special section of the movie.

In addition to declaring **secretPassword** on frame 1, we create a function that compares the user's guess to the real password. Here's our code:

```
var secretPassword;
secretPassword = "yppah";

function checkPassword() {
  if (userPassword == secretPassword) {
    gotoAndStop("accessGranted");
  } else {
    gotoAndStop("accessDenied");
  }
}
```

Suppose we ask the user to enter her password on frame 30. She enters a password into an input text field variable named **userPassword**, which we compare to our **secretPassword** variable using the *checkPassword()* function on frame 1. If our password-checking code is defined on frame 1, but **userPassword** isn't defined until frame 30, does the **userPassword** variable exist when we call our *checkPassword()* function?

The answer, again, is yes. Even though **userPassword** is defined on a later frame than our *checkPassword()* function, it is still part of the same timeline.

 Any variable declared on a timeline is available to all the scripts of its timeline for as long as that timeline exists.

Variable Accessibility (Scope)

The three scenarios presented earlier explore issues of *scope*. A variable's scope describes when and where the variable can be manipulated by the code in a movie. A variable's scope defines its life span and its accessibility to other blocks of code in our scripts. To determine a variable's scope, we must answer two questions: (a) how long does the variable exist? and (b) from where in our code can we set or retrieve the variable's value?

In traditional programming, variables are often broken into two general scope categories: *global* and *local*. Variables that are accessible throughout an entire program are called *global variables*. Variables that are accessible only to limited sections of a program are called *local variables*. Though Flash supports conventional local variables, it does not support true global variables. Let's find out why.

Movie Clip Variables

As we saw in the three earlier scenarios, a variable defined on a timeline is available to all the scripts on that timeline—from the first frame to the last frame—whether the variable is declared on a frame or a button. But what happens if we have more than one timeline in a movie, as described in Scenario 4?

Scenario 4

Suppose we have two basic geometric shapes, a square and a circle, defined as movie clip symbols.

On frame 1 of the square clip symbol, we set the variable **x** to 3:

```
var x;
x = 3;
```

On frame 1 of the circle clip symbol, we set the variable **y** to 4:

```
var y;
y = 4;
```

We place instances of those clips on frame 1, layer 1 of the main timeline of our movie and name our instances `square` and `circle`.

First question: If we attach the following code to frame 1 of the *main* movie timeline (upon which `square` and `circle` have been placed), what appears in the Output window? Here's the code:

```
trace(x);
trace(y);
```

Answer: Nothing appears in the Output window. The variables **x** and **y** are defined on the timelines of our movie clips, *not* our main timeline.

Variables attached to a movie clip timeline (like that of `square` or `circle`) have scope limited to that timeline. They are not directly accessible to scripts on other timelines, such as our main movie timeline.

Second question: If we were to place the `trace(x)` and `trace(y)` statements on frame 1 of our `square` movie clip instead of frame 1 of our main movie timeline, what would appear in the Output window?

Answer: The value of `x`, which is 3, and nothing else. The value of `x` is displayed because `x` is defined on the timeline of `square` and is therefore accessible to the *trace()* command, which also resides on that timeline. But the value of `y`, which is 4, doesn't appear in the Output window because `y` is defined in `circle`, which is a separate timeline.

You can now see why I said that ActionScript doesn't support true global variables. Global variables are variables that are accessible throughout an entire program, but in Flash, a variable attached to an individual timeline is directly accessible only to the scripts on that timeline. Since all variables in Flash are defined on timelines, no variable can be guaranteed to be directly accessible to *all* the scripts in a movie. Hence, no variable can legitimately be called *global*.

To prevent confusion, we refer to variables attached to timelines as *timeline variables* or *movie clip variables*. However, it is possible to simulate global variables using the *Object* class. To create a variable that is available on all timelines, use the following statement:

```
Object.prototype.myGlobalVariable = myValue;
```

For example:

```
Object.prototype.msg = "Hello world";
```

This technique (and the reason it works) is discussed under "The end of the inheritance chain" in Chapter 12, *Objects and Classes*.

Accessing Variables on Different Timelines

Even though variables on one timeline are not directly accessible to the scripts on other timelines, they are indirectly accessible. To create, retrieve, or assign a variable on a separate timeline, we use *dot syntax*, a standard notation common to object-oriented programming languages such as Java, C++, and JavaScript. Here's the generic dot syntax phrasing we use to address a variable on a separate timeline:

```
movieClipInstanceName.variableName
```

That is, we refer to a variable on another timeline using the name of the clip that contains the variable, followed by a dot, then the variable name itself. In our earlier scenario, for example, from the main timeline we would refer to the variable x in the square clip as:

```
square.x
```

Again, from the main timeline, we refer to the variable y in the circle clip as:

```
circle.y
```

We can use these references from our main movie timeline to assign and retrieve variables in square like this:

```
square.z = 5;       // Assign 5 to z in square
var mainZ;          // Create mainZ on the main timeline
mainZ = square.z;   // Assign mainZ the value of z in square
```

However, with just the *clip.variable* syntax alone, we can't refer to variables in square from our circle clip. If we were to put a reference to square.x on a frame in circle, the interpreter would try to find a clip called square *inside* of circle, but square lives on the main timeline. So, we need a mechanism that lets us refer to the timeline that contains the square clip (in this case, the main timeline) from the circle clip. That mechanism comes in the form of two special properties: _root and _parent.

The _root and _parent properties

The _root property is a direct reference to the main timeline of a movie. From any depth of nesting in a movie clip structure, we can always address variables on the main movie timeline using _root, like this:

```
_root.mainZ        // Access the variable mainZ on the main timeline
_root.firstName    // Access the variable firstName on the main timeline
```

We can even combine a reference to _root with references to movie clip instances, drilling down the nested structure of a movie in the process. For example, we can address the variable x inside the clip square that resides on the main movie timeline, as:

```
_root.square.x
```

That reference works from anywhere in our movie, no matter what the depth of clip nesting, because the reference starts at our main movie timeline, _root. Here's another nested example showing how to access the variable area in the instance triangle that resides on the timeline of the instance shapes:

```
_root.shapes.triangle.area
```

Any reference to a variable that starts with the `_root` keyword is called an *absolute reference* because it describes the location of our variable in relation to a fixed, immutable point in our movie: the main timeline.

There are times, however, when we want to refer to variables on other timelines without referring to the main timeline of a movie. To do so, we use the `_parent` property, which refers to the timeline upon which the current movie clip instance resides. For example, from code attached to a frame of the clip `square`, we can refer to variables on the timeline that *contains* `square` using this syntax:

```
_parent.myVariable
```

References that start with the keyword `_parent` are called *relative references* because they are resolved *relative* to the location of the clip in which they occur.

Returning to our earlier example, suppose we have a variable, `size`, defined on the main timeline of a movie. We place a clip instance named `shapes` on our main movie timeline, and on the `shapes` timeline we define the variable `color`. Also on the `shapes` timeline, we place a clip named `triangle`, as shown in Figure 2-1.

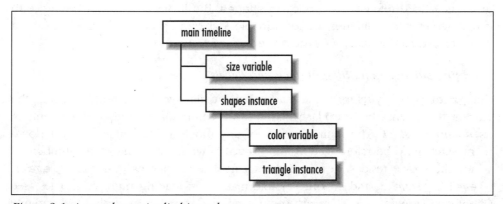

Figure 2-1. A sample movie clip hierarchy

To display the value of the variable `color` (which is in the `shapes` clip) from code attached to the timeline of `triangle`, we could use an absolute reference starting at the main timeline, like this:

```
trace(_root.shapes.color);
```

But that ties our code to the main movie timeline. To make our code more flexible, we could instead use the `_parent` property to create a relative reference, like this:

```
trace(_parent.color);
```

Our first approach (using _root) works from a top-down perspective; it starts at the main timeline and descends through the movie clip hierarchy until it reaches the color variable. The second approach (using _parent) works from a bottom-up perspective; it starts with the clip that contains the *trace()* statement (the triangle clip), then ascends one level up the clip structure where it finds the color variable.

We can use _parent twice in a row to ascend the hierarchy of clips and access our size variable on the main timeline. Here we attach some code to triangle that refers to size on the main movie timeline:

```
trace(_parent._parent.size);
```

Using the _parent property twice in succession takes us up two levels, which in this context brings us to the main timeline of the movie.

Your approach to variable addressing will depend on what you want to happen when you place instances of a movie clip symbol on various timelines. In our triangle example, if we wanted our reference to color to always point to color as defined in the shapes clip, then we would use the _root syntax, which gives us a fixed reference to color in shapes. But if we wanted our reference to color to refer to a different color variable, depending on which timeline held a given triangle instance, we would use the _parent syntax.

Accessing variables on different document levels

The _root property refers to the main movie timeline of the current level (i.e., the current document), but the Flash Player can accommodate multiple documents in its *document stack*. The main timeline of any movie loaded in the Player document stack may be referenced using _level*n*, where *n* is the level number on which the movie resides. Level numbers start with 0, such as _level0, _level1, _level2, _level3, and so on. For information on loading multiple movies, see Chapter 13, *Movie Clips*. Here are some examples showing multiple-level variable addressing:

```
_level1.firstName          // firstName on level1's main timeline
_level4.ball.area          // area in ball clip on level4's main timeline
_level0.guestBook.email    // email in guestBook clip on level0's timeline
```

When addressing variables across movie clip instance timelines using dot syntax, make sure that you have named your clip instances on the Stage and entered the names correctly when referring to them in your code. If your instances are not named, your code will not work even if it is otherwise syntactically correct. Unnamed instances and misspelled instance names are extremely common sources of problems.

Flash 4 versus Flash 5 variable access syntax

The Flash 4–style slash-colon constructions such as `/square:area` have been superseded by Flash 5's dot syntax, a much more convenient way to refer to variables and timelines. The old syntax is deprecated and no longer recommended. Table 2-1 shows equivalencies between Flash 4 and Flash 5 syntax when addressing variables. See Appendix C, *Backward Compatibility*, for other syntactical differences.

Table 2-1. Flash 4 Versus Flash 5 Variable Addressing Syntax

Flash 4 Syntax	Flash 5 Syntax	Refers to . . .
`/`	`_root`	Movie's main timeline
`/:x`	`_root.x`	Variable `x` on movie's main timeline
`/clip1:x`	`_root.clip1.x`	Variable `x` in instance `clip1` on movie's main timeline
`/clip1/clip2:x`	`_root.clip1.clip2.x`	Variable `x` in instance `clip2` within instance `clip1` within the main movie timeline
`../`	`_parent`	Timeline upon which the current clip resides (one level up from current clip timeline*)
`../:x`	`_parent.x`	Variable `x` on timeline upon which the current clip resides (one level up from current clip timeline)
`../../:x`	`_parent._parent.x`	Variable `x` on timeline that contains the clip that contains the current clip (two levels up from current clip timeline)
`clip1:x`	`clip1.x`	Variable `x` in instance `clip1`, where `clip1` resides on the current timeline
`clip1/clip2:x`	`clip1.clip2.x`	Variable `x` in instance `clip2`, where `clip2` resides within `clip1`, which, in turn, resides on current timeline
`_level1:x`	`_level1.x`	Variable `x` on the main timeline of a movie loaded onto level 1
`_level2:x`	`_level2.x`	Variable `x` on the main timeline of a movie loaded onto level 2

* The "current clip timeline" is the timeline that contains the code with the variable reference.

Movie Clip Variable Life Span

Earlier, we said that the scope of a variable answers two questions: (a) how long does the variable exist? and (b) from where in our code can we set or retrieve the variable's value? For movie clip variables, we now know the factors involved in answering the second question. But we skipped answering the first question. Let's return to it now with one final variable-coding scenario.

Scenario 5

Suppose we create a new movie with two keyframes. On frame 1, we place a clip instance, `ball`. On the `ball` timeline, we create a variable, `radius`. Frame 2 of our main timeline is blank (the `ball` instance is not present there).

From frame 1 of the main movie timeline, we can find out the value of `radius` using this code:

```
trace(ball.radius);
```

Now the question: If we move that line of code from frame 1 to frame 2 of the main timeline, what appears in the Output window when our movie plays?

Answer: Nothing appears. When the `ball` clip is removed from the main timeline on frame 2, all its variables are destroyed in the process.

 Movie clip variables last only while the clip in which they reside is present on stage. Variables defined on the main timeline of a Flash document persist within each document but are lost if the document is unloaded from the Player (either via the *unloadMovie()* function or because another movie is loaded into the movie's level).

A variable's life span is important when scripting movies that contain movie clips placed across multiple frames on various timelines. Always make sure that any clip you're addressing is present on a timeline before you try to use the variables in that clip.

Local Variables

Movie clip variables are scoped to movie clips and persist as long as the movie clip on which they are defined exists. Sometimes, that's longer than we need them to live. For situations in which we need a variable only temporarily, ActionScript offers variables with *local* scope (i.e., local variables), which live for a much shorter time than normal movie clip variables.

Local variables are used in functions and older Flash 4–style subroutines. If you haven't worked with functions or subroutines before, you can skip the rest of this section and come back to it once you've read Chapter 9, *Functions*.

Functions often employ variables that are not needed outside the function. For example, suppose we have a function that displays all of the elements of a specified array:

```
function displayElements(theArray) {
   var counter = 0;
   while(counter < theArray.length) {
      trace("Element " + counter + ": " + theArray[counter]);
      counter++;
   }
}
```

The `counter` variable is required to display the array but has no use thereafter. We could leave it defined on the timeline, but that's bad form for two reasons: (a) if `counter` persists, it takes up memory during the rest of our movie; and (b) if `counter` is accessible outside our function, it may conflict with other variables named `counter`. We would, therefore, like `counter` to die after the *displayElements()* function has finished.

To cause `counter` to be automatically deleted at the end of our function, we define it as a *local variable*. Unlike movie clip variables, local variables are removed from memory (*deallocated*) automatically by the interpreter when the function that defines them finishes.

To specify that a variable should be local, declare it with the *var* keyword from inside your function, as in the preceding *displayElements()* example.

Take heed though; when placed *outside* of a function, the *var* statement creates a normal timeline variable, not a local variable. As shown in Example 2-4, the location of the *var* statement makes all the difference.

Variables within functions need not be local. We can create or change a movie clip variable from inside a function by omitting the *var* keyword. If we do not use the *var* keyword, but instead simply assign a value to a variable, Flash treats that variable as a nonlocal variable under some conditions. Consider this variable assignment inside a function:

```
function setHeight(){
   height = 10;
}
```

The effect of the statement `height = 10;` depends on whether `height` is a local variable or movie clip variable. If `height` is a previously declared local variable (which it is not in the example at hand), the statement `height = 10;` simply modifies the local variable's value. If there is no local variable named `height`, as is the case here, the interpreter creates a movie clip (nonlocal) variable named `height` and sets its value to 10. As a nonlocal variable, `height` persists even after the function finishes.

Example 2-4 demonstrates local and nonlocal variable usage.

Example 2-4. Local and Nonlocal Variables

```
var x = 5;                          // New nonlocal variable, x, is now 5
function variableDemo(){
   x = 10;                          // Nonlocal variable, x, is now 10
   y = 20;                          // New nonlocal variable, y, is now 20
   var z = 30;                      // New local variable, z, is now 30
   trace(x + "," + y + "," + z);    // Send variable values to Output window
}
variableDemo();    // Call our function. Displays: 10,20,30
trace(x);          // Displays: 10 (reassignment in our function was permanent)
trace(y);          // Displays: 20 (nonlocal variable, y, still exists)
trace(z);          // Displays nothing (local variable, z, has expired)
```

Note that it is possible (though confusing and ill-advised) to have both a local and
a nonlocal variable that share the same name within a script but have different
scopes. Example 2-5 shows such a case.

Example 2-5. Local and Nonlocal Variables with the Same Name

```
var myColor = "blue";
function hexRed(){
   var myColor = "#FF0000";
   return myColor;
}
trace(hexRed());    // Displays: #FF0000 (the local variable myColor)
trace(myColor);     // Displays: "blue" (setting the local variable,
                    // myColor, to #FF0000 did not affect the nonlocal version)
```

Local variables in subroutines

Although functions are the preferred mechanism for producing portable code
modules, Flash 5 still supports Flash 4–style *subroutines*. In Flash 4, a subroutine
could be created by attaching a block of code to a frame with a label. Later, the
subroutine could be executed remotely via the *Call* action. But in Flash 4, any
variable declared in a subroutine was nonlocal and persisted for the lifetime of the
timeline on which it was defined. In Flash 5, you can create local variables in subroutines the same way we created them in functions—using the *var* statement.
However, variables defined with *var* in a subroutine are created as local variables
only when the subroutine is executed via the *Call* function. If the script on the
subroutine frame is executed as a result of the playhead simply entering the frame,
the *var* statement declares a normal timeline nonlocal variable. Regardless, the
more modern functions and local function variables should be used instead of subroutines.

Some Applied Examples

We've had an awful lot of variable theory. How about showing some of these concepts in use? The following examples provide three variable-centric code samples. Refer to the comments for an explanation of the code.

Example 2-6 chooses a random destination for the playhead of a movie.

Example 2-6. Send the Playhead to a Random Frame on the Current Timeline

```
var randomFrame;        // Stores the randomly picked frame number
var numFrames;          // Stores the total number of frames on the timeline
numFrames = _totalframes;   // Assign _totalframes property to numFrames

// Pick a random frame
randomFrame = Math.floor(Math.random() * numFrames + 1);

gotoAndStop(randomFrame);   // Send playhead to chosen random frame
```

Example 2-7 determines the distance between two clips. A working version of this example is available from the online Code Depot.

Example 2-7. Calculate the Distance Between Two Movie Clips

```
var c;          // A convenient reference to the circle clip object
var s;          // A convenient reference to the square clip object
var deltaX;     // The horizontal distance between c and s
var deltaY;     // The vertical distance between c and s
var dist;       // The total distance between c and s

c = _root.circle;       // Get reference to the circle clip
s = _root.square;       // Get reference to the square clip
deltaX = c._x - s._x;   // Compute the horizontal distance between the clips
deltaY = c._y - s._y;   // Compute the vertical distance between the clips

// The distance is the root of (deltaX squared plus deltaY squared).
dist = Math.sqrt((deltaX * deltaX) + (deltaY * deltaY));

// Tidy references are much more readable than the alternative:
dist = Math.sqrt(((_root.circle._x - _root.square._x) * (_root.circle._x -
_root.square._x)) + ((_root.circle._y - _root.square._y) * (_root.circle._y -
_root.square._y)));
```

Example 2-8 converts between Fahrenheit and Celsius. A working version is available in the online Code Depot.

Example 2-8. A Fahrenheit/Celsius Temperature Converter

```
var fahrenheit;         // Temperature in Fahrenheit
var celsius;            // Temperature in Celsius
var convertDirection;   // The system we are converting to.
                        // Legal values are "fahrenheit" and "celsius"
fahrenheit = 451;           // Set a Fahrenheit temperature
celsius = 20;               // Set a Celsius temperature
convertDirection = "celsius";   // Convert to Celsius in this case
```

Example 2-8. A Fahrenheit/Celsius Temperature Converter (continued)

```
if (convertDirection == "fahrenheit") {
   result = (celsius * 1.8) + 32;   // Calculate the Celsius value.
   // Display the result
   trace (celsius + " degrees Celsius is " + result + " degrees Fahrenheit.");
} else if (convertDirection == "celsius") {
   result = (fahrenheit - 32) / 1.8;   // Calculate the Fahrenheit value.
   // Display the result
   trace (fahrenheit + " degrees Fahrenheit is " + result + " degrees Celsius.");
} else {
   trace ("Invalid conversion direction.");
}
```

Onward!

Now that we know all there is to know about storing information in variables, it's time we learn something more about the content that variables store: *data*. Over the next three chapters, we'll learn what data is, how it can be manipulated, and why it's an essential part of nearly everything we build with ActionScript.

3

Data and Datatypes

Having worked with variable values in Chapter 2, *Variables*, we've already had a casual introduction to data, the information we manipulate in our scripts. In this chapter, we'll explore data in more depth, learning how ActionScript defines, categorizes, and stores data. We'll also see how to create and classify data.

Data Versus Information

In the broadest sense, *data* is anything that can be stored by a computer, from words and numbers to images, video, and sound. All computer data is stored as a sequence of ones and zeros, which you might recognize from high-tech marketing materials:

```
0101010101010101101010110110101010101010100000101010101010110101010
1010101010101010111010101010101010101010101010101011111010101010101010101
010101010101010101010101010110101010101010101010101010101010101010101010
```

Data is information in its crude state—raw and meaningless. Information, on the other hand, has meaning. Consider, for example, the number 8008898969. As raw data it isn't very meaningful, but when we classify it semantically as the telephone number (800) 889-8969, the data becomes useful information.

In this chapter we'll see how to add meaning to raw computer data so that it becomes human-comprehensible information.

Retaining Meaning with Datatypes

How do we store information as raw data in a computer without losing meaning? By categorizing our data and defining its datatype, we give it context that defines its meaning.

For example, suppose we have three numbers: 5155534, 5159592, and 4593030. By categorizing our data—as, say, a phone number, fax number, and parcel tracking number—the context (and, hence, the meaning) of our data is preserved. When categorized, each of the otherwise-nondescript seven-digit numbers becomes meaningful.

Programming languages use *datatypes* to provide rudimentary categories for our data. For example, nearly all programming languages define datatypes to store and manipulate text (a.k.a. *strings*) and numbers. To distinguish between multiple numbers, we can use well-conceived variable names, such as `phoneNumber` and `faxNumber`. In more complex situations, we can create our own custom data categories with *objects* and *object classes* as covered later. Before we think about making our own data categories, let's see which categories come built into ActionScript.

The ActionScript Datatypes

When programming, we may want to store a product name, a background color, or the number of stars to be placed in a night sky. We use the following ActionScript datatypes to store our data:

- For text sequences like "`hi there,`" ActionScript provides the *string* datatype. A *string* is a series of characters (alphanumerics and punctuation).

- For numbers, such as 351 and 7.5, ActionScript provides the *number* datatype. Numbers are used for counting and for mathematical equations.

- For logical decisions, ActionScript provides the *Boolean* datatype. With Boolean data, we can represent or record the status of some condition or the result of some comparison. Boolean data has only two legal values: `true` and `false`.

- For representing an *absence* of data, ActionScript provides two special data values: `null` and `undefined`. You can think of them as the only permissible values of the *null* and *undefined* datatypes.

- For lists of individual pieces of data, ActionScript provides the *array* datatype.

- For manipulating movie clip instances, ActionScript provides the *movieclip* datatype.

- And lastly, for arbitrary built-in or user-defined classes of data, ActionScript provides the highly powerful *object* datatype.

Every piece of data we store in ActionScript will fall into one of those categories. Before studying each datatype in Chapter 4, *Primitive Datatypes*, we'll consider the general issues that affect our use of all data.

Creating and Categorizing Data

There are two ways to create a new datum with ActionScript, both methods requiring the use of *expressions*—phrases of code that represent data in our scripts.

A *literal expression* (or *literal* for short) is a series of letters, numbers, and punctuation that *is* the datum. A data literal is a verbatim description of data in a program's source code. This contrasts with a variable, which is a container that merely holds a datum. Each datatype defines its own rules for the creation of literals. Here are some examples of literals:

```
"loading...please wait"   // A string literal
1.51                      // A numeric literal
["jane", "jonathan"]      // An array literal
```

Note that movie clips cannot be represented by literals, but are referred to by instance names.

We can also generate data programmatically with a *complex expression*. Complex expressions represent data as a phrase of code with a value that must be calculated or computed, not taken literally. The calculated value is the datum being represented. For example, each of these complex expressions results in a single datum:

```
1999 + 1        // Yields the datum 2000
"hi " + "ma!"   // Yields the datum "hi ma!"
firstName       // Yields the value of the variable firstName
_currentframe   // Yields the frame number of the playhead's current position
new Date()      // Yields a new Date object with the current date and time
```

Notice that an individual literal expression like 1999 or 1 can be a valid part of a larger complex expression, as in *1999 + 1*.

Whether we use a literal expression or a complex expression to create data, we must store every datum that we want to use later. The result of the expression **"hi" + "ma!"** is lost unless we store it, say, in a variable. For example:

```
// This datum is fleeting, and dies immediately after it's created
"hi " + "ma";

// This datum is stored in a variable and can be
// accessed later via the variable welcomeMessage
var welcomeMessage = "hi " + "ma";
```

How do we categorize data into the appropriate type? That is, how do we specify that a datum is a number, a string, an array, or whatever? In most cases, we don't categorize new data ourselves; the ActionScript interpreter automatically assigns or infers each datum's type based on a set of internal rules.

Automatic Literal Typing

The interpreter infers a literal datum's type by examining its syntax, as explained in the comments in the following code fragment:

```
"animal"       // Quotation marks identify "animal" as a string
1.35           // If it contains only integers and a decimal, it is a number
true           // Special keyword true identifies this as a Boolean
null           // Special keyword null identifies this as the null type
undefined      // Special keyword undefined identifies the undefined type

["hello", 2, true]    // Square brackets and values separated by commas
                      // indicate that this is an array

{x: 234, y: 456}      // Curly braces and property name/value pairs separated
                      // by commas indicate that this is an object
```

As you can see, using correct syntax with data literals is extremely important. Incorrect syntax may cause an error or result in the misinterpretation of a datum's content. For example:

```
animal    // Missing quotes--animal is interpreted as a variable,
          // not a string of text
"1.35"    // Numbers in quotes are treated as strings, not numbers
1. 35     // Space before the 3 causes an error
"animal   // Missing closing quotation mark causes an error
```

Automatic Complex Expression Typing

The interpreter computes an expression's value in order to determine its datatype. Consider this example:

```
pointerX = _xmouse;
```

Because **_xmouse** stores the location of the mouse pointer as a number, the type of the expression **_xmouse** will always be a number, so the variable **pointerX** also becomes a number.

Usually, the datatype automatically determined by the interpreter matches what we expect and want. However, some ambiguous cases require us to understand the rules that the interpreter uses to determine an expression's datatype (see Example 2-2 and Example 2-3). Consider the following expression:

```
"1" + 2;
```

The operand on the left of the + is a string ("1"), but the operand on the right is a number (2). The + operator works on both numbers (addition) and strings (concatenation). Should the value of the expression *"1" + 2* be the number 3, or the string "12"? To resolve the ambiguity, the interpreter relies on a fixed rule: the plus operator (+) always favors strings over numbers, so the expression *"1" + 2* evaluates to the string "12", not the number 3. This rule is arbitrary, but it provides a consistent way to interpret the code. The rule was chosen with typical uses of the plus operator in mind: if one of the operands is a string, it's likely that we want to concatenate the operands, not add them numerically, as in this case:

```
trace ("The value of x is: " + x);
```

Combining disparate types of data or using a datum in a context that does not match the expected datatype causes ambiguity. This forces the interpreter to perform an automatic datatype *conversion* according to arbitrary, but predictable, rules. Let's examine the cases in which automatic conversions will occur and what the expected results are of converting a datum from one type to another.

Datatype Conversion

Take a closer look at the example from the previous section. In that example, each datum—"1" and 2—belonged to its own datatype; the first was a string and the second a number. We saw that the interpreter joined the two values together to form the string "12". Note that the interpreter first had to *convert* the *number* 2 into the *string* "2". Only after that automatic conversion was performed could the value "2" be joined (concatenated) to the string "1".

Datatype conversion simply means changing the type of a datum. Not all datatype conversions are automatic; we may also change a datum's type explicitly in order to override the default datatyping that ActionScript would otherwise perform.

Automatic Type Conversion

Whenever we use a value in a context that does not match its datatype, the interpreter attempts a conversion. That is, if the interpreter expects data of type A, and we provide data of type B, the interpreter will attempt to convert our type B data into type A data. For example, in the following code we use the string "Flash" as the righthand operand of the subtraction operator. Since only numbers may be used with the subtraction operator, the interpreter attempts to convert the string "Flash" into a number:

```
999 - "Flash";
```

Of course, the string "Flash" can't be successfully converted into any legitimate number, so it is converted into the special numeric data value NaN (i.e., Not-a-Number). NaN is a legal value of the *number* datatype, intended specifically to handle such a situation. With "Flash" converted to NaN, our expression ends up looking like this to the interpreter (though we never see this internal step):

```
999 - NaN;
```

Both operands of the subtraction operator are now numbers, so the operation can proceed: 999 – NaN yields the value NaN, which is the final value of our expression.

An expression that yields the numeric value NaN isn't particularly useful; most conversions have more functional results. For example, if a string contains only numeric characters, it can be converted into a useful number. The expression:

```
999 - "9";   // The number 999 minus the string "9"
```

converts internally to:

```
999 - 9;     // The number 999 minus the number 9
```

which yields the value 990 when the expression is resolved. Automatic conversion is most common with the plus operator, the equality operator, the comparison operators, and conditional or loop statements. In order to be sure of the result of any expression that involves automatic conversion, we have to answer three questions: (a) what is the expected datatype of the current context? (b) what happens when an unexpected datatype is supplied in that context? and (c) when conversion occurs, what is the resulting value?

To answer the first and second questions, we need to consult the appropriate topics elsewhere in this book (e.g., to determine what datatype is expected in a conditional statement, see Chapter 7, *Conditionals*).

The next three tables, which list the rules of automatic conversion, answer the third question, "When conversion occurs, what is the resulting value?" Table 3-1 shows the results of converting each datatype to a number.

Table 3-1. Converting to a Number

Original Data	Result After Conversion
undefined	0
null	0
Boolean	1 if the original value is true; 0 if the original value is false
Numeric string	Equivalent numeric value if string is composed only of base-10 numbers, whitespace, exponent, decimal point, plus sign, or minus sign (e.g., "−1.485e2")
Other strings	Empty strings, non-numeric strings, including strings starting with "x", "0x", or "FF", convert to NaN
"Infinity"	Infinity
"-Infinity"	-Infinity
"NaN"	NaN
Array	NaN
Object	The return value of the object's *valueOf()* method
Movieclip	NaN

Table 3-2 shows the results of converting each datatype to a string.

Table 3-2. Converting to a String

Original Data	Result After Conversion
`undefined`	`""` (the empty string).
`null`	`"null"`.
Boolean	`"true"` if the original value was `true`; `"false"` if the original value was `false`.
NaN	`"NaN"`.
0	`"0"`.
`Infinity`	`"Infinity"`.
`-Infinity`	`"-Infinity"`.
Other numeric value	String equivalent of the number. For example, `944.345` becomes `"944.345"`.
Array	A comma-separated list of element values.
Object	The value that results from calling *toString()* on the object. By default, the *toString()* method of an object returns `"[object Object]"`. The *toString()* method can be customized to return a more useful result (e.g., *toString()* of a *Date* object returns: `"Sun May 14 11:38:10 EDT 2000"`).
Movieclip	The path to the movie clip instance, given in absolute terms starting with the document level in the Player. For example, `"_level0.ball"`.

Table 3-3 shows the results of converting each datatype to a Boolean.

Table 3-3. Converting to a Boolean

Original Data	Result After Conversion
`undefined`	`false`
`null`	`false`
NaN	`false`
0	`false`
`Infinity`	`true`
`-Infinity`	`true`
Other numeric value	`true`
Nonempty string	`true` if the string can be converted to a valid nonzero number, `false` if not; in ECMA-262, a non-empty string always converts to `true` (Flash 5 breaks the rules in order to maintain compatibility with Flash 4)
Empty string (`""`)	`false`
Array	`true`
Object	`true`
Movieclip	`true`

Explicit Type Conversion

If the automatic (implicit) type-conversion rules do not suit our purpose, we can manually (explicitly) change a datum's type. When we take matters into our own hands, we must remember that the rules listed in the preceding tables still apply.

Converting to a string with the toString() method

We can invoke the *toString()* method to convert any datum to a string. For example:

```
x.toString();      // Get the string value of the variable x.
(523).toString();  // Returns "523". Note that we use parentheses
                   // so that the "." isn't treated as a decimal point
```

When we invoke the *toString()* method on a number, we may also provide a numeric argument indicating the base of the number system in which we'd like the converted string to be represented. This provides a handy means of switching between hexadecimal, decimal, and octal numbers. For example:

```
var myColor = 255;
var hexColor = myColor.toString(16);  // Sets hexColor to "ff"
```

Converting to a string with the String() function

The *String()* function has the same result as the *toString()* method, but uses a different grammar:

```
String(x);    // Convert x to a string
String(523);  // Convert 523 to the string "523"
```

Don't confuse the global *String()* function with the built-in class constructor of the same name. Both are described in Part III, *Language Reference*.

Converting to a string with empty string concatenation

Because the plus operator (+) favors strings in its automatic conversion rules, adding " " to any datum converts that datum to a string.

```
x + "";    // Convert x to a string
523 + "";  // Convert 523 to the string "523"
```

Converting to a number with the Number() function

Just as the *String()* function converts data to the string type, the *Number()* function converts its argument to the *number* type. When conversion to a real number is impossible or illogical, the *Number()* function returns a special numeric value as described in Table 3-1. Some examples:

```
Number(age);      // Yields the value of age converted to a number
Number("29");     // Yields the number 29
Number("sara");   // Yields NaN
```

Don't confuse the global *Number()* function with the built-in class constructor of the same name. Both are described in Part III.

Because user input in on-screen text fields always belong to the string type, it's necessary to convert text fields to numbers when performing mathematical calculations. For example, if we want to find the sum of the text fields `price1` and `price2`, we use:

```
totalCost = Number(price1) + Number(price2);
```

Otherwise, `price1` and `price2` will be concatenated as strings, not added as numbers. For more information on text fields, see Chapter 18, *On-Screen Text Fields.*

Converting to a number by subtracting zero

To trick the interpreter into converting a datum to a number, we can subtract zero from that datum. Again, the conversion follows the rules described in Table 3-1:

```
"953" - 0      // Yields 953
"molly" - 0    // Yields NaN
x - 0          // Yields the value of x converted to a number
```

Converting to a number using the parseInt() and parseFloat() functions

The *parseInt()* and *parseFloat()* functions convert a string containing numbers and letters into a number. The *parseInt()* function extracts the first integer that appears in a string, provided that the string's first non-blank character is a legal numeric character. Otherwise, *parseInt()* yields NaN. The number extracted via *parseInt()* starts with the first non-blank character in the string and ends with the character before either the first non-numeric character or the first occurrence of a decimal point.

Some *parseInt()* examples:

```
parseInt("1a")                 // Extracts 1
parseInt("1.3a"                // Extracts 1
parseInt("    1a")             // Extracts 1
parseInt("I am 14 years old")  // Yields NaN (the first non-blank
                               // character is not a number)
parseInt("14 years old")       // Extracts 14
```

The *parseFloat()* function extracts the first floating-point number that appears in a string, provided that the string's first non-blank character is a valid numeric character. (A floating-point number is a positive or negative number that contains a decimal value, such as −10.5 or 345.678.) Like *parseInt()*, *parseFloat()* yields the special numeric value NaN if the string's first non-blank character is not a valid numeric character. The number extracted by *parseFloat()* is a series of characters that starts with the first non-blank character in the string and ends with the character before the first non-numeric character (any character other than +, -, 0–9, or a decimal point).

Some *parseFloat()* examples:

```
parseFloat("1.3a");              // Extracts 1.3
parseFloat("2.75 years old")     // Extracts 2.75
parseFloat("1nce upon a time")   // Extracts 1
parseFloat("I'm 3.5 feet tall")  // Yields NaN
```

For more information on *parseInt()* and *parseFloat()*, see Part III.

Converting to a Boolean

When we want to convert a datum to a Boolean, we can use the global *Boolean()* function, which uses similar syntax to the *String()* and *Number()* functions. For example:

```
Boolean(5);   // The result is true
Boolean(x);   // Converts value of x to a Boolean
```

Don't confuse the global *Boolean()* function with the built-in class constructor of the same name. Both are described in Part III.

Conversion Duration

All type conversions performed on variables, array elements, and object properties are temporary unless the conversion happens as part of an assignment. Here we see a temporary conversion:

```
var x = "10";       // x is a string
y = x - 5;          // y is now 5; x's value was converted to a number
trace(typeof x);    // Displays: "string"; the conversion was temporary
```

Here we see a permanent conversion that is the result of an assignment:

```
x = "10";           // x is a string
x = x - 5;          // x is converted to a number
trace(typeof x);    // Displays: "number". The conversion was permanent because
                    // it occurred as part of an assignment.
```

Flash 4-to-Flash 5 Datatype Conversion

In Flash 4, the string operators and the numeric operators were completely distinct—one set of operators worked only with numbers, and a second set worked only with strings. For example, the string concatenation operator in Flash 4 was &, but the mathematical addition operator was +. Similarly, string comparisons were done with the eq and ne operators, but numeric comparisons were accomplished via = and <>. Table 3-4 lists the Flash 5 syntax for analogous Flash 4 operators.

Table 3-4. Flash 4 Versus Flash 5 Operators

Operation	Flash 4 Syntax	Flash 5 Syntax
String concatenation	&	+ or *add*
String equality	eq	==
String inequality	ne	!=
String comparison	ge, gt, le, lt	>=, >, <=, <
Numeric addition	+	+
Numeric equality	=	==
Numeric inequality	<>	!=
Numeric comparison	>=, >, <=, <	>=, >, <=, <

Some Flash 5 operators can operate on both strings and numbers. For example, when used with strings, the + operator concatenates its operands together to form a new string. But when used with numbers, the + operator adds its two operands together mathematically. Similarly, the equality operator (==) and inequality operator (!=) in Flash 5 are used to compare strings, numbers, and other datatypes.

Because many Flash 5 operators work with multiple datatypes but Flash 4 operators do not, an ambiguity arises when a Flash 4 file is imported into Flash 5. Therefore, when importing Flash 4 files, Flash 5 automatically inserts the *Number( )* function around any numeric data that is used as an operand of the following potentially ambiguous operators (unless the operand is a numeric literal):

```
+, ==, !=, <>, <, >, >=, <=
```

Flash 4 files converted to Flash 5 will also have the string concatenation operator (&) changed to the new *add* operator. Table 3-5 contains examples of Flash 4–to–Flash 5 operator translation.

Table 3-5. Sample Flash 4–to–Flash 5 Operator Translations

Flash 4 Syntax	Flash 5 Syntax
`Loop While (count <= numRecords)`	`while (Number(count)<= Number(numRecords))`
`If (x = 15)`	`if(Number(x) == 15)`
`If (y <> 20)`	`if(Number(y) != 20)`
`Set Variable: "lastName" = "kavanagh"`	`lastName = "kavanagh"`
`Set Variable: "name" = "molly" & lastName`	`name = "molly" add lastName`

Determining the Type of an Existing Datum

To determine what kind of data is held in a given expression before, say, proceeding with a section of code, we use the *typeof* operator, as follows:

```
typeof expression;
```

The *typeof* operator returns a string telling us the datatype of **expression**, according to Table 3-6.

Table 3-6. Return Values of typeof

Original Datatype	typeof Return Value
Number	"number"
String	"string"
Boolean	"boolean"
Object	"object"
Array	"object"
null	"null"
Movieclip	"movieclip"
Function	"function"
undefined	"undefined"

Here are a few examples:

```
trace(typeof "game over");    // Displays: "string" in the Output window

var x = 5;
trace(typeof x);              // Displays: "number"

var now = new Date();
trace(typeof now);            // Displays: "object"
```

As shown in Example 3-1, when combined with a *for-in* statement, *typeof* provides a handy way to find all the movie clip instances on a timeline. Once identified, we can assign the clips to an array for programmatic handling. (If you can't follow all of Example 3-1, revisit it after completing Part I, *ActionScript Fundamentals*.)

Example 3-1. Populating an Array with Dynamically Identified Movie Clips

```
var childClip = new Array();
var childClipCount = 0;

for (i in _root) {
   thisItem = _root[i];
   if (typeof thisItem == "movieclip") {
     // Notice the use of the postfix increment operator
     childClip[childClipCount++] = thisItem;
   }
}
```

Example 3-1. Populating an Array with Dynamically Identified Movie Clips (continued)

```
// Now that our array is populated, we can use it
// to manipulate the clips it contains
childClip[0]._x = 0;   // Place the first clip on the left of the Stage
childClip[1]._y = 0;   // Place the second clip at the top of the Stage
```

Primitive Data Versus Composite Data

So far we've been working mostly with numbers and strings, which are the most common *primitive* datatypes. Primitive datatypes are the basic units of a language; each primitive value contains a single datum (as opposed to an array of multiple items) and describes that datum literally. Primitive data is very straightforward.

ActionScript supports these primitive datatypes: *number, string, boolean, undefined*, and *null*. ActionScript does not have a separate single-character datatype (i.e., *char*) as found in C/C++.

Primitive datatypes are, as their name suggests, simple. They can hold text messages, frame numbers, movie clip size values, and so on, but they don't readily accommodate higher levels of complexity. For more elaborate data handling—such as simulating the physics of a dozen bouncing balls or managing a quiz with 500 questions and answers—we turn to *composite* datatypes. Using composite data, we can manage multiple pieces of related data as a single datum.

ActionScript supports the following composite datatypes: *array, object*, and *movieclip*. Functions are technically a type of object and are therefore considered composite data, but we rarely manipulate them as such. See Chapter 9, *Functions*, for more about functions as a datatype.

Whereas a single number is a primitive datum, a list (i.e., an *array*) of multiple numbers is a *composite* datum. Here's a practical example of how composite datatypes are useful: Suppose we wanted to track the profile of a customer named Derek. We could create a series of variables that store Derek's attributes as primitive values, like this:

```
var custName = "Derek";
var custTitle = "Coding Genius";
var custAge = 30;
var custPhone = "416-222-3333";
```

However, this format gets pretty cumbersome once we add even a few more customers. We're forced to use sequentially named variables to keep track of everything—cust1Name, cust2Name, cust1Title, cust2Title, and so on. Yuck! But if we use an array, we can store our information much more efficiently:

```
cust1 = ["Derek", "Coding Genius", 30, "416-222-3333"];
```

When we want to add more customers we just create new arrays:

```
cust2 = ["Komlos", "Comic Artist", 28, "515-515-3333"];
cust3 = ["Porter", "Chef", 51, "515-999-3333"];
```

Nice and tidy. We'll learn much more about composite datatypes in the coming chapters.

Onward!

We've been introduced to data in ActionScript, and we're ready for deeper study. In Chapter 4, we'll study the *number, string, boolean, undefined,* and *null* datatypes. In Chapter 5, *Operators*, we'll learn how to manipulate data. In later chapters, we'll study the complex datatypes, such as *movieclips, arrays* and *objects.*

4

Primitive Datatypes

Primitive data consists of simple characters or keywords such as the numbers 0, 1, 2, 3, 4, 5, 6, 7, 8, 9, or the strings "a", "b", "c". As we learned in the previous chapter, the primitive datatypes supported by ActionScript are *number*, *string*, *boolean*, *undefined*, and *null*. In this chapter we'll learn how to define, examine, and change data of each type.

The Number Type

Numbers are used for counting, mathematics, and to keep track of numeric properties in our movies (like the current frame of a movie clip or its location on the Stage). Let's see how numbers are defined and manipulated in ActionScript.

Integers and Floating-Point Numbers

Most programming languages distinguish between two kinds of numbers: *integers* and *floating-point numbers*. An integer is a whole number that has no fractional component. Integers can be positive or negative and include the number 0. Floating-point numbers (*floats* for short) can include a fractional value represented after a decimal point, as in 0.56, 199.99, and 3.14159. So 1, 34523, –3, 0, and –9999999 are integers, but 223.45, –0.56, and 1/4 are floats.

Numeric Literals

We learned earlier that a *literal* is a direct representation of a single, fixed data value. The *number* type supports three kinds of literals: integer literals, floating-point literals, and special numeric values. The first two literal categories represent *real numbers* (numbers that have a fixed mathematical value); the third category comprises values that represent numeric concepts such as infinity.

Integer Literals

Integer literals such as 1, 2, 3, 99, and –200, must follow these rules:

- Integers may not contain a decimal point or fractional value.

- Integers must not exceed the minimum or maximum legal numeric values of ActionScript. See also the `MIN_VALUE` and `MAX_VALUE` properties of the *Number* object in Part III, *Language Reference*, for a discussion of legal values.

- Base-10 integer numbers must not start with a leading zero (e.g., 002, 000023, and 05).

Not all integer values are base-10 (i.e., decimal) integers. ActionScript also supports base-8 (octal) and base-16 (hexadecimal) numeric literals. For a primer on decimal, octal, and hexadecimal numbers, see:

http://www.moock.org/asdg/technotes

We use a leading zero to indicate an octal number. For example, to represent the octal number 723 in ActionScript, we use:

```
0723   // 467 in decimal (7*64 + 2*8 + 3*1)
```

To indicate a hexadecimal (*hex* for short) literal integer, we put 0x (or 0X) in front of the number, such as:

```
0x723  // 1827 in decimal (7*256 + 2*16 + 3*1)
0xFF   //  255 in decimal (15*16 + 15*1)
```

Hexadecimal numbers are often used to indicate color values, but most simple programs require only base-10 numbers. Be careful to remove unwanted leading zeros when converting strings to numbers, as shown in Example 4-1.

Example 4-1. Trim Leading Zeros

```
function trimZeros(theString) {
  while (theString.charAt(0) == "0" || theString.charAt(0) == " ") {
    theString = theString.substring(1, theString.length);
  }
  return theString;
}

testString = "00377";
trace(trimZeros(testString));  // Displays: 377
```

Floating-Point Literals

Floating-point literals represent numbers containing fractional parts. A floating-point literal may contain some or all of these four components:

- a base-10 integer
- a decimal point (.)
- a fraction (represented as a base-10 number)
- an exponent

The first three components are pretty straightforward: in the number 3.14, "3" is the base-10 integer, "." is the decimal point, and "14" is the fraction. But the fourth component (the exponent) requires a closer look.

To represent a very large positive or negative number as a float, we can attach an exponent to a number using the letter E (or e). To determine the value of a number with an exponent, multiply the number by 10 to the power specified by the exponent. For example:

```
12e2    // 1200 (10 squared is 100, times 12 yields 1200)
143E-3  // 0.143 (10 to the power -3 is .001, times 143 yields 0.143)
```

You may recognize the format as standard scientific notation. If math isn't your strong point, here's an easy conversion tip: if the exponent is positive, move the decimal point that many places to the right; if the exponent is negative, move the decimal point that many places to the left.

Sometimes ActionScript will return a number with an exponent as the result of a calculation if the result is a very large or very small value. Note, however, that the exponent E (or e) is merely a notational convenience. If we want to raise a number to an arbitrary power, we use the built-in *Math.pow()* function, which is documented in Part III.

Floating-point precision

Flash uses *double-precision* floating-point numbers, which offer precision to about 15 significant digits. (Any leading zeros, trailing zeros, and/or exponents are not counted as part of the 15 digits.) This means that Flash can represent the number 123456789012345, but not 1234567890123456. The precision doesn't limit how big a number can get, only how precise a number can be represented; 2e16 is a bigger number than 123456789012345 but employs only one significant digit.

ActionScript calculations are occasionally rounded in undesirable ways, producing numbers such as 0.14300000000000001 instead of 0.143. This happens because computers convert numbers of any base to an internal binary representation, which can lead to nonterminating fractions in binary (much like 0.3333333 in decimal). Computers have only finite precision, so they cannot perfectly represent nonterminating fractions. In order to accommodate for the minute discrepancy, you should round your numbers manually if the difference will adversely affect the behavior of your code. For example, here we round `myNumber` to three decimal places:

```
myNumber = Math.round(myNumber * 1000) / 1000;
```

And here's a reusable function to round any number to an arbitrary number of decimal places:

```
function trim(theNumber, decPlaces) {
  if (decPlaces >= 0) {
    var temp = Math.pow(10, decPlaces);
    return Math.round(theNumber * temp) / temp;
  }
}

// Round a number to two decimal places
trace(trim(1.12645, 2));  // Displays: 1.13
```

Special Values of the Number Datatype

Integer and floating-point literals account for nearly all the legal values of the number datatype, but there are special keyword values that represent these numeric concepts: Not-a-Number, Minimum Allowed Value, Maximum Allowed Value, Infinity, and Negative Infinity.

Each of the special values may be assigned to variables and properties or used in literal expressions just like any other numeric literal. More often than not, though, the special numeric values are returned by the interpreter as the result of some expression evaluation.

Not-a-Number: NaN

Occasionally, a mathematical computation or an attempted datatype conversion results in a value that is simply not a number. For example, 0/0 is an impossible calculation, and the following expression can't be converted to a finite number:

```
23 - "go ahead and try!"
```

In order to accommodate data that is of the *number* type but is not a real number, ActionScript provides the `NaN` keyword value. Though `NaN` doesn't represent a number, it is still a legal value of the *number* type as demonstrated by the following code:

```
x = 0/0;
trace(x);        // Displays: NaN
trace(typeof x); // Displays: "number"
```

Since **NaN** is not a finite numeric value, it never compares as equal to itself. If two variables hold the value **NaN**, they are considered not equal (though they may seem equal to us). As a workaround to this problem, we use the built-in function *isNaN()* to check whether a variable contains the **NaN** value:

```
x = 12 - "this doesn't make much sense";  // x is now NaN
trace(isNaN(x));                          // Displays: true
```

Minimum and maximum allowed values: MIN_VALUE and MAX_VALUE

ActionScript represents a broad but not unlimited range of numbers. The maximum allowable value is 1.7976931348623157e+308, and the minimum allowed value is 5e–324. Obviously, those numbers are a bit inconvenient, so we use the special values **Number.MAX_VALUE** and **Number.MIN_VALUE** instead.

Number.MAX_VALUE comes in handy when we are checking to see if a calculation results in a representable positive number:

```
z = x*y;
if (z <= Number.MAX_VALUE && z >= -Number.MAX_VALUE) {
  // Number is legal
}
```

Note that **Number.MIN_VALUE** is the smallest *positive* value allowed, not the largest *negative* value. The largest negative legal value is **-Number.MAX_VALUE**.

Infinity and negative infinity: Infinity and -Infinity

If a calculation results in a value larger than **Number.MAX_VALUE**, ActionScript will use the keyword **Infinity** to represent the result of the calculation. Similarly, if a calculation results in a value more negative than the largest allowable negative value, ActionScript uses **-Infinity** to represent the result. **Infinity** and **-Infinity** may also be used directly as literal numeric expressions.

Irrational numbers

In addition to the special numeric values **NaN**, **Infinity**, **-Infinity**, **Number.MAX_VALUE** and **Number.MIN_VALUE**, ActionScript provides convenient access to mathematical constants via the *Math* object. For example:

```
Math.E        // The value of E, the base of the natural logarithm
Math.LN10     // Natural logarithm of 10
Math.LN2      // Natural logarithm of 2
Math.LOG10E   // Base-10 logarithm of e
Math.LOG2E    // Base-2 logarithm of e
Math.PI       // Pi (i.e., 3.1415926...)
Math.SQRT1_2  // Square root of 1/2
Math.SQRT2    // Square root of 2 (i.e., 1.4142135...)
```

The constants are simply shorthand forms of floating-point values that approximate commonly used irrational numbers. You can use these irrational numbers just as you would any other object property:

```
area = Math.PI*(radius*radius);
```

For a complete list of supported constants, see the *Math* object in Part III.

Working with Numbers

We can manipulate numbers by combining them with operators to form mathematical expressions, and by calling built-in functions to perform complex mathematical operations.

Using Operators

Basic arithmetic—addition, subtraction, multiplication, and division—is accomplished using the +, −, *, and / operators. Operators can be used with any numeric literals or data containers such as variables. Mathematical expressions are evaluated in the order determined by the *precedence* of the operators as shown in Table 5-1. For example, multiplication is performed before addition. All of these are legitimate uses of mathematical operators:

```
x = 3 * 5;            // Assign the value 15 to x
x = 1 + 2 - 3 / 4;    // Assign the value 2.25 to x

x = 56;
y = 4 * 6 + x;        // Assign the value 80 to y
y = x + (x * x) / x;  // Assign the value 112 to y
```

Built-in Mathematical Functions

To perform advanced math, we use the built-in mathematical functions of the *Math* object. For example:

```
Math.abs(x)        // Absolute value of x
Math.min(x, y)     // The smaller of the values x and y
Math.pow(x, y)     // x raised to the power y
Math.round(x)      // x rounded to the nearest integer
```

The math functions return values that we use in expressions, just as we use real numbers. For example, suppose we want to simulate a six-sided die. We can use the *random()* function to retrieve a random float between 0 and 1:

```
dieRoll = Math.random();
```

Then we multiply that value by 6, giving us a float between 0 and 5.999, to which we add 1:

```
dieRoll = dieRoll * 6 + 1;  // Sets dieRoll to a number between 1 and 6.999
```

Finally, we use the *floor()* function to round our number down to the closest integer:

```
dieRoll = Math.floor(dieRoll);  // Sets dieRoll to a number
                                // between 1 and 6
```

Compressed into a single expression, our die roll calculation looks like this:

```
// Sets dieRoll to a number between 1 and 6
dieRoll = Math.floor(Math.random() * 6 + 1);
```

The String Type

String is the datatype used for textual data (letters, punctuation marks, and other characters). A string literal is any combination of characters enclosed in quotation marks:

```
"asdfksldfsdfeoif"   // A frustrated string
"greetings"          // A friendly string
"moock@moock.org"    // A self-promotional string
"123"                // It may look like a number, but it's a string
'singles'            // Single quotes are acceptable too
```

Before we see how to form string literals, let's examine which characters are permitted in strings.

Character Encoding

Like all computer data, text characters are stored internally using a numeric code. They are *encoded* for storage and *decoded* for display using a *character set*, which *maps* (i.e., relates) characters to their numeric codes. Character sets vary for different languages and alphabets. Older Western applications use some derivative of ASCII, a standard character set that includes only 128 characters—the English alphabet, numbers, and basic punctuation marks. Modern applications support a family of character sets known collectively as ISO-8859. Each of the ISO-8859 character sets encodes the standard Latin alphabet ('A' to 'Z') plus a varying set of letters needed in the target languages. ActionScript uses ISO-8859-1, also known as *Latin 1*, as its primary character map.

The Latin 1 character set accommodates most Western European languages—French, German, Italian, Spanish, Portuguese, and so on—but not languages such as Greek, Turkish, Slavic, and Russian. *Unicode*, the preferred international standard for character encoding that maps up to a million characters, is *not* supported in ActionScript (support for Unicode would greatly increase the Flash Player size). However, ActionScript does support a second character set for Japanese characters called *Shift-JIS*. When working with text in ActionScript, we can use any character from Latin 1 or Shift-JIS.

Even though Unicode itself isn't supported, we can use the standard Unicode escape sequences to represent any character from Latin 1 or Shift-JIS. We can also manipulate character strings with Unicode-style functions. In theory, then, Unicode support could be added to Flash at some future date without breaking old code.

Appendix B, *Latin 1 Character Repertoire and Keycodes*, lists each character's Unicode *code point*, which is the character's numeric position in the Unicode set. Later, we'll see how to use those code points to manipulate characters in our scripts.

String Literals

The most common way to make a string is to put either single or double quotation marks around a group of characters from the Latin 1 or Shift-JIS character sets:

```
"hello"
'Nice night for a walk.'
"The equation is 12 + 4 = 16, which programmers see as 12 + 4 == 16."
```

If we use a double quotation mark to start a string, we must end it with a double quotation mark as well. Likewise, if we use a single quotation mark to start a string, we must end that string with a single quotation mark. However, a double-quoted string may contain single-quoted characters and vice versa. These strings, for example, contain legal uses of single and double quotes:

```
"Nice night, isn't it?"              // Single (apostrophe) inside double quotes
'I said, "What a pleasant evening!"' // Double quotes inside single quotes
```

The empty string

The shortest possible string is the *empty string*, a string with no characters:

```
""
''
```

The empty string is occasionally handy when we're trying to detect whether a variable contains a usable string value or not:

```
if (firstName == "") {
  trace("You forgot to enter your name!");
}
```

However, comparing a variable to `""` may not always work as we desire. Remember that `""` is considered equal to the number 0 and the Boolean value **false** (see Table 3-1 and Table 3-3). So, in order to be sure we're checking for an actual empty string, we should first make sure our variable value belongs to the string datatype, like this:

```
if (typeof firstName == "string" && firstName == "") {
  trace("You forgot to enter your name!");
}
```

Escape sequences

We saw earlier that single quotes (') may be used inside double-quoted literals, and double quotes (") may be used inside single-quoted literals. But what if we want to use both? For example:

```
'I remarked "Nice night, isn't it?"'
```

As is, that line of code causes an error because the interpreter thinks that the string literal ends with the apostrophe in the word "isn't." The interpreter reads it as:

```
'I remarked "Nice night, isn'   // The rest is considered unintelligible garbage
```

To use the single quote inside a string literal delimited by single quotes, we must use an *escape sequence.*

An escape sequence represents a literal string value using a backslash character (\), followed by a code that represents the desired character or the character itself. The escape sequences for single and double quotes are:

```
\'
\"
```

So, our cordial evening greeting, properly expressed as a string literal, should be:

```
'I remarked "Nice night, isn\'t it?"'   // Escape the apostrophe!
```

Other escape sequences, which can be used to represent various special or reserved characters, are listed in Table 4-1.

Table 4-1. ActionScript Escape Sequences

Escape Sequence	Meaning
\b	Backspace character (ASCII 8)
\f	Form feed character (ASCII 12)
\n	Newline character; causes a line break (ASCII 10)
\r	Carriage return (CR) character; causes a line break (ASCII 13)
\t	Tab character (ASCII 9)
\'	Single quotation mark
\"	Double quotation mark
\\	Backslash character; necessary when using backslash as a literal character to prevent \ from being interpreted as the beginning of an escape sequence

Unicode-style escape sequences

Not all characters from Latin 1 and Shift-JIS are accessible from a keyboard. In order to include inaccessible characters in a string, we use Unicode-style escape sequences. Note that Flash does not actually support Unicode; it merely emulates its syntax.

A Unicode-style escape sequence starts with a backslash and a *lowercase u* (i.e., \u) followed by a four-digit hex number that corresponds to the Unicode character's code point, such as:

```
\u0040  // The @ sign
\u00A9  // The copyright symbol
\u0041  // The capital letter "A"
```

A *code point* is a unique identification number that is assigned to each character in the Unicode character set. See Appendix B for a list of the Unicode code points for Latin 1. The Shift-JIS code points may be found at the Unicode Consortium site:

ftp://ftp.unicode.org/Public/MAPPINGS/EASTASIA/JIS/SHIFTJIS.TXT

If we're only escaping characters from the Latin 1 character set, we may use a short form for the standard Unicode escape sequence. The short form consists of the prefix \x followed by a two-digit hexadecimal number that represents the Latin 1 encoding of the character. Since Latin 1 code points are the same as the first 256 Unicode code points, you can still use the reference chart in Appendix B, but simply remove the u00, as in the following examples:

```
\u0040  // Unicode escape sequence
\x40    // \x shortcut form
\u00A9  // Unicode...
\xA9    // ...you get the idea
```

In addition to using Unicode escape sequences, we can insert any character into a string via the more cumbersome built-in function, *fromCharCode()*, described later in "Character Code Functions." Note that with both Unicode escape sequences and the *fromCharCode()* function, Flash 5 supports only those code points that map to characters in the Latin 1 and Shift-JIS character sets. Inserting other code points will not yield the correct Unicode character unless future versions of Flash support more of Unicode's character repertoire.

Working with Strings

By manipulating strings we can program anything from a user-input validator to a word-scramble game. With a little ingenuity, we can make neat visual text effects and other fun stuff.

We can manipulate strings with both operators and built-in functions. String operators can join multiple strings together or compare the characters of two strings. Built-in functions can examine a string's properties and contents, extract a portion of a string, check a character's code point, create a character from a code point, change the case of the characters in a string, and even turn a string into a variable or property name.

Joining Strings Together

Joining strings together (creating a new string from two or more strings) is called *concatenation*. As seen earlier, we can concatenate two strings with the plus operator (+), like this:

```
"Macromedia" + "Flash"
```

That line of code yields the single string value "MacromediaFlash". Oops! We forgot to put a space between the words. To add the space, we can insert it within the quotes that define one of the strings, such as:

```
"Macromedia " + "Flash"   // Yields "Macromedia Flash"
```

But that's not always practical. In most cases we don't want to add a space to a company or a product name. So instead, we join three strings together, the middle one of which is simply an empty space:

```
"Macromedia" + " " + "Flash"    // Also yields "Macromedia Flash"
```

Note that the space character is not the same as the empty string we saw earlier because the empty string has no characters between the quotes.

We can also concatenate variables that contain string data. Consider the following code:

```
var company = "Macromedia";
var product = "Flash";

// Set the variable sectionTitle to "Macromedia Flash"
var sectionTitle = company + " " + product;
```

In lines 1 and 2, we store string values in variables. Then, we join those values together with a space. Two of our string values are contained in variables, one (the space) is a string literal. Not a problem. Happens all the time.

Occasionally, we'll want to append characters onto an existing string. For example, we could change the tone of a welcome message like this:

```
var greeting = "Hello";     // Our welcome message
greeting = greeting + "?";  // Our quizzical welcome message: "Hello?"
```

The preceding code gets the job done, but notice that we have to refer to **greeting** twice in line 2. To be more efficient, we can use the **+=** operator, which appends the string on its right to the string variable on the left:

```
var greeting = "Hello";     // Our welcome message
greeting += "?";            // Our quizzical welcome message: "Hello?"
```

The Flash 4 string concatenation operator (&) performs a *different* operation (bitwise AND) in Flash 5. If exporting a Flash 4 *.swf*, you must use the *add* operator to concatenate strings. Note that *add* is supported only for backward compatibility; the + operator is preferred in Flash 5.

The concat() function

The *concat()* function appends characters to a string, like +=. Because *concat()* is a function, it uses the dot operator, like this:

```
var product = "Macromedia".concat(" Flash");

var sentence = "How are you";
var question = sentence.concat("?")
```

Take heed though—unlike +=, the *concat()* function does not alter the string that it is applied to; it merely returns the concatenated string value. In order to make use of that value, we must assign it to a variable or other data container. Study the following code closely so you'll understand the difference between += and *concat()*:

```
var greeting = "Hello";
greeting.concat("?");
trace(greeting);  // Displays "Hello"; greeting was unaffected by concat

finalGreeting = greeting.concat("?");
trace(finalGreeting);  // Displays "Hello?"
```

The *concat()* function also accepts multiple arguments (that is, it can combine multiple comma-separated strings into one string):

```
firstName = "Karsten";

// Sets finalGreeting to "Hello Karsten?"
finalGreeting = greeting.concat(" ", firstName, "?");
```

which is the same as:

```
finalGreeting = greeting;
finalGreeting += " " + firstName + "?";
```

Comparing Strings

To check whether two strings are the same, we use the equality (==) and inequality (!=) operators. We often compare strings when executing code based on a condition. For example, if a user enters a password, we need to compare his input string with the actual password. The result of our comparison governs the behavior of our code.

Using the equality (==) and inequality (!=) operators

The equality operator takes two operands—one on its left and one on its right. The operands may be string literals or any variable, array element, object property, or expression that can be converted to a string:

```
"hello" == "goodbye"      // Compare two string literals
userGuess == "fat-cheeks" // Compare a variable with a string
userGuess == password     // Compare two variables
```

If the operand on the right has the exact same characters in the exact same order as the operand on the left, the two strings are considered equal and the result is the Boolean value `true`. However, upper- and lowercase letters have different code points in a character set, so they are not considered equal. The following comparisons all evaluate to `false`:

```
"olive-orange" == "olive orange"  // Not equal
"nighttime" == "night time"       // Not equal
"Day 1" == "day 1"                // Not equal
```

Because string comparisons result in the Boolean value `true` or `false`, we can use them as test expressions within conditional statements and loops, like this:

```
if (userGuess == password) {
  gotoAndStop("classifiedContent");
}
```

If the expression *(userGuess == password)* is `true`, then the *gotoAndStop("classifiedContent");* statement will be executed. If the expression is `false`, the *gotoAndStop("classifiedContent");* statement will be skipped.

We'll learn more about Boolean values later in this chapter. And we'll learn about conditional statements in Chapter 7, *Conditionals*.

To check whether two strings are not equal, we use the *inequality* operator, which yields a result opposite to the equality operator. For example, the following expressions represent the values `false` and `true`, respectively:

```
"Jane" != "Jane"  // false because the two strings are equal
"Jane" != "Biz"   // true because the strings are different
```

Here we use the inequality operator to take some action only if two strings are not equal:

```
if (userGender != "boy") {
  // Girls-only code goes here...
}
```

If exporting a Flash 4 *.swf*, you must use the older eq and ne operators for string equality and inequality comparisons. Although eq and ne are supported for backward compatibility, the == and != operators are preferred in Flash 5.

Character order and alphabetic comparisons

We can also compare two strings on a character-order basis. We saw earlier that each character has a numeric code point assigned to it and that those code points are ordered numerically in a character set. We can check which character comes first in the order using the *comparison* operators: greater than (>), greater than or equal to (>=), less than (<), and less than or equal to (<=). All of the comparison operators compare two operands:

```
"a" < "b"
"2" > "&"
"r" <= "R"
"$" >= "@"
```

Much like equality and inequality expressions, comparison expressions yield a Boolean value, `true` or `false`, depending on the relationship of the operands. Each operand can be anything that yields a string value.

Since the characters 'A' to 'Z' and 'a' to 'z' are grouped in alphabetic sequence in the Latin 1 character set, we frequently use character-order comparisons to determine which of two letters comes first alphabetically. Note, however, that any uppercase letter comes before all lowercase letters in the Latin 1 character set. If we forget this, we're in for some surprising results:

```
"Z" < "a"       // Evaluates to true
"z" < "a"       // Evaluates to false
"Cow" < "bird"  // Evaluates to true
```

Here's a closer look at each comparison operator; in the following descriptions, the *comparison character* is defined as the first nonidentical character found in the two operands:

Greater than (>)

Yields `true` if the comparison character of the left operand appears later in the Latin 1 or Shift-JIS character order than the comparison character of the right operand. If the two operands are completely identical, > returns `false`:

```
"b" > "a"       // true
"a" > "b"       // false
"ab" > "ac"     // false (the second character is the comparison character)
"abc" > "abc"   // false (the strings are identical)
"ab" > "a"      // true (b is the comparison character)
"A" > "a"       // false ("A" comes before "a" in the character order)
```

Greater than or equal to (>=)

Yields `true` if the comparison character of the left operand appears later in the character order than the comparison character of the right operand or if the two operands are completely identical:

```
"b" >= "a"   // true
"b" >= "b"   // true
"b" >= "c"   // false
"A" >= "a"   // false ("A" and "a" occupy different code points)
```

Less than (<)

Yields `true` if the comparison character of the left operand appears earlier in the Latin 1 or Shift-JIS character order than the comparison character of the right operand. If the two operands are completely identical, < returns `false`:

```
"a" < "b"      // true
"b" < "a"      // false
"az" < "aa"    // false (the second character is the comparison character)
```

Less than or equal to (<=)

Yields `true` if the comparison character of the left operand appears earlier in the character order than the comparison character of the right operand or if the two operands are completely identical:

```
"a" <= "b"   // true
"a" <= "a"   // true
"z" <= "a"   // false
```

To determine which of two nonalphabetic characters comes first in the Latin 1 character order, consult Appendix B.

The following example checks whether a character is a letter from the Latin alphabet (as opposed to a number, punctuation mark, or other symbol):

```
var theChar = "w";

if ((theChar >= "A" && theChar <= "Z") || (theChar >= "a" && theChar <= "z")) {
    trace("The character is in the Latin alphabet.");
}
```

Notice how the logical OR operator (||) lets us check two conditions at once. We'll study OR in Chapter 5, *Operators*.

 If exporting a Flash 4 *.swf*, you must use the older `gt`, `ge`, `lt`, and `le` string comparison operators. Although the older operators are supported for backward compatibility, the >, >=, <, and <= operators are the preferred equivalents in Flash 5.

Using Built-in String Functions

With the exception of the *concat()* function, every tool we've used so far with strings has been an operator. Now we'll see how to use built-in functions and properties to perform more advanced string manipulation.

To execute a built-in function on a string, we must perform a *function call*, which takes the form:

```
string.functionName(arguments)
```

For example, here we execute the *charAt()* function on `myString`:

```
myString.charAt(2)
```

String functions return data that relates in some way to the original string. We assign these return values to variables or object properties for future use, such as:

```
thirdCharacter = myString.charAt(2);
```

Character Indexing

Many of the string functions make use of a character's *index*—its numeric position relative to the string's first character, starting at 0, not 1. The first character is numbered 0, the second is numbered 1, the third is numbered 2, and so on. For example, in the string "red", the *r* is at index 0, the *e* is at index 1, and the *d* is at index 2.

Using character indexes we identify portions of a string. We may, for example, instruct the interpreter to "Get the characters from index 3 to index 7," or we may ask it, "What character is at index 5?"

Examining Strings

We can inspect and search within strings using the built-in `length` property or the *charAt()*, *indexOf()*, and *lastIndexOf()* functions.

The length property

The `length` property tells us how many characters are in a string. Because it is a property, not a function, we don't use parentheses or arguments when referring to it. Here we see the `length` of several strings:

```
"Flash".length          // length is 5
"skip intro".length     // length is 10 (the space is a character, and
                        // every character counts)
"".length               // The empty string contains 0 characters

var axiom = "all that glisters will one day be obsolete";
axiom.length            // 42
```

Because character indexes start at 0 (i.e., are *zero-relative*), the index of the last character is always equal to the `length` of the string minus one.

A string's `length` property can be read but not set. We can't make a string longer like this:

```
axiom.length = 100;  // Nice try, but it ain't gonna work
```

 If exporting a Flash 4 *.swf*, you must use the older *length()* function as shown next. The *length()* function is supported for backward compatibility, but the `length` property is preferred in Flash 5.

Here we use the Flash 4 *length()* function to display the number of characters in the word "obsolete":

```
trace (length("obsolete"));  // Displays: 8
```

The charAt() function

We can determine the character at any index position of a string using the *charAt()* function, which takes the form:

```
string.charAt(index)
```

where *string* may be any literal string value or an identifier that contains a string; an *index* is an integer or an expression that resolves to an integer that indicates the position of the character we want to retrieve. The value of *index* should be between 0 and *string.length - 1*. If *index* does not fall in that range, the empty string is returned. Here are some examples:

```
"It is 10:34 pm".charAt(1)  // Returns "t", the second character
var country = "Canada";
country.charAt(2);          // Returns "n", the third character
var x = 4;
fifthLetter = country.charAt(x);              // fifthLetter is "d"
lastLetter = country.charAt(country.length - 1); // lastLetter is "a"
```

The indexOf() function

We use the *indexOf()* function to search for characters in a string. If the string we're searching contains our search sequence, *indexOf()* returns the index (i.e., position) of the sequence's first occurrence in the string. Otherwise, it returns the value −1. The general form of *indexOf()* is:

```
string.indexOf(character_sequence, start_index)
```

where *string* is any literal string value or an identifier that contains a string; *character_sequence* is the string for which we're searching, which may be a string literal or an identifier that contains a string; and *start_index* is the starting position of the search. If *start_index* is omitted, the search starts at the beginning of *string*.

Let's use *indexOf()* to check whether a string contains the character *W*:

```
"GWEN!".indexOf("W");   // Returns 1
```

Yup, *W* is the second character in "GWEN!", so we get 1, the index of the *W* character. Remember, character indexes start at 0, so the second character occupies index 1.

What happens if we search for the lowercase character *w*? Let's see:

```
"GWEN!".indexOf("w");   // Returns -1
```

There is no *w* in "GWEN!" so *indexOf()* returns −1. The upper- and lowercase versions of a letter are different characters and *indexOf()* is case sensitive!

Now let's make sure that there's an @ sign in an email address:

```
var email = "daniella2dancethenightaway.ca";  // Oops, someone forgot to
                                              // press Shift!

// If there's no @ sign, warn the user via the formStatus text field
if (email.indexOf("@") == -1) {
  formStatus = "The email address is not valid.";
}
```

We don't always have to search for single characters. We can search for an entire character sequence in a string too. Let's look for "Canada" in the address of a company:

```
var iceAddress = "St. Clair Avenue, Toronto, Ontario, Canada";
iceAddress.indexOf("Canada");  // Returns 36, the index of the letter "C"
```

Notice that *indexOf()* returns the position of the first character in "Canada". Now let's compare the return value of *iceAddress.indexOf("Canada")* to −1, and assign the result to a variable that stores the nationality of the company:

```
var isCanadian = iceAddress.indexOf("Canada") != -1;
```

The value of *iceAddress.indexOf("Canada") != −1* will be **true** if *iceAddress.indexOf("Canada")* does *not* equal −1 ("Canada" is found) and **false** if *iceAddress.indexOf("Canada") does* equal −1 ("Canada" is not found). We then assign that Boolean value to the variable **isCanadian**, which we can use to create a country-specific mailing form for North America:

```
if (isCanadian) {
  mailDesc = "Please enter your postal code.";
} else {
  mailDesc = "Please enter your zip code.";
}
```

The *indexOf()* function can also help us determine which part of a string we need to extract. We'll see how that works when we learn about the *substring()* function.

The lastIndexOf() Function

The *indexOf()* function returns the location of a character sequence's *first* occurrence in a string. The *lastIndexOf()* function returns the location of a character sequence's *last* occurrence in a string, or −1 if the sequence isn't found. The general form of *lastIndexOf()* is just like that of *indexOf()*:

```
string.lastIndexOf(character_sequence, start_index)
```

The only difference being that since *lastIndexOf()* searches a string backward, `start_index` refers to the rightmost character we want included in our search (not the leftmost). If `start_index` is omitted, it defaults to `string.length - 1` (the last character in the string).

For example:

```
paradox = "pain is pleasure, pleasure is pain";
paradox.lastIndexOf("pain");      // Returns 30; indexOf() would return 0
```

The following returns 0 (the index of the first occurrence of the word "pain"), because we started the backward search before the second occurrence of "pain":

```
paradox.lastIndexOf("pain",29);   // Returns 0
```

No regular expressions

Note that regular expressions (a powerful tool used to recognize patterns in textual data) are not supported in ActionScript.

Retrieving Portions of Strings

Sometimes a long string contains a sequence of characters that we'd like to access more conveniently. In the string "Steven Sid Mumby", for example, we may want to extract the last name, "Mumby". To extract a shorter string (or *substring*) we use one of these functions: *substring()*, *substr()*, *splice()*, or *split()*.

The substring() function

We use *substring()* to retrieve a sequence of characters from a string based on starting and ending character indexes. The *substring()* function takes the following form:

```
string.substring(start_index, end_index)
```

where `string` is any literal string value or an identifier that contains a string, `start_index` is the index of the first character to include in the substring, and *end_index* is the character *after* the last character we want in our substring. If not provided, *end_index* defaults to *string*.length. Hence:

```
var fullName = "Steven Sid Mumby";
middleName = fullName.substring(7, 10);   // Assigns "Sid" to middleName
firstName = fullName.substring(0, 6);     // Assigns "Steven" to firstName
lastName = fullName.substring(11);        // Assigns "Mumby" to lastName
```

In reality, we wouldn't know where the first name, middle name, and last name begin and end, so we'd typically look for some *delimiter*, such as the space character to help us guess where the word breaks are. Here we search for the last space in the name and assume that the remainder of the string following it is the user's last name:

```
fullName = "Steven Sid Mumby";
lastSpace = fullName.lastIndexOf(" "); // Returns 10

// Characters from 11 to the end of the string are presumably the last name
lastName = fullName.substring(lastSpace+1);
trace ("Hello Mr. " + lastName);
```

If *start_index* is greater than *end_index*, the two arguments are swapped automatically before the function executes. Although the following function invocations yield the same result, you shouldn't make a habit of using *substring()* with the indexes reversed because it makes your code harder to understand:

```
fullName.substring(4, 6);  // Returns "en"
fullName.substring(6, 4);  // Returns "en"
```

The substr() function

The *substr()* function extracts a sequence of characters from a string using a starting index and a length (in contrast to *substring()*, which uses starting and ending indexes). The general form of *substr()* is:

```
string.substr(start_index, length)
```

where *string* is, as usual, any literal string value or an identifier that contains a string; *start_index* is the first character to include in the substring; *length* specifies how many characters should be included in our string, starting at *start_index* and counting to the right. If *length* is omitted, the substring starts at *start_index* and ends with the last character in the original string. Some examples:

```
var fullName = "Steven Sid Mumby";
middleName = fullName.substr(7, 3);   // Assigns "Sid" to middleName
firstName = fullName.substr(0, 6);    // Assigns "Steven" to firstName
lastName = fullName.substr(11);       // Assigns "Mumby" to lastName
```

The *start_index* can be specified relative to the *end* of a string by using a negative number. The last character is –1, the second last character is –2, and so on. So the preceding three *substr()* examples could be written as:

```
middleName = fullName.substr(-9, 3);   // Assigns "Sid" to middleName
firstName = fullName.substr(-16, 6);   // Assigns "Steven" to firstName
lastName = fullName.substr(-5);        // Assigns "Mumby" to lastName
```

A negative *length*, however, is not allowed.

 In Flash 5, the *substr()* function is the string-extraction function that most closely resembles Flash 4's *substring()* function, which also used a start index and a length to retrieve a substring.

The slice() function

Like *substring()*, *slice()* retrieves a sequence of characters from a string based on starting and ending character indexes. While *substring()* can specify only the indexes relative to the *beginning* of the original string, *slice()* can specify them relative to the string's beginning or end.

The *slice()* function takes the following form:

```
string.slice(start_index, end_index)
```

where *string* is any literal string value or an identifier that contains a string and *start_index* is the first character to include in the substring. If *start_index* is a positive integer, it is a normal character index; if *start_index* is a negative integer, the equivalent character index is determined by counting back from the end of the string (that is, *string*.length + *start_index*). Finally, *end_index* is the character *after* the last character we want in our substring. If *end_index* is not provided, it defaults to *string*.length. If *end_index* is negative, the equivalent character index is determined by counting back from the end of the string (that is, *string*.length + *end_index*).

Using nonnegative indexes with *slice()* works just like *substring()*. When using negative indexes, remember that you are not getting a substring with reversed characters, and you are not getting a string from *end_index* to *start_index* in that order. You are merely specifying the indexes relative to the end of the original string. Remember also that the last character of the string is −1, and the *end_index* argument specifies the character *after* the last character in your substring, so it's impossible to refer to the last character in the original string using a negative *end_index*. Take a careful look at how we use negative indexes to extract the following substrings:

```
var fullName = "Steven Sid Mumby";
middleName = fullName.slice(-9, -6);   // Assigns "Sid" to middleName
firstName = fullName.slice(-16, -10);  // Assigns "Steven" to firstName
lastName = fullName.slice(-5, -1);     // Assigns "Mumb" to lastName: not what
                                       // we want, but the best we can do with
```

```
                                     // a negative end_index.
lastName = fullName.slice(-5, 16)    // Assigns "Mumby" to lastName. Notice
                                     // how we combine negative and
                                     // positive indexes.
```

The split() function

So far, the string-extraction functions we've seen have retrieved only one character sequence at a time. If we want to rip out a bunch of substrings in one fell swoop, we can use the powerful *split()* function. (As the *split()* function uses arrays, you may want to skip this function for now and come back after you've read Chapter 11, *Arrays.*)

The *split()* function breaks a string up into a series of substrings and puts those substrings into an array, which it returns. The *split()* function takes the following form:

```
string.split(delimiter)
```

where **string** is any literal string value or an identifier that contains a string, and **delimiter** is the character or characters that indicate where **string** should be split. Typical delimiters are commas, spaces, and tabs. To break up a string at each comma, for example, we use:

```
theString.split(",")
```

One of the neat tricks we can pull with *split()* is to break a sentence up into individual words. In our coverage of the *substring()*, *substr()*, and *slice()* functions, we had to manually grab each name from the string "Steven Sid Mumby." Look how much easier things are when we use *split()* with a space (" ") as the **delimiter**:

```
var fullName = "Steven Sid Mumby";
var names = fullName.split(" ");  // Man that's easy!

// Now assign the names in our array to individual variables
firstName  = names[0];
middleName = names[1];
lastName   = names[2];
```

String extraction performance issues

Flash 5's *substr()* and *slice()* functions are actually implemented as veneer atop the old Flash 4 *substring()* function, and therefore take marginally longer to execute. The speed difference is on the order of milliseconds but can be noticeable in intensive string processing. When carrying out highly repetitive operations, use *substring()* for optimal performance, as follows:

```
fullName = "Steven Sid Mumby";
// Assign "Sid" to middleName using Flash 5 substr() function
middleName = fullName.substr(7, 3);
```

```
// Assign "Sid" to middleName using Flash 4 substring() function.
// Note that character indexes start at 1 with Flash 4's substring().
middleName = substring(fullname, 8, 3);
```

Combining String Examination with Substring Extraction

We've seen how to search for characters in a string and how to extract characters from a string. These two tasks are most powerful when we put them together.

Most of the examples we've seen so far use literal expressions as arguments, like this:

```
var msg = "Welcome to my website!";
var firstWord = msg.substring(0, 7);  // 0 and 7 are numeric literals
```

That's a decent demonstration of the way *substring()* works, but it doesn't represent the typical real-world use of *substring()*. More often, we don't know the content of the string in advance and we must generate our arguments dynamically. For example, instead of saying something static like, "Get me the substring from index 0 to index 7," we usually say something dynamic like, "Get me the substring starting from the first character and ending at the first occurrence of a space in this string." This more flexible approach doesn't require us to know the content of a string in advance. Here we extract the first word of the variable **msg**, by combining *substring()* with *indexOf()*:

```
var firstWord = msg.substring(0, msg.indexOf(" "));
```

The expression *msg.indexOf(" ")* evaluates to the numeric index of the first space in **msg**. Our technique will work regardless of the space's location. This allows us to work with strings that change while our program is running and saves us a lot of character counting, which is prone to error.

The combinations of string examination and string extraction are practically endless. In Example 4-2 we extract the second word of the **msg** variable without hard-coding the character indexes. In natural language we want to "Extract a substring from **msg** starting with the character after the first occurrence of a space and ending with the character before the second occurrence of a space." We store the location of the first and second spaces as variables, making what's going on more obvious.

Example 4-2. Retrieving the Second Word of a String

```
var msg = "Welcome to my website!";
firstSpace = msg.indexOf(" ");                  // Find the first space
secondSpace = msg.indexOf(" ", firstSpace + 1);  // Find the next space

// Now extract the second word
var secondWord = msg.substring(firstSpace + 1, secondSpace);
```

Character Case Conversion

We can convert a string to upper- or lowercase using the built-in *toUpperCase()* and *toLowerCase()* functions. These are typically used to display a string with nice formatting or to compare strings with different cases.

The toUpperCase() function

The *toUpperCase()* function converts all of the characters in a string to uppercase (i.e., capital letters) and returns the converted version. If no uppercase version of a given character exists, the character is returned unchanged. The general form of *toUpperCase()* is:

```
string.toUpperCase()
```

where **string** is any literal string value or an identifier that contains a string. Some examples:

```
"listen to me".toUpperCase();         // Yields the string "LISTEN TO ME"
var msg1 = "Your Final Score: 234";
var msg2 = msg1.toUpperCase();        // Set msg2 to "YOUR FINAL SCORE: 234"
```

Note that *toUpperCase()* does not affect the string it's called on; it merely returns an uppercase copy of that string. The following example shows the difference:

```
var msg = "Forgive me, I forgot to bring my spectacles.";
msg.toUpperCase();
trace(msg);     // Displays: "Forgive me, I forgot to bring my spectacles."
                // msg was unaffected by the toUpperCase() invocation
```

The toLowerCase() function

The *toLowerCase()* function changes the characters in a string from upper- to lowercase. For example:

```
// Set normal to "this sentence has mixed caps!"
normal = "ThiS SenTencE Has MixED CaPs!".toLowerCase();
```

To compare two strings in a case-insensitive manner, convert them both to the same case, such as:

```
if (userEntry.toLowerCase() == password.toLowerCase()) {
  // They get secret access
}
```

Example 4-3 shows how we can have a little fun using the case-conversion and string functions to animate text in a text field. To use it, you'll need a three-frame movie with a text field called **msgOutput** on its own layer and the code from Example 4-3 on a *scripts* layer.

Example 4-3. Character Case Animation

```
// CODE ON FRAME 1
var i = 0;
var msg = "my what fat cheeks you have";
```

Example 4-3. Character Case Animation (continued)

```
function caseAni () {
  var part1 = msg.slice(0, i);
  var part2 = msg.charAt(i);
  var part2 = part2.toUpperCase();
  var part3 = msg.slice(i+1, msg.length);
  msg = part1 + part2 + part3;
  msgOutput = msg;
  msg = msg.toLowerCase();
  i++;

  if (i > (msg.length - 1)) {
    i=0;
  }
}

// CODE ON FRAME 2
caseAni();

// CODE ON FRAME 3
gotoAndPlay(2);
```

Character Code Functions

In the earlier section, "Unicode-style escape sequences," we learned how to insert characters into a string as escape sequences. ActionScript also includes two built-in functions for working with character codes in strings: *fromCharCode()* and *charCodeAt()*.

The fromCharCode() function

We can create any character or series of characters by invoking the *fromCharCode()* function. Unlike the other string functions, *fromCharCode()* is not called on a string literal or an identifier that contains a string, but as a method of the special *String* object, like this:

```
String.fromCharCode(code_point1, code_point2, ...)
```

Every *fromCharCode()* call starts with `String.fromCharCode`. Then one or more code points (representing the characters we want to create) are supplied as arguments. Unlike Unicode-style escape sequences, the code points in a *fromCharCode()* call are expressed as decimal integers, not hexadecimal. If you're unfamiliar with hex numbers you may, therefore, find *fromCharCode()* easier to use than Unicode-style escape sequences. Here are some examples:

```
// Set lastName to "moock"
lastName = String.fromCharCode(109, 111, 111, 99, 107);

// For comparison, let's do the same thing with Unicode-style escape sequences
lastName = "\u006D\u006F\u006F\u0063\u006B"  ;

// Make a copyright symbol
copyNotice = String.fromCharCode(169) + " 2001";
```

If exporting a Flash 4 *.swf*, you must use the older Flash 4 character-creation functions, *chr()* and *mbchr()*. Although these functions are supported for backward compatibility, *fromCharCode()* is preferred in Flash 5.

The charCodeAt() function

To determine the code point of any character in a string, we use the *charCodeAt()* function, which takes the following form:

```
string.charCodeAt(index)
```

where ***string*** is any literal string value or an identifier that contains a string, and ***index*** is the position of the character we're examining. The *charCodeAt()* function returns a decimal integer that matches the Unicode code point of the character at ***index***. For example:

```
var msg = "A is the first letter of the Latin alphabet.";
trace(msg.charCodeAt(0));  // Displays: 65 (the code point for "A")
trace(msg.charCodeAt(1));  // Displays: 32 (the code point for space)
```

We normally use *charCodeAt()* to perform string handling with characters we can't type directly using a keyboard. For example, in the following code we check whether a character is the copyright symbol:

```
msg = String.fromCharCode(169) + " 2000";
if (msg.charCodeAt(0) == 169) {
  trace("The first character of msg is a copyright symbol.");
}
```

If exporting a Flash 4 *.swf*, you must use the older Flash 4 code point functions, *ord()* and *mbord()*. Although they are supported for backward compatibility, *charCodeAt()* is preferred in Flash 5.

Executing Code in a String with eval

In ActionScript, the *eval()* function converts a string to an identifier. But to thoroughly understand the ActionScript *eval()* function, we must learn how JavaScript's analogous *eval()* function works. In JavaScript, *eval()* is a top-level, built-in function that converts any string to a block of code and then executes that block of code. The syntax for JavaScript's *eval()* is:

```
eval(string)
```

When *eval()* is executed in JavaScript, the interpreter converts *string* to code, runs that code, and returns the resulting value (if a value is generated). Consider the following JavaScript examples:

```
eval("parseInt('1.5')");   // Calls the parseInt() function, which returns 1
eval("var x = 5");         // Creates a new variable named x and
                           // sets its value to 5
```

If you've never seen *eval()* before, you may be thinking, "When would I ever have a string with code in it? Why not just write the code out?" Because *eval()* lets you dynamically generate code when you need to. For example, suppose you have ten functions named sequentially: *func1*, *func2*, *func3*, ..., *func10*. You could execute those functions with 10 function-call statements:

```
func1();
func2();
func3();
// etc...
```

But you could also execute them more conveniently using *eval()* in a loop, like this:

```
for (i = 1; i <= 10; i++){
   eval("func" + i + "()");
}
```

ActionScript's *eval()* function supports a small subset of its JavaScript cousin's functionality: it works only when its argument is an identifier. Hence, Action-Script's *eval()* function can only retrieve the data associated with the specified identifier. For example:

```
var num = 1;
var person1 = "Eugene";
trace (eval("person" + num));  // Displays: "Eugene"
```

Even in this pared-back form, *eval()* is quite useful. Here we generate a series of movie clips dynamically with a loop. We place our clips in an array by using *eval()* to refer to them:

```
for (var i = 0; i < 10; i++) {
   duplicateMovieClip("ballParent", "ball" + i, i);
   balls[i] = eval("ball" + i);
}
```

Note, however, that *eval()* can be quite processor-intensive. In more demanding scenarios, we're better off using the array-access operator to generate dynamic clip references. For example:

```
duplicateMovieClip("ballParent", "ball" + i , i);
balls[ballCount] = _root ["ball" + i];
```

In Flash 4, *eval()* was used abundantly to simulate arrays through dynamic variable-name generation and referencing. This technique is not recommended or required in Flash 5 due to Flash 5's native support for arrays. See "Creating dynamically named variables" in Chapter 2, *Variables*, for more details.

Flash 4 Versus Flash 5 String Operators and Functions

Throughout the descriptions of the string operators and functions, we looked at equivalent Flash 4 techniques. When we're using Flash 5 to author Flash 4 movies, we should use the Flash 4 string operators and functions in all of our work. But when we're authoring for Flash 5, we should use the swanky Flash 5 operators. If you're accustomed to the Flash 4 syntax, see Table 4-2 for the Flash 5 equivalents.

Table 4-2. Flash 4 Operators and Functions with Flash 5 Equivalencies

Flash 4 Syntax	Flash 5 Syntax	Description
" "	" " or ' '	String literal
&	+ (or *add* for backward compatibility)	String concatenation operator
eq	==	Equality operator
ge	>=	Greater-than-or-equal-to comparison
gt	>	Greater-than comparison
le	<=	Less-than-or-equal-to comparison
lt	<	Less-than comparison
ne	!=	Inequality operator (not equal to)
chr() or *mbchr()*	*fromCharCode()**	Creates a character from an encoded number
length() or *mblength()*	length*	Function in Flash 4, property in Flash 5; gives the number of characters in a string
mbsubstring()	*substr()*	Extracts character sequence from a string
ord() or *mbord()*	*charCodeAt()**	Gives the code point of the specified character
substring()	*substr()**	Extracts character sequence from a string

* Because all the Flash 5 string operations and functions work with multibyte characters, there's no way in Flash 5 to force a single-byte operation as there was in Flash 4. The *fromCharCode()* function is, for example, as close as things get to *chr()* in Flash 5. The same is true of *mblength()* and length, *mbsubstring()* and *substr()*, and *mbord()* and *charCodeAt()*.

The Boolean Type

Boolean data is used to represent the logical states of truth and falsehood. There are, hence, only two legal values of the *boolean* datatype: `true` and `false`. Notice that there are no quotation marks around the words `true` and `false` because Boolean data is *not* string data. The keywords `true` and `false` are the reserved primitive data values and may not be used as variable names or identifiers.

We use Boolean values to add logic to the execution of code. For example, we might assign the value `true` to a variable that tracks the status of a spaceship's firepower:

```
shipHasDoubleShots = true;
```

By comparing `shipHasDoubleShots` to the Boolean literal `true`, we can then decide how much damage to inflict when a shot hits its target:

```
if (shipHasDoubleShots == true) {
  // Shoot them with twice the power.
  // This will be reached if the comparison is true.
} else {
  // Shoot them with a single dose.
  // This will be reached if the comparison is false.
}
```

When the double-shot power runs out, we can set the variable to `false`:

```
shipHasDoubleShots = false;
```

This will cause the larger expression *shipHasDoubleShots* == *true* to become `false`, causing the single-damage-dose script to execute when a shot hits its target.

All comparison operators express results with Boolean values. When we ask, "Is the user's guess the same as the password?" the answer is given as a Boolean:

```
// userGuess == password will yield either true or false
if (userGuess == password) {
  gotoAndStop("secretContent");
}
```

And when we ask, "Is the movie clip rotated greater than 90 degrees?" the answer, again, is a Boolean:

```
// myClip._rotation > 90 will yield either true or false
if (myClip._rotation > 90) {
  // Fade out the clip if it's rotated past 90 degrees
  myClip._alpha = 50;
}
```

Many internal ActionScript properties and methods describe the Flash movie environment in Boolean terms. For example, if we ask, "Is the spacebar being pressed?" the interpreter answers with a Boolean: `true` (yes) or `false` (no):

```
// Key.isDown() is a function that returns either true or false
if (Key.isDown(Key.SPACE)) {
  // Spacebar is being pressed, so make our spaceship fire
}
```

In Chapter 5, we'll learn how to phrase complex logical expressions using Boolean operators.

Using Boolean Values to Build a Preloader

Let's consider an applied Boolean example. Suppose we have a document with 500 frames and lots of content. The beginning of our opening sequence, frame 20, is labeled `intro`. We put the following code on frame 2 of that movie's main timeline:

```
if (_framesloaded >= _totalframes) {
  gotoAndPlay("intro");
} else {
  gotoAndPlay(1);
}
```

When the movie plays, the playhead enters frame 2. The ActionScript interpreter reaches the conditional statement and evaluates the Boolean expression *_framesloaded >= _totalframes*. While the movie is still loading, `_framesloaded` is less than the total number of frames in our movie (`_totalframes`). If `_framesloaded` is not greater than or equal to `_totalframes`, then the expression *_framesloaded >=_totalframes*, yields `false`. Therefore, the statement *gotoAndPlay("intro")* is skipped and the statement *gotoAndPlay(1)* is executed instead. The *gotoAndPlay(1)* statement sends the playhead back to frame 1 and plays the movie. When the playhead enters frame 2, our code is executed *again*. The playhead keeps looping in this way until the expression *_framesloaded >= _totalframes* yields the value `true` (i.e., until all the frames have loaded). At that point, the statement *gotoAndPlay("intro")*, which sends the playhead to the label `intro`, is executed. There we can safely start our movie, now that all of the frames have loaded.

Whammo! You've created a preloader based on a Boolean expression. Solid stuff. We'll learn much more about conditionals and controlling movies with Booleans in Chapter 7.

Undefined

Most of the datatypes we've explored so far have been used for storing and manipulating information. The *undefined* datatype has a more narrow purpose: it is used to check whether a variable exists or whether a variable has yet been assigned a value. The *undefined* datatype has only one legal value, the primitive value `undefined`.

When we first define a variable, it is assigned the value **undefined** by default:

```
var velocity;
```

To the interpreter, the preceding statement reads:

```
var velocity = undefined;
```

To check whether a variable has a value, we can compare the variable to **undefined**, as in:

```
if (myVariable != undefined) {
  // myVariable has a value, so proceed as desired...
}
```

Note that an **undefined** value is converted to the empty string when used as a string. For example, if `firstName` is **undefined**, the following *trace()* statement will display `""` (the empty string):

```
var firstName;
trace(firstName);  // Displays nothing (the empty string)
```

This same code in JavaScript would display the string "undefined" instead of the empty string. ActionScript converts **undefined** to `""` for the sake of backward compatibility.

Because there was no *undefined* type in Flash 4 ActionScript, many Flash 4 programs used the empty string to check whether a variable had a useful value. Code like this was common:

```
if (myVar eq "") {
  // Don't do anything yet: myVar is undefined
}
```

If Flash 5 converted **undefined** to anything other than `""` in a string context, old code like that would break in the Flash 5 player.

Note that ActionScript returns **undefined** both for variables that do not exist and variables that have been declared but have no value. This is also a departure from JavaScript, where references to variables that do not exist cause an error.

Null

Intellectually, the *null* type is nearly identical to the *undefined* type. Like the *undefined* datatype, the *null* datatype is used to represent a lack of data and has only one legal value, the primitive value `null`. The `null` value is not assigned by the interpreter automatically, but rather by us deliberately.

We assign `null` to a variable, array element, or object property to indicate that the specified data container does not contain a legal number, string, boolean, array, or object value.

Note that `null` only compares equal to itself and `undefined`:

```
null == undefined;   // true
null == null;        // true
```

Onward!

We've learned a lot more so far than you may have realized. We've built a solid foundation that will allow us to understand the advanced topics coming in later chapters. If you haven't mastered all the details yet, don't worry. Your training will come back to you when you need it. Keep the faith during the next chapter in which you'll learn how to merge and transform data. Following that we'll get into some more fully formed applied examples.

5

Operators

An *operator* is a symbol or keyword that manipulates, combines, or transforms data. If you're new to programming, you'll notice that some mathematical operators, like + (addition) and − (subtraction) are very familiar. In other cases, you'll have to learn special programming syntax even if the concepts are familiar. For example, to multiply two numbers, ActionScript uses the symbol * (the multiplication operator) instead of the X typically taught in grade school. For example, this multiplies 5 times 6:

```
5 * 6;
```

General Features of Operators

Though each operator has its own specialized task, all operators share a number of general characteristics. Before we consider the operators individually, let's see how they behave generally.

Operators and Expressions

Operators perform some action using the data values (*operands*) supplied. For example, in the operation 5 * 6, the numbers 5 and 6 are the *operands* of the multiplication operator (*). The operands can be any kind of expression, for example:

```
player1score + bonusScore;              // Operands are variables
(x + y) - (Math.PI * radius * radius);  // Operands are complex expressions
```

Observe in the second example that both the left and right operands of the − operator are expressions that themselves involve other operations. We can use complex expressions to create even larger expressions, such as:

```
((x + y) - (Math.PI * radius * radius)) / 2  // Divide the whole thing by 2
```

When expressions become very large, consider using variables to hold interim results for both convenience and clarity. Remember to name your variables descriptively, such as:

```
var radius = 10;
var height = 25;
var circleArea = (Math.PI * radius * radius);
var cylinderVolume = area * height;
```

Number of Operands

Operators are sometimes categorized according to how many operands they take. Some ActionScript operators take one operand, some take two, and one even takes three:

```
-x                                         // One operand
x * y                                      // Two operands
(x == y) ? "true result" : "false result"  // Three operands
```

Single-operand operators are called *unary* operators; operators with two operands are called *binary* operators; operators with three operands are called *ternary* operators. For our purposes, we'll look at operators according to what they do, not the number of operands they take.

Operator Precedence

An operator *precedence* determines which operation is performed first in an expression with multiple operators. For example, when multiplication and addition occur in the same expression, multiplication is performed first:

```
4 + 5 * 6  // Yields 34, because 4 + 30 = 34
```

The expression 4 + 5 * 6 is evaluated as 4 + (5 * 6) because the * operator has higher precedence than the + operator. When in doubt, or to ensure a different order of operation, use parentheses, which have the highest precedence:

```
(4 + 5) * 6  // Yields 54, because 9 * 6 = 54
```

Even if not strictly necessary, parentheses can make a complicated expression more readable. The expression:

```
// x is greater than y or y equals z
x > y || y == z
```

may be difficult to comprehend without consulting a precedence table. It's a lot easier to read with parentheses added:

```
(x > y) || (y == z)  // Much better!
```

Table 5-1 shows the precedence of each operator. Operators with the highest precedence (at the top of the table) are executed first. Operators with the same precedence are performed left to right.

Table 5-1. ActionScript Operator Associativity and Precedence

Operator	Precedence	Associativity	Description
x++	16	left to right	postfix increment
x--	16	left to right	postfix decrement
.	15	left to right	object property access
[]	15	left to right	array element access
()	15	left to right	parentheses
function()	15	left to right	function call
++x	14	right to left	prefix increment
--x	14	right to left	prefix decrement
-	14	right to left	unary negation
~	14	right to left	bitwise NOT
!	14	right to left	logical NOT
new	14	right to left	create object/array
delete	14	right to left	remove object/property/array element
typeof	14	right to left	determine datatype
void	14	right to left	return undefined value
*	13	left to right	multiply
/	13	left to right	divide
%	13	left to right	modulo division
+	12	left to right	addition or string concatenation
-	12	left to right	subtraction
<<	11	left to right	bitwise left shift
>>	11	left to right	bitwise signed right shift
>>>	11	left to right	bitwise unsigned right shift
<	10	left to right	less than
<=	10	left to right	less than or equal to
>	10	left to right	greater than
>=	10	left to right	greater than or equal to
==	9	left to right	equality
!=	9	left to right	not equal to
&	8	left to right	bitwise AND
^	7	left to right	bitwise XOR
|	6	left to right	bitwise OR

Table 5-1. ActionScript Operator Associativity and Precedence (continued)

Operator	Precedence	Associativity	Description
&&	5	left to right	logical AND
||	4	left to right	logical OR
?:	3	right to left	conditional
=	2	right to left	assignment
+=	2	right to left	add and reassign
-=	2	right to left	subtract and reassign
*=	2	right to left	multiply and reassign
/=	2	right to left	divide and reassign
%=	2	right to left	modulo division and reassign
<<=	2	right to left	bit-shift left and reassign
>>=	2	right to left	bit-shift right and reassign
>>>=	2	right to left	bit-shift right (unsigned) and reassign
&=	2	right to left	bitwise & and reassign
^=	2	right to left	bitwise XOR and reassign
|=	2	right to left	bitwise OR and reassign
,	1	left to right	comma

Operator Associativity

As we've just learned, operator precedence indicates the pecking order of operators: those with a higher precedence are executed before those with a lower precedence. But what happens when multiple operators occur together and have the same level of precedence? In such a case, we apply the rules of *operator associativity*, which indicate the direction of an operation. Operators are either left-associative (performed left to right) or right-associative (performed right to left). For example, consider this expression:

```
a = b * c / d
```

The * and / operators are left-associative, so the * operation on the left (b * c) is performed first. The preceding example is equivalent to:

```
a = (b * c) / d
```

In contrast, the = (assignment) operator is right-associative, so the expression:

```
a = b = c = d
```

says "assign d to c, then assign c to b, then assign b to a," as in:

```
a = (b = (c = d))
```

Operator associativity is fairly intuitive, but if you're getting an unexpected value from a complex expression, consult Table 5-1 or add extra parentheses. We'll note cases in which associativity is a common source of errors throughout the remainder of the chapter.

Datatypes and Operators

Some operators accept multiple datatypes as operands. Depending on the datatype of an operand, the effect of an operator may change. The + operator, for example, performs addition when used with numeric operands but concatenation when used with string operands. If operands are of different datatypes or of the wrong type, ActionScript will perform type conversion according to the rules described in Chapter 3, *Data and Datatypes*, which can have serious effects on your code.

The Assignment Operator

We've already used the assignment operator frequently. It can place a value into a variable, array element, or object property. Assignment operations take the form:

```
identifier = expression
```

The *identifier* is the variable, array element, or object property into which we want to place our value. The *expression* represents the value (i.e., data) that we want to store. For example:

```
x = 4;                    // Assign 4 to the variable x
x = y;                    // Assign the value of y to the variable x
name = "dj duong";        // Assign a string to the variable name
products[3] = "Flash";    // Assign a string to the 4th element of products

// Assign a number to the area property of square
square.area = square.width * 2;
```

We may also perform multiple assignment operations at once, like this:

```
x = y = 4;   // Set both x and y to 4
```

Remember that assignment operations have right-to-left associativity, so 4 is assigned first to y then the value of y (which is now 4) is assigned to x.

Combining Operations with Assignment

Assignment operations are often used to set a variable's new value based in part on its old value. For example:

```
counter = counter + 10;            // Add 10 to the current value of counter
xPosition = xPosition + xVelocity; // Add xVelocity to xPosition
score = score / 2;                 // Divide score by two
```

ActionScript supports a shorthand version of assignment, called *compound assignment* that combines operators such as +, −, / with the assignment operator to form a single "calculate-while-assigning" operation. So, to combine addition with assignment we use +=. To combine division with assignment, we use /=. The previous examples, hence, can be written more succinctly with compound assignment operators as follows:

```
counter += 10;
xPosition += xVelocity;
score /= 2;
```

Refer to Table 5-1 for a list of the compound assignment operators.

Arithmetic Operators

The arithmetic operators perform mathematical operations on numeric operands. If you use non-numeric operands with the arithmetic operators, ActionScript will attempt to convert the foreign data to a number. For example, `false - true` evaluates to –1 because `false` converts to the numeric value 0 and `true` converts to 1. Similarly, the expression `"3" * "5"` results in the number 15, because the strings "3" and "5" are converted to the numbers 3 and 5 before the multiplication is performed. The + operator, however, presents a special case: when used with at least one string operand, it performs a string concatenation operation, not mathematical addition.

If an attempt to convert a non-numeric operand to a number fails, the operand will be set to the special numeric value `NaN`. This results in the entire operation yielding `NaN`. Refer to Table 3-1 for details on numeric conversion.

Addition

The *addition* operator returns the sum of its two operands:

```
operand1 + operand2
```

In order to return a meaningful mathematical result, the operands of + should be expressions that yield a numeric value, such as:

```
234 + 5           // Returns 239
(2 * 3 * 4) + 5   // Returns 29
```

The addition operator is unique among the arithmetic operators in that if one or both of its operands are strings, it performs as a string concatenation. Refer to "Joining Strings Together" in Chapter 4, *Primitive Datatypes*.

Increment

A handy variation on addition, the *increment* operator accepts a single operand and simply adds 1 to its current value. Increment has two general forms, called *prefix increment* and *postfix increment*, as follows:

```
++operand     // Prefix increment
operand++     // Postfix increment
```

In both forms, increment adds 1 to a variable, array element, or object property, such as:

```
var x = 1;
x = x + 1;    // x is now 2 (the verbose syntax)
x++;          // Add 1: x is now 3
++x;          // Add 1: x is now 4
```

When used in isolation, there is no difference between postfix and prefix increment, although postfix increment is more common by convention.

However, when used in larger expressions, postfix and prefix increment have different behaviors: prefix increment adds 1 to *operand* and returns the value of *operand + 1*; postfix increment adds 1 to *operand* but returns the value of *operand* itself, not *operand + 1*:

```
var x = 1;
// Postfix increment: y is set to 1, then x is incremented to 2
var y = x++;

var x = 1;
// Prefix increment: x is incremented first, so y is set to 2
var y = ++x;
```

We'll revisit the increment operators in Chapter 8, *Loop Statements*.

Subtraction

The *subtraction* operator subtracts the second operand from the first operand. It takes the general form:

```
operand1 - operand2
```

The operands may be any valid expression. If either operand is not of the *number* type and conversion to a real number fails, the operation yields NaN:

```
234 - 5  // Yields 229
5 - 234  // Yields -229
```

To determine the absolute (i.e., positive) difference between two numbers, see the *Math.abs()* method in Part III, *Language Reference*.

Decrement

The *decrement* operator is analogous to the increment operator, but subtracts 1 from its operand's current value instead of adding 1. Like increment, decrement has two general forms, called *prefix decrement* and *postfix decrement*, as follows:

```
--operand  // Prefix decrement
operand--  // Postfix decrement
```

In both forms, it is used to subtract 1 from a variable, array element, or object property. Prefix decrement subtracts 1 from *operand* and returns the value of *operand* - 1; postfix decrement subtracts 1 from *operand* but returns the value of *operand* itself, not *operand* - 1. As with the increment operators, the form of decrement used matters only if the operand is part of a larger expression:

```
var x = 10;
var y;
x = x - 1;     // x is now 9
x--;           // x is now 8
--x;           // x is now 7
y = --x;       // y is now 6, x is now 6
y = x--;       // y is still 6, x is now 5
```

Multiplication

The *multiplication* operator multiplies two numeric operands and returns the result (i.e., the *product*). Multiplication takes the general form:

operand1 * *operand2*

The operands may be any valid expression. The * symbol used for multiplication is in lieu of the X ("times") symbol used in traditional mathematics. If either operand is not of the *number* type, and conversion to a real number fails, the operation yields NaN:

```
6 * 5  // Returns 30
```

Division

The *division* operator divides the first operand (the *numerator*) by the second operand (the *divisor*) and returns the result (the *quotient*). Division takes the general form:

operand1 / *operand2*

The operands must be valid numeric expressions. The / symbol used for division is in lieu of the ÷ symbol used in traditional mathematics. If either operand is not of the *number* type, and conversion to a real number fails, the operation yields NaN. If necessary to express a fractional result, the quotient is a floating-point number even if both operands are integers:

```
20 / 5  // Returns 4
5 / 4   // Returns 1.25; In other languages, the result may be 1, not 1.25
```

Note that some other languages, such as Director's Lingo language, return an integer unless at least one operand is a float.

If the divisor is zero, the result is Infinity. If there is any possibility of the divisor being zero, check its value before performing the division, such as:

```
if (numItems != 0) {
  trace ("Average is" + total / numItems);
else
  trace ("There are no items for which to calculate the average");
}
```

Note that in some languages, attempting to divide by zero causes an error.

Modulo Division

The *modulo* operator performs so-called *modulo division*. It returns the remainder (i.e., *modulus*) that results when the first operand is divided by the second. Modulo division takes the general form:

operand1 % operand2

For example 14 % 4 returns the value 2 because 4 divides evenly into 14 three times, with 2 being the remainder.

The operands of modulo may be any valid numeric expression, including integers and (unlike C and C++) floating-point numbers. For example, 5 % 4 is 1, and 5 % 4.5 is 0.5. If either operand is not of the *number* type, and conversion to a real number fails, the operation yields NaN.

If a number is even, the modulo will be zero when we divide the number by two. We can use the trick shown in Example 5-1 to test whether a number is even or odd.

Example 5-1. Using Modulo Division to Test for Even Numbers

```
var x = 3;
if (x%2 == 0) {
  trace("x is even");
} else {
  trace("x is odd");
}
```

Unary Negation

The *unary negation* operator takes only one operand. It switches the operand's sign (that is, positive becomes negative, negative becomes positive). Unary negation takes the general form:

-operand

The operand may be any valid expression. Here we test whether something's horizontal position is greater than the positive limit or less than the negative limit:

```
if (xPos > xBoundary || xPos < -xBoundary){
  // We've gone too far
}
```

The Equality and Inequality Operators

We use the *equality* operator (==) to test whether two expressions have the same value. The equality test takes the general form:

```
operand1 == operand2
```

where **operand1** and **operand2** may be any valid expression. The equality operator can compare operands of any type. When **operand1** and **operand2** are equal, the expression returns the Boolean value `true`; when they differ, it returns the Boolean value `false`. For example:

```
var x = 2;
x == 1       // false
x == 2       // true
```

The equality operator is created using two equal signs in a row (==). It determines whether two expressions are equal and should not be confused with the assignment operator (=) which is used to assign a variable a new value.

Consider this example:

```
if (x = 5) {
   trace ("x is equal to 5")
}
```

The preceding example does *not* check whether **x** equals 5. Instead, it *sets* **x** equal to 5. The proper expression is as follows:

```
// Use == instead of =
if (x == 5) {
   trace ("x is equal to 5")
}
```

Primitive Datatype Equality

For the primitive datatypes, the result of most equality tests is fairly intuitive. Table 5-2 lists the rules that govern equality for each primitive datatype.

Table 5-2. Equality of Primitive Datatypes

Type	Terms of Equality (both operands must be of given type)

Number	If *operand1* is the same number as *operand2*, the result is `true`. If both operands are +Infinity or both are −Infinity, the result is `true`. If both operands are either −0 or +0, the result is `true`. For all other combinations, including if *either* or *both* operands are NaN, the result is `false`:
	`1 == 4          // false`
	`4 == 4          // true`
	`NaN == NaN       // false`
	`+Infinity = -Infinity  // false`

Table 5-2. Equality of Primitive Datatypes (continued)

Type	Terms of Equality (both operands must be of given type)

String*	Performs case-sensitive string comparison. If *operand1* and *operand2* are strings of the same length that contain the exact same sequence of characters, the result is `true`; otherwise, the result is `false`:
	`"Flash" == "Flash"` `// true`
	`"O'Reilly" == "O Reilly"` `// false`
	`"Moock" == "moock"` `// false ("m" and "M" are`
	`// not the same character)`

Boolean	If both operands are `true` or both operands are `false`, the result is `true`; otherwise, the result is `false`:
	`true == true` `// true`
	`false == false` `// true`
	`true == false` `// false`

undefined	If both operands are `undefined` or one operand is `undefined` and the other is `null`, the result is `true`; otherwise, the result is `false`:
null	If both operands are `null` or if one operand is `undefined` and the other is `null`, the result is `true`; otherwise, the result is `false`:
Composite datatypes	See the following section, "Composite Datatype Equality."

* Flash 4's string equality operator was `eq`. While `eq` is supported in Flash 5 for backward compatibility, it is not recommended unless exporting to Flash 4 *.swf* format.

Composite Datatype Equality

Because variables containing composite data (objects, arrays, functions, or movie clips) store *references* to the data and not the data itself, it is possible for two variables to refer to the same underlying item. Two such operands are considered equal if and only if they refer to the same underlying composite data, not if the operands refer to two different items that contain identical contents. Even if two operands can be converted to the same primitive value they are still not necessarily considered equal.

The following examples illustrate how ActionScript compares the references that point to the composite data, not the data itself. In the first example, the operands (`nameList1` and `nameList2`) refer to arrays that have the same elements but are actually two distinct arrays. The references are therefore different and the comparison evaluates to `false`:

```
nameList1 = ["Linkovich", "Harris", "Sadler"];
nameList2 = ["Linkovich", "Harris", "Sadler"];
nameList1 == nameList2  // false
```

In this example, `cities` and `canadianCities` both refer to the same array:

```
canadianCities = ["Toronto","Montreal","Vancouver"];
cities = canadianCities;
cities == canadianCities  // true
```

In this example, `myFirstBall` and `mySecondBall` have the same constructor (i.e., are both objects derived from the same class), but they exist as separate (unequal) instances:

```
myFirstBall = new Ball();
mySecondBall = new Ball();
myFirstBall == mySecondBall  // false
```

Thus, equality tests for composite data values are said to be compared by reference, not by value. For more information on the difference, see "Copying, Comparing, and Passing Data" in Chapter 15, *Advanced Topics*.

To duplicate an array's contents without copying the array reference, we can use the *Array.slice()* method. In this example, we copy the elements from the `dishes` array into `kitchenItems`:

```
dishes = [ "cup", "plate", "spoon" ];
kitchenItems = dishes.slice(0, dishes.length);
trace(kitchenItems == dishes);  // Displays: false
```

Now `kitchenItems` and `dishes` each contains its own private copy of the array elements and can alter them without affecting each other.

Equality and Datatype Conversion

We've seen the results of equality tests when the two operands have the same datatype, but what happens when we compare operands of different datatypes, such as a string and a number, as in:

```
"asdf" == 13;
```

When the operands have disparate datatypes, the interpreter performs a type conversion before performing the comparison. Here are the rules the interpreter follows:

1. If both operands are of the same type, compare them and return the result. (If `null` is compared to `undefined`, `true` is returned.)

2. If one operand is a number and the other operand is a string, convert the string to a number and go back to step 1.

3. If one operand is a Boolean, convert the Boolean to a number (`true` = 1, `false` = 0) and go back to step 1.

4. If one operand is an object, invoke the *valueOf()* method of the object to convert it to a primitive type. Return `false` if this is not possible. Otherwise, go back to step 1.

5. Return `false` if the previous steps don't obtain a valid result.

Note that if one operand is an object and the other is a Boolean, the Boolean will be converted to a number and compared to the primitive value of the object. This means that `someObject == true` is normally `false`, even if `someObject` exists, because `someObject` is converted to a number or a string for the comparison while `true` is converted to the number 1. To force `someObject` to be treated as a Boolean in a comparison, we use the *Boolean( )* function, like this:

```
Boolean(someObject) == true    // Returns true if someObject exists,
                               // or false if it doesn't
```

Conversions caused by equality operations favor the number type. If you're wondering about the results of the various type conversions just described, see "Datatype Conversion" in Chapter 3.

Note that type conversions performed during a comparison do not alter the original item's stored value or datatype. The results of the temporary conversion are discarded once the expression has been evaluated.

The Inequality Operator

The *does-not-equal* or *not-equal-to* operator (or *inequality* operator) returns the opposite Boolean result of the equality operator. It is often more readable to say, "If x is *not* equal to y, do this," than to say, "If x is equal to y, don't do anything, otherwise do this," as shown later in Example 5-2. The inequality operator takes the general form:

```
operand1 != operand2
```

For example:

```
var a = 5;
var b = 6;
var c = 6;
a != b  // true
b != c  // false
```

The inequality operator follows the same type conversion rules as the equality operator and always yields the opposite result, including when using NaN as one operand:

```
NaN != 7    // true
NaN != NaN  // true!
```

In some languages, including Flash4 ActionScript, the <> operator is used as the inequality operator. See also the NOT operator (!) discussed later.

Common Uses of Equality Operations

We'll frequently use equality operations to form Boolean expressions within conditional statements or to assign a Boolean value to a variable. Example 5-2 shows both situations and demonstrates the != and == operators in action.

Example 5-2. Using the Equality and Inequality Operators

```
version = getVersion();        // Retrieve Player version

// Check if the string "WIN" is in version. If so,
// set isWin to true, otherwise set it to false
isWin = (version.indexOf("WIN") != -1);

// If isWin is true...
if (isWin == true) {
  // ...perform Windows-specific actions here
  trace("Please use IE4 or later on Windows.");
}
```

Experienced programmers will be quick to point out that we could have reduced *if(isWin==true)* to *if(isWin)*, because `isWin` holds a Boolean value, which is what the *if* statement expects. While that's quite right, it doesn't make for a good example of the equality operator, now does it? Also, new programmers usually find the more verbose form clearer. Both approaches are perfectly acceptable. I'll cover this topic in more detail in Chapter 7, *Conditionals*.

The Comparison Operators

The *comparison* operators (also called *relational* operators) are used to determine which of two values appears first in a given order. Like the equality and inequality operators, the comparison operators return one of the Boolean values `true` or `false` indicating whether the relationship described in the comparison is accurate (`true`) or inaccurate (`false`).

Comparison operators work only with strings and numbers. When the two operands of a comparison operator are numbers, the comparison is performed mathematically: *5 < 10* is `true`, *-3 < -6* is `false`, and so on. When the two operands of a comparison operator are strings, the comparison is performed according to character code points, as shown in Appendix B, *Latin 1 Character Repertoire and Keycodes*. See "Comparing Strings" in Chapter 4 for details on string comparisons.

The interpreter will attempt to convert any nonstring or nonnumeric data value used in a comparison operation to the *string* or *number* type. We'll consider the effect of datatype conversions on comparison operations after we discuss the comparison operators themselves.

The Less-Than Operator

The *less-than* operator takes the general form:

> operand1 < operand2

If the operands are numeric, the less-than operator returns the Boolean `true` if *operand1* is mathematically smaller than *operand2*:

```
5 < 6        // true
5 < 5        // false; they are equal, but 5 is not less than 5
-3 < -6      // false; -3 is larger than -6
-6 < -3      // true;  -6 is smaller than -3
```

If the operands are strings, the less-than operator returns `true` if *operand1* comes "alphabetically" before *operand2* (see Appendix B); otherwise, returns `false`:

```
"a" < "z"        // true; lowercase "a" comes before lowercase "z"
"A" < "a"        // true; uppercase letters come before lowercase
"Z" < "a"        // true; uppercase letters come before lowercase
"hello" < "hi"   // true; "e" is less than "i"
```

The Greater-Than Operator

The *greater-than* operator takes the general form:

> operand1 > operand2

If the operands are numeric, the greater-than operator returns the Boolean `true` if *operand1* is mathematically larger than *operand2*:

```
5 > 6        // false
5 > 5        // false; they are equal, but 5 is not greater than 5
-3 > -6      // true; -3 is greater than -6.
-6 > -3      // false; -6 is not greater than -3.
```

If the operands are strings, the greater-than operator returns `true` if *operand1* comes "alphabetically" after *operand2* (see Appendix B); otherwise, returns `false`:

```
"a" > "z"        // false; lowercase "a" comes before lowercase "z"
"A" > "a"        // false; uppercase letters don't come after lowercase
"Z" > "a"        // false; uppercase letters don't come after lowercase
"hello" > "hi"   // false; "e" is less than "i"
```

The Less-Than-or-Equal-to Operator

The *less-than-or-equal-to* operator takes the general form:

> operand1 <= operand2

If the operands are numeric, the less-than-or-equal-to operator returns the Boolean `true` if *operand1* is mathematically smaller than or equal to *operand2*:

```
5 <= 6        // true
5 <= 5        // true; note the difference from 5 < 5
-3 <= -6      // false
-6 <= -3      // true
```

If the operands are strings, this operator returns `true` if *operand1* comes "alphabetically" before *operand2* or if the operands are identical according to the rules described under "Comparing Strings" in Chapter 4; otherwise, it returns `false`:

```
"a" <= "z"        // true; lowercase "a" comes before lowercase "z"
"A" <= "a"        // true; although not equal, "A" comes before "a"
"Z" <= "a"        // true; uppercase letters come before lowercase
"hello" <= "hi"   // true; "e" is less than "i"
```

Note that the `<=` operator is written with the equal sign after the less-than sign. The following is not a valid operator: `=<`.

The Greater-Than-or-Equal-to Operator

The *greater-than-or-equal-to* operator takes the general form:

```
operand1 >= operand2
```

If the operands are numeric, the greater-than-or-equal-to operator returns the Boolean `true` if *operand1* is mathematically larger than or equal to *operand2*:

```
5 >= 6        // false
5 >= 5        // true; note the difference from 5 > 5
-3 >= -6      // true
-6 >= -3      // false
```

If the operands are strings, this operator returns `true` if *operand1* comes "alphabetically" after *operand2* or if the operands are identical according to the rules described under "Comparing Strings" in Chapter 4; otherwise, it returns `false`:

```
"a" >= "z"        // false; lowercase "a" comes before lowercase "z"
"A" >= "a"        // false; "A" comes before "a" and they are not equal
"Z" >= "a"        // false; uppercase letters come before lowercase
"hello" >= "hi"   // false; "e" is less than "i"
```

Note that the `>=` operator is written with the equal sign after the greater-than sign. The following is not a valid operator: `=>`.

Comparison Operations and Datatype Conversion

Most of the time, when we're using comparison operators we're comparing numbers. Type conversions instigated by the comparison operators, hence, favor numbers. When the two operands of any comparison operator belong to different datatypes, or when neither operand is a string or a number, a type conversion is attempted according to the following steps:

1. If both operands are numbers, compare the operands mathematically and return the result. If either number is (or both numbers are) NaN, the result of the comparison is `false` except in the case of the != operator.

2. If both operands are strings, compare the operands alphabetically using the code points shown in Appendix B and return the result.

3. If one operand is a number and the other is a string, convert the string to a number and go back to step 1.

4. If either operand is a Boolean, `null`, or `undefined`, convert the operand to a number and go back to step 1.

5. If either operand is an object, invoke its *valueOf()* method to convert the object to a primitive value and go back to step 1. If the *valueOf()* method fails or does not return a primitive value, return `false`.

6. Return `false`.

Note that type conversions performed during a comparison do not alter the original item's stored value or datatype. The results of the temporary conversion are discarded once the expression has been evaluated.

Here is a simple conversion example comparing two Booleans:

```
false < true      // true: 0 is less than 1
```

Comparison operators always convert composite datatypes to strings or numbers for comparison. In the following example, because both `someObj` and `someOtherObj` are members of the Object class, their string value, "[object Object]", is the same:

```
someObj = new Object();
someOtherObj = new Object();
someObj <= someOtherObj;    // true!
```

In the next example, even though "A" has the code point 65, converting "A" to a number yields NaN, which means the whole expression yields `false`. Use the *charCodeAt()* function to check a string's code point:

```
"A" <= 9999               // false
"A".charCodeAt(0) < 9999   // true
```

The String Operators

Special string operators—concatenation (&), equality (eq), inequality (ne), and comparison (lt, gt, le, ge)—were required when using string data in Flash 4. In Flash 5 and later, the special string operators are *deprecated* (i.e., supported but obsolete). Use ==, !=, <, >, <=, and >= for string comparisons, unless exporting to Flash 4 *.swf* format, in which case you must use the old operators (eq, ne, lt, gt, le, ge). Use + for string concatenation, unless exporting to Flash 4 format, in which case you should use add instead of & (because & is the bitwise AND operator in Flash 5 and later).

For more details and a list of Flash 4 versus Flash 5 string-operation equivalencies, see "Working with Strings" and Table 4-2 in Chapter 4.

The Logical Operators

In Chapter 4, we learned how to make logical decisions using Boolean values. The decisions we considered were based on single factors: if a movie hasn't loaded, don't start playing; if a spaceship has double-shot power, increase the damage its shots inflict, and so on. Not all programming logic is so simple. We'll often want to consider multiple factors in our *branching* (i.e., decision-making) logic.

Suppose, for example, that we are making a personalized Flash site that requires users to log in. If a user logs in as a guest, the content he can see is limited. When a registered user logs into the site, we set a variable that indicates, for the duration of our movie, that the user is allowed to see privileged content:

```
var userStatus = "registered";
```

To decide whether to allow access to a restricted area, we use a Boolean check like this:

```
if (userStatus == "registered") {
  // It's okay, let 'em in...
}
```

Suppose we want to demonstrate the site to prospective investors without forcing them to register and without showing them material reserved for registered users. We can invent a new user category, "specialGuest," that allows investors to see more than a guest but not as much as a registered user. When we want to identify someone as a special guest, we set userStatus to "specialGuest."

How do we perform a Boolean check now that there are two categories of users to allow in? We could do things the brutish, painful way by duplicating portions of our code:

```
if (userStatus == "registered") {
  // Execute legal-user code...
}

if (userStatus == "specialGuest") {
  // Execute exact same legal-user code...
}
```

Obviously, that's going to turn into a real headache to maintain. Every bit of complexity we add to our script doubles, and we end up with serious version-control problems.

We'd prefer to perform a single Boolean check that says, "If the user is registered *or* if the user is a special guest, then grant access." We can produce compound logical phrases like that with Boolean *logical operators*. Here, the logical OR operator (||) lets us check the status of multiple Boolean operations in a single expression:

```
if (userStatus == "registered" || userStatus == "specialGuest") {
    // Execute legal user code...
}
```

Nice, huh? Sometimes programming is so elegant. Such distinctive vertical lines . . . such supple parentheses . . .

Logical OR

The *logical OR* operator is most commonly used to initiate some action when at least one of two conditions is met. For example, "If I am hungry *or* I am thirsty, I'll go to the kitchen." The symbol for logical OR is made using two vertical line characters (||). The | character is typically accessible using the Shift key and the Backslash (\) key in the upper right of most keyboards, where it may be depicted as a dashed vertical line. Logical OR takes the general form:

operand1 || *operand2*

When both operands are Boolean expressions, logical OR returns `true` if either operand is `true` and returns `false` only if *both* operands are `false`. In summary:

```
true  || false   // true because first operand is true
false || true    // true because second operand is true
true  || true    // true (either operand being true is sufficient)
false || false   // false because both operands are false
```

The preceding is a simplified case in which both operands are Booleans, but the operands can be any valid expression including non-Boolean ones. In that case, the return value of a logical OR operation is not necessarily a Boolean (`true` or `false`). Technically, the first step in evaluating a logical OR is to convert `operand1` to a Boolean; if the result of such a conversion is `true`, logical OR returns `operand1`'s resolved value. Otherwise logical OR returns `operand2`'s resolved value. Some code to demonstrate:

```
null || "hi there!"  // Operand1 does not convert to true, so the
                     // operation returns operand2's value: "hi there!"

true || false        // Operand1 is true, so the operation returns
                     // operand1's value: true
```

```
"hey" || "dude"        // Operand1 is a nonempty string, so it converts to
                       // false and the operation returns
                       // operand2's value: "dude"

false || 5 + 5         // Operand1 does not convert to true so the
                       // value of operand2 (namely 10) is returned
```

In practice, we rarely make use of non-Boolean values returned by a logical OR expression. Instead, we normally use the result in a conditional statement where it is used to make a Boolean decision. Consider Example 5-3.

Example 5-3. A Logical OR Operation as a Conditional Test Expression

```
var x = 10;
var y = 15;
if (x || y) {
  trace("One of either x or y is not zero");
}
```

On line 3, we see a logical OR operation *(x || y)* being used where a Boolean is expected as the test expression of an *if* statement. Our first step in determining the value of *x || y* is to convert 10 (the value of the first operand, **x**) to a Boolean. As Table 3-3 shows, any non-zero finite number converts to the Boolean **true**. When the first operand converts to **true**, the logical OR returns the value of the first operand, in this case 10. So to the interpreter, our *if* statement looks like this:

```
if (10) {
   trace("One of either x or y is not zero");
 }
```

But 10 is a number, not a Boolean. So what happens? The *if* statement *converts* the return value of the logical OR operation to a Boolean. In this case, 10 is converted to the Boolean value **true** (again, according to the rules in Table 3-3), and the interpreter sees our code as:

```
if (true) {
   trace("One of either x or y is not zero");
 }
```

And there you have it. The test expression is **true**, so the *trace()* statement between the curly braces is executed.

Note that if the first operand in a logical OR operation resolves to **true**, it is unnecessary and therefore inefficient to evaluate the second operand. Therefore, ActionScript evaluates the second operand only if the first operand resolves to **false**. This fact is useful in cases in which you don't want to resolve the second operand unless the first operand resolves to **false**. In this example, we check if a number is out of range. If the number is too small, there is no need to perform the second test in which we check whether it is too large:

```
if (xPos < 0 || xPos > 100) {
   trace ("xPos is not between 0 and 100 inclusive.");
 }
```

Logical AND

Like the logical OR operator, *logical AND* is primarily used to execute a block of code conditionally, in this case only when both of two conditions are met. The logical AND operator takes the general form:

```
operand1 && operand2
```

Both **operand1** and **operand2** may be any valid expression. In the simplest case in which both operands are Boolean expressions, logical AND returns `false` if either operand is `false` and returns `true` only if *both* operands are `true`. In summary:

```
true  && false    // false because second operand is false
false && true     // false because first operand is false
true  && true     // true because both operands are true
false && false    // false because both operands are false (either is sufficient)
```

Let's see how the logical AND operator is used in two real examples. In Example 5-4, we execute a *trace()* statement only when two variables are both greater than 50.

Example 5-4. A Logical AND Operation as a Conditional Test Expression

```
x = 100;
y = 51;
if (x>50 && y>50) {
  trace("Both x and y are greater than 50");
}
```

Because the expressions *x>50* and *y>50* are both `true`, the *trace()* statement is executed.

In Example 5-5, we return to our web site example in which access was restricted to registered users and special guests. But this time we'll let users in only if the date is not January 1. Note the use of the *Date* object to determine the current date. Note that *getMonth()* returns 0 to indicate January.

Example 5-5. Compound Logical Expressions

```
userStatus = "registered";
now = new Date();        // Create a new Date object
day = now.getDate();     // Returns an integer between 1 and 31
month = now.getMonth();  // Returns an integer between 0 and 11

// Note the indentation style and parentheses...if statements may span
// multiple lines for the sake of readability
if ( ((userStatus == "registered") || (userStatus == "specialGuest"))
    && (month + day) > 1) {
  // Let the user in...
}
```

The technical behavior of the logical AND operator is quite similar to that of the logical OR operator. First, *operand1* is converted to a Boolean. If the result of that conversion is `false`, the value of *operand1* is returned. If the result of that conversion is `true`, the value of *operand2* is returned.

If the first operand in a logical AND operation resolves to `false`, it is unnecessary and therefore inefficient to evaluate the second operand. Therefore, ActionScript evaluates the second operand only if the first operand resolves to `true`. This fact is useful in cases in which you don't want to resolve the second operand unless the first operand resolves to `true`. In this example, we perform the division only if the divisor is nonzero:

```
if (numItems != 0 && total / numItems > 3) {
    trace ("You've averaged more than 3 dollars per transaction");
}
```

Logical NOT

The *logical NOT* operator (`!`) returns the Boolean opposite of its single operand. It takes the general form:

```
!operand
```

where *operand* may be any legal expression. If *operand* is `true`, logical NOT returns `false`. If *operand* is `false`, logical NOT returns `true`. If *operand* is not a Boolean, its value is converted to a Boolean for the sake of the operation and its opposite is returned.

Like the does-not-equal operator (`!=`), the logical NOT operator is convenient for testing what something *isn't* rather than what it *is*. Recall Example 5-5 in which we wanted to perform an action only if the date was not January 1. At first impression, this attempt might seem correct:

```
month != 0 && day != 1
```

We find, however, that *month != 0* is `true` anytime the month is not January (so far so good), but *day != 1* is actually `false` on the first day of every month. So the expression *month != 0 && day != 1* would exclude our users on the first day of any month, not just January 1. Hardly what we intended.

It's much easier to check if today *is* January 1:

```
month == 0 && day == 1
```

That expression yields `true` only on the first day of January. Once we've gotten that far, all we need is the NOT operator to determine when today is *not* January 1:

```
!(month==0 && day==1)
```

Obviously this code's intent is much clearer than the *month+day > 1* test used in Example 5-5.

Another typical usage of the NOT operator is to *toggle* a variable from `true` to `false` and vice versa. For example, suppose you have a single button that is used to turn the sound on and off. You might use code like this:

```
soundState = !soundState  // Reverse the current sound state
if (soundState) {
  // If sound is turned on, make sure sounds are audible
} else {
  // If the sound is off, set the volume to 0 to mute it
}
```

Notice that `!` is also used in the inequality operator (`!=`). As a programming *token* (i.e., symbol), the `!` character usually means *not*, or *opposite*. It is unrelated to the `!` symbol used to indicate "factorial" in common mathematic notation.

Logical Expressions and Data Values

Using logical operators to calculate a Boolean result is analogous to using arithmetic operators to calculate a numeric result. For example, the following four operands and three operators are used to calculate a single result:

```
userStatus == "registered" || userStatus == "specialGuest"
```

If the user is not registered, but is a special guest, the preceding expression reduces to:

```
false || true
```

which in turn reduces to the Boolean result `true`.

Here is an analogous arithmetic operation that reduces to a single number:

```
(1 + 2) * (3 + 4)  // Four values (1, 2, 3, 4) which become...
3 * 7              // two values (3, 7), which become...
21                 // a single value (21)
```

Remember, a complex expression that reduces to a Boolean can be used anywhere a single Boolean value is required (such as the test expression of a conditional statement).

The Grouping Operator

Aside from being used in function calls, parentheses `( )` can also be used to group a phrase of code to override the precedence of various operators. Parentheses are also required in some statements, most notably *if* statements. Parentheses take the general form:

```
(expression)
```

The *expression* within the parentheses is evaluated and returned. Here are some examples:

```
if (x == y) {                    // Syntactically required for if statement
   trace("x and y are equal");   // Required for the function call
}
(5 + 6) * 7                      // Force a nonstandard order of operation
(x >= 100) || (y <= 50)          // Parentheses not required but added for legibility
x >= 100 || y <= 50              // No parentheses...a little harder to read
```

The Comma Operator

Rarely used, the *comma* operator (,) allows us to evaluate two expressions where a single expression is expected. It takes the general form:

```
operand1, operand2
```

Both operands must be legal expressions. When a comma operation executes, *operand1* is evaluated, then *operand2* is evaluated, and then the resolved value of *operand2* is returned. In practice, the return value of the comma operator is usually ignored.

The comma operator is primarily used in *for* loops that initialize multiple variables as shown in Example 5-6. Note that in the first line of the example, the expressions i=0 and j=10 are both operands of the comma operator. (These expressions cause i and j to be initialized to 0 and 10.) The expressions i++ and j-- are both operands of a second comma operator. (These expressions cause i to be incremented and j to be decremented each time the loop executes.) The comma operator is used in order to squeeze multiple expressions within the confines of the *for* loop's syntax.

Example 5-6. Using the Comma Operator in a for Loop

```
for (var i=0, j=10; i!=j; i++, j--) {
  trace ("i: " + i + " j: " + j);
}

// Which produces this output...
 i: 0 j: 10
 i: 1 j: 9
 i: 2 j: 8
 i: 3 j: 7
 i: 4 j: 6
```

The void Operator

The *void* operator is used to evaluate an expression without returning a value. It has the syntax:

```
void expression
```

where **expression** is the expression to evaluate. In JavaScript, *void* is used to evaluate a JavaScript expression in a hypertext link without causing the result to appear in the browser's address bar. There are few, if any, such applications for *void* in ActionScript; it is included for the sake of compatibility with ECMA-262.

Other Operators

The remaining operators apply to topics considered in other chapters. We'll include them here for quick reference only and describe their usage fully in those chapters.

The Bitwise Operators

If you're planning to develop large-scale systems in which every iota of memory, calculation speed, and transfer-rate optimization makes a meaningful difference in performance, read about the bitwise operators in Chapter 15. Otherwise, use the Boolean logical operators, which perform the same tasks the bitwise operators do, albeit in a less optimized way.

The typeof Operator

The *typeof* operator is used to determine the datatype of an expression. It takes one operand, as follows:

```
typeof operand;
```

where **operand** may be any legal expression. The return value of the *typeof* operation is a string indicating the datatype of the evaluated **operand**. See Chapter 3 for more details.

The new Operator

The *new* operator creates a new composite datum—either an array or an object. The object may be a member of a built-in class or a user-defined class. The syntax for *new* is:

```
new constructor
```

where **constructor** must be a function that defines the properties of the newly created object. See Chapter 11, *Arrays*, and Chapter 12, *Objects and Classes*.

The delete Operator

We use the *delete* operator to remove an object, an object property, an array element, or variables from a script. The syntax for *delete* is:

```
delete identifier
```

If *identifier* is not a data container (variable, property, or element), the *delete* operation fails and returns the value `false`; otherwise, it returns `true`, indicating success. See Chapter 11.

Array-Element/Object-Property Operator

As we'll see in Chapters 11 and 12, we use the [ ] operator to retrieve and set the value of an array element or an object property. When accessing an array it takes the form:

```
array[element]
```

where *array* is the name of an array or an array literal and *element* is an expression that resolves to a zero-relative, non-negative integer representing the index of the array element to access.

When accessing an object, it takes the form:

```
object[property]
```

where *object* is an object name or object literal and *property* is any expression that resolves to a string representing the name of the object property to access.

When used on the left side of an assignment operator (=), the element or property is assigned the new value shown on the right side of the expression:

```
var colors = new Array();  // Create a new array
colors[0] = "orange";      // Set its first element
colors[1] = "green";       // Set its second element

var ball = new Object();   // Create a new object
var myProp = "xVelocity";  // Store a string in a variable
ball["radius"] = 150;      // Set the radius property
ball[myProp] = 10;         // Set the xVelocity property through myProp
```

When used anywhere else, the expression returns the value of the specified element or property:

```
diameter = ball["radius"] * 2;  // Sets diameter to 300
trace(colors[0]);               // Displays "orange"
```

The dot Operator

The *dot* operator is our primary means of referring to object properties and nested movie clips. Functionally, the dot operator has the exact same purpose as the [ ] operator—it lets us set and retrieve object-property values. But the two operators have syntactic differences that make them unique. The general syntax of the dot operator is:

```
object.property
```

where *object* must be the name of an object or an object literal, and *property* must be an identifier that represents a property of *object*. Note that *property* may *not* be an arbitrary expression or a string literal; it must be the name of a property. Because array elements are numbered, not named, the dot operator cannot be used to access the elements of an array.

When used as the lefthand operand of an assignment operator, the dot operator is used to set a new value for a property:

```
var ball = new Object();
ball.radius = 150;
ball.xVelocity = 10;
```

When used anywhere else, a dot operation returns the value of the named object property:

```
diameter = ball.radius;
newX = ball.xPosition + ball.xVelocity;
```

See Chapter 12, *Objects and Classes* and Chapter 13, *Movie Clips*.

The conditional Operator

The *conditional* operator is a syntactic convenience that lets us succinctly represent a simple conditional statement. This operator takes three operands, in the form:

```
condition ? result_if_true : result_if_false;
```

When a conditional operation is executed, the first operand (*condition*) is evaluated. If *condition* is **true** or can be converted to **true**, the value of the second operand (*result_if_true*) is returned. Otherwise, the value of the third operand (*result_if_false*) is returned. See Chapter 7.

The Function Call Operator

As we've seen with the *trace()* function and the string-manipulation functions, we use the function call operator, ( ), to invoke a function. A function call takes the general form:

```
function_name(argument_list)
```

The first operand, *function_name*, is the name of some function and *must* be an identifier, not an expression. The function must exist or the interpreter will produce an error. The *argument_list* is a series of zero or more arguments passed to the function, separated by commas. The return value of a function call operation is the return value supplied by the function itself.

The function call operator can call any built-in or user-defined function:

```
trace("an internal function");   // Built-in function, one argument
myClip.play();                    // Method of a movie clip, no arguments
myRectangle.area(6, 9);           // User-defined method, two arguments
init();                           // User-defined function, no arguments
```

Onward!

Like all languages, ActionScript has a grammar and different parts of speech. Over the last few chapters, you've learned the equivalent of sentence structure, nouns, adjectives, and conjunctions. Now, let's move on to statements, which, like verbs, can do things. Statements complete our ability to form sentence-like instructions.

6

Statements

We saw in earlier chapters how ActionScript stores and manipulates data. In this chapter we'll learn how to do things with that data. We'll give Flash instructions in the form of *statements*, or phrases of code that instruct the interpreter to perform some task.

To make something happen in Flash—whether stopping a sound, playing a movie, running a function, or looping some code—we use a statement. In fact, an Action-Script program can be defined as nothing more than a list of statements that tell the interpreter what we want Flash to do. Here, for example, is an entire Action-Script program, which consists of four statements and tells the interpreter to load a web page into the browser:

```
var protocol = "http";                          // Statement 1
var domain = "www.moock.org";                   // Statement 2
var path = "webdesign/flash/";                  // Statement 3
getURL(protocol + "://" + domain + "/" + path); // Statement 4
```

Scripting a movie with ActionScript is simply a matter of attaching statements to frames, movie clips, and buttons. This chapter explores the syntactic makeup of statements and lists the general statement categories. We'll touch on all the Action-Script statements in this chapter, but some of the more important ones will be examined in detail in later chapters.

Types of Statements

Conceptually speaking, there are five core types of statements:

Statements that control the execution flow of a program
  loops
  conditionals
  ifFrameLoaded

Statements that declare variables
> var
> set

Statements that declare, call, and return values from functions
> function
> function call
> call
> return

Statements that deal with objects
> with
> for . . . in

Statements that represent a data value
> any expression (especially expressions with side effects)

These informal categories help us to understand what we can tell the interpreter to do using statements. At first glance, the list may seem fairly limited. However, we'll see that there are many variations of conditionals and loops and that there are thousands of things we can do via function calls. First, let's see how statements are formed.

Statement Syntax

Statements are typically made up of *keywords* and *expressions*. We've already seen the *var* statement, which declares and optionally initializes a variable. Here's an example of the *var* statement's general syntax:

```
var numFrames;
```

The *keyword* (*var* in this case) identifies the beginning of the statement. Then comes the syntax required by the statement, which, in our example, is simply the name of a variable, **numFrames**. Finally, a semicolon marks the end of the statement.

In ActionScript, every statement should end with a semicolon. (It's good form to use semicolons, but not officially mandatory. In Chapter 14, *Lexical Structure*, I'll have more to say about semicolon usage.)

Some statements can take multiple forms. For example, we can use *var* with or without an optional initial assignment (in this case 10 is a simple expression whose value is assigned to **x**):

```
var x;        // Simple declaration
var x = 10;   // Declaration with assignment
```

We'll learn the specific syntax of each statement throughout the rest of this chapter.

Statement Blocks

Some statements actually include other statements, or *substatements*, as part of their syntax. For example, the *if* statement has this syntax:

```
if (expression) substatement;
```

The *substatement*, which is executed only if *expression* evaluates to **true**, can be a single statement such as a variable declaration statement:

```
if (x == 5) var numFrames = 2;
```

or it can be a *series* of statements grouped together as a *statement block*:

```
if (x == 5) {
  var numFrames;
  numFrames = 10;
  play();
}
```

As you can see, a statement block is any number of statements on one or more lines surrounded by curly braces:

```
{ statement1; statement2; statement3... }
```

By using a statement block as the substatement of our *if* statement, we've managed to specify many statements where normally only one is expected. Very handy.

Anywhere ActionScript expects a single statement we may use a statement block. In fact, statement blocks are sometimes required. For example, the *function* statement must always include a statement block, even if the function being declared has only one statement in its body:

```
function aheadTwoFrames() {
  gotoAndStop(_currentframe + 2);
}
```

For the sake of readability, statement blocks are typically formatted as shown here:

```
parent_syntax {
  substatement1;
  substatement2;
  substatement3;
}
```

where *parent_syntax* represents the statement for which we are defining a statement block.

Note that the opening curly brace appears at the end of the first line after `parent_ syntax`. The substatements of the statement block appear indented two spaces, each on its own line. The closing curly brace, also on its own line, is flush with the original main statement. Substatements within statement blocks should end with a semicolon, but there are no semicolons on the lines with curly braces.

The indenting format is simply a convention, not a requirement of legal syntax. This book adheres to the style used by the Flash ActionScript editor.

The ActionScript Statements

Now that you know how a typical statement is formed, skim Table 6-1 to acquaint yourself with some of the things that ActionScript statements do.

Table 6-1. The ActionScript Statements

Statement	Syntax	Use
break	`break;`	Cancels a loop
call	`call (frame);`	Executes the script on a remote frame
continue	`continue;`	Restarts the current loop

do-while	`do {`
	`  statements`
	`} while (expression);`
		A variation of a *while* loop

empty state- ment	`;`	Holds a place where a statement is expected, and used with *evaluate* in novice mode

for	`for (init; test; increment) {`
	`  statements`
	`}`
		Executes some code repetitively (a *for* loop)

for-in	`for (property in object) {`
	`  statements`
	`}`
		Enumerates the properties of an object

function	`function name(parameters) {`
	`  statements`
	`}`
		Declares a function

if-else if-else	`if (expression) {`
	`  statements`
	`} else if (expression) {`
	`  statements`
	`} else {`
	`  statements`
	`}`
		Executes some code based on a condition or a series of conditions

ifFrame- Loaded	`ifFrameLoaded (frame) {`
	`  statements`
	`}`
		Executes some code if a certain frame has loaded; deprecated in Flash 5

Table 6-1. The ActionScript Statements (continued)

Statement	Syntax	Use
return	`return;` `return expression;`	Exits a function or returns a value from a function
set	`set (variable, value);`	Assigns a value to a dynamically named variable
var	`var variableName;` `var variableName = expression;`	Declares and optionally initializes a variable

while	`while (expression) {`
	`    statements`
	`}`
		Executes some code repetitively (a *while* loop)

with	`with (objectName) {`
	`    statements`
	`}`
		Executes some code in the context of a given object

Loops and Conditionals

We've already had several informal encounters with loops and conditionals. Together, these two statement types account for the majority of complex flow in our programs. Loops allow us to execute statements repeatedly, and conditionals allow us to execute statements under only the specified circumstances. See Chapter 7, *Conditionals*, and Chapter 8, *Loop Statements*, for complete details.

Expression Statements

Although any expression can be used independently as a valid statement, if the expression performs no action and we don't do anything with the result, the exercise is rather pointless:

```
"hi there";   // This doesn't do much
345 + 5;      // Neither does this
```

Some expressions, however, have *side effects* that change the state of a system through variable or property assignments or by physically altering the Flash environment. In this example, an expression changes the value of x:

```
x = 345 + 5;  // Much more useful
```

Function calls are the most powerful type of expression statement. Even if a function doesn't return a useful value, it may have a very useful side effect. For example, *gotoAndStop()* returns the value **undefined** but has an important side effect—it moves the playhead to another frame:

```
gotoAndStop(5);   // The value of _currentframe is changed to 5.
```

We'll learn more about function calls under "Running Functions" in Chapter 9, *Functions*.

The var Statement

The *var* statement declares a new variable:

```
var x;
```

You can assign the new variable's initial value as part of a *var* statement:

```
var x = 10;
```

When used outside of a function, the *var* statement creates a variable scoped to the timeline containing the statement. When used inside a function, the *var* statement creates a variable local to that function (i.e., one that dies when the function finishes). See Chapter 2, *Variables*.

The set Statement (Set Variable)

For most variable assignments, we use an assignment expression in statement form, like this:

```
x = 30;
```

That kind of expression, however, requires us to know the name of our variable in advance. If we want to generate the name of a variable dynamically during an assignment, we can use the *set* statement, which has the following syntax:

```
set (variable, expression);
```

where *variable* is a string expression to be used as the variable name in the assignment and *expression* is the new value to assign to it. For example:

```
var x;
set ("x", 10);       // x is now 10

var firstName;
set ("first" + "Name", "jane");  // firstName is now "jane"
```

In the following, trickier example, **y** is not being set in the *set* statement. Instead, **y**'s value (**"x"**) is retrieved and that value is used as the name of the variable to set:

```
// Pay close attention to this one...
var y = "x";
var x;
set(y, 15);  // x is now 15, y is still "x".
```

In Flash 4, *set* was called *Set Variable*. In that version of ActionScript, it was often used to dynamically assign variables that had programmatically generated sequential names. This allowed programmers to simulate arrays, which were not a native part of Flash 4 ActionScript. Since arrays were added in Flash 5, *set* is rarely used. For more information on simulating arrays with *set*, see Chapter 2.

The function Statement

Just as the *var* statement is used to *declare* (i.e., create) variables, the *function* statement is used to declare functions. The *function* statement has the following syntax:

```
function funcName (param1, param2, param3,...paramn) {
  statements
}
```

The keyword **function** begins the statement; **funcName** is the name of the function being declared; **param1** through **paramn** define the parameters required by the function when it executes; **statements** is a list of one or more statements that will be executed when the function is called.

The *function* statement creates a function for later use but does not execute that function. To execute a function, we use the function's name in a *function call* statement.

Function Call Statements

A function call statement executes a built-in or user-defined function simply by using the function's name and providing the inputs that the function needs to perform its job. The terms *call, run,* and *invoke* are often used interchangeably to mean that a function's name has been used to cause it to execute. Function call statements have the following general syntax:

```
funcName (arg1, arg2, ... argn);
```

where **funcName** is the name of the function we want to execute and **arg1** through **argn** is the list of *arguments* (i.e., input values) that the function expects when it runs.

The function call statement is an extremely powerful and fundamental device; it's our primary means of controlling Flash movies. When we want to manipulate a movie in some way, we often call a function. Here are a few examples:

```
play();                        // Plays the current movie
gotoAndStop(5);                // Sends the playhead to frame 5
startDrag("crosshair", true);  // Makes the "crosshair" instance follow
                               // the mouse pointer
```

Function calls are also used with objects to invoke methods:

```
circle.area();
today.getDate();
```

Because movie clip instances are objects, we frequently use method invocation in our scripts:

```
ball.play()
intro.gotoAndStop("end");
```

We'll be learning more about using functions in Chapter 9 and we'll see how functions can become object methods in Chapter 12, *Objects and Classes.*

The call() Statement

On a simple level, a function is a series of reusable statements that can be executed at any time during the running of a program. Although Flash 4 did not support real functions, it did attempt to provide some of the portability of functions through remote script activation. In Flash 4 we could create something close to a function by attaching a list of statements to a frame with a label. A pseudofunction thus created could subsequently be executed via the *call()* statement:

```
call (frame);
```

The *call()* statement executes the script on the frame specified by **frame**, which may be any frame label or frame number. If the specified frame is not loaded, the *call()* statement fails silently.

Obviously, the pseudofunctions of Flash 4 pale in comparison with real functions, so we normally have no reason to use a *call()* statement when authoring for Flash 5 or later. But when we're authoring Flash 4 movies, we need to use the old-style subroutines and the Flash 4 *call()* statement.

The return Statement

When we call a function, we may optionally pass it one or more values (*parameters* or *arguments*) to manipulate during execution. A function may likewise send us back a *return value* (a value that results from the execution of a function and is sent back to the caller). Within the body of a function, we use the *return* statement to conclude the function's execution and optionally return a value. A *return* statement takes one of the following forms:

```
return;
return expression;
```

The optional **expression**, if included, becomes the return value of the function. A *return* statement without a return value exits the function and returns the value **undefined**. All *return* statements exit the current function. Note that *return* statements are not required in functions; a function without a *return* statement simply ends after the last statement in the function body and returns **undefined**. See Chapter 9 for more details on creating, calling, and terminating functions.

The with Statement

The *with* statement provides a shorthand way to refer to properties of an object without having to retype the object's name repeatedly. A *with* statement takes the general form:

```
with (object) {
   statements
}
```

When a property is referenced within a *with* statement block, `object` is checked for the specified property. If the property exists in `object`, then `object`'s property is used to resolve the property reference. If the property does not exist in `object`, the current timeline or function is consulted for the property in question.

The following example shows the difference between executing a statement inside a *with* statement and outside a *with* statement:

```
PI = 10;                    // Set a timeline variable, PI
with (Math) {               // Execute statements in the context of Math
   trace("pi is: " + PI);   // Displays: 3.1459... (PI is a property of Math)
}
trace("PI is: " + PI);      // Displays: 10 (Math is no longer accessed)
```

In addition to providing convenient access to object properties, *with* can be used to invoke object methods:

```
x = 10;
y = 11;
with (Math) {
   larger = max(x, y);
}
trace(larger);   // Displays: 11
```

It is not possible to define a new property on an object that is the target of a *with* statement. Notice in the previous example that the variable **larger** is *not* defined on the *Math* object, so the property reference affects the timeline or function that contains the *with* statement. The following code shows a misguided attempt to set a variable in **myClip**:

```
with (myClip) {
   var x = 10;   // x is set on the current timeline, not myClip
}
```

We can, however, legitimately use *with* to affect movie clip instances in other ways. It can provide a handy way to work with deeply nested instance structures. For example, we can change this:

```
_root.form.userProfile.userID = "U346BX";
_root.form.userProfile.gotoAndPlay("questionnaire");
```

to this:

```
with (_root.form.userProfile) {
   userID = "U346BX";              // Resets an existing variable
                                   // in userProfile instance
   gotoAndPlay("questionnaire");   // Function applied to userProfile instance
}
```

But *with* is not our only means of achieving this convenience. We could also simply assign our instance to a variable and use that variable in our references:

```
var userForm = _root.form.userProfile;
userForm.useriD = "U346BX";
userForm.gotoAndPlay("questionnaire");
```

Many developers find the variable approach easier to read and work with, but both are valid. We'll learn more about treating movie clips as objects in Chapter 13, *Movie Clips*.

The ifFrameLoaded Statement

The Flash 5 *ifFrameLoaded* statement replaces the *If Frame Is Loaded* Action used in prior versions. Like an *if* statement, *ifFrameLoaded* has a substatement that is executed only under certain circumstances. Here's the syntax:

```
ifFrameLoaded (expression) {
   statements
}
```

where **expression** must be either the number of a frame or a string indicating a frame label. If the frame indicated by **expression** has downloaded to the Player, **statements** are executed. If not, the statement block is skipped.

The *ifFrameLoaded* statement is awkward to use in preloading scripts because it lacks an *else* clause. It has, therefore, been deprecated and should be used only when authoring Flash 3 or older movies. In Flash 4 and later you should use the **_totalframes** and **_framesloaded** properties with *if-else* statements to create a more versatile preloader. For example:

```
if (_totalframes > 0 && _framesloaded == _totalframes) {
    gotoAndPlay("beginMovie");
} else {
    gotoAndPlay(_currentframe - 1);
}
```

The Empty Statement

For the sake of completeness we should mention that it is legal to issue a statement with no content via a lone semicolon:

```
;
```

The *empty statement* has very little practical application except that it can be used as a placeholder anywhere a statement is normally expected. It is not needed if you simply want to add blank lines to your code. ActionScript ignores blank vertical lines, which can be used to improve code readability.

In novice authoring mode, the lone semicolon appears when the *evaluate* Action is added to a block of code. An arbitrary statement may then be added by typing into the Expression field of the Parameters panel.

Statements Versus Actions

If you look through the Flash ActionScript editing environment, you won't find any reference to the word "statement." Even Macromedia's *Flash 5 ActionScript Reference Guide* uses the terms "Action" and "statement" interchangeably.

Using the term "Action" as a synonym for "statement" blurs the distinction between several different ActionScript tools. To see how, open the ActionScript editor and look in the Actions folder, as shown in Figure 1-2. Under the list of Actions in that folder, you'll find the statements we saw earlier in Table 6-1. Interspersed with the statements you'll also notice quite a few functions: *gotoAndPlay()*, *getURL()*, *startDrag()*, and so on. Although the functions listed as Actions can be used in statements, they're technically not unique statement types—they're just built-in functions. Statements, some built-in functions, and event handlers are all called Actions by Macromedia. Throughout this book, we do not use the generic term Action. Instead, each Action is described with the term that matches its formal role in the language: either *statement, function,* or *event handler.*

Onward!

Though we've learned a lot about statements, two important statement types— conditionals and loops—are yet to come. We'll deal with those kinds of statements in the next two chapters.

7

Conditionals

Most of the code examples we've seen so far have been very *linear*—each statement is executed in turn, starting with the first and ending with the last. Linear code always does the same thing. A *conditional*, by contrast, is a type of statement that performs an action only when a specified condition is met. In linear code, the interpreter might execute statement A, then statement B, then statement C. With conditional statements we can tell the interpreter to execute statement A, then execute *either* statement B *or* statement C, depending on condition X.

We can use conditionals to create and control situations that have more than one potential outcome. For example, suppose we want to create a password-protected site. When users attempt to log in, either the password is correct and the user is allowed to enter the site, or the password is wrong and the user sees an error message. The two outcomes require two very different blocks of code in our movie's script. One block needs to send the Flash playhead to a frame containing the site's welcome screen, and the other block needs to send the playhead to a frame with an error message. But only one of the blocks should be executed when the user attempts to log in. A conditional statement allows us to execute the appropriate block and skip the inappropriate one.

How does the interpreter know which code block to execute? When we define a conditional statement, we specify the condition that must be met in order for the *first* block of code to be executed. If the condition is not met, an alternate block of code may be executed (and that alternate block may, in turn, have its own condition). Essentially, we set up flowchart-like logic in our program that, in pseudocode, reads like this:

```
if (the first condition is met) {
  // Execute this code
} else if (the second condition is met) {
  // Execute this code
```

```
} ...otherwise {
  // Execute this code
}
```

Of course, we must describe each condition in terms the interpreter understands. Not a problem—that's just a question of syntax, which we'll learn next. Conceptually, all conditionals either allow or suppress the execution of a code block based on the specified condition. Now let's see how conditionals work in practice.

The if Statement

The *if* statement is your everyday, all-purpose conditional. We use *if* to create a two-pronged branch in our code, like a fork in the road. The *if* statement contains one or more substatements that are executed only when the specified condition is met. The *if* statement has the following syntax:

```
if (condition) {
  substatements
}
```

An *if* statement starts, not surprisingly, with the keyword if. The `condition` that must be satisfied for `substatements` to be executed is enclosed in parentheses. The `substatements` are one or more ActionScript statements. Each substatement should be on its own line and terminated with a semicolon. The entire *if* statement ends with a closing curly brace, (}), without a trailing semicolon.

The `condition` of our *if* statement can be any valid expression. When an *if* statement is executed, the interpreter checks the value of that expression (called the *test expression*). If it is true, the `substatements` are executed. Otherwise, the `substatements` are not executed. Here we use simple Boolean values as the test expression:

```
if (true) {
  trace("The condition was met!");  // This statement will be executed
}
if (false) {
  trace("The condition was met!");  // This statement is never executed
}
```

Of course, there's no practical reason to use Boolean literals as test expressions because their values never change. Instead, we'll use complex expressions that *return* Boolean values. For example, expressions that involve a comparison operation return a Boolean value, which makes them perfect for conditional test expressions:

```
var pointerX = _xmouse;  // Horizontal location of the mouse

// If pointerX > 300 yields true...
if (pointerX > 300) {
```

```
   // ...this statement is executed
   trace("The mouse is past the 300 pixel mark");
}
```

Now for the cool part: the test expression of a conditional doesn't necessarily have to evaluate to a Boolean—any expression will do. We can use a string or a number as the test expression of a conditional:

```
if ("hi") {
  trace("The condition was met!");
}
if (4) {
  trace("The condition was met!");
}
```

How does this work if the expressions "hi" and 4 are not Booleans? The answer lies in the marvels of datatype conversion as shown in Table 3-3. When the test expression of a conditional statement is not a Boolean value, the interpreter converts the expression to a Boolean. For example, the interpreter converts "hi" to **false** because all non-numeric strings convert to **false** when used in a Boolean context. So the condition is not met and the first *trace ()* statement is not executed. Similarly, the interpreter converts the number 4 to **true** (any nonzero number converts to **true**), so the second *trace ()* statement is executed.

All our earlier work learning about datatype conversion has paid off! Here are some basic applied examples. Try to guess whether each substatement will be executed:

```
x = 3;
if (x) {
  trace("x is not zero");
}
```

This example uses the OR operator, described in Chapter 5, *Operators*:

```
lastName = "";
firstName = "";
if (firstName != "" || lastName != "") {
  trace("Welcome " + firstName + " " + lastName);
}
```

Finally, we test whether a movie clip object exists:

```
if (myClip) {
  myClip._x = 0;  // If myClip exists, put it on
                  // the left edge of the Stage
}
```

The else Statement

With a lone *if* statement, we can cause a single code block to be optionally executed. By adding an *else* clause, we can choose which of two code blocks should be executed. Syntactically, an *else* statement is an extension of an *if* statement:

```
if (condition) {
  substatements1
} else {
  substatements2
}
```

where `condition` may be any valid expression. `substatements1` will be executed if `condition` is `true`; `substatements2` will be executed if `condition` is `false`. In other words, an *else* statement is perfect for depicting a mutually exclusive decision; one code block will be executed and the other will not.

Some code to demonstrate:

```
var lastName = "Grossman";
var gender = "male";
if (gender == "male") {
  trace("Good morning, Mr. " + lastName + ".");
} else {
  trace("Good morning, Ms. " + lastName + ".");
}
```

The *else* clause often acts as the backup plan of an *if* statement. Recall our password-protected web site example. If the password is correct, we let the user enter the site; otherwise, we display an error message. Here's some code we could use to perform the password check (assume that **userName** and **password** are the user's entries and that **validUser** and **correctPassword** are the correct login values):

```
if (userName == validUser && password == correctPassword) {
  gotoAndPlay("intro");
} else {
  gotoAndStop("loginError");
}
```

The Conditional Operator

Simple two-part conditional statements can be expressed conveniently with the conditional operator (?:). The conditional operator has three operands, which you'll recognize as analogous to the components of an *if-else* statement series:

```
condition ? expression1 : expression2;
```

In a conditional operation, if *condition* is `true`, *expression1* is evaluated and returned. Otherwise, *expression2* is evaluated and returned. The conditional operator is just a quicker way to write the following conditional statement:

```
if (condition) {
  expression1
} else {
  expression2
}
```

Like a conditional statement, the conditional operator can be used to control the flow of a program:

```
// If command is "go", play the movie; otherwise, stop
command == "go" ? play() : stop();
```

The conditional operator also provides a terse way to assign values to variables:

```
var guess = "c";
var answer = "d";
var response = (guess == answer) ? "Right" : "Wrong";
```

which is equivalent to:

```
var guess = "c";
var answer = "d";
if (guess == answer) {
  response = "Right";
} else {
  response = "Wrong";
}
```

The else if Statement

Using *if* and *else*, we can optionally execute one of two code blocks. By using *if* and *else if*, we can optionally execute one (or even none) of an *unlimited* number of code blocks. Like *else*, *else if* is a syntactic extension of an *if* statement:

```
if (condition1) {
  substatements1
} else if (condition2) {
  substatements2
} else if (condition3) {
  substatements3
} else {
  substatements4  // Catchall if other conditions were not met
}
```

where *condition1*, *condition2*, and *condition3* must be valid expressions. *substatements1* will be executed if *condition1* is `true`. If *condition1* is `false`, *substatements2* will be executed if *condition2* is `true`. Otherwise, *condition3* is evaluated and so on for as many *else if* statements are provided. If none of the test expressions are **true**, the statements in the final catchall *else* clause will be executed. For example, we could write a login-checking routine to provide insightful error messages, like this:

```
if (userName != validUser) {
  message = "User not found. Please try again.";
  gotoAndStop("loginError");
} else if (password != correctPassword) {
  message = "Password incorrect. Please try again.";
  gotoAndStop("loginError");
} else {
  gotoAndPlay("intro");
}
```

Note that an *else if* statement is merely a combination of an *else* with a nested *if* statement. Although the following two code segments are equivalent, the first one is much easier to read:

```
// Normal "else if" syntax
if (x > y) {
  trace("x is larger than y");
} else if (x < y) {
  trace("x is smaller than y");
} else {
  trace("x and y are equal");
}

// Expanded if/else chain
if (x > y) {
  trace("x is larger than y");
} else {
  if (x < y) {
    trace("x is smaller than y");
  } else {
    trace("x and y are equal");
  }
}
```

Simulating the switch Statement

Though *switch* statements (sometimes called *case* statements) are not supported by ActionScript, this common form of complex conditional can be emulated. A *switch* statement lets us execute only one of a series of possible code blocks based on the value of a single test expression. For example, in the following JavaScript *switch* statement, we greet the user with a custom message depending on the value of the test expression **gender**:

```
var surname = "Porter";
var gender = "male";

switch (gender) {
```

```
      case "femaleMarried" :
        alert("Hello Mrs. " + surname);
        break;
      case "femaleGeneric" :
        alert("Hello Ms. " + surname);
        break;
      case "male" :
        alert("Hello Mr. " + surname);
        break;
      default :
        alert("Hello " + surname);
    }
```

In the JavaScript example, *switch* attempts to match the value of **gender** to one of the *case* expressions: "femaleMarried", "femaleGeneric", or "male". Because **gender** matches the expression "male", the substatement *alert("Hello Mr. " + surname);* is executed. If the test expression had not matched any case, then the default statement—*alert("Hello " + surname);*—would have been executed.

In ActionScript, we can simulate a *switch* statement using a chain of *if–else if–else* statements, like this:

```
    var surname = "Porter";
    var gender = "male";

    if (gender == "femaleMarried") {
      trace("Hello Mrs. " + surname);
    } else if (gender == "femaleGeneric") {
      trace("Hello Ms. " + surname);
    } else if (gender == "male") {
      trace("Hello Mr. " + surname);
    } else {
      trace("Hello " + surname);
    }
```

In a more advanced approach, we could simulate a *switch* as a series of functions stored in the properties of a generic object. Example 7-1 shows the technique. Pay close attention to the comments to learn how it works. Also note the use of the conditional operator, which we encountered earlier.

Example 7-1.   A Simulated switch Statement

```
var surname = "Porter"; // Our user's name
var gender = "male";     // Our user's gender (the test expression)

// Create an object to act as our simulated switch statement
var mySwitch = new Object();

// Assign "case expression" properties to the mySwitch object.
// Each "case expression" property holds a function.
mySwitch.femaleMarried = function() {
  trace("Hello Mrs. " + surname);
};
```

Example 7-1.   A Simulated switch Statement (continued)

```
mySwitch.femaleGeneric = function() {
  trace("Hello Ms. " + surname);
};
mySwitch.male = function() {
  trace("Hello Mr. " + surname);
};
mySwitch.default = function() {
  trace("Hello " + surname);
};

// Now execute the appropriate function, depending on the
// value of gender (in our case, "male"). If the named
// property doesn't exist, execute the default function instead.
mySwitch[gender] ? mySwitch[gender]() : mySwitch["default"]();
```

Compact Conditional Syntax

Throughout this book we use statement blocks (statements surrounded by curly braces) with all conditional statements, even if a block contains only one statement:

```
if (x == y) {
  trace("x and y are equal");
}
```

For the sake of terseness, ActionScript does not require curly braces when a conditional has only one substatement. A single substatement may quite legitimately be placed directly after an *if* or an *else if* statement without any curly braces, like this:

```
if (x == y) trace ("x and y are equal");
```

Or like this:

```
if (x == y)
  trace ("x and y are equal");
```

For some programmers, this style can be a little slower to read and slightly more error prone, though it undeniably saves room in source code.

Onward!

Conditional statements are an immensely important component of ActionScript. They give us precise control over the execution of our code. In the next chapter, we'll examine another kind of important execution-control statement, *loops*.

8

Loop Statements

In the previous chapter, we learned that a *conditional* causes a statement block to be executed once if the value of its test expression is `true`. A *loop*, on the other hand, causes a statement block to be executed repeatedly, for as long as its test expression remains `true`.

Loops come in a variety of tasty flavors: *while*, *do-while*, *for*, and *for-in*. The first three types have very similar effects, but with varying syntax. The last type of loop, *for-in*, is a specialized kind of loop used with objects. We'll start our exploration of loops with the *while* statement, the easiest kind of loop to understand.

The while Loop

Structurally, a *while* statement is constructed much like an *if* statement: a main statement encloses a block of substatements that are executed only when a given condition is `true`:

```
while (condition) {
   substatements
}
```

If the condition is `true`, *substatements* are executed. But unlike the *if* statement, when the last substatement is finished, execution begins anew at the beginning of the *while* statement (that is the interpreter "loops" back to the beginning of the *while* statement). The second pass through the *while* statement works just like the first: the condition is evaluated, and if it is still `true`, *substatements* are executed again. This process continues until *condition* becomes `false`, at which point execution continues with any statements that follow the *while* statement in the script.

Here's an example of a very simple loop:

```
var i = 3;
while (i < 5) {
   trace("x is less than 5");
}
```

The example reliably represents the correct syntax of a *while* loop but is most likely in error. To see why, let's follow along with the interpreter as it executes the example.

We start with the statement before the *while* statement, *var i = 3*, which sets the variable i to 3. Because the variable i is used in the test expression of the loop, this step is often called the loop *initialization*. Next, we begin executing the *while* statement by resolving the test expression: *i < 5*. Because i is 3, and 3 is less than 5, the value of the test expression is `true` so we execute the *trace()* statement in the loop.

With that done, it's time to restart the loop. Once again, we check the value of the test expression. The value of the variable i has not changed, so the test expression is still `true` and we execute the *trace()* statement again. At this point, we're done executing the loop body, so it's time to restart the loop. Guess what? The variable i still has not changed, so the test expression is still `true` and we must execute the *trace()* statement again, and again, and again, forever. Because the test expression always returns `true`, there's no way to exit the loop—we're trapped forever in an *infinite loop*, unable to execute any other statements that may come after the *while* statement. In ActionScript, an infinite loop causes an error, as we'll see later.

Our loop is infinite because it lacks an *update statement* that changes the value of the variable used in the test expression. An update statement typically causes the test expression to eventually yield `false`, which terminates the loop. Let's fix our infinite loop by adding an update statement:

```
var i = 3;
while (i < 5) {
   trace("x is less than 5");
   i++;
}
```

The update statement, *i++*, comes at the end of the loop body. When the interpreter goes through our loop, it executes the *trace()* statement as before, but it also executes the statement *i++*, which adds one to the variable i. With each iteration of the loop, the value of i increases. After the second iteration, i's value is 5, so the test expression, *i < 5*, becomes `false`. The loop, therefore, safely ends.

Our loop's update statement performs a fundamental loop activity: it counts. The variable i (called a *counter*) runs through a predictable numeric sequence—perfect for methodical tasks such as duplicating movie clips or accessing the elements of an array. Here we duplicate the **square** movie clip five times without using a loop:

```
// Name each new clip sequentially and place it on its own level
duplicateMovieClip("square", "square1", 1);
duplicateMovieClip("square", "square2", 2);
duplicateMovieClip("square", "square3", 3);
duplicateMovieClip("square", "square4", 4);
duplicateMovieClip("square", "square5", 5);
```

And here we do it with a loop:

```
var i = 1;
while (i <= 5) {
  duplicateMovieClip("square", "square" + i, i);
  i++;
}
```

Imagine the difference if we were duplicating **square** 100 times!

Loops are marvelously useful for manipulating data, particularly data stored in arrays. Example 8-1 shows a loop that displays all the elements of an array to the Output window. Note that the first element is number 0, not number 1.

Example 8-1. Displaying an Array with a while Loop

```
var people = ["John", "Joyce", "Margaret", "Michael"];  // Create an array
var i = 0;
while (i < people.length) {
  trace("people element " + i + " is " + people[i]);
  i++;
}
```

The result in the Output window is:

```
people element 0 is John
people element 1 is Joyce
people element 2 is Margaret
people element 3 is Michael
```

Notice that the variable i is used both in the test expression and as the array index number, as is typical. Here we use i again as an argument for the *charAt()* function:

```
var city = "Toronto";
trace("The letters in the variable 'city' are ");
var i = 0;
while (i < city.length) {
  trace(city.charAt(i));
  i++;
}
```

The Output window shows:

```
The letters in the variable 'city' are:
T
o
r
o
n
t
o
```

Finally, instead of dissecting data, we use a loop to construct a sentence from a series of words stored in an array:

```
var words = ["Toronto", "is", "not", "the", "capital", "of", "Canada"];
var sentence;
var i = 0;
while (i < words.length) {
  sentence += words[i];       // Add the current word to the sentence.

  // If it's not the last word...
  if (i < words.length - 1) {
    sentence += " ";          // ...tack on a space.
  } else {
    sentence += ".";          // ...otherwise, end with a period.
  }
  i++;
}
trace(sentence);              // Displays: "Toronto is not the capital of Canada."
```

Nearly all loops involve some kind of counter (also sometimes called an *iterator* or *index variable*). Counters let us cycle sequentially through data. This is particularly convenient when we determine the counter's maximum limit using the `length` property of the array or string we want to manipulate, as we did in the preceding example.

It's also possible to create a loop whose end point doesn't depend on a counter. As long as the test expression of the loop eventually becomes `false`, the loop will end. Here, for example, we examine the level stack of the Flash Player to determine the first vacant level:

```
var i = 0;
while (typeof eval("_level" + i) == "movieclip") {
  i++;
}
trace("The first vacant level is " + i);

// Now load a movie into the vacant level, knowing it's free
loadMovie("myMovie.swf", i);
```

Loop Terminology

In the previous section we encountered several new terms. Let's look at these more formally, so that you'll understand them well when working with loops:

Initialization

> The statement or expression that defines one or more variables used in the test expression of a loop.

Test expression

> The condition that must be met in order for the substatements in the loop body to be executed. Often called a *condition* or *test*, or sometimes, *control*.

Update

> The statements that modify the variables used in the test expression before a subsequent test. A typical update statement increments or decrements the loop's counter.

Iteration

> One complete execution of the test expression and statements in the loop body. Sometimes referred to as one *loop* or one *pass*.

Nesting or nested loop

> A loop that contains another loop so that you can iterate through some sort of two-dimensional data. For example, you might loop through each row in a column for all the columns in a table. The outer or top-level loop would progress through the columns, and the inner loop would progress through the rows in each column.

Iterator or index variable

> A variable whose value increases or decreases with each iteration of a loop, usually used to count or sequence through some data. Loop iterators are often called *counters*. Iterators are conventionally named `i`, `j`, and `k` or sometimes `x`, `y`, and `z`. In a series of nested loops, `i` is usually the iterator of the top-level loop, `j` is the iterator of the first nested loop, `k` is the iterator of the second nested loop, and so on. You can use any variable name you like for clarity. For example, you can use `charNum` as the variable name to remind yourself that it indicates the current character in a string.

Loop body

> The block of statements that are executed when a loop's condition is met. The body may not be executed at all, or it may be executed thousands of times.

Loop header or loop control

> The portion of a loop that contains the loop statement keyword (*while*, *for*, *do-while*, or *for-in*) and the loop controls. The loop control varies with the type of

loop. In a *for* loop, the control comprises the initialization, the test, and the update; in a *while* loop, the control comprises simply the test expression.

Infinite loop

A loop that repeats forever because its test expression never yields the value `false`. Infinite loops cause an error in ActionScript as discussed later under "Maximum Number of Iterations."

The do-while Loop

As we saw earlier, a *while* statement allows the interpreter to execute a block of code repeatedly while a specified condition remains `true`. Due to a *while* loop's structure, its body will be skipped entirely if the loop's condition is not met the first time it is tested. A *do-while* statement lets us guarantee that a loop body will be executed at least once with minimal fuss. The body of a *do-while* loop *always* executes the first time through the loop. The *do-while* statement's syntax is somewhat like an inverted *while* statement:

```
do {
  substatements
} while (condition);
```

The keyword *do* begins the loop, followed by the **substatements** of the body. On the interpreter's first pass through the *do-while* statement, **substatements** are executed before `condition` is ever checked. At the end of the **substatements** block, if `condition` is `true`, the loop is begun anew and **substatements** are executed again. The loop executes repeatedly until `condition` is `false`, at which point the *do-while* statement ends. Note that a semicolon is required following the parentheses that contain the `condition`.

Obviously, *do-while* is handy when we want to perform a task at least once and perhaps subsequent times. In Example 8-2 we duplicate a series of twinkling-star movie clips from a clip called `starParent` and place them randomly on the Stage. Our galaxy will always contain at least one star, even if `numStars` is set to 0.

Example 8-2. Using a do-while Loop

```
var numStars = 5;
var i = 1;
do {
  // Duplicate the starParent clip
  duplicateMovieClip(starParent, "star" + i, i);

  // Place the duplicated clip randomly on Stage
  _root["star" + i]._x = Math.floor(Math.random() * 551);
  _root["star" + i]._y = Math.floor(Math.random() * 401);
} while (i++ < numStars);
```

Did you notice that we sneakily updated the variable i in the test expression? Remember from Chapter 5, *Operators*, that the post-increment operator both returns the value of its operand and also adds one to that operand. The increment operator is very convenient (and common) when working with loops.

The for Loop

A *for* loop is essentially synonymous with a *while* loop but is written with more compact syntax. Most notably, the loop header can contain both initialization and update statements in addition to the test expression.

Here's the syntax of the *for* loop:

```
for (initialization; condition; update) {
   substatements
}
```

The *for* loop places the key components of a loop tidily in the loop header, separated by semicolons. Before the first iteration of a *for* loop, the `initialization` statement is performed (once and only once). It is typically used to set the initial value of an iterator variable. As with other loops, if `condition` is `true`, `substatements` are executed. Otherwise, the loop ends. At the *end* of each loop iteration, the `update` statement is executed, before `condition` is tested again to see if the loop should continue. Here's a typical *for* loop that simply counts from 1 to 10:

```
for (var i = 1; i <= 10; i++) {
   trace("Now serving number " + i);
}
```

It's easier to understand how a *for* loop works when you see its equivalent constructed using the *while* loop syntax:

```
var i = 1;
while (i <= 10) {
   trace("Now serving number " + i);
   i++;
}
```

Once you're used to the *for* syntax, you'll find it saves space and allows for easy scanning of the loop's body and controls.

Multiple Iterators in for Loops

If we want to control more than one factor in a loop, we may optionally use more than one iterator variable. A *while* loop with multiple iterators may look like this:

```
var i = 1;
var j = 10;
while (i <= 10) {
```

```
      trace("Going up " + i);
      trace("Going down " + j);
      i++;
      j--;
   }
```

The same effect can be achieved in a *for* statement using the comma operator:

```
for (var i = 1, j = 10; i <= 10; i++, j--) {
   trace("Going up " + i);
   trace("Going down " + j);
}
```

The for-in Loop

A *for-in* statement is a specialized loop used to list the properties of an object. New programmers may want to skip this section for now and return to it after reading Chapter 12, *Objects and Classes*.

Rather than repeating a series of statements until a given test expression yields the value `false`, a *for-in* loop iterates once for each property in the specified object. Therefore, *for-in* statements do not need an explicit update statement because the number of loop iterations is determined by the number of properties in the object being inspected. The syntax of a *for-in* loop looks like this:

```
for (var thisProp in object) {
   substatements;  // Statements typically use thisProp in some way
}
```

The **substatements** are executed once for each property of **object**; **object** is the name of any valid object; **thisProp** is any variable name or identifier name. During each loop iteration, the **thisProp** variable temporarily holds a string that is the name of the object property currently being enumerated. That string value can be used during each iteration to access and manipulate the current property. The simplest example of a *for-in* loop is a script that lists the properties of an object. Here we create an object and then itemize its properties with a *for-in* loop:

```
var ball = new Object();
ball.radius = 12;
ball.color = "red";
ball.style = "beach";

for (var prop in ball) {
   trace("ball has the property " + prop);
}
```

Because **prop** stores the names of the properties of **ball** as strings, we can use **prop** with the [] operator to retrieve the values of those properties, like this:

```
for (var prop in ball) {
   trace("ball." + prop + " is " + ball[prop]);
}
```

Retrieving property values with a *for-in* loop also provides a super way to detect the movie clips present on a timeline. For a demonstration of the *for-in* loop used as a movie clip detector, see Example 3-1.

Note that the properties of the object being inspected in a *for-in* loop are not enumerated in any predictable order. Also, *for-in* statements do not always list every property of an object. When the object is user-defined, all properties are enumerated, including any inherited properties. But some properties of built-in objects are skipped by the *for-in* statement. Methods of built-in objects, for example, are not enumerated by a *for-in* loop. If you want to use a *for-in* statement to manipulate the properties of a built-in object, first build a test loop to determine the object's accessible properties.

 Input text fields without a default value are not enumerated by a *for-in* loop. Hence, form-validation code that detects empty text fields will not work properly unless those text fields are explicitly declared as normal variables in the timeline upon which they reside. See "Empty Text Fields and the for-in Statement" in Chapter 18.

The *for-in* statement can also be used to extract elements in an array, in which case it takes the form:

```
for (var thisElem in array) {
    substatements; // Statements typically use thisElem in some way
}
```

This example lists the elements of an array:

```
var myArr = [123, 234, 345, 456];
for (var elem in myArr) {
    trace(myArr[elem]);
}
```

Stopping a Loop Prematurely

In a simple loop, the test expression is the sole factor that determines when the loop stops. When the test expression of a simple loop yields **false**, the loop terminates. However, as loops become more complex, we may need to arbitrarily terminate a running loop regardless of the value of the test expression. To do so, we use the *break* and *continue* statements.

The break Statement

The *break* statement ends execution of the current loop. It has the modest syntax:

```
break
```

The only requirement is that *break* must appear within the body of a loop.

The *break* statement provides a way to halt a process that is no longer worth completing. For example, we might use a *for-in* loop to build a form-checking routine that cycles through the input-text variables on a timeline. If a blank input field is found, we alert the user that she hasn't filled in the form properly. We can abort the process by executing a *break* statement. Example 8-3 shows the code. Note that the example assumes the existence of a movie clip called form that contains a series of declared input variables named input01, input02, and so on.

Example 8-3. A Simple Form-Field Validator

```
for (var prop in form) {
  // If this property is one of our "input" text fields
  if (prop.indexOf("input") != -1) {
    // If the form entry is blank, abort the operation
    if (form[prop] == "") {
      displayMessage = "Please complete the entire form.";
      break;
    }
    // Any substatements following the break command are not reached
    // when the break is executed
  }
}
// Execution resumes here after the loop terminates whether
// due to the break command or the test condition becoming false
```

You can use the *break* statement to interrupt a loop that would otherwise be infinite. This allows you to perform, say, the statements in the first half of the code block without necessarily executing the statements following an *if (condition) break;* statement. The generic approach is shown in Example 8-4.

Example 8-4. Breaking out of an Infinite Loop

```
while (true) {
  // Initial statements go here
  if (condition) break;
  // Subsequent statements go here
}
```

The continue Statement

The *continue* statement is similar to the *break* statement in that it causes the current iteration of a loop to be aborted, but unlike *break*, it resumes the loop's execution with the next natural cycle. The syntax of the *continue* statement is simply:

```
continue
```

In all types of loops, the *continue* statement interrupts the current iteration of the loop body, but the resumption of the loop varies slightly depending on the type of loop statement. In a *while* loop and a *do-while* loop, the test expression is checked before the loop resumes. But in a *for* loop, the loop update is performed before the test expression is checked. And in a *for-in* loop, the next iteration begins with the next property of the object being inspected (if one exists).

Using the *continue* statement, we can make the execution of the body of a loop optional under specified circumstances. For example, here we move all the movie clip instances that aren't transparent to the left edge of the Stage, and we skip the loop body for transparent instances:

```
for (var prop in _root) {
  if (typeof _root[prop] == "movieclip") {
    if (_root[prop]._alpha < 100) {
      continue;
    }
    _root[prop]._x = 0;
  }
}
```

Maximum Number of Iterations

As noted earlier, loops are not allowed to execute forever in ActionScript. In the Flash 5 Player loops are limited to 15 seconds. The number of iterations that can be achieved in that time depends on what's inside the loop and the computer's speed. To be safe, you shouldn't create loops requiring more than even a few seconds to execute (which is eons in processing terms!). Most loops should take only milliseconds to finish. If a loop takes longer to complete (for example, because it's processing hundreds of strings while initializing a word-scramble game), it's worth rewriting the code using a timeline loop, as described in the next section. Timeline loops allow us to update the progress of a script's execution on screen and avoid the potential display of the error message shown in Figure 8-1.

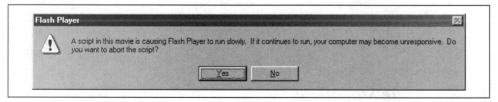

Figure 8-1. Bad loop! Down boy!

When a loop has run for more than 15 seconds in the Flash 5 Player, an alert box warns the user that a script in the movie is delaying the movie's playback. The user is offered the choice to either wait for the script to finish or to quit the script.

The Flash 4 player is even stricter—it allows only 200,000 iterations—after which all scripts are disabled without any warning.

Take special heed: the 15-second warning that users see does not mention that canceling a runaway script will actually cause all scripts in the movie to stop functioning! If a user selects "Yes" to stop a loop from continuing, all scripts in the movie are disabled.

Timeline and Clip Event Loops

All the loops we've looked at so far cause the interpreter to repeatedly execute blocks of code. Most of your loops will be of this "ActionScript-statement" type. But it's also sometimes desirable to create a *timeline loop* by looping Flash's playhead in the timeline. To do so, attach a series of statements to any frame; on the next frame, attach a *gotoAndPlay()* function whose destination is the previous frame. When the movie plays, the playhead will cycle between the two frames, causing the code on the first frame to be executed repeatedly.

We can make a simple timeline loop by following these steps:

1. Start a new Flash movie.

2. On frame 1, attach the following statement:

   ```
   trace("Hi there! Welcome to frame 1");
   ```

3. On frame 2, attach the following statements:

   ```
   trace("This is frame 2");
   gotoAndPlay(1);
   ```

4. Select Control → Test Movie.

When we test our movie, we see an endless stream of the following text:

```
Hi there! Welcome to frame 1
This is frame 2
Hi there! Welcome to frame 1
This is frame 2
```

Timeline loops can do two things ordinary loops cannot:

- They can execute a block of code an infinite number of times without causing an error.

- They can execute a block of code that requires a Stage update between loop iterations.

This second feature of timeline loops requires a little more explanation. When any frame's script is executed, the movie Stage is not updated visually until the end of the script. This means that traditional loop statements cannot be used to perform repetitive visual or audio tasks because the task results aren't rendered between each loop iteration. Repositioning a movie clip, for example, requires a Stage update, so we can't programmatically animate a movie clip with a normal loop statement.

You might assume that the following code would visually slide the `ball` movie clip horizontally across the Stage:

```
for (var i = 0; i < 50; i++) {
  ball._x += 10;
}
```

Conceptually, the loop statement has the right approach—it repetitively updates the position of `ball` by small amounts, which should give the illusion of movement. However, in practice, the `ball` doesn't move each time the `_x` position of `ball` is changed because the Stage isn't updated. Instead, we'd see the `ball` suddenly jump 500 pixels to the right—10 pixels for each of the 50 loop iterations—after the script completes.

To allow the Stage to update after each execution of the `ball._x += 10;` statement, we can use a timeline loop like this:

```
// CODE ON FRAME 1
ball._x += 10;


// CODE ON FRAME 2
gotoAndPlay(1);
```

Because Flash updates the Stage between any two frames, the `ball` will appear to animate. But the timeline loop completely monopolizes the timeline it's on. While it's running, we can't play any normal content on that timeline. A better approach is to put our timeline loop into an empty, two-frame movie clip. We'll get the benefit of a Stage update between loop iterations without freezing a timeline we may need for other animation.

Creating an Empty-Clip Timeline Loop

The following steps show how to create an empty-clip timeline loop:

1. Start a new Flash movie.
2. Create a movie clip symbol named *ball* that contains a circle shape.
3. On the main Stage, rename layer *Layer 1* to *ball*.
4. On the *ball* layer, place an instance of the *ball* symbol.
5. Name the instance of the *ball* clip, `ball`.
6. Select Insert → New Symbol to create a blank movie clip symbol.
7. Name the clip symbol `process`.

8. On frame 1 of the **process** clip, attach the following code:

```
_root.ball._x += 10;
```

9. On frame 2 of the process clip, add the following code:

```
gotoAndPlay(1);
```

10. Return to the main movie timeline and create a layer called *scripts.*

11. On the *scripts* layer, place an instance of the **process** symbol.

12. Name the instance **processMoveBall**.

13. Select Control → Test Movie.

The **processMoveBall** instance will now move **ball** without interfering with the playback of the main timeline upon which **ball** resides.

Note that step 12 isn't mandatory, but it gives us more control over our loop. By giving our timeline-loop instance a name, we can stop and start our loop by starting and stopping the playback of the instance, like this:

```
processMoveBall.play();
processMoveBall.stop();
```

Note that in this example **processMoveBall** and **ball** must both exist on the main timeline for as long as the loop is supposed to work. If we wanted to make the code more portable, we could use a relative reference to our **ball** clip in **process**:

```
_parent.ball._x += 10;
```

And if we wanted to control our ball from any timeline, we'd use an absolute reference to **ball**:

```
_root.ball._x += 10;
```

 Timeline loops can't loop on a single frame. That is, if we place a `gotoAndPlay(5)` function on frame 5 of a movie, the function will be ignored. The Player realizes that the playhead is already on frame 5 and simply does nothing.

You'll find the sample timeline loop and empty-clip loop *.fla* files in the online Code Depot.

Flash 5 Clip Event Loops

Timeline loops are effective but not necessarily elegant. In Flash 5, we can use an event handler on a movie clip to achieve the same results as a timeline loop but with more flexibility (just try to follow along with this example, or see Chapter 10, *Events and Event Handlers*, for details on movie clip event handlers).

When placed on a movie clip, an *enterFrame* event handler causes a block of code to execute every time a frame passes in a movie. We can use an *enterFrame* event handler on a single-frame empty clip to repetitively execute a block of code while allowing for a Stage update between each repetition (just as a timeline loop does). Follow these steps to try it out:

1. Follow steps 1 through 7 from the previous section.

2. On the main Stage, create a new layer called *scripts*.

3. On the *scripts* layer, place an instance of the process clip.

4. Select the process instance and attach the following code:

    ```
    onClipEvent(enterFrame) {
      _root.ball._x += 10;
    }
    ```

5. Select Control → Test Movie.

The `ball` instance should animate across the Stage.

Clip event loops free us from nesting our code inside a movie clip and don't require a two-frame loop, as timeline loops do. All the action of a clip event loop happens in a single event handler. However, the clip event example we just saw has a potential drawback: there's no way to programmatically start or stop the loop once it's started. The only way to stop the loop is to physically remove the process instance from the timeline with a blank keyframe.

To create an event loop that can be arbitrarily started and stopped, we have to create an empty clip that contains *another* empty clip that bears an event loop. We can then dynamically attach and remove the whole package whenever we want to start or stop our loop. A little convoluted, yes, but the results are quite flexible. Once again, follow the steps to try it out:

1. Follow steps 1 through 5 under "Creating an Empty-Clip Timeline Loop."

2. Select Insert → New Symbol twice to create two blank movie clip symbols.

3. Name one clip symbol process and the other eventLoop.

4. In the Library, select the process clip, then select Options → Linkage. The Symbol Linkage Properties dialog box appears.

5. Select Export This Symbol.

6. In the Identifier field, type **processMoveBall** and then click OK.

7. On frame 1 of the process clip, drag an instance of eventLoop onto the Stage.

8. Select the `eventLoop` instance, and attach the following code:

```
onClipEvent(enterFrame) {
   _parent._parent.ball._x += 10;
}
```

9. Return to the main movie timeline and attach the following code to frame 1:

```
attachMovie("processMoveBall", "processMoveBall", 5000);
```

10. Whenever you want to stop the event loop, issue the following statement:

```
_root.processMoveBall.removeMovieClip();
```

11. Select Control → Test Movie.

Once again, the **ball** instance should animate across the Stage, but this time we can start and stop it whenever we like by using the *attachMovie()* and *removeMovieClip()* functions shown in steps 9 and 10.

There are examples of regular and controllable clip event loops available from the online Code Depot.

Keeping event loops portable

Both of the clip event loops we just saw included a line of code that updates the position of the **ball** instance on the Stage. For example:

```
onClipEvent(enterFrame) {
   _parent._parent.ball._x += 10;   // Updates ball's position
}
```

Although this approach works, it's sloppy. By attaching meaningful code to our clip event, we've decentralized our code base, dispersing logic and behavior throughout our movie. In order to keep our code accessible during authoring and better structured for reuse, from within event loops, we should *only* call functions. So, instead of actually moving the **ball** clip in our example, we should call a function that moves the **ball** clip, like this:

```
onClipEvent(enterFrame) {
   _parent._parent.moveBall();
}
```

The user-defined function *moveBall()* would be defined on the same timeline we attach the **processMoveBall** clip to, like this:

```
function moveBall() {
   ball._x += 10;
}
```

We'll talk more about functions and code portability in Chapter 9, *Functions*.

If our application is simple, we may wish to forego our empty event-loop clip altogether. In some cases, we can quite legitimately attach an event loop directly to the clip being manipulated. In our `ball` example, we could avoid the need for separate empty clips by attaching the following code directly to the `ball` instance:

```
onClipEvent(enterFrame) {
  _x += 10;
}
```

This approach is ultraconvenient, but it doesn't scale very easily, and like our first example, it suffers from the inability to start and stop the loop.

Frame Rate's Effect on Timeline and Clip Event Loops

Because timeline and clip event loops iterate once per frame, their execution frequency is tied to the frame rate of a movie. If we're moving an object around the screen with a timeline or an event loop, an increase in frame rate can mean an increase in the speed of our animation.

When we programmed the movement of the `ball` clip in our earlier examples, we implicitly specified the velocity of the ball in relation to the frame rate. Our code says, "With each frame that passes, move `ball` ten pixels to the right":

```
_ball += 10;
```

The speed of `ball` is, hence, dependent on the frame rate. If our movie plays at 12 frames per second, then our `ball` clip moves 120 pixels per second. If our movie plays at 30 frames per second, our `ball` clip moves *300* pixels per second!

When timing scripted animations, it's tempting to calculate the distance to move an item in relation to the movie's frame rate. So, if a movie plays 20 frames per second, and we want an item to move 100 pixels per second, we're tempted to set the velocity of the object to 5 pixels per frame (5 pixels * 20 frames per second = 100 pixels per second). There are two serious flaws in this approach:

- By relying on the frame rate to determine the speed of an item, we make it painful to change the frame rate. If we change the frame rate, we have to recalculate our speed and edit our code accordingly.

- The Flash Player does not necessarily play movies back at the frame rate set in the Flash authoring tool; it often plays them slower. If the computer running the movie cannot render frames fast enough to keep up with the designated frame rate, the movie slows down. This slowdown can even vary depending on the system load; if other programs are running or if Flash is performing some processor-intensive task, the frame rate may drop for only a short period and then resume its normal pace.

You can test this out yourself using the time-tracker tool available at:

http://www.moock.org/webdesign/flash/actionscript/fps-speedometer

In some cases, an animation that plays back at slightly different speeds could be deemed acceptable. But when visual accuracy matters or when we're concerned with the responsiveness of an action game, it's much more appropriate to calculate the distance to move an object relative to elapsed time instead of the frame rate. Example 8-5 shows a quick-and-dirty sample of time-based animation (i.e., the `ball` speed is independent of the frame rate). The new movie would have three frames and two layers, one layer with the `ball` instance and the other with our scripts.

Example 8-5. Calculating Move Distances Based on Time, Not Frame Rate

```
// CODE ON FRAME 1
var distancePerSecond = 50;  // Pixels to move per second
var now = getTimer();        // The current time
var then = 0;                // The time when last frame was rendered
var elapsed;                 // Milliseconds between frame renders
var numSeconds;              // elapsed expressed in seconds
var moveAmount;              // Distance to move each frame

// CODE ON FRAME 2
then = now;
now = getTimer();
elapsed = now - then;
numSeconds = elapsed / 1000;
moveAmount = distancePerSecond * numSeconds;
ball._x += moveAmount;

// CODE ON FRAME 3
gotoAndPlay(2);
```

Note that our time-based movement might appear jerky if the frame rate suddenly changes. We could smooth things out by using an elapsed-time measurement that averages the time between a series of frames instead of just two.

Onward!

Well, we've come pretty far. The end of this chapter marks a milestone—it ends our examination of the ActionScript statements. That means we have variables, data, datatypes, expressions, operators, and statements under our belt. These components of the language are the foundation of all scripts. If you've read and understood everything up to this point, or at least most of it, you can officially claim that you're able to "speak" ActionScript.

In the remainder of Part I, *ActionScript Fundamentals*, we'll work on making our conversations more eloquent and our commands more powerful. We'll consider the advanced topics of how to make code portable, how to create events that initiate the execution of our code, how to manage complex data, and how to manipulate movie clips programmatically. These techniques will help us build more advanced applied examples.

9

Functions

I'm almost giddy to tell you about functions because they're such a powerful part of ActionScript. A function is simply a chunk of code that can be reused throughout a program. Not only do functions lend enormous flexibility and convenience to our scripts, they also give us control over Flash movie elements. I can hardly imagine programming without functions—they ease everything from sorting words to calculating the distance between two movie clips. We'll introduce functions in this chapter before learning how to create complex, powerful programs using functions with objects in Chapter 12, *Objects and Classes*.

We'll focus first on *program functions*—the functions we create ourselves in our scripts. By learning to create our own functions, we'll become familiar with these fundamentals:

Function declaration
　　Creating functions to use in our scripts.

Function invocation
　　Causing functions to execute. In other words, running the code in a function. Also known as *calling a function.*

Function arguments and parameters
　　Providing functions with data to manipulate upon invocation.

Function termination
　　Ending the execution of a function and optionally returning a result.

Function scope
　　Determining the availability and life span of a function, and the accessibility of variables referenced in a function body.

Once we understand those aspects of functions, we'll consider how they apply to *internal functions*, functions that come built into ActionScript. Let's get to it!

Creating Functions

To make a basic *function* we simply need a function name and a block of statements to perform, like this:

```
function funcName () {
  statements
}
```

The `function` keyword starts the *declaration* of our new function. Next comes our function name, `funcName`, which we'll use later to *invoke* our function. `funcName` must be a legal identifier.* Next, we supply a pair of parentheses, ( ), that enclose any optional parameters, which we'll discuss later. If our function does not have any parameters, we leave the parentheses empty. Finally, we provide the *function body* (i.e., statement block), which contains the code that's executed when our function is *called*.

Let's make a (very) simple function:

1. Start a new Flash movie.

2. On frame 1 of the main movie timeline, attach the following code:

```
function sayHi () {
  trace("Hi there!");
}
```

That was easy—we've just created a function named *sayHi()*. When we run it, the *trace()* statement in its body will be executed. Don't close the movie you've created, we'll learn to run our function next.

Running Functions

We run a function like a wizard invokes a spell, by proclaiming the function's name, followed by the function call operator, ( ), introduced in Chapter 5, *Operators*:

```
funcName()
```

(You can almost detect the faint odor of smoldering mandrake root in the air.)

The parentheses may contain any parameters defined by the function. If the function defines no parameters, the parentheses are left empty. Let's try invoking our

---

* See Chapter 14, *Lexical Structure*, for the rules that govern legal identifiers.

sayHi() function, which has no parameters, to get the hang of basic function invocation.

Here, again, is our *sayHi()* function declaration:

```
function sayHi () {
  trace("Hi there!");
}
```

And here's our *sayHi()* function invocation:

```
sayHi();
```

When that line is executed, *sayHi()* is invoked, so its function body runs, causing "Hi there!" to appear in the Output window.

You can see that typing *sayHi();* is more convenient than typing the whole *trace()* statement, and the function name *sayHi* is a more meaningful description of what our code does. Using thoughtful function names makes our code more readable, almost like human sentences.

Before we continue, notice the semicolon at the end of the function call:

```
sayHi();
```

We add the semicolon because a function call is a complete statement, and good form dictates that all statements should end in a semicolon.

Believe it or not, we've just learned the basics of creating and invoking functions. Not too shabby. Functions keep your code centralized and easier to maintain, especially when you need to perform the same operation repeatedly throughout your program. Functions become even more powerful when used with parameters, which we'll consider next.

Passing Information to Functions

In the last section, we created a function that executed a simple *trace()* statement—not exactly the most compelling specimen of the function species. Here's a more interesting function that moves a movie clip instance named **ball** a short distance:

```
function moveBall () {
  ball._x += 10;
  ball._y += 10;
}
```

With the function *moveBall()* defined, we can move **ball** diagonally anytime by calling the *moveBall()* function:

```
moveBall();
```

The ball moves diagonally down and to the right. (Note that the origin (0, 0) is in the upper left of the main Stage. Increasing values of _x move the ball to the right, but unlike the Cartesian coordinates, increasing values of _y move the ball *down*, not up.)

Our *moveBall()* function is convenient, but it lacks flexibility. It works only on one movie clip (`ball`), it moves `ball` in only one direction, and it always moves `ball` the same distance.

A well-designed function should define a single code segment that works in many circumstances. We can generalize our *moveBall()* function so that it can move *any* clip *any* distance in *any* direction. The first step in generalizing any function is determining what factors control its behavior. In our *moveBall()* function, the factors are the name of the movie clip to move, the distance to move it horizontally, and the distance to move it vertically. Such factors are known as the *parameters* of the function—they're the information that we'd like to be able to adjust when the function is called.

Creating Functions with Parameters

Recall the generic syntax of a simple function declaration:

```
function funcName () {
  statements
}
```

To add *parameters*, which are variables that can be used within a function, we provide a list of legal identifiers between the parentheses of a function declaration. Parameters are separated by commas as shown here:

```
function funcName (param1, param2, param3,...paramn) {
  statements
}
```

Once defined, we can access a function's parameter values from inside the function body just as we would any other variable. For example:

```
function say(msg) {                 // Define the msg parameter
  trace("The message is " + msg); // Use msg within the trace() statement
}
```

Our function declaration defines the parameter `msg`. The *trace()* statement uses the parameter as it would any variable, outputting its value to the Output window.

Let's use parameters with our *moveBall()* function so that we can set the clip's name, horizontal distance, and vertical distance differently each time it runs. Example 9-1 shows the code.

Example 9-1. A Generalized moveClip Function

```
function moveClip (theClip, xDist, yDist) {
  theClip._x += xDist;
  theClip._y += yDist;
}
```

We renamed the function from *moveBall()* to the generic name *moveClip()*. We
also defined three parameters: `theClip` (the movie clip we want to move), `xDist`
(the horizontal distance to move), and `yDist` (the vertical distance to move).
Inside the function body, we use those parameters instead of the hardcoded values in the original example, thereby allowing our function to reposition any clip
by any horizontal and vertical distance.

Invoking Functions with Parameters

When we create a function, we define the parameter names, which are essentially
placeholders; when we invoke the function, we'll provide values to be plugged in
for each of the parameters.

The words *parameters* and *arguments* are used interchangeably in this book and
in most documentation. Technically, *arguments* are the values used when invoking a function, and *parameters* are the placeholders in the function that "receive"
the arguments.

Recall the generic syntax of function invocation with no arguments:

```
funcName()
```

To supply (or *pass*) arguments to a function, we provide a list of values within the
parentheses when invoking the function:

```
funcName(arg1, arg2, arg3,...argn)
```

The values used as arguments may be any legitimate expression in ActionScript,
including compound expressions. For example, earlier we defined a simple function, *say()*, that expects a single parameter, `msg`:

```
function say(msg) {
  trace("The message is " + msg);
}
```

To invoke *say()*, we use a statement like this:

```
say("This is my first argument...how touching");
```

Or like this:

```
say(99);
```

Notice that the values, "This is my first argument . . . how touching" and 99, belong to different datatypes. ActionScript allows us to pass any data of any type to a function, as long as the function knows what to do with the passed value. (Languages such as C require that we predefine the datatype for each parameter, and they display an error if data of the wrong type is provided.)

Before each argument is passed, its value is fully resolved. We may, therefore, also invoke functions with complex expressions. For example:

```
var name = "Gula";
say("Welcome to my web site " + name);
```

Because the expression *"Welcome to my web site " + name* is evaluated before it is passed to the *say()* function, the function receives the resolved value "Welcome to my web site Gula". This means that we can programmatically generate function arguments. Powerful stuff.

To pass more than one argument to a function, we separate our arguments with commas. Recall that our *moveClip()* function from Example 9-1 accepts three parameters: `theClip`, `xDist`, `yDist`. Invoking *moveClip()*, therefore, looks like this:

```
moveClip(ball, 5, -15);
```

Each of the three arguments is assigned as the value of the corresponding parameter named in the function declaration: `ball` is assigned to `theClip`, 5 is assigned to `xDist`, and –15 is assigned to `yDist`. We can move any clip any distance by invoking our generic *moveClip()* function with different arguments. Here we move the clip instance named `square` to the right 2 pixels and down 100 pixels:

```
moveClip(square, 2, 100);
```

Exiting and Returning Values from Functions

Unless instructed otherwise, a function will end naturally when the interpreter finishes executing the last statement in the function's body. You can, however, terminate a function before the last statement is reached. Additionally, a function can return a result (send back a calculated value) to the code that invoked it. Let's see how these things work.

Terminating a Function

The *return* statement, which was introduced in Chapter 6, *Statements*, can be used to terminate a function and, optionally, to return a result. When the interpreter encounters a *return* statement during a function execution, it skips any remaining statements in the function. Consider this example:

```
function say(msg) {
  return;
  trace(msg);          // This line is never reached
}
```

The preceding example is not realistic because its *return* statement always causes the function to end before the *trace()* statement is reached. Therefore, the *return* statement is normally the last statement in a function body unless it is used inside a conditional statement. In this example, we use *return* to exit if the password is not correct:

```
var correctPass = "cactus";
function enterSite(pass) {
  if (pass != correctPass) {
    // Exit if the password is wrong
    return;
  }
  // This code is reached only if the password is correct
  gotoAndPlay("intro");
}

enterSite("hackAttack");  // Function will exit prematurely
enterSite("cactus");      // Function will end naturally
```

As its name implies, *return* tells the interpreter to return to the location of the function invocation. If no *return* statement is present, ActionScript acts as if the last line of the function body contains a *return* statement:

```
function say(msg) {
  trace(msg);
  return;                // This line is completely optional in this context
}
```

Regardless of whether the *return* statement is implied or explicit, whenever a function terminates, execution resumes at the line of code following the function-call statement. For example:

```
say ("Something");  // This executes the code in the say() function
// Execution resumes here after the say() function terminates
trace ("Something else");
```

Returning Values from Functions

As we've seen, *return* always terminates a function. But it can also be used to send a value back to the script that invoked the function, using the following syntax:

```
return expression;
```

The value of *expression* becomes the result of the function invocation. For example:

```
// Define a function that adds two numbers
function combine(a, b) {
  return a + b;  // Return the sum of the two arguments
}

// Invoke the function
var total = combine(2, 1);  // Sets total to 3
```

The expression or result returned by the *return* statement is called the *return value* of the function.

Notice that our *combine()* function merely calculates and returns the sum of two numbers (it will also concatenate two strings). It does not perform an action, as did the *sayHi()* function (which displayed a message) or the *moveClip()* function (which repositioned a movie clip). We can make use of a function's return value by assigning it to a variable:

```
var total = combine (5, 6);               // Sets total to 11
var greet = combine ("Hello ", "Cheryl")  // greet is "Hello Cheryl"
```

The result of a function call is just an ordinary expression. Therefore, it can also be used in additional expressions. This example sets **phrase** to "11 people were at the party":

```
var phrase = combine(5, 6) + " people were at the party";
```

We'll frequently use function return values as parts of compound expressions—even as arguments in another function invocation. For example:

```
var a = 3;
var b = 4;
function sqr(x) {  // Squares a number
  return x * x;
}
var hypotenuse = Math.sqrt(sqr(a) + sqr(b));
```

Notice how the example passes the return values of our *sqr()* function to the *Math.sqrt()* function! Along the same lines, our earlier example could be rewritten as:

```
var phrase = combine (combine(5,6), " people were at the party");
```

In the preceding example, the expression *combine(5,6)*, which evaluates to 11, becomes an argument to the outer *combine()* function call, where it is concatenated with the string " people were at the party".

If a *return* statement doesn't include an expression to be returned or the *return* statement is omitted entirely, a function will return the value **undefined**. In fact, this is a common source of error. For example, the following won't do anything meaningful because the *return* statement is missing:

```
function combine(a, b) {
  var result = a + b;  // The result is calculated, but not returned
}
```

Likewise, this too is incorrect:

```
function combine(a, b) {
  var result = a + b;
  return;  // You've forgotten to specify the return value
}
```

When creating a function that is supposed to return the result of a calculation, don't forget to include a *return* statement that actually returns the desired value. Otherwise, the return value will be **undefined** and any subsequent calculations based on that result will almost certainly be incorrect.

Function Literals

ActionScript allows us to create *function literals*, which are convenient when we need a function temporarily or when we'd like to use a function where an expression is expected.

Function literals have the same syntax as standard function declarations except that the function name is omitted and there's a semicolon after the statement block. The general form is:

```
function (param1, param2, ... paramn) { statements };
```

where **param1,param2,...paramn** is an optional list of parameters and **statements** is one or more statements that constitute the function body. Because it doesn't include a function name, a function literal is "lost" unless we store it in a variable (or an array element or object property). We can store a function literal in a variable for later access, like this:

```
// Store a function literal in a variable
var mouseCoords = function () { return [ _xmouse, _ymouse ]; };

// Now we can execute the function
mouseCoords();
```

Note that because ActionScript does not support JavaScript's *Function()* constructor, dynamic functions cannot be composed at runtime, as they can in JavaScript.

Function Availability and Life Span

Like variables, program functions do not live forever and are not directly accessible throughout a movie. In order to invoke functions with confidence, we need to know how to access them from different areas of our movie, and we need to be sure that they exist before we call them.

Function Availability

Program functions (the functions we create ourselves in our code) are *directly* accessible for invocation only from:

- Code attached to the timeline of the movie clip that bears the function declaration

- A button on the timeline of the movie clip that bears the function declaration

By "directly accessible," we mean that the function can be invoked simply by name, without reference to a movie clip or object, like this:

```
myFunction();
```

Functions are also *indirectly* accessible (i.e., remotely accessible) from any point in a movie using dot syntax. As when referring to variables remotely, we must include the path to the movie clip that contains the function, such as:

```
myClip.myOtherClip.myFunction();
_parent.myFunction();
_root.myFunction();
```

So, suppose a clip instance named `rectangle` on the main timeline contains a function named *area()*. We may invoke *area()* from anywhere in our movie using an absolute path to `rectangle`, like this:

```
_root.rectangle.area();
```

To reference a function from a remote movie clip timeline, we follow the same rules used when referring to remote variables, as described in Chapter 2, *Variables*. (We'll also learn more about invoking functions remotely in Chapter 13, *Movie Clips*.)

Not all functions are attached to movie clip timelines. Some program functions may be attached to user-defined or built-in objects. When attached to an object, a function is accessible only through its host object. We'll learn more about the availability and life span of *methods* (i.e., functions attached to objects) in Chapter 12.

Function Life Span

A function defined on a movie clip timeline is lost when that clip is removed from the Stage. An attempt to invoke a function that was defined in a clip that no longer exists will fail silently. Defining a function on the main movie timeline is the best way to ensure the function's permanence, because the main timeline persists throughout the movie.

Note that functions in a frame's script are initialized and become available when the playhead first enters the frame containing the script. Therefore, we may use a function invocation before the declaration of the function, as long as both are in the same script. For example:

```
// Invoke the tellTime() function before its declaration statement
tellTime();

// Declare the tellTime() function
function tellTime() {
  var now = new Date();
  trace(now);
}
```

Function Scope

ActionScript statements have a certain *scope*, or area of effect within which they are valid. When a statement is attached to a movie clip, that statement's scope is limited to the clip that bears it. For example, here we refer to a variable, **score**, in an assignment statement:

```
score = 10;
```

If that statement were attached to **clipA**, then the interpreter would set the value of **score** in **clipA**, because the statement is "scoped" to **clipA**. If that statement were attached to **clipB**, the interpreter would set the value of **score** in **clipB**, because the statement is scoped to **clipB**. The location of the statement determines its scope, and, hence, its effect.

Statements in the body of a function operate in their own, separate scope, called a *local scope*. A function's local scope is like a private phone booth for the function, distinct from the scope of the clip or object to which the function is attached. The local scope of a function is created when the function is invoked and destroyed when the function finishes executing. When resolving variables referenced in the statements of the function body, the interpreter looks first in the function's scope.

Function parameters, for example, are defined in the *local* scope of a function—not the scope of the timeline that bears the function. Parameters, hence, are accessible to the statements of a function's body only while the function is running. Statements outside the function have no access to the function's parameters.

A function's local scope provides a place for temporary variables for use solely within a function. This eliminates potential name conflicts between function variables and timeline variables, and it reduces our overall memory usage.

The Scope Chain

Even though functions operate in their own local scopes, normal timeline variables are still accessible to the statements of a function body. The local scope of a function is the *first* place the interpreter looks to resolve variable references, but if the variable reference can't be found in the local scope, the search extends to the object or movie clip that bears the function.

For example, suppose we define a variable, `firstName`, on the timeline of a movie clip, `clipA`. We also declare a function, *getName()*, on `clipA`. Inside *getName()*, we refer to the variable `firstName` in a *trace()* statement:

```
firstName = "Christine";

funtion getName () {
  trace(firstName);
}

getName();
```

When we invoke *getName()*, the interpreter must find the value of `firstName`. There is no variable called `firstName` in the local scope of *getName()*, so the interpreter checks the timeline of `clipA` for the variable `firstName`. There, the interpreter finds `firstName` and displays its value, "Christine".

Our *trace()* statement is able to refer to a timeline variable from the body of our *getName()* function because *getName()* does not, itself, define a parameter or variable called `firstName`. Now consider what happens when we add a parameter called `firstName` to the *getName()* function:

```
firstName = "Christine";

function getName (firstName) {
  trace(firstName);
}

getName("Kathy");
```

This time, when we invoke *getName()*, we assign the value "Kathy" to the parameter `firstName`. When the interpreter executes the *trace()* statement, it searches the local scope where it finds the `firstName` parameter and its value "Kathy". So the output of the function this time is "Kathy" not "Christine". Even though the timeline variable `firstName` exists, the function's local variable called `firstName` takes precedence.

Our example demonstrates the operation of the *scope chain*—the hierarchy of objects used by the interpreter to resolve references to variables and object properties. For functions attached to timelines, the scope chain has only two levels: the local scope and the scope of the movie clip that bears the function. But when we attach functions to custom objects and classes, the scope chain can involve many more levels, as we'll see in "Object Property Inheritance" in Chapter 12.

If the scope of the variables and properties we want to access from our function body differs from the statement's scope, we must use dot syntax to form an explicit reference. For example:

```
function dynamicGoto() {
  // Deliberately go outside the function's local scope
  _root.myClip.gotoAndPlay(_root.myClip.targetFrame);
}
```

Note that a function's scope chain is determined relative to the function *declaration* statement, not any function *invocation* statement. That is, the code in a function's body is scoped to the movie clip that bears the function declaration, not the movie clip that bears the statement that invokes the function.

Here's an example showing a misguided use of the scope chain:

```
// CODE ON MAIN MOVIE TIMELINE
// This function's scope chain includes the main movie
function rotate(degrees) {
  _rotation += degrees;
}
```

If we attempt to rotate `clipA` using `_root.rotate`, it rotates the entire main movie, not just `clipA`:

```
// CODE ON clipA's TIMELINE
_root.rotate(30);  // Oops! This rotates the entire movie!
```

In this situation we can fix our problem by passing the clip to be rotated as an argument to the `rotate()` function:

```
function rotate (theClip, degrees) {
    theClip._rotation += degrees;
}

// Invoke rotate() with a reference to clipA
_root.rotate(clipA, 30);
```

Local Variables

Variables assigned to a function's local scope are called *local variables*. Local variables, including parameters, are accessible only to statements in the body of the function in which they are defined and exist only while that function runs. To create a local variable (other than the parameters that automatically become local variables), we use the *var* statement inside any function, like this:

```
function funcName() {
  var temp = "just testing!";  // Declares the local variable temp
}
```

Local variables are useful for holding information temporarily. Here, for example, we use the local variable `lastSpacePlusOne` to hold an interim result. Like all local variables, it dies when the function ends:

```
function getLastWord(text) {
  var lastSpacePlusOne = text.lastIndexOf(" ") + 1;               // Local
  var lastWord = text.subString(lastSpacePlusOne, text.length);   // Local
  return lastWord;
}

// Displays: "word"
trace(getLastWord("Tell me the last word"));

// Displays: undefined. lastSpacePlusOne is local, and not
// available outside the getLastWord() function.
trace(lastSpacePlusOne);
```

When local variables expire at the end of a function, the memory associated with them is freed. By using local variables to store all temporary values, we can conserve memory in a program. Furthermore, when we declare a local variable, we need not worry that it might conflict with a timeline variable of the same name.

Of course, not all variables used in functions need to be local. Earlier we learned that we can read timeline variables from inside a function; we can also create and write to them. Variable assignment statements within a function that do not apply to a local variable are scoped to the timeline instead of the function. In this example, x is a local variable, but y and z are timeline variables:

```
var z = 1;

function createVars() {
  var x = 10;     // Create local variable x
  y = 13;         // Create timeline variable y
  z = 2;          // Alter timeline variable z
}
createVars();     // Call the function
trace(x);         // x is undefined (x dies when the function ends)
trace(y);         // y is 13 (y exists after the function ends)
trace(z);         // z is 2 (z was permanently altered by the function)
```

The rules for creating timeline variables apply even if our function is a method of an object. We won't cover objects until Chapter 12, but for those familiar with object-oriented programming, Example 9-2 shows code that proves the point. Note that x is defined on the timeline because it doesn't exist in the local scope of *newFunc()* or as a property of newObj.

Example 9-2. Variable Scope Within Object Methods

```
newObj = new Object();                 // Create an object
newObj.newFunc = function() { x = 12; };  // Attach a new method
newObj.newFunc ();                     // Call the method

// Now let's check for x
trace("x is " + x);                    // x is 12
trace("newObj.x is " + newObj.x);      // newObj.x is undefined
```

Function Parameters Revisited

Now that we're comfortable with how functions work, let's return to the topic of function parameters. Our current discussion requires a little knowledge of objects, so new programmers may want to read Chapter 12 before reading this section.

Number of Parameters

Earlier we learned that the parameters of a function are declared when the function is created. Recall the syntax:

```
function funcName (param1, param2, param3,...paramn) {
  statements
}
```

Perhaps surprisingly, the number of parameters passed to a function can differ from the number specified in the formal function declaration. Functions can accept any number of parameters, whether more than or fewer than the "expected" number. When a function is called with fewer than the declared number of parameters, the value of each missing parameter is set to **undefined**. For example:

```
function viewVars (x, y, z) {
  trace ("x is " + x);
  trace ("y is " + y);
  trace ("z is " + z);
}

viewVars(10);  // Displays: "x is 10", "y is ", and "z is " because
               // y and z are undefined (and display as blanks)
```

When a function is called with *more* parameters than the declared number, excess parameter values can be accessed using the *arguments* object. (Obviously the excess parameters can't be accessed by name like explicitly declared parameters because their names were not declared.)

The arguments Object

During the execution of any function, the built-in *arguments* object gives us access to three pieces of information: (a) the number of parameters that were passed to the function, (b) an array containing each of those parameter values, and (c) the name of the function being executed. The *arguments* object is really a special hybrid between an array and an object with some other properties.

Retrieving parameter values from the arguments array

The **arguments** array lets us check the value of any function parameter whether or not that parameter is defined formally in the function's declaration statement. To access a parameter, we examine the indexes of the **arguments** array:

```
arguments[n]
```

where *n* is the index of the parameter we're accessing. The first parameter (the leftmost parameter in the function-call expression) is stored at index 0 and is referred to as **arguments[0]**. Subsequent arguments are stored in order, proceeding to the right—so the second argument is **arguments[1]**, the third is **arguments[2]**, and so on.

From within a function, we can tell how many arguments were passed to the currently executing function by checking the number of elements in **arguments**, as follows:

```
arguments.length
```

We can easily cycle through all the parameters passed to a function and display the results in the Output window, as shown in Example 9-3.

Example 9-3. Displaying an Unknown Number of Parameters

```
function showArgs() {
  for (var i = 0; i < arguments.length; i++) {
    trace("Parameter " + (i + 1) + " is " + arguments[i]);
  }
}

showArgs(123, 23, "skip intro");

// Displays...
Parameter 1 is 123
Parameter 2 is 23
Parameter 3 is skip intro
```

The **arguments** array allows us to create very flexible functions that accept an arbitrary number of parameters.

Here's a generic function that removes any number of duplicated movie clip instances from the Stage:

```
function killClip() {
  for (var i = 0; i < arguments.length; i++) {
    arguments[i].removeMovieClip();
  }
}

  killClip(clip10, clip5, clip13);
```

Reader Exercise: Modify our earlier *combine()* function to accept an arbitrary number of inputs. What other functions might benefit from accepting an arbitrary number of parameters? How about a function that averages an arbitrary list of numbers? (Hint: sum all the arguments and then divide by the number of arguments.)

The callee property

As we've seen, the **arguments** array lets us retrieve a function's parameters. The *arguments* object has one property, **callee**, which returns a reference to the executing function. Normally, we know the name of the function we're calling, but if we are executing an anonymous function that was originally created with a function literal, the **callee** property can prove useful. Example 9-4 shows a function created with a function literal that performs recursive executions without knowing its own name. See "Recursive Functions" later in this chapter

Example 9-4. Counting Down with callee

```
count = function (x) {
  trace(x);
  if (x > 1) {
    arguments.callee(x - 1);
  }
}
count(25);
```

Obviously we can count down without using recursive anonymous functions. We'll see a more realistic example of function recursion later in this chapter.

Primitive Versus Composite Parameter Values

There's one more parameter subtlety we should consider—the difference between passing *primitive* data and *composite* data to a function.

When we pass a primitive data value as an argument to a function, the function receives a copy of the data, not the original. Changes made to a parameter in the function have no effect on the original argument outside that function. In Example 9-5, **variableName**'s value is initially set to 25. Changing its value to 10 within the *setValue()* function has no effect on **y**'s value.

Example 9-5. Primitive Data Is Passed by Value

```
var y = 25;
function setValue(variableName) {
  variableName = 10;
}
setValue(y);
trace("y is " + y);   // Displays: "y is 25"
```

Primitive data is, therefore, said to be *passed by value*. When we pass *composite* data as an argument to a function, however, the function receives a *reference* that points to the same data as the original argument, not just a duplicate of the data. Altering the data via the parameter variable affects the original data and therefore affects other variables that point to the same data, even outside of the function. Composite data, therefore, is said to be *passed by reference*.

In Example 9-6, changes to the `myArray` parameter variable affect the external `boys` array because they both point to the same data in memory.

Example 9-6. Modifying Composite Data Arguments Passed by Reference

```
// Create an array
var boys = ["Andrew", "Graham", "Derek"];

// setValue() sets the value of the first element of an array
function setValue(myArray) {
  myArray[0] = "Sid";        // Set the first element of the array
}

// Pass our array to the function
setValue(boys);

// Check the value of our array elements
trace("Boys: " + boys);  // Displays: "Boys: Sid,Graham,Derek"
```

Note that while we can overwrite individual elements of the array from inside a function, assigning a new value to a parameter will break its association with the original argument. Subsequent changes to the parameter variable will have no effect on the original argument. In Example 9-7, although the `boys` array is passed as an argument, the `myArray` parameter variable is immediately set to `girls`. Subsequent changes to `myArray` affect the `girls` array, not the `boys` array.

Example 9-7. Breaking the Association Between an Argument and a Parameter

```
// Create two arrays
var boys  = ["Andrew", "Graham",  "Derek"];
var girls = ["Alisa",  "Gillian", "Daniella"];

// setValue() ignores the passed array and modifies the girls array
function setValue(myArray) {
  myArray = girls;         // Make myArray point to girls, not boys
  myArray[0] = "Mary";  // Changes the first element of girls
}
```

Example 9-7. Breaking the Association Between an Argument and a Parameter (continued)

```
// Pass the boys array to the setValue() function
setValue(boys);

trace("Boys: " + boys);    // Displays: "Boys: Andrew,Graham,Derek"
trace("Girls: " + girls);  // Displays: "Girls: Mary,Gillian,Daniella"
```

More information on primitive and composite data can be found in Chapter 15, *Advanced Topics*.

Recursive Functions

A *recursive* function is a function that calls itself (by using its own name within its function body). Here's a simple example that shows the principle of recursion. But because the code tells the *trouble()* function to execute repeatedly (like an image reflected infinitely in two opposing mirrors), Flash will quickly run out of memory, causing an error:

```
function trouble() {
  trouble();
}
```

Practical recursive functions call themselves only while a given condition is met (thus preventing *infinite recursion*). Example 9-4 used recursion to count from a specified number down to 1, but obviously that can be accomplished without recursion.

One classic use of recursion is to calculate the mathematical *factorial* of a number. The factorial of 3 (written as 3! in mathematical nomenclature) is 3*2*1=6. The factorial of 5 is 5*4*3*2*1=120. Example 9-8 shows a factorial function that uses recursion.

Example 9-8. Calculating Factorials Using Recursion

```
function factorial(x) {
    if (x < 0) {
      return undefined;  // Error condition
    } else if (x <= 1) {
      return 1;
    } else {
      return x * factorial(x-1);
    }
}
trace (factorial(3));  // Displays: 6
trace (factorial(5));  // Displays: 120
```

As usual, there is more than one way to skin a proverbial cat. Using a loop, we can also calculate a factorial without recursion, as shown in Example 9-9.

Example 9-9. Calculating Factorials Without Recursion

```
function factorial(x) {
    if (x < 0) {
      return undefined; // Error condition
    } else {
      var result = 1;
      for (var i = 1; i <= x; i++) {
        result = result * i;
      }
      return result;
    }
}
```

Example 9-8 and Example 9-9 represent two ways of solving the same problem. The recursive method says, "The factorial of 6 is 6 multiplied by the factorial of 5. The factorial of 5 is 5 multiplied by the factorial of 4 . . . " and so on. The nonrecursive method loops over the numbers from 1 to **x** and multiplies them all together into one big number.

Which approach is better—recursive or nonrecursive—depends on the problem. Some problems are solved more easily using recursion, but recursion can be slower than nonrecursive solutions. Recursion is best used when you don't know how deeply a data structure may be nested. For example, suppose you wanted to list all the files within a subdirectory, including listing all files within any nested subdirectory, ad infinitum. You couldn't write a general solution that worked for any number of subdirectories without resorting to recursion. A recursive solution might look like this in pseudocode:

```
function listFiles (directoryName) {
    do (check the next item in directoryName) {
      if (this item is a subDirectory itself) {
        // Recursively call this function with the new subdirectory
        listFiles(subDirectoryName);
      } else {
        // Display the name of this file
        trace (filename);
      }
    } while (there are still items to check);
}
```

When we consider the *XML* object in Part III, *Language Reference*, we'll use recursion to list all the elements in an XML document.

Internal Functions

Although we've seen how to create user-defined functions, let's not forget that ActionScript comes with a bevy of built-in functions (akin to verbs in our language analogy). We've already seen some built-in functions that allow us to manipulate data. We've also touched on functions that control the Flash movie and the user environment.

For example, to manipulate the playhead of a movie clip, we can call the *gotoAndPlay()* function with a frame number as a parameter:

```
gotoAndPlay(5);
```

If you are a new programmer, you may be experiencing an epiphany. You hopefully will have noticed that you invoke built-in functions using the function-call operator (the parentheses) and a parameter list (the value 5 in this case) just like our custom user-defined functions! Built-in functions, such as *gotoAndPlay()*, are used just like the functions we've been building ourselves. Naturally, the built-in functions do different things than our custom functions, and there is no sense in writing a custom function to do something that a built-in ActionScript function already offers. But like any custom function, each built-in function has a name, optional parameters, and a return value (although sometimes it's `undefined`).

Even though Flash has long referred to *gotoAndPlay* as an "Action," we now see it in its true form, as an internal function. In Chapter 6 we learned that some Flash Actions are statements and some are functions. Now that you've studied both thoroughly, you'll be able to tell which are which.

By looking upon certain Actions as *functions*, you'll have an easier time remembering and using their syntax. For example, to load a movie into the Flash Player we need to know that a *loadMovie()* function exists and what parameters it expects. After a quick jaunt over to Part III, we find the info and can easily put together a statement like this:

```
loadMovie("myMovie.swf", 1);
```

Easy stuff once you've become comfortable with using functions.

ActionScript's built-in functions are many and varied. They give us control over the elements of a movie, empowering us to examine and change everything from the volume of a sound to the amount of text selected in an editable text field. For an exhaustive list of ActionScript's built-in functions, consult Part III. Skim it periodically to familiarize yourself with the type of functions that are available, although there is no need to memorize their specific syntax.

Internal Function Availability

Some built-in functions are universally available, while others can be invoked only through an object. If the function is a *global* function, it may be used anywhere; if the function is a *method* of an object, however, it must be used in conjunction with the appropriate object. Because we haven't covered objects yet and most of ActionScript's built-in functions are object methods, we'll delay our consideration of the built-in methods until Chapter 12.

Functions as Objects

In ActionScript, functions are technically a special type of built-in object. Let's see what that means and how it affects what you can do with functions.

Passing Functions to Functions

Perhaps surprisingly, we can use any function as an argument to another function like this:

```
function1(function2);
```

Note that if there are no parentheses following *function2*, the interpreter doesn't execute *function2()* but instead just passes its "object reference" as an argument to *function1()*. That is, *function1()* receives *function2* itself, not the return value of *function2()*. Because objects are passed by reference, we can pass a function identifier to another function and it will arrive unscathed. The passed function can be executed like this:

```
function doCommand(command) {
   command();       // Executes the passed function
}

// Some examples:
doCommand(stop);  // Pass the internal stop() function (stops the current movie)
doCommand(play);  // Pass the internal play() function (plays the current movie)
```

Because functions are a type of object, we may treat them like any other data. In the following example, we assign the internal *gotoAndPlay* function to the variable gp, which gives us a shorter way to refer to the function:

```
gp = gotoAndPlay;  // Create a shortcut reference to gotoAndPlay()
gp(25);            // Invoke gotoAndPlay() using our reference
```

In addition to passing and storing functions as objects, we can exploit the "object-ness" of functions by attaching properties to them, like this:

```
// Create a function
function myFunction () {
```

```
    trace(myFunction.x);
}

// Attach a property to it
myFunction.x = 15;

// Check the property value by invoking the function
myFunction();   // Displays: 15
```

 By attaching properties to functions, we can maintain the state of a piece of information between function executions without cluttering up a timeline with variables.

Function properties offer the benefits of local variables without expiring between function invocations. This is useful when a function needs to be invoked with a unique identifier. Here, for example, is a generic function that duplicates a movie clip and gives the duplicated clip a unique name and level:

```
makeClip.count = 0;     // Define a property of makeClip() (remember that
                        // makeClip() already exists because functions are
                        // defined before code runs)

// Duplicate a passed clip and assign the new clip an automatic name
function makeClip (theClip) {
  // Add one to our clip counter
  makeClip.count++

  // Now duplicate the clip, assigning it a unique name and depth
  theClip.duplicateMovieClip(theClip._name + makeClip.count, makeClip.count);
}

makeClip(square);   // Make a duplicate of square using makeClip()

square1._x += 100;  // Now move the duplicated square to the right
```

Centralizing Code

Probably the single most important feature of functions is their reusability—we can create reusable segments of code that can be executed from anywhere in a movie. Because functions can be executed remotely, they can be stored in a central location, easing code maintenance and upgrades.

Suppose, for example, that we have three buttons in three different movie clips, all with the same purpose. Instead of triplicating our code, we can put one copy in a function on the main timeline and invoke it from each button as needed. This saves time, reduces the potential for errors, and makes it easy to update the behavior of all three buttons at once. Because the code is centralized, testing is more reliable and troubleshooting much easier. If one button works and another doesn't, chances are that the problem is in the second button's function invocation and not in your centralized behavior.

The Multiple-Choice Quiz Revisited

In Example 1-1, we introduced new programmers to a simple scripted movie—a multiple-choice quiz. Let's revisit that quiz now to see how we can centralize its code.

Our new quiz's layer structure is set up exactly as before. We'll be changing the code on only the first frame, the `quizEnd` frame, and the buttons.

You can retrieve the *.fla* file for both the original and revised versions of the quiz from the online Code Depot.

Organizing the Quiz Code into Functions

In our first attempt at creating a multiple-choice quiz, we scattered our code around our movie. We placed the logic of our quiz in three places: on the first frame, where we initialized our quiz; on the buttons, where we tracked the user's answers; and on the `quizEnd` frame, where we tallied the user's score. We're now going to centralize the quiz logic by performing all of those tasks in the first frame. To initialize the quiz, we'll still use a simple series of statements as we did in the first version, but to track the user's answers and tally the user's score, we'll use two functions, *answer()* and *gradeUser()*.

Example 9-10 shows the code on our quiz's first frame. This is where we'll store all the logic needed to run our quiz. Take a look at the code in its entirety, then we'll dissect it.

Example 9-10. A Multiple-Choice Quiz, Version 2

```
// Stop the movie at the first question
stop ();

// Initialize main timeline variables
var displayTotal;        // Text field for displaying user's score
var numQuestions = 2;    // Number of quiz questions
var q1answer;            // User's answer for question1
var q2answer;            // User's answer for question2
var totalCorrect = 0;    // Number of questions answered correctly
var correctAnswer1 = 3;  // The correct choice for question 1
var correctAnswer2 = 2;  // The correct choice for question 2

// Function to register user's answers
function answer (choice) {
  answer.currentAnswer++;
  set ("q" + answer.currentAnswer + "answer", choice);
```

Example 9-10. A Multiple-Choice Quiz, Version 2 (continued)

```
  if (answer.currentAnswer == numQuestions) {
    gotoAndStop ("quizEnd");
  } else {
    gotoAndStop ("q" + (answer.currentAnswer + 1));
  }
}

// Function to tally user's score
function gradeUser() {
  // Count how many questions user answered correctly
  for (i = 1; i <= numQuestions; i++) {
    if (eval("q" + i + "answer") == eval("correctAnswer" + i)) {
      totalCorrect++;
    }
  }

  // Show user's score in an on-screen text field
  displayTotal = totalCorrect;
}
```

Our first chore is to stop the movie, using the *stop()* function, so that it doesn't play through all the questions. Next, we initialize our quiz's timeline variables. You'll recognize `displayTotal`, `totalCorrect`, `q1answer`, and `q2answer` from the first version of the quiz. We've also added `numQuestions` (which we'll use in our *answer()* and *gradeUser()* functions) and `correctAnswer1` and `correctAnswer2` (which we'll use when grading the quiz).

With our variables initialized, we can create the *answer()* function, which will record the user's answers and advance the playhead to the next question. The *answer()* function expects one parameter, `choice`, which is the number of the user's answer for each question, so its function declaration begins like this:

```
function answer (choice) {
```

Each time an answer is given, the function increments `currentAnswer`, a function property that tracks the question being answered:

```
answer.currentAnswer++;
```

Next, we set the user's choice in a dynamically named timeline variable that corresponds to the question being answered. We use the value of the `currentAnswer` property to determine the name of our timeline variable (`q1answer`, `q2answer`, etc.):

```
set ("q" + answer.currentAnswer + "answer", choice);
```

With the user's choice stored in the appropriate variable, if we are on the last question, we go to the end of the quiz; otherwise, we go to the next question, which is at the frame labeled *"q" + (answer.currentAnswer + 1)*:

```
if (answer.currentAnswer == numQuestions) {
  gotoAndStop ("quizEnd");
} else {
  gotoAndStop ("q"+ (answer.currentAnswer + 1));
}
```

That takes care of our question-answering logic. The *answer()* function is ready to handle answers from any question in the quiz. Now let's build the function that evaluates those answers, *gradeUser()*.

The *gradeUser()* function takes no parameters. It has to compare each user answer with each correct answer and display the user's score. We handle the comparisons in a *for* loop—we cycle through the loop body for the number of questions in the quiz:

```
for (i = 1; i <= numQuestions; i++) {
```

Inside the loop, a comparison expression tests the user's answers against the correct answers. Using *eval()*, we dynamically retrieve the value of each user-answer variable and each correct-answer variable. If the two variables are equal, `totalCorrect` is incremented:

```
if (eval("q" + i + "answer") == eval("correctAnswer" + i)) {
  totalCorrect++;
}
```

After the loop finishes, `totalCorrect` will contain the number of questions that the user answered correctly. We display that number by setting the dynamic text field `displayTotal` to `totalCorrect`:

```
displayTotal = totalCorrect;
```

Voila! With both functions in place and our quiz variables initialized, the logic of our quiz system is complete. Notice how much easier it is to follow the quiz's operation when most of the code is contained on a single frame? All that's left is to call the functions from the appropriate points in the quiz.

Calling the quiz functions

We'll call the *answer()* function from the buttons that the user clicks to indicate answers, and we'll call the *gradeUser()* function from the `quizEnd` frame.

On the first answer button of frame 1, we attach the following code:

```
on (release) {
  answer(1);
}
```

On the second button, we attach this code:

```
on (release) {
  answer(2);
}
```

And on the third button, we attach this code:

```
on (release) {
  answer(3);
}
```

Then we attach the exact same code to the three buttons at frame q2. Notice how elegant this process is. With the code needed to handle each button neatly packed into a function, our button code is kept to a bare minimum. The answer and quiz progression logic is not redundantly duplicated as it was in the earlier version of the quiz. Furthermore, creating new buttons is a simple matter of changing the number passed to the *answer()* function. We don't need to do anything special for the last question in the quiz because the *answer()* function handles that automatically.

With the button code attached, we simply need to grade the user at the end of the quiz by attaching this statement to the `quizEnd` frame:

```
gradeUser();
```

Once again, by placing our grading functionality on the first frame of our movie with the other functions, we've separated the *mechanics* of the system from the *use* of the system. Hence, we don't lose those mechanics in the maze of frames and buttons that Flash movies can often become.

Test your quiz to make sure that it works. Experiment to see what happens when you add quiz questions, remove quiz questions, and change anything else that comes to mind. As we continue, think about how the techniques we learn might be applied to our quiz example. What visible features can we add to the user experience? What invisible changes can we make to the code that will make it more flexible or elegant even if the user experience is unchanged?

Onward!

This chapter showed us one of the most powerful devices in ActionScript: functions. In the next chapter, we'll learn about a special variety of functions, called *event handlers*, that are executed automatically by the interpreter. Event handlers are one of the key building blocks of interactivity.

10

Events and Event Handlers

We've learned a lot about composing instructions for the ActionScript interpreter to execute. By now we're pretty comfortable telling the interpreter *what* we want it to do, but how do we tell it *when* to perform those actions? ActionScript code doesn't just execute of its own accord—something always provokes its execution.

That "something" is either the synchronous playback of a movie or the occurrence of a predefined asynchronous *event*.

Synchronous Code Execution

As a movie plays, the timeline's playhead travels from frame to frame. Each time the playhead enters a new frame, the interpreter executes any code attached to that frame. After the code on a frame has been executed, the screen display is updated and sounds are played. Then, the playhead proceeds to the next frame.

For example, when we place code directly on frame 1 of a movie, that code executes before the content in frame 1 is displayed. If we place another block of code on a keyframe at frame 5 of the same movie, frames 1 through 4 will be displayed, then the code on frame 5 will be executed, then frame 5 will be displayed. The code executed on frames 1 and 5 is said to be executed *synchronously* because it happens in a linear, predictable fashion.

All code attached to the frames of a movie is executed synchronously. Even if some frames are played out of order due to a *gotoAndPlay()* or *gotoAndStop()* command, the code on each frame is executed in a predictable sequence, synchronized with the movement of the playhead.

Event-Based Asynchronous Code Execution

Some code does not execute in a predictable sequence. Instead, it executes when the ActionScript interpreter notices that one of a predetermined set of *events* has occurred. Many *events* involve some action by the user, such as clicking the mouse or pressing a key. Just as the playhead entering a new frame executes synchronous code attached to the frame, events can cause *event-based* code to execute. Event-based code (code that executes in response to an event) is said to be executed *asynchronously* because the triggering of events can occur at arbitrary times.

Synchronous programming requires us to dictate, in advance, the timing of our code's execution. Asynchronous programming, on the other hand, gives us the ability to react dynamically to events as they occur. Asynchronous code execution is critical to ActionScript and to interactivity itself.

This chapter explores asynchronous (event-based) programming in Flash and catalogs the different events supported by ActionScript.

Types of Events

Conceptually, events can be grouped into two categories:

user events
> Actions taken by the user (e.g., a mouseclick or a keystroke)

system events
> Things that happen as part of the internal playback of a movie (e.g., a movie clip appearing on stage or a series of variables loading from an external file)

ActionScript does not distinguish syntactically between user events and system events. An event triggered internally by a movie is no less palpable than a user's mouseclick. While we might not normally think of, say, a movie clip's removal from the Stage as a noteworthy "event," being able to react to system events gives us great control over a movie.

ActionScript events may also be categorized more practically according to the object to which they pertain. All events happen relative to some object in the Flash environment. That is, the interpreter doesn't just say "The user clicked"; it says, "The user clicked *this button*" or "The user clicked while *this movie clip* was on stage." And the interpreter doesn't say, "Data was received"; it says, "*This movie clip* received some data." We define the code that responds to events on the objects to which the events relate.

The ActionScript objects that can receive events are:

- Movie Clips
- Buttons
- Objects of the *XML* and *XMLSocket* classes

As we'll see throughout this chapter, ActionScript actually has two different event implementations: one for events that relate to movie clips and buttons, and one for all other kinds of objects.

Event Handlers

Not every event triggers the execution of code. Events regularly occur without affecting a movie. A user may, for example, generate dozens of events by clicking repeatedly on a button, but those clicks may be ignored. Why? Because, on their own, events can't cause code to execute—we must write code to react to events explicitly. To instruct the interpreter to execute some code in response to an event, we add a so-called *event handler* that describes the action to take when the specified event occurs. Event handlers are so named because they *catch*, or *handle*, the events in a movie.

An event handler is akin to a specially named function that is automatically invoked when a particular event occurs. Creating an event handler is, hence, very much like creating a function, with a few twists:

- Event handlers have predetermined names such as *keyDown*. You can't name an event handler whatever you like; you have to use the predefined names shown later in Table 10-1 and Table 10-2.
- Event handlers are not declared with the *function* statement.
- Event handlers must be attached to buttons, movie clips, or objects, not frames.

 Most events were first introduced in Flash 5. If exporting to Flash 4 format, use only the button event handlers (only button events were supported in Flash 4), and test your work carefully in the Flash 4 Player.

Event Handler Syntax

The names of events (and their corresponding event handlers) are predetermined by ActionScript. Button event handlers are defined using *on* (*eventName*), and movie clip event handlers are defined using *onClipEvent* (*eventName*), where *eventName* is the name of the event to be handled.

Hence, all button event handlers (except *keyPress*, which also requires a *key* parameter) take the form:

```
on (eventName) {
  statements
}
```

A single button handler can respond to multiple events, separated by commas. For example:

```
on (rollover, rollOut) {
  // Invoke a custom function in response to both the rollOver and rollOut events
  playRandomSound( );
}
```

All movie clip event handlers take the form:

```
onClipEvent (eventName) {
  statements
}
```

Unlike button handlers, clip handlers can respond only to a single event.

Creating Event Handlers

To create an event handler, we define the handler and attach it to the appropriate object. We'll begin with the most common handlers—those attached to buttons and movie clips.

Attaching Event Handlers to Buttons and Movie Clips

To attach an event handler to a button or a movie clip, we must physically place the code of the handler function onto the desired button or clip. We may do so only in the Flash authoring tool, by selecting the object on stage and entering the appropriate code in the Actions panel, shown in Figure 10-1.

Let's try making a simple event handler function for both a button and a movie clip. To create a button event handler, follow these instructions:

1. Start a new Flash movie.

2. Create a button and drag an instance of it onto the main Stage.

3. With the button selected, type the following code in the Actions panel:

```
on (release) {
  trace("You clicked the button");
}
```

4. Select Control → Test Movie.

5. Click the button. The message, "You clicked the button," appears in the Output window.

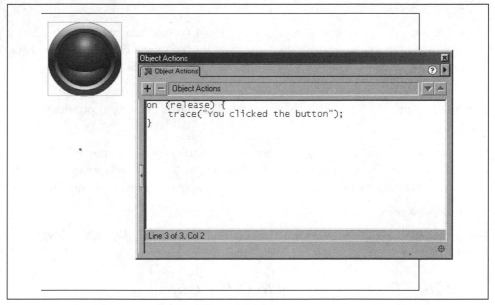

Figure 10-1. Attaching an event handler to a button

When the movie plays and we press and release the button, the *release* event is detected by the interpreter and it executes the *on (release)* event handler. Each time that we press and release the button, the message, "You clicked the button," appears in the Output window.

Now let's try making a slightly more interesting event handler on a movie clip. Once again, follow the instructions:

1. Start a new Flash movie.

2. On the main movie Stage, draw a rectangle.

3. Select Insert → Convert to Symbol.

4. In the Symbol Properties dialog box, name the new symbol `rectangle` and select Movie Clip as the Behavior.

5. Click OK to finish creating the `rectangle` movie clip.

6. Select the `rectangle` clip on stage, and then type the following in the Actions panel:

```
onClipEvent (keyDown) {
  _visible = 0;
}

onClipEvent (keyUp) {
  _visible = 1;
}
```

7. Select Control → Test Movie.

8. Click the movie to make sure it has keyboard focus, then press and hold any key. Each time you depress a key, the `rectangle` movie clip disappears. Each time you release the depressed key, `rectangle` reappears.

Notice that we don't manually issue any handler-invocation statements—the interpreter automatically invokes our event handler when the corresponding event occurs.

Flash doesn't support attaching and removing handlers via ActionScript while the movie is playing. Event handlers must be assigned to buttons and movie clips using the Flash authoring tool. The following imaginary syntax, therefore, is not legal:

```
myClip.onKeyDown = function () { _visible = 0; };
```

We'll see how to work around this shortcoming later under "Dynamic Movie Clip Event Handlers."

Attaching Event Handlers to Other Objects

In addition to movie clips and buttons, two built-in object classes—*XML* and *XMLSocket*—support event handlers. For these objects, event handlers are not added to some physical entity in the authoring tool. Rather, they are attached as methods to object instances.

For the *XML* and *XMLsocket* objects, ActionScript uses predefined properties to hold the name of the event handlers. For example, the `onLoad` property holds the name of the handler to be executed when external XML data has loaded.

To set the `onLoad` property for an *XML* object, we use the following code:

```
myDoc = new XML();
myDoc.onLoad = function () { trace("all done loading!"); };
```

Alternatively, we can define the handler function first, and then assign it to the `onLoad` property of our object:

```
function doneMsg () {
  trace("all done loading!");
}
myDoc.onLoad = doneMsg;
```

This syntax closely resembles that of JavaScript, where functions may be assigned to event handler properties, as shown in Example 10-1.

Example 10-1. Assigning a JavaScript Event Handler

```
// Assign a function literal to the onload handler in JavaScript
window.onload = function () { alert("done loading"); };

// Or, alternatively, create and then assign a function to the onload property
function doneMsg () {
  alert("done loading");
```

Example 10-1. Assigning a JavaScript Event Handler (continued)

```
}
window.onload = doneMsg;
```

In the future, more ActionScript objects may support assigning event handlers using object properties, so it's a good idea to get used to this style now. If you're not using the *XML* or *XMLSocket* objects, you can still practice making handlers in this way with HTML documents and JavaScript. The beauty of this approach is its flexibility; any event handler function may be easily reassigned or even removed during movie playback.

We'll learn more about attaching functions to objects in Chapter 12, *Objects and Classes*. Information about the events supported by the *XML* and *XMLSocket* objects may be found in Part III, *Language Reference*.

The lifespan of event handlers is tied to the life of the objects with which they are associated. When a clip or button is removed from the Stage or when an *XML* or *XMLSocket* object dies, any event handlers associated with those objects die with them. An object must be present on stage or exist on the timeline for its handlers to remain active.

Event Handler Scope

As with any function, the statements in an event handler execute within a predefined scope. Scope dictates where the interpreter looks to resolve the variables, subfunctions, objects, or properties referenced in an event handler's body. We'll consider event handler scope in relation to movie clip events, button events, and other object events.

Movie Clip Event Handler Scope

Unlike regular functions, movie clip event handlers *do not define a local scope*! When we attach a handler to a clip, the scope of the handler is the clip, not just the event handler itself. This means that all variables are retrieved from the clip's timeline. For example, if we attach an *enterFrame* event handler to a clip named **navigation** and write *trace(x);* inside the handler, the interpreter looks for the value of **x** on **navigation**'s timeline:

```
onClipEvent (enterFrame) {
   trace(x);  // Displays the value of navigation.x
}
```

The interpreter does not consult a local scope first because there is no local scope to consult. If we write *var y = 10;* in our handler, y is defined on **navigation**'s timeline, even though the *var* keyword ordinarily declares a local variable when used in a function.

The easiest way to remember the scope rules of a clip event handler is to treat the handler's statements as though they were attached to a frame of the handler's clip. For example, suppose we have a clip named **ball** that has a variable called **xVelocity** in it. To access **xVelocity** from inside a **ball** event handler, we simply refer to it directly, like this:

```
onClipEvent (mouseDown) {
  xVelocity += 10;
}
```

We don't have to supply the path to the variable as **_root.ball.xVelocity** because the interpreter already assumes we mean the variable **xVelocity** in **ball**. The same is true of properties and methods; instead of using **ball._x**, we simply use **_x**, and instead of using *ball.gotoAndStop(5)*, we simply use *gotoAndStop(5)*. For example:

```
onClipEvent (enterFrame) {
  _x += xVelocity;                  // Move the ball
  gotoAndPlay(_currentframe - 1);   // Do a little loop
}
```

We can even define a function on **ball** using a function declaration statement in a handler, like this:

```
onClipEvent (load) {
  function hideMe() {
    _visibility = 0;
  }
}
```

It's sometimes easy to forget that statements in clip event handlers are scoped to the *clip's timeline*, not the handler function's local scope and not the clip's *parent* timeline (the timeline upon which the clip resides).

For example, suppose we place our **ball** clip on the main timeline of a movie, and the main timeline (not **ball**'s timeline) has a *moveBall()* function defined on it. We may absent-mindedly call *moveBall()* from an event handler on **ball** like this:

```
onClipEvent (enterFrame) {
  moveBall();  // Does nothing! There's no moveBall() function in ball.
               // The moveBall() function is defined on _root
}
```

We have to explicitly refer to the *moveBall()* function on the main timeline using **_root** like this:

```
onClipEvent (enterFrame) {
  _root.moveBall();  // Now it works!
}
```

Occasionally, we may need to refer to the current clip object explicitly from within an event handler. We can do so using the **this** keyword, which refers to the current movie clip when used in an event handler. Hence, the following references are synonymous within a clip event handler:

```
this._x  // Same as next line
_x

this.gotoAndStop(12);  // Same as next line
gotoAndStop(12);
```

Use of **this** is most frequently required when we're dynamically generating the name of one of the current clip's properties (either a variable name or a nested clip). Here we tell one of the nested clips in the series **ball.stripe1**, **ball. stripe2**, . . . to start playing, depending on the current frame of the **ball** clip:

```
onClipEvent (enterFrame) {
  this["stripe" + _currentframe].play();
}
```

The keyword **this** is also frequently used with movie clip methods that demand an explicit reference to a movie clip object upon invocation. Any movie clip method with the same name as an ActionScript global function must be used with an explicit clip reference. The **this** keyword is therefore necessary when invoking the following functions as methods inside an event handler:

> *duplicateMovieClip()*
> *loadMovie()*
> *loadVariables()*
> *print()*
> *printAsBitmap()*
> *removeMovieClip()*
> *startDrag()*
> *unloadMovie()*

For example:

```
this.duplicateMovieClip("ball2", 1);
this.loadVariables("vars.txt");
this.startDrag(true);
this.unloadMovie();
```

We'll learn all about the dual nature of these functions in "Method versus global function overlap issues," in Chapter 13, *Movie Clips*.

Note that the **this** keyword allows us to refer to the current clip even when that clip has no assigned instance name in the authoring tool or when we don't know the clip's name. In fact, using `this`, we may even pass the current clip as a reference to a function without ever knowing the current clip's name. Here's some quite legal (and quite elegant) code to demonstrate:

```
// CODE ON MAIN TIMELINE
// Here is a generic function that moves any clip
function move (clip, x, y) {
  clip._x += x;
  clip._y += y;
}
```

```
// CODE ON CLIP
// Call the main timeline function and tell it to move the
// current clip by passing a reference with the this keyword
onClipEvent (enterFrame) {
  _root.move(this, 10, 15);
}
```

In build 30 of the Flash 5 Player, a bug prevented *gotoAndStop()* and *gotoAndPlay()* from working inside a clip handler when used with string literal labels. Such commands were simply ignored. For example, this would not work:

```
onClipEvent(load) {
  gotoAndStop("intro");  // Won't work in Flash 5 r30
}
```

To work around the bug, use a self-reflexive clip reference, as in:

```
onClipEvent(load) {
  this.gotoAndStop("intro");
}
```

Button Event Handler Scope

Button handlers are scoped to the timeline upon which the button resides. For example, if we place a button on the main timeline and declare the variable `speed` in a handler on that button, `speed` will be scoped to the main timeline (`_root`):

```
// CODE FOR BUTTON HANDLER
on (release) {
  var speed = 10;  // Defines speed on _root
}
```

By contrast, if we place a movie clip, `ball`, on the main timeline and declare the variable `speed` in a handler of `ball`, `speed` is scoped to `ball`:

```
// CODE FOR ball HANDLER
on (load) {
  var speed = 10;  // Defines speed on ball, not _root
}
```

Inside a button handler, the `this` keyword refers to the timeline on which the button resides:

```
on (release) {
  // Make the clip on which this button resides 50% transparent
  this._alpha = 50;
  // Move the clip on which this button resides 10 pixels to the right
  this._x += 10;
}
```

Other Object Event Handler Scope

Unlike movie clip and button handlers, event handlers attached to instances of built-in classes such as *XML* and *XMLSocket* are scoped exactly like functions. An *XML* or *XMLSocket* object's event handler has a scope chain that is defined when the handler function is defined. Furthermore, *XML* and *XMLSocket* event handlers define a local scope. All the rules of function scope described in "Function Scope" in Chapter 9, *Functions*, apply directly to event handler functions attached to objects that are neither buttons nor movie clips.

Button Events

Table 10-1 briefly introduces the various events available for buttons. Using button events, we can easily create code for navigation, forms, games, and other interface elements. Let's explore each button event and learn how a button can be programmed to react to mouse and keyboard events.

Each of the button events in Table 10-1 is handled by a matching button event handler of the form *on* (*eventName*). For example, the *press* event is handled using an event handler beginning with *on* (*press*). The exception is the *keyPress* event handler which takes the form *on* (*keyPress key*) where *key* is the key to detect. Button events are sent only to the button with which the mouse is interacting. If multiple buttons overlap, the topmost button receives all events; no other buttons can respond, even if the topmost button has no handlers defined. In the following descriptions, the *hit* area refers to the physical region of the button that must be under the mouse pointer in order for the button to be activated. (A button's *hit* area is defined graphically when you create the button in the Flash authoring tool.)

Table 10-1. Button Events

Button Event Name	Button Event Occurs When . . .
press	Primary mouse button is depressed while pointer is in the button's *hit* area. Other mouse buttons are not detectable.
release	Primary mouse button is depressed and then released while pointer is in the button's *hit* area.

Table 10-1. Button Events (continued)

Button Event Name	Button Event Occurs When . . .
releaseOutside	Primary mouse button is depressed while pointer is in the button's *hit* area and then released while pointer is outside of the *hit* area.
rollOver	Mouse pointer moves into the button's *hit* area without the mouse button depressed.
rollOut	Mouse pointer moves out of the button's *hit* area without the mouse button depressed.
dragOut	Primary mouse button is depressed while pointer is in the button's *hit* area, and then, while mouse button is still depressed, pointer is moved out of the *hit* area.
dragOver	Primary mouse button is depressed while pointer is in the button's *hit* area, and then, while mouse button is still depressed, pointer is moved out of, then back into, the button's *hit* area.
keyPress	Specified *key* is depressed. In most cases, the *keyDown* clip event is preferred over the *keyPress* button event.

press

A mouseclick is technically a two-step process: the mouse button is depressed (*press*) and then released (*release*). A *press* event occurs when the mouse pointer is in the *hit* area of a button and the primary mouse button is depressed. Secondary mouse buttons are not detectable. Button *press* events are appropriate for radio buttons or weapons firing in a game, but use *release* events to allow the user to change his mind before releasing the mouse.

release

The *release* button event occurs when the following sequence is detected:

1. The mouse pointer is in the *hit* area of a button.

2. The primary mouse button is pressed while the mouse pointer is still in the *hit* area of the button (at which point a *press* event occurs).

3. The primary mouse button is released while the mouse pointer is still in the *hit* area of the original button (at which point the *release* event occurs).

By using the *release* event instead of the *press* event, you give users a chance to move the pointer off of a button even after it has been clicked, thus allowing them to retract their action.

releaseOutside

The *releaseOutside* event typically indicates that the user changed his mind by clicking on a button but moving the pointer off the button before releasing the mouse button. The event is generated when the following sequence is detected:

1. The mouse pointer is in the *hit* area of a button.

2. The primary mouse button is pressed and held (the *press* event occurs).

3. The mouse pointer moves out of the button's *hit* area (the *dragOut* event occurs).

4. The primary mouse button is released while not in the *hit* area of the original button.

You will rarely bother detecting *releaseOutside* events, as they usually indicate that the user intended not to perform any action.

rollOver

The *rollOver* event occurs when the mouse pointer moves into the *hit* area of a button with no mouse buttons depressed. The *rollOver* event is rarely used in ActionScript because visual button changes are created directly in the authoring tool, not with scripting. You should use the provided *up*, *over*, and *down* frames in the authoring tool to create highlight states for buttons.

The *rollOver* event in Flash 5 provides a handy means of retrieving a text field selection. For more details, see "Selection Object" in Part III.

rollOut

The *rollOut* event is *rollOver*'s counterpart; it occurs when the mouse pointer is moved out of the *hit* area of a button with no mouse buttons depressed. As with *rollOver*, *rollOut* is rarely used because button highlight states are created directly in the authoring tool, so manual image swapping is not required in ActionScript.

dragOut

The *dragOut* event is similar to *rollOut*, except that it is generated if the mouse button is down when the pointer leaves a button's *hit* area. The *dragOut* event is followed by either the *releaseOutside* event (if the user releases the mouse button) or the *dragOver* event (if the user moves the pointer back into the button's *hit* area without having released the mouse button).

dragOver

The *dragOver* event is a seldom-seen woodland creature. It is conjured up when the following sequence is performed:

1. The mouse pointer moves into the *hit* area of a button (*rollOver* event occurs).

2. The primary mouse button is pressed and held (*press* event occurs).

3. The mouse pointer moves out of the button's *hit* area (*dragOut* event occurs).

4. The mouse pointer moves back into the button's *hit* area (*dragOver* event occurs).

Thus, the *dragOver* event indicates that the user has moved the mouse pointer out of and back into the *hit* area, all the while holding the mouse button down. Note that *dragover*, instead of the *rollOver* event, is generated if the mouse button is still down when the pointer reenters the button's *hit* area.

keyPress

The *keyPress* event is unrelated to mouse events and is instead triggered by the pressing of a specified key. We cover it here because it uses the *on* (`eventName`) syntax of other ActionScript button event handlers. This event handler requires us to specify the key that triggers the event:

```
on (keyPress key) {
   statements
}
```

where *key* is a string representing the key associated with the event. The string may be either the character on the key (such as "s" or "S"), or a keyword representing the key in the format `"<Keyword>"`. Only one key may be specified with each handler. To capture multiple keys using *keyPress*, we must create multiple *keyPress* event handlers. For example:

```
// Detects the "a" key
on (keyPress "a") {
  trace("The 'a' key was pressed");
}

// Detects the Enter key
on (keyPress "<Enter>") {
  trace("The Enter key was pressed");
}

// Detects the Down Arrow key
on (keyPress "<Down>") {
  trace("The Down Arrow key was pressed");
}
```

The legal values of *Keyword* are as follows (note that the function keys F1 . . . F12 are not supported by *keyPress*, but are detectable using the *Key* object):

```
<Backspace>
<Delete>
<Down>
<End>
<Enter>
<Home>
```

```
<Insert>
<Left>
<PgDn>
<PgUp>
<Right>
<Space>
<Tab>
<Up>
```

In Flash 4, *keyPress* was the only means we had of interacting with the keyboard. In Flash 5 and later, the *Key* object, in combination with the movie clip events *keyDown* and *keyUp* (discussed later), offer much greater control over keyboard interaction. The *keyPress* event detects the pressing of a single key at a time, whereas the *Key* object can detect the simultaneous pressing of multiple keys.

Movie Clip Events Overview

Movie clip events are generated by a wide variety of occurrences in the Flash Player, from mouseclicks to the downloading of data. Clip events can be broken into two categories: user-input events and movie-playback events. User-input events are related to the mouse and keyboard, while movie-playback events are related to the rendering of frames in the Flash Player, the birth and death of movie clips, and the loading of data.

Note that user-input clip events partially overlap the functionality of the button events described earlier. For example, a clip's *mouseDown* event handler can detect a mouse press just as a button's *press* event handler can. Movie clip events, however, are not tied to any kind of *hit* area like button events are and do not affect the look of the mouse pointer.

Let's spend some quality time with the ActionScript movie clip events, summarized in Table 10-2. We'll look at the movie-playback events first (*enterFrame*, *load*, *unload*, and *data*) and then see how the user-input events work (*mouseDown*, *mouseUp*, *mouseMove*, *keyDown*, *keyUp*). Each of the clip events is handled by a matching clip event handler of the form *onClipEvent* (`eventName`). For example, the *enterFrame* event is handled using an event handler beginning with *onClipEvent (enterFrame)*. With the exception of *load*, *unload*, and *data*, movie clip events are sent to *all* movie clips on stage even if, say, the user clicks the mouse while on top of a different movie clip (or no movie clip).

Table 10-2. Movie Clip Events

Clip Event Name	Clip Event Occurs When . . .
enterFrame	Playhead enters a frame (before frame is rendered in the Flash Player)
load	The clip first appears on the Stage
unload	The clip is removed from the Stage

Table 10-2. Movie Clip Events (continued)

Clip Event Name	Clip Event Occurs When . . .
data	Variables finish loading into a clip or a portion of a loaded movie loads into a clip
mouseDown	Primary mouse button is depressed while the clip is on stage (secondary mouse buttons are not detectable)
mouseUp	Primary mouse button is released while the clip is on stage
mouseMove	Mouse pointer moves (even a teensy bit) while the clip is on Stage, even if the mouse is not over the clip
keyDown	A key is pressed down while the clip is on Stage
keyUp	A depressed key is released while the clip is on Stage

Movie-Playback Movie Clip Events

The following events are generated without user intervention as Flash loads and plays movies.

enterFrame

If you've ever resorted to empty, looping movie clips to trigger scripts, *enterFrame* offers a welcome respite. The *enterFrame* event occurs once for every frame that passes in a movie. For example, if we place the following code on a movie clip, that clip will grow incrementally by 10 pixels per frame:

```
onClipEvent (enterFrame) {
  _height += 10;
  _width += 10;
}
```

(Notice that, as we learned earlier, the **_height** and **_width** properties are resolved within the scope of the clip to which the *enterFrame* event handler is attached, so no clip instance name is required before **_height** and **_width**.)

 The *enterFrame* event is generated before each frame is rendered even if the playhead of the clip with the *enterFrame* handler is stopped. The *enterFrame* event, hence, is always being triggered.

When displayed in the Flash Player, all Flash movies are constantly running, even when nothing is moving on screen or when a movie's playhead is stopped on a frame. An individual movie clip's *enterFrame* handler will, hence, be executed repeatedly for as long as that clip is on stage, regardless of whether the clip is playing or stopped. If a clip's playhead is moved by a *gotoAndStop()* function call, the clip's *enterFrame* event handler is still triggered with each passing frame. And if every playhead of an entire movie has been halted with a *stop()* function, all *enterFrame* event handlers on all clips will still execute.

The *enterFrame* event is normally used to update the state of a movie clip repeatedly over time. But an *enterFrame* event handler need not apply directly to the clip that bears it—*enterFrame* can be used with a single-frame, empty clip to execute code repeatedly. This technique, called a *clip event loop* (or more loosely, a *process*) is demonstrated in "Timeline and Clip Event Loops" in Chapter 8, *Loop Statements*.

Note that the code in an *enterFrame* event handler is executed *before* any code that appears on the timeline of the clip containing the handler.

With a little ambition, we can use *enterFrame* to gain extremely powerful control over a clip. Example 10-7, shown later, extends our earlier clip-enlarging code to make a movie clip oscillate in size.

load

The *load* event occurs when a movie clip is born—that is, when a movie clip appears on stage for the first time. A movie clip "appears on stage" in one of the following ways:

- The playhead moves onto a keyframe that contains a new instantiation of the clip, placed in the authoring tool.

- The clip is duplicated from another clip via the *duplicateMovieClip()* function.

- The clip is programmatically added to the Stage via the *attachMovie()* function.

- An external *.swf* file is loaded into the clip with the *loadMovie()* function.

- The contents of a clip are unloaded with the *unloadMovie()* function. (A *load* event is triggered because an empty placeholder clip is loaded into the clip when its contents are expelled.)

The body of a *load* event handler is executed *after* any code on the timeline where the movie clip first appears.

A *load* event handler is often used to initialize variables in a clip or to perform some setup task (like sizing or positioning a dynamically generated clip). A *load* handler can also provide a nice way to prevent a movie clip from automatically playing:

```
onClipEvent (load) {
    stop();
}
```

The *load* event handler might also be used to trigger some function that relies on the existence of a particular clip in order to execute properly.

The *load* event is particularly interesting when combined with the *duplicateMovieClip()* function, which creates new movie clips. In Example 10-2 we generate an entire field of `star` clips using a single *load* event handler in a cascading chain. The load handler is copied to each duplicated `star`, causing it, in turn, to duplicate itself. The process stops when the 100th clip is duplicated. The *.fla* file for Example 10-2 is available from the online Code Depot.

Example 10-2. Generating a Star Field with a load Event

```
onClipEvent (load) {
  // Place the current clip at a random position
  _x = Math.floor(Math.random() * 550);
  _y = Math.floor(Math.random() * 400);

  // Reset clip scale so we don't inherit previous clip's scale
  _xscale = 100;
  _yscale = 100;

  // Randomly size current clip between 50 and 150 percent
  randScale = Math.floor(Math.random() * 100) - 50;
  _xscale += randScale;
  _yscale += randScale;

  // If we're not at the 100th star, make another one
  if (_name != "star100") {
    nextStarNumber = number(_name.substring(4, _name.length)) + 1;
    this.duplicateMovieClip("star" + nextStarNumber, nextStarNumber);
  }
}
```

unload

The *unload* event is the opposite of the *load* event: it occurs when a movie clip expires—that is, immediately *after* the last frame in which the clip is present on stage (but *before* the first frame in which the clip is absent).

The following incidents provoke a movie clip's *unload* event:

- The playhead reaches the end of the span of frames upon which the clip resides.

- The clip is removed via the *removeMovieClip()* function (which kills clips generated by the *attachMovie()* and *duplicateMovieClip()* functions).

- A previously loaded external *.swf* file is removed from the clip via the *unloadMovie()* function.

- The clip has an external *.swf* loaded into it.

This last *unload* event trigger may seem a little odd but is actually a natural result of the way movies are loaded into Flash. Anytime a *.swf* is loaded into a movie clip, the previous contents of that clip are displaced, causing an *unload* event.

Here's an example that illustrates the behavior of the *load* and *unload* events in connection with *loadMovie()*:

1. In the Flash authoring tool, we place an empty movie clip on stage at frame 1 of a movie's main timeline. We name our clip `emptyClip`.

2. At frame 5 of the main timeline, we load the movie *test.swf* into `emptyClip` using the following code: `emptyClip.loadMovie("test.swf");`

3. We play the movie using Control → Play movie.

The results are:

1. Frame 1: The `emptyClip` clip appears, causing a *load* event.

2. Frame 5: The *loadMovie()* function is executed in two stages:

    a. The placeholder content of `emptyClip` is removed to make room for the incoming *test.swf*, causing an *unload* event.

    b. The movie *test.swf* loads, causing a *load* event.

The *unload* event is typically used to initiate housecleaning code—code that cleans up the Stage or resets the program environment in some way. An *unload* handler also provides a means for performing some action (such as playing another movie) after a movie clip ends.

data

The *data* event occurs when external data is loaded into a movie clip. The *data* event can be triggered by two quite different circumstances, according to the kind of data being loaded. We'll consider those circumstances separately.

Using a data event handler with loadVariables()

When we request a series of variables from a server using *loadVariables()*, we must wait for them to load completely before using their information. (See Part III.)

When a movie clip receives the end of a batch of loaded variables, the *data* event is triggered, telling us it's safe to execute code that relies on the variables.

For example, suppose we have a guest book movie in which visitors enter comments and we store those comments on a server. When a user attempts to view a comment, we request it from the server using *loadVariables()*. But before we can display the comment, we must pause at a loading screen until we know that the requested data is available. A *data* event handler tells us when our data has loaded, at which point we can safely display the comment to the user.

Example 10-3 is a simplified excerpt of some code from a guest book showing a data event handler used with *loadVariables()*. In the example, a button loads two

URL-encoded variables from a text file into a movie clip. The movie clip bears a *data* event handler that executes when the variables have loaded. From inside that handler, we display the values of the variables. We know the variables are safe to display because the code in the handler isn't executed until triggered by the *data* event (i.e., after the data is received).

Example 10-3. Waiting for a data Event

```
// CONTENT OF OUR guestbook.txt FILE
name=judith&message=hello

// BUTTON INSIDE OUR CLIP
on (release) {
  this.loadVariables("guestbook.txt");
}

// HANDLER ON OUR CLIP
onClipEvent (data) {
  trace(name);
  trace(message);
}
```

We'll use the *data* event again when we build a Flash form in Chapter 17, *Flash Forms*.

Using a data event handler with loadMovie()

The second use of the *data* event relates to the loading of external *.swf* files into movie clips with the *loadMovie()* function. When a *.swf* file is loaded into a host clip, by default the file begins playing immediately, even if only partially loaded. This is not always desirable—sometimes we want to guarantee that all or a certain percentage of a *.swf* has loaded before playback begins. We can make that guarantee with a *data* event handler and some preloading code.

The *data* event occurs each time a host movie clip receives a portion of an external *.swf* file. The definition of what constitutes a "portion" is more complex than you might expect. In order for a *data* event to be triggered, at least one complete new frame of the external *.swf* file must have loaded since either: (a) the last *data* event fired or (b) the *.swf* file started loading. (More than one frame of the *.swf* file may actually have loaded in that amount of time, but one frame is the minimum number required to prompt a *data* event.)

The execution of *data* event handlers is tied to the rendering of frames in the Player. With every frame rendered, the interpreter checks to see if part of an external *.swf* file has been loaded into a clip that has a *data* event handler. If part of an external *.swf* file has been loaded into such a clip, and the loaded portion contains at least one new frame, then the *data* event handler is executed. This process happens once—and only once—per frame rendered (even if the playhead is stopped).

Note that because the *data* event happens on a per-frame basis, movies with higher frame rates tend to have smoother-looking preloaders because they receive more frequent updates on the status of loading *.swf* files.

The exact number of *data* events triggered during a *loadMovie()* operation depends on the distribution of content in the *.swf* file being loaded and the speed of the connection. A single-frame *.swf* file, no matter how large, will trigger only one *data* event. On the other hand, a *.swf* file with 100 frames may trigger up to 100 separate *data* events, depending on the movie's frame rate, the byte size of each frame and the speed of the network connection. If the frames are large and the connection is slow, more *data* events will be triggered (up to a maximum of one per frame). If the frames are small and the connection is fast, fewer *data* events will be triggered (the entire 100 frames may be transferred between the rendering of two frames in the Player, prompting only one *data* event).

So how do we use a *data* event handler to build a preloader? Well, whenever a *data* event occurs due to a *loadMovie()* function call, we know that an external *.swf* file download is in progress. Therefore, from inside a *data* event handler, we can check whether enough of the file has downloaded before allowing it to play. We do so using the *getBytesLoaded()* and *getBytesTotal()* functions as shown in Example 10-4. (The `_framesloaded` and `_totalframes` movie clip properties may also be used.)

Example 10-4 also provides feedback while the movie is loading. Note that the *.swf* file being loaded should have a *stop()* function call on its first frame to prevent it from automatically playing before it is completely downloaded. A variation of Example 10-4 is available from the online Code Depot.

Example 10-4. A data Event Preloader

```
onClipEvent (data) {
    trace("data received");          // The show's about to start!

    // Turn on data-transfer light
    _root.transferIndicator.gotoAndStop("on");

    // If we're done loading, turn off transfer light, and let the movie play
    if (getBytesTotal() > 0 && getBytesLoaded() == getBytesTotal()) {
      _root.transferIndicator.gotoAndStop("off");
      play();
    }

    // Display some loading details in text field variables on the _root
    _root.bytesLoaded = getBytesLoaded();
    _root.bytesTotal = getBytesTotal();
    _root.clipURL = _url.substring(_url.lastIndexOf("/") + 1, _url.length);
}
```

The User-Input Movie Clip Events

The remainder of the movie clip events relate to user interaction. When any of the user-input clip events occurs, *all* clips on stage (no matter how deeply nested in other clips) receive the event. Hence, multiple clips may react to a single mouse-click, mouse movement, or keystroke.

To execute code based on the proximity of the mouse to a particular clip, an event handler should check the location of the mouse pointer relative to the clip. The built-in *hitTest()* function provides an easy way to check whether a mouse-click occurred within a certain region, as shown later in Example 10-9.

mouseDown

Like the *press* button event, the *mouseDown* clip event detects the downstroke of a mouseclick. The *mouseDown* event occurs each time the primary mouse button is depressed while the mouse pointer is over *any part* of the Stage.

Unlike the button *press* event, *mouseDown* is not tied to the *hit* area of a button. In combination with the *mouseUp* and *mouseMove* events and the *Mouse.hide()* method, the *mouseDown* event can be used to implement a custom mouse pointer, as we'll see later in Example 10-8.

mouseUp

The *mouseUp* event is the counterpart to *mouseDown*. It occurs each time the primary mouse button is released while the mouse pointer is over any part of the Stage. As with *mouseDown*, a clip with a *mouseUp* handler must be present on stage at the time the mouse button is released in order for the event to have any consequence. The *mouseUp, mouseDown,* and *mouseMove* events can be used to create rich levels of mouse interactivity without affecting the appearance of the mouse pointer (as a button does).

mouseMove

The *mouseMove* event lets us detect changes in the mouse pointer's position. Whenever the mouse is in motion, *mouseMove* events are issued repeatedly, as fast as the processor can generate new events. A clip with a *mouseMove* handler must be present on stage at the time the mouse is moving in order for the *mouseMove* event to have any effect.

The *mouseMove* event is useful for code that wakes up idle applications, displays mouse trails, and creates custom pointers, as we'll see later in Example 10-8.

keyDown

The *keyDown* and *keyUp* events are the keyboard analogs of *mouseDown* and *mouseUp*. Together, they provide fundamental tools for coding keyboard-based interactivity. The *keyDown* event occurs whenever a key on the keyboard is depressed. When a key is held down, *keyDown* may occur repeatedly, depending on the operating system and keyboard setup. Unlike the *keyPress* button event, *keyDown* clip events occur when any key—not just a specific key—is pressed.

To *trap* (i.e., detect or *catch*) a *keyDown* event, we must ensure that a movie clip with a *keyDown* event handler is present on stage at the time that a key is pressed. The following code does the trick:

```
onClipEvent (keyDown) {
  trace("Some key was pressed");
}
```

You'll notice that our *keyDown* handler does not tell us which key was pressed. If we're waiting for the user to press any key to continue, we might not care which key it was. But usually, we want to tie some action to a specific key. For example, we might want different keys to turn a spaceship in different directions.

To find out which keys triggered the *keyDown* event, we consult the built-in *Key* object, which describes the keyboard's state. The type of information we require depends on the interactivity we're trying to produce. Games, for example, require instant, continuous feedback from potentially simultaneous keypresses. Navigational interfaces, in contrast, may require only the detection of a single keypress (e.g., the spacebar in a slide show presentation).

The *Key* object can tell us which key was last pressed and whether a particular key is currently being pressed. To determine the state of the keyboard, we use one of the four *Key* object methods:

```
Key.getCode()          // Base-10 keycode value of last key pressed
Key.getAscii()         // Base-10 ASCII value of last key pressed
Key.isDown(keycode)    // Returns true if specified key is currently pressed
Key.isToggled(keycode) // Determines whether Caps Lock or Num Lock is toggled on
```

Example 10-5 shows a *keyDown* handler that tells us the ASCII value of the last key pressed.

Example 10-5. Checking the Last Key Pressed

```
onClipEvent (keyDown) {
  // Retrieve the ASCII value of the last key pressed and convert it to a character
  lastKeyPressed = String.fromCharCode(Key.getAscii());
  trace("You pressed the '" + lastKeyPressed + "' key.");
}
```

Example 10-6 shows a sample *keyDown* handler that checks whether the up arrow was the last key pressed.

Example 10-6. Detecting an Up Arrow Keypress

```
onClipEvent (keyDown) {
  // Check to see if the up arrow was the last key pressed.
  // The up arrow is represented by the Key.UP property.
  if (Key.getCode() == Key.UP) {
    trace("The up arrow was the last key depressed");
  }
}
```

There are several ways to query the state of the keyboard, and you must choose the one that best suits your application. For example, the *Key.getAscii()* method returns the ASCII value of the character associated with the last-pressed key, which may differ across keyboards in different languages (though, in English, the placement of the letters and numbers on a keyboard is standardized). On the other hand, the *Key.getCode()* method returns a value tied to a physical key on the keyboard, not a specific letter. *Key.getCode()* may be more useful for an international or cross-platform audience if you want to, say, use four adjacent keys for navigation regardless of the characters they represent. There's more information on this topic under "Key Object" in Part III.

You can download sample *keyDown* and *keyUp* *.fla* files from the online Code Depot.

 Event handlers that react to keystrokes are executed only if the Flash Player has mouse focus. Users must click the Stage of a movie before the movie's keystroke handlers will become active. Consider forcing users to click a button before entering any keyboard-controlled section of a movie.

Handling special keys

To disable the Flash standalone Player menu commands (Open, Close, Fullscreen, etc.), add the following line of code to the beginning of your movie:

```
fscommand("trapallkeys", "true");
```

That command also prevents the Escape key from exiting fullscreen mode in a Projector. To capture Escape in a Projector, use:

```
onClipEvent (keyDown) {
  if (Key.getCode() == Key.ESCAPE) {
    // Respond to Escape keypress
  }
}
```

Note that the Escape key cannot be trapped in all browsers. Furthermore, there is no way to disable the Alt key or the Windows Alt-Tab or Ctrl-Alt-Delete key sequences.

To capture Tab keypresses, create a button with the following handler:

```
on (keyPress "<Tab>") {
  // Respond to Tab key
}
```

In the standalone Player, the Tab key may also be captured with a clip event handler such as:

```
onClipEvent (keyDown) {
  if (Key.getCode() == Key.TAB) {
    // Respond to Tab keypress
  }
}
```

In some browsers, the Tab key can be detected only with a button *keyPress* event, and it may even be necessary to combine a *keyPress* button event with a *keyUp* clip event. The following code first traps the Tab key with *keyPress*, and then reacts to it in a *keyUp* handler. Note that we don't use *keyDown* because *Key. getCode()* for the Tab key is set only on the key upstroke in Internet Explorer:

```
// CODE ON BUTTON ON MAIN TIMELINE
on (keyPress "<Tab>") {
  // Set a dummy variable here
  foo = 0;
}

// CODE ON MOVIE CLIP ON MAIN TIMELINE
onClipEvent (keyUp) {
  if (Key.getCode() == Key.TAB) {
    // Now place the cursor in myTextField on _level0
    Selection.setFocus("_level0.myTextField");
  }
}
```

We typically trap the Tab key in order to move the insertion point to a particular text field in a form. See the example under "Selection.setFocus( ) Method*"* in Part III for details.

To capture a shortcut-key-style combination such as Ctrl-F, use an *enterFrame* handler and the *Key.isDown()* method:

```
onClipEvent (enterFrame) {
  if (Key.isDown(Key.CONTROL) && Key.isDown(70)) {
    // Respond to Ctrl-F
  }
}
```

To capture the Enter (or Return) key, use either a button handler, such as:

```
on (keyPress "<Enter>") {
  // Respond to Enter key press (e.g., submit a form)
}
```

or a *keyDown* handler, such as:

```
onClipEvent (keyDown) {
  if (Key.getCode() == Key.ENTER) {
    // Respond to Enter key press (e.g., submit a form)
  }
}
```

See "Key Object" and "Key.getCode( ) Method" in Part III for more information on capturing other special keys such as the function keys (F1, F2, etc.) or keys on the numeric keypad.

keyUp

The *keyUp* event is triggered when a depressed key is released. The *keyUp* event is an essential component of game programming because it lets us turn off something that was turned on by an earlier *keyDown* event—the classic example being a spaceship's thrust. As a further example, in the Flash authoring tool, holding down the spacebar temporarily switches to the Hand tool, and releasing the spacebar restores the previous tool. This approach can be used to show and hide things in your application, such as temporary menus.

As with *keyDown*, in order to obtain useful information from a *keyUp* event, we normally use it with the *Key* object:

```
onClipEvent (keyUp) {
  if (!Key.isDown(Key.LEFT)) {
    trace("The left arrow is not depressed");
  }
}
```

Because the *Key.isDown()* method lets us check the status of any key anytime, we may use an *enterFrame* event loop to check whether a certain key is depressed. However, *polling* the keyboard (i.e., checking the status of a key repeatedly) is less efficient than waiting until we *know* that a key has been pressed as indicated by a *keyDown* event triggering our event handler.

The approach we end up taking ultimately depends on the type of system we're building. In a system that's constantly in motion, such as a game, polling may be appropriate because we're cycling through a main game loop with every frame anyway. So, we can just check the *Key* object while we're doing the rest of our loop. For example:

```
// CODE ON EMPTY CLIP
// This keeps the game process running
```

```
onClipEvent (enterFrame) {
  _root.mainLoop();
}

// CORE GAME CODE ON MAIN TIMELINE
// This is executed once per frame
function mainLoop () {
  if (Key.isDown(Key.LEFT)) {
    trace("The left arrow is depressed");
    // Rotate the spaceship to the left
  }

  // Check the other keys, then carry on with our game cycle
}
```

In static-interface environments, there's no need to use an *enterFrame* loop to check for keypresses unless you are trying to detect specific keyboard combinations (i.e., multiple keys being pressed simultaneously). You should ordinarily use *keyDown* and *keyUp* event handlers, which are triggered precisely once for each keypress and key release. When using *keyUp* and *keyDown* event handlers, you need not concern yourself with whether the key is still being pressed at any given instant. This allows you to detect keypresses accurately even if the user releases the key between frames, and it also prevents you from checking the same key twice if it was pressed only once. In any case, you will ordinarily use the *Key.getCode()* and *Key.getASCII()* methods to check for the last key pressed within a *keyDown* or *keyUp* event handler.

Order of Execution

Some movies have code dispersed across multiple timelines and multiple clip event handlers. It's not uncommon, therefore, for a single frame to require the execution of many separate blocks of code—some in event handlers, some on frames in clip timelines, and some on the main timelines of documents in the Player. In these situations, the order in which the various bits of code execute can become quite complex and can greatly affect a program's behavior. We can prevent surprises and guarantee that our code behaves as desired by becoming familiar with the order in which event handlers execute relative to the various timelines in a movie.

Asynchronous event handlers execute independently of the code on a movie's timelines. Button event handlers, for example, are executed immediately when the event that they handle occurs, as are handlers for the *mouseDown, mouseUp, mouseMove, keyDown,* and *keyUp* events.

Handlers for the movie-playback events, however, execute in order, according to the progression of the movie, as shown in Table 10-3.

Table 10-3. Movie Clip Event Handler Order of Execution

Event Handler	Execution Timing
load	Executes in the first frame in which the clip is present on stage after parent-timeline code executes, but before clip-internal code executes, and before the frame is rendered.
unload	Executes in the first frame in which the clip is not present on stage, before parent-timeline code executes.
enterFrame	Executes in the second and all subsequent frames in which the clip is present on stage. It is executed before parent-timeline code executes and before clip-internal code executes.
data	Executes in any frame in which data is received by the clip. If triggered, it executes before clip-internal code executes and before *enterFrame* code executes.

It's easier to see the effect of the rules in Table 10-3 with a practical example. Suppose we have a single-layer movie with four keyframes in the main timeline. We attach some code to each keyframe. Then, we create a second layer where we place a movie clip at frame 1, spanning to frame 3, but not present on frame 4. We add *load*, *enterFrame*, and *unload* handlers to our clip. Finally, inside the clip, we create three keyframes, each of which also contains a block of code. Figure 10-2 shows what the movie looks like.

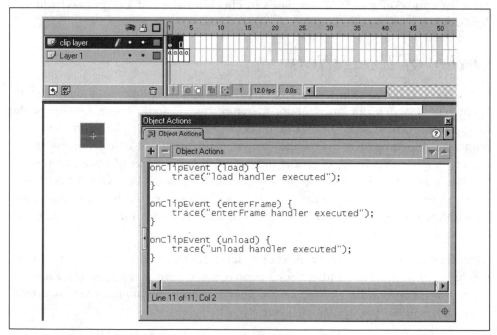

Figure 10-2. A code execution order test movie

When we play our movie, the execution order is as follows:

```
========FRAME 1=======
1) Main timeline code executed
2) load handler executed
3) Clip-internal code, frame 1, executed


========FRAME 2=======
1) enterFrame handler executed
2) Clip-internal code, frame 2, executed
3) Main timeline code executed


========FRAME 3=======
1) enterFrame handler executed
2) Clip-internal code, frame 3, executed
3) Main timeline code executed


========FRAME 4=======
1) unload handler executed
2) Main timeline code executed
```

The execution order of the code in our sample movie demonstrates some important rules of thumb to remember when coding with event handlers:

- Code in a *load* handler is executed before internal clip code, so a *load* handler may be used to initialize variables that are used immediately on frame 1 of its associated clip.

- Before a movie clip is instantiated on a frame, the code of that frame is executed. Therefore, user-defined variables and functions in a movie clip are not available to any code on its parent timeline until the frame *after* the clip first appears on stage, even if those variables and functions are declared in the clip's *load* handler.

- The *enterFrame* event never occurs on the same frame as the *load* or the *unload* event. The *load* and *unload* events supplant *enterFrame* for the frames where a clip appears on the Stage and leaves the Stage.

- On each frame, code in a clip's *enterFrame* handler is executed before code on the clip's parent timeline. Using an *enterFrame* handler, we may, therefore, change the properties of a clip's parent timeline and then immediately use the new values in that timeline's code, all on the same frame.

Copying Clip Event Handlers

A quick point that has major ramifications: movie clip event handlers are duplicated when a movie clip is duplicated via the *duplicateMovieClip()* function. Suppose, for example, we have a movie clip on stage called **square**, which has a *load* event handler defined:

```
onClipEvent (load) {
  trace("movie loaded");
}
```

What happens when we duplicate square to create square2?

```
square.duplicateMovieClip("square2", 0);
```

Because the *load* handler is copied to square2 when we duplicate square, the birth of square2 causes its *load* handler to execute, which displays "movie loaded" in the Output window. By using this automatic retention of handlers, we can create slick recursive functions with very powerful results. For a demonstration that only scratches the surface of what's possible, refer to Example 10-2.

Refreshing the Screen
with updateAfterEvent

As we learned earlier in "Order of Execution," the *mouseDown, mouseUp, mouseMove, keyDown,* and *keyUp* event handlers are executed immediately upon the occurrence of those events. Immediately means *immediately*—even if the event in question occurs between the rendering of frames.

This immediacy can give a movie great responsiveness, but that responsiveness can easily be lost. By default, the visual effects of a *mouseDown, mouseUp, mouseMove, keyDown,* or *keyUp* event handler are not physically rendered by the Flash Player until the next available frame is rendered. To really see this in action, create a single-frame movie with a frame rate of 1 frame per second, and place a movie clip with the following code on stage:

```
onClipEvent (mouseDown) {
  _x += 2;
}
```

Then, test the movie and click the mouse as fast as you can. You'll see that all your clicks are registered, but the movie clip moves only once per second. So, if you click 6 times between frames, the clip will move 12 pixels to the right when the next frame is rendered. If you click 3 times, the clip will move 6 pixels. Each execution of the *mouseDown* handler is registered between frames, but the results are displayed only when each frame is rendered. This can have dramatic effects on certain forms of interactivity.

Fortunately, we can force Flash to immediately render any visual change that takes place during a user-input event handler without waiting for the next frame to come around. We simply use the *updateAfterEvent()* function from inside our event handler, like this:

```
onClipEvent (mouseDown) {
  _x += 2;
  updateAfterEvent();
}
```

The *updateAfterEvent()* function is available for use only with the *mouseDown*, *mouseUp*, *mouseMove*, *keyDown*, and *keyUp* events. It is often essential for smooth and responsive visual behavior associated with user input. Later, in Example 10-8, we'll use *updateAfterEvent()* to ensure the smooth rendering of a custom pointer. Note, however, that button events do not require an explicit *updateAfterEvent()* function call. Buttons naturally update between frames.

Code Reusability

When using button events and movie clip events, don't forget the code-centralization principles we learned in Chapter 9. Always try to prevent unnecessary duplication and intermingling of code across movie elements. If you find yourself entering the same code in more than one event handler's body, it may not be wise to attach that code directly to the object. Try generalizing your code, pulling it off the object and placing it in a code repository somewhere in your movie; often the best place is the main timeline.

In many cases, it's a poor idea to hide statements inside a button or clip handler. Remember that encapsulating your code in a function and calling that function from your handler makes your code reusable and easy to find. This is particularly true of buttons—I rarely place anything more than a function-invocation statement directly on a button. For movie clips, you'll need to employ keener judgment, as placing code directly on clips can often be a healthy part of a clean, self-contained code architecture. Experiment with different approaches until you find the right balance for your needs and skill level. Regardless, it always pays to be mindful of redundancy and reusability issues.

For an example of the difference between attaching code to buttons versus calling functions from buttons, see "Centralizing Code" in Chapter 9.

Dynamic Movie Clip Event Handlers

Early in this chapter, we learned about two kinds of events in Flash—those that are attached to movie clips and buttons and those that are attached to other data objects such as *XML* and *XMLSocket*. To create event handlers for data objects, we assign the handler function name as a property of the object. Recall the syntax to add a function dynamically:

```
myXMLDoc.onLoad = function () { trace("all done loading!"); };
```

Dynamic function assignment lets us change the behavior of the handler during movie playback. All we have to do is reassign the handler property:

```
myXMLDoc.onLoad = function () { gotoAndPlay("displayData"); };
```

Or we can even disable the handler altogether:

```
myXMLDoc.onLoad = function () { return; };
```

Unfortunately, handlers of movie clip and button events are not nearly so flexible; they cannot be changed or removed during movie playback. Furthermore, movie clip event handlers cannot be attached to the main movie timeline of any movie! It's impossible to directly create an event handler for a movie's _root clip.

In order to work around these limitations, we can—in the case of the *enterFrame* and the user-input events—use empty movie clips to simulate dynamic event-handler removal and alteration. Empty movie clips even let us simulate _root-level events. We've already seen the technique in Chapter 8, where we learned how to create an event loop as follows:

1. Create an empty movie clip named **process**.

2. Place another empty clip called **eventClip** inside **process**.

3. On **eventClip**, attach the desired event handler. The code in the **eventClip**'s handler should target the **process** clip's host timeline, like this:

```
onClipEvent (mouseMove) {
  _parent._parent.doSomeFunction();
}
```

4. To export **process** for use with the *attachMovie()* function, select it in the Library and choose Options → Linkage. Set Linkage to Export This Symbol, and assign an appropriate identifier (e.g., "mouseMoveProcess").

5. Finally, to engage the event handler, attach the **process** clip to the appropriate timeline using *attachMovie()*.

6. To disengage the handler, remove the **process** clip using *removeMovieClip()*.

For step-by-step instructions on how to use this technique with the *enterFrame* event, see "Flash 5 Clip Event Loops" in Chapter 8.

Event Handlers Applied

We'll conclude our exploration of ActionScript events and event handlers with a few real-world examples. These are simple applications, but they give us a sense of how flexible event-based programming can be. The last two examples are available for download from the online Code Depot.

Example 10-7 makes a clip shrink and grow.

Example 10-7. Oscillating the Size of a Movie Clip

```
onClipEvent (load) {
  var shrinking = false;
```

Example 10-7. Oscillating the Size of a Movie Clip (continued)

```
  var maxHeight = 300;
  var minHeight = 30;
}

onClipEvent (enterFrame) {
  if (_height < maxHeight && shrinking == false) {
    _height += 10;
    _width  += 10;
  } else {
    shrinking = true;
  }

  if (shrinking == true) {
    if (_height > minHeight) {
      _height -= 10;
      _width  -= 10;
    } else {
      shrinking = false;
      _height += 10;      // Increment here so we don't
      _width  += 10;      // miss a cycle
    }
  }
}
```

Example 10-8 simulates a custom mouse pointer by hiding the normal system pointer and making a clip follow the mouse location around the screen. In the example, the *mouseDown* and *mouseUp* handlers resize the custom pointer slightly to indicate mouseclicks.

Example 10-8. A Custom Mouse Pointer

```
onClipEvent (load) {
  Mouse.hide();
}

onClipEvent (mouseMove) {
  _x = _root._xmouse;
  _y = _root._ymouse;
  updateAfterEvent();
}

onClipEvent (mouseDown) {
  _width  *= .5;
  _height *= .5;
  updateAfterEvent();
}

onClipEvent (mouseUp) {
  _width  *= 2;
  _height *= 2;
  updateAfterEvent();
}
```

Finally, simply to prove the power of the ActionScript movie clip event handlers, Example 10-9 turns a movie clip into a customized button using *mouseMove* to check for rollovers, *mouseDown* and *mouseUp* to check for button clicks, and the *hitTest()* function to make hit detection a snap. This example assumes that the clip with the handlers has three keyframes labeled up, down, and over (corresponding with the usual button states).

Example 10-9. A Movie Clip Button

```
onClipEvent (load) {
  stop();
}

onClipEvent (mouseMove) {
  if (hitTest(_root._xmouse, _root._ymouse, true) && !buttonDown) {
    this.gotoAndStop("over");
  } else if (!hitTest(_root._xmouse, _root._ymouse, true) && !buttonDown) {
    this.gotoAndStop("up");
  }
  updateAfterEvent();
}

onClipEvent (mouseDown) {
  if (hitTest(_root._xmouse, _root._ymouse, true)) {
    buttonDown = true;
    this.gotoAndStop("down");
  }
  updateAfterEvent();
}

onClipEvent (mouseUp) {
  buttonDown = false;
  if (!hitTest(_root._xmouse, _root._ymouse, true)) {
    this.gotoAndStop("up");
  } else {
    this.gotoAndStop("over");
  }
  updateAfterEvent();
}
```

Onward!

With statements, operators, functions, and now events and event handlers under our belt, we've learned how all of the internal tools of ActionScript work. To round out our understanding of the language, in the next three chapters we'll explore three extremely important datatypes: arrays, objects, and movie clips.

11

Arrays

Back in Chapter 3, *Data and Datatypes*, we learned that primitive datatypes—strings, numbers, Booleans, `null`, and `undefined`—represent basic information in our scripts. We also learned that ActionScript supports several *composite* datatypes, which can group several pieces of data together into a single datum.

The *array* type is the first composite datatype we'll study. Arrays are used to store and manipulate ordered lists of information and are, therefore, fundamental tools in sequential, repetitive programming. We use them to do everything from storing values retrieved via a user-input form, to generating pull-down menus, to keeping track of enemy spacecraft in a game. In its most basic form, an array is just a list of items, like your grocery list or the entries in your checkbook ledger.

What Is an Array?

An array is a data structure that can encompass multiple individual data values, just like a building is a physical structure encompassing multiple floors. Unlike a primitive datatype, an array can include more than one data value. Here is a simple example showing first, two strings, and then an array that contains two strings:

```
"oranges"               // A single primitive string value
"apples"                // Another primitive string value
["oranges", "apples"]   // A single array containing two strings
```

An array is a general-purpose container. It can contain any number of items and even items of different types. An array can even contain other arrays. Here is a simple example showing an array containing both strings and numbers. It might represent your shopping list and how many of each item you intend to buy:

```
["oranges", 6, "apples", 4, "bananas", 3]
```

Here's another analogy to make the concept of an array a little more tangible. Consider a chest of drawers. An individual drawer contains some content (socks, shirts, etc.). But the chest itself doesn't contain the *content*; it contains the *drawers*. The drawers hold the content. The chest organizes the drawers into a single unit.

When we work with an array (the chest of drawers), we are usually interested in the values within the array (the contents of the drawers). The values contained in an array are the information we want to manage. But we may also manipulate the containing structure itself. We may, for example, change an array's size (add or subtract drawers) or reorder its values (swap the contents of its drawers).

Though we speak of an array as containing many values, it's important to recognize that the array itself is a single datum the same way that a string containing multiple characters is still a single string and a number containing several digits is still a single number. As a single datum, an array may be assigned to a variable or used as part of a complex expression:

```
product = ["ladies downhill skis", 475]  // Store an array in a variable
display(product);                         // Pass that array to a function
```

The Anatomy of an Array

Each item stored in an array is called an array *element*, and each has a unique number (*index*) by which we can refer to it.

Array Elements

Like a variable, each array element can store any legal datum. An entire array, then, is akin to a collection of sequentially named variables, but instead of each item having a different name, it has an element number (the first element is number 0, not number 1).

Figure 11-1 shows, conceptually, the structure of an array that contains three elements. Element 0 stores the value "Erica", element 1 stores the value "Slavik", and element 2 stores the value "Gary".

To manipulate the values in an array's elements, we ask for them by number. In our chest of drawers analogy we might ask ActionScript to store something in the first drawer or retrieve whatever is in the second drawer for us.

Array Element Indexing

An element's position in the array is known as its *index*. Just as we can access the seventh character in a string, we can access the seventh element of an array via its index (in this case, the index is 6). We use an element's index to set or retrieve the

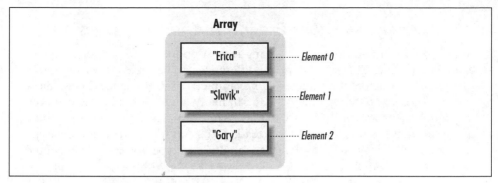

Figure 11-1. A sample array structure

element's value or to work with the element in various other ways. Some of the array-handling functions, for example, use element indexes to specify ranges of elements for processing.

We can also insert and delete elements from the beginning, end, or even middle of an array. An array can have gaps (that is, some elements may be absent). We may have elements at positions 0 and 4, but nothing in positions 1, 2, and 3. Arrays with gaps are called *sparse* arrays.

Array Size

Every array contains a specific number of elements at any given point during its life span. The number of potential elements an array can hold is called the array's *length*, which we'll discuss later.

Creating Arrays

We can create a new array with a data literal (i.e., simply typing out all the elements) or with the special built-in array constructor function, *Array()*.

The Array Constructor

To create an array with the *Array()* constructor, we use the *new* operator followed by the *Array* keyword followed by parentheses, which yields an empty array (one with no elements). We normally assign a newly created array to a variable or other data container for future reference. For example:

```
var myList = new Array();  // Store an empty array in variable myList
```

We often want to assign initial values to an array's elements. We can do so by passing parameters to the *Array()* constructor when invoking it. Depending on the parameters we supply, the constructor invocation has different effects.

Arrays in Other Programming Languages

Almost every high-level computer language supports some sort of arrays or array-like entities. That said, there are differences in the ways arrays are implemented across different languages. For example, many languages do not allow arrays to contain differing types of data. In many languages, an array can contain numbers or strings, but not both in the same array. Interestingly, in C, there is no primitive *string* datatype. Instead, C has a single-character datatype named *char*; strings are considered a complex datatype and are implemented as an array of *char*s!

In ActionScript, the size of an array will change automatically as items are added or removed. In many languages, the size of an array must be specified when the array is first *declared* or *dimensioned* (i.e., memory is *allocated* to hold the array's data). Lingo, the scripting language for Macromedia Director, refers to its arrays by the name *lists*. Like ActionScript, Lingo allows arrays to contain data values of differing types, and it will resize its arrays automatically as needed. Unlike ActionScript and C, in which the first item in an array is numbered 0 (i.e., is *zero-relative*), the first item in a Lingo list is numbered 1 (i.e., is *one-relative*).

Languages differ as to what happens when you attempt to access an element outside the bounds (limits) of the array. ActionScript and Lingo will add elements if you attempt to set a value for an element beyond the existing bounds of the array. If you attempt to access an element outside the array bounds, ActionScript returns `undefined`, whereas it causes an error in Lingo. C pays no attention to whether you are accessing a valid element number. It lets you retrieve and set elements outside the bounds of the array, which usually causes you to overwrite other data in memory or access meaningless data that is not part of the array (C gives you plenty of rope with which to hang yourself).

When we supply more than one argument to the *Array()* constructor or when we supply a single nonnumeric argument to the *Array()* constructor, each argument becomes one of the element values in our new array. For example:

```
var frameLabels = new Array("intro", "section1", "section2", "home");
```

The array stored in `frameLabels` would have the following elements:

```
0: "intro"
1: "section1"
2: "section2"
3: "home"
```

When we supply exactly one numeric argument to the *Array()* constructor, it creates an array with the specified number of empty placeholder elements:

```
var myList = new Array(14); // Creates an array with 14 empty elements
```

Arguments passed to the *Array()* constructor can be any legal expression, including compound expressions:

```
var x = 10;
var y = 5;
var myNumbers = new Array(x + 1, x * y, Math.random());
```

The **myNumbers** variable would thus store an array with the following elements:

```
0: 11
1: 50
2: a floating-point number between 0 and 1
```

Array Literals

Sometimes, it's more convenient to create arrays using array literals than to create them with the *Array()* constructor. Recall that a *literal* is a direct representation of a fixed piece of fixed data. For example:

```
"beaver"       // A string literal
234.2034       // A numeric literal
true           // A boolean literal
```

In an array literal, square brackets signal the beginning and end of the array. Inside the square brackets, a comma-separated list of expressions provides the values of the array's elements. Here's the general syntax:

```
[expression1, expression2, expression3]
```

The expressions are resolved and then stored as the elements of the array being described. Any valid expression may be used, including function calls, variables, literals, and even other arrays (an array within an array is called a *nested* array). Here are a few examples:

```
[4, 5, 63];                               // Simple numeric elements
["jeremy", "janice", "eman"]              // Simple string elements
[1, 4, 6 + 10]                            // Numeric expressions with operation
[firstName, lastName, "tall", "skinny"]   // Variables and strings as elements
["month end days", [31, 30, 28]]          // A nested array literal
```

For comparison, let's do the same thing with the *Array()* constructor:

```
new Array(4, 5, 63)
new Array("jeremy", "janice", "eman")
new Array(1, 4, 6 + 10)
new Array(firstName, lastName, "tall", "skinny")
new Array("month end days", new Array(31, 30, 28))
```

Notice that the elements of a single array in ActionScript can contain data of different types, as noted in the earlier sidebar.

Referencing Array Elements

Once we've created an array, we'll inevitably want to retrieve or change the value of its elements. To do so, we can use square brackets (i.e., the *array access operator*), [], which was introduced in Chapter 5, *Operators*.

Retrieving an Element's Value

In order to obtain an element's value, we simply refer to the element by supplying its index within square brackets, like this:

```
arrayName[elementNumber]
```

where ***arrayName*** must be an array and ***elementNumber*** can be any expression that yields a numeric value. The first element is number 0 and the last element number is one less than the array's length. Specifying an element number greater than the last valid element number causes the interpreter to return **undefined**. For example:

```
// Create an array using an array literal, and store it in trees
var trees = ["birch", "maple", "oak", "cedar"];

// Display the first element of trees in the Output window
trace(trees[0]);  // Displays: "birch"

// Assign the third element's value to the variable favoriteTree
// (remember indexes start at 0, so index 2 is the third element!!)
var favoriteTree = trees[2];  // favoriteTree becomes "oak"
```

Now the fun part. Since we can provide the index of an element as any number-yielding expression, we may use variables just as easily as we use numbers to specify an element index. For example:

```
var i = 3;
var lastTree = trees[i];  // Set lastTree to "cedar"
```

We can even use function-call expressions that have numeric return values as our array indexes:

```
// Set randomTree to a randomly picked element of trees
// by calculating a random number between 0 and 3
var randomTree = trees[Math.floor(Math.random() * 4)];
```

Hot dog, that's powerful! You might use a similar approach to pick a random question from an array of trivia questions or to pick a random card from an array that represents a deck of cards.

Note that accessing an array is very similar to accessing a variable value. Array elements can be used as part of a complex expression, as follows:

```
var myNums = [12, 4, 155, 90];
var myTotal = myNums[0] + myNums[1] + myNums[2] + myNums[3];   // Sum the array
```

The approach used in the previous example to total the values of an array's elements isn't exactly the paragon of optimized code. Later, we'll see a much faster and more convenient way to access an array's elements sequentially.

Setting an Element's Value

To set an element's value, we use *arrayName*[*elementNumber*] as the lefthand operand of an assignment expression:

```
// Make an array
var cities = ["Toronto", "Montreal", "Vancouver", "Waterloo"];
// cities is now: ["Toronto", "Montreal", "Vancouver", "Waterloo"]

// Set the value of the array's first element
// cities becomes ["London", "Montreal", "Vancouver", "Waterloo"]
cities[0] = "London";

// Set the value of the array's fourth element
// cities becomes ["London", "Montreal", "Vancouver", "Hamburg"]
cities[3] = "Hamburg";

// Set the value of the array's third element
// cities becomes ["London", "Montreal", 293.3, "Hamburg"]
cities[2] = 293.3;  // Notice that the datatype change is not a problem
```

Note that we can use any numeric expression as the index when setting an array element:

```
var i = 1;
// Set the value of element i
// cities becomes ["London", "Prague", 293.3, "Hamburg"]
cities[i] = "Prague";
```

Determining the Size of an Array

All arrays come with a built-in property named `length`, which indicates the current number of elements (including empty elements). To access an array's `length` property, we use the dot operator, like so:

```
arrayName.length
```

An array's `length` property tells us how many elements are in the array. Here are a few examples:

```
myList = [34, 45, 57];
trace(myList.length);  // Displays: 3

myWords = ["this", "that", "the other"];
trace(myWords.length);  // Displays: 3, the number of elements,
                        // not the number of words or characters
```

```
frameLabels = new Array(24);      // Note the single numeric argument
                                  // used with the Array() constructor
trace(frameLabels.length);  // Displays: 24
```

The `length` of an array is always one greater than the index of its last element. For example, an array with elements at indexes 0, 1, and 2 has a length of 3. And an array with elements at indexes 0, 1, 2, and 50 has a length of 51. 51? Yes, 51. Even though indexes 3 through 49 are empty, they still contribute to the length of the array. The last element of an array is always *myArray*[*myArray*.`length - 1`], because index numbers begin at 0, not 1.

If we add and remove elements, the array's `length` property is updated to reflect our changes. In fact, we can even set the `length` property to add or remove elements at the end of an array.

What is an array's `length` property good for, you ask? Using an array's `length` property, we can create a loop that accesses all the elements of an array as we saw in Example 8-1. Looping through an array's elements is a fundamental task in programming. To get a sense of what's possible when we combine loops and arrays, study Example 11-1, which hunts through a `soundtracks` array to find the location of the element with the value "hip hop". You should recognize the *for* loop from Chapter 8, *Loop Statements*, and the increment operator from Chapter 5. As for the array-access code, well, you just finished learning about that.

Example 11-1. Searching an Array

```
// Create an array
var soundtracks = ["electronic", "hip hop", "pop", "alternative", "classical"];

// Check each element to see if it contains "hip hop"
for (var i = 0; i < soundtracks.length; i++) {
  trace("Now examining element: " + i);
  if (soundtracks[i] == "hip hop") {
    trace("The location of 'hip hop' is index: " + i);
    break;
  }
}
```

Let's extend Example 11-1 into a generalized search function that can check *any* array for *any* matching element, as shown in Example 11-2. Our search function returns the position within the array where the element was found, or `null` if it was not found.

Example 11-2. A Generalized Array-Searching Function

```
function searchArray (whichArray, searchElement) {
  // Check each element to see if it contains searchElement
  for (var i = 0; i < whichArray.length; i++) {
    if (whichArray[i] == searchElement) {
      return i;
    }
```

Example 11-2. A Generalized Array-Searching Function (continued)

```
  }
  return null;
}
```

Here's how you might make use of our new search function to check whether or not "Fritz" is one of the names in our **userNames** array, which is an array of authorized usernames:

```
if (searchArray (userNames, "Fritz") == null) {
  trace ("Sorry, that username wasn't found");
} else {
  trace ("Welcome to the game.");
}
```

Now that's invigorating! This is one of those rewarding moments when all our hard work comes together in a single system. Seemingly trivial individual operations can combine to form extremely powerful and flexible programs. Like the letters in the alphabet or the amino acid sequences in a strand of DNA, you can construct anything imaginable from the simple building blocks at your disposal. The remainder of this chapter explains more about the mechanics of manipulating arrays, including the use of built-in functions that already perform some common functions for you. As you encounter needs not met by the built-in functions, consider writing your own custom functions, such as the *searchArray()* function in the preceding example.

Named Array Elements

Elements are usually numbered but can also be named. Using named elements we can emulate so-called *associative arrays* or *hashes*. Note that named array elements cannot be manipulated by the Array methods (*push()*, *pop()*, etc., covered later) and are not considered part of the numbered element list. An array with one named element and two numbered elements will have a **length** of 2, not 3. To access all the named elements in an array, therefore, we must use a *for-in* loop (discussed in Chapter 8), which lists both named and numbered elements.

Creating and Referencing Named Array Elements

To add an element that can later be retrieved by name, we use the familiar square brackets, with a string instead of a number, on an existing array:

```
arrayName[elementName] = expression
```

where *elementName* is a string. For example:

```
var importantDates = new Array();
importantDates["dadsBirthday"] = "June 1";
importantDates["mumsBirthday"] = "January 16";
```

We may also use the dot operator, as follows:

```
arrayName.elementName = expression
```

In this case, *elementName* must be an identifier, *not* a string. For example:

```
var importantDates = new Array();
importantDates.dadsBirthday = "June 1";
importantDates.mumsBirthday = "January 16";
```

Assuming that we know an element's identifier (for example, `dadsBirthday` in the `importantDates` array), we can access it in one of two ways:

```
var goShopping = importantDates["dadsBirthday"];
var goShopping = importantDates.dadsBirthday;
```

Just as is the case when assigning a value to a named element, when accessing an element with square brackets, *elementName* must be a string or an expression that yields a string. Likewise, when used with the *dot* operator, *elementName* must be an *identifier* (i.e., the element's name without quotes), not a string.

Removing Named Elements

To rid an array of an unwanted named element, we use the *delete* operator, which was introduced in Chapter 5:

```
delete arrayName.elementName
```

Deleting a named element destroys both the element value and the element container, freeing up any memory being occupied by the element and its contents. (Contrast this with the *delete* operator's behavior for *numbered* elements, where it simply clears the value but leaves the container intact.)

Adding Elements to an Array

You can add elements to an array by specifying a value for a new element, increasing the array's `length` property, or using one of the built-in array functions.

Adding New Elements Directly

We can add a new element to an existing array at a specific index by simply assigning a value to that element:

```
// Create an array, and assign it three values
var myList = ["apples", "oranges", "pears"];

// Add a fourth value
myList[3] = "tangerines";
```

The new element does not need to be placed immediately after the last element of the old array. If we place the new element more than one element beyond the end of the array, ActionScript automatically creates empty elements for the intervening indexes:

```
// Leave indexes 4 to 38 empty
myList[39] = "grapes";

trace (myList[12]); // Display is empty because element 12 is undefined
```

Adding New Elements with the length Property

To extend an array without assigning values to new elements, we can simply increase the `length` property and ActionScript will add enough elements to reach that length:

```
// Create an array with three elements
var myColors = ["green", "red", "blue"];

// Add 47 empty elements, numbered 3 through 49, to the array
myColors.length = 50;
```

You might use this approach to create a number of empty elements to hold some data you expect to accumulate, such as student test scores.

Adding New Elements with Array Methods

We can use built-in array methods to handle more complex element-addition scenarios. (We'll learn in Chapter 12, *Objects and Classes*, that a *method* is a function that operates on an object.)

The push() method

The *push()* method appends one or more elements to the end of an array. It automatically appends the data after the last element of the array, so we don't need to worry about how many elements already exist. The *push()* method can also append multiple elements to an array at once. To invoke *push()* on an array, we use the array name followed by the dot operator, by the keyword *push*, and zero or more parameters in parentheses:

```
arrayName.push(item1, item2,...itemn);
```

where *item1*, *item2*,...*itemn* are a comma-separated list of items to be appended to the end of the array as new elements. Here are some examples:

```
// Create an array with two elements
var menuItems = ["home", "quit"];

// Add an element
// menuItems becomes ["home", "quit", "products"]
menuItems.push("products");
```

```
// Add two more elements
// menuItems becomes ["home", "quit", "products", "services", "contact"]
menuItems.push("services", "contact");
```

When invoked with no arguments, *push()* appends an empty element:

```
menuItems.push();  // Increase array length by one

// Same as
menuItems.length++;
```

The *push()* method returns the new length of the updated array:

```
var myList = [12, 23, 98];
trace(myList.push(28, 36));  // Appends 28 and 36 to myList, and displays: 5
```

Note that the items added to a list can be any expression. The expression is resolved before being added to the list:

```
var temperature = 22;
var sky = "sunny";
var weatherListing = new Array();
weatherListing.push(temperature, sky);
trace (weatherListing); // Displays: "22,sunny", not "temperature,sky"
```

The unshift() method

The *unshift()* method is much like *push()*, but it adds one or more elements to the *beginning* of the array, bumping all existing elements further along (i.e., the indexes of existing elements increase to accommodate the new elements at the beginning of the array). The syntax of *unshift()* follows the same style as all array methods:

```
arrayName.unshift(item1, item2,...itemn);
```

where *item1, item2,...itemn* are a comma-separated list of items to be added to the beginning of the array as new elements. Note that multiple items are added in the order that they were supplied. Here are some examples:

```
var flashVersions = new Array();
flashVersions[0] = 5;
flashVersions.unshift(4);     // flashVersions is now [4, 5]
flashVersions.unshift(2,3);   // flashVersions is now [2, 3, 4, 5]
```

The *unshift()* method, like *push()*, returns the new length of the array being enlarged.

The splice() method

The *splice()* method can add elements to, or remove elements from, an array. It is typically used to squeeze elements into the middle of an array (latter elements are renumbered to make room) or to delete elements from the middle of an array (latter elements are renumbered to close the gap). When *splice()* performs both of

Pushing, Popping, and Stacks

The *push()* method takes its name from a programming concept called a *stack*. A stack can be thought of as a vertical array, like a stack of dishes. If you frequent cafeterias or restaurants with buffets, you'll be familiar with the spring-loaded racks that hold plates for the diners. When clean dishes are added, they are literally *pushed* onto the top of the stack and the older dishes sink lower into the rack. When a customer *pops* a dish from the stack, he is removing the dish that was most recently pushed onto the stack. This is known as a last-in-first-out (LIFO) stack and is typically used for things like history lists. For example, if you hit the Back button in your browser, it will take you to the previous web page you visited. If you hit the Back button again, you'll be brought to the page before that, and so on. This is achieved by *pushing* the URL of each page you visit onto the stack and *popping* it off when the Back button is clicked.

LIFO stacks can also be found in real life. The last person to check her luggage on an airplane usually receives her luggage first when the plane lands because the luggage is unloaded in the reverse order from which it was loaded. The early bird who checked his luggage first is doomed to wait the longest at the luggage conveyor belt after the plane lands. A first-in-first-out (FIFO) stack is more egalitarian—it works on a first-come-first-served basis. A FIFO stack is like the line at your local bank. Instead of taking the last element in an array, a FIFO stack deals with the first element in an array next. It then deletes the first element in the array and all the other elements "move up," just as you move up in line when the person in front of you is deleted (i.e., she is either served and then leaves, or chooses to leave in disgust because she is tired of waiting). Therefore, the word *push* generally implies that you are using a LIFO stack, whereas the word *append* implies that you are using a FIFO stack. In either case, elements are added to the "end" of the stack; the difference lies in from which end of the array the element for the next operation is taken.

these tasks in a single invocation, it effectively replaces some elements with new elements (though not necessarily the same number of elements). Here's the syntax for *splice()*:

```
arrayName.splice(startIndex, deleteCount, item1, item2,...itemn)
```

where **startIndex** is a number that specifies the index at which element removal and optional insertion should commence (remember that the first element's index is 0); **deleteCount** is an optional argument that dictates how many elements should be removed (including the element at **startIndex**). When **deleteCount** is omitted, every element after *and including* **startIndex** is removed. The optional parameters **item1**, **item2**,...**itemn** are a comma-separated list of items to be added to the array as elements starting at **startIndex**.

Example 11-3 shows the versatility of the *splice()* method.

Example 11-3. Using the splice() Array Method

```
// Make an array...
months = new Array("January", "Friday", "April", "May", "Sunday", "Monday", "July");
// Hmmm. Something's wrong with our array. Let's fix it up.
// First, let's get rid of "Friday"
months.splice(1,1);
  // months is now:
  // ["January", "April", "May", "Sunday", "Monday", "July"]

// Now, let's add the two months before "April".
// Note that we won't delete anything here (deleteCount is 0).
months.splice(1, 0, "February", "March");
  // months is now:
  // ["January", "February", "March", "April", "May", "Sunday", "Monday", "July"]

// Finally, let's remove "Sunday" and "Monday" while inserting "June"
months.splice(5, 2, "june");
  // months is now:
  // ["January", "February", "March", "April", "May", "June", "July"]

// Now that our months array is fixed, let's trim it
// so that it contains only the first quarter of the year
// by deleting all elements starting with index 3 (i.e., "April")
months.splice(3); // months is now: ["January", "February", "March"]
```

Another useful feature of *splice()* is that it returns an array of the elements it *removes*. Thus it can be used to extract a series of elements from an array:

```
myList = ["a", "b", "c", "d"];
trace(myList.splice(1, 2));  // Displays: "b, c"
                             // myList is now ["a", "d"]
```

If no elements are removed, *splice()* returns an empty array.

The concat() method

Like *push()*, *concat()* adds elements to the end of an array. Unlike *push()*, *concat()* does not modify the array on which it is invoked—instead, *concat()* returns a new array. Furthermore, *concat()* can break arrays supplied as arguments into individual elements, allowing it to combine two arrays into a single, new array. Here's the syntax for *concat()*:

```
origArray.concat(elementList)
```

The *concat()* method appends the elements contained in `elementList`, one by one, to the end of `origArray` and returns the result as a *new* array, leaving `origArray` untouched. Normally, we'll store the returned array in a variable. Here, simple numbers are used as the items to be added to the array:

```
var list1 = new Array(11, 12, 13);
var list2 = list1.concat(14, 15);  // list2 becomes [11, 12, 13, 14, 15]
```

In this example, we use *concat()* to combine two arrays:

```
var guests = ["Panda", "Dave"];
var registeredPlayers = ["Gray", "Doomtrooper", "TRK9"];
var allUsers = registeredPlayers.concat(guests);
// allUsers is now: ["Gray", "Doomtrooper", "TRK9", "Panda", "Dave"]
```

Notice that *concat()* separated the elements of the **guests** array in a way that *push()* would not have. If we had tried this code:

```
var allUsers = registeredPlayers.push(guests);
```

we'd have ended up with this nested array:

```
["Gray", "Shift", "TRK9", ["Panda", "Dave"]]
```

Furthermore, *push()* would have altered the **registeredPlayers** array, whereas *concat()* does not.

Note, however, that *concat()* does *not* break apart *nested* arrays (elements that are themselves arrays within the main array), as you can see from the following code:

```
var x = [1, 2, 3];
var y = [[5, 6], [7, 8]];
var z = x.concat(y);  // Result is [1, 2, 3, [5, 6], [7, 8]].
                      // Elements 0 and 1 of y were not "flattened."
```

Removing Elements from an Array

You can remove elements from an array using the *delete* operator, by reducing the **length** property of an array, or using one of the built-in array methods.

Removing Elements with the delete Operator

The *delete* operator sets an array element to **undefined**, using the following syntax:

```
delete arrayName[index]
```

where **arrayName** is any array, and **index** is the number or name of the element we want to set to **undefined**. The name *delete* is misleading, frankly. It does *not* remove an element from the array; it merely sets the target element's value to **undefined**. A *delete* operation, therefore, is identical to assigning the **undefined** value to an element. We can verify this by checking the **length** property of an array after deleting one of its elements:

```
var myList = ["a", "b", "c"];
trace(myList.length);  // Displays: 3
delete myList[2];
trace(myList.length);  // Still displays 3...the element at index 2 is undefined
                       // instead of "c", but it still exists
```

To truly delete elements, use *splice()* (to delete them from the middle of an array), or use *shift()* and *pop()* (to delete them from the beginning or end of an array). Note that *delete* behaves differently with object properties and named elements than with numbered elements. Using *delete* on them permanently destroys properties and named elements, leaving no trace of them.

Removing Elements with the length Property

Earlier we used the `length` property to add elements to an array. We can also set the array's `length` property to a number smaller than the current length in order to delete elements from the array (i.e., truncate the array):

```
var toppings = ["pepperoni", "tomatoes", "cheese", "green pepper", "broccoli"];
toppings.length = 3;
trace(toppings);  // Displays: "pepperoni,tomatoes,cheese"
                  // We trimmed elements 3 and 4 (the last two).
```

Removing Elements with Array Methods

Arrays come equipped with several built-in methods for removing elements. We've already seen how *splice()* can delete a series of elements from the middle of an array. The *pop()* and *shift()* methods are used to prune elements from the end or beginning of an array.

The pop() method

The *pop()* method is the antithesis of *push()*—it removes the last element of an array. The syntax of *pop()* is simple:

```
arrayName.pop()
```

(I don't know why, but I always think that "popping" an array is kinda funny.) Anyway, *pop()* decrements the array's `length` by 1 and returns the value of the element it removes. For example:

```
x = [56, 57, 58];
x.pop();     // x is now [56, 57]
```

As we learned earlier, *pop()* is often used in combination with *push()* to perform LIFO stack operations. In Example 11-4, we use the `siteHistory` array to track a user's navigation through a site. When the user navigates to a new frame, we add his location to the array using *push()*. When the user navigates back, we *pop()* his last location off of `siteHistory`, and send him to the preceding location. Example 11-4 may be downloaded from the online Code Depot.

Example 11-4. A Back Button with History

```
// CODE ON FRAME 1 OF OUR MOVIE
stop();
var siteHistory = new Array();
```

Example 11-4. A Back Button with History (continued)

```
function goto(theLabel) {
  // If we're not already at the requested frame...
  if (theLabel != siteHistory[siteHistory.length - 1]) {
    // ...add the request to the history, then go to the requested frame
    siteHistory.push(theLabel);
    gotoAndStop(siteHistory[siteHistory.length - 1]);
  }
  trace(siteHistory);
}

function goBack() {
  // Remove the last item in the history
  siteHistory.pop();
  // If there is anything left in the history...
  if (siteHistory.length > 0) {
    // ...go to the most recent frame
    gotoAndStop(siteHistory[siteHistory.length - 1]);
  } else {
    // ...otherwise go home
    gotoAndStop("home");
  }
  trace(siteHistory);
}

// CODE ON A NAVIGATION BUTTON
on (release) {
  goto("gallery");
}

// CODE ON THE BACK BUTTON
on (release) {
  goBack();
}
```

The shift() method

Remember *unshift()*, the method we used to add an element to the beginning of an array? Meet its alter ego, *shift()*, which removes an element from the beginning of an array:

```
arrayName.shift()
```

Not as funny as *pop*. Oh well.

Like *pop()*, *shift()* returns the value of the element it removes. The remaining elements all move up in the pecking order toward the beginning of the array. For example:

```
var sports = ["hackey sack", "snowboarding", "inline skating"];
sports.shift();  // Now ["snowboarding", "inline skating"]
sports.shift();  // Now ["inline skating"]
```

Because *shift()* truly deletes an element, it is more useful than *delete* for removing the first element of an array. We can also use *shift()* to limit the range of a list. For example, suppose we're calculating the frame rate of a movie. We *push()* the current time onto an array after each frame renders. To limit the size of our array to the most recent 10 time samples, we *shift()* the oldest time off as necessary. To find the frame rate, we average the times in our array. Example 11-5 shows the technique.

Example 11-5. Calculating the Frame Rate of a Movie

```
// Create our time measurement array in a movie clip
onClipEvent(load) {
  var elapsedTime = new Array();
}

// Use an enterFrame clip event to measure the time after each frame
onClipEvent(enterFrame) {
  // Add the current time to elapsedTime
  elapsedTime.push(getTimer());

  // If we have enough samples to calculate an average...
  if (elapsedTime.length > 10) {
    // ...remove the oldest time from elapsedTime
    elapsedTime.shift();

    // Average the number of elapsed milliseconds per frame
    elapsedAverage = (elapsedTime[elapsedTime.length - 1] -
                elapsedTime[0]) / elapsedTime.length;

    // To find the frames per second, divide 1 second by the elapsed average
    fps = 1000 / elapsedAverage;
    trace("current fps " + fps);
  }
}
```

The splice() method

Earlier we learned that *splice()* can both remove elements from and add elements to an array. Since we've already looked at *splice()* in detail, we won't reexamine it here. However, given our current context, we should specifically demonstrate *splice()*'s element-removal capabilities:

```
var x = ["a", "b", "c", "d", "e", "f"];
x.splice(1,3);  // Removes elements 1, 2, and 3, leaving ["a", "e", "f"]
x.splice(1);    // Removes elements 1 through the end leaving just ["a"]
```

General Array-Manipulation Tools

Earlier we saw how array methods can be used to remove elements from and add elements to arrays. ActionScript also offers built-in methods for reordering and sorting elements, converting array elements to strings, and extracting arrays from other arrays.

The reverse() Method

As its name suggests, the *reverse()* method reverses the order of the elements of an array. Simple, but impressive. Here's the syntax:

```
arrayName.reverse()
```

And here are the impressive results:

```
var x = [1, 2, 3, 4];
x.reverse();
trace(x);  // Displays: "4,3,2,1"
```

We typically use *reverse()* to reorder a sorted list. For example, if we have a list of products sorted by ascending price, we can display them from least to most expensive, or we can reverse the list to display them from most to least expensive.

Reader Exercise: Try to write your own custom function to reverse the elements in an array. Not only is it harder than it looks, you'll most likely find that the built-in *reverse()* method is substantially faster.

The sort() Method

The *sort()* method rearranges the sequence of elements in an array according to an arbitrary rule that we provide. If we provide no rule, *sort()* places the elements in (roughly) alphabetical order by default. Sorting an array alphabetically is really easy, so let's see how that works first:

```
arrayName.sort()
```

When we invoke an array's *sort()* method with no arguments, its elements are temporarily converted to strings and sorted according to their code points as shown in Appendix B, *Latin 1 Character Repertoire and Keycodes* (see "Character order and alphabetic comparisons" in Chapter 4, *Primitive Datatypes*, for important details):

```
// This works as expected...
var animals = ["zebra", "ape"];
animals.sort();
trace(animals);  // Displays: "ape,zebra"
                 // Cool! What a handy little method.

// Watch out, the sort order is not strictly alphabetical...The
// capital "Z" in zebra comes before the lowercase "a" in "ape".
var animals = ["Zebra", "ape"];
animals.sort();
trace(animals);  // Displays: "Zebra,ape". Oops. See Appendix B.
```

We can also use *sort()* to organize array elements according to a rule of our own choosing. This technique is a little trickier to work with, but quite powerful. We start by creating a *compare function* that dictates how the interpreter should sort any two elements of an array. We then pass that function to the *sort()* method when we call it, like this:

```
arrayName.sort(compareFunction)
```

where **compareFunction** is the name of the function that tells the interpreter how to make its sorting decisions.

To build a compare function, we start with a new function that accepts two arguments (these represent any two elements in the array). In the function's body, we determine, however we see fit, which of the elements we'd like to appear earlier in the element list after a *sort()*. If we want the first element to appear *before* the second element, we return a *negative* number from our function. If we want the first element to appear *after* the second element, we return a *positive* number from our function. If we want the elements to be left in the same positions, we return 0 from our function. In pseudocode, the approach generically looks like this:

```
function compareElements (element1, element2) {
  if (element1 should appear before element2) {
    return -1;
  } else if (element1 should appear after element2) {
    return 1;
  } else {
    return 0;   // The elements should be left alone
  }
}
```

For example, to put elements in ascending numeric order, we could use a function like this:

```
function sortAscendingNumbers (element1, element2) {
  if (element1 < element2) {
    return -1;
  } else if (element1 > element2) {
    return 1;
  } else {
    return 0;   // The elements are equal
  }
}

// Now that our compare function is ready, let's try it out
var x = [34, 55, 33, 1, 100];
x.sort(sortAscendingNumbers);
trace(x);     // Displays: "1,33,34,55,100"
```

Numeric-sort functions can actually be phrased much more succinctly. The preceding *sortAscendingNumbers()* function could be written as:

```
function sortAscendingNumbers (element1, element2) {
  return element1 - element2;
}
```

In our optimized version, a negative number is returned if `element1` is less than `element2`, a positive number is returned if `element1` is greater than `element2`, and a 0 is returned if the two are equal. Now that's elegant! Here is a version to perform a descending sort:

```
function sortDescendingNumbers (element1, element2) {
  return element2 - element1;
}
```

Example 11-6 shows a compare function that adjusts the default alphabetic comparison behavior of *sort()* so that upper- and lowercase letters are sorted without regard to case.

Example 11-6. A Case-Insensitive Alphabetic Array Sort

```
var animals = ["Zebra", "ape"];

function sortAscendingAlpha (element1, element2) {
    return (element2.toLowerCase() < element1.toLowerCase());
}

animals.sort(sortAscendingAlpha);
trace(animals);  // Displays: "ape,Zebra"
```

Of course, the comparison does not always have to involve simple strings and numbers. Here we sort an array of movie clips in ascending order, according to their pixel area:

```
var clips = [square1, square2, square3];

function sortByClipArea (clip1, clip2) {
  clip1area = clip1._width * clip1._height;
  clip2area = clip2._width * clip2._height
  return clip1area - clip2area;
}

clips.sort(sortByClipArea);
```

That's a mighty fine sortin' machine!

The slice() Method

Something of a subset of *splice()*, *slice()* retrieves a series of elements from an array. Unlike *splice()*, *slice()* only *retrieves* elements. It creates a new array and does not affect the array on which it is invoked. The *slice()* method has the following syntax:

```
origArray.slice(startIndex, endIndex)
```

where **startIndex** specifies the first element to retrieve and **endIndex** specifies the element *after* the last element we want to retrieve. The *slice()* method returns a new array containing a copy of the series of elements from *origArray*[*startIndex*] to *origArray*[*endIndex* - 1]. If *endIndex* is omitted, it defaults to *origArray*.length and the returned array contains the elements from *origArray*[*startIndex*] through *origArray*[*origArray*.length-1]. Here are a couple of examples:

```
var myList = ["a", "b", "c", "d", "e", "f"];
myList.slice(1, 3);  // Returns ["b", "c"], not ["b", "c", "d"]
myList.slice(2);     // Returns ["c", "d", "e", "f"]
```

The join() Method

We can use *join()* to produce a string that represents all the elements of an array. The *join()* method starts by converting each element of the specified array to a string. Empty elements are converted to the empty string (""). Then *join()* concatenates all the strings into one long string, separating them with a character (or series of characters) called a *delimiter*. Finally, *join()* returns the resulting string. The syntax of *join()* is:

```
arrayName.join(delimiter)
```

where *delimiter* is the string used to separate the converted elements of *arrayName*. If unspecified, *delimiter* defaults to a comma. The result of a *join()* statement is easiest to understand through an example:

```
var siteSections = ["animation", "short films", "games"];

// Sets siteTitle to "animation>> short films>> games"
var siteTitle = siteSections.join(">> ");

// Sets siteTitle to "animation:short films:games"
var siteTitle = siteSections.join(":");
```

Note that *join()* does not modify the array upon which it is invoked. Instead, it returns a string based on that array.

When called without a delimiter argument, *join()* behaves exactly like *toString()*. Because *toString()* does not add a space after the comma it uses to delimit elements, we may wish to use *join()* if we want nicely formatted output:

```
var x = [1, 2, 3];
trace(x.join(", "));  // Displays: "1, 2, 3" instead of "1,2,3"
```

The *join()* method has a potentially surprising result when used on an array that contains elements which are *themselves* arrays. Since *join()* converts elements to strings, and arrays are converted to strings via their *toString()* method, nested arrays are converted to strings using a comma delimiter, not the delimiter supplied to *join()* as an argument. In other words, any delimiter supplied to *join()* doesn't affect nested arrays. For example:

```
var x = [1, [2, 3, 4], 5];
x.join("|");  // Returns "1|2,3,4|5"
```

The toString() Method

As we'll learn in Chapter 12, *toString()* is a universal object method that returns a string representation of any object upon which it is invoked. In the case of an *Array* object, the *toString()* method returns a list of the array's elements converted to strings and separated by commas. The *toString()* method may be called explicitly:

```
arrayName.toString()
```

Typically, we don't use *toString()* explicitly; rather, it is invoked automatically whenever **arrayName** is used in a string context. For example, when we write *trace(arrayName)*, a list of comma-separated values appears in the Output window; *trace(arrayName)* is equivalent to *trace(arrayName.toString())*. The *toString()* method is often helpful during debugging when we need a quick, unformatted look at the elements of an array. For example:

```
var sites = ["www.moock.org", "www.macromedia.com", "www.oreilly.com"];
// Display our array in a text field
debugOutput = "the sites array is " + sites.toString();
```

Arrays as Objects

Once you've read Chapter 12, you should recognize that arrays are a type of object, specifically instances of the *Array* class. As with other objects, array objects can have properties added to them. When we add named elements to an array, we're really just adding properties to an *Array* object. However, as we learned earlier, to use the built-in methods of the *Array* class we must work with numbered elements.

In Chapter 9, *Functions*, we saw a useful "array-object" hybrid, the *arguments* object, that combined numbered elements with properties. (Recall that the *arguments* object has a `callee` property and also stores an array of parameters as array elements.) Now we can see that all arrays contain their numbered list of elements, plus the built-in property `length`, plus any custom properties we add.

Multidimensional Arrays

So far we've limited our discussion to *one-dimensional* arrays, which are akin to a single row or a single column in a spreadsheet. But what if we want to create the equivalent of a spreadsheet with both rows and columns? We need a second dimension. ActionScript natively supports only one-dimensional arrays, but we can simulate a multidimensional array by creating arrays within arrays. That is, we can create an array that contains elements that are themselves arrays (sometimes called *nested* arrays).

The simplest type of multidimensional array is a two-dimensional array, in which elements are organized conceptually into a grid of rows and columns—the rows are the first dimension of the array, and the columns are the second.

Let's consider how a two-dimensional array works with a practical example. Suppose we're processing an order that contains three products, each with a quantity and a price. We want to simulate a spreadsheet with three rows (one for each product) and two columns (one for the quantity and one for the price). We create a separate array for each row, treating the elements as columns:

```
var row1 = [6, 2.99];    // Quantity 6, Price 2.99
var row2 = [4, 9.99];    // Quantity 4, Price 9.99
var row3 = [1, 59.99];   // Quantity 1, Price 59.99
```

Next, we place the rows into a container array named `spreadsheet`:

```
var spreadsheet = [row1, row2, row3];
```

Now we can find the total cost of the order by multiplying the quantity and price of each row and adding them all together. We access a two-dimensional array's elements using two indexes (one for the row and one for the column). The expression `spreadsheet[0]`, for example, represents the first row's two-column array. Hence, to access the second column in the first row of `spreadsheet`, we use `spreadsheet[0][1]`:

```
// Create a variable to store the total cost of the order
var total;

// Now find the cost of the order. For each row, multiply the columns
// together, and add that to the total.
for (var i = 0; i < spreadsheet.length; i++) {
    total += spreadsheet[i][0] * spreadsheet[i][1];
}

trace(total);  // Displays: 117.89
```

Aside from storage and access, multidimensional arrays behave just like normal arrays. We may happily use all of the *Array* methods to manipulate data stored in multidimensional arrays.

The Multiple-Choice Quiz, Take 3

In Example 9-10, we revised the multiple-choice quiz from Example 1-1. At that time, we improved the quiz code by creating reusable, centralized functions. Now that we've studied arrays, we can return to the quiz to make a few more improvements. This time, we'll see how to use arrays to store both the user's answers and the correct answers for each question, making our code more succinct, legible, and easier to extend if we want to add new questions.

All the changes we need to make to the quiz this time take place on the *scripts* layer of frame 1, where our main quiz code is located. Both the previous version and this updated version of the quiz can be found in the online Code Depot. To see what improvements we'll make this time around, read through the code in Example 11-7, paying special attention to the comments.

Example 11-7. A Multiple-Choice Quiz, Version 3

```
stop();
//  *** Init main timeline variables
var displayTotal;            // Text field for displaying user's final score
var numQuestions = 2;        // Number of questions in the quiz
var totalCorrect = 0;        // Number of correct answers
var userAnswers = new Array(); // Array containing user's guesses
var correctAnswers = [3, 2];   // Array containing each question's correct answer
// Notice that we no longer need to maintain two long lists of variables
// named q1answer, q2answer, etc., and correctAnswer1, correctAnswer2, etc.
// We now store that information conveniently in an array.

// *** Function to register the user's answers
function answer (choice) {
  // Since we can now check how many answers have been given via the
  // length property of userAnswers, we no longer need to manually track
  // that information with the answer.currentAnswer property. Note also
  // that we have done away with the unwieldy set statement that previously
  // assigned the user's answer to a dynamically named variable.

  // Tack the user's answer onto our array
  userAnswers.push(choice);
  // Do a little navigation, baby
  if ((userAnswers.length) == numQuestions) {
    gotoAndStop ("quizEnd");
  } else {
    gotoAndStop ("q"+ (userAnswers.length + 1));
  }
}

// *** Function to tally the user's score
function gradeUser() {
  // Count how many questions were answered correctly. Our
  // userAnswer/correctAnswer element comparison is much cleaner than the
  // snake pit of eval() functions we used to do the same job in the previous version.
  for (var i = 0; i < userAnswers.length; i++) {
    if (userAnswers[i] == correctAnswers[i]) {
      totalCorrect++;
    }
  }
  // Show the user's score in a dynamic text field
  displayTotal = totalCorrect;
}
```

Reader Exercise: Try generalizing our array-based version of the quiz by using `correctAnswers.length` in place of the variable `numQuestions`.

Onward!

This chapter gave you an introduction to—and considerable practice using—your first composite datatype, arrays. Now that you understand how multiple pieces of data can be represented within a single container, you have a solid foundation to take into the next chapter. There we'll explore an even more powerful type of composite data—and a fundamental component of ActionScript—*objects*.

12

Objects and Classes

This chapter covers so-called *object-oriented programming (OOP)*, which is new territory for many readers. We'll cover some of the terminology and show some applied examples to make it all concrete. You may have heard that OOP is some big mystery or that it's difficult to understand. Quite the contrary, the concepts are highly intuitive and the OOP process much easier than you may have been led to believe. At its heart, OOP simply means that you treat portions of your program as self-contained objects. This is easy to grasp once you realize that everything you deal with in the real world is a self-contained object. Your dog, your parents, your car, and your computer are all self-contained objects meaning that they do some things independently and do other things at your request even if you don't know the inner details of how they work.

You don't have to be a biologist to get your dog to fetch a stick; you don't need to be a mechanical engineer to drive your car; you don't need to be a psychoanalyst to interact with your parents; and rumors to the contrary, you don't need to be a computer scientist to check your email. All you need to know is the commands an object is willing to obey (which are called *methods*) and the results those commands produce. For example, if you press the gas pedal of your car, you can expect it to accelerate. If you tell your dog to sit, you can expect him to sit. Armed with this commonsense context of what an object is in the real world, let's see how to relate these concepts to ActionScript.

The classic example of a programming *object* is a bouncing ball. Like a real ball, a ball object can have *properties* that represent its attributes, such as its radius, color, mass, position, and bounciness (elasticity). To represent our bouncing ball in a program, we'll create a `ball` object with a `radius` property and so forth. The properties of an object represent its state at any given time, but some of its properties change over time. For example, to make our ball move, we need to simulate

Newton's laws of motion. That is, we need to describe in computer terms how a ball moves over time. In the simplest case, recalling that speed multiplied by time equals distance, we can determine a ball's horizontal position in the future using this pseudoequation:

```
ball.xPosition += ball.xVelocity * (elapsedTime)
```

This equation starts with the ball's current position and adds the distance it has traveled (based on its velocity and the elapsed time) to come up with the new position. An object's *behaviors* are simply the rules that govern it, like our equation for calculating the position of the ball over time. We generally wrap these behaviors in so-called *methods,* which are simply *the functions that implement an object's behaviors.* For example, we might create a *move()* method that uses the preceding equation.

Therefore, methods can be thought of as the commands that an object obeys. Of course, an object can have multiple methods. Let's say we want to make our ball bounce. We can create a *bounce()* method that reverses the ball's direction and reduces its speed (our ball isn't perfectly elastic). The *bounce()* method might implement this equation:

```
ball.xVelocity =  -(ball.xVelocity) * 0.95    // Ball is 95% elastic
```

Before getting into the esoterica of how to create objects, add properties, and implement methods, let's formalize some of our definitions. An *object* is technically a data structure that groups together related *properties* and *methods* (functions). An object typically *encapsulates* its behaviors, meaning that the internal details of how it performs its functions are not necessarily visible outside the object. Instead, a program can interact with an object via its so-called *interfaces* (i.e., methods that are publicly accessible outside the object). The rest of the program typically doesn't have to worry about how an object does what it does; instead, the program merely provides *inputs* to the object and checks the *outputs* (results) when applicable. You'll also hear talk of *classes* and *instances.* A *class* is simply a generic object category, and an *instance* is simply a specific case (i.e., a copy) of the object. For example, your particular pet dog is an instance of the generic *Dog* class. All dogs in the *Dog* class bark and have four legs, but your specific dog has its own particular values for the height, weight, and color properties used to describe dogs.

Object-oriented programming (OOP) is merely the name given to programs that make use of objects. Objects and OOP are so intrinsic to ActionScript that we've already used them, perhaps without your realizing it. A movie clip is a familiar object in Flash, and like all objects it is implemented as a collection of properties and methods. When we determine the height of a movie clip using `someClip._height`, we're accessing that clip object's `_height` property. And when we tell a movie clip to play using `someClip.play()`, we're invoking that clip object's *play()* method.

 Typically, all instances of an object class share the same methods and property names; it is the property *values* of each instance that distinguish it from other instances of the same class.

Whether we create objects ourselves or use those built into ActionScript, OOP keeps the components of a program cleanly separated from one another (*encapsulated*) and allows them to interoperate without knowing the details of other objects. This allows an object to change its internal functionality without adversely affecting other portions of the program that rely on the object, so long as the object's methods (i.e., its interfaces to the outside world) don't change. Returning to our `ball` object, for example, we don't care if the laws of physics change the behavior of our ball's motion. We just call the ball's *move()* method and let the object itself worry about the details.

Another nice feature of OOP is that we can treat *different* objects that have *different* behaviors in a uniform manner as long as they implement methods of the same name. For example, suppose we have a `circle` object and a `square` object. As long as both objects implement an *area()* method that returns the shape's area, we can call their *area()* methods without worrying about how each object calculates its own area.

In this chapter, we'll learn how to make a basic object, and we'll learn how to define a category of objects (i.e., a class). Once we're comfortable with the basics, we'll see how to share common characteristics between classes and objects (i.e., create a family tree) using *inheritance*. For example, we might implement a *Horse* class that along with our *Dog* class are descendants of the *Mammal* class. The *Mammal* class could implement methods and properties common to all mammals, such as the fact that they have hair, give milk, and are warm-blooded. Finally, we'll learn how OOP is used to control the Flash environment through ActionScript's built-in objects and classes.

I hope that this introduction has shed some light on objects and OOP. Let's dive in to the specifics.

The Anatomy of an Object

Like an array, an individual object is a container of containers. An array holds multiple data values in individual *elements*; an object, analogously, holds multiple data values in individual *properties*. The properties of an object, however, are *named*, not numbered. An array stores a group of elements in a numbered list, but an object stores properties according to unique identifiers that are not arranged in any specific order. To access an array element, we need to know its numeric position, but to access an object property, we need to know its name (i.e., *identifier*).

Figure 12-1 depicts the properties of a sample object called `ball`. The `ball` object contains two properties: `radius` and `color`. The values of those properties are 50 and 0xFF0000 (the hex value of red). The properties are named with unique identifiers, much like variables. Even though each property has its own name, all are contained by the single encompassing object, `ball`.

BALL OBJECT

PROPERTY NAME	PROPERTY VALUE
radius	50

PROPERTY NAME	PROPERTY VALUE
color	0xFF0000

Ball Object Properties

Figure 12-1. A sample object structure

Obviously an object typically defines properties that are meaningfully related. More specifically, the properties of an object should be chosen in such a way that they would help distinguish one instance of the object from another. Movie clip objects, for example, have properties specific to movie clips, such as their number of frames (`_totalframes`) and position (`_x` and `_y`).

Because object properties are named, not numbered, objects do not have any of the element-management tools of arrays (*shift()*, *unshift()*, *push()*, *splice()*, etc.). Object properties are traditionally set via methods of the object to preserve the encapsulated nature of an object. That is, in strict OOP, an object should set its own properties. If an outside entity wants to set an object's property, it should be done by calling an appropriate method of the object. For example, a purist would frown on setting the `length` property of an array directly. That purist would argue that it is best to let the *Array* object set the `length` property itself, and that code outside of the object should do so only indirectly, by calling one of the *Array* object's methods. In that case, the maintainer of the *Array* class could change the name of the `length` property to `len` without adversely affecting other users.

Instantiating Objects

Although it may sound backward, let's assume that we have already created an object class. This assumption isn't too ludicrous, because ActionScript provides many built-in classes, and the custom classes we'll build will behave similarly. Assuming we have an object class, we have to create a specific object *instance* (i.e., a copy) based on the class. For example, ActionScript provides the *Array* object class, but it is up to us to create individual arrays.

To create an instance of an object (i.e., *instantiate* the object), we use the *new* operator with a *constructor function*, which is used to initialize the object. The general syntax is:

```
new ConstructorFunction()
```

Let's instantiate our first object using a constructor that's already built into Action-Script: the *Object()* constructor. The *Object()* constructor creates a completely generic object (hence its name), the foundation object type upon which all other object types are based. The following code creates a new generic object:

```
new Object()
```

When we instantiate an object, we normally store the resulting instance in a variable, array element, or object property for later access. For example:

```
var myObject = new Object();
```

Instantiating an object in this manner gives us an empty object with no properties and only two very general methods. Generic objects, hence, are of limited use—the real power of objects comes with specialized object classes. Before we learn how to make our own classes, we'll see how to use object properties and methods with objects of existing classes.

Object Properties

Properties are named data containers associated with an object. They are defined by an object's class and then set individually for each object instance. Like variables, object properties can contain any kind of data—strings, numbers, Booleans, null, undefined, functions, arrays, movie clips, or even other objects.

Referring to Properties

The familiar dot operator gives us access to an object's properties. We separate the name of the property from the object it belongs to using a dot (a period), as follows:

```
objectName.propertyName
```

where *objectName* is the name of our object and *propertyName* must be a legal identifier that matches the name of some property of *objectName*.

For example, if we have a `ball` object instance with a `radius` property, we can access `radius` using:

```
ball.radius
```

Alternatively, we may refer to a property using the `[]` operator, as follows:

```
objectName[propertyName]
```

The `[]` operator allows us to compose a property name using any expression that resolves to a string. For example:

```
trace(ball["radius"]);

var prop = "radius";
trace(ball[prop]);  // prop resolves to "radius"
```

Built-in ActionScript properties are accessed in exactly the same way. Recall the syntax for retrieving the value of pi:

```
Math.PI
```

In that expression, we're accessing the built-in `PI` property of the `Math` object. However, in pure OOP, we'll nearly never access an object's properties directly; instead, we'll use methods to access property values. For example, to check the `volume` property of an instance of the built-in *Sound* class, we use:

```
trace(mySound.getVolume());
```

not:

```
trace(mySound.volume);
```

Using a for-in Loop to Access an Object's Properties

In Chapter 8, *Loop Statements*, we learned that a *for-in* loop can be used to enumerate the properties of an object. Now that we know a little more about objects, it's worth returning to the *for-in* statement briefly to review how it can be used to manipulate an object's properties.

Like all loops, the *for-in* statement includes a header and a body. The body of a *for-in* statement is automatically executed once for each property in the specified object. We don't need to know the number of properties or their names, because as each cycle of the loop executes, our "iterator" variable automatically becomes the name of the next property. We can therefore access the properties of the object, like this:

```
// List all the properties of the ball object
for (var prop in ball) {
  trace("Property " + prop + " has the value " + ball[prop]);
}
```

Note that the iterator variable, `prop`, in the preceding example is not an integer as it would be in a *for* loop. That is, don't confuse a standard *for* loop, typically used for accessing numbered array elements, with a *for-in* loop used to access an object's properties. For more information on *for-in* loops, see Chapter 8.

Methods

Methods are functions that are associated with objects and are typically used to perform a task or access an object's data. We invoke methods with the function call operator, (), using the dot operator to separate the method name from its object:

```
objectName.methodName()
```

For example:

```
ball.getArea();  // Call the getArea() method of ball
```

As with properties, methods are defined for a class and then invoked on individual object instances. However, before we see how to create methods within a class, we're going to bend the rules of good object-oriented programming and attach a method to an individual object instance of the built-in *Object* class. Once we understand how a single method works on an isolated object, we'll apply the concept correctly to a class of our own.

A method is essentially just a function stored in an object property. By assigning a function to an object property, we turn that function into a method of the object:

```
// Create an object
myObject = new Object();

// Create a function
function greet () {
  trace("hello world");
}

// Now assign greet to the property sayHello
myObject.sayHello = greet;
```

Once a function resides in an object property, we may invoke that function as a method, like this:

```
myObject.sayHello();  // Displays: "hello world"
```

Truth be known, you can also assign a function to an array element (instead of to an object property) and invoke that function using the call operator, like this:

```
var myList = new Array();
myList[0] = greet;
myList[0]();            // Displays: "hello world"
```

But when a function is invoked as a *method* of an object, something very special happens to the function—it gains the ability to retrieve or set the properties of the object to which it is attached. Let's see how this works with our `sayHello` property. First, we add a `msg` property to our generic object (again, we're bending the OOP rules for the sake of the demonstration . . . it's bad form to attach a custom property to an individual object instance):

```
myObject.msg = "Nice day, isn't it?";
```

Now we adjust *greet()* so that it displays the value of `msg`:

```
function greet () {
  trace(this.msg);
}

// Now invoke sayHello again
myObject.sayHello();  // Displays: "Nice day, isn't it?"
```

Notice the keyword `this` at the end of line 2? That's our connection to `myObject`. When executed as a method of `myObject`, *sayHello()* is effectively passed an invisible argument called `this` containing a reference to `myObject`. In the body of the function, we use `this` to access `myObject`'s `msg` property as `this.msg`. When we invoke *myObject.sayHello()*, the expression `this.msg` resolves to `myObject.msg`, which becomes "Nice day, isn't it?".

A method can both retrieve and set the value of its host object's properties. Example 12-1 demonstrates a method that retrieves the value of two properties of an object, performs a calculation based on those values, and then sets the value of a third, new property. (Once again, because our current focus is methods, the object we're using is only an object instance. In the next section we'll learn how to add object methods properly with a class.)

Example 12-1. Implementing a Method that Sets a Property

```
// Make a new object and store it in rectangle
var rectangle = new Object();
rectangle.width = 10;
rectangle.height = 5;

// Define a function to calculate a rectangle's area, and
// set a corresponding property. Note the use of the this keyword.
function rectArea() {
  this.area = this.width * this.height;
}

// Assign the function as a method of rectangle
rectangle.setArea = rectArea;

// Now invoke rectangle's setArea() method
rectangle.setArea();    // Sets rectangle.area to 50

// Finally, examine the new property generated by setArea()
trace(rectangle.area);  // Displays: 50
```

It's more typical to have a method return a value instead of setting a property. Let's revise our `rectangle`'s *setArea()* method to do just that, as shown in Example 12-2.

Example 12-2. Returning a Value from a Method

```
// Create and set up our rectangle. Note that it's legal to assign
// the area method before the rectArea function appears in our code.
var rectangle = new Object();
rectangle.width = 10;
rectangle.height = 5;
rectangle.area = rectArea;

// This time, just return the area, don't assign it to a property
function rectArea() {
  return this.width * this.height;
}

// Now it's even easier to use
trace("The area of rectangle is: " + rectangle.area());

// Displays: "The area of rectangle is: 50"
```

The `this` keyword can be a tricky concept because it involves some sleight of hand by the interpreter. To illustrate how the preceding code works, consider Example 12-3, which exposes the implied relationship of `this` to its object and method. (Example 12-3 is fictitious because `this` is a reserved keyword and would cause an error if used as shown.)

Example 12-3. A Fictitious Example Using this Explicitly

```
// Create and set up our rectangle object
var rectangle = new Object();
rectangle.width = 10;
rectangle.height = 5;
rectangle.area = rectArea;

// Specifically require this as an argument of our rectArea() function
function rectArea(this) {
  return this.width * this.height;
}

// Call the method with an explicit reference to the rectangle object
trace("The area of rectangle is: " + rectangle.area(rectangle));
```

Methods may also be assigned to object properties as function literals. By using a function literal to create a method, we avoid the work of first creating our function and then assigning it to a property. Example 12-4 reworks our rectangle object from Example 12-2 showing the use of a function literal.

Example 12-4. Implementing Methods with Function Literals

```
var rectangle = new Object();
rectangle.width = 10;
```

Example 12-4. Implementing Methods with Function Literals (continued)

```
rectangle.height = 5;

// Here's the function literal assignment
rectangle.area = function () {
  return this.width * this.height;
};   // Using a semicolon is good form at the end of the literal

// We can still invoke the function as before
trace("The area of rectangle is: " + rectangle.area());
```

Methods give us enormous control over objects. When used with built-in objects, methods are one of our primary tools for controlling the Flash movie environment.

In this section we've seen both how to store a function in a property (thereby making it a method) and also how to invoke a function through a property. These two endeavors have very similar syntax, but very different results. It's crucial to understand the difference.

When *assigning* a method to a property, *omit* the parentheses:

```
myObj.myMethod = someFunction;
```

When *invoking* a method, *include* the parentheses:

```
myObj.myMethod();
```

The difference in syntax is subtle. Make sure to get it right.

Classes and Object-Oriented Programming

It's not uncommon to create dozens of complex objects that store rich information about everything from products in a shopping-cart system to bad guys with artificial intelligence in a video game. To expedite the creation of objects and to define object hierarchies (relationships between objects), we use object *classes*. A *class* is a template-style definition of an entire category of objects. As we learned in the introduction, classes describe the general features of a specific breed of objects, such as "all dogs have four legs."

Object Classes

Before we see how to use classes, let's see how things work when we *don't* use them. Suppose we want a `ball` object, but instead of using a class to generate it, we simply adapt a generic object of the built-in *Object* class. We give the object these properties: `radius`, `color`, `xPosition`, and `yPosition`. Then we add two methods—*moveTo()* and *area()*—used to reposition the object and to determine the amount of space it occupies.

Here's the code:

```
var ball = new Object();
ball.radius = 10;
ball.color = 0xFF0000;
ball.xPosition = 59;
ball.yPosition = 15;
ball.moveTo = function (x, y) { this.xPosition = x; this.yPosition = y; };
ball.area = function () { return Math.PI * (this.radius * this.radius); };
```

That approach gets the job done but has limitations; every time we want a new ball-like object, we have to repeat the `ball`-initializing code, which is tedious and error-prone. In addition, creating many ball objects in this way redundantly duplicates the identical *moveTo()* and *area()* function code on each object, unnecessarily taking up memory.

To efficiently create a series of objects that have common properties, we should create a *class*. Using a class, we can define the properties that all `ball` objects should possess. Furthermore, we can share any properties with fixed values across all instances of the `ball` class. In natural language our *Ball* class would be described to the interpreter as follows:

> A *Ball* is a type of object. All `ball` object instances have the properties `radius`, `color`, `xPosition`, `yPosition`, which are set individually for each `ball`. All `ball` objects also share the methods *moveTo()* and *area()*, which are identical across all members of the *Ball* class.

Let's see how this theory works in practice.

Making a Class

There is no specific "class declaration" device in ActionScript; there is no "class" statement that creates a new class akin to the *var* statement, which creates new variables. Instead, we define a special type of function, called a *constructor* function, that will generate a new instance of our class. By defining the constructor function, we are effectively creating our class template or class definition.

Syntactically, constructor functions (or simply, *constructors*) are formed just like normal functions. For example:

```
function Constructor () {
  statements
}
```

The name of a class's constructor function may be any valid function name, but it is capitalized by convention to indicate that it is a class constructor. A constructor's name should describe the class of objects it creates, as in *Ball*, *Product*, or *Vector2d*. The `statements` of a constructor function initialize the objects it creates.

We'll make our *Ball* constructor function as simple as possible to start. All we want it to do so far is create empty objects for us:

```
// Make a Ball constructor
function Ball () {
  // Do something here
}
```

That didn't hurt much. Now let's see how to generate `ball` objects using our *Ball* constructor function.

Creating members of a class

A constructor function both defines our class and is used to instantiate new instances of the class. As we learned earlier, when invoked in combination with the *new* operator, a constructor function creates *and then returns* an object instance. Recall the general syntax for creating a new object based on a constructor function:

```
new Constructor();    // Returns an instance of the Constructor class
```

So, to create a `ball` object (an *instance*) using our *Ball* class, we write:

```
myBall = new Ball();  // Stores an instance of the Ball class in myBall
```

Our *Ball* class still doesn't add properties or methods to the objects it creates. Let's take care of that next.

Assigning custom properties to the objects of a class

To customize an object's properties during the object-creation stage, we again turn to the special `this` keyword. Within a constructor function, the `this` keyword stores a reference to the object currently being generated. Using that reference, we can assign whatever properties we like to the embryonic object. The following syntax shows the general technique:

```
function Constructor () {
  this.propertyName = value;
}
```

where `this` is the object being created, `propertyName` is the property we want to attach to that object, and `value` is the data value we're assigning to that property.

Let's apply this technique to our *Ball* example. Earlier, we proposed that the properties of the *Ball* class should be `radius`, `color`, `xPosition`, and `yPosition`.

Here's how the *Ball* class constructor might assign those properties to its instances (note the use of the **this** keyword):

```
function Ball () {
  this.radius = 10;
  this.color = 0xFF0000;
  this.xPosition = 59;
  this.yPosition = 15;
}
```

With the *Ball* constructor thus prepared, we can create object instances (i.e., members of the class) bearing the predefined properties—radius, color, xPosition, and yPostion—by invoking *Ball()* with the *new* operator, just as we did earlier. For example:

```
// Make a new instance of Ball
bouncyBall = new Ball();

// Now access the properties of bouncyBall that were set when it was
// made by the Ball() constructor.
trace(bouncyBall.radius);      // Displays: 10
trace(bouncyBall.color);       // Displays: 16711680
trace(bouncyBall.xPosition);   // Displays: 59
trace(bouncyBall.yPosition);   // Displays: 15
```

Now wasn't that fun?

Unfortunately, our *Ball()* constructor uses fixed values when it assigns properties to the objects it creates (e.g., **this.radius = 10**). Every object of the *Ball* class, therefore, would have the same property values, which is antithetical to the goal of object-oriented programming (we have no need for a class that generates a bunch of identical objects; it is their differences that make them interesting).

To dynamically assign property values to instances of a class, we adjust our constructor function so that it accepts arguments. Let's consider the general syntax, then get back to the *Ball* example:

```
function Constructor (value1, value2, value3) {
  this.property1 = value1;
  this.property2 = value2;
  this.property3 = value3;
}
```

Inside the **Constructor** function, we refer to the object being created with the **this** keyword, just as we did earlier. This time, however, we don't hardcode the object properties' values. Instead, we assign the values of the arguments *value1*, *value2*, and *value3* to the object's properties. When we want to create a new, unique member of our class, we pass our class constructor function the initial property values for our new instance:

```
myObject = new Constructor (value1, value2, value3);
```

Let's see how this applies to our *Ball* class, shown in Example 12-5.

Example 12-5. A Generalized Ball Class

```
// Make the Ball() constructor accept property values as arguments
function Ball (radius, color, xPosition, yPosition) {
  this.radius = radius;
  this.color = color;
  this.xPosition = xPosition;
  this.yPosition = yPosition;
}

// Invoke our constructor, passing it arguments to use as
// our object's property values
myBall = new Ball(10, 0x00FF00, 59, 15);

// Now let's see if it worked...
trace(myBall.radius);  // Displays: 10,  :) Pretty cool...
```

We're almost done building our *Ball* class. But you'll notice that we're still missing the *moveTo()* and *area()* methods discussed earlier. There are actually two ways to attach methods to a class's objects. We'll learn the simple, less efficient way now and come back to the topic of method creation later when we cover *inheritance*.

Assigning methods to objects of a class

The simplest way to add a method to a class is to assign a property that contains a function within the constructor. Here's the generic syntax:

```
function Constructor() {
  this.methodName = function;
}
```

The *function* may be supplied in several ways, which we'll examine by adding the *area()* method to our *Ball* class. Note that we've removed the `color`, `xPosition`, and `yPosition` properties from the class for the sake of clarity.

The *function* can be a function literal, as in:

```
function Ball (radius) {
  this.radius = radius;
  // Add the area method...
  this.area = function () { return Math.PI * this.radius * this.radius; };
}
```

Alternatively, the *function* can be declared *inside* the constructor:

```
function Ball (radius) {
  this.radius = radius;
  // Add the area method...
  this.area = getArea;
  function getArea () {
    return Math.PI * this.radius * this.radius;
  }
}
```

Finally, the *function* can be declared *outside* the constructor but assigned *inside* the constructor:

```
// Declare the getArea() function
function getArea () {
  return Math.PI * this.radius * this.radius;
}

function Ball (radius) {
  this.radius = radius;
  // Add the area method...
  this.area = getArea;
}
```

There's no real difference between the three approaches—all are perfectly valid. Function literals often prove the most convenient to use but are perhaps not as reusable as defining a function outside of the constructor so that it can also be used in other constructors. Regardless, all three approaches lack efficiency.

So far we've been attaching unique property values to each object of our *Ball* class. Each `ball` object needs its own `radius` and `color` property values to distinguish one `ball` from the next. But when we assign a fixed method to the objects of a class using the techniques we've just seen, we are unnecessarily duplicating the method on *every object* of our class. The *area* formula is the same for every `ball`, and hence the code that performs this task should be centralized and generalized.

To more efficiently attach any property or method with a fixed value to a class, we use *inheritance*, our next topic of study.

Object Property Inheritance

Inherited properties are not attached to the individual object instances of a class. They are attached once to the class constructor and borrowed by the objects as necessary. These properties are said to be *inherited* because they are passed down to objects instead of being defined within each object. An inherited property appears to belong to the object through which it is referenced but is actually part of the object's class constructor.

Figure 12-2 demonstrates the general model for inherited properties using our *Ball* class as an example. Because the *moveTo()* and *area()* methods of *Ball* do not vary among its instances, those methods are best implemented as inherited methods. They belong to the class itself, and each `ball` object accesses them only by reference. On the other hand, the `radius`, `color`, `xPosition`, and `yPosition` properties of our *Ball* class are assigned to each object as normal properties because each `ball` needs its own value for those properties.

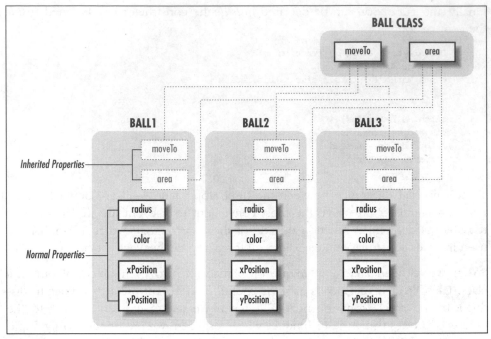

Figure 12-2. Inherited and normal properties

Inheritance works in a hierarchical chain, like a family tree. When we invoke a method of an individual object, the interpreter checks to see if that object implements the method. If the method isn't found, the interpreter then looks at the class for the method.

For example, if we execute `ball1.area()`, the interpreter checks whether `ball1` defines an *area()* method. If the `ball1` object lacks an *area()* method, the interpreter checks whether the *Ball* class defines an *area()* method. If it does, the interpreter then invokes *area()* as though it were a method of the `ball1` object, not the *Ball* class. This allows the method to operate on the `ball1` object (rather than the class), retrieving or setting `ball1`'s properties as necessary. This is one of the key benefits of OOP; we *define* the function in one place (the *Ball* class) but *use* it from many places (any `ball` object).

Unlike normal properties, inherited properties may only be *retrieved* through an object, not set.

Time for a little code to breathe some life into these principles.

Creating inherited properties with the prototype property

We start the process of creating inherited properties by creating a class constructor function, such as that of our *Ball* class in Example 12-5:

```
function Ball (radius, color, xPosition, yPosition) {
  this.radius = radius;
  this.color = color;
  this.xPosition = xPosition;
  this.yPosition = yPosition;
}
```

Remember from Chapter 9, *Functions*, that functions double as objects and can therefore take properties.

 When a constructor function is created, the interpreter automatically assigns it a property called `prototype`. In the `prototype` property, the interpreter places a generic object. Any properties attached to the `prototype` object are inherited by all instances of the constructor function's class.

To create a property that will be inherited by all the objects of a class, we simply assign that property to the prefabricated `prototype` object of the class's constructor function. Here's the general syntax:

```
Constructor.prototype.propName = value;
```

where *Constructor* is our class's constructor function (*Ball* in our example); `prototype` is the automatically generated property we use to house inherited properties; *propName* is the inherited property name, and *value* is that inherited property's value. For example, here's how we would add a global `gravity` property to our entire class of *Ball* objects:

```
Ball.prototype.gravity = 9.8;
```

With the `gravity` property in place, we can then access `gravity` from any member of the *Ball* class:

```
// Create a new instance of the Ball class
myBall = new Ball(5, 0x003300, 34, 220);

// Now display the value of the inherited gravity property
trace(myBall.gravity);  // Displays: 9.8
```

The `gravity` property is accessible through `myBall` because `myBall` inherits the properties of *Ball*'s `prototype` object.

Because the same methods are ordinarily shared by every instance of a class, they are typically stored in inherited properties. Let's add an inherited *area()* method to our *Ball* class:

```
Ball.prototype.area = function () {
  return Math.PI * this.radius * this.radius;
};  // Semicolon required because this is a function literal
```

That was so much fun, let's add an inherited *moveTo()* method, this time using a predefined function instead of a function literal:

```
function moveTo (x, y) {
  this.xPosition = x;
  this.yPosition = y;
}

Ball.prototype.moveTo = moveTo;
```

Once a function is defined as an inherited property, we can invoke it like any other method:

```
// Make a new ball
myBall = new Ball(15, 0x33FFCC, 100, 50);

// Now invoke myBall's inherited area() method
trace(myBall.area());  // Displays: 706.858347057703
```

Note that it's also possible to replace a constructor's **prototype** object entirely with a new object, thereby adding many inherited properties in a single gesture. Doing so, however, alters the inheritance chain, which we'll learn about later under "Superclasses and Subclasses."

Overriding inherited properties

To customize an inherited property for a single object, we can set a property on that object using the same name as the inherited property. For example, we might want to give one ball lower gravity than all other balls:

```
// Create our Ball class constructor
function Ball ( radius, color, xPosition, yPosition ) { ... } // Not shown

// Assign an inherited gravity property
Ball.prototype.gravity = 9.8;

// Create a Ball object
lowGravBall = new Ball ( 200, 0x22DD99, 35, 100 );

// Override the inherited gravity property
lowGravBall.gravity = 4.5;
```

A property set on an object always overrides any inherited property by the same name. This is simply a result of the way the inheritance chain works. Likewise, method definitions local to an object will override those in its class. If we execute **ball1.area()** and **ball1** defines an *area()* method, that method is used; the interpreter never bothers looking at the *Ball* class's **prototype** to see if it also defines an *area()* method.

The constructor property

When a constructor's `prototype` object is created, the interpreter automatically assigns it a special property called `constructor`. The `constructor` property is a reference to the `prototype`'s class constructor function. For example, the following expressions both yield a reference to the *Ball* constructor function:

```
trace(Ball);                      // Displays: [Function]
trace(Ball.prototype.constructor);  // Also displays: [Function]
                                  // Same reference as above
```

Note that the `constructor` property contains a *reference* to a constructor function, not a string representing the function's name.

The __proto__ property

When any object is created, the interpreter automatically assigns it a special property called `__proto__` (note the *two* underscores on either side of the name). The `__proto__` property of an object is a reference to the `prototype` property of that object's constructor function. For example, when we create an instance of *Ball* called `myBall`, `myBall.__proto__` is set to `Ball.prototype`:

```
myBall = new Ball(6, 0x00FF00, 145, 200);
trace(myBall.__proto__ == Ball.prototype);  // Displays: true
```

The `__proto__` property is used primarily by the ActionScript interpreter to look up an object's inherited properties. For example, when we invoke the inherited method *area()* through `myBall`, as in *myBall.area()*, ActionScript accesses the *Ball.prototype.area* method via `myBall.__proto__`.

We may also use `__proto__` directly to check whether an object belongs to a specified class, as shown in Example 12-6.

Example 12-6. Determining the Class of an Object

```
function MyClass (prop) {
  this.prop = prop;
}
myObj = new MyClass();
if (myObj.__proto__ == MyClass.prototype) {
  trace("myObj is an instance of MyClass");
}
```

Superclasses and Subclasses

One of the crucial features of classes in advanced object-oriented programming is their ability to share properties. That is, an entire class may inherit properties from, and pass properties on to, other classes. In complex situations, multiclass inheritance can be indispensable. (Even if you don't use multiclass inheritance yourself, understanding it will help you work with the built-in ActionScript classes.)

We've seen how objects inherit properties from the `prototype` object of their class constructors. Inheritance is not limited to that single object/class relationship. A class itself may inherit properties from other classes. For example, we may have a class called *Circle* that defines a general method, *area()*, used to find the area of all circular objects. Instead of defining a separate *area()* method in a class like *Ball*, we may simply make *Ball* inherit the *area()* method already available from *Circle*. Instances of *Ball*, hence, inherit the *Circle's area()* method through *Ball*. Notice the hierarchy—the simplest class, *Circle*, defines the most general methods and properties. Another class, *Ball*, builds on that simple *Circle* class, adding features specific to *Ball*-class instances but relying on *Circle* for the basic attributes that all circular objects share. In traditional object-oriented programming, the *Ball* class would be said to *extend* the *Circle* class. That is, *Ball* is a *subclass* of *Circle*, while *Circle* is a *superclass* of *Ball*.

Making a superclass

Earlier we learned to define inherited properties on the `prototype` object of a class's constructor function. To create a *superclass* for a given class, we completely *replace* the class's `prototype` object with a new instance of the desired superclass. Here's the general syntax:

```
Constructor.prototype = new SuperClass();
```

By replacing `Constructor`'s `prototype` object with an instance of `SuperClass`, we force all instances of `Constructor` to inherit the properties defined on instances of `SuperClass`. In Example 12-7, we first create a class, *Circle*, which assigns an *area()* method to all its instances. Then we assign an instance of *Circle* to `Ball.prototype`, causing all `ball` objects to inherit *area()* from *Circle*.

Example 12-7. Creating a Superclass

```
// Create a Circle (superclass) constructor
function Circle() {
  this.area = function () { return Math.PI * this.radius * this.radius; };
}

// Create our usual Ball class constructor
function Ball ( radius, color, xPosition, yPosition ) {
  this.radius = radius;
  this.color = color;
  this.xPosition = xPosition;
  this.yPosition = yPosition;
}

// Here we make the superclass by assigning an instance of Circle to
// the Ball class constructor's prototype
Ball.prototype = new Circle();

// Now let's make an instance of Ball and check its properties
myBall = new Ball ( 16, 0x445599, 34, 5);
```

Example 12-7. Creating a Superclass (continued)

```
trace(myBall.xPosition);    // 34, a normal property of Ball
trace(myBall.area());       // 804.24..., area() was inherited from Circle
```

However, our class hierarchy now has poor structure—*Ball* defines radius, but radius is actually a property common to all circles, so it belongs in our *Circle* class. The same is true of xPosition and yPosition. To fix the structure, we'll move radius, xPosition, and yPosition to *Circle*, leaving only color in *Ball*. (For the sake of the example, we'll treat color as a property only balls can have.)

Conceptually, here's the setup of our revised *Circle* and *Ball* constructors:

```
// Create the Circle (superclass) constructor
function Circle ( radius, xPosition, yPosition ) {
  this.area = function () { return Math.PI * this.radius * this.radius; };
  this.radius = radius;
  this.xPosition = xPosition;
  this.yPosition = yPosition;
}

// Create the Ball class constructor
function Ball ( color ) {
  this.color = color;
}
```

Having moved the properties around, we're faced with a new problem. How can we provide values for radius, xPosition, and yPosition when we're creating objects using *Ball* and not *Circle*? We have to make one more adjustment to our *Ball* constructor code. First, we set up *Ball* to receive all the required properties as parameters:

```
function Ball ( color, radius, xPosition, yPosition ) {
```

Next, within our *Ball* constructor, we define the *Circle* constructor as a method of the ball object being instantiated:

```
this.superClass = Circle;
```

Finally, we invoke the *Circle* constructor on the ball object, and pass it values for radius, xPosition, and yPosition:

```
this.superClass(radius, xPosition, yPosition);
```

Our completed class/superclass code is shown in Example 12-8.

Example 12-8. A Class and Its Superclass

```
// Create a Circle (superclass) constructor
function Circle ( radius, xPosition, yPosition) {
  this.area = function () { return Math.PI * this.radius * this.radius; };
  this.radius = radius;
  this.xPosition = xPosition;
  this.yPosition = yPosition;
}
```

Example 12-8. A Class and Its Superclass (continued)

```
// Create our Ball class constructor
function Ball ( color, radius, xPosition, yPosition ) {
  // Define the Circle superclass as a method of the ball being instantiated
  this.superClass = Circle;
  // Invoke the Circle constructor on the ball object, passing values
  // supplied as arguments to the Ball constructor
  this.superClass(radius, xPosition, yPosition);
  // Set the color of the ball object
  this.color = color;
}

// Assign an instance of our Circle superclass to our
// Ball class constructor's prototype
Ball.prototype = new Circle();

// Now let's make an instance of Ball and check its properties
myBall = new Ball ( 0x445599, 16, 34, 5);
trace(myBall.xPosition);    // 34
trace(myBall.area());       // 804.24...
trace(myBall.color);        // 447836
```

Note that the word **superClass** in *Ball* is not reserved or special. It's simply an apt name for the superclass constructor function. Furthermore, *Circle*'s *area()* method could have been defined on `Circle.prototype`. When you start programming with classes and objects in the real world, you'll undoubtedly notice that there's a certain amount of flexibility in the tools ActionScript provides for building class hierarchies and implementing inheritance. You'll likely need to adapt the approaches described in this chapter to suit the subtleties of your specific application.

Polymorphism

Inheritance makes another key OOP concept, *polymorphism*, possible. Polymorphism is a fancy word meaning "many forms." It simply means that you tell an object what to do, but leave the details up to the object (a.k.a. "Different strokes for different folks"). It is best illustrated with an example. Suppose you are creating a cops and robbers game. There are multiple cops, robbers, and innocent bystanders displayed on the screen simultaneously, all moving independently according to different rules. The cops chase the robbers, the robbers run away from the cops, and the innocent bystanders move randomly, confused and frightened. In the code for this game, suppose we create an object class to represent each category of person:

```
function Cop() { ... }
function Robber() { ... }
function Bystander() { ... }
```

In addition, we create a superclass, *Person*, that classes *Cop*, *Robber*, and *Bystander* all inherit from:

```
function Person() { ... }
Cop.prototype       = new Person();
Robber.prototype    = new Person();
Bystander.prototype = new Person();
```

On each frame of the Flash movie, every person on the screen should move according to the rules for their class. To make this happen, we define a method *move()* on every object (the *move()* method is customized for each class):

```
Person.prototype.move = function () { ... default move behavior ... }
Cop.prototype.move = function () { ... move to chase robber ... }
Robber.prototype.move = function () { ... move to run away from cop ... }
Bystander.prototype.move = function () { ... confused, move randomly ... }
```

On each frame of the Flash movie, we want every person on the screen to move. To manage all the people, we create a master array of *Person* objects. Here's an example of how the **persons** array might be populated:

```
// Create our cops
cop1 = new Cop();
cop2 = new Cop();

// Create our robbers
robber1 = new Robber();
robber2 = new Robber();
robber3 = new Robber();

// Create our bystanders
bystander1 = new Bystander();
bystander2 = new Bystander();

// Create an array populated with cops, robbers, and bystanders
persons = [cop1, cop2, robber1, robber2, robber3, bystander1, bystander2];
```

In every frame of the Flash movie, we call the function *moveAllPersons()*, which is defined as follows:

```
function moveAllPersons() {
  for (var i=0; i < persons.length; i++) {
    persons[i].move();
  }
}
```

When *moveAllPersons()* is invoked, all of the cops, robbers, and bystanders will move according to the individual rules associated with their class as defined by its *move()* method. This is polymorphism in action—objects with common characteristics can be organized together, but they retain their individual identities. The cops, robbers, and bystanders have much in common, embodied by the superclass *Person*. They have operations in common, like knowing how to move. However, they may implement the common operations differently and may support other class-specific operations and data. Polymorphism permits dissimilar objects to be treated uniformly. We use the *move()* function to cause all the people to move, even though the *move()* function for each class is unique.

Determining whether an object belongs to a superclass

Suppose we have a *Shape* class and a *Rectangle* class that has *Shape* as its super-class. To check whether an object is a descendant of *Shape*, we must refine the method in Example 12-6, to walk the chain of prototype objects (called the *prototype chain*). Example 12-9 shows the technique.

Example 12-9. Walking the Prototype Chain

```
// This function checks if theObj is a descendant of theClass
function objectInClass(theObj, theClass) {
  while (theObj.__proto__ != null) {
    if (theObj.__proto__ == theClass.prototype) {
      return true;
    }
    theObj = theObj.__proto__;
  }
  return false;
}


// Make a new instance of Rectangle
myObj = new Rectangle();

// Now check if myRect inherits from Shape
trace (objectInClass(myRect, Shape)); // Displays: true
```

The end of the inheritance chain

All objects descend from the top-level *Object* class. Hence, all objects inherit the properties defined in the *Object* constructor—namely the *toString()* and *valueOf()* methods. We can, therefore, add new properties to *every* object in a movie by adding new properties to the *Object* class. Properties attached to `Object.prototype` will proliferate throughout the entire class hierarchy, including all internal objects and even *movieclip* objects! This approach can generate a type of truly global variable or method. In the following code, for example, we hardcode a stage width and height dimension into the *Object* class `prototype`. We can then access that information from any movie clip:

```
Object.prototype.mainstageWidth = 550;
Object.prototype.mainstageHeight = 400;
trace(anyClip.mainstageWidth);  // Displays: 550
```

`Object.prototype` properties are inherited not only by movie clips but by every object, so even our own custom objects and instances of other built-in classes such as *Date* and *Sound* will inherit properties assigned to `Object.prototype`.

Reader Exercise: We can attach new properties and methods to any built-in class. Try adding the case-insensitive alphabetical sort function from Example 11-6 to the *Array* class as an inherited method.

Comparing Java terminology

In our survey of classes and class hierarchies, we've come across properties defined on objects, class constructors, and class prototypes. In Java and C++, there are specific names for the various types of class and object properties. For the benefit of Java programmers, Table 12-1 outlines the rough equivalencies between Java and ActionScript.

Table 12-1. Java and ActionScript Property Equivalencies

Java	Description	ActionScript	ActionScript Example
Instance variables	Variables local to an object instance	Properties defined in a class constructor function and copied to objects	```function Square (side) { this.side = side; }```
Instance methods	Methods invoked on an object instance	Methods defined on the prototype object of a class constructor function, and accessed automatically through prototype when invoked on an instance	```Square.prototype.area = squareArea; mySquare.area();```
Class variables	Variables with the same value across all object instances of a class	Properties defined as function properties on a class constructor function	```Square.numSides = 4;```
Class methods	Methods invoked through a class	Methods defined as function properties on a class constructor function	```Square.findSmaller = function (square1, square2) { ... }```

Object-Oriented Programming Summary

Classes and inheritance open up a world of potential for sharing common information among many objects. Object-oriented programming is the basis of all ActionScript. Whether or not you use every aspect of classes and objects in your scripts, understanding the general concepts involved is an essential part of understanding the Flash programming environment. As we'll see in the last section of this chapter, our confidence with object-oriented programming greatly influences our confidence with ActionScript in general.

For further advanced reading on object-oriented programming with ECMA-262–derived languages, see Netscape's documentation for JavaScript, *Details of the Object Model*:

> *http://developer.netscape.com/docs/manuals/js/core/jsguide/obj2.htm*

David Flanagan's canonical text, *JavaScript: The Definitive Guide* (O'Reilly & Associates, Inc.) also provides valuable information on OOP in JavaScript. For a general introduction to OOP from a Java perspective, see Sun's *Object Oriented Programming Concepts* (from The Java^tm Tutorial):

> *http://java.sun.com/docs/books/tutorial/java/concepts*

Built-in ActionScript Classes and Objects

We've really come a long way since Chapter 1, *A Gentle Introduction for Non-Programmers*. Our first exposure to the components of ActionScript was a simple perusal of the items under the + button in the Actions panel. Since then, we've learned about data and expressions, operators, statements, and functions, and now we've explored the concept of classes and objects. It's time to put the final brush strokes on the picture we've been painting of the ActionScript language.

ActionScript comes with a variety of syntactic tools: *expressions* contain data; *operators* manipulate data; *statements* give instructions; and *functions* group instructions into portable commands. These are tools, but they are *just* tools. They're the grammar we use to compose instructions in our scripts. What we're still missing is *subject matter*. By now we know perfectly well how to speak ActionScript, but we have nothing to talk about. The built-in classes and objects of ActionScript fill that void.

Built-in Classes

Just as we define our own classes to describe and manipulate objects created according to our specifications, ActionScript defines its own classes of data. A variety of prefabricated classes, including the *Object* class, are built right into the ActionScript language. The built-in classes can control the physical environment of a Flash movie.

For example, one of the built-in classes, the *Color* class, defines methods that can detect or set the color of a movie clip. To use these methods, we first create a *Color* object using the *Color()* class constructor, as follows:

```
clipColor = new Color(target);
```

where *clipColor* is the variable, array element, or object property that stores our *Color* object. The *Color()* constructor takes one argument, `target`, which specifies the name of the movie clip whose color we want to set or examine.

So, suppose we have a movie clip named **square**, and we want to change its color. We create a new *Color* object like this:

```
squareColor = new Color(square);
```

Then, to set our **square** clip's color, we invoke one of the *Color* methods on our **squareColor** object:

```
squareColor.setRGB(0x999999);
```

The *setRGB()* method sets the RGB color value of our *Color* object's **target**, which in this case is **square**, so the previous method invocation would set the color of **square** to gray.

Because the *Color* object is a built-in class, it can directly set the color of a movie clip. Still other classes give us control over sounds, the date, and XML documents. We'll learn all about the built-in classes in Part III, *Language Reference.*

Built-in Objects

Like built-in classes, built-in objects let us control the movie environment. The *Key* object, for example, defines a series of properties and methods that tell us about the state of a computer's keyboard. To use these properties and methods, we don't instantiate a *Key* object, we simply use the *Key* object directly. Built-in objects are made automatically by the interpreter when the Flash Player starts and are always available throughout a movie.

Here, for example, we display the keycode of the currently depressed key by invoking the *Key* object's *getCode()* method:

```
trace(Key.getCode());
```

And here, we check whether the spacebar is depressed using the *isDown()* method and supplying the spacebar's keycode as an argument:

```
trace(Key.isDown(Key.SPACE));
```

In Part III we'll learn about the other built-in objects—*Math*, *Mouse*, and *Selection*—which provide access to mathematical information, the mouse pointer, and text field selections.

Learning the Ropes

Learning to write valid ActionScript code is only half the job of learning to program in Flash. The other half comes with learning the available built-in classes and objects and their many wonderful properties and methods. We'll undertake that task in Part III. However, it's not necessary to study all the classes and objects in one sitting. Learn about movie clips to start and then branch out as you need to.

Over time, you'll come to know what's essential to get your particular job done. What's important is that you understand the general structure of object-oriented programming. Once you know the rules of the system, learning a new object or a new class is a simple matter of looking up its method and property names.

Onward!

We've certainly come a long way, and I hope you're still as enthusiastic about the journey as I am. Next we'll explore the most important class of objects available in ActionScript, the movie clip.

13

Movie Clips

Every Flash document contains a Stage—on which we place shapes, text, and other visual elements—and a main timeline, through which we define changes to the Stage's contents over time. The Stage (i.e., the *main movie*) may contain independent submovies, christened *movie clips* (or *clips* for short). Each movie clip has its own independent timeline and *canvas* (the Stage is the canvas of the main movie) and can even contain other movie clips. A clip that contains another clip is referred to as that clip's *host clip* or *parent clip*.

A single Flash document can contain a hierarchy of interrelated movie clips. For example, the main movie may contain a mountainous landscape. A separate movie clip containing an animated character can be moved across the landscape to give the illusion that the character is walking. Another movie clip inside the character clip can be used to independently animate the character's blinking eyes. When the independent elements in the cartoon character are played back together, they appear as a single piece of content. Furthermore, each component can react intelligently to the others—we can tell the eyes to blink when the character stops moving or tell the legs to walk when the character starts moving.

ActionScript offers detailed control over movie clips; we can play a clip, stop it, move its playhead within its timeline, programmatically set its properties (like its size, rotation, transparency level, and position on the Stage) and manipulate it as a true programming object. As a formal component of the ActionScript language, movie clips may be thought of as the raw material used to produce programmatically generated content in Flash. For example, a movie clip may serve as a ball or a paddle in a pong game, as an order form in a catalog web site, or simply as a container for background sounds in an animation. At the end of this chapter we'll use movie clips as the hands on a clock and the answers in a multiple-choice quiz.

The "Objectness" of Movie Clips

As of Flash 5, movie clips can be manipulated like the objects we learned about in Chapter 12, *Objects and Classes*. We may retrieve and set the properties of a clip, and we may invoke built-in or custom methods on a clip. Unlike other objects, an operation performed on a clip may have a visible or audible result in the Player.

Movie clips are not truly a type of object; there is no *MovieClip* class or constructor, nor can we use an object literal to instantiate a movie clip in our code. So what, then, are movie clips if not objects? They are members of their very own object-like datatype, called *movieclip* (we can prove it by executing *typeof* on a movie clip, which returns the string "movieclip"). The main difference between movie clips and true objects is how they are allocated (created) and deallocated (disposed of, or freed). For details, see Chapter 15, *Advanced Topics*. Despite this technicality, however, we nearly always treat movie clips exactly like objects.

So how does the "objectness" of movie clips affect our use of them in Action-Script? Most notably, it dictates the way we control clips and examine their properties. Movie clips can be controlled directly through built-in methods. For example:

```
eyes.play();
```

We can retrieve and set a movie clip's properties using the dot operator, just as we would access the properties of any object:

```
ball._xscale = 90;
var radius = ball._width / 2;
```

A variable in a movie clip is simply a property of that clip, and we can use the dot operator to set and retrieve variable values:

```
myClip.myVariable = 14;
x = myClip.myVariable;
```

Submovie clips can be treated as object properties of their parent movie clips. We therefore use the dot operator to access "nested" clips:

```
clipA.clipB.clipC.play();
```

and we use the reserved **_parent** property to refer to the clip containing the current clip:

```
_parent.clipC.play();
```

Treating clips as objects affords us all the luxuries of convenient syntax and flexible playback control. But our use of clips as objects also lets us manage clips as data; we can store a movie clip in an array element or a variable and even pass a clip reference to a function as an argument! Here, for example, is a function that moves a clip to a particular location on the screen:

```
function moveClip (clip, x, y) {
  clip._x = x;
  clip._y = y;
}
moveClip(ball, 14, 399);
```

Throughout the rest of this chapter, we'll learn the specifics of referencing, controlling, and manipulating movie clips as data objects.

Types of Movie Clips

Not all movie clips are created equal. In fact, there are three distinct types of clips available in Flash:

* Main movies

* Regular movie clips

* Smart Clips

In addition to these three official varieties, we may define four further subcategories, based on our use of regular movie clips:

* Process clips

* Script clips

* Linked clips

* Seed clips

While these latter unofficial categories are not formal terms used in ActionScript, they provide a useful way to think about programming with movie clips. Let's take a closer look at each movie clip type.

Main Movies

The *main movie* of a Flash document contains the basic timeline and Stage present in every document. The main movie is the foundation for all the content in the document, including all other movie clips. We sometimes call the main movie the *main timeline*, the *main movie timeline*, the *main Stage*, or simply the *root*.

Main movies may be manipulated in much the same way as regular movie clips, however:

* A main movie cannot be removed from a *.swf* file (although a *.swf* file, itself, may be removed from the Flash Player).

* The following movie clip methods do not work when invoked on a main movie: *duplicateMovieClip()*, *removeMovieClip()*, *swapDepths()*.

- Event handlers cannot be attached to a main movie.

- Main movies can be referenced through the built-in, global `_root` and `_leveln` properties.

Note that while each *.swf* file contains only one main movie, more than one *.swf* may reside in the Flash Player at once—we may load multiple *.swf* documents (and therefore multiple main movies) onto a stack of *levels* via the *loadMovie()* and *unloadMovie()* functions, which we'll study later.

Regular Movie Clips

Regular movie clips are the most common and fundamental content containers; they hold visual elements and sounds and can even react to user input and movie playback through event handlers. For JavaScript programmers who are used to working with DHTML, it may be helpful to think of the main movie as being analogous to an HTML document object and regular movie clips as being analogous to that document's layer objects.

Smart Clips

Introduced in Flash 5, a *Smart Clip* is a regular movie clip that includes a graphical user interface used to customize the clip's properties in the authoring tool. Smart Clips are typically developed by advanced programmers to provide an easy way for less-experienced Flash authors to customize a movie clip's behavior without knowing how the code of the clip works. We'll cover Smart Clips in detail in Chapter 16, *ActionScript Authoring Environment*.

Process Clips

A *process clip* is a movie clip used not for content but simply to repeatedly execute a block of code. Process clips may be built with an *enterFrame* event handler or with a timeline loop as we saw under "Timeline and Clip Event Loops" in Chapter 8, *Loop Statements*.

Process clips are ActionScript's unofficial alternative to the *setTimeout()* and *setInterval()* methods of the JavaScript window object.

Script Clips

Like a process clip, a *script clip* is an empty movie clip used not for content but for tracking some variable or executing some script. For example, we may use a script clip to hold event handlers that detect keypresses or mouse events.

Linked Clips

A *linked clip* is a movie clip that either exports from or imports into the Library of a movie. Export and import settings are available through every movie clip's Linkage option, found in the Library. We most often use linked clips when dynamically generating an instance of a clip directly from a Library symbol using the *attachMovie()* clip method, as we'll see later.

Seed Clips

Before the *attachMovie()* method was introduced in Flash 5, we used the *duplicateMovieClip()* function to create new movie clips based on some existing clip, called a *seed clip*. A *seed clip* is a movie clip that resides on stage solely for the purpose of being copied via *duplicateMovieClip()*. With the introduction of *attachMovie()*, the need for seed clips has diminished. However, we still use seed clips and *duplicateMovieClip()* when we wish to retain a clip's event handlers and transformations in the process of copying it.

In a movie that makes heavy use of *duplicateMovieClip()* to dynamically generate content, it's common to see a row of seed clips on the outskirts of the movie canvas. The seed clips are used only to derive duplicate clips and are, therefore, kept off stage.

Creating Movie Clips

We usually treat movie clips just like data objects—we set their properties with the dot operator; we invoke their methods with the function-call operator (parentheses); and we store them in variables, array elements, and object properties. We do not, however, create movie clips in the same way we create objects. We cannot literally describe a movie clip in our code as we might describe an object with an object literal. And we cannot generate a movie clip with a movie clip constructor function, like this:

```
myClip = new MovieClip();  // Nice try buddy, but it won't work
```

Instead, we create movie clips directly in the authoring tool, by hand. Once a clip is created, we can use commands such as *duplicateMovieClip()* and *attachMovie()* to make new, independent duplicates of it.

Movie Clip Symbols and Instances

Just as all object instances are based on one class or another, all movie clip instances are based on a template movie clip, called a *symbol* (sometimes called a *definition*). A movie clip's symbol acts as a model for the clip's content and structure. We must always have a movie clip symbol before we may generate a specific clip object. Using a symbol, we can both manually and programmatically create clips to be rendered in a movie.

A movie clip that is rendered on the Stage is called an *instance*. Instances are the individual clip objects that can be manipulated with ActionScript; a *symbol* is the mold from which all instances of a specific movie clip are derived. Movie clip symbols are created in the Flash authoring tool. To make a new, blank symbol, we follow these steps:

1. Select Insert → New Symbol. The Symbol Properties dialog box appears.
2. In the Name field, type an identifier for the symbol.
3. Select the Movie Clip radio button.
4. Click OK.

Normally, the next step is to fill in the symbol's canvas and timeline with the content of our movie clip. Once a symbol has been created, it resides in the Library, waiting for us to use it to fashion an actual movie clip instance. It is, however, also possible to convert a group of shapes and objects that already exist on stage into a movie clip symbol. To do so, we follow these steps:

1. Select the desired shapes and objects.
2. Select Insert → Convert to Symbol.
3. In the Name field, type an identifier for the symbol.
4. Select the Movie Clip radio button.
5. Click OK.

The shapes and objects we selected to create the new movie clip symbol will be replaced by an unnamed instance of that new clip. The corresponding movie clip symbol will appear in the Library, ready to be used to create further instances.

Creating Instances

There are three ways to create a new instance based on a movie clip symbol. Two of these are programmatic; the other is strictly manual and is undertaken in the Flash authoring tool.

Manually creating instances

We can create movie clip instances manually using the Library in the Flash authoring environment. By physically dragging a movie clip symbol out of the Library and onto the Stage, we generate a new instance. An instance thus created should be named manually via the Instance panel. (We'll learn more about instance names later.) Refer to "Using Symbols and Instances" in the Macromedia Flash Help if you've never worked with movie clips in Flash.

Creating instances with duplicateMovieClip()

Any instance that already resides on the Stage of a Flash movie can be duplicated with ActionScript. We can then treat that independent copy as a completely separate clip. Both manually created and programmatically created clip instances may be duplicated. In other words, it's legal to duplicate a duplicate.

In practice, there are two ways to duplicate an instance using *duplicateMovieClip()*:

- We can invoke *duplicateMovieClip()* as a global function, using the following syntax:

  ```
  duplicateMovieClip(target, newName, depth);
  ```

  where **target** is a string indicating the name of the instance we want to duplicate. The **newName** parameter is a string that specifies the identifier for the new instance, and **depth** is an integer that designates where, in the stack of programmatically generated clips, we want to place the new instance.

- We can also invoke *duplicateMovieClip()* as a method of an existing instance:

  ```
  myClip.duplicateMovieClip(newName, depth);
  ```

  where **myClip** is the name of the clip we wish to duplicate, and **newName** and **depth** both operate as before.

When created via *duplicateMovieClip()*, an instance is initially positioned directly on top of its seed clip. Our first post-duplication task, therefore, is usually moving the duplicated clip to a new position. For example:

```
ball.duplicateMovieClip("ball2", 0);
ball2._x += 100;
ball2._y += 50;
```

Duplicated instances whose seed clips have been transformed (e.g., colored, rotated, or resized) via ActionScript or manually in the Flash authoring tool inherit the initial transformation of their seed clips. Subsequent transformations to the seed clip do not affect duplicated instances. Likewise, each instance can be transformed separately. For example, if a seed clip is rotated 45 degrees and then an instance is duplicated, the instance's initial rotation is 45 degrees:

```
seed._rotation = 45;
seed.duplicateMovieClip("newClip", 0);
trace(newClip._rotation);  // Displays: 45
```

If we then rotate the instance by 10 degrees, its rotation is 55 degrees, but the seed clip's rotation is still 45 degrees:

```
newClip._rotation += 10;
trace(newClip._rotation);  // Displays: 55
trace(seed._rotation);     // Displays: 45
```

By duplicating many instances in a row and adjusting the transformation of each duplicate slightly, we can achieve interesting compound transformations (the technique is shown under the *load* event in Example 10-2).

Using *duplicateMovieClip()* to duplicate clips via ActionScript offers other advantages over placing clips manually in a movie, such as the ability to:

- Control exactly when a clip appears on the Stage relative to a program's execution.

- Control exactly when a clip is removed from the Stage relative to a program's execution.

- Assign the layer depth of a duplicated clip relative to other duplicated clips. (This was more of a concern in Flash 4, which did not allow the layer stack of a movie to be altered.)

- Copy a clip's event handlers.

These abilities give us advanced programmatic control over the content in a movie. A salient example is that of a spaceship game in which a missile movie clip might be duplicated when the ship's fire button is pressed. That missile clip might be moved programmatically, then placed behind an obstacle in the movie, and finally, be removed after colliding with an enemy craft. Manual clips do not offer that kind of flexibility. With a manually created clip, we must preordain the birth and death of the clip using the timeline and, in Flash 4, we couldn't change the clip's layer.

Creating instances with attachMovie()

Like *duplicateMovieClip()*, the *attachMovie()* method lets us create a movie clip instance; however, unlike *duplicateMovieClip()* it does not require a previously created instance—it creates a new instance directly from a symbol in a movie's Library. In order to use *attachMovie()* to create an instance of a symbol, we must first export that symbol from the Library. Here's how:

1. In the Library, select the desired symbol.

2. In the Library's Options menu, select Linkage. The Symbol Linkage Properties dialog box appears.

3. Select the Export This Symbol radio button.

4. In the Identifier field, type a unique name for the clip symbol. The name may be any string—often simply the same name as the symbol itself—but should be different from all other exported clip symbols.

5. Click OK.

Once a clip symbol has been exported, we may attach new instances of that symbol to an existing clip by invoking *attachMovie()* with the following syntax:

```
myClip.attachMovie(symbolIdentifier, newName, depth);
```

where **myClip** is the name of the clip to which we want to attach the new instance. If **myClip** is omitted, *attachMovie()* attaches the new instance to the current clip (the clip on which the *attachMovie()* statement resides). The **symbolIdentifier** parameter is a string containing the name of the symbol we're using to generate our instance, as specified in the Identifier field of the Linkage options in the Library; **newName** is a string that specifies the identifier for the new instance we're creating; and **depth** is an integer that designates where in the host clip's layered stack to place the new instance.

When we attach an instance to another clip, that instance is positioned in the center of the clip, among the clip's layered stack (we'll discuss clip stacks soon). When we attach an instance to the main movie of a document, that instance is positioned in the upper-left corner of the Stage, at coordinates (0, 0).

Instance Names

When we create instances, we assign them identifiers, or *instance names*, that allow us to refer to them later. Notice how this differs from regular objects. When we create a normal data object (not a movie clip), we must assign that object to a variable or other data container in order for the object to persist and in order for us to refer to it by name in the future. For example:

```
new Object();              // Object dies immediately after it's created,
                           // and we can't refer to it
var thing = new Object();  // Object reference is stored in thing,
                           // and can later be referred to as thing
```

Movie clip instances need not be stored in variables in order for us to refer to them. Unlike normal data objects, clip instances are accessible in ActionScript via their instance names as soon as they are created. For example:

```
ball._y = 200;
```

Each clip's instance name is stored in its built-in property, **_name**, which can be both retrieved and set:

```
ball._name = "circle";  // Change ball's name to circle
```

When we change an instance's **_name** property, all future references to the instance must use the new name. For example, after the previous code executes, the **ball** reference ceases to exist, and we'd subsequently use **circle** to refer to the instance.

The manner in which an instance initially gets its instance name depends on how it was created. Programmatically generated instances are named by the function that creates them. Manually created instances are normally assigned explicit instance names in the authoring tool through the Instance panel, as follows:

1. Select the instance on stage.

2. Select Modify → Instance.

3. Enter the instance name into the Name field.

If a manually created clip is not given an instance name, it is assigned one automatically by the Flash Player at runtime. Automatic instance names fall in the sequence `instance1`, `instance2`, `instance3`...`instancen`, but these names don't meaningfully describe our clip's content (and we must guess at the automatic name that was generated).

Because instance names are identifiers, we must compose them according to the rules for creating a legal identifier, as described in Chapter 14, *Lexical Structure*. Most notably, instance names should not begin with a number, nor include hyphens or spaces.

Importing External Movies

We've discussed creating movie clip instances within a single document, but the Flash Player can also display multiple *.swf* documents simultaneously. We can use *loadMovie()* (as either a global function or a movie clip method) to import an external *.swf* file into the Player and place it either in a clip instance or on a numbered level above the base movie (i.e., in the foreground relative to the base movie). By managing content in separate files, we gain precise control over the download process. Suppose, for example, we have a movie containing a main navigation menu and five subsections. Before the user can navigate to section five, sections one through four must have finished downloading. But if we place each section in a separate *.swf* file, the sections can be loaded in an arbitrary order, giving the user direct access to each section.

When an external *.swf* is loaded into a level, its main movie timeline becomes the root timeline of that level, and it replaces any prior movie loaded in that level. Similarly when an external movie is loaded into a clip, the main timeline of the loaded movie replaces that clip's timeline, unloading the existing graphics, sounds, and scripts in that clip.

Like *duplicateMovieClip()*, *loadMovie()* may be used both as a standalone function and an instance method. The standalone syntax of *loadMovie()* is as follows:

```
loadMovie(URL, location)
```

where *URL* specifies the address of the external *.swf* file to load. The `location` parameter is a string indicating the path to an existing clip or a document level that should host the new *.swf* file (i.e., where the loaded movie should be placed). For example:

```
loadMovie("circle.swf", "_level1");
loadMovie("photos.swf", "viewClip");
```

Because a movie clip reference is converted to a path when used as a string, `location` may also be supplied as a movie clip reference, such as `_level1` instead of `"_level1"`. Take care when using references, however. If the reference supplied does not point to a valid clip, the *loadMovie()* function has unexpected behavior—it loads the external *.swf* into the *current* timeline. See Part III, *Language Reference* for more details, or see "Method versus global function overlap issues," later in this chapter.

The clip method version of *loadMovie()* has the following syntax:

```
myClip.loadMovie(URL);
```

When used as a method, *loadMovie()* assumes we're loading the external *.swf* into `myClip`, so the `location` parameter required by the standalone *loadMovie()* function is not needed. We, therefore, supply only the path to the *.swf* to load via the *URL* parameter. Naturally, *URL* can be a local filename, such as:

```
viewClip.loadMovie("photos.swf");
```

When placed into a clip instance, a loaded movie adopts the properties of that clip (e.g., the clip's scale, rotation, color transformation, etc.).

Note that `myClip` must exist in order for *loadMovie()* to be used in its method form. For example, the following attempt to load *circle.swf* will fail if `_level1` is empty:

```
_level1.loadMovie("circle.swf");
```

Load movie execution order

The *loadMovie()* function is not immediately executed when it appears in a statement block. In fact, it is not executed until *all* other statements in the block have finished executing.

We cannot access an externally loaded movie's properties or methods in the same statement block as the *loadMovie()* invocation that loads it into the Player.

Using loadMovie() with attachMovie()

Loading an external *.swf* file into a clip instance with *loadMovie()* has a surprising result—it prevents us from attaching instances to that clip via *attachMovie()*. Once a clip has an external *.swf* file loaded into it, that clip may no longer bear attached movies from the Library from which it originated. For example, if *movie1.swf* contains an instance named `clipA`, and we load *movie2.swf* into `clipA`, we may no longer attach instances from *movie1.swf*'s Library to `clipA`.

Why? The *attachMovie()* method works only within a *single* document. That is, we can't attach instances from one document's Library to another document. When we load a *.swf* file into a clip, we are populating that clip with a new document and, hence, a new (different) Library. Subsequent attempts to attach instances from our original document to the clip fail because the clip's Library no longer matches its original document's Library. However, if we unload the document in the clip via *unloadMovie()*, we regain the ability to attach movies to the clip from its own document Library.

Similarly, loading a *.swf* file into a clip with *loadMovie()* prevents us from copying that clip via *duplicateMovieClip()*.

Because *loadMovie()* loads an external file (usually over a network), its execution is *asynchronous*. That is, *loadMovie()* may finish at any time, depending on the speed of the file transfer. Therefore, before we access a loaded movie, we should always check that the movie has finished transferring to the Player. We do so with what's commonly called a *preloader*—a simple bit of code that checks how much of a file has loaded before allowing some action to take place. Preloaders can be built with the **_totalframes** and **_framesloaded** movie clip properties and the *getBytesLoaded()* and *getBytesTotal()* movie clip methods. See the appropriate entries in Part III for sample code. See also Example 10-4, which shows how to build a preloader using the *data* clip event.

Movie and Instance Stacking Order

All movie clip instances and externally loaded movies displayed in the Player reside in a visual stacking order akin to a deck of cards. When instances or externally loaded *.swf* files overlap in the Player, one clip (the "higher" of the two) always covers up the other clip (the "lower" of the two). Simple enough in principle, but the main stack, which contains *all* the instances and *.swf* files, is actually divided into many smaller substacks. We'll look at these substacks individually first, then see how they combine to form the main stack. (The stack in this discussion has no direct relation to the LIFO and FIFO stacks discussed in Chapter 11, *Arrays.*)

The Internal Layer Stack

Instances created *manually* in the Flash authoring tool reside in a stack called the *internal layer stack*. This stack's order is governed by the actual layers in a movie's timeline; when two manually created instances on separate timeline layers overlap, the instance on the uppermost layer obscures the instance on the lowermost layer.

Furthermore, because multiple clips may reside on a single timeline layer, each layer in the internal layer stack actually maintains its *own* ministack. Overlapping clips that reside on the same layer of a timeline are stacked in the authoring tool via the Modify → Arrange commands.

As of Flash 5, we can swap the position of two instances in the internal layer stack using the *swapDepths()* method, provided they reside on the same timeline (that is, the value of the two clips' **_parent** property must be the same). Prior to Flash 5, there was no way to alter the internal layer stack via ActionScript.

The Programmatically Generated Clip Stack

Programmatically generated instances are stacked separately from the *manually* created instances held in the internal layer stack. Each instance has its own *programmatically generated clip stack* that hold clips created via *duplicateMovieClip()* and *attachMovie()*. The stacking order for these clips varies depending on how they were created.

How clips generated via attachMovie() are added to the stack

A new instance generated via *attachMovie()* is always stacked above (i.e., in the foreground relative to) the clip to which it was attached. For example, suppose we have two clips—X and Y—in the internal layer structure of a movie and that X resides on a layer above Y. Now further suppose we attach a new clip, A, to X and a new clip, B, to Y:

```
x.attachMovie("A", "A", 0);
y.attachMovie("B", "B", 0);
```

In our scenario, the clips would appear from top to bottom in this order: A, X, B, Y, as shown in Figure 13-1.

Once a clip is generated, it too provides a separate space above its content for more programmatically generated clips. That is, we may attach clips to attached clips.

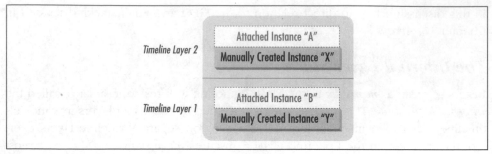

Figure 13-1. A sample instance stack

Clips attached to the `_root` movie of a Flash document are placed in the `_root` movie's programmatically generated clip stack, which appears in front of *all* clips in the `_root` movie, even those that contain programmatically generated content.

Let's extend our earlier example. If we were to attach clip C to the `_root` of the movie that contained clips X, Y, A, and B, then clip C would appear in front of all the other clips. Figure 13-2 shows the extended structure.

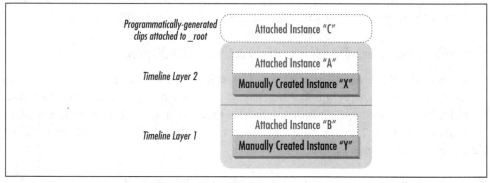

Figure 13-2. An instance stack showing a clip attached to _root

How clips generated via duplicateMovieClip() are added to the stack

Each instance duplicated via *duplicateMovieClip()* is assigned to a programmatic stack in accordance with how that instance's seed clip was created:

- If the instance's seed clip was created manually (or was duplicated using *duplicateMovieClip()* from a clip that was created manually), then the new instance is placed in the stack above `_root`.

- If, on the other hand, the instance's seed clip was created with *attachMovie()*, then the new instance is placed in its seed clip's stack.

Let's return to our example to see how this works. If we create clip D by duplicating clip X (which was created manually), then clip D is placed in the stack above `_root`, with clip C. Similarly, if we create clip E by duplicating clip D (which is derived from clip X, which was created manually), then E is also placed in the stack above _root, with C and D. *But* if we create clip F by duplicating clip A (which was created with *attachMovie()*), then F is placed in the stack above X, with clip A. Figure 13-3 is worth a thousand words.

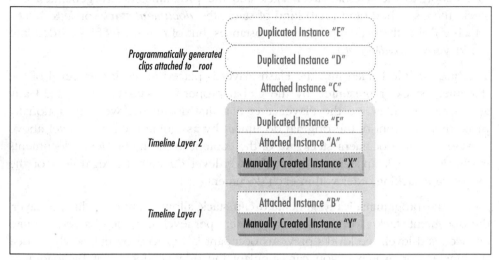

Figure 13-3. An instance stack showing various duplicated clips

Assigning depths to instances in the programmatically generated clip stack

You may be wondering what determines the stacking order of clips C, D, and E, or of clips A and F in Figure 13-3. The stacking order of a programmatically generated clip is determined by the *depth* argument passed to the *attachMovie()* or *duplicateMovieClip()* function, and can be changed at any time using the *swapDepths()* function. Each programmatically generated clip's *depth* (sometimes called its *z-index*) determines its position within a particular stack of programmatically generated clips.

The *depth* of a clip may be any integer and is measured from the bottom up, so −1 is lower than 0; 1 is higher than (i.e., in front of) depth 0; depth 2 is higher still, and so on. When two programmatically generated clips occupy the same position on screen, the one with the *greater depth* value is rendered in front of the other.

Layers are single-occupant dwellings. Only one clip may occupy a layer in the stack at a time—placing a clip into an occupied layer displaces (and deletes) the layer's previous occupant.

It's okay for there to be gaps in the depths of clips; you can have a clip at depth 0, another at depth 500, and a third one at depth 1000. There's no performance hit or increase in memory consumption that results from having gaps in your depth assignments.

The .swf Document "_level" Stack

In addition to the internal layer stack and the programmatically generated clip stack, there's a third (and final) kind of stack, the *document stack* (or *level stack*), which governs the overlapping not of instances, but of entire .*swf* files loaded into the Player via *loadMovie()*.

The first .*swf* file loaded into the Flash Player is placed in the lowest level of the document stack (represented by the global property _level0). If we load any additional .*swf* files into the Player after that first document, we may optionally place them in front of the original document by assigning them to a level above _level0 in the document stack. All of the content in the higher-level documents in the level stack appears in front of lower-level documents, regardless of the movie clip stacking order within each document.

Just as the programmatically generated clip stack allows only one clip per layer, the document stack allows only one document per level. If we load a .*swf* file into an occupied level, the level's previous occupant is replaced by the newly loaded document. For example, you can supplant the original document by loading a new .*swf* file into _level0. Loading a new .*swf* file into _level1 would visually obscure the movie in _level0, but not remove it from the Player.

Figure 13-4 summarizes the relationships of the various stacks maintained by the Flash Player.

Stacks and Order of Execution

The layering of movie clips and timeline layers affects code execution order. The rules are as follows:

- Code on frames in different timeline layers always executes from top to bottom.

- When manually created instances are initially loaded, code in their timeline and *load* event handlers executes according to the Load Order set in the Publish Settings of a Flash document—either Bottom Up, which is the default, or Top Down.

  For example, suppose we have a timeline with two layers, *top* and *bottom*, where *top* is above *bottom* in the layer stack. We place clip X on layer *top* and clip Y on layer *bottom*. If the Load Order of the document is set to Bottom Up, then the code in clip Y will execute before the code in clip X. If, on the other hand, the Load Order of the document is set to Top Down, then the code in

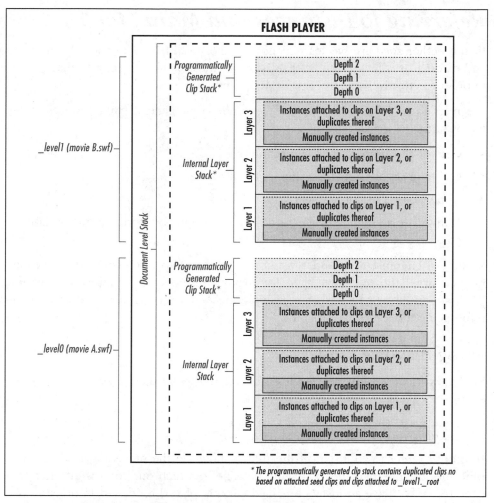

Figure 13-4. The complete Flash Player movie clip stack

clip X will execute before the code in clip Y. This execution order applies *only* to the frame on which X and Y appear for the first time.

- Once loaded, all instances of a movie are added to an execution order, which is the reverse of the load order; the last instance added to the movie is always the first to have its code executed.

Use caution when relying on these rules. Layers are mutable, so you should avoid producing code that relies on their relative position. Strive to create code that executes safely without relying on the execution order of the clips in the stack. We can avoid some of the issues presented by the execution stack by keeping all our code on a *scripts* layer at the top of each code-bearing timeline.

Referring to Instances and Main Movies

In the earlier sections, we learned how to create and layer movie clip instances and external *.swf* files in the Flash Player. We must be able to refer to that content in order to effectively control it with ActionScript.

We refer to instances and main movies under four general circumstances, when we want to:

- Get or set a property of a clip or a movie

- Create or invoke a method of a clip or a movie

- Apply some function to a clip or a movie

- Manipulate a clip or a movie as data, for example, by storing it in a variable or passing it as an argument to a function

While the circumstances under which we refer to clip instances and movies are fairly simple, the tools we have for making references are many and varied. We'll spend the rest of this section exploring ActionScript's instance- and movie-referencing tools.

Using Instance Names

Earlier, we learned that movie clips are referred to by their *instance names*. For example:

```
trace(myVariable);  // Refer to a variable
trace(myClip);      // Refer to a movie clip
```

In order to refer to an instance directly (as shown in the preceding *trace()* example), the instance must reside on the timeline to which our code is attached. For example, if we have an instance named `clouds` placed on the main timeline of a document, we may refer to `clouds` from code attached to the main timeline as follows:

```
// Set a property of the instance
clouds._alpha = 60;
// Invoke a method on the instance
clouds.play();
// Place the instance in an array of other related instances
var background = [clouds, sky, mountains];
```

If the instance we want to reference does not reside on the same timeline as our code, we must use a more elaborate syntax, as described later under "Referring to Nested Instances."

Referring to the Current Instance or Movie

We don't always have to use an instance's name when referring to a clip. Code attached to a frame in an instance's timeline may refer to that instance's properties and methods directly, without any instance name.

For example, to set the `_alpha` property of a clip named `cloud`, we could place the following code on a frame in the `cloud` timeline:

```
_alpha = 60;
```

Similarly, to invoke the *play()* method on `cloud` from a frame in the `cloud` timeline, we could simply use:

```
play();
```

This technique may be used on any timeline, including timelines of main movies. For example, the following two statements would be synonymous if attached to a frame on the main timeline of a Flash document. The first refers to the main movie implicitly, whereas the second refers to the main movie explicitly via the global `_root` property:

```
gotoAndStop(20);
_root.gotoAndStop(20);
```

As we learned in Chapter 10, *Events and Event Handlers*, code in an instance's event handler may, like timeline code, also refer to properties and methods directly. For example, we could attach the following event handler to `cloud`. This handler sets a property of, and then invokes a method on, `cloud` without referring to the `cloud` instance explicitly:

```
onClipEvent (load) {
  _alpha = 60;
  stop();
}
```

However, not all methods may be used with an implicit reference to a movie clip. Any movie clip method that has the same name as a corresponding global function (such as *duplicateMovieClip()* or *unloadMovie()*) must be invoked with an explicit instance reference. Hence, when in doubt, use an explicit reference. We'll have more to say about method and global function conflicts later in "Method versus global function overlap issues."

Self-references with the this keyword

When we want to *explicitly* refer to the current instance from a frame in its timeline or from one of its event handlers, we may use the `this` keyword. For example, the following statements would be synonymous when attached to a frame in the time-line of our `cloud` instance:

```
_alpha = 60;       // Implicit reference to the current timeline
this._alpha = 60;  // Explicit reference to the current timeline
```

There are two reasons to use `this` to refer to a clip even when we can just refer to the clip directly. When used without an explicit instance reference, certain movie clip methods are mistaken for global functions by the interpreter. If we omit the `this` reference, the interpreter thinks we're trying to invoke the analogous global function and complains that we're missing the "target" movie clip parameter. To work around the problem, we use `this`, as follows:

```
this.duplicateMovieClip("newClouds", 0);  // Invoke a method on an instance

// If we omit the this reference, we get an error
duplicateMovieClip("newClouds", 0);  // Oops!
```

Using `this`, we can conveniently pass a reference to the current timeline to functions that operate on movie clips:

```
// Here's a function that manipulates clips
function moveTo (theClip, x, y) {
  theClip._x = x;
  theClip._y = y;
}

// Now let's invoke it on the current timeline
moveTo(this, 150, 125);
```

If you do a lot of object-oriented programming, be cautious when using the `this` keyword to refer to instances and movies. Remember that inside a custom method or an object constructor, `this` has a very different meaning and is not a reference to the current timeline. See Chapter 12 for details.

Referring to Nested Instances

As we learned in the introduction to this chapter, movie clip instances are often nested inside of one another. That is, a clip's canvas may contain an instance of another clip, which may itself contain instances of other clips. For example, a game's `spaceship` clip may contain an instance of a `blinkingLights` clip or a `burningFuel` clip. Or a character's `face` clip may include separate `eyes`, `nose`, and `mouth` clips.

Earlier, we saw briefly how we could navigate up or down from any point in the hierarchy of clip instances, much like you might navigate up and down a series of subdirectories on your hard drive. Let's examine this in more detail and see some more examples.

Let's first consider how to refer to a clip instance that is nested *inside* of the current instance. When a clip is placed on the timeline of another clip, it becomes a property of that clip, and we can access it as we would access any object property (with the dot operator). For example, suppose we place clipB on the canvas of clipA. To access clipB from a frame in clipA's timeline, we use a direct reference to clipB:

```
clipB._x = 30;
```

Now suppose clipB contains another instance, clipC. To refer to clipC from a frame in clipA's timeline, we access clipC as a property of clipB like this:

```
clipB.clipC.play();
clipB.clipC._x = 20;
```

Beautiful, ain't it? And the system is infinitely extensible. Because every clip instance placed on another clip's timeline becomes a property of its host clip, we can traverse the hierarchy by separating the instances with the dot operator, like so:

```
clipA.clipB.clipC.clipD.gotoAndStop(5);
```

Now that we've seen how to navigate down the instance hierarchy, let's see how we navigate *up* it to refer to the instance or movie that contains the current instance. As we saw earlier, every instance has a built-in _parent property that refers to the clip or main movie containing it. We use the _parent property like so:

```
myClip._parent
```

Recalling our recent example with clipA on the main timeline, clipB inside clipA, and clipC inside clipB, let's see how to use _parent and dot notation to refer to the various clips in the hierarchy. Assume that the following code is placed on a frame of the timeline of clipB:

```
_parent        // A reference to clipA
this           // A reference to clipB (the current clip)
this._parent   // Another reference to clipA

// Sweet Sheila, I love this stuff! Let's try some more...
_parent._parent // A reference to clipA's parent (clipB's grandparent),
                // which is the main timeline in this case
```

Note that although it is legal to do so, it is unnecessarily roundabout to traverse *down* the hierarchy using a reference to the clipC property of clipB only to traverse back *up* the hierarchy using _parent. These roundabout references are unnecessary but do show the flexibility of dot notation:

```
clipC._parent     // A roundabout reference to clipB (the current timeline)
clipC._parent._parent._parent  // A roundabout reference to the main timeline
```

Notice how we use the dot operator to descend the clip hierarchy and use the _parent property to ascend it. If this is new to you, you should probably try building the clipA, clipB, clipC hierarchy in Flash and using the code in our example. Proper instance referencing is one of the fundamental skills of a good ActionScript programmer.

Note that the hierarchy of clips is like a family tree. Unlike a typical family tree of a sexually reproducing species in which each offspring has two parents, our clip family tree expands asexually. That is, each household is headed by a single parent who can adopt any number of children. Any clip (i.e., any *node* in the tree) can have one and only one parent (the clip that contains it) but can have multiple *children* (the clips that it contains). Of course, each clip's parent can in turn have a single parent, which means that each clip can have only one grandparent (not the four grandparents humans typically have). See Figure 13-5.

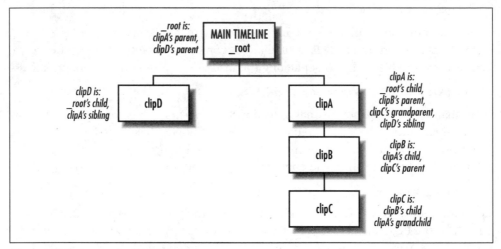

Figure 13-5. A sample clip hierarchy

Therefore, no matter how far you go down the family tree, if you go back up the same number of steps you will always end up in the same place you started. It is therefore pointless to go down the hierarchy only to come back up. However, it is *not* pointless to go up the hierarchy and then follow a *different* path back down. For example, suppose that the main timeline also contains clipD, which would make clipD a "sibling" of clipA because both would have the main timeline as their _parent. In that case, you can refer to clipD from a script attached to clipB as follows:

```
_parent._parent.clipD    // This refers to clipD, a child of the main
                         // timeline (clipA's _parent) and therefore
                         // a sibling of clipA
```

Note that the main timeline does not have a _parent property (main movies are the top of any clip hierarchy and cannot be contained by another timeline); references to _root._parent yield undefined.

Referring to Main Movies with _root and _leveln

Now that we've seen how to navigate up and down the clip hierarchy *relative* to the current clip, let's explore other ways to navigate along *absolute* pathways and even among other documents stored in other levels of the Player's document stack. In earlier chapters, we saw how these techniques applied to variables and functions; here we'll learn how they can be used to control movie clips.

Referencing the current level's main movie using _root

When an instance is deeply nested in a clip hierarchy, we can repeatedly use the **_parent** property to ascend the hierarchy until we reach the main movie timeline. But in order to ease the labor of referring to the main timeline from deeply nested clips, we can also use the built-in global property **_root**, which is a shortcut reference to the main movie timeline. For example, here we play the main movie:

```
_root.play();
```

The **_root** property is said to be an *absolute* reference to a known point in the clip hierarchy because unlike the **_parent** and **this** properties, which are relative to the current clip, the **_root** property is the same no matter which clip it is referenced from. These are all equivalent:

```
_parent._root
this._root
_root
```

Therefore, you can and should use **_root** when you don't know where a given clip is nested within the hierarchy. For example, consider the following hierarchy in which **circle** is a child of the main movie timeline and **square** is a child of **circle**:

```
main timeline
   circle
      square
```

Now consider this script attached to a frame in both **circle** and **square**:

```
_parent._x += 10  // Move this clip's parent clip 10 pixels to the right
```

When that code is executed from within **circle**, it will cause the main movie to move 10 pixels to the right. When it is executed from within **square**, it will cause **circle** (not the main movie) to move 10 pixels to the right. In order for the script to move the main movie 10 pixels regardless of where the script is executed from, it should be rewritten as:

```
_root._x += 10    // Move the main movie 10 pixels to the right
```

Furthermore, the `_parent` property is not valid from within the main timeline; the version of the script using `_root` would be valid when used in a frame of the main timeline.

The `_root` property may happily be combined with ordinary instance references to descend a nested-clip hierarchy:

```
_root.clipA.clipB.play();
```

References that start with `_root` refer to the same, known, starting point from anywhere in a document. There's no guessing required.

Referencing other documents in the Player using _leveln

If we have multiple *.swf* files loaded in the document stack of the Flash Player, we may refer to the main movie timelines of the various documents using the built-in series of global properties `_level0` through `_leveln`, where *n* represents the level of the document we want to reference.

Therefore, `_level0` represents the document in the lowest level of the document stack (documents in higher levels will be rendered in the foreground). Unless a movie has been loaded into `_level0` via *loadMovie()*, `_level0` is occupied by the movie that was initially loaded when the Player started.

Here is an example that plays the main movie timeline of the document in level 3 of the Player's document stack:

```
_level3.play();
```

Like the `_root` property, the `_leveln` property may be combined with ordinary instance references via the dot operator:

```
_level1.clipA.stop();
```

As with references to `_root`, references to `_leveln` properties are called *absolute references* because they lead to the same destination from any point in a document.

Note that `_leveln` and `_root` are not synonymous. The `_root` property is always the *current* document's main timeline, regardless of the level on which the current document resides, whereas the `_leveln` property is a reference to the main timeline of a specific document level. For example, suppose we place the code `_root.play()` in *myMovie.swf.* When we load *myMovie.swf* onto level 5, our code plays `_level5`'s main movie timeline. By contrast, if we place the code `_level2.play()` in *myMovie.swf* and load *myMovie.swf* into level 5, our code plays `_level2`'s main movie timeline not `_level5`'s. Of course, from within level 2, `_root` and `_level2` are equivalent.

Authoring Instance References with Insert Target Path

When the instance structure of a movie gets very complicated, composing references to movie clips and main movies can be laborious. We may not always recall the exact hierarchy of a series of clips, and, hence, may end up frequently selecting and editing clips in the authoring tool just to determine their nested structure. The ActionScript editor provides an Insert Target Path tool (shown in Figure 13-6) which lets us generate a clip reference visually, relieving the burden of creating it manually.

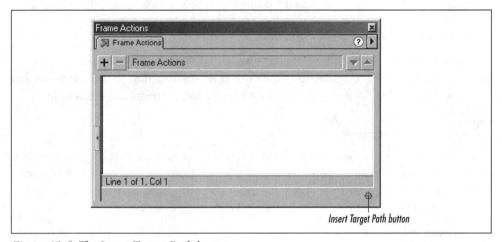

Figure 13-6. The Insert Target Path button

To use Insert Target Path, follow these steps:

1. Position the cursor in your code where you want a clip reference to be inserted.

2. Click the Insert Target Path button, shown in Figure 13-6.

3. In the Insert Target Path dialog box, select the clip to which you want to refer.

4. Choose whether to insert an *absolute reference*, which begins with _root, or a *relative reference*, which expresses the reference to the target clip in relation to the clip that contains your code.

5. If you are exporting to Flash 4 format, choose the Slashes Notation button for Flash 4 compatibility. (The Dot Notation button, selected by default, composes references that won't work in Flash 4). See Table 2-1.

The Insert Target Path tool cannot generate references that ascend a hierarchy of clips. That is, the tool cannot be used to refer to a clip that contains the current clip (unless you want to begin the path from _root and proceed downward). To create references that ascend the clip hierarchy, we must manually type the appropriate references in our code using the `_parent` property.

Dynamic References to Clip Objects

Normally, we know the name of the specific instance or movie we are manipulating, but there are times when we'd like to control a clip whose name we don't know. We may, for example, want to scale down a whole group of clips using a loop or create a button that refers to a different clip each time it is clicked. To handle these situations, we must create our clip references dynamically at runtime.

Using the array-element access operator

As we saw in Chapter 5, *Operators*, and Chapter 12, *Objects and Classes*, the properties of an object may be retrieved via the dot operator or through the array-element access operator, `[]`. For example, the following two statements are equivalent:

```
myObject.myProperty = 10;
myObject["myProperty"] = 10;
```

The array-element access operator has one important feature that the dot operator does not; it lets us (indeed requires us to) refer to a property using a *string expression* rather than an *identifier*. For example, here's a string concatenation expression that acts as a valid reference to the property **myProperty**:

```
myObject["myProp" + "erty"];
```

We can apply the same technique to create our instance and movie references dynamically. We already learned that clip instances are stored as properties of their parent clips. Earlier, we used the dot operator to refer to those instance properties. For example, from the main timeline we can refer to **clipB**, which is nested inside of another instance, **clipA**, as follows:

```
clipA.clipB;        // Refer to clipB inside clipA
clipA.clipB.stop(); // Invoke a method on clipB
```

Because instances are properties, we can also legitimately refer to them with the `[]` operator, as in:

```
clipA["clipB"];        // Refer to clipB inside clipA
clipA["clipB"].stop(); // Invoke a method on clipB
```

Notice that when we use the `[]` operator to refer to **clipB**, we provide the name of **clipB** as a string, not an identifier. That string reference may be any valid string-yielding expression. For example, here's a reference to **clipB** that involves a string concatenation:

```
var clipCount = "B";
clipA["clip" + clipCount];         // Refer to clipB inside clipA
clipA["clip" + clipCount].stop();  // Invoke a method on clipB
```

We can create clip references dynamically to refer to a series of sequentially named clips:

```
// Stop clip1, clip2, clip3, and clip4
for (var i = 1; i <= 4; i++) {
  _root["clip" + i].stop();
}
```

Now that's powerful!

Storing references to clips in data containers

I started this chapter by saying that movie clips are effectively data objects in ActionScript. We can store a reference to a movie clip instance in a variable, an array element, or an object property.

Recall our earlier example of a nested instance hierarchy (clipC nested inside clipB nested inside clipA) placed on the main timeline of a document. If we store those various clips in data containers, we can control them dynamically using the containers instead of explicit references to the clips. Example 13-1, which shows code that would be placed on a frame in the main timeline, uses data containers to store and control instances.

Example 13-1. Storing Clip References in Variables and Arrays

```
var x = clipA.clipB;   // Store a reference to clipB in the variable x
x.play();              // Play clipB

// Now let's store our clips in the elements of an array
var myClips = [clipA, clipA.clipB, clipA.clipB.clipC];
myClips[0].play();     // Play clipA
myClips[1]._x = 200;   // Place clipB 200 pixels from the Stage's left edge

// Stop all the clips in our array using a loop
for (var i = 0; i < myClips.length; i++) {
  myClips[i].stop();
}
```

By storing clip references in data containers, we can manipulate the clips (such as playing, rotating, or stopping them) without knowing or affecting the document's clip hierarchy.

Using for-in to access movie clips

In Chapter 8, we learned how to enumerate an object's properties using a *for-in* loop. Recall that a *for-in* loop's iterator variable automatically cycles through all the properties of the object, so that the loop is executed once for each property:

```
for (var prop in someObject) {
  trace("the value of someObject." + prop + " is " + someObject[prop]);
}
```

Example 13-2 shows how to use a *for-in* loop to enumerate all the clips that reside on a given timeline.

Example 13-2. Finding Movie Clips on a Timeline

```
for (var property in myClip) {
  // Check if the current property of myClip is a movie clip
  if (typeof myClip[property] == "movieclip") {
    trace("Found instance: " + myClip[property]._name);

    // Now do something to the clip
    myClip[property]._x = 300;
    myClip[property].play();
  }
}
```

The *for-in* loop gives us enormously convenient access to the clips contained by a specific clip instance or main movie. Using *for-in* we can control any clip on any timeline, whether we know the clip's name or not and whether the clip was created manually or programmatically.

Example 13-3 shows a recursive version of the previous example. It finds all the clip instances on a timeline, plus the clip instances on all nested timelines.

Example 13-3. Recursively Finding All Movie Clips on a Timeline

```
function findClips (myClip, indentSpaces) {
  // Use spaces to indent the child clips on each successive tier
  var indent = " ";
  for (var i = 0; i < indentSpaces; i++) {
    indent += " ";
  }
  for (var property in myClip) {
    // Check if the current property of myClip is a movie clip
    if (typeof myClip[property] == "movieclip") {
      trace(indent + myClip[property]._name);
      // Check if this clip is parent to any other clips
      findClips(myClip[property], indentSpaces + 4);
    }
  }
}
findClips (_root, 0); // Find all clip instances descended from main timeline
```

For more information on function recursion, see "Recursive Functions" in Chapter 9, *Functions*.

The _name property

As we learned earlier in "Instance Names," every instance's name is stored as a string in the built-in property **_name**. We can use that property, as we saw in Example 13-2, to determine the name of the current clip or the name of some other clip in an instance hierarchy:

```
_name;              // The current instance's name
_parent._name       // The name of the clip that contains the current clip
```

The **_name** property comes in handy when we want to perform conditional operations on clips according to their identities. For example, here we duplicate the **seedClip** clip when it loads:

```
onClipEvent (load) {
  if (_name == "seedClip") {
    this.duplicateMovieClip("clipCopy", 0);
  }
}
```

By checking explicitly for the **seedClip** name, we prevent infinite recursion—without our conditional statement, the *load* handler of each duplicated clip would cause the clip to duplicate itself.

The _target property

Every movie clip instance has a built-in **_target** property, which is a string specifying the clip's absolute path using the deprecated Flash 4 "slash" notation. For example, if **clipB** is placed inside **clipA**, and **clipA** is placed on the main timeline, the **_target** property of those clips is as follows:

```
_root._target              // Contains: "/"
_root.clipA._target        // Contains: "/clipA"
_root.clipA.clipB._target  // Contains: "/clipA/clipB"
```

The targetPath() function

The *targetPath()* function returns a string that contains the clip's absolute reference path, expressed using dot notation. The *targetPath()* function is the Flash 5–syntax equivalent of **_target**. It takes the form:

```
targetPath(movieClip)
```

where **movieClip** is the identifier of the clip whose absolute reference we wish to retrieve. Here are some examples, using our now familiar example hierarchy:

```
targetPath(_root);             // Contains: "_level0"
targetPath(_root.clipA);       // Contains: "_level0.clipA"
targetPath(_root.clipA.clipB); // Contains: "_level0.clipA.clipB"
```

The *targetPath()* function gives us the complete path to a clip, whereas the **_name** property gives us only the name of the clip. (This is analogous to having a complete file path versus just the filename.) So, we can use *targetPath()* to compose code that controls clips based not only on their name but also on their location. For example, we might create a generic navigational button that, by examining its *targetPath()*, sets its own color to match the section of content within which it resides. See the example under "Selection.setSelection( ) Method" in Part III for a demonstration of *targetPath()* in action.

Whither Tell Target?

In Flash 4, *Tell Target* was our main tool for referring to movie clips. *Tell Target*, bless its soul, was an unwieldy tool and is rendered obsolete by the much more elegant object model introduced in Flash 5. The *Tell Target* function has been deprecated (i.e., retired from recommended use). Although we may still use the *tellTarget()* function to code in a Flash 4 manner, *tellTarget()* will likely disappear in the future.

Consider the following code, which uses *Tell Target* to play an instance named `closingSequence`:

```
Begin Tell Target ("closingSequence")
  Play
End Tell Target
```

As of Flash 5, we simply invoke the much more convenient and readable *play()* method on the `closingSequence` instance:

```
closingSequence.play();
```

Tell Target could also perform multiple operations on an instance within a code block, like so:

```
Begin Tell Target ("ball")
  (Set Property: ("ball", x Scale) = "5")
  Play
End Tell Target
```

As of Flash 5, the *with()* statement, described in Chapter 6, *Statements*, is the preferred way to achieve similar results:

```
with (ball) {
  _xscale = 5;
  play();
}
```

See Appendix C, *Backward Compatibility*, for more details on deprecated Flash 4 ActionScript and the preferred equivalents in Flash 5.

Removing Clip Instances and Main Movies

We've learned to create and refer to movie clips; now let's see how to turn them into so many recycled electrons (in other words, blow 'em away).

The manner in which we created an instance or a movie determines the technique we use to remove that instance or movie later. We can explicitly remove movies and instances using *unloadMovie()* and *removeMovieClip()*. Additionally, we may evict a clip implicitly by loading, attaching, or duplicating a new clip in its stead. Let's look at these techniques individually.

Using unloadMovie() with Instances and Levels

The built-in *unloadMovie()* function can remove any clip instance or main movie—both those created manually and those created via *loadMovie()*, *duplicateMovieClip()*, and *attachMovie()*. It can be invoked both as a global function and as a method:

```
unloadMovie(clipOrLevel);    // Global function
clipOrLevel.unloadMovie();   // Method
```

In global function form, `clipOrLevel` is a string indicating the path to the clip or level to unload. And due to automatic value conversion, `clipOrLevel` may also be a movie clip reference (movie clips are converted to paths when used as strings). In method form, `clipOrLevel` must be a reference to a movie clip object. The exact behavior of *unloadMovie()* varies according to whether it is used on a level or an instance.

Using unloadMovie() with levels

When applied to a level in the document stack (e.g., `_level0`, `_level1`, `_level2`), *unloadMovie()* completely removes the target level and the movie that the level contains. Subsequent references to the level yield **undefined**. Removing document levels is the most common use of the *unloadMovie()* function:

```
unloadMovie("_level1");
_level1.unloadMovie();
```

Using unloadMovie() with instances

When applied to an instance (whether manually or programmatically created), *unloadMovie()* removes the *contents* of the clip, *but it does not remove the clip itself!* The timeline and canvas of the clip are removed, but an empty shell remains on stage. That shell can be referenced until the instance is permanently removed via *removeMovieClip()* (or until the span of frames on which the instance resides ends). Furthermore, any clip event handlers on the shell remain active.

This partial deletion of instances presents an interesting possibility; it lets us maintain a generic container clip whose contents can be repeatedly changed via *loadMovie()* and *unloadMovie()*. For example, we may quite legitimately invoke the following function series on an instance called `clipA` (though in a real application, these statements would include the appropriate preloader code):

```
clipA.loadMovie("section1.swf");   // Load a document into clipA
clipA.unloadMovie();               // Unload the document, leaving clipA intact
clipA.loadMovie("section2.swf");   // Load another document into clipA
```

One note of caution with this approach. When used on an instance, *unloadMovie()* removes all custom properties of the clip contained by the instance. Physical properties, such as _x and _alpha persist, but custom variables and functions are lost.

If you use the global function form of *unloadMovie()* with a non-existent clip or level instance as its argument, the clip from which you invoked the *unloadMovie()* function will, itself, unload.

For example, if _level1 is undefined, and we issue the following code from the main timeline of _level0, then _level0 will unload:

```
unloadMovie(_level1);
```

Yes, there's some logic to this behavior, but we'll cover that later under "Method versus global function overlap issues." You can avoid the problem by using a string when specifying the *clipOrLevel* argument of *unloadMovie()* or by checking explicitly that *clipOrLevel* exists before unloading it. Here's an example of each approach:

```
unloadMovie("_level1");   // clipOrLevel specified as a string
if (_level1) {            // Explicit check to make sure level exists
  unloadMovie(_level1);
}
```

Using removeMovieClip() to Delete Instances

To delete attached and duplicated instances from the Player, we can use *removeMovieClip()*. Note that *removeMovieClip()* works on duplicated or attached instances only. It cannot delete a manually created instance or a main movie. Like *unloadMovie()*, *removeMovieClip()* may be used in both method and global function form (though the syntax is different, the effect is the same):

```
removeMovieClip(clip)     // Global function
clip.removeMovieClip( )   // Method
```

In global function form, *clip* is a string indicating the path to the clip to remove. Due to automatic value conversion, *clip* may also be a movie clip reference (movie clips are converted to paths when used as strings). In method form, *clip* must be a reference to a movie clip object.

Unlike *unloadMovie()*, deleting an instance via *removeMovieClip()* completely obliterates the entire clip object, leaving no shell or trace of the clip and its properties. When we execute *clip*.removeMovieClip(), future references to *clip* yield undefined.

Removing Manually Created Instances Manually

Clip instances created manually in the Flash authoring tool also have a limited life span—they are removed when the playhead enters a keyframe that does not include them. Manually created movie clips, hence, live in fear of the almighty blank keyframe.

Remember that when a movie clip disappears from the timeline, it ceases to exist as a data object. All variables, functions, methods, and properties that may have been defined inside it are lost. Therefore, if we want a clip's information or functions to persist, we should be careful about removing the clip manually and should ensure that the span of frames on which the clip resides extends to the point where we need that clip's information. (In fact, to avoid this worry entirely, we should attach most permanent code to a frame in the main movie timeline.) To hide a clip while it's present on the timeline, simply position the clip outside the visible area of the Stage, and set the clip's `_visible` property to `false`. Setting a clip's `_x` property to a very large positive number or very small negative number should also suffice to hide it from the user's view without removing it from memory.

Built-in Movie Clip Properties

Unlike generic objects of the *Object* class, which have few built-in properties, each movie clip comes equipped with a slew of built-in properties. These properties describe, and can be used to modify, the clip's physical features. They are fundamental tools in the ActionScript programmer's toolkit.

All built-in movie clip property names begin with an underscore, which sets them apart from user-defined or custom properties. Built-in properties take the format:

    _property

Built-in property names should be written in lowercase. However, because identifiers are case insensitive in ActionScript, it is possible—though not good form—to capitalize property names.

We're not going to go into heavy descriptions of the built-in properties right now; that information is listed in Part III. However, to get us thinking about properties and what they offer, Table 13-1 provides a list of the built-in movie clip properties and basic descriptions of their functions.

Table 13-1. The Built-in Movie Clip Properties

Property Name	Property Description
_alpha	Transparency level
_currentframe	Position of the playhead

Table 13-1. The Built-in Movie Clip Properties (continued)

Property Name	Property Description
_droptarget	Path to the clip or movie on which a dragged clip was dropped
_framesloaded	Number of frames downloaded
_height	Physical height, in pixels (of instance, not original symbol)
_name	Clip's identifier, returned as a string
_parent	Object reference to the timeline containing this clip
_rotation	Angle of rotation (in degrees)
_target	Full path to the clip, in slash notation
_totalframes	Number of frames in the timeline
_url	Network location of .*swf*
_visible	Boolean indicating whether movie clip is displayed
_width	Physical width, in pixels (of instance, not original symbol)
_x	Horizontal position, in pixels, from the left of the Stage
_xmouse	Horizontal location of the mouse pointer in the clip's coordinate space
_xscale	Horizontal size, as a percentage of the original symbol (or main timeline for movies)
_y	Vertical position, in pixels, from the top of the Stage
_ymouse	Vertical location of the mouse pointer in the clip's coordinate space
_yscale	Vertical size, as a percentage of the original symbol (or main timeline for movies)

There's no direct color property attached to instances or main movies. Instead of controlling color through a property, we must use the *Color* class to create an object that is used to control the color of a clip. The methods of a *Color* object let us set or examine the RGB values and transformations of a particular clip. To learn the specific details, see the "Color Class" in Part III.

Movie Clip Methods

In Chapter 12, we learned about a special type of property called a *method*, which is a function attached to an object. Methods are most commonly used to manipulate, interact with, or control the objects to which they are attached. To control movie clips in various programmatic ways, we may use one of the built-in movie clip methods. We may also define our own movie clip methods in an individual instance or in the Library symbol of a movie clip.

Creating Movie Clip Methods

To add a new method to a movie clip, we define a function on the clip's timeline (or in one of the clip's event handlers) or we assign a function to a property of the clip. For example:

```
// Create a method by defining a function on the timeline of a clip
function halfSpin() {
  _rotation += 180;
}
// Create a method by assigning a function literal to a property of a clip
myClip.coords = function() { return [_x, _y]; };
// This method applies a custom transformation to a clip
myClip.myTransform = function () {
  _rotation += 10;
  _xscale -= 25;
  _yscale -= 25;
  _alpha -= 25;
}
```

Invoking Movie Clip Methods

Invoking a method on a movie clip works exactly like invoking a method on any object. We supply the name of the clip and the name of the method, as follows:

```
myClip.methodName();
```

If the method requires arguments, we pass them along during invocation:

```
_root.square(5);    // Provide 5 as an argument to the square() method
```

As we learned earlier, when we're working on the timeline of a clip or in a clip's event handler, we may invoke most methods on the current clip directly, without specifying an instance identifier:

```
square(10);         // Invoke the custom square() method of the current clip
play();             // Invoke the built-in play() method of the current clip
```

But some built-in methods require an instance identifier; see "Method versus global function overlap issues."

Built-in Movie Clip Methods

Recall that the generic *Object* class equips all its member objects with the built-in methods *toString()* and *valueOf()*. Recall similarly that other classes define built-in methods that can be used by their member objects: *Date* objects have a *getHours()* method, *Color* objects have *setRGB()*, *Array* objects have *push()* and *pop()*, and so on. Movie clips are no different. They come equipped with a series of built-in methods that we use to control movie clips' appearance and behavior, to check their characteristics, and even to create new movie clips. The movie clip methods are one of the central features of ActionScript. Table 13-2 gives an overview of the movie clip methods that are covered in depth in Part III.

Table 13-2. The Built-in Movie Clip Methods

Method Name	Method Description
attachMovie()	Creates a new instance
duplicateMovieClip()	Creates a copy of an instance
getBounds()	Describes the visual region occupied by the clip
getBytesLoaded()	Returns the number of downloaded bytes of an instance or a movie
getBytesTotal()	Returns the physical byte size of an instance or a movie
getURL()	Loads an external document (usually an *.html* file) into the browser
globalToLocal()	Converts main Stage coordinates to clip coordinates
gotoAndPlay()	Moves the playhead to a new frame and plays the movie
gotoAndStop()	Moves the playhead to a new frame and halts it there
hitTest()	Indicates whether a point is within a clip
loadMovie()	Brings an external *.swf* file into the Player
loadVariables()	Brings external variables into a clip or movie
localToGlobal()	Converts clip coordinates to main Stage coordinates
nextFrame()	Moves the playhead ahead one frame
play()	Plays the clip
prevFrame()	Moves the playhead back one frame
removeMovieClip()	Deletes a duplicated or attached instance
startDrag()	Causes the instance or movie to physically follow the mouse pointer around the Stage
stop()	Halts the playback of the instance or movie
stopDrag()	Ends any drag operation currently in progress
swapDepths()	Alters the layering of an instance in an instance stack
unloadMovie()	Removes an instance or main movie from a document level or host clip
valueOf()	A string representing the path to the instance in absolute terms, using dot notation

Method versus global function overlap issues

As we've mentioned several times during this chapter, some movie clip methods have the same name as equivalent global functions. You can see this for yourself in the Flash authoring tool. Open the Actions panel, make sure you're in Expert Mode, and then take a look in the Actions folder. You'll see a long list of Actions including *gotoAndPlay()*, *gotoAndStop()*, *nextFrame()*, and *unloadMovie()*. Those Actions are also available as movie clip methods. The duplication is not purely a matter of categorization; the Actions are global functions, fully distinct from the corresponding movie clip methods.

So, when we execute:

```
myClip.gotoAndPlay(5);
```

we're accessing the *method* named *gotoAndPlay()*. But when we execute:

```
gotoAndPlay(5);
```

we're accessing the *global function* called *gotoAndPlay()*. These two commands have the same name, but they are not the same thing. The *gotoAndPlay()* global function operates on the current instance or movie. The *gotoAndPlay()* method operates on the clip object through which it is invoked. Most of the time, the subtle difference is of no consequence. But for some overlapping method/function pairs, the difference is potentially quite vexing.

Some global functions require a parameter called `target` that specifies the clip on which the function should operate. This `target` parameter is not required by the comparable method versions because the methods automatically operate on the clips through which they are invoked. For example, *unloadMovie()* in its method form works like this:

```
myClip.unloadMovie();
```

As a method, *unloadMovie()* is invoked without parameters and automatically affects `myClip`. But in its global function form, *unloadMovie()* works like this:

```
unloadMovie(target);
```

The global function requires `target` as a parameter that specifies which movie to unload. Why should this be a problem? Well, the first reason is that we may mistakenly expect to be able to unload the current document by using the global version of *unloadMovie()* without any parameters, as we'd use *gotoAndPlay()* without parameters:

```
unloadMovie();
```

This format does *not* unload the current clip. It causes a "Wrong number of parameters" error. The second reason that `target` parameters in global functions can cause problems is a little more complex and can be quite a pain to track down if you're not expecting it. To supply a `target` clip to a global function that requires a `target` parameter, we may use either a string, which expresses the path to the clip we wish to affect, or a clip reference. For example:

```
unloadMovie(_level1);     // Target clip is a reference
unloadMovie("_level1");   // Target clip is a string
```

We may use a reference simply because references to clip objects are converted to movie clip paths when used in a string context. Simple enough, but if the *target* parameter resolves to an empty string or an **undefined** value, the *function operates on the current timeline*! For example:

```
unloadMovie(x);    // If x doesn't exist, x yields undefined, so
                   // the function operates on the current timeline

unloadMovie("");   // The target is the empty string, so the function operates
                   // on the current timeline
```

This can cause some quite unexpected results. Consider what happens if we refer to a level that doesn't exist:

```
unloadMovie(_level1);
```

If **_level1** is empty, the interpreter resolves the reference as though it were an undeclared variable. This yields **undefined**, so the function operates on the current timeline, not _level1! So, how do we accommodate this behavior? There are a few options. We may check for the existence of our target before executing a function on it:

```
if (_level1) {
  unloadMovie(_level1);
}
```

We may choose to always use a string to indicate the path to our target. If the path specified in our string does not resolve to a real clip, the function fails silently:

```
unloadMovie("_level1");
```

In some cases, we may use the equivalent numeric function for our operation:

```
unloadMovieNum(1);
```

Or, we may choose to avoid the issue altogether by always using methods:

```
_level1.unloadMovie();
```

For reference, here are the troublemakers (the Flash 5 ActionScript global functions that take *target* parameters):

duplicateMovieClip()
loadMovie()
loadVariables()
print()
printAsBitmap()
removeMovieClip()
startDrag()
unloadMovie()

If you're experiencing unexplained problems in a movie, you may want to check that list to see if you're misusing a global function. When passing a clip reference as a *target* parameter, be sure to double-check your syntax.

Applied Movie Clip Examples

We've now learned the fundamentals of movie clip programming. Let's put our knowledge to use by creating two very different applications, both of which exemplify the typical role of movie clips as basic content containers.

Building a Clock with Clips

In this chapter we learned how to create movie clips with *attachMovie()* and how to set movie clip properties with the dot operator. With these relatively simple tools and a little help from the *Date* and *Color* classes, we have everything we need to make a clock with functional hour, minute, and second hands.

First, we'll make the face and hands of the clock with the following steps (notice that we don't place the parts of our clock on the main Stage—our clock will be generated entirely through ActionScript):

1. Start a new Flash movie.

2. Create a movie clip symbol named `clockFace` that contains a 100-pixel-wide black circle shape.

3. Create a movie clip symbol named **hand** that contains a 50-pixel-long, vertical red line.

4. Select the line in **hand**, then choose Window → Panels → Info.

5. Position the bottom of the line at the center of the clip by setting the line's x-coordinate to 0 and its y-coordinate to –50.

Now we have to export our `clockFace` and **hand** symbols so that instances of them can be attached dynamically to our movie:

1. In the Library, select the `clockFace` clip, then select Options → Linkage. The Symbol Linkage Properties dialog box appears.

2. Select Export This Symbol.

3. In the Identifier box, type **clockFace** and then click OK.

4. Repeat steps 1 through 3 to export the **hand** clip, giving it the identifier **hand**.

The face and hands of our clock are complete and ready to be attached to our movie. Now let's write the script that places the clock assets on stage and positions them with each passing second:

1. Add the script shown in Example 13-4 to frame 1 of *Layer 1* of the main timeline.

2. Rename *Layer 1* to *scripts*.

Skim Example 13-4 in its entirety first, then we'll dissect it.

Example 13-4. An Analog Clock

```
// Create clock face and hands
attachMovie("clockFace", "clockFace", 0);
attachMovie("hand", "secondHand", 3);
attachMovie("hand", "minuteHand", 2);
attachMovie("hand", "hourHand", 1);

// Position and size the clock face
clockFace._x = 275;
clockFace._y = 200;
clockFace._height = 150;
clockFace._width = 150;

// Position, size, and color the clock hands
secondHand._x = clockFace._x;
secondHand._y = clockFace._y;
secondHand._height = clockFace._height / 2.2;
secondHandColor = new Color(secondHand);
secondHandColor.setRGB(0xFFFFFF);
minuteHand._x = clockFace._x;
minuteHand._y = clockFace._y;
minuteHand._height = clockFace._height / 2.5;
hourHand._x = clockFace._x;
hourHand._y = clockFace._y;
hourHand._height = clockFace._height / 3.5;

// Update the rotation of hands with each passing frame
function updateClock() {
  var now = new Date();
  var dayPercent = (now.getHours() > 12 ?
                    now.getHours() - 12 : now.getHours()) / 12;
  var hourPercent = now.getMinutes()/60;
  var minutePercent = now.getSeconds()/60;
  hourHand._rotation = 360 * dayPercent + hourPercent * (360 / 24);
  minuteHand._rotation = 360 * hourPercent;
  secondHand._rotation = 360 * minutePercent;
}
```

That's a lot of code, so let's review it.

We attach the `clockFace` clip first and assign it a depth of 0 (we want it to appear behind our clock's hands):

```
attachMovie("clockFace", "clockFace", 0);
```

Next we attach three instances of the `hand` symbol, assigning them the names `secondHand`, `minuteHand`, `hourHand`. Each hand resides on its own layer in the programmatically generated clip stack above the main timeline. The `secondHand` (depth 3) sits on top of the `minuteHand` (depth 2), which sits on top of the `hourHand` (depth 1):

```
attachMovie("hand", "secondHand", 3);
attachMovie("hand", "minuteHand", 2);
attachMovie("hand", "hourHand", 1);
```

At this point our code would place the clock in the top-left corner of the Stage. Next, we move the `clockFace` clip to the center of the Stage and make it larger using the `_height` and `_width` properties:

```
clockFace._x = 275;        // Set the horizontal location
clockFace._y = 200;        // Set the vertical location
clockFace._height = 150;   // Set the height
clockFace._width = 150;    // Set the width
```

Then we move the `secondHand` clip onto the clock and make it almost as long as the radius of the `clockFace` clip:

```
// Place the secondHand on top of the clockFace
secondHand._X = clockFace._x;
secondHand._y = clockFace._y;
// Set the secondHand's size
secondHand._height = clockFace._height / 2.2;
```

Remember that the line in the `hand` symbol is red, so all our `hand` instances thus far are red. To make our `secondHand` clip stand out, we color it white using the *Color* class. Note the use of the hexadecimal color value 0xFFFFFF (see the "Color Class" in Part III for more information on manipulating color):

```
// Create a new Color object to control secondHand
secondHandColor = new Color(secondHand);
// Assign secondHand the color white
secondHandColor.setRGB(0xFFFFFF);
```

Next we set the position and size of the `minuteHand` and `hourHand`, just as we did for the `secondHand`:

```
// Place the minuteHand on top of the clockFace
minuteHand._x = clockFace._x;
minuteHand._y = clockFace._y;
// Make the minuteHand shorter than the secondHand
minuteHand._height = clockFace._height / 2.5;
```

```
// Place the hourHand on top of the clockFace
hourHand._x = clockFace._x;
hourHand._y = clockFace._y;
// Make the hourHand the shortest of all
hourHand._height = clockFace._height / 3.5;
```

Now we have to set the rotation of our hands on the clock according to the current time. However, we don't just want to set the rotation once. We want to set it repetitively so that our clock animates as time passes. Therefore, we put our rotation code in a function called *updateClock()*, which we'll call repeatedly:

```
function updateClock() {
  // Store the current time in now
  var now = new Date();
  // getHours() works on a 24-hour clock. If the current hour is greater
  // than 12, we subtract 12 to convert to a regular 12-hour clock.
  var dayPercent = (now.getHours() > 12 ?
                    now.getHours() - 12 : now.getHours()) / 12;
  // Determine how many minutes of the current hour have passed, as a percentage
  var hourPercent = now.getMinutes()/60;
  // Determine how many seconds of the current minute have passed, as a percentage
  var minutePercent = now.getSeconds()/60;
  // Rotate the hands by the appropriate amount around the clock
  hourHand._rotation = 360 * dayPercent + hourPercent * (360 / 24);
  minuteHand._rotation = 360 * hourPercent;
  secondHand._rotation = 360 * minutePercent;
}
```

The first task of *updateClock()* is to retrieve and store the current time. This is done by creating an instance of the *Date* class and placing it in the local variable **now**. Next we determine, as a percentage, how far around the clock each hand should be placed—much like determining where to slice a pie. The current hour always represents some portion of 12, while the current minute and second always represent some portion of 60. We assign the **_rotation** of each hand based on those percentages. For the **hourHand**, we reflect not only the percent of the day but also the percent of the current hour.

Our clock is essentially finished. All that's left to do is call the *updateClock()* function with each passing frame. Here's how:

1. Add two keyframes to the *scripts* layer.

2. On frame 2, add the following code: **updateClock();**

3. On frame 3, add the following code: **gotoAndPlay(2);**

Test the movie and see if your clock works. If it doesn't, compare it to the sample clock *.fla* file provided at the online Code Depot or check your code against Example 13-4. Think of ways to expand on the clock application: Can you convert the main timeline loop (between frames 2 and 3) to a clip event loop? Can you make the clock more portable by turning it into a Smart Clip? How about dynamically adding minute and hour markings on the `clockFace`?

The Last Quiz

Here's one final version of the multiple-choice quiz we started way back in Chapter 1, *A Gentle Introduction for Non-Programmers*. This updated version of the quiz dynamically generates all of the quiz's questions and answers using movie clips, so our quiz is infinitely scalable and highly configurable. In fact, we're not far off from making the entire quiz a Smart Clip that could be customized by non-programmers.

The code for the quiz is shown in Example 13-5 and available from the online Code Depot. Because the quiz is now completely dynamically generated, 99% of the code fits entirely on one frame; we no longer need to fill a timeline with questions. (All we're missing is a preloader to ensure smooth playback over a network.) Note that we've used `#include` to import a block of code from an external text file. For more information on `#include`, see Part III, and see "Externalizing Action-Script Code" in Chapter 16. As an exercise, try adding new questions to the quiz by creating new objects and placing them in the questions array.

Though the code for the final quiz is relatively short, it's packed full of important techniques. With the exception of `#include`, we've seen all of them in isolation before, but this extended real-world example shows how they can all fit together. Study the comments carefully—when you understand this version of the quiz in its entirety you'll be well-equipped to create advanced applications with ActionScript.

A longer explanation of the code in this quiz is available at:

http://www.moock.org/webdesign/lectures/ff2001sfWorkshop

Example 13-5. The Multiple-Choice Quiz, One Last Time

```
// CODE ON FRAME 1 OF THE MAIN TIMELINE
//  Stop the movie
stop();

//  Init main timeline variables
var displayTotal;              // Text field for user's final score
var totalCorrect = 0;          // Number of questions answered correctly
var userAnswers = new Array(); // Array containing the user's guesses
var currentQuestion = 0;       // Number of the question the user is on

// Import the source file containing our array of question objects
// See explanation later in this example
#include "questionsArray.as"

// Begin the quiz
makeQuestion(currentQuestion);
```

Example 13-5. The Multiple-Choice Quiz, One Last Time (continued)

```
// The Question() constructor
function Question (correctAnswer, questionText, answers) {
  this.correctAnswer = correctAnswer;
  this.questionText = questionText;
  this.answers = answers;
}

// Function to render each question to the screen
function makeQuestion (currentQuestion) {
  // Clear the Stage of the last question
  questionClip.removeMovieClip();

  // Create and place the main question clip
  attachMovie("questionTemplate", "questionClip", 0);
  questionClip._x = 277;
  questionClip._y = 205;
  questionClip.qNum = "question\n  " + (currentQuestion + 1);
  questionClip.qText = questionsArray[currentQuestion].questionText;

  // Create the individual answer clips in the question clip
  for (var i = 0; i < questionsArray[currentQuestion].answers.length; i++) {
    // Attach our linked answerTemplate clip from the Library;
    // It contains a generalized button and a text field for the question
    questionClip.attachMovie("answerTemplate", "answer" + i, i);
    // Place this answer clip in line below the question
    questionClip["answer" + i]._y += 70 + (i * 15);
    questionClip["answer" + i]._x -= 100;
    // Set the text field in the answer clip to the appropriate element of this
    // question's answer array
    questionClip["answer" + i].answerText =
        questionsArray[currentQuestion].answers[i];
  }
}

// Function to register the user's answers
function answer (choice) {
  userAnswers.push(choice);
  if (currentQuestion + 1 == questionsArray.length) {
    questionClip.removeMovieClip();
    gotoAndStop ("quizEnd");
  } else {
    makeQuestion(++currentQuestion);
  }
}

// Function to tally the user's score
function gradeUser() {
  // Count how many questions the user answered correctly
  for (var i = 0; i < questionsArray.length; i++) {
    if (userAnswers[i] == questionsArray[i].correctAnswer) {
      totalCorrect++;
    }
  }
```

Example 13-5. The Multiple-Choice Quiz, One Last Time (continued)

```
  // Show the user's score in an onscreen text field
  displayTotal = totalCorrect + "/" + questionsArray.length;
}

// CODE ON THE DYNAMICALLY GENERATED ANSWER BUTTONS
// Answer clips are generated dynamically and named in the series
// "answer0", "answer1",..."answern". Each answer clip contains a
// button that, when clicked, checks the name of the answer clip it's
// in to determine the user's choice.
on (release) {
  // Trim the prefix "answer" off this clip's name
  choice = _name.slice(6, _name.length);
  _root.answer(choice);
}


// CODE ON THE quizEnd FRAME
gradeUser();
```

The contents of the *questionsArray.as* file are as shown here:

```
  // CODE IN THE questionsarray.as FILE
  // ------------------------------------------------
  // Contains an array of question objects that
  // populate the questions and answers of a multiple-
  // choice quiz. Compose new question objects according
  // to the following example.

  /************** EXAMPLE QUESTION OBJECT **************
    // Invoke the Question constructor with three arguments:
    //    a zero-relative number giving the correct answer,
    //    a string giving the question text, and
    //    an array containing the multiple-choice answers
    new Question
    (
      1,
      "question goes here?",
      ["answer 1", "answer 2", "answer 3"]
    )
  ****************************************************/
  // Remember to place a comma after each object in the array except the last
  questionsArray = [new Question (2,
    "Which version of Flash first introduced movie clips?",
    ["version 1", "version 2", "version 3",
    "version 4", "version 5", "version 6"]),

    new Question (2,
      "When was ActionScript formally declared a scripting language?",
      ["version 3", "version 4", "version 5"]),

    new Question (1,
      "Are regular expressions supported by Flash 5 ActionScript?",
      ["yes", "no"]),
```

```
new Question (0,
  "Which sound format offers the best compression?",
  ["mp3","aiff", "wav"]),

new Question (1,
  "True or False: The post-increment operator (++) returns the
  value of its operand + 1.",
  ["true", "false"]),

new Question (3,
  "Actionscript is based on...",
  ["Java", "JavaScript", "C++", "ECMA-262", "Perl"])];
```

Onward!

We've come so far that there's not much more to move on to! Once you understand objects and movie clips thoroughly, you can tackle most ActionScript projects on your own. But there's still some interesting ground ahead: the next chapter teaches "lexical structure" (the finicky details of ActionScript syntax). In the chapter following that, we'll consider a variety of advanced topics. Finally, it's on to Part II, *Applied ActionScript* and Part III, *Language Reference.*

14

Lexical Structure

The *lexical structure* of a language is the set of rules that govern its syntactic composition. We must follow these rules when writing the source code of our scripts.

Whitespace

The tab, space, and carriage return (i.e., line break) characters are used in Action-Script just like they are in English to separate words from each other so that they don't all runtogetherlikethis. In programmer-speak, these characters are known as *whitespace* and are used in source code to separate *tokens* (the keywords, identifiers, and expressions roughly akin to words, phrases, and sentences in English). Here is an example of incorrect and correct whitespace usage:

```
varx    // Oops! No whitespace between the keyword var and the variable x.
var x   // That's better...because of the whitespace the interpreter
        // can now read our code.
```

Whitespace is optional when there is some other *delimiter* (separator) that tells ActionScript where one token ends and another begins. The following code is quite legitimate because the operators =, +, and / separate x, 10, 5, and y from one another:

```
x=10+5/y;       // Crowded, but legitimate
x = 10 + 5 / y; // Easier to read, but the same as above
```

Similarly, whitespace is optional when there are other characters such as square brackets, parentheses, curly braces, commas, and greater-than or less-than signs to act as delimiters. These are all perfectly legal if somewhat claustrophobic:

```
for(var i=0;i<10;i++){trace(i);}
if(x==7){y=[1,2,3,4,5,6,7,8,9,10];}
myMeth=function(arg1,arg2,arg3){trace(arg1+arg2+arg3);};
```

Extra whitespace is simply a matter of style, because it is ignored by the Action-Script interpreter. That said, there are conventions you should follow to make your code more readable. For example, the following is another legitimate way to rewrite the earlier assignment expression, but it is obviously harder to read:

```
x =
  10
  + 5
  / y;
```

Notice that the statement is terminated by the *semicolon* not the line breaks. In nearly all cases, line breaks are inconsequential and do not act as statement termi-nators. Hence, we often use one or more line breaks (in concert with spaces or tabs) to make complex statements easier to read:

```
myNestedArray = [[x, y, z],
                 [1, 2, 3],
                 ["joshua davis", "yugo nakamura", "james patterson"]];
// Much nicer than:
myNestedArray = [[x, y, z], [1, 2, 3],["joshua davis","yugo nakamura",
"james patterson"]];
// And also nicer than:
myNestedArray = [[x, y, z],
[1, 2, 3],
["joshua davis","yugo nakamura","james patterson"]];
```

You don't need to do anything special if you want to break a statement onto more than one line. Simply add a carriage return and keep typing. For good advice on making your code more readable, see *Code Complete* by Steve McConnell (Microsoft Press). There are, however, times when line breaks may be misinter-preted as statement terminators, as we'll see in the next section.

Note that whitespace *within* the quotes that delimit a string is relevant whereas whitespace *outside* the quotes is ignored. Compare these two examples:

```
x = 5;
trace("The value of x is"  +   x);   // Displays: "The value of x is5"
trace("The value of x is "+x);       // Displays: "The value of x is 5"
```

Statement Terminators (Semicolons)

As we learned in Chapter 6, *Statements*, the semicolon terminates an ActionScript statement. Although by convention you should always end your statements with semicolons, they are not strictly required in ActionScript. The interpreter attempts to infer the end of a statement if the semicolon is omitted. For example:

```
// These are preferred
var x = 4;
var y = 5;
// But these are also legal
```

```
var x = 4
var y = 5
```

The ActionScript interpreter assumes that the line breaks in the preceding code are intended as statement terminators. (Compilers in stricter languages like C would complain.) However, omitting semicolons from statements in code is somewhat like omitting periods from sentences in normal writing—the reader will probably understand most of your sentences, but there will always be cases that lead to confusion. Not to mention it's more taxing to read. For example, consider what happens when we omit a semicolon after the **return** statement:

```
function addOne (value) {
  return
  value + 1
}
```

ActionScript will assume that we meant to write this:

```
function addOne (value) {
  return;
  value + 1;
}
```

Instead of returning **value + 1**, the function will always return **undefined**, because the keyword **return** alone is a legal statement. Even if **return** appears alone on a line, and even if we add a semicolon after **value + 1**, the **return** statement is still treated as a complete statement.

To avoid this type of ambiguity, it's good practice to include semicolons. Furthermore, in the specific case of the **return** statement, don't separate the keyword **return** from its expression with a line break, as that alters the statement's meaning. Therefore, the preceding example should be written as:

```
function addOne (value) {
  return value + 1;
}
```

Note that semicolons terminate individual statements but are not required where statement block delimiters (curly braces) occur. For example:

```
for (var i=0;i<10;i++) {   // No semicolon here
  trace(i);                // Semicolon here
}                          // No semicolon here

if(x == 10) {              // No semicolon here
  trace("x is ten");       // Semicolon here
} else {                   // No semicolon here
  trace("x is not ten");   // Semicolon here
}                          // No semicolon here

on (release) {             // No semicolon here
  trace("Click");          // Semicolon here
}                          // No semicolon here
```

However, the semicolon is mandatory following a function literal:

```
function (param1, param2, ... paramn) { statements };
```

The special `#include` directive does not allow a semicolon and will cause an error if used with one. See `#include` in Part III, *Language Reference.*

Comments

So-called *comments* are text that is ignored by the interpreter but entered by the programmer specifically for the benefit of humans reading the code. Comments should be used liberally to explain what the code does, provide version control information, or describe other relevant information such as how a data structure is being used or why certain programming choices were made. Comments should describe your code at the conceptual level, not merely mirror the syntax of the code itself. For example, the following comment is useless:

```
// Set i equal to 5
i = 5;
```

whereas the following comment tells us *why* we're setting `i` to 5, which helps us follow the flow of the code:

```
// Initialize our counter, used to search
// the password string starting at index 5
var i = 5;
```

Note that you can go a long way toward making your code "self-commenting" by using descriptive variable names and handler names. Which of the following is clearer:

```
x = y / z;                     // This is very cryptic
average = sum / numberOfItems; // This hardly needs explanation
```

ActionScript supports both one-line comments and extended, multiline comments. One-liners as we've seen throughout this book, begin with two forward slashes (//):

```
// Ah, human contact...this will never be read by the interpreter
```

One-line comments are automatically terminated by the line break at the end of the line. You must repeat the `//` characters to add more comment text on the following line:

```
// Here is the start of a comment...
// ...and here's some more of it.
```

One-line comments can also follow real code on the same line:

```
var x;    // This is a valid comment on the same line as code
```

ActionScript also supports multiline comments, used to accommodate larger blocks of code commentary, that are *not* terminated by line breaks. Multiline comments start with the two-character sequence /* and continue until the terminating two-character sequence */ is encountered, as in:

```
/* -----BEGIN VERSION CONTROL INFO----
   Name: MyApplication, Version 1.3.1
   Author: Killa Programma
   Last Modified: August 07, 2000
      ------END VERSION CONTROL INFO-----
*/
```

Multiline comments are available only in Expert Mode in the Flash 5 ActionScript editor or in external .*as* source files included via the #include directive. Multiline comments are converted to single-line comments when you switch from Expert Mode to Normal Mode. Note that nested comments are legal:

```
/* This is
/* a nested // comment */
```

The following is not used by convention, but it is valid:

```
/* This comment is followed by real code */ var x = 5;
```

It is common practice to include your initials and the date of the change in a comment whenever making major (or even minor) revisions to some code, such as this:

```
// Fixed error in financial calculation. BAE 12-04-00. V1.01
```

Comments let us temporarily disable code (or permanently disable old code) instead of deleting it. Disabling code by making it into a comment is known as *commenting out* the code. It is easy to re-enable the code by removing the comment delimiters:

```
/* Disable this block of code until I change my mind
duplicateMovieClip("character", "newCharacter", 1);
newCharacter._rotation = 90;
*/
```

You can disable a single line of code by simply preceding it with two slashes:

```
// newCharacter._rotation = 90;
```

Reserved Words

Some *reserved words* are used by the ActionScript interpreter to denote specific built-in language features such as statements and operators. They are reserved for use by the interpreter, and we must avoid using them as identifiers in our code. Using a reserved word for a purpose other than its reserved internal purpose causes an error in most cases. The reserved words of ActionScript are listed in Table 14-1.

Table 14-1. ActionScript's Reserved Words

add*	for	lt*	tellTarget*
and*	function	ne*	this
break	ge*	new	typeof
continue	gt*	not*	var
delete	if	on	void
do	ifFrameLoaded*	onClipEvent	while
else	in	or*	with
eq*	le*	return	

* Flash 4 reserved words deprecated in Flash 5.

You should also try to avoid using the keywords listed in Table 14-2. They are not part of ActionScript in Flash 5 but may become a part of the language in the future because they are slated for potential use by ECMA-262.

Table 14-2. Potential Future Reserved Words

abstract	extends	private
boolean	final	protected
byte	finally	public
case	float	short
catch	goto	static
char	implements	super
class	import	switch
const	instanceof	synchronized
debugger	int	throws
default	interface	transient
double	long	try
enum	native	volatile
export	package	

In addition to the formally defined keywords, you should also avoid using the names of built-in properties, methods, and objects as identifiers in your code. Doing so overrides the default behavior of the property, method, or object in question. For example:

```
Date = new Object();  // Oops! We just disabled the Date() constructor
```

Now we can no longer create *Date* objects:

```
var now = new Date();  // Sets now to undefined
trace(now);            // Displays the empty string, not the current time and date
```

Identifiers

All variables, functions, and object properties are named with identifiers. Action-Script identifiers must be composed according to the following rules:

- Identifiers must include only letters (A–Z or a–z), numbers, underscores, and dollar signs. Be especially careful never to use spaces, periods, backslashes, or other punctuation in identifiers.

- Identifiers must start with a letter, underscore, or dollar sign (not a number).

- Identifiers may not be identical to reserved words.

Though not strictly required, it's also good practice to follow the preceding rules when composing movie clip instance names, frame labels, and layer names.

Case Sensitivity

When a language is fully case sensitive, every token in the language—including all identifiers and keywords—must be entered with the correct capitalization. For example, in case-sensitive languages, the statement:

```
If (x == 5) {
   x = 10;
}
```

would cause an error because the keyword `if` is improperly capitalized as `If`. Furthermore, in case-sensitive languages, the following two statements would declare two separate variables (one named `firstName` and a second one named `firstname`):

```
var firstName = "doug";
var firstname = "terry";
```

The ECMA-262 specification, upon which ActionScript is based, demands complete case sensitivity. ActionScript, however, diverges from the standard in the area of case sensitivity in order to maintain backward compatibility with Flash 4 movies. In ActionScript, the keywords in Table 14-1 are case sensitive, but identifiers are not. For example, in the following, the `onClipEvent` keyword is incorrectly capitalized as `onclipevent` and would cause an error:

```
onclipevent (enterFrame)  // Should be onClipEvent (enterFrame)
```

But unlike keywords, identifiers are not case sensitive in ActionScript, so the following statements assign a value to the *same* variable:

```
var firstName = "margaret";
var firstname = "michael";
trace(firstName);   // Yields "michael"
trace(firstname);   // Also yields "michael" (the variables are the same)
```

Even internal identifiers, such as property names and function names, are not case sensitive in ActionScript. The following line would cause an error in JavaScript but would successfully create an array in ActionScript:

```
myList = new array();   // Should preferably be new Array();
```

This can present problems when porting JavaScript code to ActionScript or for Java-Script programmers learning ActionScript. Case sensitivity is often used in JavaScript to apply the same name to different purposes. For example, the statement:

```
date = new Date();   // Works in JavaScript but not ActionScript
```

will have destructive effects in ActionScript where the identifier **date** is not distin-guished from the object class *Date*. In ActionScript, the preceding code would dis-able the built-in *Date* class. We must, therefore, ensure that our identifiers are distinguished by more than just case from one another and from any predefined identifiers like *Date* or *Array*. Here's how we'd rewrite the previous code in ActionScript:

```
myDate = new Date(); // Use this in ActionScript
```

The key in all situations is to be consistent—even when consistency is not strictly required by the language. Capitalizing variables, functions, instances, and other items consistently makes our code easier to read and prevents future changes in ActionScript's case rules from breaking our hard work.

Onward!

As far as ActionScript language fundamentals go, we've reached the end of the road. You're now fully equipped to both read and write ActionScript. The next chapter covers some more advanced and esoteric topics that didn't warrant dis-tracting us in our earlier discussions.

15

Advanced Topics

This chapter collects a variety of advanced ActionScript programming techniques and issues.

Copying, Comparing, and Passing Data

There are three fundamental ways to manipulate data. We may *copy* it (e.g., assign the value of variable x to variable y), we may *compare* it (e.g., check whether x equals y), and we may *pass* it (e.g., supply a variable to a function as an argument). Primitive data values are copied, compared, and passed quite differently than composite data. When primitive data is copied to a variable, that variable gets its own unique and private copy of the data, stored separately in memory. The following lines of code would, hence, cause the string "Dave" to be stored twice in memory, once in the memory space reserved for name1 and again in the space reserved for name2:

```
name1 = "Dave";
name2 = name1;
```

We say that primitive data is copied *by value* because the data's literal value is stored in the memory space allotted to the variable. In contrast, when composite data is copied to a variable, only a *reference* to the data (and not the actual data) is stored in the variable's memory slot. That reference tells the interpreter where the actual data is kept (i.e., its address in memory). When a variable that contains composite data is copied to another variable, it is the *reference* (often called a *pointer*) and not the data itself that is copied. Composite data is, hence, said to be copied *by reference*.

This makes good design sense because it would be grossly inefficient to duplicate large arrays and other composite datatypes. But it has important consequences for our code. When multiple variables are assigned the same piece of composite data as their value, each variable does *not* store a unique copy of the data (as it would if the data were primitive). Rather, only one copy of the data exists and all the variables point to it. If the value of the data changes, *all* the variables are updated.

Let's see how this affects a practical application. When two variables refer to the same primitive data, each variable gets its own copy of the data. Here we assign the value 12 to the variable x:

```
var x = 12;
```

Now let's assign the value of x to a new variable, y:

```
var y = x;
```

As you can guess, y is now equal to 12. But y has its own copy of the value 12, distinct from the copy in x. If we change the value of x, the value of y is unaffected:

```
x = 15;
trace(x); // Displays 15 in the Output window
trace(y); // Displays 12 in the Output window
```

The value of y did not change when x changed because when we assigned x to y, y received its own copy of the number 12 (i.e., the *primitive* data contained by x).

Now let's try the same thing with *composite* data. We'll create a new array with three elements and then assign that array to the variable x:

```
var x = ["first element", 234, 18.5];
```

Now, just as we did before, we'll assign the value of x to y:

```
var y = x;
```

The value of y is now the same as the value of x. But what is the value of x? Remember that because x refers to an array, which is a composite datum, the value of x is not literally the array ["first element", 234, 18.5] but merely a reference to that datum. Hence, when we assign x to y, what's copied to y is not the array itself, but the reference contained in x that points to the array. So both x *and* y point to the same array, stored somewhere in memory.

If we change the array through the variable x, like this:

```
x[0] = "1st element";
```

the change is also reflected in y:

```
trace(y[0]);  // Displays: "1st element"
```

Similarly, if we modify the array through y, the change can be seen via x:

```
y[1] = "second element";
trace (x[1]);  // Displays: "second element"
```

To break the association, use the *slice()* function to create an entirely new array:

```
var x = ["first element", 234, 18.5];
// Copy each element of x to a new array stored in y
var y = x.slice(0);
y[0] = "hi there";

trace(x[0]);  // Displays: "first element" (not "hi there")
trace(y[0]);  // Displays: "hi there" (not "first element")
```

Let's extend our example to see how primitive and composite data values are *compared*. Here we assign x and y an identical primitive value, then we compare the two variables:

```
x = 10;
y = 10;
trace(x == y);  // Displays: true
```

Because x and y contain primitive data, they are compared by value. In a value-based comparison, data is compared literally. The number 10 in x is considered equal to the number 10 in y because the numbers are made up of the same bytes.

Now, let's assign x and y identical versions of the same composite data and compare the two variables again:

```
x = [10, "hi", 5];
y = [10, "hi", 5];
trace(x == y);  // Displays: false
```

This time, x and y contain composite data, so they are compared by reference. The arrays we assigned to x and y have the same byte values, but the variables x and y are not equal because they do not store a reference to the same composite datum. However, watch what happens when we copy the reference in x to y:

```
x = y;
trace(x == y);  // Displays: true
```

Now that the references are the same, the values are considered equal. Thus, the result of the comparison depends on the references in the variables, not the actual byte values of the arrays.

Primitive and composite data are also treated differently when passed to functions, as discussed under "Primitive Versus Composite Parameter Values" in Chapter 9, *Functions*. Most notably, when a primitive variable is passed as an argument to a function, any changes to the datum within the function are not reflected in the original variable. However, when passing a composite variable, changes within the function *do* affect the original variable. That is, if you pass an integer variable x to a function, changes to it within the function don't affect its original value. But if you pass an array y to a function, any changes to that array within the function *will* alter the original value of y outside the function (because changes to the array affect the data to which y points).

Bitwise Programming

Switching gears, let's examine an unrelated, esoteric topic—bitwise programming with bitwise operators. This discussion was too obscure for Chapter 5, *Operators*, but we'll cover it now for experienced programmers and braver beginners.

In order to track and manipulate a series of options in a highly optimized way, we can use the bitwise operators. Technically, the bitwise operators are mathematical operators, but they're typically used in a logical, not mathematical, context. Bitwise operators can access the individual binary digits (*bits*) in an integer. To understand how this works, you need to know how numbers are represented in binary format.

A binary number is stored as a sequence of ones and zeros that represent the number in the base-2 number system (i.e., the *binary system*). Each column in a number represents the base of the number system to some power. Binary uses the number 2 as its base, so the first four columns of a binary number represent, from right to left, the 1's column (2^0), the 2's column (2^1), the 4's column (2^2), and the 8's column (2^3). Here are some sample binary numbers with explanations of how their column values can be used to calculate their base-10 (decimal) equivalent:

```
1      // The base-10 number  1: (1 x 1) is 1
10     // The base-10 number  2: (1 x 2) + (0 x 1) is 2
11     // The base-10 number  3: (1 x 2) + (1 x 1) is 3
100    // The base-10 number  4: (1 x 4) + (0 x 2) + (0 x 1) is 4
1000   // The base-10 number  8: (1 x 8) + (0 x 4) + (0 x 2) + (0 x 1) is 8
1001   // The base-10 number  9: (1 x 8) + (0 x 4) + (0 x 2) + (1 x 1) is 9
```

In binary, the *columns* we've been discussing are referred to as *bits* (short for "binary digit"). A *four-bit* number, for example, is a number with four digits (each of which may contain a one or a zero). The rightmost bit is considered bit 0; the bit to its left is bit 1, and so on. Following is an 8-bit number with a 1 in bits 0, 6, and 7; the bits are labeled above the number:

```
bit: 76543210
     11000001
```

As with all numbering systems, the largest value for a single digit is one less than the base (also known as the *radix*). For example, in base-10 (decimal), the largest single digit is 9. Notice that because we're using 2 as our base, each binary digit must be either a 0 or a 1. We know that the numbers 1 and 0 are equivalent to the Boolean values `true` and `false`, so it is very convenient to use binary numbers as a series of *on* and *off* switches! That's precisely what the bitwise operators let us do.

A bit that has the value 1 is said to be *set* (i.e., on or `true`). A bit that has the value 0 is said to be *cleared* (i.e., off or `false`). Each bit is sometimes thought of as a *flag* or *switch*, which means it indicates something that has two possible states (such as on/off or true/false).

Bitwise programming nearly always involves situations in which a series of properties can be turned on or off. Using bitwise operators, we can concisely represent many options within a single numeric value instead of using multiple variables. This provides better performance and lower memory consumption.

Suppose we're building a Flash site that sells cars. For the sake of simplicity, let's say there's only one kind of car for sale, but users can customize their car with any combination of four options: air-conditioning, a CD player, a sunroof, and leather seats. It's the job of our Flash program to come up with a total price for the car including all the options, and it's the job of a server-side program to track that information as part of the user's profile.

We could store the car's options with four separate Boolean variables, like this:

```
var hasAirCon = true;
var hasCD = true;
var hasSunRoof = true;
var hasLeather = true;
```

Essentially, we've got four switches—one for each optional component of the car—each requiring a variable. That works fine, but it means we need four variables in memory and four fields in the user-profile database on the server. When we record the car's options as individual binary digits, we can store all four options in a single 4-bit number: air-conditioning is bit 0 (the 1's column), the CD player is bit 1 (the 2's column), the sunroof is bit 2 (the 4's column), and the leather seats are bit 3 (the 8's column). Here are some sample configurations that show how a single number can represent any combination of the four options:

```
var options;
options = 1    // 1 is 0001; bit 0 is on: air-conditioning only
options = 2    // 2 is 0010; bit 1 is on: CD player only
options = 4    // 4 is 0100; bit 2 is on: sunroof only
options = 8    // 8 is 1000; bit 3 is on: leather seats only

// Here's the cool part: combining options
options = 5    // 5  is 0101: air-conditioning (1) and a sunroof (4)
options = 10   // 10 is 1010: CD player (2) and leather (8)
options = 15   // 15 is 1111: fully loaded baby!
```

Whenever we want to add or remove options, we just add or subtract the value of the appropriate bit:

```
var options = 0;   // No options to start
options += 4;      // Add sunroof (options is 4, or 0100)
options += 1;      // Add air-conditioning (options is 5, or 0101)
options += 2;      // Add CD player (options is 7, or 0111)
options -= 4;      // Remove the sunroof (options is 3, or 0011)
options += 8;      // Add leather seats (options is 11, or 1011)
```

So now we know how to store multiple options as a series of bits in a single number. How do we examine those bits to calculate the cost of the car? We need to use the bitwise operators. We'll run through the operators first and come back to the car example after we're done.

Bitwise AND

The bitwise AND operator (&) combines the bits of two numbers by performing a logical AND operation on each bit of the numbers. The operation returns the result of the combination as a number.

A bitwise AND expression takes the form:

    operand1 & operand2

The operands of bitwise AND can be any numbers, but they are converted to 32-bit binary integers before the operation occurs. If an operand has a fractional value such as 2.5, the fraction is discarded.

Note that the *bitwise* AND uses the single-character operator, &, and operates on the individual bits within its operands, whereas the *logical* AND operator discussed in Chapter 5 uses the two-character operator, &&, and treats each operand as a whole.

Bitwise AND returns a number whose value is determined by comparing the individual bits in the numeric operands, *operand1* and *operand2*, one at a time. If a bit contains a 1 in both operands, the corresponding bit will also be set to 1 in the result; otherwise, the bit will be a 0 in the result.

Bitwise AND operations are most easily pictured by arranging the binary equivalents of the decimal operands vertically and lining up their bit columns. In this format, it is easy to tell which bits of the operands both contain 1s.

In this example, bit 2 (the third bit from the right) is 1 in both operands and is therefore set to 1 in the result. Other bits are set to 0 in the result:

```
  1111
& 0100
------
  0100
```

In this example, bits 0 and 3 are 1 in both operands and are therefore set to 1 in the result. Bits 1 and 2 are set to 0 in the result:

```
  1101
& 1011
------
  1001
```

ActionScript uses decimal (base-10) numbers instead of binary numbers, which makes it harder to visualize bitwise operations. Here is what the previous operations look like in real code:

```
15 & 4   // Result is 4
13 & 11  // Result is 9
```

In practice, the bitwise AND operator is used to check whether a particular flag or set of flags (i.e., bits) is `true` or `false`.

The following example checks whether bit 2 (which has the value 4) is set to `true`:

```
if (x & 4) {
  // Do something
}
```

Or, we can check whether either bit 2 or bit 3 (which has the value 8) is set to `true`:

```
if (x & (4|8)) {
  // Do something
}
```

Note that the preceding example checks whether bit 2 *or* bit 3 is set using the | operator discussed next. To check whether both bits 2 *and* 3 are set, we can use:

```
if (x & (4|8) == (4|8)) {
  // Do something
}
```

The bitwise AND operator is also used to set individual bits in a number to `false`; see the section on the bitwise NOT operator later in this chapter.

Bitwise OR

The Bitwise OR operator (|) combines the bits of two numbers by performing a logical OR operation on each bit of the numbers. Like bitwise AND, bitwise OR returns the result of the combination as a number. A bitwise OR expression takes the form:

operand1 | *operand2*

The operands can be any numbers, but they are converted to 32-bit binary integers before the operation occurs. The fractional portion of an operand, if any, is discarded.

Note that the *bitwise* OR uses the single-character operator, |, and operates on individual bits within a number, whereas the *logical* OR operator discussed in Chapter 5 uses the two-character operator, ||, and treats each operand as a whole.

Each bit in the result is determined by taking the logical OR of the bits of the two operands. Therefore, if a bit is set to 1 in either (or both) *operand1* or *operand2*, that bit will be set to 1 in the result. Compare the following pseudoexamples to those shown earlier for the bitwise AND operator.

In this example, only bit 1 is set to 0 in the result because bit 1 is 0 in both operands. The other bits are set to 1:

```
  1101
| 0100
------
  1101
```

In this example, all bits are set to 1 in the result because each bit contains a 1 in at least one of the two operands:

```
  1101
| 1011
------
  1111
```

In real code, this reads:

```
13 | 4     // Result is 13
13 | 11    // Result is 15
```

In practice, we often use bitwise OR to combine multiple numbers that represent individual options into a single numeric value that represents all the options of a system. For example, the following code combines bit 2 (value 4) and bit 3 (value 8):

```
options = 4 | 8;
```

The bitwise OR operator is also used to set an option to **true** in an existing value. The following example sets the option represented by bit 3 (value 8) to **true**. If the value in bit 3 is already **true**, it is untouched:

```
options = options | 8;
```

Multiple bits can also be set at once:

```
options = options | 4 | 8;
```

Bitwise XOR

We're officially getting into weird punctuation symbols for our operators. The bitwise XOR (eXclusive OR) operator is the caret symbol, ^ (created using Shift-6 on most keyboards). A bitwise XOR expression takes the form:

```
operand1 ^ operand2
```

The operands can be any numbers, but they are converted to 32-bit binary integers before the operation occurs. The fractional portion of an operand, if any, is discarded.

The bitwise XOR operator differs from the bitwise OR operator in that the result contains a 0, not a 1, for any bit containing a 1 in *both* its operands. In other words, the XOR result contains a 0 for any bits that are the same in both operands and contains a 1 for any bits that differ between the two operands.

In this example, bits 0 and 3 match in both operands, so those bits are set to 0 in the result. Bits 1 and 2 differ in the two operands, so they are set to 1 in the result:

```
   1011
 ^ 1101
 ------
   0110
```

In this example, all the bits match in both operands, so the result is all zeros:

```
   0010
 ^ 0010
 ------
   0000
```

In this example, bits 0, 2, and 3 differ in the two operands, so those bits are set to 1 in the result. Bit 1 is the same in both operands, so it is set to 0 in the result:

```
   0110
 ^ 1011
 ------
   1101
```

Translated to decimal numbers, the preceding examples become:

```
11 ^ 13    // Result is 6
2 ^ 2      // Result is 0
6 ^ 11     // Result is 13
```

The bitwise XOR operator is typically used to toggle options between 1 and 0 (**true** and **false**). To toggle the option indicated by bit 2 (whose value is 4), we could use:

```
options = options ^ 4;
```

Bitwise NOT

Unlike bitwise AND, OR, and XOR, which all produce a number resulting from two other numbers, bitwise NOT changes the bits of a single number. It uses the tilde symbol (~) found in the upper left of most keyboards and takes the form:

```
~operand
```

The operand can be any number, but it is converted to a 32-bit binary integer before the operation occurs. Any fractional portion of the operand is discarded.

Bitwise NOT simply inverts the bits in its operand. For example:

```
~00000000000000000000000000000010
  // Result is 11111111111111111111111111111101

~11111111111111111111111111111010
  // Result is 00000000000000000000000000000101
```

which, in decimal, read:

```
~2    // Result is -3. See the following explanation.
~-6   // Result is 5. See the following explanation.
```

It's impractical to go into a lesson on negative binary-number representation systems here, but advanced programmers should note that bitwise operations represent negative binary integers using the twos-complement system. To those unfamiliar with this notation, simply remember that the return value of a bitwise NOT operation is one less than the value obtained by taking the negative of the original operand. For example:

```
~-10  // Change the sign of -10 to 10, then subtract 1. Result is 9.
```

The bitwise NOT operator is typically used with the bitwise AND operator to clear specific bits (i.e., set them to 0). For example, to clear bit 2, we could use:

```
options = options & ~4;
```

The expression ~4 returns a 32-bit integer containing all 1s, except for a 0 in bit 2. By bitwise ANDing that number with the **options** variable, **options**' bit 2 is cleared and other bits are left unchanged. The preceding can be written more succinctly as:

```
options &= ~4;
```

The same technique can be used to clear multiple bits at once; the following example clears bits 2 and 3:

```
options &= ~(4 | 8);
```

The Bitwise Shift Operators

As we've seen, bitwise programming treats binary numbers as a series of *switches*. It's frequently useful to move those switches around. For example, if we have bit 0 on and we decide we want to turn it off and turn bit 2 on, we could simply move bit 0 left two places. Or if we want to know whether or not the bit 5 of a number is on, we could move that bit right five places and then check bit 0's value. The bitwise shift operators let us perform such movements.

Bitwise shift operators also allow us to rapidly multiply and divide by multiples of 2. If you wanted to divide a decimal (base-10) number by 10, you could simply shift the decimal point one position to the left. Likewise, to multiply by 10, you simply shift the decimal place one position to the right, and to multiply by 10^3 (i.e., 1000) you would shift the decimal place three positions to the right. The bitwise shift operators let us perform an analogous operation with binary numbers. Shifting bits to the right divides a number by 2 for each position shifted. Shifting bits to the left multiplies a number by 2 for each position shifted.

Signed right shift

The signed right shift operator can be used to divide a number by some power of 2. It uses the >> symbol (created using two successive greater-than signs) and takes the general form:

```
operand >> n
```

where *n* specifies how many places to the right to shift *operand*'s bits. The result is equivalent to dividing **operand** by 2^n. The remainder, if any, is discarded. Here's how it works:

All bits are shifted right by the number of positions specified by *n*. Any bits shifted off the righthand side of the number are discarded. New bits are added on the left side to fill the void created by the shift operation. If *operand* is positive, the newly added bits are 0s. If *operand* is negative, the newly added bits are 1s (because negative numbers are represented in twos-complement). Here's an example in pseudocode:

```
// The right-most bit (0) is lost and 0s fill in on the left
// The result is 00000000000000000000000000000100
00000000000000000000000000001000 >> 1
```

Shifting a number right one bit is like dividing it by 2^1 (i.e., 2). In decimal this reads:

```
8 >> 1  // The result is 4
```

Note that any remainder is discarded:

```
9 >> 1 // The result is still 4
```

For negative numbers, >> still divides by 2 for each bit position shifted:

```
-16 >> 2  // The result is -4 (-16 divided by 2 squared)
```

Unsigned right shift

The unsigned right shift operator, created using three successive greater-than signs (>>>), takes the form:

```
operand >>> n
```

It works like the signed right shift operator except that bits vacated by the shift are always filled with 0s (regardless of whether *operand* is positive or negative). For positive numbers, it is no different than the signed right shift operator.

Left shift

The left shift operator can be used to multiply a number by some power of 2. It uses the << symbol (created using two successive less-than signs) and takes the general form:

```
operand1 << n
```

where *n* specifies how many places to the left to shift *operand*'s bits. The result is equivalent to multiplying **operand** by 2^n. Here's how it works:

All bits are shifted left by the number of positions specified by *n*. Any bits shifted off the lefthand side of the number are discarded. The empty bits created by the shift on the right are filled in with 0s. For example:

```
01000000000000000000000000001001 << 4
  // Result is 00000000000000000000000010010000
```

Shifting a number left by 4 bits is equivalent to multiplying it by 2^4 (i.e., 16). In decimal, this reads:

```
9 << 4  // Result is 9 * 16, i.e., 144
```

Notice that in prior examples, we "manually" specified the value associated with a particular bit: 1 for bit 0, 2 for bit 1, 4 for bit 2, 8 for bit 3, and so on. The left shift operator is very handy for calculating a bit position's equivalent value:

```
(1 << 0)    // Bit 0 equals 1
(1 << 1)    // Bit 1 equals 2
(1 << 2)    // Bit 2 equals 4
(1 << 3)    // Bit 3 equals 8
(1 << 15)   // Much easier than remembering bit 15 equates to 32768!
```

The left shift operator is also handy for dynamically selecting bits by numeric index rather than bit value. Example 15-1 counts up all the 1s in a number.

Example 15-1. Using Left Shift to Count Bits That Are Set

```
myNumber = 27583;  // The number whose 1s we'll count
count = 0;
for (var i=0; i < 32; i++) {
  if (myNumber & (1 << i)) {
    count++;
  }
}
```

Example 15-2 is a variation on Example 15-1 using the right shift operator. We can repeatedly right-shift the value and check its rightmost bit (bit 0), instead of using the left shift operator to calculate the bit value associated with each bit.

Example 15-2. Counting Bits Using Right Shift

```
myNumber = 27583;
count = 0;
temp = myNumber;     // Make a copy for temporary use
for (var i = 0; i < 32; i++) {
  if (temp & 1) {
    count++;
  }
  temp = temp >> 1;
}
```

The variable myNumber is copied into the temporary variable temp because the right shift is destructive; the variable temp ends up with a final value of 0.

Bitwise Operations Applied

We began our look at bitwise operators using the example of a Flash site that sells cars. Now that we've seen how bitwise operators work, let's use them to determine the cost of a car, as shown in Example 15-3. You can download the *.fla* file for this example from the online Code Depot.

Example 15-3. Real-Life Bitwise Operations

```
// First, set the options (usually by adding and subtracting numbers
// based on the selections of a fill-in form, but we hardcode them here)
var hasAirCon   = (1<<0)    // Bit 0: 0 means no, 1 means yes
var hasCDplayer = (0<<1)    // Bit 1: 0 means no, 2 means yes
var hasSunRoof  = (1<<2)    // Bit 2: 0 means no, 4 means yes
var hasLeather  = (1<<3)    // Bit 3: 0 means no, 8 means yes

// Now combine the options into a single number using bitwise OR
var carOptions = hasAirCon | hasCDplayer | hasSunRoof | hasLeather;

// Here's a function that calculates the price
function totalPrice(carOptions) {
  var price = 0;
  if (carOptions & 1) {  // If the first bit is set
    price += 1000;       // add $1000
  }
  if (carOptions & 2) {  // If the second bit is set
    price += 500;        // add $500
  }
  if (carOptions & 4) {  // If the third bit is set
    price += 1200;       // add $1200
  }
  if (carOptions & 8) {  // If the fourth bit is set
    price += 800;        // add $800
  }
```

Example 15-3. Real-Life Bitwise Operations (continued)

```
  return price;
}

// Everything's set to go: let's call the function and see if it works!
trace(totalPrice(carOptions));  // Returns 3000. Cool...
```

To avoid hardcoded bit values throughout your code, it's good practice to store the bit values corresponding to specific options in variables, such as:

```
    var airConFLAG   = 1 << 0;  // Bit 0, whose value is 1
    var cdPlayerFLAG = 1 << 1;  // Bit 1, whose value is 2
    var sunroofFLAG  = 1 << 2;  // Bit 2, whose value is 4
    var leatherFLAG  = 1 << 3;  // Bit 3, whose value is 8
```

Reader Exercise: Rewrite Example 15-3 using variables and the left shift operator instead of hardcoded bit values to represent the options.

Why bitwise?

Although Example 15-3 would be easier to understand as a series of Boolean operations, bitwise operations are extremely fast and compact. Anytime we can speak to a computer in its native binary tongue, we save room and gain speed.

For the sake of comparison, consider a situation in which we're tracking a user's profile, and each user has 32 settings that can be on or off. In a normal database, we'd need 32 fields for each user. If we have a million users, that's a million copies of 32 fields. But when we use bitwise programming we can store the 32 settings in a single number, requiring only one field in the database for each user! Not only does this save disk space, but every time we access a user's profile, we need transfer only a single integer, not 32 Boolean values. If we are processing millions of transactions, saving a few milliseconds per transaction can measurably improve system performance.

For further study, see Gene Myers' excellent article for C programmers, *Becoming Bit Wise*, posted at *http://www.cscene.org/CS9/CS9-02.html*.

Advanced Function Scope Issues

This section describes another advanced topic that was too esoteric for our initial discussion about function scope. Let's revisit it here now that we've learned about movie clips, function scope, and objects.

We learned in Chapter 9 that a function's scope chain is normally determined relative to the function's declaration statement. There is, however, a subtle extension to this rule. When a function from one timeline is assigned to a variable in a different movie clip's timeline, that *assignment* also affects the function's scope chain. If the original function is invoked directly, its scope chain includes its original time-line, but if the function is invoked through the variable, its scope chain includes the *variable's* timeline.

For example, suppose we create a function called *transformClip()* that rotates and scales the current clip. We set the amount to rotate and scale the clip in the variable's `rotateAmount` and `widthAmount`:

```
var rotateAmount = 45;
var widthAmount = 50;

function transformClip () {
    _rotation = rotateAmount;
    _xscale = widthAmount;
}

// Invoke the function
transformClip();
```

Next we assign `transformClip` to a variable, `tc`, in a clip called `rect`:

```
rect.tc = transformClip;
```

When we invoke `transformClip` through `rect.tc`, as follows, nothing happens:

```
rect.tc();
```

Why? The function stored in `tc` has a scope chain that includes `rect`, not our original function's timeline, so `rotateAmount` and `widthAmount` are not found. But when we add `rotateAmount` and `widthAmount` variables to `rect`, the function can find the variables, so it works:

```
rect.widthAmount = 10;
rect.rotateAmount = 15;
rect.tc();  // Sets rect to 10 percent width, and 15 degrees rotation
```

In contrast, when regular data objects on the same timeline are involved in function assignment, the assigned function's scope chain is not altered; rather, the function's scope chain is permanently determined relative to the function declaration. Example 15-4 demonstrates.

Example 15-4. The Fixed Scope of Object Methods

```
// Set our variables
var rotateAmount = 45;
var widthAmount = 50;

// Create a transformClip() function
// that prints the value of rotateAmount and widthAmount
function transformClip () {
    trace(rotateAmount);
    trace(widthAmount);
}
```

Example 15-4. The Fixed Scope of Object Methods (continued)

```
// Create an object that corresponds with
// the rect clip in the previous example
var rectObj = new Object();

// Copy transformClip to a property of rectObj
rectObj.tc = transformClip;

// Set rotateAmount and widthAmount properties on rectObj
rectObj.rotateAmount = 15;
rectObj.widthAmount = 10;

// Now invoke rectObj.tc
rectObj.tc();   // Displays 45 and 50, not 15 and 10. The scope of
                // rectObj.tc is the same as transformClip().
```

When assigned to an object property, a function is scoped to the timeline that bears the function declaration. However, when assigned to a remote movie clip, a function is scoped to the timeline of the remote clip.

Note that this behavior is actually a departure from JavaScript, in which functions are permanently scoped to objects based on the function declaration. For example, if we assume the frames of an HTML frameset to be roughly analogous to the clips in a Flash movie, then we can see the discrepancy; in JavaScript, a function assigned to a remote frame is still scoped to the frame with the function declaration, not the remote frame, as shown in Example 15-5.

Example 15-5. JavaScript's Static Function Scope

```
// CODE ON FRAME 0 OF A FRAMESET
// Assign a variable in frame 0
var myVar = "frame 0";

// Set a function in frame 1 of the frameset, and copy that
// function back to frame 0
parent.frames[1].myMeth = function () { alert(myVar); };
myMeth = parent.frames[1].myMeth;

// Invoke myMeth() from frame 0
myMeth(); // displays "frame 0"

// CODE ON A BUTTON IN FRAME 1 OF THE SAME FRAMESET
<FORM>
  <INPUT type="button" value="click me" onClick="myMeth();">
</FORM>

// Now click the button to invoke myMeth() from frame 1.
// "frame 0" is displayed.
// myMeth() is not scoped to frame 1, but to frame 0, where
// the declaration statement occurred.
```

The movieclip Datatype

Again let's revisit another esoteric topic, having mastered the fundamentals of ActionScript. In Chapter 13, *Movie Clips*, we learned that movie clips behave, for the most part, exactly like objects. However, movie clips are not just another class—they are their own distinct datatype. Gary Grossman, the creator of Action-Script, explains the difference between the internal implementation of the *movieclip* and *object* datatypes as follows:

> Movie clips are implemented separately from objects internally in the Player, although both manifest almost identically in ActionScript. The primary difference lies in the way that they are allocated and deallocated. Regular objects are *reference-counted* and *garbage-collected*, whereas the lifetime of movie clips is timeline-controlled or explicitly controlled with the *duplicateMovieClip()* and *removeMovieClip()* functions.

> If you declare an array using x = new Array() and then set x = null, Action-Script will immediately detect that there are no remaining references to the *Array* object (i.e., no variables referring to it), and garbage-collect it (i.e., free the memory it used). Periodic mark-and-sweep garbage collection eliminates objects containing circular references. (That is, advanced techniques are used to ensure that memory is freed when two unused objects refer to each other.)

> Movie clips don't behave the same way. They come into and go out of existence depending on the placement of objects on the timeline. If they are created dynamically (e.g., with *duplicateMovieClip()*) they are disposed of only when *removeMovieClip()* is used on them.

> References to objects are *pointers* (memory address references); reference-tracking and garbage-collection protect the user from dangling pointers and memory leakage. References to movie clips, however, are *soft* references—the reference actually contains an absolute target path. If you have a movie clip named foo, and then set x = foo (which makes x a reference to clip foo), and then delete foo using *removeMovieClip()*, and then create *another* clip named foo, the reference x will again be valid (it will point to the new foo clip).

> Regular objects are different—the existence of a reference to an object prevents that object from being removed in the first place. So if movie clips were objects, *removeMovieClip()* wouldn't remove the object from memory so long as the variable x made reference to it. Furthermore, if you create a second movie clip named foo, the old foo and the new foo can exist simultaneously, although the old foo would no longer be rendered.

> So, a separate *movieclip* type is appropriate because of its important differences from the *object* type. For similar reasons, the *typeof* operator reports "function" for functions, even though functions are also akin to objects in many ways.

Onward!

Thus endeth Part I, *ActionScript Fundamentals*. In Part II, *Applied ActionScript*, we'll learn some important practical authoring techniques, plus how to make a Flash form and how to debug code. To speak ActionScript like a native, you should also expand your vocabulary by browsing Part III, *Language Reference*, which describes the built-in functions, properties, objects, and classes of ActionScript.

II

Applied ActionScript

This part describes some of the more practical sides of programming in Flash, such as using the authoring environment and the debugger. Part II also examines two specific areas of Flash programming: building Flash forms and using on-screen text fields.

- Chapter 16, *ActionScript Authoring Environment*
- Chapter 17, *Flash Forms*
- Chapter 18, *On-Screen Text Fields*
- Chapter 19, *Debugging*

16

ActionScript Authoring Environment

This chapter examines the practical details of authoring ActionScript code. We'll cover the following topics:

- Using the Actions panel to place code on buttons, movie clips, and frames
- Loading code from an external file
- Packaging code as a reusable authoring component with Smart Clips

The Actions Panel

The *Actions panel* is Flash's ActionScript-editing environment. Every script in a movie is created in the Actions panel, which is accessed via Window → Actions.

The Actions panel is divided into two sections: the Toolbox pane (on the left) and the Script pane (on the right), as shown in Figure 16-1.

The Script pane houses code attached to the currently selected frame, button, or movie clip. The Toolbox acts both as a quick reference guide and as a means of adding code to the Script pane. Double-clicking any item in the Toolbox adds that item to the Script pane. Items may also be dragged from the Toolbox into the Script pane.

The Actions panel's title indicates whether our current code lives on a frame (Frame Actions) or on a button or movie clip (Object Actions). When we select a frame, the Actions panel's title changes automatically to Frame Actions; when we select either a movie clip or a button, the Actions panel's title changes to Object Actions.

The organization of the items in the Toolbox differs somewhat from the categories used to describe the features of ActionScript in this book. Most notably, in the

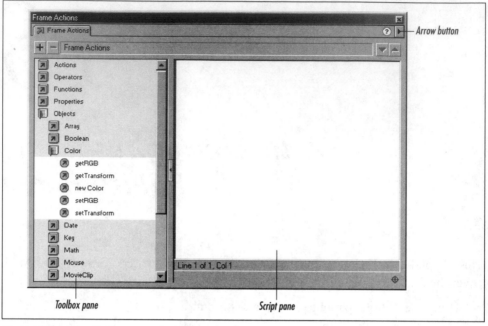

Figure 16-1. The Actions panel

Toolbox, *statements* are not separated into their own folder, and classes and objects are grouped together under the *Objects* folder. In this book we distinguish between statements, classes, and objects in keeping with more formal programming terminology.

Editing Modes

The Actions panel has two different modes of operation, Normal Mode and Expert Mode, which govern how we add code to the Script pane.

Normal Mode

In Normal Mode, the Toolbox is used to build new statements, and the Script pane is used as a viewer for those statements. To add a new statement to the Script pane in Normal Mode, we double-click the desired Action or drag an Action from the Toolbox to the Script pane. To add a statement of arbitrary code, we select the *evaluate* Action and enter the statement into the Expression field of the Parameters pane (not shown in the figure) at the bottom of the Actions panel.

After adding a statement to the Script pane, we may customize it via the Parameters pane at the bottom of the Actions panel. The layout and contents of the Parameters pane changes to suit the statement selected in the Script pane. Notice that when the Actions panel is operating in Normal Mode, code may *not* be typed into the Script pane. In Normal Mode, the Script pane is not a text-editing environment, but rather a read-only list of statements; alterations to statements in the Script pane are performed through the Parameters pane.

Although Flash 5's Normal Mode may look similar to the Actions panel in Flash 4, it should not be misconstrued as a backward-compatibility mode. To the contrary, it is quite possible to create code in either editing mode that wouldn't be Flash 4 compatible (see Appendix C, *Backward Compatibility*). Normal Mode is comforting for new programmers but constricting for most nontrivial programming projects. In this book, therefore, we use only the Expert Mode to author code. However, with the exception of multiline comments (which may be used only in Expert Mode), any code produced in one mode may also be produced in the other.

Expert Mode

In Expert Mode the Script pane functions as a traditional text-editing window. When authoring or changing code in Expert Mode, we type directly into the Script pane. We may, however, still double-click items in the Toolbox to add them to the Script pane. The Parameters pane is not used in Expert Mode; instead, parameters are typed directly into the Script pane.

Setting the editing mode

The editing mode of the Actions panel is set on a per-frame and per-object basis. That is, Flash remembers the Actions panel editing mode chosen for every object and frame in a movie. If we select Normal Mode for frame 2 and Expert Mode for frame 3, the Actions panel will automatically switch to Normal Mode when we edit the code on frame 2 and Expert Mode when we edit the code on frame 3.

To select the mode for an individual frame or an object, we choose Expert Mode or Normal Mode from the arrow button in the top-right corner of the Actions panel (see Figure 16-1). To select the default mode for *all* frames and objects of a movie, we choose Expert Mode or Normal Mode under Edit → Preferences → General → Actions Panel → Mode. Note that the default mode setting affects only those frames and objects for which an editing mode has not already been set. Therefore, the default mode should be set at the beginning of movie production. There is no way to globally override the individual mode previously set explicitly for existing frames and objects.

Switching from Expert Mode to Normal Mode destroys all source-code formatting. The code is reformatted according to Flash's standard formatting rules—extra whitespace is lost, comments are placed on their own line, and statement block indentation is adjusted to match the style shown throughout this book.

Adding Scripts to Frames

Flash documents are fundamentally structured around the concept of animation. Every Flash document comprises a linear sequence of *frames*, or slices of visual and audio content. A great deal of ActionScript code is tied to this frame-based structure. By placing a code block on a frame, we stipulate the timing of that block's execution relative to the playback of the movie. Whenever we add code to a frame, we must always consider not only what we want the code to do, but *when* we want the code to execute.

For example, we may want to write some code that places a new movie clip on stage when the 20th frame of a movie is displayed:

```
_root.attachMovie("myClip", "clip1", 0);
```

In order for that code to execute when the 20th frame is displayed, we must attach it to a keyframe at frame 20 of the movie. To attach code to a keyframe, we select the keyframe in the timeline, open the Actions panel, and then add the desired code to the Script pane. During playback, code on a keyframe is executed before the content of the frame is displayed.

Code on keyframes is used to perform tasks synchronized to the movie's playback and to establish program elements such as variables, functions, and objects for use throughout a movie clip or movie. A timeline loop is a simple example of a synchronized task. Suppose we attach the following code to frame 15 of a movie:

```
gotoAndPlay(10);
```

When the playhead of the movie reaches frame 15, the code executes and the movie begins playing back at frame 10 again. When frame 15 is reached for the second time, the code is executed again and the movie once again starts playing at frame 10. This causes the movie to cycle endlessly between frames 10 and 15.

However, code on keyframes does not always control or synchronize with a movie's playhead. We may also use keyframes simply as storage devices for functions, variables, objects, and other program entities. For example, we may attach the function *moveTo()* to frame 1 of a movie clip and then invoke *moveTo()* from a button later in the movie:

```
function moveTo (x, y) {
  _x = x;
  _y = y;
}
```

One caution: because the execution of code on frames is dictated by the playback of a movie, we must always ensure that variables, functions, and other program elements are available before they are accessed. We can't, for example, invoke a function at frame 3 if that function isn't defined until frame 10. Code used globally throughout a movie should, therefore, be placed on the first frame of the main timeline.

We must also ensure that no code attempts to access portions of a movie that have not yet loaded. To check whether a specific portion of a movie has loaded, we use either the movie clip `_framesloaded` property or the *getBytesLoaded()* method. For sample code, see the entry for *Movieclip.*`_framesloaded` in Part III, *Language Reference*.

Adding Scripts to Buttons

We add code to a button in order to tie the execution of that code to a user event. For example, if we want the clicking of a button to advance the playhead of a movie to a frame labeled `section1`, we add the following code to that button:

```
on (release) {
  gotoAndStop("section1");
}
```

To add code to a button, we select the button on the Stage and then add the code to the Script pane of the Actions panel. Code on buttons must *always* be placed in an event handler that identifies the circumstances under which the code should execute. For example, the event that triggers most button actions is *release*. We might also use the *rollOver* event, causing code to execute when the mouse moves over the button, not when the button is pressed:

```
on (rollOver) {
  gotoAndStop("section1");
}
```

For a complete description of button event handlers see Chapter 10, *Events and Event Handlers*.

Though it is legal to place thousands of lines of code on a button, it's often a bad idea to overload a button with code. Whenever possible, generalize and package the behavior of button code into functions attached to the button's timeline. For example, we *could* add the following code to a button:

```
on (release) {
  title._xscale = 20;
  title._yscale = 20;
  title._alpha  = 50;
  title._gotoAndPlay("fadeout");
}
```

But we're better off placing that code in a function and calling the function from the button:

```
// CODE ON FRAME 1 OF THE BUTTON'S TIMELINE
function transformClip(clip, scale, transparency, framelabel) {
```

```
    clip._xscale = scale;
    clip._yscale = scale;
    clip._alpha = transparency;
    clip.gotoAndPlay(framelabel);
}
// CODE ON BUTTON
on (release) {
    transformClip(title, 20, 50, "fadeout");
}
```

This approach keeps all of our code centralized and easy to maintain and allows us to quickly apply the button's behavior to many buttons with minimal effort.

> Button code must be attached to a button object on stage, and must include an event handler. Button code without an event handler will cause an error, and it's not possible to attach code to the internal UP, OVER, DOWN, and HIT frames of a button symbol.

Adding Scripts to Movie Clips

We've already learned that we can attach code to the frames of a movie clip's timeline. It is also possible to attach code to a movie clip object itself. To do so, we select the movie clip instance on stage and then add our code to the Script pane of the Actions panel. As with buttons, all code attached to movie clip objects must be contained within event handlers. Event handlers tell the interpreter when to execute the movie clip code. For example, the following code sets the variable x to 10 when a movie clip loads:

```
onClipEvent (load) {
    var x = 10;
}
```

Movie clip event handlers can react to mouse and keyboard activity, data loading, frames rendering, and the birth and death of movie clips. For complete coverage of movie clips and event handlers, see Chapter 10, *Events and Event Handlers* and Chapter 13, *Movie Clips.*

Where's All the Code?

Even for experienced Flash users, locating the code in a movie can sometimes be challenging. Because code may be attached to any frame in any timeline, to any button, or to any movie clip on stage, it is often lost in a sea of content. Obviously, a highly organized structure and thorough code documentation can mean dozens or hundreds of hours saved over the life span of a project. But if you're faced with a movie that seems to be mysteriously missing important code, open the Actions panel and try these techniques for finding it:

- Click on any frame that has a little circle icon on it in the timeline. A circle indicates the presence of ActionScript code.

- Look for, and select, any white circle with a black outline on stage. These circles indicate empty movie clips, which often contain nothing but code. If there's no code on the empty clip itself, double-click the clip to edit it and investigate its frames.

- Select each button in the movie, one at a time. Some programmers tend not to centralize code and place long, important scripts directly on buttons.

- Check the timeline for hidden or masked layers. A layer with a red X icon next to it is hidden during authoring but may contain clips and buttons with code that appear during movie playback. Similarly, masked layers may contain obscured objects that bear code. Unlock masked layers to reveal their contents.

- Unlock all layers. Empty movie clips (the little circles with black outlines) are hidden when the layer they're on is locked.

Sometimes even these techniques can fail us. If someone's determined to hide some code, there are lots of places in Flash to do it. An empty clip, for example, can be placed far beyond the limits of the Stage, making it nearly impossible to find. Fortunately, when all seems lost, our code isn't—we can always use the Movie Explorer to hunt down any script in a movie. Select Window → Movie Explorer for a bird's-eye view of all the assets in a movie, including any scripts attached to a frame, button, or movie clip. Scripts are marked with a blue arrow Actions icon that matches the icon on the items in the Actions panel Toolbox. You can even filter the display to show only scripts; select the Actions icon under the Show menu at the top of the Explorer panel, and unselect all other icons.

Productivity

Here are some tips to streamline ActionScript source code authoring:

- Keep all timeline scripts on an independent layer called *scripts*. Do not place any content on the *scripts* layer; use it exclusively for code. Store this layer at the top of your layer structure so that its code executes after all other layers have loaded (or at the bottom if you set your Load Order to Top Down). If you always keep the *scripts* layer in the same place, it's easy to find your code. (We know from the previous section how valuable that can be!)

- Keep all frame labels on an independent layer called *labels*. Do not place any content on the *labels* layer; use it exclusively for frame labels.

- Take a look under the arrow button in the top-right corner of the Actions panel. You'll find handy tools such as search and replace, source code printing, and Script pane font control.

- When working with code libraries used on multiple projects, save code in external files. See the next section, "Externalizing ActionScript Code," for details.

- To save typing, use the shortcut keys provided for Actions (for example, Esc-G-P for *gotoAndPlay()*). Shortcut sequences are listed under the plus (+) button in the Actions panel.

- Reconfigure the Actions panel to place it with the other code-centric panels: Instance, Frame, and Text Options. Simply open up any panel under Window → Panels, and then drag the Actions panel onto it.

- Notice that the Toolbox is resizable. To save space while coding, you can hide the Toolbox, partially or completely, by dragging the border between the Toolbox and the Script pane.

Externalizing ActionScript Code

ActionScript code can be saved in external text files (which use the *.as* extension by convention) or *.swf* files and imported into a Flash document. By maintaining code in external files, we facilitate the use of standard code libraries across many projects. We can import external code into Flash using Import From File, using the `#include` directive, or using a shared library.

Import From File (Author-Time Import)

While editing a *.fla* file, we may bring code into the Action panel's Script pane using Import From File, found under the arrow button in the top-right corner of the Actions panel (see Figure 16-1). Import From File is a one-time operation that copies the contents of the external file into the Actions panel, *replacing* any script currently there. Code imported via Import From File is not persistently linked to the *.fla* file in any way. To append or insert script text instead of replacing it, you need to manually cut and paste the text from an external text-editing application.

#include (Compile-Time Import)

When we export (*compile*) a *.swf* file from a *.fla* file, we may import code from an external text file using the `#include` directive. For information on using `#include`, see Part III.

Shared Library (Runtime Import)

To import code from an external source while a movie is actually playing, we must create a shared library *.swf* file with a movie clip containing the code to import. Runtime import offers the most flexible approach to sharing code across movies because it does not require recompilation of the movies that import the shared code; when the shared library *.swf* file is updated, the movies that link to it automatically reflect the update.

The following procedures describe how to share a simple test function from a movie called *codeLibrary.swf* to a movie called *myMovie.swf*. We'll create the *codeLibrary.swf* movie first:

1. Create a new Flash document.

2. Create a new movie clip symbol named `sharedFunctions`.

3. On frame 1 of the `sharedFunctions` clip, add the following code:

```
function test () {
  trace("The shared function, test, was called.");
}
```

4. Select the `sharedFunctions` clip in the Library.

5. From the Library panel, select Options → Linkage.

6. Select Export This Symbol.

7. In the Identifier box, type **sharedFunctions**.

8. Save the document as *codeLibrary.fla*.

9. Use File → Export Movie to create *codeLibrary.swf* from *codeLibrary.fla*.

10. Close the *codeLibrary.swf* and *codeLibrary.fla* files.

Now, we'll create the *myMovie.swf* file, which will execute the code imported from *codeLibrary.swf*:

1. Create a new Flash document.

2. Save the new document as *myMovie.fla* in the same folder as *codeLibrary.fla*.

3. Rename *Layer 1* to *sharedCode*.

4. Select File → Open As Shared Library, and choose *codeLibrary.fla*. The *codeLibrary.fla* Library appears.

5. Drag an instance of the `sharedFunctions` clip from the *codeLibrary.fla* Library onto the Stage of frame 1 of *myMovie.fla*.

6. Select the instance on stage, then select Modify → Instance.

7. Name the instance `sharedFunctions`.

8. On the main timeline of *myMovie.fla*, create a new layer called *scripts*.

9. Add a keyframe to the *scripts* layer at frame 2.

10. Add a new frame to the *sharedCode* layer.

11. On frame 2 of the *scripts* layer, attach the following code:

```
stop();
sharedFunctions.test();
```

12. Export *myMovie.swf*.

13. The following text appears in the Output window: "The shared function, test, was called."

Note that a shared library is a linked asset, much like a *.gif* image is linked to an *.html* file. Shared library *.swf* files must, therefore, always be uploaded correctly with the files that use them. To change the location of a link from an imported symbol to a shared library, follow these steps:

1. Select the symbol in the Library.

2. From the Library panel, select Options → Linkage.

3. Under Import This Symbol from URL, set the new location.

Packaging Components as Smart Clips

A *Smart Clip* is a movie clip that allows some of its variables to be assigned through a special graphical user interface in the Flash authoring tool. Smart Clips allow non-programmers to customize programmatically-controlled movie clips. Smart Clips separate the behavior-determining variables from the code of a clip, which lets people treat them as "black boxes"—their operation can remain mysterious as long as their inputs, outputs, and behavior are known.

Normally, variable initialization occurs in the source code of a movie clip. For example, here we set up the variables used to control a fireworks effect:

```
// User-defined variables
var numSparks = 10;          // Number of spark clips in the explosion
var randomDispersion = true; // Explosion style (true for random,
                             // false for uniform)
var duration = 1300;         // Length of explosion, in milliseconds
```

Modifying source code of this sort can be intimidating for non-programmers. But if we build our system as a Smart Clip, non-programmers can configure the fireworks effect through a familiar application-style interface. Figure 16-2 shows a Smart Clip interface equivalent to our variable-initialization code.

In a Smart Clip interface, each variable appears with its name and value clearly distinguished in separate rows and columns. Variable names cannot be edited, so

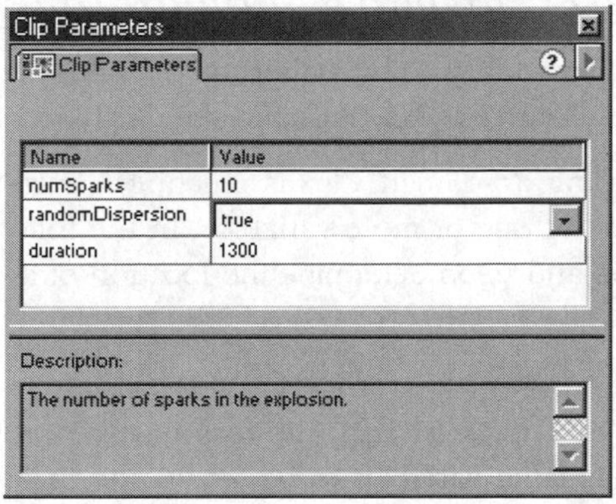

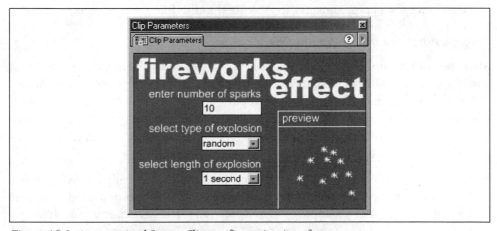

Figure 16-2. A sample Smart Clip–configuration interface

there's no chance of inadvertent typos breaking the system. Each variable also has its own verbose description explaining exactly what it does and how it should be set. Finally, variables with a limited set of legal values (such as `randomDispersion`) may be assigned via drop-down menus.

For non-programmers, the interface shown in Figure 16-2 is certainly more approachable than source code. But Smart Clips can actually be made even more user friendly. We may replace the default Smart Clip interface with our own custom interface, such as the one shown in Figure 16-3. Notice how the custom Smart Clip interface hides our system's variables entirely, allowing the non-programmer to tailor each instance of the fireworks effect with text fields and pull-down menus. The interface even provides a live preview of the effect in action!

Figure 16-3. A customized Smart Clip-configuration interface

Let's see how all this works.

Building a Smart Clip with a Standard Interface

As we've just learned, Smart Clips have either the default system interface or a customized interface. We'll learn how to build the standard kind first.

The first step in building any Smart Clip is creating a regular movie clip that is controlled by the value of one or more variables. In the following code, for example, the variables xPos and yPos determine the location of a clip on stage:

```
_x = xPos;
_y = yPos;
```

When we build a movie clip as a Smart Clip for ourselves or someone else to use, we expect certain designated variables to be set via the Smart Clip interface when the clip is placed on stage. Those variables are known as *clip parameters*. Once we've created a clip with behavior dictated by one or more clip parameters, we must give the clip a Smart Clip interface through which those parameters can be set.

Adding a standard interface to a Smart Clip

To add a default Smart Clip interface to a movie clip, follow these steps:

1. Select the clip in the Library.

2. Choose Options → Define Clip Parameters. (The Define Clip Parameters dialog box appears.)

3. In the Parameters pane, click the plus (+) button to add a clip parameter.

4. Repeat step 3 for each parameter in the Smart Clip.

5. Configure the clip parameters, as described in the following section.

Configuring standard clip parameters

After we add a clip parameter to a Smart Clip, we must assign the parameter a name and, optionally, a default value. Like variables, clip parameters can contain different types of data. The datatypes supported by clip parameters are, however, not quite the same as those supported by variables. Clip parameters may contain *strings, numbers, arrays, objects,* and *lists*. These differ from the datatypes supported by variables in two ways:

- Clip parameters support an interface-only type of value called a *list*. A *list* is used to limit the assignment of a parameter's value to one of a predetermined set of options. For example, a parameter named difficulty may have its value set to the list: "hard", "normal", "easy". Lists prevent users of a Smart Clip from supplying an invalid value for a clip parameter.

- The primitive types `Boolean`, `null`, and `undefined` may not be set directly as the value of a clip parameter. This is a limitation of the Smart Clip interface, not the clip parameter itself; code *inside* the clip may assign `Boolean`, `null`, or `undefined` values to a variable initialized as a clip parameter. To simulate the Boolean values `true` and `false` with clip parameters, we use the numbers 1 and 0, not the strings "true" and "false". The numbers 1 and 0 convert to the `Boolean` values `true` and `false`, respectively, when used in a Boolean context.

To give a clip parameter a name and optional default value, follow these steps:

1. Double-click the parameter name, and type a legal identifier for the parameter.

2. Double-click the parameter type, and then select one of the following:

   a. Default for parameters with string or numeric values

   b. Array for parameters with array values

   c. Object for parameters with object values

   d. List for parameters with a predetermined set of possible string or numeric values

3. Double-click the parameter value, and enter the default value, if one is required. This value will appear in the Smart Clip interface as the initial value for the parameter. The manner in which default values are entered depends on the type of parameter:

   a. For Default parameters, double-click the parameter value and type the string or number.

   b. For Array, Object, and List parameters, double-click the parameter value. In the Values dialog box, add, remove, and arrange items using the plus, minus, and arrow buttons. Click OK to accept your settings.

4. To add information about the parameter's purpose, enter an explanation in the Description box.

5. To prevent the parameter's name from being changed by the Smart Clip user, select Lock in Instance.

6. In the Define Clip Parameters dialog box, click OK to finalize your parameter settings.

Removing and reordering standard clip parameters

Sometimes you'll want to remove or rearrange your Smart Clip's parameters.

To remove a clip parameter, follow these steps:

1. In the Library, select the Smart Clip to modify.

2. Select Options → Define Clip Parameters.

3. Select the parameter to remove.

4. Click the minus (–) button.

5. Click OK.

To rearrange clip parameters, follow these steps:

1. In the Library, select the Smart Clip to modify.

2. Select Options → Define Clip Parameters.

3. Select the parameter to move.

4. Click the arrow buttons until the parameter is in the desired location.

5. Click OK.

Building a Smart Clip with a Customized Interface

To build a Smart Clip with a customized interface, we first create a regular movie clip whose behavior is governed by a series of clip parameters as described earlier. Next, we create an independent *.swf* file (the so-called *interface .swf*) that will be used as the Clip Parameters panel interface. We'll typically create a *.swf* file with a graphical interface that allows the user to enter parameter values (via text boxes, menus, buttons, etc.). Those values are automatically collected and passed to the Smart Clip as parameters.

The Smart Clip communicates with the interface *.swf* via the xch instance (short for *exchange*), a specially named instance in the interface *.swf*. (We'll see how to create the xch instance in a minute.) Figure 16-4 shows how parameter names and values are sent from the interface *.swf* to the Smart Clip.

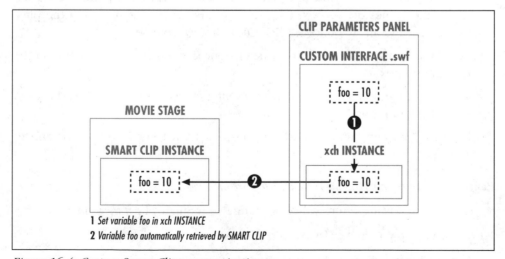

Figure 16-4. Custom Smart Clip communication

Communication between the interface *.swf* and the Smart Clip occurs in a cycle. When a Smart Clip instance is selected on stage, the corresponding interface *.swf* loads into the Clip Parameters panel. The current parameters in the Smart Clip instance are then passed to the *.swf* file's xch instance. The *.swf* file is expected to retrieve those parameters and set the interface state accordingly. Subsequent variables set in xch by the *.swf* file are automatically passed to the Smart Clip as parameters. When the Smart Clip instance is unselected, the interface *.swf* is removed from the Clip Parameters panel. However, the parameter values are not lost, they are retained by the Smart Clip. Each time the Smart Clip instance is selected, it passes its parameters back to the *.swf* file's xch clip. This cycle allows the interface *.swf* file to stay synchronized with the Smart Clip parameters.

The following sections explain how to create the custom interface *.swf* and associate it with a Smart Clip. A sample Smart Clip with a customized user interface is available under "Playhead Control" from the online Code Depot.

Creating a custom interface .swf file

To create a *.swf* file for use as the custom interface of a Smart Clip, follow these steps:

1. Start a new Flash document.
2. Create a new layer named *xchLayer*.
3. Select Insert → New Symbol to create a blank movie clip symbol.
4. Name the new symbol xchClip.
5. On the *xchLayer* layer, place an instance of the xchClip symbol.
6. Name the instance xch.
7. Provide a series of buttons, text fields, and other interface elements used to set variable values.
8. Variables set in the xch instance will automatically be added to the Smart Clip as parameters. For example, here is how you'd set values for two custom parameters:

```
xch.param1 = value1;   // Values may be of any datatype
xch.param2 = value2;
```

9. To read the value of an existing Smart Clip parameter within a custom interface *.swf*, refer to that parameter as a property of xch. For example, the following initializes the **param1Input** text field with the value of **param1** from the Smart Clip:

```
param1Input = xch.param1;
```

10. Export the *.swf* file.

Adding a custom interface to a Smart Clip

Now that we've seen how to create the interface *.swf*, let's add it to a Smart Clip as follows:

1. Close the custom interface *.swf* and return to the original *.fla* file containing the Smart Clip.

2. Select the Smart Clip in the Library.

3. Choose Options → Define Clip Parameters. The Define Clip Parameters dialog box appears.

4. In the Link to Custom UI box, type the location of the *.swf* file to use as the custom interface, relative to the current *.fla* file. (You may also select the *.swf* file using the folder button.)

Using Smart Clips

Once clip parameters have been assigned to a movie clip, the movie clip officially becomes a "Smart Clip." Smart Clips are identified in the Library with a special icon, ▓.

To use a Smart Clip instance in a movie, follow these steps:

1. Drag the Smart Clip from the Library onto the Stage.

2. Select Window → Panels → Clip Parameters.

3. If the clip has a standard interface, set each parameter value as follows:

    a. For Default parameters, double-click the parameter value and type the string or number.

    b. For Array parameters, double-click the parameter value. In the Values dialog box, double-click each array element value and type a string or number. Click OK to accept your array element values.

    c. For Object parameters, double-click the parameter value. In the Values dialog box, double-click each object property value and type a string or a number. Click OK to accept your Object properties.

    d. For List parameters, double-click the parameter value, and then select an option.

4. If the clip has a custom interface, use the tools provided in the custom interface to set the clip's parameters.

Onward!

In the next chapter we'll integrate ActionScript with a simple server application to produce a Flash form.

17

Flash Forms

Interactivity on the Web reaches perhaps its loftiest status in the guise of the fill-in form. Okay, that might sound a little hyperbolic, but it's not meant to be. Forms may appear trivial on the surface, but they are at the heart of online communities (chat rooms and message boards), the persistence of data (personalization), and of course, the saliva-in-the-jaws-of-business, e-commerce (buying and selling online).

Flash 4 was the first version of Flash to include forms support. Since then, Flash has gained many powerful means of communicating with a server. This chapter explores the basics of using forms in Flash, from capturing user input and displaying output within Flash, to sending data to a server and receiving the server's response. More advanced topics, such as XML handling, are covered in Part III, *Language Reference*.

The Flash Form Data Cycle

Before we delve into the particulars, let's take a macroscopic look at the typical steps in a form submission process:

1. Flash receives data as user input.
2. Flash prepares data for submission to the web server (collects and validates variables).
3. Flash sends data to the web server via HTTP (or, optionally, HTTPS).
4. The web server receives data, passes it to a server-side data-handling application (e.g., Perl script, PHP script, Cold Fusion, or ASP).
5. The data-handling application parses and processes submitted data.

6. The data-handling application passes results to the web server, which sends results to Flash.

7. Flash stores and optionally displays results.

Therefore, a functioning Flash form requires:

- A frontend (what the user sees)

- Some Flash scripting that submits the form's contents to a server-side script or application

- A server-side script or application

- Some Flash scripting that handles data returned from the server

Let's examine these components in a little more detail.

Flash Client-Side User Input

To supply input, users typically type text into text fields and then click the form's Submit button. Only text fields are supplied as prebuilt form components; we have to build everything else, including the Submit button, manually (as we'll see later). See "User-Input Text Fields" in Chapter 18, *On-Screen Text Fields*, for information on text fields.

Because Flash has a full scripting language, you can create intelligent forms that preprocess data before it's submitted to the server. We validate the user's entries before sending them to the web server to ensure that our data-handling application always receives usable data. Common validations include checking that all required fields have been filled out and verifying that the correct type of data has been entered. For example, an email address should include a name, followed by an @ symbol, followed by a domain name.

Transmitting Data for Server-Side Processing

Once our data is validated, we may safely pass it to the web server. ActionScript provides several tools for transferring form-based data to a web server:

- The *loadVariables()* function, described later in this chapter

- The *XML* class's *send()* and *sendAndLoad()* methods, described in Part III

- The global function *getURL()*, described in Part III

The web server passes the Flash data to the server-side application that will process the data, typically a middleware database (e.g., Allaire's ColdFusion or Microsoft's ASP) or a CGI script (e.g., a Perl or PHP script or a Java servlet).

In describing the web client/server data cycle, we make a point of distinguishing between the web server and a data-handling application. Often, this distinction is implicit—the client always has to make an HTTP request in order to send data to the data-handling application, so it naturally follows that a web server is involved. In Flash form development, however, we must remain aware of the invisible hand-off between the web server and the data-handling application. Data moves from Flash to the server either on the end of a URL (using GET) or in a stream of variable names and values (using POST). When a web server error is encountered, Flash does not display the HTTP error messages that the server sends (as a browser would). For example, if the web server can't find a CGI script, it sends a "404 Not Found" message, but Flash doesn't display it. Similarly, if a CGI script's permissions aren't set correctly, we don't see any execution-failure error message. In order to isolate client/server problems when working with Flash, it's useful to monitor the web server's HTTP error log while attempting to run scripts. You may find that the web server is trying to tell you something that Flash can't express.

The Data-Handling Application

Upon receiving a body of data, the data-handling application must *parse* it (i.e., interpret it intelligently and, if necessary, split it out into manageable pieces). After the data is parsed, it can be manipulated in an endless number of ways by the server application. Usually data processing involves saving content to a database or flat text file for future retrieval.

Once data processing is complete, the data-handling application produces a result to pass back to Flash. That result can be anything from a simple confirmation message ("Thank you for submitting your information") to a list of records from a database or the current price of a product.

The application passes the result to the web server, which will forward it on to Flash for storage or display.

Data-handling application developers should note that their application must set the MIME type of the result to "application/x-www-url-form-encoded". If that MIME type is missing, the result will likely be unusable when it reaches Flash.

Flash Receives and Interprets Results

We're nearing the end of the Flash form cycle, but we're not done yet. For one thing, we have to make sure that Flash waits patiently while the server-side application processes the data and transmits the result. Consider a movie that looks up stock prices. The user enters a stock ticker symbol and clicks the Get Stock Price button. Before the price can be displayed, the stock-retrieval application must identify and return the price. While the movie is waiting, it displays a "Loading" message. When the price is received, the movie springs back into action.

Data received by Flash in response to a *loadVariables()* invocation is stored in a specified target clip or level. Once that data has been received, the Flash form cycle is complete, and we're free to do whatever we like with our precious, well-traveled bytes of content. Let's now put our knowledge to practice by creating a simple fill-in form.

Creating a Flash Fill-in Form

Our example includes all of the necessary components of a Flash form, cited earlier, but stripped down to the simplest level. This tutorial demonstrates how to send a single text field variable from Flash to a Perl script, named *echo.pl*, and how to receive a response in Flash back from *echo.pl*. Functioning versions of the example files are available from the online Code Depot. Let's get to it, shall we?

Building the Frontend

Unlike HTML, Flash does not have an integrated mechanism for the creation of forms. In HTML, creating pull-down menus and radio buttons is simply a matter of using the `<SELECT>`, `<OPTION>`, and `<INPUT TYPE="RADIO">` tags. In Flash, those devices must be built by hand. Flash's only built-in form device is the user-input text field (the equivalent of HTML's `<INPUT TYPE="TEXT">` or `<INPUT TYPE="TEXTAREA">`).

 Though form widgets are not built directly into the Flash authoring tool, radio buttons, checkboxes, and pull-down menus are available as Smart Clips included with the product. To access the form-widget Smart Clips, choose Window → Common Libraries → Smart Clips.

In our form, we'll have a user-input text field and a Submit button. We'll place these two elements into a movie clip so that we can easily identify the variables to send to the server. First, we'll create a new document and the `formClip` movie clip, as follows:

1. Start a new Flash document.

2. Select Insert → New Symbol. The Symbol Properties dialog box appears.

3. In the Name box, type **formClip**.

4. Click OK.

5. From the Library, drag an instance of formClip onto the main Stage.

Next, we'll add a user-input text field to formClip by following these steps:

1. In the Library, double-click the formClip symbol to edit the clip.

2. Select the Text tool.

3. On the clip canvas, drag a rectangle big enough for a user to enter a single line of text.

4. Select Window → Panels → Text Options.

5. For Text Type, select Input Text.

6. For Line Display, select Single Line.

7. In the Variable box, type **input**.

8. Select Border/Bg.

Now we'll assign our input text field a default value, ensuring that it will be sent to the server even if the user doesn't enter any data:

1. In the formClip timeline, select frame 1.

2. In the Actions panel, enter the following code: **input = "";**.

Finally, we add a Submit button to formClip by following these steps:

1. Select Window → Common Libraries → Buttons.

2. From the *Buttons.fla* library, drag an instance of the *Push Bar* button onto the formClip stage.

Sending Data to the Server

There are many ways to send data from Flash to a server application, including the *loadVariables()*, *getURL()*, *loadMovie()*, *XML.load()*, *XML.sendAndLoad()*, and *XMLSocket.send()* methods. In our example, we'll use the *loadVariables()* method. For information on the others, see Part III.

In the previous section, we placed a user-input text field and a Submit button in the movie clip formClip. To make that Submit button send formClip's variables to *echo.pl* when clicked, follow these steps:

1. In the Library, double-click the formClip symbol (this edits the clip).

2. Select the *Push Bar* button instance.

3. Select Window → Actions.

4. Enter the following code in the Actions panel:

```
on (release, keyPress "<Enter>") {
  loadVariables ("http://www.yourserver.com/cgi-bin/echo.pl",
                 "_root.response",
                 "GET");

  _root.response.gotoAndStop("loading");
}
```

The code on our Submit button uses *loadVariables()* to send the variables of `formClip` to *echo.pl*, and it causes our **response** clip to display a loading message. We'll build the **response** clip a little later. For now, let's examine how the *loadVariables()* invocation works.

The first parameter of the *loadVariables()* invocation should specify the location of *echo.pl* on your server (server-side scripts are typically stored in a folder named *cgi-bin*). Be sure to set the location correctly according to your server's domain name and directory structure. When *loadVariables()* executes, all the variables in `formClip` are sent to that location.

The second parameter of the *loadVariables()* invocation indicates the path to the clip in which we will store the return value sent by *echo.pl*, namely `"_root.`
`response"`.

The third parameter of the *loadVariables()* invocation specifies the HTTP method we're using to submit `formClip`'s variables to the server—the GET method in this case. ActionScript supports both GET and POST operations, as described under *loadVariables()* in Part III.

The Perl Script, echo.pl

When the user clicks the Submit button in our movie's `formClip`, Flash initiates an HTTP GET request. This request executes the Perl script *echo.pl*. In order for our form to work, *echo.pl* must be placed in a CGI-enabled directory of a web server and configured by the server's administrator as follows:

- The script must be executable (typically, this means setting the file permissions to 755).

- On Unix, the path to the Perl interpreter must be set in the script.

Example 17-1 shows the source code for *echo.pl*. Note that the # character indicates a comment in Perl.

Example 17-1. The Source Code of echo.pl

```perl
#! /usr/local/bin/perl
#-------------------------------------------------------------------------------
#  Name:       Simple Flash Echo
#  Version:    1.2.0
#  Author:     Derek Clayton  derek_clayton@iceinc.com
#  Description:  Echoes back name/value pairs received from a Flash GET or POST.
#-------------------------------------------------------------------------------
# MAIN
#-------------------------------------------------------------------------------
use CGI;                   # Use the CGI.pm for easy parsing
$query = new CGI;          # Query object
$echoString = "output=";   # Initialize our output string
&getInput;                 # Get the input received from Flash
&writeResponse;            # Write the response back to Flash
exit;                      # Exit the script
#-------------------------------------------------------------------------------
sub getInput {
  # For each key get the associated value and add to the echo string
  foreach $key ($query->param) {
    $value = $query->param($key);
    $echoString .= "$key:$value\n";
  }
  # Remove the trailing newline (\n) before writing response
  chomp($echoString);
}

sub writeResponse {
  # Set content type for Flash
  print "Content-type: application/x-www-urlform-encoded\n\n";
  # Write the output
  print $echoString;
}
```

The *echo.pl* script performs three general tasks:

* It accepts data sent by Flash and parses that data into a series of variable names and values.

* It assembles those variable names and values into a string to return to Flash. The string has the following format:

  output=*name1:value1*\n*name2:value2*\n...*namen:valuen*

* It returns the string to Flash.

Upon receiving the string returned by *echo.pl*, Flash automatically interprets it as a series of URL-encoded variables (as described in the entry for *loadVariables()* in Part III). Hence, **output** becomes a variable on the **response** clip's timeline. By examining the value of **output** in our Flash movie, we can see which variable names and values were originally sent to *echo.pl*.

Obviously *echo.pl* is not the most interesting web application in the world. It is only a proof of concept. When applied, however, the concept can have interesting and powerful results. For an example of a more fully developed Perl system, see the flat file database sample available at the online Code Depot under "Server Communication."

Receiving Results from the Server

Recall that when we sent the variables of `formClip` to *echo.pl*, we requested that *echo.pl*'s return value be stored in the movie clip `response`:

```
loadVariables ("http://www.yourserver.com/cgi-bin/echo.pl",
               "_root.response",
               "GET");
```

We'll now build that `response` clip; it has three states: *idle, loading,* and *done loading.* In the *idle* state, `response` is invisible to the user, waiting for data to begin loading. In the *loading* state, `response` indicates to the user that data has been submitted to the server and that Flash is waiting for a reply. In the *done loading* state, `response` has received the server's reply and displays that reply to the user via a text field. The three states of `response` govern its timeline structure. Each state is represented by a labeled keyframe: `idle`, `loading`, and `doneLoading`. The frame displayed is dictated as follows:

- When the movie loads, `response` displays the `idle` frame.

- When variables are submitted, the Submit button sends `response` to the `loading` frame.

- When variables are received, `response`'s *data* event handler (which we'll create) sends `response` to the `doneLoading` frame.

To build `response`, we follow these steps:

1. Select Insert → New Symbol. The Symbol Properties dialog box appears.

2. In the Name box, type **responseClip**.

3. Click OK.

4. From the Library, drag an instance of `responseClip` onto the main Stage.

5. Name the `responseClip` instance `response`.

6. In the Library, double-click the `responseClip` symbol (this edits the clip).

7. Create four timeline layers named, from top to bottom, *scripts, labels, loading,* and *outputField.*

8. Create three keyframes on each layer.

9. On the *labels* layer, for frames 1, 2, and 3, add the labels `idle`, `loading`, and `doneLoading`, respectively.

10. On the *scripts* layer, at frame 1, add the following code: **stop();**.

11. On the *loading* layer, at frame 2, add the static text, **"loading, please wait"**.

12. Select the Text tool.

13. On the *outputField* layer, at frame 3, draw a text box.

14. Select Window → Panels → Text Options.

15. For Text Type, select Dynamic Text.

16. For Line Display, select Multiline.

17. In the Variable box, type **outputField**.

Now let's add the *data* event handler that will be triggered when the server has finished sending its data to Flash. Follow these steps:

1. On the main Stage, select the **response** instance.

2. Select Window → Actions.

3. Enter the following code in the Actions panel:

```
onClipEvent (data) {
  this.gotoAndStop("doneLoading");
  outputField = output;
}
```

When Flash receives the content sent by *echo.pl*, **response**'s *data* event handler executes automatically. In the *data* handler, we move **response**'s playhead to the `doneLoading` frame, and then we display the value of `output` (supplied by *echo.pl*) in `outputField`. Our use of the *data* event handler ensures that the `output` variable will always be loaded before we attempt to display its value in the `outputField` text field.

All that's left to do is try your form out! Export your movie, enter some text in the `input` text field, and click the Submit button. If the form doesn't work the first time, make sure your server script is configured properly. And remember, you can study the functional version posted at the online Code Depot.

Reader Exercise: Try adding a Reset button to your form that clears the value of its input field. Create a new button in the `formClip` and attach the following code to it:

```
on (release) {
  input = "";
}
```

Also, try adding more than one input field to your form; the Perl script will faithfully return as many variables as you send it. Can you split them up and display each one's value separately?

Onward!

Well, I'd say our work in this chapter wasn't too shabby. Think of all the powerful things you can do with Flash forms, like remembering a user's preferences, providing a discussion forum, or loading dynamic product information for a catalog. The flat file Perl database in the online Code Depot will take you further down the road toward building those kinds of applications. In the next chapter, we'll study the intricacies of text fields and their application within Flash forms.

18

On-Screen Text Fields

Because Flash is fundamentally a visual environment, movies often present on-screen information to users. Similarly, because Flash is an interactive environment, movies often retrieve information from users through a GUI. To display the value of a variable on screen or to allow a user to type data into a Flash movie, we use *text fields*.

Text fields provide a means of both setting and retrieving the values of variables that have a visual representation. Text fields come in two varieties—dynamic text fields, which we use to display information to the user, and user-input text fields, which we use to retrieve information from the user.

Dynamic Text Fields

A dynamic text field is like a variable viewport—it displays the value of a specified variable as a text string. Dynamic text fields are created using the Text tool in Flash. However, unlike regular static text, the content of a dynamic text field is connected to a variable and can be changed or retrieved via ActionScript.

By retrieving a text field's value, we can capture on-screen information for use in a script. By setting a text field's value, we cause that value to display on screen.

Creating a Dynamic Text Field

To make a new dynamic text field, follow these steps:

1. Select the Text tool.
2. Click and drag a rectangle on the Stage. The outline that you create will define the size of the new text field.

3. Select Text → Options. The Text Options panel appears.

4. In the Text Type menu, choose Dynamic Text (the other options are Static Text and Input Text).

5. Under Variable, type a name for the dynamic text field, following the rules we learned in Chapter 2, *Variables*, for constructing legal variable names.

After creating a dynamic text field, you'd normally set the new field's options, as described later.

Changing the Content of a Dynamic Text Field

Once a text field is created, we can use it to display a value on the screen. For example, if we create a dynamic text field named `myText`, we can set the content of that text field using the following statements:

```
myText = 10;                          // Display a number in the text field myText
myText = "Welcome to my web site"; // Display a string instead

var msg = "Please make a selection";
myText = msg;                         // Display the value of msg in myText
```

Whenever the value of the variable `myText` changes, the content of the `myText` dynamic text field updates to reflect the change. However, before a value is sent to a dynamic text field for display, it is first converted to a string. The actual content is therefore governed by string-conversion rules described in Table 3-2.

Like normal variables, text fields are tied to the movie clip timeline on which they reside. To access a dynamic text field in a remote movie clip timeline, we use the techniques described in Chapter 2 under "Accessing Variables on Different Timelines."

Retrieving the Value of a Dynamic Text Field

We can retrieve a dynamic text field's value by simply using its name. For example, if `myTextField` were a dynamic text field in our movie, we could retrieve and assign its value to another variable like so:

```
welcomeMessage = myTextField;
```

Text field assignment and retrieval are often combined in one statement. You can use the `+=` operator to append text to a text field's current contents:

```
// Set a text field's value
myTextField = "Today's Headlines...";
// Create a new message
var newText = "Update! The Party Has Been Cancelled!"
// Add the new message to the existing text field content
myTextField += newText;
```

User-Input Text Fields

User-input text fields differ from dynamic text fields only in that they may be edited by the user while the movie is playing. That is, a user can type into a user-input text field to change its value. ActionScript can then retrieve and manipulate the user-entered value. User-input text fields are useful for guest books, order forms, password-entry fields, or anywhere you request information from the user.

Creating a User-Input Text Field

To create a user-input text field, follow the same steps described earlier under "Creating a Dynamic Text Field," but choose Input Text instead of Dynamic Text from the Text Type menu.

Changing the Content of an Input Text Field

Like dynamic text fields, user-input text fields may be changed at any time simply by setting the value of the named text field with an assignment statement:

```
myInputText = "Type your name here";
```

Because user-input text fields are normally used to accept data rather than display data, we don't usually set their contents except to provide a default value for the user's input.

Retrieving and Using the Value of an Input Text Field

You can retrieve the value of a text field by simply referring to it by name in a script. For example, to display the value of an input text field called **myInput**, use:

```
trace(myInput);
```

Because data entered by the user into a user-input text field is always a string datatype, we should convert it explicitly before using it in a non-string context, as demonstrated in this simple calculator example that totals two user-input text fields:

```
// Suppose the user sets myFirstInput to 5 and mySecondInput to 10,
then we total the fields
// WRONG: "Adding" the fields together sets myOutput to "Total: 510"
// because the + operator is interpreted as a string concatenator
myOutput = "Total: " + (myFirstInput + mySecondInput);
// RIGHT: Convert the fields to numbers first in order to get the right result
myOutput = "Total: " + (parseFloat(myFirstInput) + parseFloat(mySecondInput));
```

User-Input Text Fields and Forms

User-input text fields are often used for fill-in forms submitted to a server-side application such as a Perl script. When variables are submitted to a server via *loadVariables()*, only the variables defined in the current movie clip are sent. Hence, when a form contains user-input text fields, the fields should be stored in a single, separate movie clip so that they can be submitted easily as a group to a server. See Chapter 17, *Flash Forms*, and Part III, *Language Reference* for additional details on *loadVariables()*.

Text Field Options

Dynamic text fields and user-input text fields share most, but not all, options used to configure their display and input features. Figure 18-1 shows the Text Options panel for user-input and dynamic text fields.

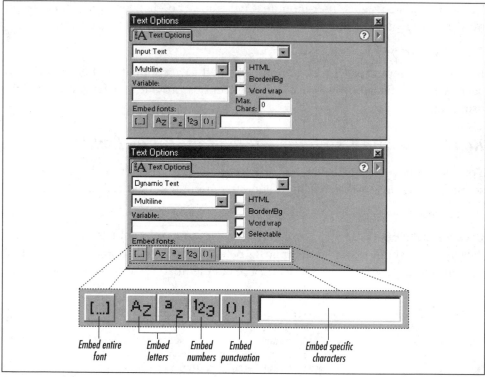

Figure 18-1. The Text Options panel

Line Display

To set the layout and input style of a text field or to disguise the user's input, we use the Line Display menu. There are three Line Display options:

Single Line

The Single Line option prevents users from entering more than one line of text in the field, effectively disabling the Enter key during text entry.

The Single Line setting also affects text entered without line breaks in the authoring tool; text that "soft wraps" automatically during authoring will not wrap in the Player. Instead, the text will be displayed on one line, even if it overflows the field to the right. Hard carriage returns entered during authoring, however, are unaffected by the Single Line setting; text with hard returns will display in the Player as it appeared in the authoring tool.

The Single Line option applies primarily to user-input text fields. When used with dynamic text fields, its behavior is the same as that of a Multiline dynamic text field unless the Word Wrap option is also selected.

Both the `\n` escape sequence and the `newline` keyword insert line breaks despite the Single Line setting. For example, if we set a text field variable to the value `"this is\na test"`, the text `"this is"` and `"a test"` will be displayed on separate lines.

Multiline

The Multiline setting allows users to enter more than one line of text in the text field. Carriage returns are permitted in user input when Multiline is selected.

Multiline has no effect on the output of a dynamic text field unless used in combination with the Word Wrap option. If Word Wrap is not on, Multiline text fields behave exactly like Single Line text fields.

Password

The Password option is used to conceal characters entered into a form and applies only to user-input text fields. It behaves like a Single Line text field except that all characters, including spaces, are masked with asterisks (*). For example, the words `"hi there"` would be displayed as `"********"`.

It is possible to cause the words in a Password text field to wrap due to a quirk in the Flash interface. If you set Line Display to Multiline and select Word Wrap, and then set the Line Display to Password, the Word Wrap setting will be retained. However, Multiline password entry is not advised as it is confusing to most users.

Variable

The Variable option in the Text Options panel is used to name a dynamic or user-input text field. Text fields *must* be named in order to be manipulated with Action-Script. When naming text fields, follow the rules for constructing legal variable names described in Chapter 2, *Variables*, and Chapter 14, *Lexical Structure*.

Border/Bg

When set in the Text Options panel, the Border/Bg option causes a black outline to be displayed around a text field and a white background to be placed behind the viewable region of the field. These colors and styles are not customizable. To produce a custom background for a text field, unset the Border/Bg option and manually draw a shape behind the text field.

Word Wrap

When used in conjunction with the Multiline setting of the Line Display option, Word Wrap soft wraps lines of text that would otherwise exceed the width of the field. This setting applies to both text entered by users and text displayed via ActionScript.

If you set the Word Wrap option while Multiline is selected and then choose Single Line, the Word Wrap setting will still apply. Be sure to unset Word Wrap if you do not want text to wrap at the end of each line.

Selectable

The text in a dynamic text field may be selected by the user only if the field's Selectable option is set. Even then, the dynamic text may be copied but not cut or edited. User-input text fields are always selectable, and their text can always be copied, cut, or edited.

 Text must be copied, cut, and pasted via the Windows right-click context menu in Flash (or Ctrl-click on Macintosh). Keyboard accelerators such as Ctrl-C and Ctrl-V (in Windows) or Cmd-C and Cmd-V (on Macintosh) are ignored.

Max Characters

Used only with user-input text fields, the Max Characters option limits the amount of text a user can enter into a text field. By default, Max Characters is set to 0, which allows an unlimited amount of text to be entered. Other settings allow the specified number of characters to be entered.

Max Characters is often used with forms that require a certain format for their data. For example, we could use it to limit a date entry to a two-digit day, a two-digit month, and a four-digit year.

Embed Fonts

By default, all dynamic and input text fields use *device fonts* (the fonts installed on the user's system). When device fonts are used, if the user has the font specified in the Character panel for the text field, the text appears on the user's system as it appeared during authoring (but without antialiasing). If the user does not have the font, an alternative font is used, which is not always desirable.

To ensure that text will render in a particular font, we embed that font in the movie using the Embed Fonts options, shown enlarged in Figure 18-1.

We can:

- Embed the entire font using the [...] button.
- Embed any combination of the letters, numbers, or punctuation using the AZ, az, 123, and () ! buttons.
- Embed specific characters by typing them into the field provided.

Embedding a complete Roman font typically adds 20–30 KB to a movie (Asian fonts can be much larger). If we're using only a subset of the characters, we can save file space by embedding only the characters we need. Characters that we don't embed cannot be entered by the user or displayed via ActionScript. We can use this to our advantage to restrict text entry to certain characters.

You must set the Embed Fonts option separately for *every* text field that uses a particular font, even if multiple text fields use the same font. However, file size is not affected when multiple text fields embed the same font—only one copy of the font is downloaded with the movie. To apply the same Embed Fonts option to many text fields at once, select the desired fields and then set the Embed Fonts option as usual.

Text displayed in text fields with embedded fonts is always antialiased. Therefore, using embedded fonts with sizes smaller than 10 point is not recommended, because antialiased text becomes unreadable below 10 point in most fonts. To prevent a font from antialiasing, use device fonts (i.e., system fonts) by unselecting all Embed Fonts options. Device fonts are never antialiased.

The contents of a text field that is rotated or masked will not show up on screen unless its font is embedded. That is, you can't rotate or mask text fields that use device fonts.

See "Using HTML as Output" later in this chapter for more important details on fonts in text fields.

Text Field Properties

When the body of text in a text field spans more lines than can be accommodated by the physical viewable region of the field, extra lines of text are hidden. The extra lines, however, are still part of the text field. To view those lines, we can click in the field and press the down arrow key until the excess lines appear. Obviously, we can't expect users to use the arrow keys to scroll through text in a text field. Instead, we should provide buttons that scroll the text using the `scroll` and `maxscroll` properties, both of which use an index number to refer to the lines in a text field. The top line is number 1, and line numbers increase for every line in the text field, including those that exceed the viewable boundaries of the field. Figure 18-2 shows a sample text field's line index values.

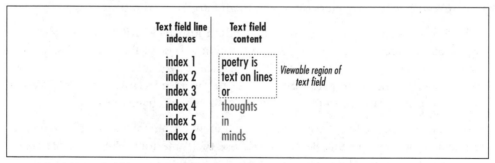

Figure 18-2. Text field line indexes

The scroll Property

The `scroll` property represents the line number of the topmost line currently displayed in a text field and can be accessed using *textFieldName*.`scroll`.

When a text field contains more lines than it can display at once, we can change which lines are shown in the field's viewable region by setting the `scroll` property. For example, if we were to set the `scroll` property of the text field shown in Figure 18-2 to 3, the text field would display:

```
or
thoughts
in
```

The maxscroll Property

The `maxscroll` property tells us how far a field can be scrolled (i.e., how far it must be scrolled until the last line becomes visible). It is always the index of the field's last line minus the number of lines that can be displayed in the viewable region at once, plus one. For example, the `maxscroll` property of the text field in Figure 18-2 would be 4 (the last line is 6, minus 3 lines in viewable region, plus 1). Note that `maxscroll` is *not* equal to the number of text lines.

We can retrieve (but not set) the `maxscroll` property using *textFieldName*.`maxscroll`.

Typical Text-Scrolling Code

In combination, the `scroll` and `maxscroll` properties can be used to scroll a text field. This code scrolls text down one line for each click of a button:

```
on (press) {
  if (textField.scroll < textField.maxscroll) {
    textField.scroll++;
  }
}
```

And here's how we scroll text up one line with each click:

```
on (press) {
  if (textField.scroll > 1) {
    textField.scroll--;
  }
}
```

For an example of simple scroll buttons used in a movie, download the sample scrollers posted at the online Code Depot.

Build 30 of the Flash 5 Player, released with the Flash 5 authoring tool, had a text field display bug. When antialiased text fields were scrolled, remnants of the scrolled text did not always disappear. To work around the problem, place a border around your text field to cover up the residual text. This bug was fixed in build 41 of the Flash 5 Player, released in December 2000. Use the global *getVersion()* function to check the version of the Player.

The _changed Event

In Flash 4 and Flash 5, changes to the content of a user-input text field can be detected via the undocumented *_changed* event. The *_changed* event triggers a specially-named Flash 4-style subroutine whenever the user adds text to or deletes text from a user-input text field. To create a *_changed* event for a text field, follow these steps:

1. Create an input text field on any timeline.

2. Name the text field `myField`.

3. On the same timeline as the text field, label a frame `myField_changed`.

4. Attach any code to the frame `myField_changed`. For example:

   ```
   trace("myField was changed");
   ```

5. Export the movie using Control → Test Movie.

6. Type characters into the `myField` text field. The code on the frame `myField_changed` is executed, and "myField was changed" appears in the Output window.

Of course, the name `myField` is arbitrary; you can use whatever text field name you like as long as the corresponding frame label is set to the same name. Note that setting the value of a text field with ActionScript does not trigger the field's *_changed* event. Only user keystrokes trigger *_changed*.

The *_changed* event is an undocumented feature. In future versions of Flash, a new, more standard method of event handling for text fields will likely be adopted.

HTML Support

The Character panel lets us set a text field's font size, font face, and font style, but it sets the attributes of the entire text field only. To set styles on a character-by-character basis and to add hypertext links, use HTML (which was added as a text field feature in Flash 5).

Though HTML can be used with both dynamic text fields and user-input text fields, we normally use HTML text fields for display purposes only. To add HTML support to a text field, select the HTML option in the Text Options panel.

The set of HTML tags supported by text fields is limited to: <B>, <I>, <U>, <FONT>, <P>, <BR>, and <A>.

<B> (Bold)

The <B> tag renders text in bold, provided that a boldface exists for the font in question:

```
<B>This is bold text</B>
```

<I> (Italics)

The `<I>` tag renders text in italics, provided that an italic face exists for the font in question:

```
<I>This is italic text</I>
```

<U> (Underline)

The `<U>` tag renders the tagged text with an underline beneath it. For example:

```
<U>This is underlined text</U>
```

Because linked text is not underlined in Flash, you should use the `<U>` tag to identify hyperlinks:

```
<A HREF="http://www.thesquarerootof-1.com"><U>Click here</U>
</A> to visit a neat site.
```

<FONT> (Font Control)

The `<FONT>` tag supports the following three attributes:

FACE

> The `FACE` attribute specifies the name of the font to use. Note that a list of multiple font faces is not supported in Flash as it is in HTML. Flash attempts to render only the first font listed in the `FACE` attribute. For example, in the code `<FONT FACE="Arial, Helvetica">my text</FONT>`, Flash will not render "my text" in Helvetica if Arial is missing. Instead, text will be rendered in the default font.

SIZE

> The `SIZE` attribute specifies the size of the tagged text as a fixed point size (such as `<FONT SIZE="18">`) or as a relative size. Relative point sizes are preceded by a + or − sign and are specified relative to the text size in the Character panel. For example, if the point size is 14 in the Character panel, then `<FONT SIZE="-2">` displays the tagged text at 12 point.

COLOR

> The `COLOR` attribute specifies the color of the tagged text, as a hexadecimal number, preceded by the pound sign (#). For example: `<FONT COLOR="#FF0000">this is red text</FONT>`. Specify the hexadecimal number as an RGB series of three two-digit numbers from 00 to FF. Note that Flash's implementation of the `COLOR` attribute is more strict than HTML's—the pound sign (#) is required, and color names such as `"green"` and `"blue"` cannot be used as `COLOR` values.

Here are some <FONT> examples:

```
<FONT FACE="Arial">this is Arial</FONT>
<FONT FACE="Arial" SIZE="12">this is 12pt Arial</FONT>
<FONT FACE="Lucida Console" SIZE="+4" COLOR="#FF0000">this is red,
+4pt Lucida Console</FONT>
```

See "Using HTML as Output" later in this chapter for more important details on fonts in Flash.

<P> (Paragraph Break)

The <P> tag demarcates paragraphs, but in Flash it behaves quite differently than its HTML counterpart. First of all, unterminated <P> tags do not cause line breaks in Flash as they do in regular HTML. Note the difference between Flash and web browser output:

```
I hate filling out forms. <P>So sometimes I don't.
// Flash output:
I hate filling out forms. So sometimes I don't.
// Web browser output:
I hate filling out forms.
So sometimes I don't.
```

Closing </P> tags are required by Flash in order for line breaks to be added. For example:

```
<P> I hate filling out forms.</P> So sometimes I don't.
```

Furthermore, in Flash, <P> causes a single line break, exactly like <BR>, whereas in web browsers, <P> traditionally causes a double line break. Consider the following:

```
<P>This is line one.</P><P>This is line two.</P>
```

In Flash, that code would be rendered with no gap between the lines, as in:

```
This is line one.
This is line two.
```

In a web browser, the code would be rendered with a gap between the lines, as in:

```
This is line one.

This is line two.
```

Because Flash's <P> tag behavior differs from web browsers, we often use the <BR> tag instead. However, the ALIGN attribute of the <P> tag is still useful to center, right-justify, or left-justify text, as follows:

```
<P ALIGN="CENTER">Centered text</P>
<P ALIGN="RIGHT">Right-justified text</P>
<P ALIGN="LEFT">Left-justified text</P>
```

*
 (Line Break)*

The `<BR>` tag causes a line break in a body of text and is functionally equivalent to the `\n` escape sequence or the `newline` keyword. Consider the following:

```
This is line one. <BR>This is line two.
This is line one. \nThis is line two.
```

Both would be rendered in Flash as:

```
This is line one.
This is line two.
```

<A> (Anchor or Hypertext Link)

The `<A>` tag creates a hypertext link. When the user clicks text tagged with `<A>`, the document specified in the `HREF` attribute of the tag loads into the browser. If the Player is running in standalone mode, the default web browser on the system is launched and the document is loaded into that browser.

The generic syntax of the `<A>` tag is:

```
<A HREF="documentToLoad.html">linked text</A>
```

For example, to link to a good video game, we could use:

```
<A HREF="http://www.quake3arena.com/">nice game</A>
```

As with HTML, the URL can be absolute or relative to the current page. Normally, links followed via an anchor tag cause the current movie to be replaced with the document specified in the `HREF` of the anchor tag. However, an anchor tag may also cause a secondary browser window to launch. Using the `TARGET` attribute, we can specify the name of a window into which to load the linked document, as follows:

```
<A HREF="documentName" TARGET="windowName">linked text</A>
```

If a window named *windowName* does not already exist, the browser launches a new window and assigns it the name *windowName*. To launch each document in its own, anonymous window, we can use the `_blank` keyword, as in:

```
<A HREF="mypage.html" TARGET="_blank">linked text</A>
```

Note that when we launch windows through the `TARGET` attribute, we have no control over the size or toolbar arrangement of the new window. To launch specifically sized windows from a link, we must use JavaScript. Techniques for launching customized secondary windows with JavaScript are described at:

http://www.moock.org/webdesign/flash

For more information on communicating with JavaScript from ActionScript, see the global functions *fscommand()* and *getURL()* in Part III, and "Executing JavaScript from HTML Links" later in this chapter.

The `TARGET` attribute can also be used to load documents into frames, as in:

```
<A HREF="documentName" TARGET="frameName">linked text</A>
```

Flash anchor tags do not always behave exactly like HTML anchor tags. We cannot, for example, use the `NAME` attribute of the anchor tag in Flash, so internal links within a body of text are not possible. Furthermore, Flash links are not underlined or highlighted in any way. Link underlines and colors must be inserted manually with the `<U>` and `<FONT>` tags described earlier.

Anchor Tag Tab Order

In Flash 5, anchor tags are not added to the tab order of the movie and are therefore not accessible via the keyboard. If your content must be accessible to keyboards and alternative input devices, you should use buttons, not anchor tags, for links.

Quoting Attribute Values

Outside Flash, HTML attribute values may be quoted with single quotes, double quotes, or not at all. The following tags are all valid in most web browsers:

```
<P ALIGN=RIGHT>
<P ALIGN='RIGHT'>
<P ALIGN="RIGHT">
```

But in Flash, unquoted attribute values are not allowed. For example, the syntax `<P ALIGN=RIGHT>` is illegal in Flash. However, both single and double quotes may be used to delimit attribute values. When composing text field values that include HTML attributes, we must be careful to quote our attributes correctly, using one type of quote to demarcate the string itself and another to demarcate attribute values. For example:

```
// These examples are both valid
myText = "<P ALIGN='RIGHT'>hi there</P>";
myText = '<P ALIGN="RIGHT">hi there</P>';
// This example would cause an error because double quotation marks are
// used to demarcate both the string and the attribute
myText = "<P ALIGN="RIGHT">hi there</P>";
```

For more information on using quotation marks to form strings, see "String Literals" in Chapter 4, *Primitive Datatypes*.

Unrecognized Tags and Attributes

Like web browsers, Flash ignore tags and attributes it does not recognize. For example, if we assign the following value to an HTML text field in Flash:

```
<P>Please fill in and print this form</P>
<FORM><INPUT TYPE="TEXT"></FORM>
<P>Thank you!</P>
```

The output would be:

```
Please fill in and print this form
Thank you!
```

The **FORM** and **INPUT** elements are not supported by Flash so both are ignored. Similarly, if we use container elements such as **<TD>**, the content is preserved but the markup is ignored. For example:

```
myTextField = "<TABLE><TR><TD>table cell text</TD></TR></TABLE>";
```

outputs the following line without table formatting:

```
table cell text
```

Using HTML as Output

HTML text entered manually into a text field using the Text tool will not be rendered as HTML. To display HTML-formatted text on screen, we must assign HTML text to a dynamic text field via ActionScript. For example:

```
myTextField = "<P><B>Error!</B> You <I>must</I> supply an email address!</P>";
```

Embedding a font for an HTML text field embeds only a single style of a single font. For example, a text field set to bold Arial in the Character panel will only support characters of the Arial bold typeface. If we use HTML to assign a different style of Arial (such as italic) or a different typeface altogether (such as Garamond), the tagged text will be invisible unless the appropriate fonts are embedded with the movie!

Suppose, for example, that we create a text field called output. In the Character panel for our output text field we select Arial set to Italic. In the Text Options panel, we embed the entire Arial italic font. Then we set output to display HTML. Finally, we assign the following value to our text field:

```
output = '<P><I>My</I>, what <B>lovely</B>'
       + '<FONT SIZE="24">eyes</FONT> you have!</P>';
```

When the movie plays, the following text will appear in the text field:

My

Everything else we assigned to output is missing! Only the italic text in the HTML can be rendered. The rest of the text requires other variations of the Arial font that we didn't embed—"what", "eyes", and "you have" are all nonitalic, and "lovely" is bold.

For every font face and variation we use in an HTML text field, we must embed the appropriate font. We have two means of doing so:

- Make a dummy text field, hidden from view, with the desired font selected in the Character panel and embedded in the Text Options panel.

- Add a new font symbol to the movie's Library and export the font with the movie.

Here are the steps for embedding Arial bold in a movie for use with a text field:

1. Select Window → Library.

2. Select Options → New Font. The Font Symbol Properties dialog box appears.

3. Under Font, select Arial.

4. Under Style, select Bold.

5. Under Name, type **ArialBold** (this is a cosmetic name, used only in the Library).

6. In the Library, select the `ArialBold` font symbol.

7. Select Options → Linkage.

8. In the Symbol Linkage Properties dialog box, select Export This Symbol.

9. In the Identifier box, type **ArialBold**. For our purposes, the name we type here doesn't matter. Exported symbol identifiers are used only for shared libraries.

Note that every variation of a font style must be embedded individually. If we use Arial bold, Arial italic, and Arial bold italic in a text field, then we must embed all three font variations. Underline is not considered a font variation, nor is font size or color.

If, however, we do not enable *any* of the Embed Fonts options in the Text Options panel, then Flash relies entirely on the user's system for fonts, in which case normal, bold, and italic text will be rendered only if users have the appropriate font variant installed on their systems.

To ensure that text will display consistently across all platforms and user systems, you should embed all the fonts required for your text field.

Using HTML as Input

Whereas HTML is normally used with text fields for display purposes, it may also be entered into a movie via an HTML-enabled or a regular (non-HTML) user-input text field.

When regular text is entered into an HTML-enabled user-input text field, HTML markup tags are added automatically. For example, the text "Hi there" would be converted to the HTML value:

```
'<P ALIGN="LEFT"><FONT FACE="Arial" SIZE="10" COLOR="#000000">Hi there</FONT></P>'
```

When HTML tags are typed into an HTML-enabled user-input text field, the < and > characters are converted to > and <. For example, the text "<B>hi there</B>" would be converted to the value:

```
'<P ALIGN="LEFT"><FONT FACE="Arial" SIZE="10"
COLOR="#000000">&lt;B&gt;hi there&lt;/B&gt;</FONT></P>'
```

HTML-enabled user-input text fields may be used to create a very simple HTML data entry system.

When regular or HTML text is typed into a normal (non-HTML) user-input text field, no modification of the entered text occurs. Regular user-input text fields allow raw HTML code to be entered into a movie without distortion.

An example showing HTML-enabled and regular user-input text field data entry is available from the online Code Depot.

Executing JavaScript from HTML Links

In most JavaScript-capable web browsers, it is possible to execute JavaScript statements from an anchor tag using the `javascript:` protocol as the value of the `HREF` attribute. For example:

```
<A HREF="javascript:square(5);">find the square of 5</A>
```

In ActionScript, we can also execute JavaScript statements from an <A> tag, like this:

```
myTextField = "<A HREF='javascript:alert(5);'>display the number 5</A>";
```

However, to include string values in JavaScript statements, we must use the HTML entity `&quot;` for quotation marks, as in:

```
myTextField = "<A HREF='javascript:alert(&quot;hello world&quot;);'>"
              + "display hello world</A>";
```

Calling ActionScript Functions from HTML Links

Though arbitrary statements of ActionScript code cannot be executed from a Flash <A> tag, ActionScript *functions* can. To invoke an ActionScript function from an anchor tag, we use the following syntax:

```
<A HREF="asfunction:myFunctionName">invoke the function</A>
```

The function invocation operator ( ) is not allowed and should not be used when invoking an ActionScript function from an anchor tag. In addition to calling an ActionScript function from an anchor tag, we may also pass one parameter to that function using the syntax:

```
<A HREF="asfunction:myFunctionName,myParameter">invoke the function</A>
```

where *myParameter* is the value of the parameter to pass. Inside the invoked function, *myParameter* is always a string. To pass more than one piece of information to a function from an anchor, we use a delimiter in the *myParameter* value and dissect the string ourselves in the function. For example, here's a function invocation that passes two values, separated by a | character, to the *roleCall()* function:

```
<A HREF="asfunction:roleCall,megan|murray">invoke the function</A>
```

And here's the *roleCall()* function. Notice how it separates the values with the *split()* method:

```
function roleCall (name) {
  var bothNames = name.split("|");
  trace("first name: " + bothNames[0]);
  trace("last name: " + bothNames[1]);
}
```

Working with Text Field Selections

When a user selects a portion of a dynamic or user-input text field, the positions of the selected characters are stored in a special built-in object called the *Selection* object. Using the *Selection* object, we can check which part of a text field a user has selected or even select a part of a text field programmatically. The *Selection* object can also tell us which of a series of text fields is currently selected by the user. Finally, we can use the *Selection* object to give keyboard focus to a particular text field, prompting a user to type in a suggested location.

To learn how to work with text field selections, see the *Selection* object in Part III.

Empty Text Fields and the for-in Statement

To check all the values of the variables on a timeline, we can use the *for-in* statement as described in Chapter 6, *Statements*. Undefined text fields (those that appear on screen but contain the **undefined** value), however, are not enumerated by the *for-in* statement. (Fields containing the empty string (`""`) or only spaces are not considered empty and are therefore enumerated.)

The invisibility of undefined text fields in *for-in* loops can cause problems for error-checking scripts. Scripts that use a *for-in* loop to cycle through a series of text fields must be written to account for undefined text fields. For example, here we attempt to check a movie clip called **formClip** to see if any of its variables contain the empty string:

```
for (i in formClip) {
  if (formClip[i] == "") {
    trace(i + " is empty! don't submit the form!");
    break;
  }
}
```

As is, that code would not function as desired because undefined text fields would not be enumerated by the loop and would never be checked. To force an undefined text field to be enumerated in a *for-in* loop, we must deliberately assign the empty string to a corresponding timeline variable. For example, we would attach this script to a frame of **formClip** in order to fix our previous example:

```
// Assign our text fields the empty string so that
// they show up in our for-in loop
formField1 = "";
formField2 = "";
```

Onward!

We're almost at that inevitable stage where the guided tour ends and you head off to explore your own projects and ideas. The previous two chapters have taught us how to create forms, display information on screen, and retrieve user input. Our last stop before the reference section—debugging code—teaches survival techniques to use in your uncharted journeys ahead.

19

Debugging

So far we've explored a lot of techniques and also the syntax to accomplish many goals. Inevitably, however, when you begin writing your own ActionScript, you'll encounter innumerable errors (especially at first when you are still making syntax and conceptual errors). Do not lose heart! Even experienced programmers spend a lot of time *debugging* (fixing broken code).

It is important that you test your product thoroughly so that you can find the bugs in the first place. This means testing in various browser brands and versions of those brands on all platforms that you intend to support. Test under different flavors of Windows and, if applicable, older versions of the Flash plug-in, which you can find at:

http://www.macromedia.com/support/flash/ts/documents/oldplayers.htm

A discussion of testing and quality assurance (QA) is beyond the scope of this book. Suffice to say that you should have a testing and QA process in place and a bug report form on which you can receive reports with sufficient detail (such as the platform, browser version, Flash plug-in version, and reproducible steps) for you to reproduce the error, which is the first step toward fixing it.

Debugging is an essential part of programming and what sets great programmers apart from average ones. Beginners are often happy if a bug that was seen earlier inexplicably disappears. Experienced programmers know that the bug will undoubtedly resurface at the most inopportune time, and although it is intermittent (perhaps especially so), it warrants further investigation. On the other hand, inexperienced programmers tend to shy away from error messages or be unnerved by obvious errors, whereas skilled programmers rely heavily on error messages and know that easily reproducible errors are the easiest kind to fix.

Successful debugging requires logical, disciplined investigative skills and a decent understanding of troubleshooting tools. In this chapter, we'll briefly consider the basics of debugging tools and some general techniques for solving code problems. Remember that debugging is characterized by the systematic challenging of our assumptions. Any given problem is often caused by some other problem upstream (i.e., the disease). We'll use the debugging tools to investigate whether things are in fact operating as designed, and that will lead to an understanding and resolution of the manifest bug (i.e., the symptom).

Debugging Tools

ActionScript comes equipped with the following debugging tools:

- The *trace()* function
- The List Variables command
- The List Objects command
- The Bandwidth Profiler
- The Debugger

All of these tools are used in Test Movie mode. To enter Test Movie mode, we export a movie from the authoring tool using Control → Test Movie.

In addition to these formal debugging tools, Flash also sends error messages to the Output window when a movie is exported or Check Syntax is performed. (Check Syntax is a command listed under the arrow button in the top right of the Actions panel.) Error messages often identify the exact cause of a problem down to the problematic line number in a block of source code. Comprehensive explanations for the various error messages are provided in Macromedia's ActionScript Reference Guide.

Note that not all bugs cause error messages. For example, a calculation that yields the wrong result is a bug even if it doesn't crash your browser. Also note that there are two types of error messages, so-called *compile-time* error messages that occur when you try to export your scripts and so-called *runtime* error messages that don't occur until you run your Flash movie and reach the point that causes the error. Compile-time errors indicate some sort of syntax problem such as a missing parenthesis or unclosed quotation. Refer to Part III, *Language Reference*, for the exact syntax needed for each command, and refer to Chapter 14, *Lexical Structure*, for an explanation of proper ActionScript syntax.

Runtime errors can take a wide variety of forms and may not indicate a problem with the current code under examination but rather may be caused by using the incorrect result of an earlier operation. For example, suppose you try to use the values received back from a *loadVariables()* command sent to a web server. If the Perl script responding to the command didn't supply the correct data in the correct format, you need to correct the Perl script. Your Flash script may be perfectly correct and yet fail because it received incorrect input.

Which brings up an important technique—defensive programming. You can avoid a lot of errors and potential errors by always checking for potential problematic conditions, which is known as *error checking* (or sometimes *data validation* if it pertains to user input). For example, before trying to display the questions of a quiz, you might check that those questions loaded properly. You might also check each question to be sure it's in the correct format for display. If the provided data was improperly entered, you should display an appropriate error message that allows the programmer or the user to take corrective action.

The trace() Function

In ActionScript, one of the most effective tools for identifying the source of a bug is also one of the simplest—the *trace()* function. As we've seen throughout this book, *trace()* sends the value of an expression to the Output window in Test Movie mode. For example, if we add the following code to a movie:

```
trace("hello world");
```

the text "hello world" appears in the Output window. Similarly, here we *trace()* the value of a variable:

```
var x = 5;
trace(x);   // Displays 5 in the Output window
```

Using *trace()* we may check the status of variables, properties, and objects, and we may track the progression of our code. Often by confirming the result of each operation in a script, we can figure out where a problem lies. For example, suppose a function is supposed to return a value but we find, using the *trace()* command, that the return value is undefined (i.e., it prints out as nothing in the Output window). We'd know that we have to examine the function in more detail and make sure that it is properly using a *return* command to pass back a meaningful value.

The List Variables Command

When a movie is running in Test Movie mode, we can check the value of current variables defined in the movie via the Debug → List Variables command. List Variables tells us the name and location of all the variables currently active in our movie and also reports their values. Because functions and movie clips are stored in variables, the List Variables command also shows us the functions and movie clips of a movie.

Example 19-1 shows sample output from List Variables. Notice that the variable `rate` is shown as declared but `undefined`. This subtlety is often difficult to detect with *trace()* because *trace()* converts the value `undefined` to the empty string (`" "`).

Example 19-1. List Variables Sample Output

```
Level #0:
  Variable _level0.$version = "WIN 5,0,30,0"
  Variable _level0.calcDist = [function]
  Variable _level0.deltaX = 194
  Variable _level0.deltaY = 179
  Variable _level0.rate = undefined
  Variable _level0.dist = 264
Movie Clip:  Target="_level0.clip1"
Movie Clip:  Target="_level0.clip2"
```

Note that both *trace()* and the List Variables command give only a snapshot in time. Often, you'll want to monitor the value of a variable over time or check it repeatedly. The Debugger (discussed later) allows you to track the value of a variable as it changes.

The List Objects Command

The List Objects command produces a catalog of text, shapes, graphics, and movie clips defined in a movie. To execute it, select Debug → List Objects while in Test Movie mode. Note that List Objects does not include a list of data objects (instances of a class) in a program; those are reported by List Variables.

Example 19-2 shows some sample output from List Objects. Notice that editable text fields are clearly labeled and that automatically named movie clip instances are revealed (e.g., `_level0.instance1`).

Example 19-2. List Objects Sample Output

```
Level #0: Frame=1
  Shape:
  Text: Value = "variables functions clip events startDrag stopDrag Math"
  Text: Value = "this movie demonstrates a little math, variables, movie clip events"
  Text: Value = "draggable distance"
  Text: Value = "calculator"
  Movie Clip: Frame=1 Target="_level0.instance1"
    Shape:
  Text: Value = "distance between clipstotal:horizontal:vertical:"
  Edit Text: Variable=_level0.dist Text="222"
  Edit Text: Variable=_level0.deltaX Text="174"
  Edit Text: Variable=_level0.deltaY Text="138"
  Movie Clip: Frame=1 Target="_level0.obj1"
    Shape:
  Movie Clip: Frame=1 Target="_level0.obj2"
    Shape:
```

Again, List Objects provides only a snapshot in time. You need to run it again to get the current value of objects whenever they may have changed.

The Bandwidth Profiler

The Bandwidth Profiler is used to simulate movie download at various modem speeds. Using the Bandwidth Profiler, we may gauge the performance of a movie, test preloading code, and track the position of the main movie's playhead during movie playback. Here's how to turn the Bandwidth Profiler on:

1. While in Test Movie mode, select View → Bandwidth Profiler.

2. Under the Debug menu, select the desired download rate.

3. To simulate the download of a movie at that rate, select View → Show Streaming.

There are many things that can affect Flash performance, such as the assets in use and the rendering demands on the Player. For example, using large bitmaps, rendering complex shapes with many curves, and excessive use of alpha channels can all degrade performance. Asset downloading and rendering times usually dwarf the bandwidth and processor time required for ActionScript to execute. That said, ActionScript is generally much slower than compiled languages such as C.

From an ActionScript perspective, the most time-consuming operations are those that either must wait for data to be uploaded or downloaded or those that are performed repetitively (such as examining a large array).

 Displaying items in the Output window is very slow compared to "invisible" operations in ActionScript. If a simple movie seems excessively choppy, try disabling all *trace()* statements, or play the movie outside Test Movie mode.

A discussion of writing optimized code is beyond the scope of this book, but some quick tips should suffice:

- Don't perform an operation repeatedly within a loop if it can be performed once outside of a loop with no loss of functionality.

- Don't wait in a loop for some event to occur. The event may take a long time or may never occur, causing your performance to slow or your application to lock up entirely. Instead, rely on event handlers, such as *on (load)* to be triggered when an event occurs or completes.

- Generalize your code wherever possible (perhaps even use Smart Clips to do so). This reduces the size of the code that needs to be downloaded. For example, instead of writing two nearly identical routines that are each 5 KB long, you can save 5 KB by writing one generalized routine and calling it twice with different parameters. (Generalizing code is explained in Chapter 9, *Functions*, and Smart Clips are explained in Chapter 16, *ActionScript Authoring Environment*).

- If you're using the Flash 5 Player and optimized ActionScript performance is critical to your project, try using old-style Flash 4 syntax instead of newer techniques. In Flash 5, certain operations are faster when phrased with Flash 4 syntax. For example, Flash 4's *substring()* function is faster than Flash 5's *substring()* and *substr()* methods, and Flash 4's *Tell Target* is faster than Flash 5's dot notation.

- Export your movies without *trace()* statements by selecting Publish Settings → Flash → Options → Omit Trace Actions.

- Remember that removing and reattaching a clip is more costly than moving an existing one; reuse your movie assets whenever possible.

- For a list of general Flash optimization techniques, see *http://www.macromedia. com/support/flash/publishexport/stream_optimize/stream_optimize.html.*

The Debugger

The Debugger is a highly useful tool that gives us organized access to the values of properties, objects, and variables in a movie and even allows us to change variable values at runtime.

To enable the Debugger, select Control → Debug Movie in the Flash authoring tool (*not* in Test Movie mode). You may also use the Debugger in a web browser, provided that:

- The movie being viewed was originally exported with debugging permitted.
- The Player being used to view the movie is a debugging Player.
- The Flash authoring tool is running when you attempt to debug.

To export a movie with in-browser debugging permitted, select File → Publish Settings → Flash → Debugging Permitted, then optionally provide a password to prevent prying eyes from snooping around your code. To install a debugging Player in your browser, use the installers provided in the */Players/Debug/* folder where you installed Flash on your hard drive. To enable debugging while viewing a movie, right-click in Windows (Ctrl-click on Macintosh) on the movie and select Debugger.

Not all versions of the Flash Player have a corresponding debugging Player. Check Macromedia's support site for the newest versions of the debugging Player, *http://www.macromedia.com/support/flash*.

The top half of the Debugger (the Display List) shows the movie clip hierarchy of the movie. To inspect the properties and variables of a specific movie clip, select it in the Display List. The bottom half of the Debugger contains three tabs, Properties, Variables, and Watch, which update dynamically to show the properties and variables for the selected clip. To set the value of any property or variable, double-click its value and enter the new data. To single out one or more items for convenient scrutiny, select them in the Properties or Variables tab, then choose Add Watch from the arrow button in the upper-right corner of the Debugger. All "watched" variables are added to the Watch tab (this lets us view variables in different movie clips simultaneously).

For more information about the mechanics of using the Flash Debugger, consult Macromedia's thorough documentation under "Troubleshooting ActionScript" in the ActionScript Reference Guide. If you've lost your Reference Guide, remember that it's available on Macromedia's web site at *http://www.macromedia.com/support/flash* and also under the Help menu in the Flash authoring tool.

Debugging Methodology

Let's take a quick look at some techniques involved in code debugging. Debugging can be broken into three stages:

- Recognizing and reproducing a problem
- Identifying the source of the problem
- Fixing the problem

Recognizing Bugs

Very often, we recognize code problems as part of the active process of programming. That is, we write some code, test our movie, and find that the movie doesn't work properly. Problem recognized.

The earlier a problem is discovered, the better. The process of writing code should therefore be a constant ebb and flow of writing and testing—write a few lines, export the movie, make sure the lines work as expected, then write a few more lines, export the movie, and so on. Make sure each component of a program works on its own before testing the program as a whole. Try not to get carried away writing a complex body of code without testing it frequently along the way.

Don't assume your movie is perfect just because you can't find any bugs on your own. Always schedule time for external testing by target users, particularly if the code you are delivering is part of a product or a service intended for a client. As described earlier, implement error checking to head off possible problems with incorrect data input. For example, if you write a function that expects an integer argument, you might use the *typeof* operator to verify that the input parameters are of the correct type. Also test *end conditions* such as extremely large, small, and negative values, including zero.

Don't underestimate the value of finding the *minimum reproducible steps* that replicate the problem. These should be the fewest steps that recreate the error reliably. A bug report such as, "I played it for an hour and then it froze" is not very helpful. Useful bug reports include numbered steps such as:

1. Enter 0 for the number of years.
2. Click the Calculate button.
3. The results field shows "NaN" instead of a dollar amount.

Identifying the Source of a Bug

Once we've recognized a bug, our quest for a solution has only begun. Our first task is to find the source of the bug, however far upstream that may be. A bug can be thought of like a heart attack that was caused by bad dietary habits years earlier. The heart attack is merely the most manifest symptom, but you must often correct something earlier in the process. Most bugs are caused by false assumptions; we assume we've typed the name of a variable correctly but we haven't, or we assume a text field stores numeric data but it doesn't. By executing a series of *trace()* statements or using the Debugger or List Variables command, we can test our assumptions against the interpreter's understanding of our code.

Here, for example, is some code with a bug. It incorrectly sets **status** to "equal":

```
var x = 11;
isTen(x);
function isTen(val) {
  if (val = 10) {
    status = "equal";
  }
}
```

To find out what's wrong with the code, we compare what we *think* the code should be doing against what it *actually* is doing, one step at a time:

```
// This should set x to 11
var x = 11;

// Let's see if it really does
trace(x);      // Yup...this displays: 11

// This should invoke the isTen() function
isTen(x);

// Now on to our function
function isTen(val) {
  // Let's make sure our function is being called
  trace("isTen was called");   // Yup...this displays: "isTen was called"

  // Now let's make sure our parameter was passed correctly
  trace("val is " + val);       // Yup...this displays: "val is 11"
```

Let's pause here for a second. Notice what's happened—we've made it most of the way through our code and so far everything has worked as expected. Our variable was set correctly; *isTen()* was called and received its argument properly.

 Many errors occur because the code that you think is being executed has never even been reached! We can use *trace()* statements to verify that a particular portion of our code is reached.

By process of elimination, we already know that our code's problem must lie either in the conditional statement `if(val = 10)` or in the text field assignment `status = "equal"`. We next check our conditional statement by using *trace()* to display the value of its test expression (we're expecting either `true` or `false`):

```
trace(val = 10);
```

Eureka! The Output window displays 10, not `true` or `false` as we had expected.

On closer inspection, we see that the test expression is an assignment statement, not a comparison statement! We forgot an equal sign in our equality comparison operator. The expression `if(val = 10)` should be `if(val == 10)`.

Obviously, not all bugs are as simple as our conditional statement bug (which is an exceedingly common error), but the approach we used is applicable to most bug hunts: execute a series of *trace()* functions to create a running, step-by-step report on the actual behavior of a movie's code and use the Debugger as explained in the Macromedia documentation.

Common Sources of Bugs

Table 19-1 lists some common sources of bugs in ActionScript.

Table 19-1. ActionScript Gotchas

Problem	Description
Code in the wrong place	All code must be attached to a movie clip, frame, or button. Take care that your code is actually attached to what you intend by observing the title of the Actions panel—when attaching code to a frame, the Actions panel's title reads Frame Actions; when attaching code to a movie clip or button, the Actions panel title reads Object Actions. If you want a script to be on a particular frame, make sure that frame is selected in the timeline before you start coding, and that there's a keyframe where you want to place your code. If you want a script to be on a movie clip or button, make sure that object is selected on stage before you start coding. Use the Movie Explorer (Window → Movie Explorer) to keep track of exactly where code is attached.

Missing event handler	Code attached to movie clips and buttons *must* be contained by an event handler. For movie clips, use:
	
	```\nonClipEvent (event) {\n // statements\n}\n```
	
	For buttons, use:
	
	```\non (event) {\n // statements\n}\n```
	
	where *event* is the name of the event to handle. The error, "Statement must appear within on handler," indicates that you're missing an event handler. See Chapter 10.

Bad movie clip reference	A movie clip that doesn't exist is referenced, or a reference to a movie clip is malformed. Check that all instances are named, and that instance names match the reference supplied. See "Referring to Nested Instances" in Chapter 13 for information on composing valid movie clip references.
Unexpected type conversion	The result of a data conversion yields an unexpected result. For example, 3 + "4" yields the string "34", not the number 7. Similarly, the string "true" converts to the Boolean value `false`! Study type conversion rules in Chapter 3. Check datatypes using the *typeof* operator.
Missing semicolon	A statement ends prematurely because a semicolon is missing. See Chapter 14 for proper semicolon usage.
Problem quotation mark	A string includes an unescaped quotation character that interferes with the string literal. See "String Literals" in Chapter 4.
Bad text field data usage	A text field is treated as a number or other datatype, not a string. User input in text fields is always a string value and should be converted manually before being treated as any other type.

Table 19-1. ActionScript Gotchas (continued)

Problem	Description
Scope problems	A variable, property, clip, or function is referenced in the wrong scope. For example, a statement in a clip handler attempts to invoke a function scoped to that clip's parent time-line. See "Event Handler Scope" in Chapter 10, "Variable Scope" in Chapter 2, and "Function Availability and Life Span" in Chapter 9.
Global function versus method confusion	Some global functions have the same name as movie clip methods. Occasionally, this overlap causes problems. See "Method versus global function overlap issues," in Chapter 13.
Content not yet loaded	A reference to a clip, property, function, or variable can't be resolved because the content is not yet loaded. Be sure all content is loaded by checking the *MovieClip._framesloaded* property as shown in Part III.
Incorrect capitalization	Some keywords are case sensitive in ActionScript. If you mis-capitalize *onClipEvent* as *onclipevent*, ActionScript will think you are trying to call a custom function named *onclipevent* instead of using the built-in *onClipEvent* handler keyword. As such, it will give you an error when it encounters the { at the beginning of the *onClipEvent* statement block (it expects a semicolon indicating the end of what it perceives to be an *onclipevent* function call). See "Case Sensitivity" in Chapter 14.

Fixing Bugs

In some cases, the fix for an identified bug is self-evident. For example, if we discover a bug caused by a missing quotation mark on a string, we fix the bug by adding the quotation mark.

In more involved programs, fixing bugs can be a serious challenge. If a bug is proving difficult to fix, consider the following:

- Don't be afraid to rewrite code. In many cases the best way to fix overly complicated code is to rearchitect the system and start from scratch. Recreating a program nearly always goes faster and smoother than creating the program in the first place. Most experts agree on this one (for example, Quake III was a complete rewrite of the Quake II engine). That said, new code still needs to be debugged. Don't throw out perfectly good code close to a deadline. Keep what's good and rewrite only the problematic code.

- Break problematic components out into separate test movies. Work on each aspect of a system in complete isolation, then integrate working sections one at a time.

- Have a peer review your code. Don't be afraid. We're all embarrassed by the code we wrote a year earlier.

- Ask for help at one of the resources cited in Appendix A, *Resources*. For example, the FlashCoders mailing list is devoted entirely to ActionScript questions.

For lots of good advice on programming techniques, see *Extreme Programming Explained* by Kent Beck (Addison Wesley) and *Code Complete* by Steve McConnell (Microsoft Press).

Onward!

Our ActionScript conversation is over, but yours has just begun. By reading Part I, *ActionScript Fundamentals* and Part II, *Applied ActionScript*, you've learned to speak ActionScript—now it's time to apply that knowledge to your own projects. Before you embark, here are a few parting thoughts:

- As with any art form, learning to program is a process not an event. For as long as you program, you'll learn more about programming. Consider the multiple-choice quiz example from Chapters 1, 9, 11, and 13—we rebuilt it four times! Each time we refined our approach, added features, and learned something we hadn't considered before. Just as each painting teaches the painter something new about her subject matter, so creating and recreating applications will reveal new approaches to you.

- There's practical help in Part III, which contains detailed descriptions of ActionScript's built-in functions, properties, classes, and objects. While you may not want to read it from start to finish, you should definitely skim each topic so you have a sense of ActionScript's capabilities.

- Revisit this book and Part III often. You'll pick up new insights each time through because you'll be considering the information with a higher level of understanding and will be able to relate concepts to real-world experiences. Treat Part III as a dictionary and keep it by your side while you work.

- There's a thriving community of Flash developers out there offering ideas and solutions and—most importantly—sharing source code! Dissect as much as you can. Identify the things you can't understand and look those topics up in this book. Macromedia maintains a list of web sites and mailing lists devoted to Flash at *http://www.macromedia.com/support/flash/ts/documents/flash_websites.htm*.

- Don't limit your exploration of ActionScript to this book. Look at things from multiple angles by consulting other sources of knowledge and inspiration, such as those listed in Appendix A and the Preface. You'll also find a long list of Flash resources at *http://www.moock.org/moockmarks* and reviews of worthwhile Flash books at *http://www.moock.org/webdesign/books.*

- Finally, remember to drop by the ActionScript Definitive Guide support site, *http://www.moock.org/asdg,* for lots of code samples, tech notes, and discussions of new topics.

With that, I wish you happy coding! Throw an extra iteration into a *while* loop for me sometime. :)

III

Language Reference

This part explains how to use each built-in class, object, function, property, and event handler supported by ActionScript. You'll use Part III regularly to accomplish specific tasks in your daily programming work.

- ActionScript Language Reference

ActionScript Language Reference

This *Language Reference* documents all the supported classes and objects of ActionScript, explaining their general purpose, usage, properties, methods, and event handlers. Also covered are the *global functions* and *global properties* (those not attached to a class or an object, but available in standalone form, throughout a movie).

All entries in the *Language Reference* are alphabetized. For example, the global function *duplicateMovieClip()* is listed after the *Date* class (not, say, in a separate "Global Functions" section). However, each entry title clearly indicates the type of item being described so that there can be no confusion between overlapping items. For example, *duplicateMovieClip()* comes in both global function and movie clip method form, so you'll find it listed as both *duplicateMovieClip() Global Function* and *MovieClip.duplicateMovieClip() Method*. If you're unsure of where to find an item, consult the index at the back of the book.

Global Functions

Global functions are built-in functions that are available throughout an entire movie—they may be invoked from any frame, button, or event handler in a movie (unlike methods, which must be invoked using a reference to a specific object).

Table R-1 lists the global functions available in Flash 5 ActionScript.

Table R-1. ActionScript Global Functions

Boolean()	*call()*	*Date()*
duplicateMovieClip()	*escape()*	*eval()*
fscommand()	*getProperty()*	*getTimer()*
getURL()	*getVersion()*	*gotoAndPlay()*
gotoAndStop()	*#include*	*int()**
isFinite()	*isNaN()*	*loadMovie()*
loadMovieNum()	*loadVariables()*	*loadVariablesNum()*
maxscroll	*newline*	*nextFrame()*

Table R-1. ActionScript Global Functions (continued)

nextScene()	*Number()*	*parseFloat()*
parseInt()	*play()*	*prevFrame()*
prevScene()	*print()*	*printAsBitmap()*
printAsBitmapNum()	*printNum()*	*random()**
removeMovieClip()	*scroll*	*setProperty()*
startDrag()	*stop()*	*stopAllSounds()*
stopDrag()	*String()*	*targetPath()*
*tellTarget()**	*toggleHighQuality()**	*trace()*
unescape()	*unloadMovie()*	*unloadMovieNum()*
updateAfterEvent()		

*Deprecated in Flash 5.

Global Properties

Global properties, like global functions, may be accessed from any script in a movie. They store information that is generally useful, from any point in our code. Many of them affect the entire Flash Player, not just a particular movie clip or movie.

Table R-2 lists the global properties available in Flash 5.

Table R-2. ActionScript Global Properties

Property Name	Description
_focusrect	The highlight state of buttons activated via the keyboard
_highquality	The rendering quality of the Player*
Infinity	A constant representing the Infinity value of the *number* type
-Infinity	A constant representing the −Infinity value of the *number* type
_level*n*	A document level in the Player
NaN	Not-A-Number; the value of the *number* type representing invalid numeric data
_quality	The rendering quality of the Player
_root	A reference to the main movie timeline of the current level
_soundbuftime	Number of seconds of a streaming sound to preload
$version*	The version of the Flash Player

*Deprecated in Flash 5.

Built-in Classes and Objects

This *Language Reference* assumes that you understand the terms *class*, *object*, and *instance* as discussed exhaustively in Chapter 12, *Objects and Classes*. The built-in classes of Action-

Script are used to create objects that can control a movie and manipulate data. The built-in ActionScript classes are *Array, Boolean, Color, Date, MovieClip, Number, Object, Sound, String, XML, XMLNode,* and *XMLSocket.* To create an instance of a particular class, we use the class's *constructor* function with the *new* operator. For example, to make a new object of the *Color* class, we use the *Color* constructor as follows:

```
myColor = new Color(_root);
```

For each class in the *Language Reference*, the *Constructor* entry shows how to create new objects of that particular class (i.e., it demonstrates each class's constructor function syntax). The properties, methods, and event handlers available for objects in the class are also summarized along with a description of the class's purpose and typical use. Some classes also define methods or properties that are accessed through the class constructor itself, not individual instances. These methods and properties are listed as *Class Methods* and *Class Properties.* Full details for each class's properties, methods, and event handlers are given in an alphabetical list after each class's general introduction.

ActionScript's special built-in objects—*Arguments, Key, Math, Mouse* and *Selection*—are interspersed alphabetically with the class descriptions in this book but are distinguished by the word *Object* (e.g., *Math Object*). Unlike true classes, which use a constructor function to instantiate multiple objects, these standalone objects are never instantiated (i.e., they are not constructed with the *new* operator). Rather, they are predefined objects that exist solely to collect related functionality into a single package. The *Math* object, for example, provides convenient access to common mathematical functions and constants.

Entry Headings

The headings used to document each item of the *Language Reference* are described in Table R-3.

Table R-3. Language Reference Headings

Heading	Description
Availability	Indicates when the item was added to ActionScript (or became an Action, if the item predates formal ActionScript). Also summarizes backward-compatibility and deprecation status.
Synopsis	Illustrates the abstract syntax required by the item. Italicized code indicates text that must be provided by the programmer.
Arguments	Applies to method and function entries only. Describes the parameters used with the method or function, as listed in the Synopsis.
Returns	Applies to method and function entries only. Describes the return value of the method, if any. If the method does not have a return value, this heading is omitted.
Access	Applies to property entries only. Describes whether the property value may be retrieved ("Read-only") or both retrieved and assigned ("Read/write").
Description	Explains how the item works and how it might be used in a practical scenario.
Usage	Describes noteworthy peculiarities of the item.

Table R-3. Language Reference Headings (continued)

Heading	Description
Bugs	Describes known problems associated with the item.
Example	Offers sample code showing the item in use.
See Also	Lists cross-references to related topics.

Alphabetical Language Reference

The following entries document ActionScript's objects and classes. Refer to the index for the operators and statements covered elsewhere in this book.

Arguments Object   access to function parameters and the current function

Availability   Flash 5

Synopsis   `arguments[elem]`
                  `arguments.propertyName`

Properties

callee   A reference to the function being executed.

length   The number of parameters passed to the function being executed.

Description

The *Arguments* object is stored in the local **arguments** variable of every function and is accessible only while a function is executing. *Arguments* is both an array and an object. As an array, **arguments** stores the values of the parameters passed to the currently executing function. For example, **arguments[0]** is the first passed parameter, **arguments[1]** is the second passed parameter, and so on. As an object, *Arguments* stores the **callee** property, which can be used to identify or invoke the current function.

See Also

"The arguments Object" in Chapter 9, *Functions*

---

arguments.callee Property   a reference to the function being executed

Availability   Flash 5

Synopsis   `arguments.callee`

Access   Read/write

Description

The **callee** property stores a reference to the function currently executing. We may use this reference to execute the current function again or to identify the current function through comparison.

Example

```
function someFunction () {
  trace(arguments.callee == someFunction);    // Displays: true
}

// An unnamed recursive function
countToTen = function () {
  i++;
  trace(i);
  if (i < 10) {
    arguments.callee();
  }
};
```

arguments.length Property

the number of parameters passed to an argument

Availability	Flash 5
Synopsis	`arguments.length`
Access	Read/write

Description

The `length` property stores an integer representing the number of elements in the `arguments` array, which equates to the number of parameters passed to the currently executing function.

Example

We can use the `length` property of **arguments** to determine whether a function was invoked with the correct number of parameters. The following example checks whether two arguments have been passed to *someFunction()*. Checking whether the passed arguments are of the correct type is left as an exercise to the reader. (Hint: see the *typeof* operator.) Here's the code:

```
function someFunction (y, z) {
  if (arguments.length != 2) {
    trace("Function invoked with wrong number of parameters");
    return;
  }
  // Proceed with normal function body...
}
```

Array Class

support for ordered lists of data

Availability	Flash 5

Constructor	`new Array()`
	`new Array(len)`
	`new Array(element0, element1, element2,...elementn)`

Arguments

len	A non-negative integer specifying the size of the new array.

element0,...elementn

A list of one or more initial values to be assigned as elements of the array.

Properties

length   The number of elements in an array (including empty elements).

Methods

concat()   Create a new array by appending additional elements to an existing array.

join()   Convert an array to a string.

pop()   Remove and return the last element of an array.

push()   Add one or more elements to the end of an array.

reverse()   Reverse the order of elements in an array.

shift()   Remove and return the first element of an array.

slice()   Create a new array using a subset of elements from an existing array.

sort()   Sort the elements of an array according to the specified rule.

splice()   Remove elements from, and/or add elements to, an array.

toString()   Convert an array to a string of comma-separated element values.

unshift()   Add one or more elements to the beginning of an array.

Description

We use the properties and methods of the *Array* class to manipulate the data stored in the elements of an array object. See Chapter 11, *Arrays*, for exhaustive details on what arrays are and how you can use them, plus detailed definitions of the terminology used in this section. See also the [] and . operators, which are used to access array elements as described in Chapter 5, *Operators*.

Usage

If the *Array* constructor is invoked with a single integer argument, that argument is used to set the length of the new array, not the value of the first element. If two or more arguments are supplied to the constructor or if a single non-numeric argument is supplied to the constructor, the arguments are used as the initial values for elements in the array, and the length of the array is determined by the number of arguments specified.

Array.concat( ) Method   *create a new array by extending an existing array*

Availability   Flash 5

Synopsis   `array.concat(value1, value2, value3,...valuen)`

Arguments
value1,...valuen   A list of expressions to be added to the end of *array* as new elements.

Returns

A new array containing all the elements of *array* followed by the elements *value1,...valuen*.

Description

The *concat()* method returns a new array created by appending new elements to the end of an existing array. The original *array* is left unchanged. Use the *push()*, *splice()*, or *shift()* method to modify the original array.

If an array is used as an argument to *concat()*, each element of that array is appended separately. That is, the result of *arrayX.concat(arrayY)* will be an array formed by appending each element of **arrayY** to the end of **arrayX**. The resulting array will have a `length` equal to `arrayY.length + arrayX.length`. Nested arrays, however, are not similarly flattened.

Example

```
// Create an array
myListA = new Array("apples", "oranges");

// Set myListB to ["apples", "oranges", "bananas"]
myListB = myListA.concat("bananas");

// Create another new array
myListC = new Array("grapes", "plums");

// Set myListD to ["apples", "oranges", "bananas", "grapes", "plums"]
myListD = myListB.concat(myListC);

// Set myListA to ["apples", "oranges", "bananas"]
myListA = myListA.concat("bananas");

// Create an array
settings  = ["on", "off"];
// Append an array containing a nested array
options = settings.concat(["brightness", ["high", "medium", "low"]]);
// Sets options to: ["on", "off", "brightness", ["high", "medium", "low"]]
// not: ["on", "off", "brightness", "high", "medium", "low"]
```

See Also

Array.push(), *Array.shift()*, *Array.splice()*; "The concat() method" in Chapter 11

Array.join( ) Method   convert an array to a string

Availability   Flash 5

Synopsis   `array.join()`
                `array.join(delimiter)`

Arguments
delimiter   An optional string to be placed between elements in the newly created string. Defaults to a comma if not supplied.

Returns

A string composed of all the elements of **array** converted to strings and separated by *delimiter*.

Description

The *join()* method returns a string created by combining all the elements of an array, as follows:

1. Convert each element in the array to a string (empty elements are converted to the empty string).

2. Add `delimiter` to the end of each converted-element string, except the last one.

3. Concatenate the converted-element strings into one long string.

Note that elements that are themselves arrays are converted to strings via the *toString()* method, so nested array elements are always delimited by commas, not the delimiter used in the *join()* invocation.

Example

```
fruit = new Array("apples","oranges","bananas","grapes","plums");
// Set fruitString to "apples,oranges,bananas,grapes,plums"
fruitString = fruit.join();
// Set fruitString to "apples-oranges-bananas-grapes-plums"
fruitString = fruit.join("-");
```

See Also

Array.toString(), *String.split()*; "The join() Method" in Chapter 11

Array.length Property   the number of elements in an array

Availability   Flash 5

Synopsis   `array.length`

Access   Read/write

Description

The `length` property is a non-negative integer specifying the number of elements in an array. An array with no elements has a length of 0, an array with 2 elements has a length of 2. Note that the index number of the first element in an array is 0, so `length` is always one greater than the index of the last element in the array.

The `length` property of an array indicates how many numbered elements the array currently contains, including empty elements (those containing `null` or `undefined`). For example, an array may have values for elements 0, 1, 2, and 9, but elements 3 through 8 may be empty. Such an array has a length of 10 because it has 10 element positions (0 through 9) even though only 4 positions are occupied by useful values.

Setting the `length` of an array changes the number of elements in the array. If we increase `length`, empty elements are added to the end of the array; if we decrease `length`, existing elements are removed from the end of the array. The `length` property changes automatically whenever any elements are added or removed via the *Array* class methods. The `length` property reflects numbered elements only; it does not include named array elements, which are treated as properties of the array.

Example

```
myList = new Array("one", "two", "three");
trace(myList.length);  // Displays: 3

// Loop through the array's elements
for (var i = 0; i < myList.length; i++) {
  trace(myList[i]);
}
```

See Also

"Determining the Size of an Array" in Chapter 11

Array.pop( ) Method   remove the last element of an array

Availability   Flash 5

Synopsis   `array.pop()`

Returns

The value of the last element of **array**, which is also deleted.

Description

The *pop()* method deletes the *last* element of an array, reduces the array's `length` by 1, and returns the value of the deleted element. Compare with the *shift()* method, which deletes the *first* element of an array.

Example

```
myList = new Array("one", "two", "three");
trace ("Now deleting " + myList.pop());  // myList is now: ["one", "two"]
```

See Also

Array.push(), *Array.shift()*, *Array.splice()*; "Removing Elements from an Array" in Chapter 11, "The delete Operator" in Chapter 5

Array.push( ) Method   add one or more elements to the end of an array

Availability   Flash 5

Synopsis   `array.push(value1, value2,...valuen)`

Arguments

value1,...valuen   A list of one or more values to be added to the end of **array**.

Returns

The new `length` of **array**.

Description

The *push()* method appends a list of values to the end of an array as new elements. Elements are added in the order provided. It differs from *concat()* in that *push()* modifies the original array, whereas *concat()* creates a new array. It differs from *unshift()* in that it adds elements at the end of an array, not the beginning.

Example

```
myList = new Array (5, 6);
myList.push(7);              // myList is now [5, 6, 7]
myList.push(10, 8, 9);      // myList is now [5, 6, 7, 10, 8, 9]
```

See Also

Array.concat(), *Array.pop()*, *Array.unshift()*; "Adding Elements to an Array" in Chapter 11

Array.reverse( ) Method   reverse the order of elements in an array

Availability   Flash 5

Synopsis   `array.reverse()`

Description

The *reverse* method reverses the order of elements in an array, swapping the last element with the first element, the second-to-last element with the second element, and so on.

Example

```
myList = new Array(3, 4, 5, 6, 7);
myList.reverse();                        // myList is now [7, 6, 5, 4, 3]
```

See Also

Array.sort()

Array.shift( ) Method   remove the first element of an array

Availability   Flash 5

Synopsis   `array.shift()`

Returns

The value of the first element of *array*, which is also deleted.

Description

The *shift()* method deletes the *first* element of an array and then moves all the remaining elements of the array up one position. The affected array's `length` is reduced by 1. Note that *shift()* differs from the *pop()* method, which deletes the *last* element of an array.

Example

```
myList = new Array ("a", "b", "c");
myList.shift();                          // myList becomes ["b", "c"]
```

See Also

Array.pop(), *Array.splice()*, *Array.unshift()*; "Removing Elements from an Array" in Chapter 11

Array.slice( ) Method

create a new array using a subset
of elements from an existing array

Availability   Flash 5

Synopsis   `array.slice(startIndex, endIndex)`

Arguments

startIndex   A zero-relative integer specifying the first element in **array** to add to the new array. If negative, `startIndex` indicates an element number counting backward from the end of **array** (–1 is the last element, –2 is the second-to-last element, etc.).

endIndex   An integer specifying the element *after* the last element in **array** to add to the new array. If negative, `endIndex` counts backward from the end of **array** (–1 is the last element, –2 is the second-to-last element, etc.). If omitted, `endIndex` defaults to `array.length`.

Returns

A new array containing the elements of **array** from `startIndex` to `endIndex-1`.

Description

The *slice()* method creates a new array by extracting a series of elements from an existing array. The new array is a subset of the elements of the original **array**, starting with `array[startIndex]` and ending with `array[endIndex-1]`.

Example

```
myList = new Array("a", "b", "c", "d", "e");

// Set myOtherList to ["b", "c", "d"]
myOtherList = myList.slice(1, 4);

// Set anotherList to ["d", "e"]
anotherList = myList.slice(3);

// Set yetAnotherList to ["c", "d"]
yetAnotherList = myList.slice(-3, -1);
```

See Also

Array.splice(); "The slice() Method" in Chapter 11, "The delete Operator" in Chapter 5

Array.sort( ) Method

sort the elements of an array

Availability   Flash 5

Synopsis   `array.sort()`
        `array.sort(compareFunction)`

Arguments

compareFunction A function that dictates how to sort **array**.

Description

When invoked without any arguments, the *sort()* method temporarily converts the elements of *array* to strings and orders the elements according to the code points of those strings (approximately alphabetical order). Alphabetic comparisons and code points are described in "Character order and alphabetic comparisons" in Chapter 4, *Primitive Datatypes*.

When invoked with a *compareFunction* argument, *sort()* reorders the elements of *array* according to the return value of *compareFunction*, which is a user-defined function that dictates how to arrange any two values in the array. Your user-defined *compareFunction* should be designed to accept two array elements as arguments. It should return a negative number if the first element should come before the second element; it should return a positive number if the first element should come after the second element; and it should return a 0 if the elements should not be reordered. If additional elements are added to the array after it has been sorted, they are *not* added in sorted order. You must resort the array to reorder any newly added elements. Note that numbers are sorted according to their Latin 1 code points by default. Chapter 11 explains how to sort numbers by their numeric values.

Example

The following example sorts an array of movie clips according to their horizontal location on screen:

```
var clips = [clip1, clip2, clip3, clip4];

function compareXposition (element1, element2) {
  if (element1._x < element2._x) {
    return -1;
  } else if (element1._x > element2._x) {
    return 1;
  } else {
    return 0;  // The clips have the same x position
  }
}

clips.sort(compareXposition);
```

See Also

Array.reverse(); "The sort() method" in Chapter 11

Array.splice( ) Method   remove elements from, and/or add elements to, an array

Availability   Flash 5

Synopsis   *array*.splice(*startIndex*)
                    array.splice(*startIndex*, *deleteCount*)
                    array.splice(*startIndex*, *deleteCount*, *value1*,...*valuen*)

Arguments
startIndex   The zero-relative element index at which to start element deletion and optional insertion of new elements. If negative, *startIndex* specifies an element counting back from the end of *array* (–1 is the last element, –2 is the second-to-last element, etc.).

deleteCount	An optional non-negative integer representing the number of elements to remove from *array*, including the element at *startIndex*. If 0, no elements are deleted. If omitted, all elements from *startIndex* to the end of the array are removed.
value1,...valuen	An optional list of one or more values to be added to *array* at index *startIndex* after the specified elements have been deleted.

Returns

A new array containing the *deleted* elements (the original *array* is modified separately to reflect the requested changes).

Description

The *splice()* method removes the elements from *array*[*startIndex*] to *array*[*startIndex* + *deleteCount*-1] and then optionally inserts new elements starting at *startIndex*. The *splice()* method does not leaves gaps in *array*; it moves elements up or down to ensure the contiguity of elements in the array.

Example

```
myList = new Array (1, 2, 3, 4, 5);
// Deletes the second and third elements from the list
// and insert the elements "x", "y", and "z" in their place.
// This changes myList to [1, "x", "y", "z", 4, 5].
myList.splice(1, 2, "x", "y", "z");
```

See Also

Array.slice(); "The splice() method" in Chapter 11

Array.toString( ) Method

convert an array to a string of comma-separated element values

Availability	Flash 5
Synopsis	`array.toString()`

Returns

A comma-separated list of *array*'s elements converted to strings.

Description

The *toString()* method creates a string representation of *array*. The string returned by *toString()* is a list of array elements converted to strings and separated by commas (the same as is returned by the *join()* method when *join()* is invoked without parameters). An array's *toString()* method is automatically invoked whenever the array is used in a string context. Therefore, it is rarely necessary to manually execute *toString()* on an array. Normally, when we want a precise string representation of an array, we use the *join()* method, which offers us more control over the string we're creating.

Example

```
myList = new Array("a", "b", "c");           // Create an array
trace(myList.toString());                    // Displays: "a","b","c"
myList = new Array([1, 2, 3], "a", "b", "c"); // Create a nested array
trace(myList.toString());                    // Displays: "1,2,3,a,b,c"
```

See Also

Array.join()

Array.unshift( ) Method   add one or more elements to the beginning of an array

Availability   Flash 5

Synopsis   `array.unshift(value1, value2,...valuen)`

Arguments

value1,...valuen   A list of one or more element values to be added to the beginning of `array`.

Returns

The new `length` of `array`.

Description

The *unshift()* method adds a series of elements to the beginning of an array. Elements are added in the order specified. To add elements at the end of an array, use *push()*.

Example

```
myList = new Array (5, 6);
myList.unshift(4);          // myList becomes [4, 5, 6]
myList.unshift(7, 1);          // myList becomes [7, 1, 4, 5, 6]
```

See Also

Array.push(), *Array.shift()*; "Adding Elements to an Array" in Chapter 11

Boolean( ) Global Function   convert a value to the *boolean* datatype

Availability   Flash 5

Synopsis   `Boolean(value)`

Arguments

value   An expression containing the value to be converted to a Boolean.

Returns

The result of converting `value` to a primitive Boolean (either `true` or `false`).

Description

The *Boolean()* global function converts its argument to a primitive Boolean value and returns that converted value. The results of converting various types of data to a primitive Boolean are described in Table 3-3. It's normally not necessary to use the *Boolean()* function; ActionScript automatically converts values to the *boolean* type when appropriate.

Usage

Be sure not to confuse the global *Boolean()* function with the *Boolean* class constructor. The *Boolean()* function converts its argument to the *boolean* datatype, whereas the *Boolean* class constructor creates a new Boolean object. Note that in ECMA-262, all nonempty strings convert to `true`. In Flash 5, only strings that can be converted to a valid nonzero number convert to `true`. Therefore, even the string "true" converts to the Boolean `false`.

Example

```
var x = 1;
if (Boolean(x)) {
  trace("x is true");
}
```

See Also

The *Boolean* class; "Datatype Conversion" in Chapter 3, *Data and Datatypes*

Boolean Class   wrapper class for primitive Boolean data

Availability   Flash 5

Constructor   new Boolean(*value*)

Arguments
value   An expression to be resolved and, if necessary, converted to a Boolean value, then wrapped in a *Boolean* object.

Methods

toString()   Convert the value of a *Boolean* object to a string.

valueOf()   Retrieve the primitive value of a *Boolean* object.

Description

The *Boolean* class creates a *Boolean* object which contains a primitive Boolean value in an inaccessible, internal property. *Boolean* objects are used purely for the sake of manipulating and examining primitive Boolean values using methods of the *Boolean* class. A *Boolean* object is, hence, known as a *wrapper object* because it simply packages a primitive Boolean value, giving it some object-like methods. Compare the *Boolean* class with the *String* and *Number* classes, which similarly wrap *string* and *number* primitive values, but with more useful results.

For the most part, *Boolean* objects are used internally. They are created automatically by the interpreter whenever a method is invoked on a primitive Boolean value and are deleted automatically after each use. We can create *Boolean* objects ourselves using the *Boolean* constructor, but there is seldom reason to do so.

Usage

Note that in practice it is much more common to use the *Boolean()* global function as a datatype-conversion tool than it is to use the *Boolean* class.

See Also

Boolean() global function; "The Boolean Type" in Chapter 4

Boolean.toString( ) Method   the value of the Boolean object converted to a string

Availability   Flash 5

Synopsis   `booleanObject.toString()`

Returns

The string "true" if the primitive value of *booleanObject* is `true`; "false" if the primitive value of *booleanObject* is `false`. The value of the Boolean object is specified when the object is constructed and stored internally thereafter. Although the internal value of a Boolean object is inaccessible, we can use *toString()* to convert it to its string equivalent.

Description

The *toString()* method retrieves the primitive value of a Boolean object, converts that value to a string, and returns the resulting string.

Example

```
x = new Boolean(true);
trace(x.toString());  // Displays: "true"
```

See Also

Object.toString()

Boolean.valueOf( ) Method   the primitive value of the Boolean object

Availability   Flash 5

Synopsis   `booleanObject.valueOf()`

Returns

The Boolean value `true` if the primitive value of *booleanObject* is `true`; `false` if the primitive value of *booleanObject* is `false`. The value of the Boolean object is specified when the object is constructed and stored internally thereafter.

Description

The *valueOf()* method returns the primitive Boolean datum associated with a Boolean object. Although the internal value of a Boolean object is inaccessible, we can use *valueOf()* to convert it to its primitive equivalent.

Example

```
x = new Boolean(0);
trace(x.valueOf());  // Displays: false
```

See Also

Object.valueOf()

Call( ) Global Function   execute the script of a remote frame

Availability   Flash 4; deprecated in Flash 5

| *Synopsis* | `call(frameLabel)` |
| | `call(frameNumber)` |

Arguments

| *frameLabel* | A string representing the label of the frame whose script should be executed. |
| *frameNumber* | The number of the frame whose script should be executed. |

Description

The *call()* function executes the script attached to the frame at `frameLabel` or `frameNumber`. For example, the following code runs the script on frame 20 of the current timeline:

```
call(20);
```

In Flash 4, *call()* was used to create a crude kind of reusable subroutine (one that could not accept parameters or return any value). In Flash 5, the *function* statement is preferred.

Note that in Flash 5, when a script is executed remotely via *call()*, any variables declared with the *var* keyword are considered local to that execution and expire after the script completes. To create nonlocal variables in a remotely-executed script, omit the *var* keyword:

```
var x = 10;   // Local variable; dies after script completes
x = 10;       // Timeline variable; persists after script completes
```

To invoke *call()* on frames outside the current timeline, use the *tellTarget()* function. The following example executes the script on frame 10 of the **box** clip:

```
tellTarget ("box") {
  call(10);
}
```

See Also

Chapter 9, *Functions*; Appendix C, *Backward Compatibility*

Color Class   control over movie clip color values

| *Availability* | Flash 5 |
| *Constructor* | `new Color(target)` |

Arguments

| *target* | A string or reference indicating the path to the movie clip or document level whose color will be controlled by the new object (references are converted to paths when used in a string context). |

Methods

| *getRGB()* | Retrieve the current offset values for Red, Green, and Blue. |
| *getTransform()* | Retrieve the current offset and percentage values for Red, Green, Blue, and Alpha. |

setRGB()   Assign new offset values for Red, Green, and Blue, while reducing per-
                    centage values to 0.

setTransform()   Assign new offset and/or percentage values for Red, Green, Blue, and
                    Alpha.

Description

We use objects of the *Color* class to programmatically dictate the color and transparency of
a movie clip or main movie. Once we've created an object of the *Color* class for a specific
target, we can then invoke the methods of that object to affect its target's color and
transparency. For example, suppose we have a clip instance named `ball` that we want to
make red. We first make a *Color* object with a target of `ball` and store it in the variable
`ballColor`. Then we use *ballColor.setRGB()* to assign `ball` the color red, as follows:

```
var ballColor = new Color("ball");
ballColor.setRGB(0xFF0000);  // Pass setRGB() the hex value for red
```

The preceding example provides color control for simple applications. But to handle more
complex scenarios, we need to know more about how color is represented in Flash. Every
individual color displayed in a movie clip is defined by four separate components: Red,
Green, Blue, and Alpha (or transparency). Those four components are combined in different
amounts to generate each color we see on screen. The amount of Red, Green, Blue, and
Alpha in a given color is described as a number between 0 and 255. The higher the value of
Red, Green, or Blue, the more each of those colors contributes to the final color. However,
remember that computer color is additive, not subtractive like paint, so higher values tend
to be brighter, not darker. If all three RGB components are equal, the result is a shade of
gray; if they are all 0, the result is black; if they are all 255, the result is white. The higher
the value of Alpha, the more opaque the final color will be. (A color with an Alpha of 0 is
completely transparent, and a color with an Alpha of 255 is completely opaque.)

For example, pure red would be described by the following values:

```
Red: 255, Green: 0, Blue: 0, Alpha: 255
```

whereas a partially transparent red might have the values:

```
Red: 255, Green: 0, Blue: 0, Alpha: 130
```

For the purposes of this discussion, we adopt the so-called *RGB triplet* notation (*Red,
Green, Blue*) when talking about color values. Although ActionScript doesn't support
decimal RGB triplets such as (255, 0, 255), it does support the hexadecimal equivalent form
0xRRGGBB, where *RR*, *GG*, and *BB* are two-digit hex numbers representing Red, Green and
Blue. We'll also adopt the *RGBA quadlet* notation (*Red, Green, Blue, Alpha*) for convenience only in the following discussion.

The initial Red, Green, Blue, and Alpha values for each color in a movie clip are set in the
Flash authoring tool using the Mixer panel. (In the Mixer panel, Alpha is shown as a
percentage, not a number from 0 to 255.) To alter *all* the colors in a movie clip via Action-
Script, we make universal adjustments (known as *transformations*) to the Red, Green, Blue,
and Alpha components of the clip's color.

We have two means of setting transformations for each color component:

- We may set the *percentage* of the component's original value to a number between –100
  and 100. For example, we may say "set all red used in this clip to 80% of its original
  value."

- We may specify an amount to *offset* the component's original value. The offset is a number between –255 and 255. For example, we may say, "add 20 to all blue values in this clip," or, using a negative number we may say, "subtract 30 from all blue values in this clip."

The final value of a color in a transformed clip is determined by combining its original (author-time) color component values with the transformation percentages and offsets set through the *Color* object, as follows:

```
R = originalRedValue   * (redTransformPercentage/100)   + redTransformOffset
G = originalGreenValue * (greenTransformPercentage/100) + greenTransformOffset
B = originalBlueValue  * (blueTransformPercentage/100)  + blueTransformOffset
A = originalAlphaValue * (alphaTransformPercentage/100) + alphaTransformOffset
```

If no transformations have been performed through ActionScript, the initial transformation *percentage* for each component defaults to 100, while the initial *offset* defaults to 0.

Let's look at how color transformations work with a practical example. Suppose that a clip contains an opaque red triangle (R:255, G:0, B:0, A:255) and an opaque green circle (R:0, G: 255, B:0, A:255). Now further suppose that we apply a universal transformation to the clip, setting the percentage of Green to 50, the percentage of Alpha to 80, and the offset of Blue to 100 but leaving the other offsets and percentages at their defaults (0 or 100). Here's how the universal transformation affects our red triangle:

```
R == 255 * (100/100) +   0 == 255      // No change to Red
G ==   0 *  (50/100) +   0 == 0        // Green reduced to 50%
B ==   0 * (100/100) + 100 == 100      // Blue offset by 100
A == 255 *  (80/100) +   0 == 204      // Alpha reduced to 80%
```

The final transformed red triangle has the color value (R:255, G:0, B:100, A:204). Now here's how the transformation affects our green circle:

```
R ==   0 * (100/100) +   0 == 0        // No change to Red
G == 255 *  (50/100) +   0 == 127.5    // Green reduced to 50%
B ==   0 * (100/100) + 100 == 100      // Blue offset by 100
A == 255 *  (80/100) +   0 == 204      // Alpha reduced to 80%
```

The final transformed green circle has the color value (R:0, G:127.5, B:100, A:204).

To actually apply our hypothetical color transformations to a real clip, we use a *Color* object as we saw earlier. To set a clip's universal color *offset* and *percentage* values we use the *setRGB()* or the *setTransform()* methods (see the entries for those methods for example code). Conversely, to examine the current color transformations of a clip, we use the *getRGB()* and *getTransform()* methods. The *Color* class methods can produce animated color effects such as fade-ins, fade-outs, and tinting. Furthermore, because we can apply tints to each clip instance individually, the *Color* class provides a very efficient way to create diverse graphics with minimal assets. For example, we could create a scene full of balloons from a single movie clip that was colorized and tinted in myriad ways, as shown under the Example heading that follows.

Usage

Some points of interest for *Color* objects:

- Changing the color of a movie clip with a *Color* object will break a tween and place the movie clip under ActionScript's control, meaning that some authoring-time behaviors applied to the clip may cease functioning.

- Setting the `_alpha` property of a clip affects the clip's Alpha percentage as reflected by the `aa` property of the object returned by *getTransform()*.

- Color transformations do not affect the background color of a movie or a movie clip. They apply only to solid shapes placed on the Stage.

- Manual color transformations may be applied to movie clips in the authoring tool via the Effect panel (Window → Panels → Effect). All such transformations are reflected in the properties of the object returned by *getTransform()*. The Effect panel serves as an excellent tool for viewing and choosing color transformations while authoring a movie.

Example

The first example shows how to generate a series of randomly colored balloon movie clips based on an existing clip called `balloon`:

```
// Loop to make 20 duplicates of the clip balloon
for (var i = 0; i < 20; i++) {
  // Duplicate this balloon
  balloon.duplicateMovieClip("balloon" + i, i);

  // Position this balloon on stage
  this["balloon" + i]._x = Math.floor(Math.random() * 550);
  this["balloon" + i]._y = Math.floor(Math.random() * 400);

  // Create a Color object for this balloon
  balloonColor = new Color(this["balloon" + i]);
  // Randomly assign this balloon's color using the setRGB() method
  balloonColor.setRGB(Math.floor(Math.random() * 0xFFFFFF));
}
```

By setting the Red, Green, and Blue offsets to the same value, we can effectively brighten or darken a movie clip. For example, the following code darkens `myClip`:

```
brightness = new Color("myClip");
brightnessTransform = new Object();
brightnessTransform.rb = -30;
brightnessTransform.bb = -30;
brightnessTransform.gb = -30;
brightness.setTransform(brightnessTransform);
```

This last example contains code that brightens and darkens a clip according to the mouse position:

```
onClipEvent (load) {
  var brightness = new Color(this);
  var brightnessTransform = new Object();
  var stageWidth = 550;
}

onClipEvent (mouseMove) {
  brightnessAmount = -255 + (_root._xmouse / stageWidth) * 510;
  brightnessTransform.rb = brightnessAmount;
  brightnessTransform.bb = brightnessAmount;
  brightnessTransform.gb = brightnessAmount;
  brightness.setTransform(brightnessTransform);
  updateAfterEvent();
}
```

Color.getRGB( ) Method   retrieve the current offset values for Red, Green, and Blue

Availability   Flash 5

Synopsis   `colorObj.getRGB()`

Returns

A number representing the current RGB offsets of `colorObj`'s target.

Description

The *getRGB()* method returns a number ranging from –16777215 to 16777215 that represents the current color offsets for the Red, Green, and Blue components in a clip; to retrieve the color percentages, you must use *getTransform()*. Because color offset values normally range from 0 to 255, it's convenient to work with the return value of *getRGB()* in hexadecimal, where each color offset can be represented by a two-digit hex number. To decipher the number returned by *getRGB()*, we treat it as a six-digit hex number of the form 0x*RRGGBB*, where *RR* is the Red offset, *GG* is the Green offset, and *BB* is the Blue offset. For example, if *getRGB()* returns the number 10092339, we convert it to the hex number 0x99FF33 from which we derive the color offsets R:153, G:255, B:51. Or if *getRGB()* returns the number 255, we convert it to the hex number 0x0000FF from which we derive the color offsets R:0, G:0, B:255. The return value of *getRGB()* can be converted to hexadecimal with *toString()*, as follows:

```
// Create a Color object
myColor = new Color("myClip");
// Set the Red offset to 255 (FF in hex)
myColor.setRGB(0xFF0000);
// Retrieve the RGB offset and convert it to hexadecimal
hexColor = myColor.getRGB().toString(16);
trace(hexColor);  // Displays: ff0000
```

Hexadecimal color values are familiar to most web developers, as they are often used in HTML tags. For example, here we use a hexadecimal number to specify the background color of a page (full values for red and blue combine to form pink):

```
<BODY BGCOLOR="#FF00FF">
```

The hex color format used in HTML tags is, in fact, the same as the format used by *getRGB()* and *setRGB()*. However, it's not mandatory to use hexadecimal to interpret the return value of *getRGB()*; we may also extract the individual Red, Green and Blue color offsets from the return value of *getRGB()* using the bitwise operators:

```
var rgb = myColorObject.getRGB();
var red = (rgb >> 16) & 0xFF;   // Isolate the Red offset and assign it to red
var green = (rgb >> 8) & 0xFF;  // Isolate the Green offset and assign it to green
var blue  = rgb & 0xFF;         // Isolate the Blue offset and assign it to blue
```

With the offset values separated into individual variables, we may examine and manipulate them individually as decimal numbers. However, when we want to apply any offset value changes to a *Color* object, we must reassemble the offsets into a single number, as shown under the entry for the *setRGB()* method.

Usage

The *getRGB()* and *setRGB()* methods are convenient when we're directly assigning new colors to a clip without reference to the clip's original color values. However, the *getTransform()* and *setTransform()* methods are better suited to modifying the RGB components of a clip's color transformation in relation to the clip's original colors.

Color offsets are most easily read using *getTransform()*, which returns each component separately rather than as a lump sum as *getRGB()* does. This is especially true when setting negative offsets with *setTransform()* due to the way that negative numbers are represented in binary.

Example

```
// Create a new Color object for a clip named box
boxColor = new Color("box");
// Set a new RGB offset for "box"
boxColor.setRGB(0x333366);
// Check the RGB offset for "box"
trace(boxColor.getRGB());        // Displays: 3355494
```

See Also

Color.getTransform(), *Color.setRGB()*

Color.getTransform( ) Method
retrieve both the current offset and percentage values for a clip's Red, Green, Blue, and Alpha components

Availability   Flash 5

Synopsis   `colorObj.getTransform()`

Returns

An object whose properties contain the color transformation values for the target clip of `colorObj`.

Description

The *getTransform()* method returns an object with properties that tell us which transformations are currently applied to the target of a *Color* object. The property names and values of the returned object are described in Table R-4.

Table R-4. Properties of Object Returned by getTransform()

Property Name	Property Value	Property Description
ra	−100 to 100	The Red transformation percentage
rb	−255 to 255	The Red offset amount
ga	−100 to 100	The Green transformation percentage
gb	−255 to 255	The Green offset amount
ba	−100 to 100	The Blue transformation percentage
bb	−255 to 255	The Blue offset amount
aa	−100 to 100	The Alpha transformation percentage
ab	−255 to 255	The Alpha offset amount

Usage

Note in Table R-4 that both the percentage and the offset can have negative values; however, these are only one factor in calculating the RGB color components, which always range from 0 to 255. Values outside that range are clipped to the allowable range. See the *Color* class description for an explanation of the calculation used to determine final RGB and Alpha color components.

Example

We can use *getTransform()* in combination with *setTransform()* to modify the Red, Green, Blue, or Alpha components of a color transformation individually. For example, in the following code, we adjust the Red and Alpha components of a clip named **box**:

```
// Create a new Color object for a clip named box
boxColor = new Color("box");

// Assign the return object of getTransform() to boxTransform
boxTransform = boxColor.getTransform();

// Now, make some modifications to the transform object's properties
boxTransform.rb = 200;      // Set Red offset to 200
boxTransform.aa = 60;       // Set Alpha percentage to 60

// Apply the new transformations to box via boxColor
boxColor.setTransform(boxTransform);
```

See Also

Color.setTransform()

Color.setRGB( ) Method   assign new offset values for Red, Green, and Blue

Availability   Flash 5

Synopsis   *colorObj*.setRGB(*offset*);

Arguments

offset   A number in the range 0 to 16777215 (0xFFFFFF), representing the new RGB offsets of *colorObj*'s target clip. May be a decimal integer or a hexadecimal integer.

                       Numbers outside the allowed range are converted to numbers within the allowed range (using the rules of twos-complement binary notation). Therefore, *setRGB()* cannot be used to set negative offset values (as *setTransform()* can).

Description

The *setRGB()* method assigns new transformation offsets for a movie clip's RGB components. The new *offset* is most easily specified as a six-digit hexadecimal number of the form 0x*RRGGBB*, where *RR*, *GG*, and *BB* are two-digit numbers between 00 and FF representing the Red, Green, and Blue components. For example, the RGB triplet (51, 51, 102) is equivalent to the hexadecimal value:

```
0x333366
```

Hence, to assign a gray RGB offset to a clip named menu, we could use:

```
var menuColor = new Color("menu");
menuColor.setRGB(0x999999);
```

Web developers comfortable with six-digit hexadecimal color values in HTML will have an easy time using *setRGB()* using the preceding hexadecimal format. For a primer on decimal, octal, and hexadecimal numbers see *http://www.moock.org/asdg/technotes*.

Note that in addition to setting offsets, *setRGB()* also automatically sets the Red, Green, and Blue percentages of a clip's color transformation to 0, meaning that color changes performed via *setRGB()* behave as direct color assignments (not adjustments of the original colors in the clip). To adjust the color of a movie clip in relation to the clip's original colors, we must use the *setTransform()* method.

Example

Here's a handy technique for generating a number to use with the *setRGB()* method. Our custom *combineRGB()* function shifts the **red** and **green** numbers into the proper position in a 24-bit number and then combines the **red**, **green**, and **blue** values using the bitwise OR operator (|). We use the result to assign a color value to the movie clip **box**:

```
function combineRGB (red, green, blue) {
  // Combine the color values into a single number
  var RGB = (red<<16) | (green<<8) | blue;
  return RGB;
}
// Create the Color object
var boxColor = new Color("box");
// Set the color of box to the RGB triplet (201, 160, 21)
boxColor.setRGB(combineRGB(201, 160, 21));
```

For more information on bitwise operations, see Chapter 15, *Advanced Topics*.

See Also

Color.getRGB(), *Color.setTransform()*

Color.setTransform( ) Method

assign new offset and/or percentage values for Red, Green, Blue, and Alpha

Availability   Flash 5

Synopsis   `colorObj.setTransform(transformObject)`

Arguments
transformObject   An object whose properties contain the new color transformation values for the target clip of `colorObj`.

Description

The *setTransform()* method gives us precise control over the percentage and offset of the Red, Green, Blue, and Alpha components of a movie clip's color. To use *setTransform()*, we must first create an object with a series of predefined properties. The transformation we wish to apply to our *Color* object is expressed using those properties, which are listed in

Table R-4 for the *getTransform()* method (except that *setTransform()* specifies their values rather than reading their values).

Once we have created an object with the properties described in Table R-4, we pass that object to the *setTransform()* method. The values of the properties on our `transformObject` become the new offset and percentage transform values of `colorObj` and, hence, `colorObj`'s target movie clip. The final color values in the clip are then determined according to the calculation discussed under the *Color* class.

To examine the current offsets and percentages of a particular *Color* object, we use the *getTransform()* method.

Example

```
// Create a new Color object for the box clip
boxColor = new Color("box");

// Create a new anonymous object and store it in boxTransform
boxTransform = new Object();

// Assign the required properties of boxTransform, setting our
// transformation values as desired
boxTransform.ra = 50;      // Red percentage
boxTransform.rb = 0;       // Red offset
boxTransform.ga = 100;     // Green percentage
boxTransform.gb = 25;      // Green offset
boxTransform.ba = 100;     // Blue percentage
boxTransform.bb = 0;       // Blue offset
boxTransform.aa = 40;      // Alpha percentage
boxTransform.ab = 0;       // Alpha offset

// Now that our transform object has been
// prepared, pass it to setTransform()
boxColor.setTransform(boxTransform);
```

The preceding approach to creating a transform object is fairly labor-intensive. We may generate a new transform object more easily using the *getTransform()* method, as follows:

```
// Create a new Color object for the box clip
boxColor = new Color("box");

// Invoke getTransform() on boxColor, retrieving an appropriately
// constructed transform object
boxTransform = boxColor.getTransform();

// Now alter only the desired properties of boxTransform,
// leaving the others unchanged
boxTransform.rb = 51;      // Red offset
boxTransform.aa = 40;      // Alpha percentage

// Use our transform object with setTransform()
boxColor.setTransform(boxTransform);
```

See Also

Color.getTransform()

Date( ) Global Function

a string representing the current date and time

Availability Flash 5

Synopsis Date()

Returns

A string containing the current date and time.

Description

The *Date()* function returns a human-readable string that expresses the current date and time relative to the local time zone. The string also includes the GMT offset (the number of hours difference between local time and Greenwich Mean Time).

Be sure not to confuse the global *Date()* function with the *Date()* class constructor. The *Date()* function returns the date formatted as a standard, if terse, string. It is convenient for humans but not very useful inside a program where you need to manipulate dates and times. For that purpose, you are better off using objects of the *Date* class, which allow convenient independent access to the year, month, day, and time.

Example

To place the current time and date in a text field with minimal fuss, we can use the *Date()* function as follows:

```
myTextField = Date();

// Sets myTextField to a string formatted as follows:
// "Mon Aug 28 16:23:09 GMT-0400 2000"
```

See Also

The *Date* class, *Date.UTC()*

Date Class

current time and structured support for date information

Availability Flash 5

Constructor
```
new Date()
new Date(milliseconds)
new Date(year, month, day, hours, minutes, seconds, ms)
```

Arguments

milliseconds The number of milliseconds between the new date and midnight of January 1, 1970 UTC (Coordinated Universal Time, akin to GMT). Positive if after; negative if before. Any required local time zone adjustment is made after the date in UTC time is determined. For example, specifying a *milliseconds* argument of 1000 in Eastern Standard Time would create a date 1 second past midnight on January 1, 1970 in UTC time, which translates to 7:00:01 p.m. on December 31, 1969 in EST time (5 hours behind UTC time).

year An integer specifying the year. Required when using the *year, ...ms* constructor format. If *year* is one or two digits, it is treated as the number of years since 1900 (e.g., a *year* of 11 always refers to the year 1911,

	not 2011). Use four-digit numbers to specify year 2000 or later (e.g., use 2010, not 10). Three-digit years are treated as pre-1000 A.D. Note that when *year* is negative or less than 800, the calculation is unreliable. To specify dates prior to 1000 A.D., it's safest to use the single *milliseconds* constructor format.
month	An integer specifying the month, from 0 (January) to 11 (December), not from 1 to 12. Required when using the *year, ...ms* constructor format. Out-of-range months are carried over to the next or previous year. For example, a *month* of 13 is treated as February of the following year.
day	An optional integer specifying the day, from 1 to 31. Defaults to 1 if not specified. Out-of-range days are carried over to the next or previous month. For example September 31 is treated as October 1 and September 0 is treated as August 31.
hours	An optional integer specifying the hour, from 0 (midnight) to 23 (11 p.m.). Defaults to 0 if not specified. AM and PM notation are not supported. Out-of-range hours are carried over to the next or previous day. For example, an *hour* of 25 is treated as 1 a.m. of the following day.
minutes	An optional integer specifying the minute, from 0 to 59. Defaults to 0 if not specified. Out-of-range minutes are carried over to the next or previous hour. For example, a *minute* of 60 is treated as the first minute of the following hour.
seconds	An optional integer specifying the seconds, from 0 to 59. Defaults to 0 if not specified. Out-of-range seconds are carried over to the next or previous minute. For example, a *second* of –1 is treated as the last second of the previous minute.
ms	An optional integer specifying the milliseconds, from 0 to 999. Defaults to 0 if not specified. Out-of-range milliseconds are carried over to the next or previous second. For example, an *ms* of 1005 is treated as 5 milliseconds into the following second.

Class Methods

UTC()	Retrieve the number of milliseconds between January 1, 1970 and a supplied UTC date.

Methods

getDate()	Retrieve the day of the month, from 1 to 31.
getDay()	Retrieve the day of the week, as a number from 0 (Sunday) to 6 (Saturday).
getFullYear()	Retrieve the four-digit year.
getHours()	Retrieve the hour of the day from 0 to 23.
getMilliseconds()	Retrieve the milliseconds.
getMinutes()	Retrieve the minutes.
getMonth()	Retrieve the month of the year, as a number from 0 (January) to 11 (December).
getSeconds()	Retrieve the seconds.

getTime()	Retrieve the date in internal format (i.e., the number of milliseconds between the date and January 1, 1970).
getTimezoneOffset()	
	Retrieve the number of minutes between UTC and local time.
getUTCDate()	Retrieve the day of the month in UTC time.
getUTCDay()	Retrieve the day of the week in UTC time.
getUTCFullYear()	Retrieve the four-digit year in UTC time.
getUTCHours()	Retrieve the hour of the day in UTC time.
getUTCMilliseconds()	
	Retrieve the milliseconds in UTC time.
getUTCMinutes()	Retrieve the minutes in UTC time.
getUTCMonth()	Retrieve the month of the year in UTC time.
getUTCSeconds()	Retrieve the seconds in UTC time.
getYear()	Retrieve the year, relative to 1900.
setDate()	Assign the day of the month.
setFullYear()	Assign the year in four-digit format.
setHours()	Assign the hour of the day.
setMilliseconds()	Assign the milliseconds.
setMinutes()	Assign the minutes.
setMonth()	Assign the month of the year.
setSeconds()	Assign the seconds.
setTime()	Assign the date in internal format (i.e., the number of milliseconds between the date and January 1, 1970).
setUTCDate()	Assign the day of the month in UTC time.
setUTCFullYear()	Assign the year in four-digit format in UTC time.
setUTCHours()	Assign the hour of the day in UTC time.
setUTCMilliseconds()	
	Assign the milliseconds in UTC time.
setUTCMinutes()	Assign the minutes in UTC time.
setUTCMonth()	Assign the month of the year in UTC time.
setUTCSeconds()	Assign the seconds in UTC time.
setYear()	Assign the year in four-digit, or in two-digit format for the 20th century.
toString()	A human-readable string representing the date.
valueOf()	The number of milliseconds between the date and midnight of January 1, 1970 UTC.

Description

We use objects of the *Date* class as a mechanism by which to determine the current time and date and as a means of storing arbitrary dates and times in a structured format.

In ActionScript, a specific date is represented by the number of milliseconds before or after midnight of January 1, 1970. If the number of milliseconds is positive, the date comes after midnight, January 1, 1970; if the number of milliseconds is negative, the date comes before midnight, January 1, 1970. For example, if a date value is 10000, the date being described is 12:00:10, January 1, 1970. If a date value is –10000, the date being described is 11:59:50, December 31, 1969.

Normally, however, we needn't worry about calculating the number of milliseconds to a particular date; the ActionScript interpreter takes care of that for us. When we construct a *Date* object, we simply describe our date as a year, month, day, hour, minute, second, and millisecond. The interpreter then converts that point in time to the internal milliseconds-from-1970 format. We may also ask the interpreter to create a new *Date* object using the current time. Once a *Date* object is created, we can use the *Date* class's methods to retrieve and set the date's year, month, day, hour, minute, second, and millisecond.

There are three ways to make a new *Date* object:

- We may invoke the *Date()* constructor with no arguments. This sets the new *Date* object to the current time.

- We may invoke the *Date()* constructor with one numeric argument: the number of milliseconds between midnight, January 1, 1970 and the date we're creating.

- We may invoke the *Date()* constructor with from two to seven numeric arguments, corresponding to the year and month (mandatory) and (optionally) the day, hour, minute, second, and millisecond of the date we're creating.

Because dates are stored internally as a single number, objects of the *Date* class do not have properties to retrieve and set. Rather, they have methods that we use to access the various components of a date in human-readable terms (i.e., in more convenient units). For example, to determine the month of a particular *Date* object, we use:

```
myMonth = myDate.getMonth();
```

We cannot use:

```
myMonth = myDate.month;  // There's no such property! We have to use methods.
```

Many *Date* methods contain the letters "UTC," which is an abbreviation for Coordinated Universal Time. For most purposes, UTC time is directly synonymous with the more colloquial Greenwich Mean Time, or GMT—the time as measured on the Greenwich meridian. UTC is simply a newer standard that is less ambiguous than GMT, which has had several meanings over history. The UTC methods allow us to work with times directly in Coordinated Universal Time without converting between time zones. The equivalent non-UTC methods all generate values based on local, adjusted time zones.

Usage

All dates and times are determined according to the settings on the operating system on which the Flash movie is running (not the web server) and include regional offsets. Times and dates, therefore, are only as accurate as the user's system.

Note that the *Date()* constructor may also be used as a global function to generate a string expressing the current time in the same format as would be returned by `myDate.toString()`.

In Flash 5 ActionScript, it is not possible to convert a string into a *Date* object, as is possible in JavaScript.

Example

Dates can be added and subtracted to come up with cumulative times or elapsed times. Suppose our friend Graham decides to go traveling for a little less than a year. While he's gone, we want to keep track of how many days he's been away and how many days we have to wait for him to return. The following code takes care of our countdown:

```
// Assign the current time to now
var now = new Date();

// Graham leaves September 7, 2000 (remember, months start at 0
// so September is 8, not 9)
var departs = new Date(2000,8,7);

// Graham comes back August 15, 2001
var returns = new Date(2001,7,15);

// Convert the times to milliseconds for easy comparison.
// Then check how many milliseconds have elapsed between the two times.
var gone = now.getTime() - departs.getTime();

// Divide the difference between departure date and now by the number
// of milliseconds in a day. This tells us how many days we've been waiting.
var numDaysGone = Math.floor(gone/86400000);

// Use the same technique to determine how many days we have left to wait
var left = returns.getTime() - now.getTime();
var numDaysLeft = Math.floor(left/86400000);

// Display our days in text fields
goneOutput = numDaysGone;
leftOutput = numDaysLeft;
```

When adding a day to, or subtracting a day from, an existing date, we normally assign the number of milliseconds in a day (86400000) to a variable for convenient use. The following code adds one day to the current date:

```
oneDay = 86400000;
now = new Date();
tomorrow = new Date(now.getTime() + oneDay);

// We could also add one day to the date in now like this
now.setTime(now.getTime() + oneDay);
```

To apply custom formatting to a date, we must manually map the return values of *getDate()*, *getDay()*, *getHours()*, and so on to custom strings as shown in the following example:

```
// Takes any Date object and returns a string of the format:
// Saturday December 16
function formatDate(theDate) {
  var months = ["January", "February", "March", "April",
              "May", "June", "July", "August", "September",
              "October", "November", "December"];
  var days = ["Sunday", "Monday", "Tuesday", "Wednesday", "Thursday",
            "Friday", "Saturday"];
  var dateString = days[theDate.getDay()] + " "
```

```
                              + months[theDate.getMonth()] + " "
                              + theDate.getDate();
        return dateString;
    }

    now = new Date();
    trace("Today is " + formatDate(now));
```

The next example shows how to convert the 24-hour clock return value of *getHours()* to a 12-hour clock with AM and PM:

```
    // Takes any Date object and returns a string of the format:
    // "2:04PM"
    function formatTime(theDate) {
      var hour = theDate.getHours();
      var minute = theDate.getMinutes() > 9 ?
                   theDate.getMinutes() : "0" + theDate.getMinutes();
      if (hour > 12) {
        var timeString = (hour - 12) + ":" + minute + "PM";
      } else {
        var timeString = hour + ":" + minute + "AM";
      }
      return timeString;
    }

    now = new Date();
    trace("The time is " + formatTime(now));
```

For an example using the *Date* class to create an analog-style clock, see "Building a Clock with Clips" in Chapter 13, *Movie Clips*. Note that programming time-based behavior such as a 10-second pause in a movie is often accomplished more easily with the global *getTimer()* function.

See Also

Date(), *Date.UTC()*, *getTimer()*

Date.getDate( ) Method   the day of the month

Availability   Flash 5

Synopsis   `date.getDate()`

Returns

An integer from 1 to 31, representing the day of the month for *date*.

Date.getDay( ) Method   the day of the week

Availability   Flash 5

Synopsis   `date.getDay()`

Returns

An integer from 0 (Sunday) to 6 (Saturday), representing the day of the week for *date*.

Example

The following code loads a *.swf* file specific to the current day of the week into the movie clip welcomeHeader (the seven *.swf* files are named in the series *sun.swf, mon.swf,* and so on):

```
now = new Date();
today = now.getDay();
days = ["sun", "mon", "tue", "wed", "thu", "fri", "sat"];
welcomeHeader.loadMovie(days[today] + ".swf");
```

Date.getFullYear( ) Method   the four-digit year

Availability   Flash 5

Synopsis   date.getFullYear()

Returns

A four-digit integer representing the year for *date*, for example 1999 or 2000.

Date.getHours( ) Method   the hour of the day

Availability   Flash 5

Synopsis   date.getHours()

Returns

An integer from 0 (midnight) to 23 (11 p.m.) representing the hour of the day for *date*. A.M. and P.M. notation are not supported but can be constructed manually as shown in the *Date* class examples.

Date.getMilliseconds( ) Method   the milliseconds of a date

Availability   Flash 5

Synopsis   date.getMilliseconds()

Returns

An integer from 0 to 999 representing the milliseconds of *date*. Note that it does not represent the milliseconds from 1970 (see *getTime( )*), but rather the fractional remainder of the seconds indicated by the specified *Date* object.

See Also

Date.getTime( )

Date.getMinutes( ) Method   the minutes of a date

Availability   Flash 5

Synopsis   `date.getMinutes()`

Returns

An integer from 0 to 59 representing the minutes of the hour of `date`.

Date.getMonth( ) Method   the month of the year

Availability   Flash 5

Synopsis   `date.getMonth()`

Returns

An integer from 0 (January) to 11 (December), not 1 to 12, representing the month of the year of `date`.

Usage

Be careful not to assume that 1 is January! The return value of *getMonth()* starts at 0, not 1.

Example

Here we convert the number returned by *getMonth()* to a human-readable abbreviation:

```
var months = ["Jan", "Feb", "Mar", "Apr", "May", "Jun",
              "Jul", "Aug", "Sept", "Oct", "Nov", "Dec"];
myDateObj = new Date();
trace ("The month is " + months[myDateObj.getMonth()]);
```

Date.getSeconds( ) Method   the seconds of a date

Availability   Flash 5

Synopsis   `date.getSeconds()`

Returns

An integer from 0 to 59 representing the seconds of the minute of `date`.

Date.getTime( ) Method   retrieve the number of milliseconds between
January 1, 1970 and the time of a date object

Availability   Flash 5

Synopsis   `date.getTime()`

Returns

An integer expressing the number of milliseconds between the time of `date` and midnight, January 1, 1970. Positive if after January 1, 1970; negative if before.

Description

Internally, all dates are represented as a single number—the number of milliseconds between the time of the `date` and midnight, January 1, 1970. The *getTime()* method gives us access to that number of milliseconds so that we may use it to construct other dates or to compare the elapsed time between two dates.

Example

Suppose we place the following code on the 10th frame of a movie:

```
time1 = new Date();
```

Then we place the following code on the 20th frame of a movie:

```
time2 = new Date();
```

With the following code, we can determine the amount of time that elapsed, in milliseconds, between the 10th and 20th frames of our movie:

```
elapsedTime = time2.getTime() - time1.getTime();
```

Note that Flash's global *getTimer()* function also gives us access to elapsed time in a movie.

See Also

Date.setTime(), *getTimer()*

Date.getTimezoneOffset( ) Method

the number of minutes between
local time and UTC (a.k.a. GMT)

Availability   Flash 5

Synopsis   `date.getTimezoneOffset()`

Returns

An integer representing the current number of *minutes* between the local time zone and the actual UTC (Greenwich meridian) time. Positive if local time is behind UTC; negative if local time is ahead of UTC. Includes adjustments for local daylight saving time depending on the day of the year.

Example

When invoked in Eastern Daylight Time (EDT) during daylight savings, the following code returns the value 240 (240 minutes is 4 hours):

```
myDate = new Date();
trace(myDate.getTimezoneOffset());  // Displays: 240
```

However, when invoked in EDT, during non–daylight savings times of year, the same code returns 300 (300 minutes is 5 hours), which is the real offset between Eastern Standard Time (EST) and UTC.

Date.getUTCDate( ) Method

the day of the month (UTC time)

Availability   Flash 5

Synopsis   `date.getUTCDate()`

Returns

An integer from 1 to 31, representing the day of the month for `date`, where `date` is treated as a UTC time.

Date.getUTCDay( ) Method   the day of the week (UTC time)

Availability   Flash 5

Synopsis   `date.getUTCDay()`

Returns

An integer from 0 (Sunday) to 6 (Saturday), representing the day of the week for *date*, where *date* is treated as a UTC time.

Date.getUTCFullYear( ) Method   the four-digit year (UTC time)

Availability   Flash 5

Synopsis   `date.getUTCFullYear()`

Returns

A four-digit integer representing the year for *date*, where *date* is treated as a UTC time, for example 1999 or 2000.

Date.getUTCHours( ) Method   the hour of the day (UTC time)

Availability   Flash 5

Synopsis   `date.getUTCHours()`

Returns

An integer from 0 (midnight) to 23 (11 p.m.) representing the hour of the day for *date*, where *date* is treated as a UTC time.

Date.getUTCMilliseconds( ) Method   the milliseconds of a date (UTC time)

Availability   Flash 5

Synopsis   `date.getUTCMilliseconds()`

Returns

An integer from 0 to 999 representing the milliseconds of *date*, where *date* is treated as a UTC time.

Date.getUTCMinutes( ) Method   the minutes of a date (UTC time)

Availability   Flash 5

Synopsis   `date.getUTCMinutes()`

Returns

An integer from 0 to 59 representing the minutes of the hour of *date*, where *date* is treated as a UTC time.

Date.getUTCMonth( ) Method   the month of the year (UTC time)

Availability   Flash 5

Synopsis   `date.getUTCMonth()`

Returns

An integer from 0 (January) to 11 (December), not 1 to 12, representing the month of the year of *date*, where *date* is treated as a UTC time.

Usage

Be careful not to assume that 1 is January! The return value of *getUTCMonth()* starts at 0, not 1.

Date.getUTCSeconds( ) Method   the seconds of a date (UTC time)

Availability   Flash 5

Synopsis   `date.getUTCSeconds()`

Returns

An integer from 0 to 59 representing the seconds of the minute of *date*, where *date* is treated as a UTC time.

Date.getYear( ) Method   the year, relative to 1900

Availability   Flash 5

Synopsis   `date.getYear()`

Returns

The value of `date.getFullYear()` −1900. For example, *getYear()* of 1999 is 99, *getYear()* of 2001 is 101, and *getYear()* of 1800 is −100. This function is most useful for dates in the 20th century.

Date.setDate( ) Method   assign the day of the month

Availability   Flash 5

Synopsis   `date.setDate(day)`

Arguments

day   An integer from 1 to 31, representing the new day of the month for *date*. If you specify a day greater than the number of days in the current month, it will cause the month to increment accordingly. For example, if the current *month* is 8 (September) and you specify 31 for the new *day*, it will be treated as October 1. The *day* will become 1 and the *month* will become 9 (October).

Returns

An integer representing the number of milliseconds between the new date and midnight, January 1, 1970.

See Also

Date.getDate( )

Date.setFullYear( ) Method   assign the century and year in four-digit format

Availability   Flash 5

Synopsis   `date.setFullYear(year, month, day)`

Arguments

year   A four-digit integer representing the new year for *date*, for example 1999 or 2000.

month   An optional integer from 0 (January) to 11 (December), not 1 to 12, representing the new month of the year of *date*. Defaults to 0 if not specified.

day   An optional integer from 1 to 31 representing the new day of the month of *date*. Defaults to 1 if not specified.

Returns

An integer representing the number of milliseconds between the new date and midnight, January 1, 1970.

See Also

Date.setYear( ), Date.getFullYear( )

Date.setHours( ) Method   assign the hour of the day

Availability   Flash 5

Synopsis   `date.setHours(hour)`

Arguments

hour   An integer from 0 (midnight) to 23 (11 p.m.) specifying the new hour of the day for *date*.

Returns

An integer representing the number of milliseconds between the new date and midnight, January 1, 1970.

See Also

Date.getHours( )

Date.setMilliseconds( ) Method   assign the milliseconds of a date

Availability   Flash 5

Synopsis   date.setMilliseconds(*ms*)

Arguments

ms   An integer from 0 to 999 representing the new milliseconds of *date* not
                      the number of milliseconds since 1970. Values above 999 or below 0 are
                      carried over to the seconds of *date*.

Returns

An integer representing the number of milliseconds between the new date and midnight,
January 1, 1970.

See Also

Date.getMilliseconds( ), Date.setTime( )

Date.setMinutes( ) Method   assign the minutes of a date

Availability   Flash 5

Synopsis   date.setMinutes(*minute*)

Arguments

minute   An integer from 0 to 59 representing the new minutes of the hour of
                      date. Values above 59 or below 0 are carried over to the hours of *date*.

Returns

An integer representing the number of milliseconds between the new date and midnight,
January 1, 1970.

See Also

Date.getMinutes( )

Date.setMonth( ) Method   assign the month of the year

Availability   Flash 5

Synopsis   date.setMonth(*month*)

Arguments

month   An integer from 0 (January) to 11 (December), not from 1 to 12, repre-
                      senting the new month of the year of *date*. Values above 11 or below 0
                      are carried over to the year of *date*.

Returns

An integer representing the number of milliseconds between the new date and midnight,
January 1, 1970.

Usage

Be careful not to assume that 1 is January! Months start at 0, not 1.

See Also

Date.getMonth( )

Date.setSeconds( ) Method   assign the seconds of a date

Availability   Flash 5

Synopsis   `date.setSeconds(second)`

Arguments
second   An integer from 0 to 59 representing the new seconds of the minute of
                       `date`. Values above 59 or below 0 are carried over to the minutes of
                       `date`.

Returns

An integer representing the number of milliseconds between the new date and midnight,
January 1, 1970.

See Also

Date.getSeconds()

Date.setTime( ) Method   assign a new date based on the number of milliseconds
                                          between January 1, 1970 and the new date

Availability   Flash 5

Synopsis   `Date.setTime(milliseconds)`

Arguments
milliseconds   An integer expressing the number of milliseconds between the new
                       desired date and midnight, January 1, 1970. Positive if after January 1,
                       1970; negative if before.

Returns

The value of `milliseconds`.

Description

Internally, all dates are represented as the number of milliseconds between the time of the
date and midnight, January 1, 1970. The *setTime()* method specifies a new date using the
internal millisecond representation. Setting a date using milliseconds from 1970 is often
handy when we're determining differences between multiple dates and times using
getTime().

Example

Using *setTime()* in concert with *getTime()* we can adjust the time of an existing date by
adding or subtracting milliseconds. For example, here we add one hour to a date:

```
now = new Date();
now.setTime(now.getTime() + 3600000);
```

And here we add one day:

```
now = new Date();
now.setTime(now.getTime() + 86400000);
```

To improve the readability of our code, we create variables representing the number of milliseconds in an hour and milliseconds in a day:

```
oneDay = 86400000;
oneHour = 3600000;
now = new Date();
// Subtract one day and three hours.
now.setTime(now.getTime() - oneDay - (3 * oneHour));
```

See Also

Date.getTime(), *Date.setMilliseconds()*, *Date.UTC()*, *getTimer()*

Date.setUTCDate( ) Method   assign the day of the month (UTC time)

Availability   Flash 5

Synopsis   `date.setUTCDate(day)`

Arguments

day   An integer from 1 to 31, representing the new day of the month for *date* in UTC time. If you specify a day greater than the number of days in the current month, it will cause the month to increment accordingly. For example, if the current *month* is 8 (September) and you specify 31 for the new *day*, it will be treated as October 1. The *day* will become 1 and the *month* will become 9 (October).

Returns

An integer representing the number of milliseconds between the new date and midnight, January 1, 1970 in UTC time.

Date.setUTCFullYear( ) Method   assign the century and year in
                                                  four-digit format (UTC time)

Availability   Flash 5

Synopsis   `date.setUTCFullYear(year)`

Arguments

year   A four-digit integer representing the new year for *date* in UTC time, for example 1999 or 2000.

Returns

An integer representing the number of milliseconds between the new date and midnight, January 1, 1970 in UTC time.

Date.setUTCHours( ) Method   assign the hour of the day (UTC time)

Availability   Flash 5

Synopsis   `date.setUTCHours(hour)`

Arguments

hour   An integer from 0 (midnight) to 23 (11 p.m.) representing the new hour
                   of the day for *date* in UTC time.

Returns

An integer representing the number of milliseconds between the new date and midnight,
January 1, 1970 in UTC time.

Date.setUTCMilliseconds( ) Method   assign the milliseconds of a date (UTC time)

Availability   Flash 5

Synopsis   `date.setUTCMilliseconds(ms)`

Arguments

ms   An integer from 0 to 999 representing the new milliseconds of *date* in
                   UTC time.

Returns

An integer representing the number of milliseconds between the new date and midnight,
January 1, 1970 in UTC time.

Date.setUTCMinutes( ) Method   assign the minutes of a date (UTC time)

Availability   Flash 5

Synopsis   `date.setUTCMinutes(minute)`

Arguments

minute   An integer from 0 to 59 representing the new minutes of the hour of
                   date in UTC time.

Returns

An integer representing the number of milliseconds between the new date and midnight,
January 1, 1970 in UTC time.

Date.setUTCMonth( ) Method   assign the month of the year (UTC time)

Availability   Flash 5

Synopsis   `date.setUTCMonth(month)`

Arguments

month   An integer from 0 (January) to 11 (December), not from 1 to 12, repre-
                   senting the new month of the year of *date* in UTC time.

Returns

An integer representing the number of milliseconds between the new date and midnight,
January 1, 1970 in UTC time.

Usage

Be careful not to assume that 1 is January! Months start at 0, not 1.

Date.setUTCSeconds( ) Method   assign the seconds of a date (UTC time)

Availability   Flash 5

Synopsis   `date.setUTCSeconds(second)`

Arguments
second   An integer from 0 to 59 representing the new seconds of the minute of
                      `date` in UTC time.

Returns

An integer representing the number of milliseconds between the new date and midnight,
January 1, 1970 in UTC time.

Date.setYear( ) Method   assign the year, relative to 1900

Availability   Flash 5

Synopsis   `date.setYear(year, month, day)`

Arguments
year   A required integer specifying the new year of `date`. If one or two digits
                      are supplied, the year is assumed to be in the 20th century. For example,
                      1 is the year 1901, and 99 is the year 1999. Three-digit years are assumed
                      to be pre–1000 A.D. Use four digits to specify the year 2000 and later.

month   An optional integer from 0 (January) to 11 (December), not from 1 to 12,
                      representing the new month of the year of `date`.

day   An optional integer from 1 to 31 representing the new day of the month
                      of `date`.

Returns

An integer representing the number of milliseconds between the new date and midnight,
January 1, 1970.

Description

setYear() is identical to *setFullYear()* except that it interprets one- and two-digit years as
being relative to 1900 whereas *setFullYear()* interprets them as being relative to 0 A.D.

See Also

Date.getYear(), Date.setFullYear()

Date.toString( ) Method   a human-readable string representing the date

Availability   Flash 5

Synopsis   `date.toString()`

Returns

A string giving the current time and date of `date` in human-readable format, including the
UTC (GMT) offset. To compose customized representations of the date, use the methods for

retrieving the day, hours, minutes, and so on, and map those values onto your own strings, as shown earlier in the example under *Date* class.

Example

```
trace (myDate.toString()); // Displays a date in the format:
                           // Wed Sep 15 12:11:33 GMT-0400 1999
```

Date.UTC( ) Class Method

retrieve the number of milliseconds between
January 1, 1970 and a supplied UTC date

Availability   Flash 5

Synopsis   Date.UTC(*year, month, day, hours, minutes, seconds, ms*)

Arguments

year,...ms   A series of numeric values describing the date and time but supplied in UTC time, not local time. For descriptions of each argument see the *Date()* constructor.

Returns

The number of milliseconds between the specified date and midnight, January 1, 1970.

Description

The *Date.UTC()* method takes the same arguments as the *Date()* constructor, but instead of returning an object for the specified date, *Date.UTC()* returns a number indicating the date in the internal milliseconds-from-1970 format. The returned number is typically used to construct a new *Date* object in UTC or to assign a UTC time to an existing *Date* object via the *setTime()* method.

Example

The following code shows how to measure the milliseconds elapsed between midnight 1970 and midnight 2000 in UTC time:

```
trace(Date.UTC(2000, 0) + " milliseconds passed between 1970 and 2000.");
// Displays: "946684800000 milliseconds passed between 1970 and 2000."
```

Here we use those elapsed milliseconds to construct a UTC-time-based *Date* object:

```
nowUTC = new Date(Date.UTC(2000, 0));
```

If that code were invoked in EST (Eastern Standard Time), which is 5 hours behind UTC, nowUTC would represent the local time 7p.m. on December 31, 1999. When we check the hour using the non-UTC method *getHours()*, we get the local hour, 19 (7p.m. in a 24-hour clock):

```
trace(nowUTC.getHours());  // Displays: 19
```

But when we check the hour using the UTC method *getUTCHours()*, we get the correct UTC hour, 0 (midnight in a 24-hour clock):

```
trace(nowUTC.getUTCHours());  // Displays: 0
```

See Also

Date(), *Date.setTime()*, the *Date* class

Date.valueOf( ) Method   the number of milliseconds between January 1, 1970
                                                     and the time of the *Date* object

Availability   Flash 5

Synopsis   date.valueOf( )

Returns

An integer expressing the number of milliseconds between the time of the *Date* object and midnight, January 1, 1970. Positive if after January 1, 1970; negative if before.

Description

In practice, *Date.valueOf()* is equivalent to *Date.getTime()*.

See Also

Date.toString()

---

duplicateMovieClip( ) Global Function   create a copy of a movie clip

Availability   Flash 4 and later

Synopsis   duplicateMovieClip(*target, newName, depth*)

Arguments

target   A string indicating the path to the movie clip to duplicate (known as the *seed clip*). Nested clips may be referred to with dot syntax, as in *duplicateMovieClip("_root.myClip", "myClip2", 0)*. Because a movie clip reference is converted to a path when used in a string context, target may also be a movie clip object reference, as in *duplicateMovieClip(myClip, "myClip2", 0)*.

newName   A string that will become the instance name of the duplicated clip. The string used must adhere to the rules for creating an identifier outlined in "Identifiers" in Chapter 14, *Lexical Structure*.

depth   An integer indicating the level in the programmatic clip stack on which to place the duplicated clip. Clips on lower levels are placed visually behind clips on higher levels. The movie clip with the highest depth in a stack obscures all the clips below it. For example, a clip on depth −1 appears behind a clip on depth 0, which appears behind a clip on depth 1. If the assigned depth is occupied, the occupant clip is removed, and the new duplicate takes its place. See Chapter 13 for additional details. Negative depths are functional, but not officially supported by ActionScript; to ensure future compatibility, use depths of 0 or greater.

Description

The *duplicateMovieClip()* function is one way to create a new movie clip during movie playback (the other is *attachMovie()*). *duplicateMovieClip()* creates an identical copy of target and places the copy in target's clip stack on layer depth. The duplicated clip begins playing at frame 1 no matter what the frame of target is when duplication occurs.

A duplicated clip inherits any transformations (rotation, scale, etc.) that had been applied to target but does not inherit the timeline variables of target. The global function *duplicateMovieClip()* is also available as a movie clip method, though when used in that form, the *target* argument is not used.

Example

```
// Copies the ball clip and names the copy ball2
duplicateMovieClip(ball, "ball2", 0);
// Moves the new ball2 clip over so we can see it
ball2._x += 100;
```

See Also

MovieClip.duplicateMovieClip(), *removeMovieClip()*; "Creating instances with duplicateMovieClip()," "How clips generated via duplicateMovieClip() are added to the stack," and "Method versus global function overlap issues" in Chapter 13

---

escape( ) Global Function   encode a string for safe network transfer

Availability   Flash 5

Synopsis   escape(*string*)

Arguments
string   A string (or an expression that yields a string) to be encoded.

Returns

An (almost) URL-encoded version of *string*.

Description

The *escape()* function creates a new encoded string based on a supplied string. The new string contains a hexadecimal escape sequence in place of any character in the supplied string that is not a digit or a basic, unaccented Latin letter between A and Z or a and z. The replacement hexadecimal escape sequences take the format %xx, where xx is the hexadecimal value of the character's code point in the Latin 1 character set. Shift-JIS double-byte characters are converted to two hexadecimal escape sequences of the form %xx%xx.

The *escape()* function effectively URL-encodes a string, except that space characters are converted to %20, not +. *escape()* is sometimes used when a Flash movie sends information to server applications or writes cookies in a browser.

To decode an encoded string, we use the global *unescape()* function.

Example

```
var phoneNumber = "(222) 515-1212"
escape(phoneNumber);  // yields %28222%29%20515%2D1212
```

See Also

unescape(); Appendix B, *Latin 1 Character Repertoire and Keycodes*

---

eval( ) Global Function   convert a string to an identifier

Availability   Flash 4 and later

Synopsis   eval(*stringExpression*)

Arguments

stringExpression A string or an expression that yields a string. Should match the name of
                    some identifier.

Returns

The value of the variable represented by *stringExpression* or a reference to the object,
movie clip, or function represented by *stringExpression*. If *stringExpression* does
not represent a variable or a movie clip, undefined is returned.

Description

The *eval()* function provides a means of constructing a dynamic reference to an identifier
based on a string of text. *eval()* converts a string to a variable, movie clip, object property,
or other identifier and then evaluates that identifier. For example, here we use the return
value of *eval()* to set the value of a variable:

```
name1 = "Kathy";
count = 1;
currentName = eval("name" + count);      // Sets currentName to "Kathy"
```

And here we control a dynamically-named movie clip, star1:

```
eval("star" + count)._x += 100;          // Move star1 right 100 pixels
```

But we may also use an *eval()* invocation in place of an identifier that is the lefthand
operand of an assignment expression, as in:

```
eval("name" + count) = "Simone";         // Sets name1 to "Simone"
```

Note that, unlike its JavaScript cousin, *eval()* in ActionScript does not allow for the
compiling and execution of arbitrary blocks of code in a string. Full support of *eval()*
would require an ActionScript compiler in the Player, which would cause too great an
increase in the Player size.

Usage

As of Flash 5, *eval()* is rarely needed for dynamic variable access. When managing multiple
pieces of data, use arrays and objects instead.

Example

The *eval()* function is often used to convert the *MovieClip.*_droptarget string property to
a movie clip object reference. In the following example, suppose we have a series of
cartoon face clips. When the user drops a food clip onto one of the faces, we retrieve the
path to the face in question using _droptarget, then we use *eval()* to retrieve an object
reference to that face. Finally, we send the face to a frame showing the mouth full of food:

```
// Convert _droptarget string to a reference
theFace = eval(food._droptarget);
// Control appropriate face clip using converted reference
theFace.gotoAndStop("full");
```

See Also

See "Executing Code in a String with eval" in Chapter 4

_focusrect Global Property

the highlight state used for buttons
activated via the keyboard

Availability   Flash 4 and later

Synopsis   _focusrect

Access   Read/write

Description

When the mouse hovers over a button in Flash, the content of the button's Over state is displayed. Buttons can also gain keyboard focus when the user presses the Tab key. When a button has keyboard focus, Flash places a yellow rectangle over that button, which is not always aesthetically desirable. You can turn off the yellow highlight rectangle using the _focusrect global property, like so:

```
_focusrect = false;
```

When _focusrect is set to false, Flash displays the Over state of keyboard-focused buttons. When _focusrect is set to true (its default), Flash displays the yellow rectangle.

Usage

Though _focusrect is used in a Boolean sense, it actually stores a number, not a Boolean. Although there's rarely a reason to do so, if we examine the value of _focusrect, it returns either 1 (indicating true) or 0 (indicating false).

fscommand( ) Global Function

send a message to the standalone Player
or to the Player's host application

Availability   Flash 3 and later (enhanced in Flash 5 to include trapallkeys)

Synopsis   fscommand(command, arguments)

Arguments

command   A string passed to the host application, often the name of a JavaScript function.

arguments   A string passed to the host application, often an argument to the function named by *command.*

Description

With the *fscommand()* function, a Flash movie can communicate with the standalone Player or with the Player's host application—the environment in which the Flash Player is running (e.g., a web browser or Macromedia Director). The *fscommand()* function is typically used in one of three ways:

* To send one of a limited set of built-in commands to the standalone Flash Player
* To send commands to a scripting language such as JavaScript or VBScript in a web browser
* To communicate with Lingo in a Macromedia Director movie

When used with the standalone Player, *fscommand()* takes one of the built-in sets of command/argument pairs, as shown in Table R-5.

Table R-5. command/argument Pairs in Standalone Player

Command	Argument	Description
"allowscale"	"true" or "false"	When "false", prevents the contents of a movie from growing or shrinking in relation to the window size of the Player. "allowscale" is often used in combination with "fullscreen" to create a Projector that occupies the entire screen while maintaining the movie's original size.
"exec"	"application_name"	Launches an external application. The path to the application is specified in the string *application_name*. The path is resolved relative to the Flash movie unless *application_name* is specified as an absolute path such as: "C:/WINDOWS/ NOTEPAD.EXE". Note that the path uses *forward slashes* (/), not backslashes (\ ).
"fullscreen"	"true" or "false"	When "true", causes the Player window to maximize, filling the user's entire screen.
"quit"	not applicable	Closes the movie and exits the Flash projector (standalone Player).
"showmenu"	"true" or "false"	When "false", suppresses the display of the controls in the context menu of the Player, leaving only the About Macromedia Flash Player option. The context menu is accessed via right-click on Windows and Ctrl-click on Macintosh.
"trapallkeys"	"true" or "false"	When "true", causes all keystrokes— even keyboard shortcuts—to be sent to the Flash movie. trapallkeys is used to disable the control keys in the standalone Player (e.g., Ctrl-F or Command-F for Full Screen mode, Ctrl-Q or Command-Q for Exit, Esc for Stop/exit Full Screen mode, etc.). Added to *fscommand* in Flash 5.

When used in a browser, the execution of an *fscommand()* function in a movie causes the invocation of a special JavaScript function (Netscape) or VBScript function (Internet Explorer) on the page that contains the movie. The name of this special function takes the general form *movieID_DoFSCommand* where *movieID* is the name specified in the movie's OBJECT ID attribute (Internet Explorer) or EMBED NAME attribute (Netscape) from the host HTML document. When *movieID_DoFSCommand()* is invoked, the values of the *fscommand()*'s command and arguments parameters are passed to the *movieID_DoFSCommand()* function as arguments. If no *movieID_DoFSCommand()* function exists in the host page, *fscommand()* fails silently.

Note that in order for *fscommand()* to work with Netscape, the swLiveConnect attribute of the movie's EMBED tag must be set to "true". For example:

```
<EMBED
  NAME="testmovie"
  SRC="myMovie.swf"
  WIDTH="100%"
  HEIGHT="100%"
  swLiveConnect="true"
  PLUGINSPAGE="http://www.macromedia.com/go/flashplayer/"
</EMBED>
```

Usage

It is *not* possible to communicate with a browser via *fscommand()* under the following system configurations:

- Internet Explorer on the Macintosh OS
- Any browser running on a 68K-series Macintosh
- Any browser running on Windows 3.1
- Netscape 6

Note that *fscommand()* does not always provide the best means of communicating with a Director movie from Flash. The preferred director communication device is a *getURL()* function with either the **event:** or **lingo:** protocol. For details, see the *getURL()* function or the following Macromedia tech notes:

> *http://www.macromedia.com/support/director/ts/documents/flash_xtra_sending_events. htm*
> *http://www.macromedia.com/support/director/ts/documents/flash_xtra_lingo.htm*
> *http://www.macromedia.com/support/director/ts/documents/flash_tips.htm*

Example

To quit a standalone Projector, use:

```
fscommand("quit");
```

To create a standalone Projector that runs fullscreen, use:

```
fscommand("fullscreen", "true");
```

To create a standalone Projector that runs fullscreen but maintains the original movie's size, use:

```
fscommand("fullscreen", "true");
fscommand("allowscale", "false");
```

For information on launching a movie in a fullscreen web browser window, see *http://www. moock.org/webdesign/flash/launchwindow/fullscreen.*

To launch Notepad on most Windows systems, use:

```
fscommand("exec", "C:/WINDOWS/NOTEPAD.EXE");
```

The following code shows an HTML page with the JavaScript and VBScript needed to respond to a simple *fscommand()* from a movie. Notice that the VBScript function simply calls the JavaScript function; this allows us to handle both Internet Explorer and Netscape with a single JavaScript function:

```
<HTML>
<HEAD>
<TITLE>fscommand demo</TITLE>

<SCRIPT LANGUAGE="JavaScript">
<!--
function testmovie_DoFSCommand(command, args) {
  alert("Here's the Flash message " + command + ", " + args);
}
//-->
</SCRIPT>

<SCRIPT LANGUAGE="VBScript">
<!--
Sub testmovie_FSCommand(ByVal command, ByVal args)
    call testmovie_DoFSCommand(command, args)
end sub
//-->
</SCRIPT>

</HEAD>

<BODY BGCOLOR="#FFFFFF">

<OBJECT
  ID="testmovie"
  CLASSID="clsid:D27CDB6E-AE6D-11cf-96B8-444553540000"
  WIDTH="100%"
  HEIGHT="100%"
  CODEBASE="http://download.macromedia.com/pub/shockwave/cabs/flash/swflash.cab">
  <PARAM NAME="MOVIE" VALUE="flash-to-javascript.swf">

  <EMBED
    NAME="testmovie"
    SRC="flash-to-javascript.swf"
    WIDTH="100%"
    HEIGHT="100%"
    swLiveConnect="true"
    PLUGINSPAGE="http://www.macromedia.com/go/flashplayer/"
  </EMBED>
</OBJECT>

</BODY>
</HTML>
```

To invoke the preceding *testmovie_DoFSCommand()* JavaScript function from the *flash-to-javascript.swf* movie, we'd use:

```
fscommand("hello", "world");
```

See Also

For more information on *fscommand()* and controlling Flash with JavaScript, see:

http://www.moock.org/webdesign/flash/fscommand
http://www.macromedia.com/support/flash/publishexport/scriptingwithflash

getProperty( ) Global Function

retrieve the value of a movie clip property

Availability   Flash 4; deprecated in Flash 5

Synopsis   getProperty(*movieClip, property*)

Arguments

movieClip   An expression that yields a string indicating the path to a movie clip. In Flash 5, this may also be a movie clip reference because movie clip references are converted to paths when used in a string context.

property   The name of the built-in property to retrieve. Must be an identifier, not a string (e.g., _x, not "_x").

Returns

The value of *movieClip*'s *property.*

Description

The *getProperty()* function retrieves the value of one of a movie clip's built-in properties. Though *getProperty()* was the only way to access object properties in Flash 4, the . and [] operators are the preferred property-access tools in Flash 5 and later.

Example

Each of the following *getProperty()* invocations retrieve the values of the _x property of a movie clip named **ball** on the main movie timeline:

```
getProperty(ball, _x);              // Relative movie clip reference
getProperty(_root.ball, _x);        // Absolute movie clip reference
getProperty("ball", _x);            // Relative path in string
getProperty("_root.ball", _x);      // Dot path in string
getProperty("/ball", _x);           // Slash path in string
```

The following code shows similar property access using the dot and [] operators:

```
ball._x;
_root.ball._x;
ball["_x"];
_root["ball"]["_x"];
```

See Also

setProperty(); "The "Objectness" of Movie Clips" in Chapter 13

---

getTimer( ) Global Function

determine the age of a movie, in milliseconds

Availability   Flash 4 and later

Synopsis   getTimer()

Returns

The number of milliseconds that have passed since the movie started playing.

Description

The *getTimer()* function indicates how long a movie has been playing, in milliseconds. We can use multiple *getTimer()* checks to govern the timed execution of a block of code or to add time-based features to a movie, such as a countdown in a video game. For example, when attached to a movie clip that contains a text field named `counterOutput`, the following code counts down from 60 to 0:

```
onClipEvent (load) {
  // Record the current time
  var startTime = getTimer();
  // Set the number of seconds to count down
  var countAmount = 60;
  // Initialize a variable to keep track of how much time has passed
  var elapsed = 0;
}

onClipEvent (enterFrame) {
  // Check how much time has passed
  elapsed = getTimer() - startTime;
  // If the time passed is less than the length of our countdown...
  if (elapsed < countAmount * 1000) {
    // ...set the text field to show the amount of time left
    counterOutput = countAmount - Math.floor(elapsed / 1000);
  } else {
    // ...otherwise, our countdown is done, so tell the user
    counterOutput = "Time's UP!";
  }
}
```

To determine the number of full seconds that have passed in a movie (rather than milliseconds), divide the return of *getTimer()* by 1000 and trim off the decimal portion with either *Math.floor()*, *Math.round()*, or *Math.ceil()*. For example:

```
numSeconds = Math.floor(getTimer()/1000);
```

Example

The following code loops between two frames until a movie is more than 10 seconds old and then plays the movie:

```
now = getTimer();
if (now > 10000) {
  play();
} else {
  gotoAndPlay(_currentframe - 1);
}
```

See Also

Date(), the *Date* class

---

getURL( ) Global Function   load a document into a browser, execute server-side scripts, or trigger Macromedia Director events

Availability   Flash 2 and Flash 3; enhanced in Flash 4 to include *method* parameter; Flash 5

Synopsis

```
getURL (URL)
getURL (URL, window)
getURL (URL, window, method)
```

Arguments

URL

A string specifying the absolute or relative location of the document to load or external script to run.

window

An optional string specifying the name of the browser window or frame into which to load the document. May be a custom name or one of the four presets: `"_blank"`, `"_parent"`, `"_self"`, or `"_top"`.

method

An optional string specifying the method by which to send the current timeline's variables to an external script—either `"GET"` or `"POST"`. This parameter must be a literal string, not a variable or other expression. The standalone version of the Flash Player always uses the `"GET"` method, regardless of the *method* specified.

Description

The *getURL()* function is used to:

- Load a document (usually a web page) into a web browser frame or window
- Execute a server-side script and receive the results in a browser frame or window
- Execute JavaScript code in a web browser
- Trigger events from Flash assets imported as sprites into Director

To load a document into the current window or frame, simply specify the URL of the document without supplying a *window* or *method* argument. Naturally, Flash supports absolute URLs (those that contain a protocol such as "http:" plus a server name or hardware device) and relative URLs (those that are relative to the current location):

```
getURL("http://www.moock.org/");                // Absolute URL to web page
getURL("file:///C|/WINDOWS/Desktop/index.html"); // Absolute URL to local file
getURL("/whatever/index.html");                  // Relative URL, http protocol
                                                 //is assumed
```

To load a document into a named window or frame, supply the window or frame name as the *window* argument. For example:

```
getURL("http://www.moock.org/", "contentFrame"); // Load into named frame
getURL("http://www.moock.org/", "remoteWin");    // Load into named window
```

To replace the frameset that contains the current movie, use `"_parent"` as the value of the *window* argument. For example:

```
getURL("http://www.moock.org/", "_parent");
```

To replace *all* framesets in a web page with a loaded document, use `"_top"` as the value of the *window* argument. For example:

```
getURL("http://www.moock.org/", "_top");
```

To open a loaded document in a new, anonymous browser window, use `"_blank"` as the value of the *window* argument. For example:

```
getURL("http://www.moock.org/", "_blank");
```

Note that launching a new window with `"_blank"` does not give us any control over the appearance of the new window (size, toolbar configuration, location, etc.). To launch customized windows with *getURL()*, we must invoke a JavaScript function on the movie's host page. JavaScript window-launching techniques are described at *http://www.moock.org/ webdesign/flash*.

The *getURL()* function may also be used to send variables to a remote server application or script. To send the current movie clip's timeline variables to an external script, specify the name of the script as the *URL* argument, and use either `"GET"` or `"POST"` as the value of the *method* argument. For example:

```
getURL("http://www.someserver.com/cgi-bin/search.pl", "resultsFrame", "GET");
```

When invoked as a movie clip method, *getURL()* sends the timeline variables of that clip, as in:

```
// Sends myClip's variables to search.pl
myClip.getURL("http://www.server.com/cgi-bin/search.pl", "resultsFrame", "GET");
```

The results of the script execution will appear in the window or frame specified in the *getURL()*'s *window* argument (which is required when variables are submitted).

To load the results of a script execution into the current frame or window, use `"_self"` as the *window* argument value, as in:

```
getURL("http://www.someserver.com/cgi-bin/search.pl", "_self", "GET");
```

When the *method* argument is `"GET"`, the current movie clip timeline variables are sent as a query string attached to the script URL in an HTTP GET request. Query strings are composed of variable name/value pairs, separated by ampersands (&). For example:

```
http://www.someserver.com/cgi-bin/search.pl?term=javascript&scope=entiresite
```

When the *method* argument is `"POST"`, the current movie clip timeline variables are sent to the script as a separate block of data after the HTTP POST-request header (exactly like a regular HTML form that uses the POST method). Note that `"POST"` is not available in the standalone Flash Player.

Because most web servers restrict the length of URLs to between 255 and 1024 characters, use `"POST"` instead of `"GET"` to transfer larger amounts of data.

Note that any returned information sent by a script invoked by *getURL()* is displayed as regular web content in the browser, not in Flash. To accept the results of a script execution into Flash, use *loadVariables()*.

The *getURL()* function can also be used with protocols other than "http:" as shown in Table R-6.

Table R-6. Supported Protocols for getURL

Protocol	Format	Purpose
event	`"event: eventName params"`	Send an event to Director if the Flash asset is a Director sprite.
file	`"file:///driveSpec/folder/filename"`	Access a local file.

Table R-6. Supported Protocols for getURL (continued)

Protocol	Format	Purpose
ftp	"ftp://server.domain.com/folder/filename"	Access a remote file via FTP (file transfer protocol).
http	"http://server.domain.com/folder/filename"	Access remote file via HTTP (hypertext transfer protocol).
javascript	"javascript: *command*"	Perform JavaScript command in browser.
lingo	"lingo: *comand*"	Perform Lingo command if Flash asset is a Director sprite.
print	"print:", "*targetClip*"	Prints in Flash 4, prior to the availability of the *print()* function in Flash 5.
vbscript	"vbscript: *command*"	Perform VBScript command in browser.

As Table R-6 shows, if the Flash asset is imported into a Macromedia Director file, *getURL()* can be used to trigger Lingo events or execute a Lingo command. (Lingo is Director's scripting language, akin to ActionScript). For example, you can add a frame event of this form:

```
getURL ("event: eventName params");
```

which will cause the Lingo event handler named *on eventName* to be called in Director. Here is a *getURL()* statement that generates an event named "myEvent" and passes it the string "A". Note that the " character is escaped using the sequence \":

```
getURL ("event: myEvent \"A\"");  // Send an event to Director
```

Here is the Lingo *sprite* event handler that should be attached to the Flash sprite asset in Director in order to receive the event. Note that a Director sprite is roughly equivalent to a Flash movie clip instance; the Lingo keyword *put* is akin to ActionScript's *trace()* command, and && is Lingo's string concatenation operator:

```
on myEvent msg
  put "The message received from Flash was " && msg
end
```

You can also trigger Lingo to be executed from a Flash sprite within Director using the `"lingo:"` keyword, such as:

```
getURL ("lingo: beep");  // Tell Director to play a beep sound
```

Note that Director 8.0 cannot import Flash 5 *.swf* files, but an updated Flash asset Xtra is expected to be available by the time you read this.

Finally, *getURL()* can also be used to execute JavaScript code. Here we invoke a simple JavaScript *alert* using *getURL()*:

```
getURL ("javascript: alert('hello world');");
```

Note that execution of JavaScript code from a URL does not work in Internet Explorer 4.5 for Macintosh.

Example

Here's the code for a standard button that links to a web page:

```
on (release) {
  getURL("http://www.macromedia.com/");
}
```

Bugs

Internet Explorer 4.5 (IE 4.5) and older versions on Macintosh do not support the `"POST"` method of a *getURL()* call. To service those browsers, use `"GET"` instead of `"POST"` (subject to the length limitations cited earlier).

In most browsers, *getURL()* relative links are resolved relative to the HTML file that contains the *.swf* file. In IE 4.5 and older versions on Macintosh, relative links are resolved relative to the location of the *.swf* file, not the HTML file, which causes problems when the two are in different directories. To avoid the problem, either place the *.swf* and the *.html* file in the same directory or use absolute URLs when invoking *getURL()*, such as:

```
getURL ("http://www.someserver.com/")
```

See Also

loadVariables(), MovieClip.getURL(), movieClip.loadVariables(); "<A> (Anchor or Hypertext Link)" in Chapter 18, *On-Screen Text Fields*

---

getVersion( ) Global Function   examine the platform and version of the Flash Player

Availability   Flash 5

Synopsis   `getVersion()`

Returns

A string containing version and platform information for the Flash Player hosting the current movie.

Description

The *getVersion()* function tells us the platform and Flash Player version being used to view a movie. It can be used to conditionally execute different code for specific versions of the Flash Player or on certain operating systems. The string returned by *getVersion()* takes the form:

```
platform majorVersion,minorVersion,buildNumber,patch
```

Where **platform** is a code indicating the platform (`"WIN"`, `"MAC"`, or `"UNIX"`), followed by the major version number, the minor version number, and the build (a.k.a. revision) number. The last item, **patch**, is typically 0. For example:

```
WIN 5,0,30,0    // Version 5.0, Build 30 (5.0r30) on Windows
MAC 5,0,41,0    // Version 5.0, Build 41 (5.0r41) on Macintosh
UNIX 4,0,12,0   // Version 4.0, Build 12 (4.0r12) on Unix
```

Despite the Macromedia documentation's claim to the contrary, *getVersion()* does work in the Flash authoring tool's Test Movie mode. It reports the version number of the *Player* embedded in the authoring tool (which is not the same as the version of the authoring tool itself). For example, the Flash 5 authoring tool embeds the 5.0 r30 version of the Player, so its *getVersion()* function reports:

```
WIN 5,0,30,0
or
MAC 5,0,30,0
```

Any time a major or minor version of the authoring tool is created, the `buildNumber` restarts at 0. However, in the typical development cycle of the Flash authoring tool, many builds of the Flash Player are produced before the final version of the authoring tool is released. The build number of the first new major version of a Player is, hence, usually greater than 0. For example, the Flash 5 Player was first officially released at Build 30. Presumably, when Flash 6 is introduced, the Flash 6 Player will return something like:

```
WIN 6,0,xx,0
```

but if a movie created in Flash 6 is played back in the Flash 5 Player, *getVersion()* would still return:

```
WIN 5,0,30,0
```

Typically, we're concerned with only the platform, the major version, and the build number of a Player. To extract the portion of the *getVersion()* string we're after, we may use the string manipulation tools described in Chapter 4, *Primitive Datatypes*, or we may construct a custom object with each component of the *getVersion()* string assigned to a property of that object as shown in the next example.

Unless we need to produce internal blocks of ActionScript code for a specific version of the Flash Player, JavaScript and VBScript provide better tools for version detection, browser sniffing, and automatic page redirection. Furthermore, you can't use *getVersion()* unless the user already has version 5.0 or later of the Player. For details on detecting the Flash Player's presence and version with JavaScript and VBScript, see *http://www.moock.org/webdesign/ flash/detection/moockfpi*.

Example

The following code extracts the various portions of the string returned by *getVersion()* and stores them as the properties of an object for easy access:

```
// Split up the getVersion() string into usable pieces
var version = getVersion();
var firstSpace = version.indexOf(" ");
var tempString = version.substring(firstSpace + 1, version.length);
var tempArray = tempString.split(",");

// Assign the various parts of the getVersion() string to our object.
// Note that we convert the version number portions to integers.
var thePlayer = new Object();
thePlayer.platform = version.substring(0,firstSpace);
thePlayer.majorVersion = parseInt(tempArray[0]);
thePlayer.minorVersion = parseInt(tempArray[1]);
thePlayer.build = parseInt(tempArray[2]);
thePlayer.patch = parseInt(tempArray[3]);

// Now use our object to perform version-specific code
if (thePlayer.platform == "WIN") {
```

```
    // Perform Windows-specific code here.
  } else if (thePlayer.platform == "MAC") {
    // Perform Mac-specific code here.
  } else if (thePlayer.platform == "UNIX") {
    // Perform Unix-specific code here.
  }

  if ((thePlayer.majorVersion == 5) && (thePlayer.build == 30)) {
    trace ("I recommend upgrading your player to avoid text display bugs");
  }
```

See Also

$version; Appendix C, *Backward Compatibility*

---

gotoAndPlay( ) Global Function

move the playhead to a given frame, then play the current clip or movie

Availability	Flash 2 and later
Synopsis	gotoAndPlay(*frameNumber*)
	gotoAndPlay(*frameLabel*)
	gotoAndPlay(*scene, frameNumber*)
	gotoAndPlay(*scene, frameLabel*)

Arguments

frameNumber A positive integer indicating the number of the frame to which the play-head of the current timeline should proceed before playing. If frameNumber is less than 1 or greater than the number of frames in the timeline, the playhead is sent to either the first or last frame, respectively.

frameLabel A string indicating the label of the frame to which the playhead of the current timeline should proceed before playing. If *frameLabel* is not found, the playhead is sent to the first frame of the timeline.

scene An optional string indicating the name of the scene that contains the specified *frameNumber* or *frameLabel*. If not supplied, the current scene is assumed.

Description

When invoked without a *scene* argument, *gotoAndPlay()* sends the playhead of the current timeline to the frame specified by either the *frameNumber* or *frameLabel* and then plays the timeline from that point. The "current timeline" is the movie clip or movie from which the *gotoAndPlay()* function is invoked.

If two arguments are specified in the *gotoAndPlay()* function call, the first argument is assumed to be the *scene*. If only one argument is specified, it is treated as a *frameNumber* or *frameLabel*, and the current scene is assumed.

When invoked with a *scene* argument, *gotoAndPlay()* moves the playhead to the frame number or label in the specified scene and then plays that scene. If a *scene* argument is used, the *gotoAndPlay()* function *must* be invoked from the _root timeline; otherwise, the operation fails silently and the playhead is not sent to the destination frame. Note that scenes are flattened into a single timeline during movie playback. That is, if scene 1's timeline contains 20 frames, and scene 2's timeline contains 10 frames, then we can send the playhead to frame 5 of scene 2 using `gotoAndPlay(25);`.

 I recommend against using scenes when working with ActionScript-intensive movies. Unlike movie clips, scenes are not represented by objects and cannot be manipulated directly by most built-in functions. It's normally better to use labels and movie clips as pseudo-scenes in your timeline instead of Flash's scene feature.

The global *gotoAndPlay()* function affects only the current timeline. The frames or state of other movie clips within the current timeline are not affected. To cause other movie clips to play, you must issue a separate *play()* or *gotoAndPlay()* command for each movie clip. To apply the *gotoAndPlay()* function to a clip other than the current movie clip, use the movie clip method form, `myClip.gotoAndPlay()`.

Bugs

In Build 5.0r30 of the Flash Player, *gotoAndPlay()* did not work when used in an *onClipEvent()* handler with a string literal for *frameLabel*. To work around the bug, use the movie clip variation of the function using `this` to indicate the current clip, as in `this.gotoAndPlay("myLabel")`, rather than `gotoAndPlay("myLabel")`.

Example

```
// Go to frame 5 of the current timeline and play it
gotoAndPlay(5);
// Go to frame 10 of the exitSequence scene, and play it
gotoAndPlay("exitSequence", 10);
// Go to frame "goodbye" of the exitSequence scene, and play it
gotoAndPlay("exitSequence", "goodbye");
// Caution! This plays the frame labeled "exitSequence" in the current scene.
gotoAndPlay("exitSequence");
// This plays frame 1 of the exitSequence scene
gotoAndPlay("exitSequence", 1);
```

See Also

gotoAndStop(), *MovieClip.gotoAndPlay()*, *play()*, *stop()*

---

gotoAndStop( ) Global Function

move the playhead to a given frame
and stop the current clip

Availability	Flash 2 and later
Synopsis	gotoAndStop(*frameNumber*)
	gotoAndStop(*frameLabel*)
	gotoAndStop(*scene, frameNumber*)
	gotoAndStop(*scene, frameLabel*)

Arguments

frameNumber   A positive integer indicating the number of the frame to which the playhead of the current timeline should proceed. If `frameNumber` is less than

1 or greater than the number of frames in the timeline, the playhead is sent to either the first or last frame, respectively.

frameLabel   A string indicating the label of the frame to which the playhead of the current timeline should proceed. If `frameLabel` is not found, the playhead is sent to the first frame of the timeline.

scene   An optional string indicating the name of the scene that contains the specified `frameNumber` or `frameLabel`. If not supplied, the current scene is assumed.

Description

When invoked without a *scene* argument, *gotoAndStop()* sends the playhead of the current timeline to the frame specified by either the `frameNumber` or `frameLabel` argument. The "current timeline" is the movie or movie clip from which the *gotoAndStop()* function is invoked. The playhead will stop at the target frame; it will not advance automatically after arriving at the target frame.

If two arguments are specified in the *gotoAndStop()* function call, the first argument is assumed to be the *scene*. If only one argument is specified, it is treated as a `frameNumber` or `frameLabel`, and the current scene is assumed.

When invoked with a *scene* argument, *gotoAndStop()* moves the playhead to the frame number or label in the specified scene and then halts playback. If a *scene* argument is used, the *gotoAndStop()* function *must* be invoked from the `_root` timeline; otherwise, the operation fails silently and the playhead is not sent to the destination frame.

The global *gotoAndStop()* function affects only the current timeline. The frames or state of other movie clips within the current timeline are not affected. To move the playhead of other movie clips, you must issue a separate *gotoAndStop()* command for each movie clip. To apply the *gotoAndStop()* function to a clip besides the current movie clip, use the movie clip method of the form `myClip.gotoAndStop()`.

Bugs

In Build 5.0r30 of the Flash 5 Player, *gotoAndStop()* did not work when used in an *onClipEvent()* handler with a string literal for `frameLabel`. To work around the bug, use the movie clip variation of the function using `this` to indicate the current clip, as in `this.gotoAndStop("myLabel")`, rather than `gotoAndStop("myLabel")`.

Example

```
// Go to frame 5 of the current timeline and stop there
gotoAndStop(5);
// Go to frame 20 of the introSequence scene and stop there
gotoAndStop("introSequence", 20);
// Go to frame "hello" of the introSequence scene, and stop there
gotoAndStop("introSequence", "hello")
// Caution! This goes to the frame labeled "introSequence" in the current scene
gotoAndStop("introSequence")
// This goes to frame 1 of the introSequence scene
gotoAndStop("introSequence", 1)
```

See Also

gotoAndPlay(), *MovieClip.gotoAndStop()*, *play()*, *stop()*

_highquality Global Property   the rendering quality of the Player

Availability   Flash 4; deprecated in Flash 5 in favor of _quality

Synopsis   _highquality

Access   Read/write

Description

The _highquality global property stores an integer between 0 and 2 that dictates the rendering quality of the Flash Player as follows:

0

Low quality. Neither bitmaps nor vectors are antialiased (smoothed).

1

High quality. Vectors are antialiased. Bitmaps are antialiased when no animation is occurring.

2

Best quality. Both bitmaps and vectors are always antialiased.

As of Flash 5, _highquality has been superceded by _quality, which may be used to set a movie's quality to "Medium", as well as "Low", "High", and "Best".

See Also

_quality, *toggleHighQuality()*

#include Directive   import the text of an external ActionScript file

Availability   Flash 5

Synopsis   #include *path*

Arguments
path   A string indicating the name and location of the script file to import, which may be specified relative to the *.fla* file or as an absolute path (see samples under Example). Note that forward slashes, not backslashes should be used in the path. Script files should be named with the *.as* file extension.

Description

The #include directive brings script text from an external text file (preferably one with the *.as* extension) into the current script, placing it directly where the #include command occurs in the script. The *#include* operation is performed at compile time, meaning that the text included in a movie is the text that existed at the time the movie was tested, exported, or published from the authoring tool. If the external file changes after the movie is exported, the changes will not be reflected in the movie. In order for the changes to be added to the movie, the movie must be re-exported.

The #include directive is used to incorporate the same block of code in multiple scripts or across Flash projects (much as you'd use an external asset library). You would do this in order to centralize your code, when maintaining code in a version-control system tool (such as CVS or Microsoft Visual Source Safe), or when using an external text editor that you prefer over the ActionScript editor. It is also handy when a programmer is working separately from, say, a graphic artist creating the Flash animations. External files lend themselves well to code repositories, such as a library of functions that are independent of the current timeline or movie clip. They tend to be less useful for code that needs to be tightly integrated with the Flash file.

Usage

Note that an `#include` directive begins with a pound sign (#), does not use parentheses, and must *not* end in a semicolon. Any `#include` statements that end in a semicolon will cause an error and will not successfully import an external script. If the file can't be found at the specified path, the directive will cause an error and no external text will be included. The text in the external file is also checked when performing a syntax check using the Check Syntax command (Ctrl-T or Command-T) in the Actions panel menu (found under the arrow button in the upper-right corner of the panel).

Example

The following code imports an external *.as* file named *myScript.as* into the current *.fla* file. When using a relative path, *myScript.as* would have to be in the same folder as the *.fla* file containing the include directive:

```
#include "myScript.as"
```

We can construct a relative path including a subdirectory. The following assumes that *myScript.as* is one level down from the current *.fla* file in a subdirectory named *includes*:

```
#include "includes/myScript.as"
```

Use two dots to indicate the folder above the current folder. The following assumes that *myScript.as* is one level *up* from the current *.fla* file:

```
#include "../myScript.as"
```

The following assumes that *myScript.as* is in a subdirectory named *includes* adjacent to the subdirectory containing the current *.fla* file:

```
#include "../includes/myScript.as"
```

You can also specify an absolute path to any folder, such as:

```
#include "C:/WINDOWS/Desktop/myScript.as"
```

but absolute paths are not cross-platform and may need to be changed if you compile the *.fla* file on a different machine with different directories. Note the differences in the drive letter specification:

```
#include "C:/WINDOWS/Desktop/myScript.as"               // Windows
#include "Mac HD/Desktop folder/working/myScript.as"    // Macintosh
```

See Also

See "Externalizing ActionScript Code" in Chapter 16

Infinity Global Property   a constant representing an infinite number

Availability   Flash 5

Synopsis   Infinity

Access   Read-only

Description

Any number in ActionScript that exceeds the maximum allowed numeric range is represented by the numeric constant Infinity. The largest value allowed in ActionScript is
represented by Number.MAX_VALUE (1.7976931348623157e+308).

Example

The result of a calculation that exceeds the largest allowed number is Infinity. For
example:

```
Number.MAX_VALUE * 2;    // Yields Infinity
```

Infinity also results when dividing a positive number by zero:

```
1000 / 0;                // Yields Infinity
```

Usage

Infinity is shorthand for Number.POSITIVE_INFINITY.

See Also

–Infinity, Number.POSITIVE_INFINITY; "Special Values of the Number Datatype" in
Chapter 4

–Infinity Global Property   a constant representing an infinitely negative number

Availability   Flash 5

Synopsis   –Infinity

Access   Read-only

Description

Any number in ActionScript that exceeds the allowed *negative* numeric range is represented by the numeric constant –Infinity. The smallest negative value (the one with the
largest absolute value) allowed in ActionScript is –Number.MAX_VALUE, which is equivalent
to –1.7976931348623157e+308.

Example

The result of a calculation that is smaller than (i.e., more negative than) the smallest
allowed negative number is –Infinity. For example:

```
-Number.MAX_VALUE * 2;    // Yields -Infinity
```

–Infinity also results when dividing a negative number by zero:

```
-1000 / 0;                // yields -Infinity
```

Usage

–Infinity is shorthand for Number.NEGATIVE_INFINITY.

See Also

Infinity, Number.NEGATIVE_INFINITY; "Special Values of the Number Datatype" in Chapter 4

---

int( ) Global Function   truncate the decimal portion of a number

Availability   Flash 4; deprecated in Flash 5 in favor of analogous *Math* methods

Synopsis   int(*number*)

Arguments

number   A number or an expression that yields a number, typically a number with a fractional (decimal) portion.

Returns

The integer portion of *number*.

Description

The *int()* function was used in Flash 4 as a brute-force means of extracting the integer portion of a number. It effectively rounds positive numbers down and rounds negative numbers up. The *int()* function works only for numbers in the range -2147483648 (-2^{31}) to 2147483647 ($2^{31}-1$); it produces undefined results for numbers outside this range. If *number* is a string composed of only numbers, *int()* converts the string to a number before operating on it. If *number* is the Boolean value true, *int()* returns the value 1. For all other non-numeric data (including undefined and null), *int()* returns the value 0.

Usage

The *int()* function has been deprecated in favor of the more precise and standard *Math. floor()*, *Math.ceil()*, and *Math.round()* methods. Use *parseInt()* or *Number()* to convert non-numeric data to an integer or number.

Example

```
int(4.5)      // Yields 4
int(-4.5)     // Yields -4
int(3.999)    // Yields 3
```

The *int()* function is useful to check if a number is a whole number by comparing the original number to the result of the *int()* function:

```
if (int(x) != x) {
   trace ("Please enter a whole number for your age in years");
}
```

See Also

Math.ceil(), *Math.floor()*, *Math.round()*, *Number()*, *parseFloat()*, *parseInt()*

---

isFinite( ) Global Function   check if a number is less than Infinity
                                                        and greater than –Infinity

Availability   Flash 5

Synopsis   `isFinite(number)`

Arguments

number   Any numeric value or expression that yields a numeric value.

Returns

A Boolean value; `true` if the number falls between `Number.MAX_VALUE` and `–Number.MAX_VALUE` (inclusive), `false` if not. If *number* does not belong to the *number* datatype, *number* is converted to the *number* type before *isFinite()* executes.

Description

The *isFinite()* function simply checks if a number is in the legal numeric value range of ActionScript. Use *isFinite()* before executing code that requires a legitimate number to operate properly.

Example

```
if (!isFinite(x * y)) {          // Test if the number is not finite
  trace ("The answer is too large to display. Try again.");
}
isFinite(-2342434);             // Yields true
isFinite(Math.PI);              // Yields true
isFinite(Number.MAX_VALUE * 2)  // Yields false
```

See Also

`–Infinity`, `Infinity`, *isNan()*, `Number.MAX_VALUE`, `Number.MIN_VALUE`; "Special Values of the Number Datatype" in Chapter 4

---

isNaN( ) Global Function   equality test for the special NaN value

Availability   Flash 5

Synopsis   `isNaN(value)`

Arguments

value   The expression to test.

Returns

A Boolean value: `true` if *value* is the special numeric value `NaN`; otherwise, `false`.

Description

To test whether or not a value is equal to the special numeric value `NaN`, we must use the *isNaN()* function because `NaN` does not test equal to itself in an ordinary equality test. For example, the expression:

```
NaN == NaN;
```

yields the value `false`. The *isNaN()* function is often used to check whether a mathematical error (such as zero divided by itself) has occurred in a phrase of code or whether converting a value to a legitimate number has failed. Because *isNaN()* returns `true` when the expression is *not* a valid numeric expression, you'll often use the logical NOT operator (`!`) along with *isNaN()* (something that is *not* not a number *is* a number). Note that 0/0 yields NaN, but all positive numbers divided by 0 yield Infinity, and all negative numbers divided by 0 yield -Infinity.

Example

```
// Set a value
var x = "test123";
// Check if x is a legitimate number before using it is in a math expression.
// This is a handy technique for user input in text fields, which always a string.
if (!isNaN(parseFloat(x))) {
  var y = parseFloat(x) * 2;
}
```

See Also

isFinite(), NaN; "Special Values of the Number Datatype" in Chapter 4

Key Object   determine the state of keys on the keyboard

Availability   Flash 5

Synopsis   Key.*property*
                     Key.*methodName ()*

Properties

Table R-7 lists the properties of the *Key* object.

Table R-7. Key Object Keycode Properties

Property	Equivalent Keycode	Property	Equivalent Keycode
BACKSPACE	8	INSERT	45
CAPSLOCK	20	LEFT	37
CONTROL	17	PGDN	34
DELETEKEY	46	PGUP	33
DOWN	40	RIGHT	39
END	35	SHIFT	16
ENTER	13	SPACE	32
ESCAPE	27	TAB	9
HOME	36	UP	38

Methods

getAscii()   Returns the ASCII value of the last key pressed

getCode()   Returns the keycode of the last key pressed

isDown()   Checks if a specific key is currently depressed

isToggled()   Checks if the Num Lock, Caps Lock, or Scroll Lock keys are activated

Description

The *Key* object is used to determine which keys are currently depressed and which key was last depressed. We can use it to build interfaces controlled by the keyboard, such as a game with a spaceship moved via the arrow keys.

Because not all keyboards are identical, keyboard-controlled interfaces can sometimes be tricky to create. By choosing our scripting tools correctly, however, we can ensure that all users have the same experience.

There are two general approaches to detecting keyboard commands:

* We may check if a key is currently depressed via the *isDown()* method. This is recommended for cases in which keyboard input is constantly required, such as in video games.

* We may check which key was last depressed using the *getCode()* and *getAscii()* methods. This is recommended for typical keyboard-driven interfaces in which specific operations are performed when keys are pressed. You would ordinarily use these methods within a *keyDown* event handler in order to distinguish between different keys. There is no need to constantly check (i.e., *poll*) for the last key pressed. In fact, doing so would lead to erroneously repeating some operation even if a key wasn't pressed repeatedly. That is, you should generally check *getCode()* and *getAscii()* within a *keyDown* event handler only because the handler is guaranteed to be called once and only once for each keystroke.

The so-called *Windows virtual keycode* (or simply, *keycode*) returned by *getCode()* and required by *isDown()* is a number representing the physical keys on the keyboard, not the symbols on those keys. By using the keycode, we can identify keys even when a movie is running on different operating systems or when two keyboards use different languages or have different symbol layouts.

On most keyboards the keycodes of the keys A to Z are the same as the code points (65–90) for the equivalent uppercase Latin 1 letters. The keycodes of the keys 0 to 9 are, likewise, the same as the Latin 1 values for those numbers (48–57). The key codes of other keys do not match Latin 1 code points. However, many of the non-letter and non-number keycodes are available as properties of *Key*. For example, we don't have to remember that the up arrow uses keycode 38, we simply use the `Key.UP` property. The following code checks whether the up arrow key is currently depressed:

```
if (Key.isDown(Key.UP)) {
  trace("The up arrow is being pressed");
}
```

When working with a keycode that is not a letter or a number and is not available as a property of *Key*—such as those of the function keys (F1, F2, etc.)—it's safest to create a quick test movie to check the keycode of the desired key, as follows:

```
trace(Key.getCode());
```

The keycodes are listed in Appendix B.

See Also

"keyUp" and "keyDown" in Chapter 10, and Appendix B, *Latin 1 Character Repertoire and Keycodes*

Key.getAscii( ) Method   returns the ASCII value of the last key pressed

Availability   Flash 5

Synopsis   `Key.getAscii()`

Returns

An integer representing the ASCII value of the last key pressed.

Description

The *getAscii()* method returns the ASCII value of the last key that was pressed. Since not all keys have an ASCII value, *getAscii()* is normally used for detecting letters and numbers from the Latin 1 character set (Western European languages). Unlike *getCode()*, *getAscii()* distinguishes between upper- and lowercase letters. But unlike *getCode()*, it cannot differentiate between two keys with the same ASCII value, such as the 8 key on the main keyboard and the 8 key on the numeric keypad.

To detect the pressing of specific keys relative to their physical location on a keyboard rather than their ASCII value (such as would be desirable when using four keys in a diamond pattern to control game play), use *getCode()*.

Example

The following example demonstrates keystroke detection for a simple hangman word game. It uses a *keyDown* event handler to identify the pressing of a key and adds that key to a list of user guesses:

```
onClipEvent (keyDown) {
  var lastKey = Key.getAscii();
  guessNum++;
  userGuesses[guessNum] = String.fromCharCode(lastKey);
}
```

See Also

Key.getCode(); Appendix B, and "keyDown" in Chapter 10

Key.getCode( ) Method   returns the keycode of the last key pressed

Availability   Flash 5

Synopsis   `Key.getCode()`

Returns

An integer representing the keycode of the last key pressed.

Description

The *getCode()* method returns the keycode of the last key that was pressed, which is an arbitrary number representing the physical location of a key on the keyboard. On non-Windows operating systems, the native keycode system is translated automatically by Flash to the Windows equivalent, so *getCode()* provides a cross-platform means of referring to specific keys. The *getCode()* method can also be used to differentiate between two keys with the same ASCII value. For example, it can differentiate between the 8 key on the main keyboard and the 8 key on the numeric keypad, whereas *getAscii()* cannot. However, *getCode()* cannot differentiate between upper- and lowercase letters (for example, *A* and *a* use the same keycode because they are produced using the same key).

Many common keycode values are available as properties of the *Key* object (e.g., `Key.UP`, `Key.BACKSPACE`). To determine the keycode of a particular key, see Appendix B or construct a keycode tester as follows:

1. Create a new Flash document.
2. At frame 2 of the timeline, add a frame.
3. On frame 1, add the following code:

   ```
   trace(Key.getCode());
   ```
4. Select Control → Test Movie.
5. Click the movie's Stage.
6. Press a key. The key code for that key will appear in the Output window.

Example

Unlike *isDown()*, *getCode()* is useful for creating interfaces where an individual key press has a single, direct result. For example, the user may be able to skip a movie's intro by pressing the spacebar. When the spacebar is depressed, we send the playhead to the main interface of the movie (on the main timeline) as follows:

```
// Code on intro clip
onClipEvent (keyDown) {
  if (Key.getCode() == Key.SPACE) {
    _root.gotoAndStop("mainInterface");
  }
}
```

See Also

Key.getAscii(), Key.isDown(); Appendix B, and "keyDown" in Chapter 10

Key.isDown( ) Method   check whether a specific key is currently depressed

Availability   Flash 5

Synopsis   `Key.isDown(keycode)`

Arguments
keycode   A number representing the keycode of the key to check. May also be one of the *Key* constants (e.g., `Key.UP`, `Key.BACKSPACE`).

Returns

A Boolean indicating whether the key specified by *keycode* is pressed (`true`) or not pressed (`false`).

Description

The *isDown()* method tells us whether the key specified by *keycode* is currently being pressed. It offers arbitrary, immediate access to the state of the keyboard and is best used with systems that require constant key-based input or that detect the pressing of simultaneous keys.

One important advantage of *isDown()* over *getCode()* and *getAscii()* is its ability to detect the simultaneous pressing of multiple keys. By checking for both Key.UP and Key.RIGHT, for example, we may determine that a spaceship in a game should be moved diagonally. Depending on the placement of the specific keys being tested, the maximum number of keys that can be simultaneously detected may be as low as three.

Example

The *isDown()* method is normally used to create systems that undergo a constant update with each passing frame. In the following code, we rotate and thrust a spaceship on any frame where the appropriate arrow keys are being pressed. Note that if you need to detect two keys simultaneously, you should use separate *if* statements. In this example, the state of the right arrow key is ignored if the left arrow key is also being depressed. But regardless, the state of the up arrow key is always checked in a separate *if* statement. A working version of this spaceship example is available from the online Code Depot:

```
// Code on a spaceship clip
onClipEvent (enterFrame) {
  if (Key.isDown(Key.LEFT)) {        // Left arrow
    _rotation -= 10;
  } else if (Key.isDown(Key.RIGHT)) { // Right arrow
    _rotation += 10;
  }
  if (Key.isDown(Key.UP)) {          // Up arrow
    thrust += 10;
  }
}
```

See Also

Key.getCode(); "keyDown" in Chapter 10

Key.isToggled( ) Method

check whether the Caps Lock, Num Lock, or Scroll Lock keys are activated

Availability　　　Flash 5

Synopsis　　　`Key.isToggled(keycode)`

Arguments

keycode　　　An integer keycode, usually the keycode of the Caps Lock key (20), Num Lock key (144), or Scroll Lock key (145). May also be the key constant `Key.CapsLock`.

Returns

A Boolean indicating whether the key specified by *keycode* is on (`true`) or off (`false`).

Description

The *isToggled()* method detects the state of the special Caps Lock, Num Lock, or Scroll Lock keys. Unlike other keys, these keys have an "on" state and an "off" state indicating whether or not the feature they represent is active. The return of *isToggled()* tells us if the key's feature is in effect or not. (Though *isToggled()* actually works for any keycode, its return value is useful only for special keys that support a toggle feature. To detect the state of other keys, use *isDown()*, *getCode()*, or *getAscii()*.)

_leveln Global Property   a document level in the Player

Availability   Flash 3 and later

Synopsis   _level0
            _level1
            _level2
            . . .
            _leveln

Access   Read-only

Description

Multiple *.swf* files may be loaded into the Flash Player for simultaneous display. Each loaded *.swf* resides on its own level in the document level stack. (A *.swf* file on a higher level number will obscure lower levels if they occupy the same portion of the Stage.) The _leveln property stores a reference to the main timeline of a *.swf* loaded into a document level in the Player. Each document level is represented by a numbered property, such as _level0, _level1, _level2, and so on.

The original document loaded into any Flash Player is considered _level0.

Example

A _leveln reference is normally used to control movies on other levels of the document stack. For example, here we play the movie on level 2:

```
_level2.play();
```

We can also use _leveln in combination with movie clip references to control clips contained by a movie on any level in the document stack. For example:

```
_level1.orderForm.titleBar.play();
```

A _leveln reference may also be used as the value of the *target* argument of several functions, including *loadMovie()*, *unloadMovie()*, *loadVariables()* and *print()*. If the level does not yet exist, you should specify the level reference within quotes. If used without quotes, a nonexistent level is considered **undefined** and may cause the command to operate on the current timeline instead of the new, undefined level. For example, when executed from the main timeline of _level0, the following will replace the movie in _level0 if _level1 has not yet been defined:

```
loadMovie("myMovie.swf", _level1);
```

The following is a safer approach if you can't guarantee that the level already exists:

```
loadMovie("myMovie.swf", "_level1");  // Works even if _level1 doesn't exist
```

Of course, from other levels, you may wish to refer to the original level, using _level0, such as:

```
startDrag(_level0, true);
```

See Also

loadMovie(), *unloadMovie()*, **_root**; "Importing External Movies" and "Movie and Instance Stacking Order" in Chapter 13

loadMovie( ) Global Function   load an external *.swf* file into the Player

Availability   Flash 4 and later. The *loadMovie()* function in Flash 5 corresponds to the Flash 4 *Load Movie* with a target path.

Synopsis   `loadMovie(URL, target)`
`loadMovie(URL, target, method)`

Arguments
URL   A string specifying the absolute or relative file path to the external *.swf* file to load. All URLs must use forward slashes, and absolute URLs must include either the `http://` or `file|///` protocol reference.

target   A string indicating the movie clip or document level that will host the external *.swf* file. May also be a reference to an existing movie clip or document level (references are converted to paths when used in a string context).

method   An optional string indicating the method by which to send variables to an external script. The legal values for *method* are `"GET"` and `"POST"`. This parameter must be a literal, not a variable or other expression. The standalone version of the Flash Player always uses the `"GET"` method regardless of the *method* specified.

Description

The *loadMovie()* function imports the *.swf* file located at *URL* into the Flash Player.

If *target* is a reference to an existing movie clip or a string indicating the path to a movie clip, the loaded *.swf* file is placed into the specified clip (causing the eviction of any previous content). To load a movie into the *current* movie clip, use the empty string as the *target* parameter, as in:

```
loadMovie("myMovie.swf", "")
```

If *target* is a reference to an existing document level (such as _level2) or a string indicating the path to a document level (such as `"_level2"`), then the *.swf* is placed into the specified document level. Loading a movie into `_level0` clears the Player of all content and places the new *.swf* file into `_level0`.

It is possible to send variables along with a *loadMovie()* invocation, in which case *URL* is normally the location of a script that returns a *.swf* file based on the variables sent. To send variables with a *loadMovie()* call, we include the *method* argument (set to either `"GET"` or `"POST"`). `"GET"` sends the current movie clip timeline variables as a query string attached to the script *URL*. `"POST"` sends the current movie clip timeline variables after the HTTP POST-request header. The `"POST"` method is not available in the standalone Flash Player. Because most web servers restrict the length of URLs to between 255 and 1024 characters, use `"POST"` instead of `"GET"` to transfer larger amounts of data.

Over a web server, *loadMovie()* invocations that use the `"GET"` method can pass variables to a loaded movie without the help of an intervening script. Here, we load the external movie *myMovie.swf* into level 1 of the Player document stack, passing it the variables from the current timeline:

```
loadMovie("myMovie.swf", "_level1", "GET");
```

Variables passed to the loaded movie are defined on that movie's main timeline. This technique works only when the *loadMovie()* request is handled by a web server. Attempts to use the `"GET"` method with *loadMovie()* using local files will cause an "Error opening URL" error.

Usage

Be careful when using movie clip and level references as the *target* argument of *loadMovie()*. If a *loadMovie()*'s `target` argument yields `undefined`, the *loadMovie()* function uses the current timeline as its *target*. Similarly, *target* references that yield the empty string cause *loadMovie()* to operate on the current timeline. In particular, this causes problems for loading movies onto new, unoccupied levels. Consider the following code:

```
loadMovie("myMovie.swf", _level1);
```

If no `_level1` object exists prior to the execution of that statement, that code will load *myMovie.swf* into the timeline that contains the *loadMovie()* statement, not `_level1`! To avoid the problem, you can use *loadMovieNum()* instead. Alternatively, you can use a string for the *target* parameter to *loadMovie()*, as in:

```
loadMovie("myMovie.swf", "_level1");
```

In that case, the level will be created if it doesn't already exist (only `_level0` exists by default in all movies). For more information, see "Method versus global function overlap issues" in Chapter 13.

Example

```
loadMovie("myMovie.swf", "_level1");       // Place myMovie.swf on level 1
loadMovie("myMovie.swf", "_level0");       // Place myMovie.swf on level 0
loadMovie("myMovie.swf", "myClip");        // Place myMovie.swf into myClip
// Replace the contents of the Player with
// coolmovie.swf, using an absolute path
loadMovie("http://www.yourflashsite.com/coolmovie.swf", "_level0");
// Load a movie into level 1 from the Windows desktop. Note the
// file:/// protocol and the forward slashes.
loadMovie("file:///C|/WINDOWS/Desktop/animation.swf", "_level1");
```

See Also

loadMovieNum(), *MovieClip.loadMovie()*, *unloadMovie()*; "Importing External Movies" lin Chapter 13

---

loadMovieNum( ) Global Function   load an external *.swf* file into a document level

Availability   Flash 3; enhanced in Flash 4 to include the *method* parameter; available in Flash 5. The *loadMovieNum()* function corresponds with Flash 3's *Load Movie,* which accepted only level numbers.

Synopsis
```
loadMovieNum(URL, level)
loadMovieNum(URL, level, method)
```

Arguments
URL   A string specifying the absolute or relative file path of the external *.swf* file to load.

level	A non-negative integer, or an expression that yields one, indicating the document level that will host the external *.swf* file.
method	An optional string indicating the method by which to send variables to an external script. The legal values for *method* are "GET" and "POST". This parameter must be a literal, not a variable or other expression. The standalone version of the Flash Player always uses the "GET" method regardless of the *method* specified.

Description

The *loadMovieNum()* function is nearly identical to *loadMovie()* except that it requires the target *level* of the load operation to be specified as a number rather than as a string. This means that *loadMovieNum()* can load movies only into document levels, not host clips. If the specified level doesn't exist, it will be created. If the specified level does exist, its occupant is replaced by the new *.swf* file. It is valid to load a movie into _level2 even if _level1 hasn't been created.

The *loadMovieNum()* function can be used when we wish to dynamically assign the level of a loaded movie, as in:

```
var x = 3;
loadMovieNum("myMovie.swf", x);
```

which could also be achieved via a string concatenation expression with the regular *loadMovie()* function:

```
loadMovie("myMovie.swf", "_level" + x);
```

See Also

loadMovie(), MovieClip.loadMovie()

---

loadVariables( ) Global Function   retrieve an external set of variables

Availability	Flash 4 and later
Synopsis	loadVariables(*URL*, *target*) loadVariables(*URL*, *target*, *method*)
Arguments	
URL	A string specifying the path to a variable source—either a server-side script that returns variables or a text file containing variables.
target	A string indicating the path to the movie clip or document level on which the loaded variables will be defined. May also be a reference to a movie clip or document level (references are converted to paths when used in a string context).
method	An optional string indicating the method by which to send variables to an external script. If specified, the variables from the current timeline are sent to the script and *target* receives the loaded variables. If omitted, variables are retrieved but none are sent. The legal values for *method* are "GET" and "POST". This parameter must be a literal, not a variable or other expression. The standalone version of the Flash Player always uses the "GET" method regardless of the *method* specified.

Description

Normally, we define variables inside our movies using ActionScript. However, using *loadVariables()*, we may also import variables into a movie from a text file or a server-side application such as a Perl script. Variables loaded via *loadVariables()* are scoped to the movie clip or level specified by `target` and are always of the *string* datatype. To attach loaded variables to the current timeline, use the empty string as the value of the `target` argument. For example:

```
loadVariables("myVars.txt", "");  // Loads the variables from myVars.txt onto
                                   // the current timeline
```

Whether the variables to be loaded reside in a text file or are composed by a script, they must be formatted according to the rules of URL encoding, as follows:

- Every variable name should be separated from its value with an equals sign, without spaces, as in `firstName=stephen`.

- Multiple variable name/value pairs should be separated by ampersands (&), as in `firstName=stephen&lastName=burke`.

- Spaces should be replaced with plus (+) signs.

- Any character that is not a space, a number (1–9), or an unaccented Latin 1 letter (a–z, A–Z) should be replaced by a hexadecimal escape sequence of the form `%xx`, where `xx` is the hex Latin 1 code point of the character.

For example, the following code shows the contents of a text file to be imported into Flash via *loadVariables()*. The imported variables are **name** and **address**, which have the values `"stephen"` and `"65 nowhere st!"`, respectively:

```
name=stephen&address=65+nowhere+st%21
```

A text file for use with *loadVariables()* is simply a regular text file containing URL-encoded variables, as shown previously. To load variables from an external text file, we specify the path of the file as the *URL* argument in our *loadVariables()* function invocation. For example:

```
// Load the variables from myVariables.txt into the main movie timeline
loadVariables("myVariables.txt", "_root");
```

loadVariables() may also be used with a script or server application that outputs URL-encoded variables. When a script sends data to a Flash movie in response to a *loadVariables()* function, the script should set the MIME type of the data as: `"application/x-www-urlform-encoded"`. Here's a typical MIME-setting statement from a Perl script:

```
print "Content-type: application/x-www-urlform-encoded\n\n";
```

Though the name *loadVariables()* suggests only a single direction of variable transmission, it may also be used to *send* variables to a server-side script. To send all the variables defined on the current timeline to a script, we set the `method` argument of a *loadVariables()* function invocation to either `"GET"` or `"POST"`. Variables are sent in URL-encoded format. If `method` is set to `"GET"`, the variables are sent as a query string of the script *URL*. If `method` is set to `"POST"`, the variables are sent after the HTTP POST-request header. The `"POST"` method is not available in the standalone Flash Player. Because most web servers restrict the length of URLs to between 255 and 1024 characters, use `"POST"` instead of `"GET"` to transfer larger amounts of data.

For security reasons, *loadVariables()* works only with hosts in the domain from which the movie was downloaded. The rules that govern *loadVariables()* usage are listed in Table R-8. These security measures affect the Flash Player browser plugins and ActiveX controls only; variables may be loaded from any domain in the standalone Player.

Table R-8. Domain-Based loadVariables() Security Restrictions

Domain of Movie Origin	Host to Connect to	Permitted?
www.somewhere.com	*www.somewhere.com*	Yes
www.somewhere.com	*other.somewhere.com*	Yes
www.somewhere.com	*www.somewhere-else.com*	No
www.somewhere.com	*somewhere.com*	Yes
somewhere.com	*www.somewhere.com*	Yes

Domain restriction is an intentional security feature of Flash, but it can be circumvented with either a proxy script running on siteX that acts as a go-between for Flash and siteY, or a DNS alias on siteX that points to siteY. For more information, see:

> *http://www.macromedia.com/support/flash/ts/documents/loadvars_security.htm*

Usage

The results of multiple *loadVariable()* calls to the same script URL may be cached on some browsers to the point that new data is never loaded from the server. To avoid this problem, append a dummy variable to each *loadVariables()* call so that the URL is unique. For example, here we generate a unique URL by appending the time in milliseconds:

```
loadVariables("http://www.mysite.com/cgi-bin/myScript.pl?cacheKiller="
              + getTimer(), serverResponse);
```

Bugs

The POST method is not supported by Internet Explorer 4.5 on Macintosh. This problem was fixed in Version 5 of the browser.

See Also

loadVariablesNum(), *MovieClip.loadVariables();* Chapter 17, *Flash Forms*

---

loadVariablesNum( ) Global Function

attach an external set of variables
to a document level

Availability   Flash 5. Use the *Load Variables* Action in Flash 4 to place variables on a document level.

Synopsis   `loadVariablesNum(URL, level)`
               `loadVariablesNum(URL, level, method)`

Arguments
URL   A string specifying the path to a variable source—either a server-side script that returns variables or a text file containing variables.

level   A non-negative integer, or an expression that yields one, indicating the document level on which the loaded variables will be defined.

method	An optional string indicating the method by which to send variables to an external script. If specified, the variables from the current timeline are sent to the script, and `level` receives the loaded variables. If omitted, variables are retrieved but none are loaded. The legal values for *method* are `"GET"` and `"POST"`. This parameter must be a literal, not a variable or other expression. The standalone version of the Flash Player always uses the `"GET"` method regardless of the *method* specified.

Description

The *loadVariablesNum()* function is nearly identical to *loadVariables()* except that it requires the target `level` to be specified as a number rather than as a string. This means that *loadVariablesNum()* can attach variables to document levels only, not movie clips. The target `level` can be specified dynamically, as in:

```
var myLevel = 2;
loadVariablesNum("myVars.txt", myLevel);
```

A similar effect could be achieved using string concatenation with the regular *loadVariables()* function:

```
loadVariables("myVars.txt", "_level" + myLevel);
```

See Also

loadVariables()

Math Object
access to mathematical functions and constants

Availability	Flash 5
Synopsis	`Math.propertyName` `Math.methodName()`

Properties

E	The constant *e*, the base of natural logarithms, approximately 2.71828.
LN10	The natural logarithm of 10 ($\log_e 10$), approximately 2.30259.
LN2	The natural logarithm of 2 ($\log_e 2$), approximately 0.69315.
LOG10E	The base-10 logarithm of *e*, approximately 0.43429.
LOG2E	The base-2 logarithm of *e*, approximately 1.44270. See bug noted in detailed listing.
PI	The ratio of a circle's circumference to its diameter, approximately 3.14159.
SQRT1_2	The reciprocal of the square root of 2, approximately 0.70711.
SQRT2	Square root of 2, approximately 1.41421.

Methods

abs()	Compute the absolute value of a number.
acos()	Compute the arc cosine of a number.
asin()	Compute the arc sine of a number.
atan()	Compute the arc tangent of a number.

atan2()	Compute the angle of a point, relative to the x-axis.
ceil()	Round a number up to the next integer.
cos()	Compute the cosine of an angle.
exp()	Raise *e* to a specified power.
floor()	Return the closest integer less than or equal to the input.
log()	Compute the natural logarithm of a number.
max()	Determine the larger of two numbers.
min()	Determine the smaller of two numbers.
pow()	Raise a number to a specified power.
random()	Retrieve a random floating-point number between 0 and 1.
round()	Calculate the closest integer to a number.
sin()	Compute the sine of an angle.
sqrt()	Compute the square root of a number.
tan()	Compute the tangent of an angle.

Description

The *Math* object provides access to built-in mathematical functions (accessed through methods) and constant values (accessed through properties). These functions and constants are used to perform potentially complex calculations with relative ease.

Note that the properties and methods of the *Math* object may be used in movies exported to the Flash 4 format, in which case Flash will approximate the calculations. The resulting values are reasonable approximations but not necessarily identical to the native Flash 5 functions. The Flash 4 values are sufficiently accurate for "close-enough" applications such as graphics display but are not accurate enough for critical financial or engineering calculations.

Note that the trigonometric functions require angles to be measured in radians whereas Flash's *MovieClip.*`_rotation` property is measured in degrees. There are 2π radians in a circle (1 radian is approximately 57.3 degrees). To convert from radians to degrees, use the formula:

```
degrees = (radians / Math.PI) * 180;
```

To convert from degrees to radians, use the formula:

```
radians = (degrees / 180) * Math.PI;
```

See Also

Math.atan2(), *Math.cos()*; "The Number Type" in Chapter 4

Math.abs( ) Method   compute the absolute value of a number

Availability   Flash 5; may be used when exporting Flash 4 movies

Synopsis   Math.abs (*x*)

Arguments

x   A positive or negative number.

Returns

The absolute value of *x* (a positive number of magnitude *x*).

Description

The *abs()* method calculates the distance between *x* and 0 (also known as the *absolute value* of *x*). It leaves positive numbers unchanged and converts negative numbers into positive numbers of the same magnitude. It is useful for calculating the difference between two numbers without regard to which is larger than the other. For example, it is useful when calculating the distance between two points because distances are always positive.

Example

```
Math.abs(-5);  // Returns 5

// Calculate the difference between two numbers
function diff (num1, num2) {
  return Math.abs(num1-num2);
}

diff(-5, 5);  // Returns 10
```

Math.acos( ) Method   compute the arc cosine of a number

Availability   Flash 5; may be used when exporting Flash 4 movies

Synopsis   Math.acos(*x*)

Arguments

x   A number between −1.0 and 1.0 (the cosine of an angle).

Returns

The angle, in radians, whose cosine is *x*. If *x* is not in the range −1.0 to 1.0, returns NaN.

Description

The arc cosine function (sometimes written as cos[-1]) is the inverse of the cosine function. It returns the angle whose cosine has the specified value, in radians. The return value is in the range 0 to π (i.e., 0 to 3.14159...).

Example

```
trace (Math.acos(1.0));  // Displays: 0
trace (Math.acos(0.0));  // Displays: 1.5707... (i.e., pi/2)
```

See Also

Math.asin(), Math.atan(), Math.cos()

Math.asin( ) Method   compute the arc sine of a number

Availability   Flash 5; may be used when exporting Flash 4 movies

Synopsis   `Math.asin(x)`

Arguments

x   A number between −1.0 and 1.0 (the sine of an angle).

Returns

The angle, in radians, whose sine is *x*. If *x* is not in the range −1.0 to 1.0, returns `NaN`.

Description

The arc sine function (sometimes written as sin[-1]) is the inverse of the sine function. It returns the angle whose sine has the specified value, in radians. The return value is in the range $-\pi/2$ to $\pi/2$ radians.

Example

```
trace (Math.asin(1.0));  // Displays: 1.5707...  (i.e., pi/2)
trace (Math.asin(0.0));  // Displays: 0
```

See Also

Math.acos, Math.atan, Math.sin

Math.atan( ) Method   compute the arc tangent of a number

Availability   Flash 5; may be used when exporting Flash 4 movies

Synopsis   `Math.atan(x)`

Arguments

x   A number between −`Infinity` and `Infinity`, inclusive (the tangent of some angle).

Returns

The angle, in radians, whose tangent is *x*.

Description

The arc tan function (sometimes written as tan[-1]) is the inverse of the tangent function. It returns the angle whose tangent has the specified value, in radians. The return value is in the range $-\pi/2$ to $\pi/2$.

Example

```
trace (Math.atan(1.0));        // Displays: 0.78539...
trace (Math.atan(0.0));        // Displays: 0
trace (Math.atan(-Infinity));  // Displays: -1.5707... (i.e., -pi/2)
```

See Also

Math.acos(), Math.asin(), Math.tan()

Math.atan2( ) Method   determine an angle based on a point

Availability   Flash 5; may be used when exporting Flash 4 movies

Synopsis   Math.atan2(*y*, *x*)

Arguments

y   The y-coordinate of the point.

x   The x-coordinate of the point.

Returns

The angle, in radians, of the point (*x*, *y*) from the center of a circle, measured counterclockwise from the circle's positive horizontal axis (i.e., the X-axis). Ranges from π to $-\pi$. (Negative values indicate angles below the X-axis).

Description

The *atan2()* method, like *atan()*, performs an arc tangent calculation but uses x- and y-coordinates, rather than their ratio, as arguments. That is, calculating an arc tangent with *atan2()* as:

```
Math.atan2(9, 3);  // Yields 1.24904577239825
```

is equivalent to calculating the arc tangent with *atan()*, using the ratio of 9/3 (or 3), as follows:

```
Math.atan(3);       // Same thing
```

Usage

Note that the *y*-coordinate is passed as the first argument to *atan2()*, whereas the *x*-coordinate is passed as the second argument. This is intentional and required. It mirrors the structure of tangent, which is the ratio of the side opposite an angle (y) divided by the side adjacent to the angle (x).

Example

The *atan2()* method can be used to make a movie clip point toward a moving target. The following example, available at the online Code Depot, shows code that rotates the current clip toward the mouse pointer. It can be used to orient an enemy spaceship toward a player's spaceship:

```
// Rotate movie clip toward mouse
onClipEvent (load) {
  // Convert radians to degrees. There are 2*pi radians per 360 degrees.
  function radiansToDegrees(radians) {
    return (radians/Math.PI) * 180;
  }
}

onClipEvent (enterFrame) {
  // Create a point object that stores the x- and y- coordinates of
  // this clip relative to its parent's registration point
  point = {x:_x, y:_y};
  // Convert our local (parent) coordinates to global (Stage) coordinates
  _parent.localToGlobal(point);
  // Measure the distance between the registration
  // point of this clip and the mouse
  deltaX = _root._xmouse - point.x;
  deltaY = _root._ymouse - point.y;
```

```
    // Calculate the angle of the line from the registration point
    // of this clip to the mouse
    rotationRadian = Math.atan2(deltaY, deltaX);
    // Convert the radian version of the angle to degrees
    rotationAngle = radiansToDegrees(rotationRadian); // See earlier function
    // Update the rotation of this clip to point to the mouse
    this._rotation = rotationAngle;
}
```

Math.ceil( ) Method   round a number up to the next integer

Availability   Flash 5; may be used when exporting Flash 4 movies

Synopsis   `Math.ceil(x)`

Arguments
x   A number.

Returns

The next integer greater than or equal to *x*.

Description

The *ceil()* (i.e., ceiling) method converts a floating-point number to the first integer greater than or equal to *x*.

Example

```
    Math.ceil(1.00001);   // Returns 2
    Math.ceil(5.5);       // Returns 6
    Math.ceil(-5.5);      // Returns -5
```

See Also

Math.floor(), *Math.round()*

Math.cos( ) Method   compute the cosine of an angle

Availability   Flash 5; may be used when exporting Flash 4 movies

Synopsis   `Math.cos(theta)`

Arguments
theta   An angle, in radians (not degrees), in the range 0 to 2π.

Returns

The cosine of *theta* (the result is in the range −1.0 to 1.0).

Description

The *cos()* function returns the trigonometric cosine of an angle. In a right triangle, the cosine of an angle is the result of dividing the length of the side adjacent to the angle by the triangle's hypotenuse.

Usage

Note that *cos()* expects angles to be provided in radians, not degrees.

Example

```
trace (cos(0));           // Displays: 1.0
trace (cos(Math.PI));     // Displays: -1.0
```

The *cos()* function can be used along with *sin()* to calculate a point on a circle, which we use in the following example to move a movie clip in a circular path. Given the radius of a circle, *r*, and an angle, θ, measured counterclockwise from the positive horizontal axis, a point's location is (r*cosθ, r*sinθ):

```
// CODE ON FRAME 1
var radius = 100;         // Radius of circle path
var centerX = 275;        // Horizontal center of circle path
var centerY = 200;        // Vertical center of circle path
var rotAngleDeg = 0;      // Angle of object in degrees, measured
                          //   counterclockwise from the horizon (x-axis)
var rotAngRad;            // Radian version of rotAngleDeg

// Convert degrees to radians. There are 2*pi radians per 360 degrees.
function degreesToRadians(degrees) {
  return (degrees/180) * Math.PI;
}

// CODE ON FRAME 2
// Increase the rotation angle by 5 degrees
rotAngleDeg += 5;

// Place the object. Note that Flash inverts the Y-axis of Cartesian coordinates
// so we decrement y to obtain our new location
rotAngRad= degreesToRadians(rotAngleDeg);
ball._x = centerX + Math.cos(rotAngRad) * radius;
ball._y = centerY - Math.sin(rotAngRad) * radius;

// CODE ON FRAME 3
// Go back to frame 2 where we move the ball again
gotoAndPlay(2);
```

See Also

Math.acos(), Math.sin(), Math.tan()

Math.E Property   the constant *e* (the base of the natural logarithm)

Availability   Flash 5; may be used when exporting Flash 4 movies

Synopsis   `Math.E`

Description

The E property stores an approximation of the natural logarithmic base (roughly 2.71828), which in mathematics is represented by the symbol *e*. It is a transcendental number like π, used in mathematical equations involving growth or change. Don't confuse it with the E that is used for exponential notation as described in "Floating-Point Literals" in Chapter 4. The two are unrelated.

See Also

Math.log(), Math.LN10(), Math.LN2()

Math.exp( ) Method   raise the constant *e* to a specified power

Availability   Flash 5; may be used when exporting Flash 4 movies

Synopsis   `Math.exp(x)`

Arguments

x   The exponent to which to raise `Math.E`.

Returns

`Math.E` to the power *x*.

Math.floor( ) Method   round a number to down to the previous integer

Availability   Flash 5; may be used when exporting Flash 4 movies

Synopsis   `Math.floor(x)`

Arguments

x   A number.

Returns

The closest integer less than or equal to *x*.

Description

The *floor* method converts a floating-point number to the first integer less than or equal to *x*.

Example

```
Math.floor(1.99999);  // Returns 1
Math.floor(5.5);      // Returns 5
Math.floor(-5.5);     // Returns -6

function minutesToHHMM (minutes) {
  var hours = Math.floor(minutes/60);
  minutes -= hours * 60;
  minutes = minutes < 10 ? "0" + minutes : minutes;
  return hours + ":" + minutes;
}
```

See Also

Math.ceil(), Math.round()

Math.LN10 Property   natural logarithm of 10 ($\log_e 10$), approximately 2.30259

Availability   Flash 5; may be used when exporting Flash 4 movies

Synopsis   `Math.LN10`

Description

The `LN10` property represents the natural logarithm of 10 (the base-*e* logarithm of 10), a constant equaling approximately 2.30259.

Math.LN2 Property   natural logarithm of 2 ($\log_e 2$), approximately 0.69315

Availability   Flash 5; may be used when exporting Flash 4 movies

Synopsis   `Math.LN2`

Description

The `LN2` property represents the natural logarithm of 2 (the base-*e* logarithm of 2), a constant equaling approximately 0.69315

Math.log( ) Method   compute the natural logarithm of a number

Availability   Flash 5; may be used when exporting Flash 4 movies

Synopsis   `Math.log(x)`

Arguments
x   A positive integer.

Returns

The natural logarithm of **x**.

Description

The *log()* method calculates the natural logarithm (i.e., the base-*e* logarithm) of a number. See the following example to calculate the base-10 logarithm.

Example

```
trace (Math.log(Math.E));   // Displays: 1

// Compute the base-10 logarithm of a number
function log10 (x) {
  return (Math.log(x) / Math.log(10));
}
```

Math.LOG10E Property   base-10 logarithm of *e*, approximately 0.43429

Availability   Flash 5; may be used when exporting Flash 4 movies

Synopsis   `Math.LOG10E`

Description

The `LOG10E` property represents the common logarithm of *e* (the base-10 logarithm of *e*), a constant equaling approximately 0.43429.

Math.LOG2E Property   base-2 logarithm of *e*, approximately 1.44270

Availability   Flash 5; may be used when exporting Flash 4 movies

Synopsis   `Math.LOG2E`

Description

The `LOG2E` property represents the base-2 logarithm of *e* ($\log_2 e$), a constant equaling approximately 1.44270.

Bugs

In Flash 5r30, `LOG2E` erroneously returns the value of `LN2` (0.69315).

Math.max( ) Method   determine the larger of two numbers

Availability   Flash 5; may be used when exporting Flash 4 movies

Synopsis   `Math.max(x, y)`

Arguments

x   A number.

y   A number.

Returns

The larger of *x* and *y*.

Example

```
Math.max(5, 1);    // Returns 5
Math.max(-6, -5);  // Returns -5
```

This example constrains a value to the specified range:

```
function constrainToRange (checkVal, minVal, maxVal) {
  return Math.min(Math.max(checkVal, minVal), maxVal);
}
// Constrain the slider to the stage area
mySlider._x = constainToRange (mySlider._x, 0, 550);
```

This example returns the maximum value in an array:

```
function maxInArray (checkArray) {
  maxVal = -Number.MAX_VALUE;  // Initialize maxVal to a very small number
  for (var i = 0; i < checkArray.length; i++) {
    maxVal = Math.max(checkArray[i], maxVal);
  }
  return maxVal;
}

trace(maxInArray([2,3,66,4,342,-90,0]));  // Displays: 342
```

See Also

Math.min( )

Math.min( ) Method   determine the smaller of two numbers

Availability   Flash 5; may be used when exporting Flash 4 movies

Synopsis   Math.min(*x*, *y*)

Arguments
x   A number.
y   A number.

Returns

The smaller of *x* and *y*.

Example

```
Math.min(5, 1);    // Returns 1
Math.min(-6, -5);  // Returns -6
```

Reader Exercise: Modify the example under *Math.max()* to return the minimum value in an array rather than the maximum.

See Also

Math.max()

Math.PI Property   the ratio of a circle's circumference to
                                             its diameter, approximately 3.14159

Availability   Flash 5; may be used when exporting Flash 4 movies

Synopsis   Math.PI

Description

The PI property represents the constant π, the ratio of the circumference of a circle to its diameter.

Example

Math.PI is most famously used in calculating the area of a circle:

```
function circleArea (radius) {
  // PI times the radius squared could also be
  // written as Math.PI * Math.pow(radius, 2)
  return Math.PI * (radius * radius);
}
```

Math.pow( ) Method   raise a number to a specified power

Availability   Flash 5; may be used when exporting Flash 4 movies

Synopsis   Math.pow(*base*, *exponent*)

Arguments
base   A number representing the base of the exponential expression.
exponent   A number representing the power (i.e., exponent) to which to raise *base*.

Returns

The *base* raised to the power *exponent*.

Description

The *pow()* method can be used to raise any number to any power. If *exponent* is negative, *pow()* returns $1 / (base^{abs(exponent)})$. If *exponent* is a fraction, *pow()* can be used to take, say, the square root or cube root of a number (in which case it returns the positive root, although, mathematically, there may also be a negative root).

Example

```
Math.pow(5, 2);     // Returns 25 (5 squared)
Math.pow(5, 3);     // Returns 125 (5 cubed)
Math.pow(5, -2);    // Returns 0.04 (1 divided by 25)
Math.pow(8, 1/3);   // Returns 2 (cube root of 8)
Math.pow(9, 1/2);   // Returns 3 (square root of 9)
Math.pow(10, 6);    // Returns 1000000 (can also be written as 1e6)
```

Bugs

Build 30 of the Flash 5 Player did not correctly calculate *Math.pow()* for negative values of *base*. For example, `Math.pow(-2, 2)` was calculated as `NaN` whereas it should be 4.

See Also

Math.exp(), *Math.sqrt()*, `Math.SQRT2`, `Math.SQRT1_2`

Math.random( ) Method   generate a random number from 0 to 1.0

Availability   Flash 5; may be used when exporting Flash 4 movies

Synopsis   `Math.random()`

Returns

A floating-point number greater than or equal to 0.0 and less than 1.0.

Description

The *random()* method provides a way to produce random numbers, which can be used to choose randomly between actions in a script. The *random()* method generates a random value between 0 and .99999... inclusive, which we can scale according to our needs. For example, to obtain a random number between 0 and 5, we use:

```
Math.floor(Math.random() * 6)
```

And to obtain a random number between 1 and 6, we use:

```
Math.floor(Math.random() * 6) + 1
```

This custom function returns an integer number in a specified range rather than a floating-point number in the range 0 to 1:

```
// Returns a number in the range minVal to maxVal, inclusive
function myRandom (minVal, maxVal) {
  return minVal + Math.floor(Math.random() * (maxVal + 1 - minVal));
}
```

```
// Invoke the function
dieRoll = myRandom(1, 6);   // Emulates a six-sided die
trace(dieRoll);

// Note that to simulate two dice, you can use this:
twoDice = myRandom(2, 12);   // The minimum value is 2, not 1

// To return the die values separately, use an array
function rollTwoDice () {
  return [myRandom(1, 6), myRandom(1, 6)];
}
```

Due to a bug in Build 30 of the Flash 5 Player, this approach is prone to an extremely rare, but potentially important inaccuracy. In Build 30, *random()* generates values in the range 0.0 to 1.0, inclusive. When we multiply the return of *random()* by an integer, *n*, we produce values in the range 0.0 to *n*. In our example, we multiplied *Math.random()* by 6, so that the returned value ranges from 0.0 to 6.0. By invoking *floor()* on the adjusted value, we produce integers in the range 0 to *n* (0 to 6 in our example). This leads to an inaccurate distribution of random numbers—the chance of producing *n* is much smaller than the chance of producing any other number in the series.

The following version of the *myRandom()* function avoids the problem by simply discarding the value 1.0 if it happens to be chosen by *Math.random()*:

```
// Returns an integer in the range minVal to maxVal, inclusive
function myRandom (minVal, maxVal) {
  do {
    r = Math.random();   // Keep picking a number until it is not 1.
  } while (r == 1);
  return minVal + Math.floor(r * (maxVal + 1 - minVal));
}

// Invoke the function
dieRoll = myRandom(1, 6);   // Emulates a six-sided die safely in Build 30
                            // of the Flash 5 Player
```

Usage

Math.random() replaces the deprecated Flash 4 *random* function.

Example

Math.random() is often used to cause the playhead to jump to a random frame in the timeline. The following code invokes the *myRandom()* function from the preceding example and then sends the playhead to the randomly chosen frame:

```
// Invoke the function; pick a random number between 10 and 20
var destinationFrame = myRandom(10, 20);

// Now send the playhead to that frame
gotoAndStop(destinationFrame);
```

Math.round( ) Method   calculate the closest integer to a number

Availability   Flash 5; may be used when exporting Flash 4 movies

Synopsis   `Math.round(x)`

Arguments

x   A number.

Returns

The integer mathematically closest to *x* (or *x* itself, if *x* is an integer). If the fractional component of *x* is exactly 0.5 (*x* is equidistant from the two closest integers), *round()* returns the first integer greater than *x.*

Description

The *round()* method performs traditional rounding; it converts a floating-point number to the nearest integer. Positive numbers with a fractional portion *less* than 0.5 and negative numbers with a fractional portion *greater* than 0.5 are rounded *down*. Positive numbers with a fractional portion *greater* than or equal to 0.5 and negative numbers with a fractional portion *less* than or equal to 0.5 are rounded *up*.

Example

```
Math.round(1.4);      // Returns 1
Math.round(1.5);      // Returns 2
Math.round(1.6);      // Returns 2
Math.round(-5.4);     // Returns -5
Math.round(-5.5);     // Returns -5
Math.round(-5.6);     // Returns -6
```

See Also

int(), Math.ceil(), Math.floor()

Math.sin( ) Method   compute the sine of an angle

Availability   Flash 5; may be used when exporting Flash 4 movies

Synopsis   `Math.sin(theta)`

Arguments

theta   An angle, in radians (not degrees), in the range 0 to 2π.

Returns

The sine of *theta* (the result is in the range −1.0 to 1.0).

Description

The *sin()* method returns the trigonometric sine of an angle. In a right triangle, the sine of an angle is the result of dividing·the length of the side opposite the angle by the triangle's hypotenuse.

Usage

Note that *sin()* expects angles to be provided in radians, not degrees.

Example

```
trace (Math.sin(0));          // Displays: 0
trace (Math.sin(Math.PI/2));  // Displays: 1.0
```

The *sin()* function can be used along with *cos()* to calculate a point on a circle. See the example under *Math.cos()*.

See Also

Math.asin(), Math.cos(), Math.tan()

Math.sqrt( ) Method   calculate the square root of a number

Availability   Flash 5; may be used when exporting Flash 4 movies

Synopsis   `Math.sqrt(x)`

Arguments

x   A non-negative integer.

Returns

The square root of *x*, or NaN if *x* is less than 0.

Description

The *sqrt()* method returns the positive root of its operand (even though there may also be a mathematically valid negative root). It is equivalent to:

```
Math.pow(x, 0.5)
```

Example

```
Math.sqrt(4);    // Returns 2, although -2 is also a valid root
Math.sqrt(36);   // Returns 6, although -6 is also a valid root
Math.sqrt(-20);  // Returns NaN
```

See Also

Math.pow(), `Math.SQRT2`, `Math.SQRT1_2`

Math.SQRT1_2 Property   the reciprocal of the square root of 2, approximately 0.70711

Availability   Flash 5; may be used when exporting Flash 4 movies

Synopsis   `Math.SQRT1_2`

Description

The `SQRT1_2` property is a constant approximating the value `1/Math.SQRT2` (the reciprocal of the square root of 2), equaling approximately 0.70711.

See Also

`Math.SQRT2`

Math.SQRT2 Property   the square root of 2, approximately 1.41421

Availability   Flash 5; may be used when exporting Flash 4 movies

Synopsis   Math.SQRT2

Description

The SQRT2 property is a constant approximating the square root of 2, an irrational number, equaling approximately 1.41421.

See Also

Math.SQRT1_2

Math.tan( ) Method   compute the tangent of an angle

Availability   Flash 5; may be used when exporting Flash 4 movies

Synopsis   Math.tan(*theta*)

Arguments
theta   An angle, in radians (not degrees), in the range $-\pi/2$ to $\pi/2$.

Returns

The tangent of *theta* (the result is in the range -Infinity to Infinity).

Description

The *tan()* method returns the trigonometric tangent of an angle. In a right triangle, the tangent of an angle is the result of dividing the length of the side opposite the angle by the length of the side adjacent to the angle. This is also the same as the ratio *Math.sin(theta)/Math.cos(theta)*, so as *cos(theta)* approaches zero, *tan(theta)* approaches Infinity. Therefore, *tan(theta)* is not calculable for the values $-\pi/2$, $\pi/2$, $-3\pi/2$, $3\pi/2$, etc.

Example

```
trace (Math.tan(0));        // Displays: 0
trace (Math.tan(Math.PI/4));  // Displays: 1
```

See Also

Math.atan(), Math.cos(), Math.sin()

---

maxscroll Property   the last legal top line of a text field

Availability   Flash 4 and later

Synopsis   *textField*.maxscroll

Returns

A positive integer representing the line number of the last legal top line of a text field.

Description

The maxscroll property tells us the largest allowed scroll value for a text field. It represents the number of the last line in a text field that may be used as the top line in its viewable region.

The `maxscroll` property can be used with the `scroll` property to manage a scrolling-text field.

See Also

`scroll`; "The maxscroll Property" in Chapter 18

Mouse Object   hide or reveal the mouse pointer

Availability   Flash 5

Synopsis   `Mouse.`*methodName*

Methods

hide()   Hides the mouse pointer.

show()   Enables the mouse pointer.

Description

The *Mouse* object has only two methods and no properties. We use *Mouse.hide()* to conceal the system mouse pointer, usually in order to replace it with a customized mouse pointer as shown later. It may also be desirable to hide the mouse pointer in fullscreen, keyboard-controlled movies or for touch-screen kiosks.

Note that the *Mouse* object does not tell us the location of the mouse pointer. That information is stored in the `_xmouse` and `_ymouse` properties of each movie clip object. Use `_root._xmouse` and `_root._ymouse` to determine the mouse pointer's location on the main Stage.

See Also

`MovieClip._xmouse`, `MovieClip._ymouse`

Mouse.hide( ) Method   make the mouse pointer disappear

Availability   Flash 5

Synopsis   `Mouse.hide()`

Description

The *hide()* method causes the normal mouse pointer (usually an arrow) to disappear when the mouse is over any part of the Player. The normal system pointer reappears when the mouse passes outside the Flash Player's active stage area.

Usage

Note that in Flash 5, even after *Mouse.hide()* has been invoked, the normal system text I-beam cursor will appear when the mouse hovers over a text field.

Example

The *hide()* method is used to conceal the default system mouse pointer, typically in order to replace it with a custom pointer. In Flash, a custom pointer is nothing more than a movie clip that follows the mouse. Using the *mouseMove* event, we can cause a movie clip to

follow the mouse by updating the clip's _x and _y properties with each passing frame. The
following code demonstrates the technique:

```
// Code on the clip that acts as the custom pointer
onClipEvent (load) {
  Mouse.hide();
}

onClipEvent (mouseMove) {
  _x = _root._xmouse;
  _y = _root._ymouse;
  updateAfterEvent();
}
```

It may also be desirable to hide the custom pointer when the mouse is inactive, say,
because the pointer has left the Flash Player's active stage area, in which case the system
pointer appears and there are two pointers on screen. The following code shows how to
adapt the previous code to hide the cursor after 5 seconds of inactivity:

```
onClipEvent (load) {
  Mouse.hide();
}

onClipEvent (enterFrame) {
  if (getTimer() - lastMove > 5000) {
    _visible = false;
  } else {
    _visible = true;
  }
}

onClipEvent (mouseMove) {
  _x = _root._xmouse;
  _y = _root._ymouse;
  lastMove = getTimer();
  updateAfterEvent();
}
```

To change a custom pointer to a custom "hand" icon when the mouse hovers over a
button, use the button's *rollOver* event to set the custom pointer clip to a frame containing
the custom hand, and use the *rollOut* event to set the custom pointer back to the default, as
follows:

```
on (rollOver) {
  _root.customPointer.gotoAndStop("hand");
}

on (rollOut) {
  _root.customPointer.gotoAndStop("default");
}
```

In all cases, remember to place the custom pointer on the top layer of your movie so it
appears above all other content. Alternatively, use *duplicateMovieClip()* or *attachMovie()* to
dynamically generate the custom pointer clip and assign it a very high depth.

See Also

Mouse.show(), `MovieClip._xmouse`, `MovieClip._ymouse`

Mouse.show( ) Method   make the mouse pointer appear

Availability   Flash 5

Synopsis   `Mouse.show()`

Description

The *show()* method causes the default system mouse pointer to reappear after *Mouse.hide()* has been invoked. It can be used to provide a normal pointer at necessary times in a movie, such as when the user is expected to fill in a form. This is one way to handle the unfortunate appearance of the text I-beam when the system pointer is hidden.

See Also

Mouse.hide()

MovieClip "Class"   class-like datatype for main movies and movie clips

Availability   Flash 3 and later

Constructor

None. Movie clip symbols are created manually in the Flash authoring tool. Movie clip instances can be created with *attachMovie()* and *duplicateMovieClip()*.

Properties

Movie clip properties provide descriptions of, and control over, various physical features of movie clips and main movies. Properties are accessed using the dot operator, as with any object. See "The "Objectness" of Movie Clips" in Chapter 13, *Movie Clips*, for details on using movie clip properties.

Two property-related issues to note:

- Changing a physical property of a *MovieClip* object places that clip under programmatic control, breaking the internal timeline's hold on it. This halts any tween currently in progress.

- Some *MovieClip* properties appear to be floating-point numbers but are mapped to other formats internally. The `_alpha` property, for example, is mapped to an integer between 0 and 255 internally. This results in a loss of precision between setting and retrieving values of certain properties. We may, for example, set a property value to 90 and then immediately retrieve the value back as 89.84375. If minor variations in property values make a difference to a script, we must manually round those values using *Math.round()*, *Math.floor()*, or *Math.ceil()* after retrieval, or we must store the original value in a variable separate from the property.

Table R-9 lists the movie clip properties. Note that all built-in movie clip properties begin with an underscore. This make them easy to distinguish from custom properties that you can add to your movie clip and which by convention should not begin with an underscore. In the *Access* column of Table R-9, *R/W* indicates that a property's value may be both retrieved and set (i.e., read/write), and *RO* indicates that it can be retrieved but not set (i.e., read-only). Some read-only properties can sometimes be set indirectly through the authoring tool or via some related function (e.g., *gotoAndStop()* sets the _currentframe property), but only read/write properties can be set directly via ActionScript. The *Type* column describes the datatype of each property's value. The *Property Description* column gives a quick summary of the property's purpose, but the full descriptions that follow later provide important details. With the exception of the _name and _parent properties, the properties in Table R-9 apply to both movie clip instances and the main movie (i.e., _root). However, a property's value may differ markedly depending on whether it is checked from a movie clip instance or the main movie and may also differ depending on where the clip is attached. For example, a movie clip's _x property differs depending on whether it is attached to the main timeline or as a child of a parent clip. Furthermore, all properties of the current timeline may be accessed without an explicit reference to it, as in _alpha versus myClip._alpha.

Table R-9. Movie Clip Property Summary

Property Name	Access	Type	Property Description
_alpha	R/W	number	Opacity percentage: 0 is transparent; 100 is opaque
_currentframe	RO	number	Frame number at which playhead resides
_droptarget	RO	string	Target path of the clip over which a dragged clip hovers or has been dropped, in slash notation
_framesloaded	RO	number	Number of frames that have been down-loaded
_height	R/W	number	Height, in pixels, of the current contents
_name*	R/W	string	Identifier of an instance as a string (not a reference)
_parent*	RO	MovieClip reference	A reference to the instance or movie that contains the current instance
_rotation	R/W	number	Degrees of rotation
_target	RO	string	Target path in absolute terms, in slash notation
_totalframes	RO	number	Number of frames in the timeline
_url	RO	string	Disk or network location of the source *.swf* file
_visible	R/W	boolean	Visibility: true if shown; false if hidden
_width	R/W	number	Width, in pixels, of the current contents
_x	R/W	number	Horizontal position, in pixels
_xmouse	RO	number	Horizontal location of mouse pointer, in pixels
_xscale	R/W	number	Horizontal scaling percentage
_y	R/W	number	Vertical position, in pixels
_ymouse	RO	number	Vertical location of mouse pointer, in pixels
_yscale	R/W	number	Vertical scaling percentage

*Applies to movie clip instances; does not apply to the main timeline.

Methods

Movie clip methods may be invoked on any movie clip instance and, in most cases, on any main movie timeline. Many of the movie clip methods provide the same functionality as analogous global functions but simply use the convenient `MovieClip.method()` dot syntax format. Those that do not correspond to a global function may be applied to the current clip without an explicit reference to it, as in `attachMovie()` versus `myClip.attachMovie()`. Table R-10 lists the movie clip methods.

Table R-10. Movie Clip Method Summary

Method Name	Method Description
attachMovie()	Creates a new instance based on an exported symbol from the current document's Library. Places the new instance in the host clip or the movie's programmatically generated clip stack.
*duplicateMovieClip()**	Creates a copy of the current instance and places the copy in the appropriate programmatic ally generated clip stack (see "How clips generated via duplicateMovieClip() are added to the stack" in Chapter 13.)
getBounds()	Returns an object whose properties give the coordinates of the bounding box that defines the visual region occupied by the clip.
getBytesLoaded()	Returns the number of downloaded bytes of an instance or a movie. Not applicable for use with internal clips.
getBytesTotal()	Returns the physical byte size of an instance or a main movie.
getURL()	Loads an external document (usually a web page) into the browser.
globalToLocal()	Converts the properties of a *coordinates* object from Stage coordinates to instance coordinates. Has no effect when invoked on a main movie object (such as `_root`), because the original and target coordinate spaces are identical.
gotoAndPlay()	Moves the playhead of an instance or movie to a specific frame, and then plays the instance or movie.
gotoAndStop()	Moves the playhead of an instance or movie to a specific frame and then stops the playhead.
hitTest()	Returns a Boolean indicating whether or not a clip intersects with a given point or another clip.
loadMovie()	Brings an external *.swf* file into the Player.
loadVariables()	Retrieves external data composed of variable names and values and converts that data into equivalent ActionScript variables.
localToGlobal()	Converts the properties of a *coordinates* object from an instance's coordinates to main movie coordinates.
nextFrame()	Moves the playhead of instance or movie ahead one frame and stops it there.
play()	Starts the playhead of instance or movie in motion (i.e., plays the clip).

Table R-10. Movie Clip Method Summary (continued)

Method Name	Method Description
prevFrame()	Moves the playhead of instance or movie back one frame and stops it there.
removeMovieClip()*	Deletes a duplicated or attached instance.
startDrag()	Causes instance or movie to physically follow the mouse pointer.
stop()	Halts the playback of instance or movie.
stopDrag()	Ends any drag operation currently in progress.
swapDepths()*	Alters the position of an instance in an instance stack.
unloadMovie()	Removes an instance or main movie from a document level or host clip.
valueOf()	Represents the path to the instance in absolute terms, using dot notation.

*Applies to movie clip instances; does not apply to the main timeline.

Events

Movie clip instances support *event handlers,* which respond automatically to a predefined set of events (e.g., mouse or keyboard interaction or movie playback). The supported movie clip event handlers are listed in Table R-11. See Chapter 10, *Events and Event Handlers,* for details on each.

Table R-11. Movie Clip Event Handler Summary

Clip Event Handler	Clip Event Occurs When...
onClipEvent (enterFrame)	A frame passes in the Flash Player
onClipEvent (load)	The clip first appears on the Stage
onClipEvent (unload)	The clip is removed from the Stage
onClipEvent (data)	The clip receives the end of a stream of loaded variables, or a portion of a loaded movie
onClipEvent (mouseDown)	Primary mouse button is depressed while the clip is on stage
onClipEvent (mouseUp)	Primary mouse button is depressed and then released while the clip is on stage
onClipEvent (mouseMove)	Mouse pointer moves (even a teensy bit) while the clip is on stage
onClipEvent (keyDown)	A key is pressed down while the clip is on stage
onClipEvent (keyUp)	A depressed key is released while the clip is on stage

Description

MovieClip is not actually a class in ActionScript but rather a unique ActionScript datatype used to represent information about, and allow control of, movies and movie clips. For most purposes, we treat movie clips and movies as objects; we may create and access movie clip properties, and we may create and invoke movie clip methods.

Because *MovieClip* is not a true class, we do not use a constructor to create new *MovieClip* instances. Instead, we create movie clip symbols in the authoring tool and place instances on the Stage manually. Some methods, however, allow us to copy existing clips (*duplicateMovieClip()*), or add new clips to the Stage programmatically (*attachMovie()*).

Not all *MovieClip* objects are equal; some *MovieClip* methods and properties apply only to movie clip instances, not to main movies (a main movie is the `_root` timeline of a *.swf* document). In our consideration of the *MovieClip* properties and methods, we'll note cases in which functionality is limited to one type of *MovieClip* object. Note that we use the word *MovieClip* to refer to the "class" of the objects, and the word *movieclip* (lowercase) to refer to the ActionScript datatype; we use *movie clip*, *clip*, or *instance* to refer to a particular movie clip, and we use *movie* to refer to the main movie of a *.swf* file. In the synopsis for each detailed property and method entry, the abbreviation *mc* stands in for the name of a clip or main movie. For many properties and methods, *mc* is optional—if omitted, the current timeline is used.

Throughout this *MovieClip* section, when talking about coordinates, we need to refer to the location of movie clips. We measure the position of a clip in reference to one representative point, its so-called *registration point*, as marked by a crosshair in the clip's Library symbol.

When a clip resides on the main Stage, we describe its location relative to the top-left corner of the Stage, which corresponds to the point (0,0). When a clip resides within another clip, we describe its location relative to the registration point of the parent clip, which again corresponds to the point (0,0). The point (0,0) in both cases is the origin point (or simply *origin*) of the coordinate space being used to plot the location of the clip. We'll see how the *localToGlobal()* and *globalToLocal()* methods can convert between these two coordinate spaces.

 Flash's coordinate system inverts the Y-axis of Cartesian coordinates; that is, y values increase in a downward direction, not upward. For example, a y-coordinate of 100 indicates a point 100 pixels *below* the X-axis.

We'll often use the coordinate-related properties and methods to move a clip, determine where a clip is, or determine whether it intersects another object or point. The last technique is referred to as *collision detection* because it is often used to determine whether to change the direction in which a clip is animating, as if it bounced off another object (see the *MovieClip.hitTest()* method).

Note that ActionScript doesn't have a native datatype to represent a *point* (i.e., an x- and y-coordinate). See *MovieClip.globalToLocal()* for an explanation of how to create a point object from a generic object.

See Also

For a full consideration of the *MovieClip* class, see Chapter 13

MovieClip._alpha Property   opacity of a clip or movie

Availability   Flash 4 and later

Synopsis   mc._alpha

Access   Read/write

Description

The floating-point _alpha property specifies the opacity (or conversely the transparency) of *mc* as a percentage—0 is completely transparent whereas 100 is completely opaque. Setting the _alpha of *mc* affects the visual transparency of all clips nested inside *mc* but does not affect their _alpha properties. That is, if we have a clip, square, that contains another clip, circle, and we set square._alpha to 50, then circle will be 50% transparent on-screen but will have an _alpha of 100.

Usage

Note that setting the _alpha of a movie clip affects the aa property of the object returned by *Color.getTransform( )*.

Example

```
ball._alpha = 60;    // Make ball partially transparent
ball._alpha = 0;     // Make ball invisible
```

The following clip event handler makes a clip more transparent as the mouse moves down on the screen:

```
onClipEvent(enterFrame) {
  _alpha = 100 - (_root._ymouse / 400) * 100;
}
```

See Also

The *Color* Class; *MovieClip._visible*

MovieClip.attachMovie( ) Method   create a new movie clip instance from
                                          an exported Library symbol

Availability   Flash 5

Synopsis   mc.attachMovie(*symbolIdentifier*, *newName*, *depth*)

Arguments

symbolIdentifier   A string specifying the linkage identifier of an exported movie clip symbol, as set in the Library under Options → Linkage.

newName   A string specifying the new instance name of the clip being created. The name must adhere to the rules for creating an identifier outlined under "Identifiers" in Chapter 14, *Lexical Structure*.

depth   An integer specifying the level on which to place the new clip in the programmatic clip stack above *mc*. A depth of −1 is below 0, 1 is in front of 0, 2 is in front of 1, and so on. See "How clips generated via attachMovie( ) are added to the stack" in Chapter 13 for more details. Negative depths are functional but not officially supported by ActionScript; to ensure future compatibility, use depths of 0 or greater.

Description

The *attachMovie()* method creates a new instance called *newName* based on the exported movie clip symbol specified by *symbolIdentifier*. If *mc* is the main movie, the new instance is placed in the top-left corner of the Stage. If *mc* is a movie clip instance, the new instance is placed on *mc*'s registration point. In either case, the new instance is placed above *mc* in a stack of programmatically-generated clips.

See Also

duplicateMovieClip(), *MovieClip.duplicateMovieClip()*; "Creating instances with attachMovie()" and "How clips generated via attachMovie() are added to the stack" in Chapter 13

MovieClip._currentframe Property

the frame number of the playhead of a clip or movie

Availability   Flash 4 and later

Synopsis   mc._currentframe

Access   Read-only

Description

The integer _currentframe property represents the frame number at which the playhead of *mc* currently resides. Note that the first frame is 1, not 0; therefore, _currentframe ranges from 1 to *mc*._totalframes.

Example

```
// Send a playhead back two frames from its current location
gotoAndStop(_currentframe - 2);
```

See Also

MovieClip.gotoAndPlay(), *MovieClip.gotoAndStop()*

MovieClip._droptarget Property

the path to the clip or movie on which a dragged clip was dropped

Availability   Flash 4 and later

Synopsis   mc._droptarget

Access   Read-only

Description

If *mc* is being dragged, _droptarget stores a string indicating the path to the clip over which *mc* hovers (if any). If *mc* is not hovering over a clip, _droptarget stores undefined. If *mc* was previously dragged and then dropped on a clip, _droptarget stores a string indicating the path to the clip upon which *mc* was dropped. The path is provided in slash notation. A movie clip is considered to be "over" another clip if the registration point of the dragged clip overlaps any portion of the target clip.

Example

The `_droptarget` property is convenient for creating drag-and-drop interfaces. The following example demonstrates how to create a simple shopping-basket interface using `_droptarget` (when an `item` clip is dropped onto the `basket` clip, the `item` is allowed to stay in the `basket`; otherwise, the `item` is returned to its original location):

```
// CODE ON FRAME ONE OF item
var origX = _x;
var origY = _y;

function drag() {
  this.startDrag();
}

function drop() {
  stopDrag();
  if (_droptarget != "/basket") {
    _x = origX;
    _y = origY;
  }
}

// CODE ON A BUTTON IN item
on (press) {
  drag();
}

on (release) {
  drop();
}
```

Note that `_droptarget` stores a string, not a clip reference. To convert a `_droptarget` string to a movie clip reference, use the technique shown in the example for *eval()*.

See Also

MovieClip.startDrag(), MovieClip.stopDrag()

MovieClip.duplicateMovieClip( ) Method   create a copy of a movie clip

Availability Method form introduced in Flash 5 (global form introduced in Flash 4)

Synopsis   `mc.duplicateMovieClip(`*newName, depth*`)`

Arguments

newName   A string that will become the instance name of the duplicated clip. The name must adhere to the rules for creating an identifier outlined under "Identifiers" in Chapter 14.

depth   An integer specifying the level on which to place the new clip in the programmatically generated clip stack above *mc*. A depth of –1 is below 0, 1 is in front of 0, 2 is in front of 1, and so on. See "How clips generated via duplicateMovieClip() are added to the stack" in Chapter 13 for more details. Negative depths are functional but not officially supported by ActionScript; to ensure future compatibility, use depths of 0 or greater.

Description

The *MovieClip.duplicateMovieClip()* method is an alternative to the global *duplicateMovieClip()* function. When invoked as a *MovieClip* method, *duplicateMovieClip()* takes no `target` parameter—it duplicates *mc*. The method syntax is less prone to user error than its global function counterpart.

For usage instructions, see the global *duplicateMovieClip()* function.

See Also

MovieClip.attachMovie(), *duplicateMovieClip()*

MovieClip._framesloaded Property

the number of frames of a clip or movie
that have downloaded to the Player

Availability	Flash 4 and later
Synopsis	`mc._framesloaded`
Access	Read-only

Description

The integer `_framesloaded` property indicates how many frames of *mc* have been loaded into the Player (from 0 to *mc._totalframes*). It is normally used to create preloaders that pause playback until a sufficient number of frames have downloaded. For a movie clip, the `_framesloaded` property always equals `_totalframes` (because clips are loaded in their entirety before playing) *unless* the instance is in the process of loading an external *.swf* file due to a *loadMovie()* invocation. The `_framesloaded` property is, therefore, useful only with main movies or external *.swf* files loading into instances or levels.

Preloader code is traditionally placed directly on the main timeline of the movie being preloaded. A simple approach is to loop between frames 1 and 2 until the movie has loaded, at which point we go to the movie's start frame. For example:

```
// CODE ON FRAME 1
if (_framesloaded > 0 && _framesloaded == _totalframes) {
  gotoAndPlay("beginMovie");
}
```

```
// CODE ON FRAME 2
gotoAndPlay(1);
```

In Flash 5 and later, we may alternatively use the *enterFrame* movie clip event handler to build a more portable preloader. In the movie we wish to preload, at the frame where we want preloading to start, we invoke the *stop()* function. Then we place a movie clip with the following code on that movie's timeline:

```
onClipEvent (enterFrame) {
  loaded = _parent._framesloaded;
  if (loaded > 0 && loaded == _parent._totalframes && loading != "done") {
    _parent.gotoAndPlay("beginMovie");
    loading = "done";
  }
}
```

In the preceding example, the clip tracks its parent's load progress and starts its parent playing when loading is finished. By using a movie clip as a preloader, we circumvent the need for a loop on the preloading movie's timeline. A movie clip preloader could even be turned into a Smart Clip, providing easier workflow for less experienced developers.

Notice that in our preloader examples, we checked whether _framesloaded > 0 in addition to whether _framesloaded == _totalframes. This is necessary because when a movie is unloaded from a clip, that clip has a _totalframes of 0. Hence, if _framesloaded is 0 (as it might be on a very slow connection), the comparison _framesloaded == _totalframes can return true even when no frames have yet loaded. Our check prevents the movie from skipping ahead before the appropriate content has loaded. This precaution is not necessary with main movie preloaders for *.swf* files loaded onto levels, because their _totalframes property is never zero.

Example

Preloaders often include a horizontal loading bar and a text field indicating the percentage of a movie that has downloaded. Loading bars are implemented as clips sized with either the _width property or the _xscale property. However, note that a clip scales about its registration point (proportionately on the right and left sides of the clip's registration point). Therefore, to size a clip from one side only, we must place all of the clip's content on one side of the registration point in the clip's symbol. The following example shows how to add a loading bar and a status text field to our earlier clip handler code:

```
// A Portable Preloader with a Status Bar
onClipEvent (enterFrame) {
  // Measure how many frames have loaded
  loaded = _parent._framesloaded;
  // If all the frames have finished loading...
  if (loaded > 0 && loaded == _parent._totalframes && loading != "done") {
    // ...play the movie and make a note that we're done loading
    _parent.gotoAndPlay("beginMovie");
    loading = "done";
  }
  // Determine the percentage of bytes that have loaded
  percentDone = Math.floor((_parent.getBytesLoaded()
                            / _parent.getBytesTotal()) * 100);
  // Display the percentage of loaded bytes in the text field loadStatus
  loadStatus =  percentDone + "% complete";
  // Set the size of our loadBar clip
  loadBar._xscale = percentDone;
}
```

Use the Bandwidth Profiler in Test Movie mode to simulate movie download for preloader testing.

See Also

MovieClip.getBytesLoaded(), *MovieClip._totalframes*; "data" in Chapter 10, and "The Bandwidth Profiler" in Chapter 19

MovieClip.getBounds( ) Method   determine the bounding box of a clip or movie

Availability   Flash 5

Synopsis   `mc.getBounds(targetCoordinateSpace)`

Arguments

targetCoordinateSpace

> A string indicating the path to the movie or clip in which space *mc*'s dimensions are measured. Because a movie clip reference is converted to a path when used in a string context, `targetCoordinateSpace` may also be a movie clip object reference, as in `mc.getBounds(_root)` versus `mc.getBounds("_root")`. Defaults to *mc* if not specified.

Returns

An object whose properties—**xMin**, **xMax**, **yMin**, **yMax**—describe the bounding box of the space occupied by *mc*. These four properties of the object respectfully specify the leftmost, rightmost, topmost, and bottommost pixel coordinates of *mc*.

Description

The *getBounds()* method returns an anonymous object with properties that define the rectangular area occupied by *mc* (i.e., *mc*'s *bounding box*). To retrieve the values stored in the returned object, we must access that object's properties as shown in the next example.

The dimensions of the bounding box of a clip may be measured relative to any other clip or movie. Using the `targetCoordinateSpace` argument, we may pose the question, "If *mc* resided on `targetCoordinateSpace`'s canvas, what area would it occupy?" The answer will be different depending on whether `targetCoordinateSpace` is a main movie or a clip instance; the origin point of the main movie's coordinate space is the top-left corner of the Stage, but the origin point of an instance's coordinate space is its registration point as marked in the clip's Library symbol (shown as a crosshair).

The *getBounds()* method can be used to perform basic collision detection between a movie or clip and some other point (though *MovieClip.hitTest()* serves this purpose better). It might also be used to identify a rectangular region in which to place a clip added to a movie with *MovieClip.attachMovie()*.

Example

```
var clipBounds = this.getBounds();
var leftX   = clipBounds.xMin;
var rightX  = clipBounds.xMax;
var topY    = clipBounds.yMin;
var bottomY = clipBounds.yMax;
```

See Also

MovieClip.hitTest()

MovieClip.getBytesLoaded( ) Method

check the number of bytes that have
downloaded to the Player

Availability   Flash 5

Synopsis   `mc.getBytesLoaded()`

Returns

An integer representing the number of bytes of *mc* that have finished downloading to the Player. (Divide by 1024 to convert to kilobytes.)

Description

The *getBytesLoaded()* method tells us the number of bytes of a movie that have downloaded into the Flash Player. However, *getBytesLoaded()* measures bytes in whole-frame chunks only. So if a movie's first frame is 200 bytes in size and its second frame is 3000 bytes in size, *getBytesLoaded()* will return 200 and 3200 but never any increment in between. Until *all* of a given frame has downloaded, the return value of *getBytesLoaded()* does not change. The *getBytesLoaded()* method may, therefore, be thought of as a "bytes version" of the `_framesloaded` property.

Note that internal movie clips are always entirely loaded before they are displayed, so the return value of *getBytesLoaded()* on an internal movie clip will always be the same as *getBytesTotal()* (unless the movie clip is currently loading an external *.swf* file in response to *loadMovie()*). Therefore, *getBytesLoaded()* is effective only when used with a main movie or an external *.swf* file being loaded into an instance or level.

Like `_framesloaded`, *getBytesLoaded()* is normally used to build preloaders. It can be used in concert with *getBytesTotal()* to create a more accurate progress bar than is possible with `_framesloaded` and `_totalframes` (because the byte size of each frame may not be equal—a movie with 10 frames is not 30% loaded when three frames are loaded if the frames differ widely in size).

Example

```
// CODE ON FRAME 1
if (_framesloaded > 0 && _framesloaded == _totalframes) {
  gotoAndPlay("beginMovie");
} else {
  // Show the load progress in text fields. Divide by 1024 to convert to KB.
  loadProgressOutput = this.getBytesLoaded()/1024;
  loadTotalOutput = this.getBytesTotal()/1024;
}

// CODE ON FRAME 2
gotoAndPlay(1);
```

See Also

MovieClip._framesloaded, *MovieClip.getBytesTotal()*

MovieClip.getBytesTotal( ) Method   check the size of a clip or movie, in bytes

Availability   Flash 5

Synopsis   `mc.getBytesTotal()`

Returns

An integer representing the size of *mc*, in bytes. Divide by 1024 to convert to kilobytes.

Description

The *getBytesTotal()* method tells us the size, in bytes, of a clip instance or the main movie. When invoked on the main movie, *getBytesTotal()* reports the size of the entire *.swf*. It is normally used in concert with *getBytesLoaded()* to produce preloaders for main movies and *.swf* files loaded into instances or levels.

See Also

MovieClip.getBytesLoaded(), `MovieClip._totalframes`

MovieClip.getURL( ) Method   load a document into a browser window

Availability   Method form introduced in Flash 5 (global form supported by Flash 2, enhanced in Flash 4 to include the *method* argument)

Synopsis   `mc.getURL(URL, window, method)`

Arguments

URL   A string specifying the location of the document to load or external script to run.

window   An optional string, specifying the name of the browser window or frame into which to load the document. May be a custom name or one of the four presets: `"_blank"`, `"_parent"`, `"_self"`, or `"_top"`.

method   An optional string literal specifying the method by which to send the variables from *mc* to an external script. Must be either the literal `"GET"` or `"POST"`; no other expression is allowed.

Description

The *MovieClip.getURL()* method is an alternative to the global *getURL()* function. Its method form is useful only when variables are being sent, in which case *getURL()* sends the variables from *mc*, which does not have to be the current timeline.

See Also

For general usage instructions, see the global *getURL()* function.

MovieClip.globalToLocal( ) Method   convert a point on the main Stage to clip coordinates

Availability   Flash 5

Synopsis   `mc.globalToLocal(point)`

Arguments

point   A reference to an object with two properties, `x` and `y`, that describe a point on the main Stage of the Player (i.e., on `_root`). Both `x` and `y` may be any floating-point number.

Description

The *globalToLocal()* method converts the `x` and `y` properties of *point* from coordinates on the main Stage to coordinates in the coordinate space of *mc*. Note that *globalToLocal()* does not return a new object, it merely modifies the existing `x` and `y` values of *point*.

To use *globalToLocal()*, we must first create an object with `x` and `y` properties. For example:

```
var myPoint = new Object();
myPoint.x = 10;
myPoint.y = 20;
```

The x and y properties of our object are positions on the horizontal and vertical axes of the main Stage, relative to its top-left corner. For example, an x of 10 is 10 pixels to the right of the Stage's left edge, and a y of 20 is 20 pixels below the Stage's top border. With our object created and our x and y properties set, we then pass the object to the *globalToLocal()* method, as in:

```
myClip.globalToLocal(myPoint);
```

When *globalToLocal()* is executed, the values of myPoint's x and y properties are transformed to represent a point in the space of myClip, measured from myClip's registration point. By examining the new values of our myPoint object's properties, we answer the question, "Where does the point *(x, y)* of the main Stage appear in myClip?" For example:

```
xInClip = myPoint.x;
yInClip = myPoint.y;
```

Example

The following example calculates the offset from the upper-left corner of the main Stage to the registration point of the current clip:

```
pt = new Object();        // Create generic object to hold our point
pt.x = 0;                 // Left border of main Stage
pt.y = 0;                 // Top border of main Stage
this.globalToLocal(pt);   // Convert pt to local coordinates

trace("From the current clip, the top-left corner of the main Stage is at ");
trace("x: " + pt.x + "y: " + pt.y);
```

See Also

MovieClip.localToGlobal()

MovieClip.gotoAndPlay( ) Method   jump to a given frame, then play

Availability	Method form introduced in Flash 5 (global form supported by Flash 2 and later)
Synopsis	*mc*.gotoAndPlay(*frameNumber*) *mc*.gotoAndPlay(*frameLabel*)

Arguments

frameNumber   A positive integer indicating the number of the frame to which the playhead of *mc* should jump before playing. If *frameNumber* is less than 1 or greater than the number of frames in *mc*'s timeline, the playhead is sent to either the first or last frame, respectively.

frameLabel   A string indicating the label of the frame to which the playhead of *mc* should jump before playing. If *frameLabel* is not found, the playhead is sent to the first frame of *mc*'s timeline.

Description

The *MovieClip.gotoAndPlay()* method is an alternative to the global *gotoAndPlay()* function. Use the method form to control remote movie clips or movies, specified by *mc*.

For general usage instructions, see the global *gotoAndPlay()* function.

Example

```
// Send the part1 clip to the label intro, then play part1
part1.gotoAndPlay("intro");
```

MovieClip.gotoAndStop( ) Method   jump to a given frame, and stop the playhead

Availability   Method form introduced in Flash 5 (global form supported by Flash 2 and later)

Synopsis   `mc.gotoAndStop(frameNumber)`
                `mc.gotoAndStop(frameLabel)`

Arguments
frameNumber   A positive integer indicating the number of the frame to which the playhead of *mc* should jump. If `frameNumber` is less than 1 or greater than the number of frames in *mc*'s timeline, the playhead is sent to either the first or last frame, respectively.

frameLabel   A string indicating the label of the frame to which the playhead of *mc* should jump. If `frameLabel` is not found, the playhead is sent to the first frame of *mc*'s timeline.

Description

The *MovieClip.gotoAndStop()* method is an alternative to the global *gotoAndStop()* function. Use the method form to control remote movie clips or main movies specified by *mc*.

For general usage instructions, see the global *gotoAndStop()* function.

Example

```
// Send the mainMenu clip to frame 6 and stop the playhead there
mainMenu.gotoAndStop(6);
```

MovieClip._height Property   height of a clip or movie, in pixels

Availability   Flash 4; enhanced in Flash 5

Synopsis   `mc._height`

Access   Read-only in Flash 4; read/write in Flash 5

Description

The floating-point `_height` property is a non-negative number specifying the height of *mc*, in pixels. If *mc* has no content, `_height` is 0. The `_height` property measures the content of a clip as the distance between the highest occupied pixel and the lowest occupied pixel, even if there is empty space between those pixels. An *occupied pixel* is a pixel that contains a shape, graphic, button, movie clip, or other content element. Changes made to a clip's height in the authoring tool or via `_yscale` are reflected by `_height`.

We may set the value of _height in order to vertically resize a movie clip. Attempts to set _height to a negative value are ignored. Setting a clip's _height to 0 does not make it invisible; rather, the clip becomes a one-pixel horizontal line.

The _height of the main movie (either _root._height or _level*n*._height) is not the Stage height as specified under Modify → Movie → Dimensions in the authoring tool but rather the height of the contents of the main movie. There is no explicit Stage height property; if required, we must provide the Stage height manually as a variable. For example, if a movie's Stage has a height of 400, we could add the following variable:

```
_root.stageHeight = 400;
```

To make that value available on the timeline of any clip, use:

```
Object.prototype.stageHeight = 400;
```

Usage

Note that when we set the height of a movie clip, lines are scaled proportionally, losing their original point size as set in the Stroke panel. However, the point size of lines set to Hairline in the Stroke panel is not scaled when a movie clip is resized. That is, use hairlines to prevent your strokes from appearing fat or distorted when a clip is scaled.

Example

```
ball._height = 20;          // Set the height of ball to 20 pixels
ball._height /= 2;          // Reduce the height of ball by a factor of 2
```

See Also

MovieClip._width, *MovieClip._yscale*

MovieClip.hitTest( ) Method   check whether a point is in a clip or two clips intersect

Availability   Flash 5

Synopsis   *mc*.hitTest(*x, y, shapeFlag*)
                   mc.hitTest(*target*)

Arguments
x   The horizontal coordinate of the point to test.

y   The vertical coordinate of the point to test.

shapeFlag   An optional Boolean value indicating whether the collision test should detect against the bounding box of *mc* (false) or the actual pixels of *mc* (true). Defaults to false if not supplied. Note that *shapeFlag* may be used only with the *x* and *y* arguments, not the *target* argument. It is meaningful only when *mc* has an irregular contour or a hole like a donut; it has no effect if *mc* is a solid rectangular object.

target   A string indicating the path to the movie clip to test for collision with *mc*. Because movie clip references are converted to paths when used in a string context, *target* may also be a movie clip object reference, as in *mc*.hitTest(ball) versus *mc*.hitTest("ball").

Returns

A Boolean indicating the result of the collision-detection test. The result is `true` under any of the following circumstances:

- The point *(x, y)* on the main Stage intersects with any occupied pixel of *mc*. An occupied pixel is one that contains a visual element, such as a shape or text.

- The *shapeFlag* property is `false` and the point *(x, y)* on the main Stage intersects with any pixel in the bounding box of *mc*. The bounding box of *mc* is the smallest rectangle that can encompass every occupied pixel of *mc*.

- Any pixel in the bounding box of *target* intersects any pixel in the bounding box of *mc*.

The result is `false` under any of the following circumstances:

- The *shapeFlag* property is `true` and the point *(x, y)* on the main Stage does not intersect with any occupied pixel of *mc*. An occupied pixel is one that contains a visual element, such as a shape or text.

- The point *(x, y)* on the main Stage does not intersect with any pixel in the bounding box of *mc*. The bounding box of *mc* is the smallest rectangle that can encompass every occupied pixel of *mc*.

- No pixels in the bounding box of *target* intersect with any pixel in the bounding box of *mc*.

Description

The *hitTest()* method is used to determine whether a movie clip or specific point intersects with (i.e., "hits") *mc*.

When checking to see if a point intersects *mc*, we provide *hitTest()* with the *x* and *y* coordinates of the point to check (relative to the main Stage). We may also provide the optional *shapeFlag* argument, which indicates whether the collision test should use the actual pixels of *mc*, or just *mc*'s bounding box (the smallest rectangle that can encompass every occupied pixel of *mc*). Checking the actual pixels of *mc* allows us to determine whether the point *(x, y)* is an occupied pixel inside the contour of *mc*, not merely whether it is any point inside *mc*'s bounding box.

When we're checking to see if a movie clip intersects *mc*, we provide *hitTest()* with the *target* argument specifying the clip to check. Collision detection between *target* and *mc* always uses the bounding boxes of the clips; *hitTest()* does not support pixel-perfect clip-versus-clip detection. Manual pixel-perfect collision-detection routines can be difficult to create and processor-intensive to run. In many situations—for example, a simple spaceship game—it's common practice to detect against a bounding circle rather than exact pixels.

Usage

Note that collision is always tested relative to the location of *mc* on the main Stage of the Player. Therefore, when *hitTest()* is used with a single point, the arguments x and y should always describe a point using Stage coordinates. See *MovieClip.localToGlobal()* for information on converting clip coordinates to Stage coordinates. In clip-versus-clip detection, the coordinates of clips on different timelines are automatically converted to global (i.e., Stage) coordinates.

Example

This example shows how to manually detect the intersection of two circles without using *hitTest()*:

```
// Check the distance between two circular clips on both axes
var deltaX = clip1._x - clip2._x;   // Horizontal distance
var deltaY = clip1._y - clip2._y;   // Vertical distance

// Store the radius of each circle in a convenient property
var radius1 = clip1._width / 2;
var radius2 = clip2._width / 2;

// If the distance between the circles' centers squared is less
// than or equal to the total length of the two radii squared,
// an intersection occurs.
if ((deltaX * deltaX) + (deltaY * deltaY)
    <= (radius1 + radius2) * (radius1 + radius2)) {
  trace("intersecting");
} else {
  trace("not intersecting");
}
```

Here we check whether `paddle` intersects `ball` using *hitTest()*:

```
if (paddle.hitTest("ball")) {
  trace("The paddle hit the ball.");
}
```

Here we check whether the mouse pointer is over an occupied pixel within `tractor`'s contour. Notice that the coordinates of the pointer are given in relation to `_root` (the main Stage). Gaps in a movie clip are detectable when *shapeFlag* is `true`; for example, if the `tractor` uses empty space to represent its windows, then *hitTest()* will return `false` when the pointer is over a window:

```
if (tractor.hitTest(_root._xmouse, _root._ymouse, true)) {
  trace("You're pointing to the tractor.");
}
```

See Also

MovieClip.getBounds(), MovieClip.localToGlobal()

MovieClip.loadMovie( ) Method   load an external *.swf* file into the Player

Availability   Method form introduced in Flash 5 (global form supported by Flash 4)

Synopsis   `mc.loadMovie(URL)`
            `mc.loadMovie(URL, method)`

Arguments
URL   A string specifying the location of the external *.swf* file to load.

method   An optional string literal indicating the method by which to send variables to an external script. Must be either the literal `"GET"` or `"POST"`; no other expression is allowed.

Description

The *MovieClip.loadMovie()* method is an alternative to the global *loadMovie()* function. When invoked as a *MovieClip()* method, *loadMovie()* takes no `target` parameter; it loads the *.swf* at *URL* into *mc*. The method syntax is less prone to user error than its global function counterpart.

For usage instructions, see the global *loadMovie()* function.

See Also

loadMovie(); "Method versus global function overlap issues" in Chapter 13

MovieClip.loadVariables( ) Method — retrieve an external set of variables

Availability   Method form introduced in Flash 5 (global form supported by Flash 4 and later)

Synopsis
```
mc.loadVariables(URL)
mc.loadVariables(URL, method)
```

Arguments

URL   A string specifying the path to one of two variable sources: a script that produces variables as output or a text file containing variables.

method   An optional string literal indicating the method by which to send the variables from *mc* to an external script. If specified, variables are both sent and loaded. If omitted, variables are loaded only. Must be either the literal `"GET"` or `"POST"`; no other expression is allowed.

Description

The *MovieClip.loadVariables()* method is an alternative to the global *loadVariables()* function. When invoked as a *MovieClip* method, *loadVariables()* takes no `target` parameter; it loads the variables at *URL* into *mc*. The method syntax is less prone to user error than its global function counterpart.

For usage instructions, see the global *loadVariables()* function.

See Also

loadVariables(); "Method versus global function overlap issues" in Chapter 13

MovieClip.localToGlobal( ) Method — convert a point in a clip to main Stage coordinates

Availability   Flash 5

Synopsis
```
mc.localToGlobal(point)
```

Arguments

point   A reference to an object with two properties, **x** and **y**, that describe a point in *mc*'s coordinate space. Both **x** and **y** may be any floating-point number.

Description

The *localToGlobal()* method converts the x and y properties of *point* from coordinates given in *mc*'s coordinate space to coordinates on the main Stage of the Player. Note that *localToGlobal()* does not return a new object, it merely modifies the existing x and y values of *point*.

To use *localToGlobal()*, we must first create a so-called *point* or *coordinates* object with x and y properties. To do so, we'll simply create a generic object from the *Object* class, and add x and y properties to it:

```
myPoint = new Object();
myPoint.x = 10;
myPoint.y = 20;
```

The x and y properties of our object are positions on the horizontal and vertical axes of *mc*, relative to *mc*'s registration point (shown as a crosshair in *mc*'s Library symbol). For example, an x of 10 is 10 pixels to the right of *mc*'s registration point, and a y of 20 is 20 pixels below *mc*'s registration point. With our object created and our x and y properties set, we then pass the object to the *localToGlobal()* method, as in:

```
myClip.localToGlobal(myPoint);
```

When *localToGlobal()* is executed, the values of myPoint's x and y properties are transformed to represent the corresponding point on the main Stage, measured from the Stage's upper-left corner. By examining the new values of our myPoint object's properties, we answer the question "Where does the point *(x, y)* of the movie clip appear on the main Stage?" For example:

```
mainX = myPoint.x;
mainY = myPoint.y;
```

Example

The following example determines the location of a clip's registration point relative to the main Stage:

```
pt = new Object();
pt.x = 0;                  // Horizontal registration point of clip
pt.y = 0;                  // Vertical registration point of clip
this.localToGlobal(pt);    // Convert pt to main Stage coordinates

trace("On the main Stage, the registration point of the current clip is at: ");
trace("x: " + pt.x + "y: " + pt.y);
```

The *localToGlobal()* method can be used to convert a point to Stage coordinates for use with the *hitTest()* method, which expects points to be supplied in the Stage's coordinate space. It can also be used to compare points in two different movie clips using a common coordinate space.

See Also

MovieClip.globalToLocal(), *MovieClip.hitTest()*

MovieClip._name Property   the identifier of a clip instance, as a string

Availability   Flash 4 and later

Synopsis	`mc._name`
Access	Read/write

Description

The `_name` property specifies the instance name of a movie clip instance as a string. Because it initially reflects the instance name set in the Instance panel during authoring, the `_name` property doesn't apply to main movies (the main movie is most easily referred to by the global property `_root`).

Example

We can use `_name` to determine whether or not to perform some manipulation of a given clip, as we did when generating a series of star movie clips in Example 10-2.

The `_name` property may also be used to reassign the identifier of a clip. For example:

```
// Change ball to circle
ball._name = "circle";

// Now control the former ball as circle
circle._x = 500;
```

See Also

`MovieClip._target`, *targetPath()*; "Instance Names" in Chapter 13

MovieClip.nextFrame( ) Method

advance a clip or movie's playhead one frame and stop it

Availability	Method form introduced in Flash 5 (global form supported by Flash 2 and later)
Synopsis	`mc.nextFrame()`

Description

The *MovieClip.nextFrame()* method is an alternative to the global *nextFrame()* function. Use the method form to control remote movie clips or main movies specified by *mc*.

For general usage instructions, see the global *nextFrame()* function.

Example

```
// Advance slideshow one frame and stop the playhead
slideshow.nextFrame();
```

See Also

MovieClip.prevFrame(), *nextFrame()*

MovieClip._parent Property

a reference to the host clip or movie containing this clip

Availability	Flash 4 and later

Synopsis   `mc._parent`

Access   Read-only

Description

The `_parent` property stores a reference to the clip object upon whose timeline *mc* resides. Main movies don't support the `_parent` property because they are at the top level (conveniently referred to as `_root`). References to `_root._parent` return `undefined`. The `_parent` property gives us the powerful ability to manipulate clips in relation to the current clip.

Bugs

Though it is possible in Flash 5 to reassign the `_parent` property to another clip, doing so has little purpose—only the reference is changed, not the physical structure of the clips. This unintentional behavior will likely be changed in the future.

Example

If *mc* resides on the main timeline of a movie, we can play the main timeline from *mc* using:

```
_parent.play();
```

We may also set the parent timeline's properties, as in:

```
_parent._alpha = 50;
```

The `_parent` property may also be used in succession; that is, we may access the `_parent` of a `_parent`, as follows:

```
_parent._parent.play();  // Play the clip two clips above the current clip
```

See Also

`_root`; "Referring to Nested Instances" in Chapter 13

MovieClip.play( ) Method   begin the sequential display of frames in a clip or movie

Availability   Method form introduced in Flash 5 (global form supported by Flash 2 and later)

Synopsis   `mc.play()`

Description

The *MovieClip.play()* method is an alternative to the global *play()* function. Use the method form to control remote movie clips or main movies specified by *mc*.

For general usage instructions, see the global *play()* function.

Example

```
// Begin playing clip intro
intro.play();
```

See Also

MovieClip.stop(), *play()*

MovieClip.prevFrame( ) Method   send a clip or movie's playhead
                                                    back one frame and stop it

Availability   Method form introduced in Flash 5 (global form supported by Flash 2
                   and later)

Synopsis   `mc.prevFrame()`

Description

The *MovieClip.prevFrame()* method is an alternative to the global *prevFrame()* function.
Use the method form to control remote movie clips or main movies specified by *mc*.

For general usage instructions, see the global *prevFrame()* function.

Example

```
// Rewind slideshow one frame and stop it
slideshow.prevFrame();
```

See Also

MovieClip.nextFrame(), prevFrame()

MovieClip.removeMovieClip( ) Method   delete a movie clip from the Flash Player

Availability   Method form introduced in Flash 5 (global form supported by Flash 4
                   and later)

Synopsis   `mc.removeMovieClip()`

Description

The *MovieClip.removeMovieClip()* method is an alternative to the global *removeMovieClip()*
function. When invoked as a *MovieClip* method, *removeMovieClip()* takes no `target`
parameter; it removes *mc*. The method syntax is less prone to user error than its global
function counterpart.

For usage instructions, see the global *removeMovieClip()* function.

See Also

duplicateMovieClip(), MovieClip.attachMovie(), MovieClip.duplicateMovieClip(); "Method
versus global function overlap issues" in Chapter 13

MovieClip._rotation Property   rotation, in degrees, of a clip or movie

Availability   Flash 4 and later

Synopsis   `mc._rotation`

Access   Read/write

Description

The floating-point `_rotation` property specifies the number of degrees *mc* is rotated from
its original orientation (if *mc* is a clip, the *original orientation* is that of its symbol in the

Library). Both authoring tool and programmatic adjustments are reflected in _rotation. Numbers in the range 0 to 180.0 rotate the clip clockwise. Numbers in the range 0 to –180.0 rotate the clip counter-clockwise. The same effect is achieved when rotating a clip *n* degrees or *n–360* degrees (where *n* is positive). For example, there is no difference between rotating a clip +299.4 degrees or –60.6 degrees. Likewise, when *n* is negative, there is no difference between *n* degrees and *n+360* degrees. For example, rotating a clip –90 degrees is the same as rotating it +270 degrees.

When _rotation is set to anything outside the range of –180 to 180, the value is brought into the proper range according to the following calculation:

```
x = newRotation % 360;
if (x > 180) {
  x -= 360;
} else if (x < -180) {
  x += 360;
}
_rotation = x;
```

Bugs

In the Flash 4 Player, setting the _rotation of a clip reduces the scale of that clip by a fractional amount. Over many _rotation settings, a clip will actually shrink noticeably. To account for this bug, set the _xscale and _yscale of the clip to 100 whenever setting the _rotation.

Example

Placing the following code on a clip causes the clip to rotate 5 degrees clockwise each time a frame is rendered:

```
onClipEvent (enterFrame) {
  _rotation += 5;
}
```

MovieClip.startDrag( ) Method   make a movie or movie clip follow the mouse

Availability	Method form introduced in Flash 5 (global form supported by Flash 4 and later)

Synopsis	`mc.startDrag()`
	`mc.startDrag(lockCenter)`
	`mc.startDrag(lockCenter, left, top, right, bottom)`

Arguments	
lockCenter	A Boolean indicating whether the registration point of *mc* should be centered under the mouse pointer (`true`) or dragged relative to its original location (`false`).
left	A number specifying the x-coordinate to the left of which *mc*'s registration point may not be dragged.
top	A number specifying the y-coordinate above which *mc*'s registration point may not be dragged.

right   A number specifying the x-coordinate to the right of which *mc*'s registration point may not be dragged.

bottom   A number specifying the y-coordinate below which *mc*'s registration point may not be dragged.

Description

The *MovieClip.startDrag( )* method is an alternative to the global *startDrag( )* function. When invoked as a *MovieClip* method, *startDrag( )* takes no **target** parameter; it drags *mc*. The method syntax is less prone to user error than its global function counterpart.

For usage instructions, see the global *startDrag( )* function.

Bugs

Note that the correct order of the constraining rectangular coordinates is left, top, right, bottom but that the Flash 5 ActionScript Dictionary lists them in the wrong order under *MovieClip.startDrag( )*.

Example

```
// Button code to drag and drop the current clip or movie
on (press) {
  this.startDrag(true);
}

on (release) {
  stopDrag();
}
```

See Also

MovieClip.stopDrag( ), *startDrag( )*, *stopDrag( )*; "Method versus global function overlap issues" in Chapter 13

MovieClip.stop( ) Method   pause a clip or movie

Availability   Method form introduced in Flash 5 (global form supported by Flash 2 and later)

Synopsis   `mc.stop()`

Description

The *MovieClip.stop( )* method is an alternative to the global *stop( )* function. Use the method form to control remote movie clips or main movies specified by *mc*.

For general usage instructions, see the global *stop( )* function.

Example

```
// Halt the playback of spinner
spinner.stop();
```

See Also

MovieClip.play( ), *stop( )*

MovieClip.stopDrag( ) Method   end a drag operation in progress

Availability   Method form introduced in Flash 5 (global form supported by Flash 4 and later)

Synopsis   `mc.stopDrag()`

Description

The *MovieClip.stopDrag()* method is an alternative to the global *stopDrag()* function. However, there is no need to use the method form; *stopDrag()* cancels any drag operation in progress, whether invoked through a movie clip or as a global function.

See Also

MovieClip.startDrag(), stopDrag()

MovieClip.swapDepths( ) Method   change the graphic layering of an instance
in the instance stack

Availability   Flash 5

Synopsis   `mc.swapDepths(target)`
`mc.swapDepths(depth)`

Arguments
target   A string indicating the path to the movie clip to be swapped with *mc*. Because movie clip references are converted to paths when used in a string context, `target` may also be a movie clip object reference, as in `mc.swapDepths(window2)` versus `mc.swapDepths("window2")`.

depth   An integer specifying a level in *mc*'s parent's clip stack. A depth of −1 is below 0, 1 is in front of 0, 2 is in front of 1, and so on. See "Movie and Instance Stacking Order" in Chapter 13 for more details. Negative depths are functional, but not officially supported by ActionScript; to ensure future compatibility, use depths of 0 or greater.

Description

All movie clip instances in a *.swf* document reside in a stack that governs the visual layering of instances in the Player. The stack is structured like a deck of cards; clips in higher positions in the stack appear in front of clips in lower positions. The position of an instance in the stack is initialized when the clip is created (either in the Flash authoring tool or via *attachMovie()* or *duplicateMovieClip()*). Using *swapDepths()*, we can change the position of an instance in the stack.

The *swapDepths()* method takes two forms. When used with a `target` argument, *swapDepths()* trades the stack position of *mc* and `target`, provided that *mc* and `target` share the same parent clip (reside on the same timeline). When used with a `depth` argument, *swapDepths()* places *mc* in a new position in *mc*'s parent stack. If that position is occupied, the previous occupant is moved to *mc*'s old position. Note that *swapDepths()* cannot be used to move a clip outside of the stack maintained by its parent. For information on how movies and movie clips are stacked in the Player, see "Movie and Instance Stacking Order" in Chapter 13.

Bugs

Note that swapping a duplicated or attached instance with a manually created instance via the `depth` argument can cause redraw problems in the Flash 5 Player. Treat the `depth` argument with prudence, and always test depth-swapping code extensively.

See Also

"Movie and Instance Stacking Order" in Chapter 13

MovieClip._target Property — the target path of a clip or movie, in slash syntax

Availability   Flash 4 and later

Synopsis   `mc._target`

Access   Read-only

Description

The `_target` property represents the path to *mc* in a Flash 4-style slash notation string. For example, if a clip, `ball`, resides on the main movie timeline, `ball`'s `_target` property is `"/ball"`. A clip, `stripe`, inside `ball` would have a `_target` of `"/ball/stripe"`.

To retrieve a string giving the path to a clip in dot notation, use the *targetPath( )* function.

See Also

targetPath( )

MovieClip._totalframes Property — the total number of frames in a clip or movie timeline

Availability   Flash 4 and later

Synopsis   `mc._totalframes`

Access   Read-only

Description

The integer `_totalframes` property represents the number of frames in *mc*'s timeline, where *mc* is a movie clip or main movie. A new clip or main movie always has a `_totalframes` of 1. But if the contents of a clip are unloaded via *unloadMovie()*, `_totalframes` becomes 0. It may also be 0 momentarily while the current clip is unloaded before a new clip is loaded during a *loadMovie()* operation over a slow connection. The `_totalframes` property is most often used along with `_frameloaded` to create preloaders as shown in the entry for `MovieClip._framesloaded`.

See Also

`MovieClip._framesloaded`

MovieClip.unloadMovie( ) Method   remove a movie or movie clip from the Player

Availability   Method form introduced in Flash 5 (global form supported by Flash 3 and later)

Synopsis   `mc.unloadMovie()`

The *MovieClip.unloadMovie()* method is an alternative to the global *unloadMovie()* function. When invoked as a *MovieClip* method, *unloadMovie()* takes no `target` parameter; it unloads *mc*. The method syntax is less prone to user error than its global function counterpart.

For usage instructions, see the global *unloadMovie()* function.

Example

```
// Removes a loaded document from level 1
_level1.unloadMovie();
```

See Also

MovieClip.loadMovie(), *unloadMovie()*; "Method versus global function overlap issues" in Chapter 13

MovieClip._url Property   the network address from which a clip or movie was loaded

Availability   Flash 4 and later

Synopsis   `mc._url`

Access   Read-only

Description

The `_url` property represents the URL (Uniform Resource Locator) indicating the Internet or local disk location from which the content of *mc* was loaded, as a string. The `_url` property is always an absolute URL, never a relative one. For main movies, `_url` is simply the location of the current *.swf* file. The `_url` of all movie clips in a *.swf* file is the same as the main movie of that file unless external *.swf* files have been loaded into individual clips via *MovieClip.loadMovie()*. The `_url` of a clip that hosts an externally loaded *.swf* file is the location of the externally loaded file.

The `_url` property is sometimes used to create simple security systems that prevent a movie from playing when displayed in a unwanted location.

Example

The value of `_url` in a movie loaded from a web site looks like this:

```
"http://www.moock.org/gwen/meetgwen.swf"
```

The value of `_url` in a movie loaded from a local PC hard drive looks like this:

```
"file:///C|/data/flashfiles/movie.swf"
```

Here we check whether a movie is hosted in the desired location (if not, we display a frame that contains an error):

```
    if (_url != "http://www.moock.org/gwen/meetgwen.swf") {
      trace ("This movie is not running from its intended location.";
      gotoAndStop("accessDenied");
    }
```

See Also

MovieClip.loadMovie()

MovieClip.valueOf( ) Method   the path of a clip or movie, as a string

Availability   Flash 5

Synopsis   `mc.valueOf( )`

Returns

A string containing the full path to *mc*, using dot syntax. For example:

```
"_level1.ball"
"_level0"
"_level0.shoppingcart.product1"
```

Description

The *valueOf()* method returns a string representing the absolute path to *mc* using dot syntax notation. The *valueOf()* method is automatically invoked whenever a *MovieClip* object is used where a string is called for. For example, `trace(mc)` will generate the same result as `trace(mc.valueOf())`. It is, therefore, rarely necessary to invoke *valueOf()* explicitly.

See Also

Object.valueOf(), targetPath()

MovieClip._visible Property   whether a clip or movie is shown or hidden

Availability   Flash 4 and later

Synopsis   `mc._visible`

Access   Read/write

Description

The Boolean `_visible` property indicates whether *mc* is currently shown (`true`) or hidden (`false`). We use `_visible` as a quick means of hiding a movie clip or movie from view. Note that hidden clips may still be controlled via ActionScript and still play, stop, receive events, and otherwise operate as normal. Hidden clips are simply not displayed on screen.

The initial value of the `_visible` property for all movie clips is `true`, even for movie clips that are fully transparent or completely off stage. The `_visible` property changes only when deliberately modified by a script; think of it as a way to programmatically show and hide clips, not a reflection of all factors such as position and transparency that can affect a clip's visibility.

Hiding a movie clip using the `_visible` property is preferred to setting it to fully transparent or moving it off stage because the Flash Player does not attempt to draw the graphics in movie clips with `_visible` set to `false`, thus improving rendering performance.

Example

The following button code hides the current clip when the button is depressed and reveals it when the button is released:

```
on (press) {
  this._visible = false;
}

on (release) {
  this._visible = true;
}
```

See Also

MovieClip._alpha

MovieClip._width Property   width of a clip or movie, in pixels

Availability   Flash 4; enhanced in Flash 5

Synopsis   *mc*._width

Access   Read-only in Flash 4; read/write in Flash 5

Description

The floating-point `_width` property stores a non-negative number specifying the current width of *mc*, in pixels. If *mc* has no content, `_width` is 0. The `_width` property measures the content of a clip or movie as the distance between the leftmost occupied pixel and the rightmost occupied pixel, even if there is empty space between those pixels. An *occupied pixel* is a pixel that contains a shape, graphic, button, movie clip, or other content element. Changes made to a clip's width in the authoring tool or via `_xscale` are reflected by `_width`.

We may set the value of `_width` in order to horizontally resize a movie clip. Attempts to set `_width` to a negative value are ignored. Setting a clip's `_width` to 0 does not hide the clip, it turns it into a one-pixel vertical line.

The `_width` of the main movie (either `_root._width` or `_leveln._width`) is not the Stage width as specified under Modify → Movie → Dimensions in the authoring tool but rather the width of the contents of the main movie. There is no explicit Stage width property; if required, we must provide the Stage width manually as a variable. For example, if a movie's Stage has a width of 550, we could add the following variable:

```
_root.stageWidth = 550;
```

To make that value available on the timeline of any clip, use:

```
Object.prototype.stageWidth = 550;
```

Usage

Note that when we set the width of a movie clip, lines are scaled proportionally, losing their original point size as set in the Stroke panel. However, the point size of lines set to

Hairline in the Stroke panel is not scaled when a movie clip is resized. That is, use hairlines to prevent your strokes from appearing fat or distorted when a clip is scaled.

Example

```
ball._width = 20;       // Set the width of ball to 20 pixels
ball._width *= 2;       // Double the width of ball
```

See Also

MovieClip._height, *MovieClip._xscale*

MovieClip._x Property   horizontal location of a clip or movie, in pixels

Availability   Flash 4 and later

Synopsis   *mc._x*

Access   Read/write

Description

The floating-point _x property always indicates the horizontal position of *mc*'s *registration point,* but it is measured relative to one of three possible coordinate spaces:

- If *mc* resides on the main timeline, _x is measured relative to the *Stage's left edge.* For example, an _x of 20 would indicate that the registration point of *mc* is 20 pixels to the right of the Stage's left edge; –20 would indicate 20 pixels to the left.

- If *mc* resides on another movie clip instance's timeline, _x is measured relative to the *registration point* of that parent instance. For example, an _x of 20 would indicate that the registration point of *mc* is 20 pixels to the right of its parent instance's registration point; –20 would indicate 20 pixels to the left.

- If *mc* is the main movie, _x is the horizontal offset of the entire *.swf* document relative to the Stage's left edge. For example, an _x of 200 would indicate that the contents of the Stage are offset 200 pixels to the right of their author-time position; –200 would indicate 200 pixels to the left.

The _x property (along with all horizontal coordinates in Flash) increases to the right and decreases to the left. Fractional _x values are approximated in Flash with antialiasing (blurring).

If *mc* is contained by an instance that is scaled and/or rotated, the coordinate space it inhabits is also scaled and/or rotated. For example, if *mc*'s parent is scaled by 200% and rotated 90 degrees clockwise, _x will increase in the downward direction rather than to the right, and a single unit of _x will actually be 2 pixels instead of 1.

Because switching between instance and main movie coordinate spaces can be cumbersome, the *MovieClip* object provides the *localToGlobal()* and *globalToLocal()* methods for performing coordinate-space transformations.

Example

Placing the following code on a clip causes it to move 5 pixels to the right with each passing frame (assuming that its coordinate space hasn't been altered by transformations to its parent):

```
onClipEvent (enterFrame) {
  _x += 5;
}
```

Positioning clips via _x and _y is a fundamental task in visual ActionScript programming. The following example shows clip event handlers that cause a clip to follow the mouse at a fixed rate of speed (many other motion samples may be obtained from the online Code Depot):

```
// Make a clip follow the mouse
onClipEvent(load) {
  this.speed = 10;

  // Moves clip toward the point (leaderX, leaderY)
  function follow (clip, leaderX, leaderY) {
    // Move only if we're not at the destination
    if (clip._x != leaderX || clip._y != leaderY) {
      // Determine the distance between clip and leader
      var deltaX = clip._x - leaderX;
      var deltaY = clip._y - leaderY;
      var dist = Math.sqrt((deltaX * deltaX) + (deltaY * deltaY));

      // Allocate speed between X and Y axes
      var moveX = clip.speed * (deltaX / dist);
      var moveY = clip.speed * (deltaY / dist);

      // If the clip has enough speed to overshoot the destination,
      // just go to the destination. Otherwise move according to
      // the clip's speed.
      if (clip.speed >= dist) {
        clip._x = leaderX;
        clip._y = leaderY;
      } else {
        clip._x -= moveX;
        clip._y -= moveY;
      }
    }
  }
}

onClipEvent(enterframe) {
  follow(this, _root._xmouse, _root._ymouse);
}
```

See Also

MovieClip.globalToLocal(), MovieClip.localToGlobal(), `MovieClip._y`

MovieClip._xmouse Property
horizontal location of the mouse pointer

Availability   Flash 5

Synopsis   `mc._xmouse`

Access   Read-only

Description

The floating-point _xmouse property indicates the horizontal location of the mouse pointer's hotspot relative to the coordinate space of *mc*. If *mc* is a main movie, _xmouse is measured from the Stage's left edge. If *mc* is an instance, _xmouse is measured from the instance's registration point. To obtain a consistent _xmouse coordinate that is always measured relative to the Stage, use _root._xmouse.

Example

Placing the following code on a clip causes it to mirror the mouse pointer's horizontal position relative to the Stage (it moves left and right in a straight line):

```
onClipEvent (enterFrame) {
  _x = _root._xmouse;
}
```

See Also

MovieClip._ymouse

MovieClip._xscale Property   width of a clip or movie, as a percentage

Availability   Flash 4 and later

Synopsis   mc._xscale

Access   Read/write

Description

The floating-point _xscale property specifies the width of *mc* relative to its original width, expressed as a percentage. If *mc* is an instance, its "original width" is the width of the instance's symbol in the Library. If *mc* is a main movie, its "original width" is the width of the movie at authoring time.

When the current width of *mc* is the same as its original width, _xscale is 100. An _xscale of 200 doubles *mc*'s width relative to its original width. An _xscale of 50 halves *mc*'s width relative to its original width.

The _xscale property scales a clip about its registration point (proportionately on the right and left sides of the clip's registration point). To size a clip from one side only, place all of the clip's content on one side of the registration point in the clip's symbol (this is a useful technique for creating horizontal preloader bars). When a clip's _xscale is set to a negative value, the clip is flipped horizontally as if across a vertical mirror running through its registration point (i.e., it becomes a mirror image of itself), after which the negative value is treated as a positive. To flip a clip horizontally without resizing it, set the clip's _xscale to −100.

Example

```
// Double the width of ball (the height remains unchanged)
ball._xscale *= 2;

// Create a mirror image of ball
ball._xscale = -100;
```

See Also

MovieClip._yscale

MovieClip._y Property   vertical location of a clip or movie, in pixels

Availability   Flash 4 and later

Synopsis   mc._y

Access   Read/write

Description

The floating-point _y property always indicates the vertical position of *mc*'s *registration point,* but it is measured relative to one of three possible coordinate spaces.

- If *mc* resides on the main timeline, _y is measured relative to the *Stage's top edge.* For example, a _y of 20 would indicate that the registration point of *mc* is 20 pixels below the Stage's top edge; –20 would indicate 20 pixels above.

- If *mc* resides on another movie clip instance's timeline, _y is measured relative to the *registration point* of that parent instance. For example, a _y of 20 would indicate that the registration point of *mc* is 20 pixels below its parent instance's registration point; –20 would indicate 20 pixels above.

- If *mc* is the main movie, _y is the vertical offset of the entire *.swf* document relative to the Stage's top edge. For example, a _y of 200 would indicate that the contents of the Stage are offset 200 pixels below their author-time position; –200 would indicate 200 pixels above.

The _y property (along with all vertical coordinates in Flash) increases downward and decreases upward—the opposite of the Cartesian coordinate system. Fractional _y values are approximated in Flash with antialiasing (blurring).

If *mc* is contained by an instance that is scaled and/or rotated, the coordinate space it inhabits is also scaled and/or rotated. For example, if *mc*'s parent is scaled by 200% and rotated 90 degrees clockwise, _y will increase toward the left rather than downward, and a single unit of _y will actually be 2 pixels instead of 1.

Because switching between instance and main movie coordinate spaces can be cumbersome, the *MovieClip* object provides the *localToGlobal()* and *globalToLocal()* methods for performing coordinate-space transformations.

Example

Placing the following code on a clip causes the clip to move down 5 pixels with each passing frame (assuming that its coordinate space hasn't been altered by transformations to its parent):

```
onClipEvent (enterFrame) {
   _y += 5;
}
```

See Also

MovieClip.globalToLocal(), *MovieClip.localToGlobal()*, MovieClip._x

MovieClip._ymouse Property   vertical location of the mouse pointer

Availability   Flash 5

Synopsis   `mc._ymouse`

Access   Read-only

Description

The floating-point `_ymouse` property indicates the vertical location of the mouse pointer's hotspot relative to the coordinate space of *mc*. If *mc* is a main movie, `_ymouse` is measured from the Stage's top edge. If *mc* is an instance, `_ymouse` is measured from the instance's registration point. To obtain a consistent `_ymouse` coordinate that is always measured relative to the Stage, use `_root._ymouse`.

Example

Placing the following code on a clip causes it to mirror the mouse pointer's vertical position relative to the Stage (it moves up and down in a straight line):

```
onClipEvent (enterFrame) {
  _y = _root._ymouse;
}
```

See Also

`MovieClip._xmouse`

MovieClip._yscale Property   height of a clip or movie, as a percentage

Availability   Flash 4 and later

Synopsis   `mc._yscale`

Access   Read/write

Description

The floating-point `_yscale` property specifies the height of *mc* relative to its original height, expressed as a percentage. If *mc* is an instance, its "original height" is the height of the instance's symbol in the Library. If *mc* is a main movie, the "original height" is the height of the movie at authoring time.

When the current height of *mc* is the same as its original height, `_yscale` is 100. A `_yscale` of 200 doubles *mc*'s height relative to its original height. A `_yscale` of 50 halves *mc*'s height relative to its original height.

The `_yscale` property scales a clip about its registration point (proportionately above and below the clip's registration point). To size a clip from above or below only, place all of the clip's content above or below the registration point in the clip's symbol (this is a useful technique for creating vertical preloader bars). When a clip's `_yscale` is set to a negative value, the clip is flipped vertically as if across a horizontal mirror running through its registration point (i.e., it becomes a vertical mirror image of itself), after which the negative value is treated as a positive. To flip a clip vertically without resizing it, set the clip's `_yscale` to –100.

Example

```
// Double the height of ball (the width remains unchanged)
ball._yscale *= 2;
// Flip ball vertically
ball._yscale = -100;
```

See Also

`MovieClip._xscale`

NaN Global Property   constant representing invalid numeric data (Not-a-Number)

Availability	Flash 5
Synopsis	NaN
Access	Read-only

Description

NaN is a special numeric constant used to represent invalid numeric data (NaN is an acronym for "Not-a-Number"). Numeric operations that cannot be resolved to a legitimate number yield the value NaN. For example:

```
Math.sqrt(-1);       // An imaginary number that cannot be represented
15 - "coffee cup";   // "coffee cup" cannot be converted to a number.
```

Note that NaN is still numeric data, even though it is not a calculable number:

```
typeof NaN;     // Yields "number"
```

Usage

The value NaN is hardly ever used directly in source code but rather serves as a way for an operation to return an error condition. Because NaN does not compare equal to itself, the only way you can detect it is with the global function *isNaN()*. NaN is shorthand for `Number.NaN`.

See Also

isNaN(), `Number.NaN`; "Special Values of the Number Datatype" in Chapter 4

---

newline Constant   insert a line break

Availability	Flash 4 and later
Synopsis	newline

Returns

A newline character.

Description

The constant `newline` represents a standard line break character (ASCII 10). It is synonymous with the escape sequence `"\n"` and is used to force a line break in a block of text (usually for display in a text field variable).

Usage

Though `newline` was a function in Flash 4, it became a constant in Flash 5 and has a syntax that resembles a property or variable. Note that parentheses are not used following `newline`.

Example

```
myOutput = "hello" + newline + "world";
```

See Also

See "Escape sequences" in Chapter 4

---

nextFrame( ) Global Function

advance a movie or movie clip's
playhead one frame and stop it

Availability   Flash 2 and later

Synopsis   `nextFrame()`

Description

The *nextFrame()* function moves the playhead of the current timeline ahead one frame and stops it there. The "current timeline" is the timeline from which the *nextFrame()* function is invoked. The *nextFrame()* function is synonymous with *gotoAndStop(_currentFrame + 1);*. If invoked on the last frame of a timeline, *nextFrame()* simply stops the playhead on that frame unless another scene follows the current scene, in which case *nextFrame()* moves the playhead to frame 1 of the next scene.

See Also

gotoAndStop(), MovieClip.nextFrame(), nextScene(), prevFrame()

---

nextScene( ) Global Function

advance a movie's playhead
to frame 1 of the next scene

Availability   Flash 2 and later

Synopsis   `nextScene()`

Description

The *nextScene()* function moves the main playhead of a movie to frame 1 of the scene following the current scene and stops the main movie timeline. The "current scene" is the scene from which the *nextScene()* function is invoked. It must be invoked on a scene's main timeline in order to have an effect; that is, *nextScene()* does not work inside a movie clip or *onClipEvent()* handler. If invoked from the last scene in a movie, *nextScene()* sends the playhead to frame 1 of that scene and halts movie playback.

See Also

nextFrame(), prevScene()

Number( ) Global Function   convert a value to the *Number* datatype

Availability   Flash 5

Synopsis   Number(`value`)

Arguments
value   An expression containing the value to be converted to a number.

Returns

The result of converting `value` to a primitive number.

Description

The *Number()* function converts its argument to a primitive numeric value and returns that converted value. The results of converting various types of data to a primitive number are described in Table 3-1. It's often not necessary to use the *Number()* function; ActionScript automatically converts values to the *number* type when appropriate.

Be sure not to confuse the global *Number()* function with the *Number* class constructor. The former is a function that converts a value to the *number* type, whereas the latter is the class used to wrap a primitive numeric datum in an object that can take properties and methods.

Usage

Note that the *Number()* function frequently appears in Flash 4 *.fla* files that have been converted to the Flash 5 format. For information on how datatypes are handled when Flash 4 files are converted to Flash 5, see "Flash 4–to–Flash 5 Datatype Conversion" in Chapter 3.

See Also

The *Number* class, *parseFloat()*, *parseInt()*; "Explicit Type Conversion" in Chapter 3

Number Class   wrapper class for primitive numeric data

Availability   Flash 5

Constructor   new Number(`value`)

Arguments
value   An expression to be resolved and, if necessary, converted to a numeric value, then wrapped in a *Number* object.

Class Properties

The following properties are accessed directly as properties of the *Number* class, using Number.*propertyName*. To access them you do not need to instantiate a new *Number* object (i.e., there is no need for the constructor function). Some of these properties, such as NaN don't even require the Number.*propertyName* notation. You can simply use NaN as shorthand for Number.NaN (details for each property follow later).

MAX_VALUE	The largest representable positive number in ActionScript.
MIN_VALUE	The smallest representable positive number in ActionScript.
NaN	Special Not-a-Number value indicating invalid numeric data.

NEGATIVE_INFINITY
> Any number more negative than –MAX_VALUE.

POSITIVE_INFINITY
> Any number larger than MAX_VALUE.

Methods

toString()   Convert a number to a string.

Description

The *Number* class has two purposes:

- It gives us access to built-in properties that represent special numeric values—MIN_VALUE, MIN_VALUE, NaN, NEGATIVE_INFINITY, and POSITIVE_INFINITY—that can be used to check whether numeric data is valid.

- It can be used to convert between different number systems, such as base-10 (decimal) and base-16 (hexadecimal). Refer to *Number.toString()* method.

Usage

There is no need to create a new *Number* object if you simply want to access the numeric properties it defines. In fact, where applicable, it is easier to use global property equivalents (NaN, Infinity, and –Infinity). Frankly, it is rare that you'll need the *Number* class properties at all.

On the other hand, the *Number* class's *toString()* method is used with an instantiated *Number* object. However, the interpreter takes care of creating a *Number* object for us whenever we invoke a method on a primitive numeric value. For example:

```
x = 102;
x.toString(16);  // x is automatically converted to a Number object
                 // for the sake of this operation.
```

You might do this in order to, say, use *toString()* to convert between various number systems. Again, frankly, this is a fairly rare task, so you probably won't be using the *Number* class much.

See Also

The *Math* object; "The Number Type" in Chapter 4

Number.MAX_VALUE Property

the largest representable positive
number in ActionScript

Availability   Flash 5

Synopsis   Number.MAX_VALUE

Access   Read-only

Description

The MAX_VALUE property stores the largest representable positive number in ActionScript (1.7976931348623157e+308). It is convenient when you'd like to start with a very large value, as shown in the following example. Any number greater than MAX_VALUE can't be represented by ActionScript and is therefore considered to be POSITIVE_INFINITY.

Example

Here we are looking for a minimum value in an array. We initialize the minVal variable to MAX_VALUE, knowing that any subsequent value will be less than it:

```
var myArray = [-10, 12, 99]
var minVal = Number.MAX_VALUE
for (thisValue in myArray) {
  if (myArray[thisValue] < minVal) {
    minVal = myArray[thisValue];
  }
}
trace ("The minimum value is " + minVal);
```

See Also

Number.MIN_VALUE; Number.POSITIVE_INFINITY; "Special Values of the Number Datatype" in Chapter 4

Number.MIN_VALUE Property   the smallest representable positive
                                                        number in ActionScript

Availability   Flash 5

Synopsis   Number.MIN_VALUE

Access   Read-only

Description

The MIN_VALUE property stores the smallest representable positive number in ActionScript, 5e-324 (not to be confused with -Number.MAX_VALUE, the most-negative number allowed in ActionScript).

See Also

Number.MAX_VALUE; "Special Values of the Number Datatype" in Chapter 4

Number.NaN Property   constant representing invalid numeric
                                                        data (Not-a-Number)

Availability   Flash 5

Synopsis   Number.NaN

Access   Read-only

Description

The NaN property stores the special "invalid number" value of the *number* datatype. It is used to represent the result of an illogical mathematical calculation (e.g., 0/0) or an attempted data conversion that does not yield a legitimate number.

Number.NaN is normally used in its more convenient global property form, NaN.

Usage

The value NaN is hardly ever used directly in source code but rather serves as a way for an operation to return an error condition. The only way you can detect NaN is with the global function *isNaN()*.

See Also

isNaN(), NaN; "Special Values of the Number Datatype" in Chapter 4

Number.NEGATIVE_INFINITY Property   constant representing any number more negative than -Number.MAX_VALUE

Availability   Flash 5

Synopsis   Number.NEGATIVE_INFINITY

Access   Read-only

Description

The NEGATIVE_INFINITY property stores a special numeric value used to represent values more negative than -Number.MAX_VALUE (the most-negative number representable in ActionScript). This is known as an *underflow condition* and is typically caused by a mathematical error.

Number.NEGATIVE_INFINITY is normally used in its more convenient global property form, -Infinity.

See Also

-Infinity, *isFinite()*, Number.MAX_VALUE; "Special Values of the Number Datatype" in Chapter 4

Number.POSITIVE_INFINITY Property   constant representing any number greater than Number.MAX_VALUE

Availability   Flash 5

Synopsis   Number.POSITIVE_INFINITY

Access   Read-only

Description

The POSITIVE_INFINITY property stores a special numeric value used to represent values greater than Number.MAX_VALUE (the largest number representable in ActionScript). This is known as an *overflow condition* and is usually caused by some sort of mathematical error.

Number.POSITIVE_INFINITY is normally used in its more convenient global property form, Infinity.

Example

```
if (score == Number.POSITIVE_INFINITY) {
  trace ("You've achieved the highest possible score.");
}
```

See Also

Infinity, *isFinite()*, Number.MAX_VALUE; "Special Values of the Number Datatype" in Chapter 4

Number.toString( ) Method   convert a Number to a string

Availability   Flash 5

Synopsis   *numberObject*.toString(*radix*)

Arguments

radix   An integer between 2 and 36 specifying the base of the number system used to represent *numberObject* in string format. This argument is optional; if omitted, it defaults to 10.

Returns

The value of *numberObject* converted to a string.

Description

The *toString()* method retrieves the value of a *Number* object, converts that value to a string, and returns that string. We may use the *radix* argument to convert numeric values between different bases (e.g., binary, octal, decimal, and hexadecimal). The letters A–Z are used to represent digits with the value 10–35, respectively, although ordinarily only A through F are used (to represent the hex digits equivalent to 10 through 15).

To use *Number.toString()* with a primitive numeric value, surround the value with parentheses, as in:

```
(204).toString(16);
```

Example

```
x = new Number(255);
trace(x.toString());        // Displays: "255" (i.e., decimal)
trace(x.toString(16));      // Displays: "ff" (i.e., hexadecimal)
trace(x.toString(2));       // Displays: "11111111" (i.e., binary)

// Convert a hex literal to decimal
trace((0xFFFFFF).toString(10));  // Displays: "16777215"
```

See Also

Number (), *Object.toString()*, *parseInt()*; See "Integer Literals" in Chapter 4

Object Class   the basis for all other classes and for generic objects

Availability   Flash 5

Constructor   new Object( )

Properties

constructor   A reference to the class constructor function used to create the object.

__proto__   A reference to the **prototype** property of the object's constructor function.

Methods

toString()   Convert the value of the object to a string.

valueOf()   Retrieve the primitive value of the object, if one exists.

Description

The *Object* class is the base class of the ActionScript object model. *Object* is used for two general purposes: (a) as a constructor for creating new, generic objects, and (b) as a superclass upon which to base new classes. All classes in ActionScript, whether user-defined or built-in are descendants of the *Object* class. All objects of all classes therefore inherit the properties of *Object* (though some classes override those properties).

To create a generic object of the Object class directly in our code without using a constructor, we can use an object literal just as we might use a string literal or an array literal. An object literal is a series of comma-separated property name/value pairs, enclosed in curly braces. Here's the general syntax:

```
{ property1: value1, property2: value2, property3: value3 }
```

The names of properties in an object literal must be legal identifiers as described in Chapter 14, *Lexical Structure*. The values may be any valid expression. For example:

```
// An object literal with two numeric properties
myObject = { x: 30, y: 23 };
// Set the x property value using a complex expression
myOtherObject = { x: Math.floor(Math.random() * 50 + 1) };
```

Because object literals always create generic, anonymous objects, they are used only when we need object-formatted data temporarily, such as when, say, invoking *Sound. setTransform()*, *Color.setTransform()*, or *MovieClip.localToGlobal()*.

See Also

Chapter 12, *Objects and Classes*

Object.constructor Property

a reference to the class constructor function used to create the object

Availability   Flash 5

Synopsis   *someObject*.constructor

Access   Read/write (overwriting an object's constructor property is not recommended as it alters the natural structure of class inheritance).

Description

The constructor property stores a reference to the constructor function that was used to create *someObject*. For example, the constructor property of a *Date* object is the *Date* constructor function:

```
now = new Date();
now.constructor == Date;        // Yields true
```

See Also

"The constructor property" in Chapter 12

Object.__proto__ Property

a reference to the object's constructor's
prototype property

Availability   Flash 5

Synopsis   `someObject.__proto__`

Access   Read/write (Overwriting an object's `__proto__` property is not recom-
                  mended as it alters the natural structure of class inheritance.)

Description

The `__proto__` property stores a reference to the automatically-assigned `prototype`
property of *someObject*'s constructor function, which is used to transfer properties down
through a class hierarchy. An object's `__proto__` property is mostly used internally by
the interpreter to look up inherited properties for an object, but we can also use it to
determine the class of an object, as shown in Example 12-6 and Example 12-9. Note that
`__proto__` begins and ends with *two* underscore characters.

See Also

"The `__proto__` property" in Chapter 12

Object.toString( ) Method

the value of the object, as a string

Availability   Flash 5

Synopsis   `someObject.toString()`

Returns

An internally defined string that describes or otherwise represents the object.

Description

The *toString()* method returns a string description for *someObject*. By default,
`someObject.toString()` returns the expression:

```
"[object " + class + "]"
```

where *class* is the internally defined name of the class to which *someObject* belongs. The
ActionScript interpreter automatically invokes the *toString()* method whenever *someObject*
is used in a string context. For example:

```
x = new Object();
trace(x);        // Displays: "[object Object]"
```

Most classes overwrite the default *toString()* method of *Object* in order to provide more
meaningful information about each member of the class. For example, the *Date.toString()*
method returns the date and time, and the *Array.toString()* method returns a comma-separated list of array elements. We may do the same when constructing our own classes.

Example

This example shows how to provide a custom *toString()* method for the *Ball* class that we
created in Chapter 12:

```
// Add a Custom toString() method
// Make the Ball constructor
function Ball (radius, color, xPosition, yPosition) {
  this.radius = radius;
  this.color = color;
  this.xPosition = xPosition;
  this.yPosition = yPosition;
}

// Assign a function literal to the Ball class prototype's toString() method
Ball.prototype.toString = function () {
  return "A ball with the radius " + this.radius;
};

// Create a new ball object
myBall = new Ball(6, 0x00FF00, 145, 200);

// Now check myBall's string value
trace(myBall);   // Displays: "A ball with the radius 6"
```

See Also

Array.toString(), Date.toString(), Number.toString(), Object.valueOf()

Object.valueOf( ) Method   the primitive value of the object

Availability   Flash 5

Synopsis   *someObject*.valueOf()

Returns

The internally defined primitive value of *someObject*, if a primitive value is associated with *someObject*. If no primitive value is associated with *someObject*, then *someObject* itself is returned.

Description

The *valueOf()* method returns the primitive datum associated with an object, if such an association exists. This method is mostly commonly used with objects of the *Number, String,* and *Boolean* classes, which all have associated primitive data. The *MovieClip. valueOf()* method returns a string representing the path to the clip.

Note that it's rarely necessary to invoke *valueOf()* explicitly; it is automatically invoked by the interpreter whenever *someObject* is used where a primitive is expected.

See Also

Boolean.valueOf(),   MovieClip.valueOf(),   Number.valueOf(),   Object.toString(),   String. valueOf()

---

parseFloat( ) Global Function   extract a floating-point number from a string

Availability   Flash 5

Synopsis   parseFloat(*stringExpression*)

Arguments
stringExpression   The string from which a floating-point number is to be extracted.

Returns

The extracted floating-point number. Or, if extraction was unsuccessful, the special numeric value NaN.

Description

The *parseFloat()* function converts a string to a floating-point number (a number with a fractional portion). It works only with strings that contain a valid string representation of a floating-point number; otherwise, NaN is returned. The string must be of the following form:

- Optional leading whitespace
- Optional sign indicator + or –
- At least one digit from 0–9 and an optional decimal point
- Optional exponent starting with e or E followed by integer exponent

Trailing characters that cannot be parsed as part of the preceding numeric form are ignored.

Usage

Because user input data entered into text fields always belongs to the *string* datatype, we often use *parseFloat()* to extract numeric data from user-entered text. Note that *parseFloat()* can extract numbers from strings that contain both numbers and non-numeric characters, whereas *Number()* cannot.

Examples

```
parseFloat("14.5 apples");   // Yields 14.5
parseFloat(".123");          // Yields 0.123
var x = "15, 4, 23, 9";
parseFloat(x);               // Yields 15
```

See Also

isNaN(), NaN, *Number()*, *parseInt()*; "Explicit Type Conversion" in Chapter 3; "Integers and Floating-Point Numbers" in Chapter 4

---

parseInt( ) Global Function

extract an integer from a string or convert numbers to base-10.

Availability   Flash 5

Synopsis   parseInt(*stringExpression*)
                  parseInt(*stringExpression*, *radix*)

Arguments
stringExpression   The string from which an integer is to be extracted.

radix   An optional integer, between 2 and 36, specifying the base (or *radix*) of the integer to be extracted. If not specified, the default radix depends on the contents of *stringExpression* (as described later).

Returns

The extracted integer value, as a base-10 number regardless of the original *radix*. Or, if extraction was unsuccessful, the special numeric value NaN.

Description

The *parseInt()* function converts a string expression to an integer. It works only with strings that contain a valid string representation of an integer using the specified radix. The string must be of the following form:

- Optional leading whitespace
- Optional + or –
- One or more digits that are valid in the number system of the specified radix

Trailing characters that cannot be parsed as part of the preceding numeric form are ignored.

The number derived from the supplied string starts with the first nonblank character in the string and ends with the character before the first character that is not a legitimate digit in the supplied *radix*. For example, in the base-10 system, the letter *F* is not a valid digit, so the following expression yields the number 2:

```
parseInt("2F", 10);
```

But in the base-16 system (hexadecimal), the characters *A, B, C, D, E,* and *F are* valid numerals, so the following expression yields the number 47:

```
parseInt("2F", 16);   // 2F in hexadecimal is 47 in base-10
```

The *radix* argument of *parseInt()* specifies the base of the number as it exists in the string. In other words, using the *radix* argument we may say to the interpreter "Treat this string as a base-16 number" or "Treat this string as a base-2 number."

parseInt() also interprets the prefix 0x to indicate a hexadecimal (a.k.a. hex) number (as if a *radix* of 16 was specified) and a leading 0 to indicate an octal number (as if a *radix* of 8 was specified):

```
parseInt("0xFF");     // Parsed as hex, yields 255
parseInt("FF", 16);   // Parsed as hex, yields 255
parseInt("0377");     // Parsed as octal, yields 255 = (3 * 64) + (7 * 8) + (7 * 1)
parseInt("377", 8);   // Parsed as octal, yields 255
```

An explicit radix overrides any implicit radix:

```
parseInt ("0xFF", 10)    // Parsed as decimal, yields 0
parseInt ("0x15", 10)    // Parsed as decimal, yields 0 (not 15, and not 21)
parseInt ("0377", 10)    // Parsed as decimal, yields 377
```

Note that the *parseInt()* function extracts integer values only, unlike *parseFloat()* which can also extract fractional values but may be used only with base-10 numbers.

Example

We primarily use *parseInt()* to extract integers from a string that contains both numbers and text or to remove the decimal place from a number (similar to *Math.floor()*).

```
parseInt("Wow, 20 people were there");  // Yields NaN
parseInt("20 people were there");       // Yields 20
parseInt("1001", 2);                    // Yields 9 (1001 evaluated in binary)
parseInt(1.5);  // Yields 1 (the number 1.5 is converted to the string
           // "1.5" before the parseInt operation proceeds)
```

See Also

Math.floor(), NaN, *parseFloat()*; "Explicit Type Conversion" in Chapter 3; "Integers and Floating-Point Numbers" in Chapter 4

---

play( ) Global Function   begin the sequential display of frames in a movie

Availability   Flash 2 and later

Synopsis   play()

Description

Invoking the *play()* function initiates the sequential display of the frames in the current main movie or movie clip. The "current" movie or movie clip is the one that bears the *play()* function invocation statement. Frames are displayed at a rate dictated by the frames per second (or FPS) setting of the entire movie, which is set under the Movie Properties (Modify → Movie → Frame Rate).

Once started, the playback of a movie or movie clip continues until another function invocation specifically stops the playback. All movie clips loop (begin playing again at frame 1) when the playhead reaches the end of the timeline. In a browser, however, main movies loop only if the code used to embed the movie in the HTML page specifies that the movie should loop, as determined by the LOOP attribute. (If you're using the Publish command to embed your movie in an HTML page, set the LOOP attribute by selecting File → Publish Settings → HTML → Playback → Loop.)

See Also

gotoAndPlay(), *MovieClip.play()*, *stop()*

---

prevFrame( ) Global Function   send a movie's playhead back one frame and stop it

Availability   Flash 2 and later

Synopsis   prevFrame()

Description

The *prevFrame()* function moves the playhead of the current timeline back one frame and stops it there. The "current timeline" is the timeline from which the *prevFrame()* function is invoked. The *prevFrame()* function is synonymous with *gotoAndStop(_currentFrame - 1);*. If invoked on the first frame of a timeline, *prevFrame()* simply stops the playhead on that frame unless another scene precedes the current scene, in which case *prevFrame()* moves the playhead to the last frame of the previous scene.

See Also

gotoAndStop(), *MovieClip.prevFrame()*, *nextFrame()*, *prevScene()*

---

prevScene( ) Global Function   send a movie's playhead to frame 1
of the previous scene

Availability   Flash 2 and later

Synopsis prevScene()

Description

The *prevScene()* function moves the main playhead of a movie to frame 1 of the scene before the current scene and stops the main movie timeline. The "current scene" is the scene from which the *prevScene()* function is invoked. It must be invoked on a scene's main timeline in order to have an effect; that is, *prevScene()* does not work inside a movie clip or *onClipEvent()* handler. If invoked from the first scene in a movie, *prevScene()* sends the playhead to frame 1 of that scene and halts movie playback.

See Also

nextScene(), *prevFrame()*

---

print( ) Global Function
print the frames of a movie or movie clip using vectors

Availability Flash 5

Synopsis print(*target*, *boundingBox*)

Arguments

target A string or reference indicating the path to the movie clip or document level to print (references are converted to paths when used in a string context).

boundingBox A string indicating how the printed frames of *target* should be cropped when printed. Cropping is defined by a bounding box that represents the entire printed page. The region of *target* included in the printed page can be set using one of three legal values for *boundingBox* (which must be a literal string):

"bframe"

The bounding box for each printed frame is set individually to match the size of each frame's contents. Hence, every printed frame's content is scaled to fill the entire printed page.

"bmax"

The area occupied by the content of all printed frames is combined to form a general bounding box. Each printed frame's content is scaled and placed on the printed page relative to the general bounding box.

"bmovie"

The bounding box for all printed frames is set to the size of a single, designated frame in the *target* clip. Content of printed frames is cropped to the bounding box of that designated frame. To designate a frame as the bounding box, assign it the label #b.

Description

Printing a Flash movie using a web browser's built-in print function behaves inconsistently and often results in poor quality printouts. Using the *print()* function, we can print the contents of a movie with accuracy and quality, directly from Flash. By default, *print()* causes all of the frames of *target*'s timeline to be sent to the printer, one frame per page, cropped according to the *boundingBox* argument. To designate only specific frames for printing, we assign the label #P to the desired frames.

The *print()* function sends vectors directly to PostScript printers and vectors converted to bitmaps to non-PostScript printers. Because *print()* uses vectors, it cannot be used to print movies with alpha transparency or color transformations. To print movies that have color effects, use *printAsBitmap()*.

Usage

In Flash 4 r20 and above, the features of the various Flash 5 *print()* functions are available as a modified *getURL()* Action. For more details, see Macromedia's Flash Printing SDK, available at:

> *http://www.macromedia.com/software/flash/open/webprinting/authoring.html*

Example

```
// Print every frame in the main movie timeline,
// sizing each individually to fill the page
print("_root", "bframe");

// Print every frame in the main movie timeline,
// sizing each frame relative to the combined size of all frames
print("_root", "bmax");
```

When a button with the following code is clicked, Flash prints all frames in the button's timeline, cropped to the bounding box of the frame with the label #b and sized to fill the page:

```
on (release) {
  print(this, "bmovie");
}
```

See Also

getURL(), *printAsBitmap()*, *printAsBitmapNum()*, *printNum()*

---

printAsBitmap( ) Global Function

print the frames of a movie
or movie clip as bitmaps

Availability   Flash 5

Synopsis   printAsBitmap(*target*, *boundingBox*)

Arguments

target   A string or reference indicating the path to the movie clip or document level to print (references are converted to paths when used in a string context).

boundingBox   A string indicating how the printed frames of *target* should be cropped when printed, as described earlier under *print()*.

Description

The *printAsBitmap()* function is functionally identical to *print()*, except that it outputs rasterized content to the printer, not vectors. It can, therefore, successfully print movies with color transformations but produces poorer quality for vector-based artwork.

Usage

See Usage notes under the *print()* function.

See Also

print(), printAsBitmapNum(), printNum()

---

printAsBitmapNum( ) Global Function

print the frames of a document
level as bitmaps

Availability   Flash 5

Synopsis   `printAsBitmapNum(level, boundingBox)`

Arguments
level   A non-negative integer or an expression that yields a non-negative inte-
              ger, indicating the document level to print.

boundingBox   A string indicating how the printed frames of `target` should be cropped
              when printed, as described earlier under *print()*.

Description

The *printAsBitmapNum()* function is nearly identical to *printAsBitmap()* except that it
requires the target `level` of the print operation to be specified as a number rather than as a
string. This means that *printAsBitmapNum()* can print only document levels, not movie
clips. It is normally used when we wish to dynamically assign the level of a movie to print,
as in:

```
var x = 3;
printAsBitmapNum(x, "bmax");
```

which could also be achieved using string concatenation with the regular *printAsBitmap()*
function:

```
printAsBitmap("_level" + x, "bmax");
```

Usage

See Usage notes under the *print()* function.

See Also

print(), printAsBitmap(), printNum()

---

printNum( ) Global Function

print the frames of a document level

Availability   Flash 5

Synopsis   `printNum(level, boundingBox)`

Arguments
level   A non-negative integer or an expression that should be cropped
              ger indicating the document level to print

boundingBox   A string indicating how the printed fr
              when printed, as described earlier

Description

The *printNum()* function is nearly identical to *print()* except that it requires the target `level` of the print operation to be specified as a number rather than as a string. This means that *printNum()* can print only document levels, not movie clips. It is normally used when we wish to dynamically assign the level of a movie to print, as in:

```
var x = 3;
printNum(x, "bmax");
```

which could also be achieved using string concatenation with the regular *print()* function:

```
print("_level" + x, "bmax");
```

Usage

See Usage notes under the *print()* function.

See Also

print(), *printAsBitmap()*, *printAsBitmapNum()*

_quality Global Property   the rendering quality of the Player

Availability   Flash 5

Synopsis   `_quality`

Access   Read/write

Description

The `_quality` property stores a string that dictates the rendering quality of the Flash Player as follows:

"LOW"	Low quality. Neither bitmaps nor vectors are antialiased (smoothed).
"MEDIUM"	Medium quality. Vectors are moderately antialiased.
"HIGH"	High quality. Vectors are highly antialiased. Bitmaps are antialiased when no animation is occurring.
"BEST"	Best quality. Both bitmaps and vectors are always antialiased.

Lower rendering quality means that fewer calculations are required to draw a frame of the movie, resulting in faster performance. The typical setting of `_quality` for most movies is "HIGH".

Ex

Here

slowest the rendering quality of a movie to the best it can be (which also causes the `_quack`):

See Also   "EST";

`_highQual`

HighQuality()

random( ) Global Function   generate a random number

Availability   Flash 4; deprecated in Flash 5 in favor of *Math.random()*

Synopsis   random(*number*)

Arguments
number   A positive integer.

Returns

A random integer greater than or equal to 0 and less than *number*.

Description

The deprecated *random()* function was used in Flash 4 to generate random numbers. This function has been retired from the language and is available only for the sake of backward compatibility. In Flash 5 and higher, use the preferred *Math.random()* method. Note that *random()* generated integers from 0 to **number** –1, whereas *Math.random()* generates floats from 0.0 to .999.

See Also

Math.random()

---

removeMovieClip( ) Global Function   delete a movie clip from the Flash Player

Availability   Flash 4; enhanced in Flash 5 to apply to instances created with *attachMovie()*

Synopsis   removeMovieClip(*target*)

Arguments
target   A string or reference indicating the path to the movie clip instance to be removed from the Player (references to movie clips are converted to paths when used in a string context).

Description

The *removeMovieClip()* function deletes the specified movie clip from the Player, leaving no trace of the clip's contents or shell. Subsequent references to the clip or any of its variables or properties yield **undefined**.

The *removeMovieClip()* function may be used only on movie clip instances that were originally created via *duplicateMovieClip()* or *attachMovie()*. It has no effect on movie clips created in the authoring tool.

See Also

attachMovie(), *duplicateMovieClip()*, *MovieClip().removeMovieClip()*; "Removing Clip Instances and Main Movies" in Chapter 13

_root Global Property   a reference to the main timeline of the movie in the current level

Availability   Flash 5 (same as "/" in Flash 4 movies)

Synopsis   _root

Access   Read-only

Description

The _root property stores a reference to the main timeline of the current document level. We use _root to invoke methods on the main movie or to retrieve and set the main movie's properties. For example:

```
_root.play();       // Play the main timeline
_root._alpha = 40;  // Make the whole movie partially transparent
```

The _root property may also be used to refer to nested clips. For example:

```
_root.myClip.play();
_root.shapes.square._visible = false;
```

The _root property provides access to a movie clip in absolute terms. That is, a reference that starts with _root is valid (and invariant) from anywhere in a movie.

See Also

_level*n*; _parent; "Referring to Main Movies with _root and _leveln" in Chapter 13 and "Accessing Variables on Different Timelines" in Chapter 2

---

scroll Property   the current top line displayed in a text field

Availability   Flash 4 and later

Synopsis   `textfield.scroll`

Returns

A positive integer representing the number of the topmost viewable line of a text field.

Description

The `scroll` text field property can be both retrieved and set. When we retrieve the value of a text field's `scroll` property, it indicates the number of the line currently displayed as the first line in the field's viewable region. When we set the value of `scroll`, it scrolls the text field, making the supplied line number the top line in the field's viewable region. The `scroll` property is normally used with `maxscroll` to create text-scrolling interfaces as described under "Typical Text-Scrolling Code" in Chapter 18, *On-Screen Text Fields*.

Usage

Though `scroll` is listed as a function in Flash, it is effectively used as a property of a text field variable. Notice that parentheses are not used when `scroll` is invoked.

Bugs

In Build 5.0 r30 of the Flash Player, when a text field's font is embedded, using `scroll` may cause some text to be displayed outside the visual region of the field. Some text may not be removed as the text in the field scrolls. To work around the problem, use a mask over the text field layer. This problem was fixed in Build 5.0 r41.

Example

```
// Sets x to the index of the top line displayed in myField
var x = myField.scroll;
// Scrolls the text in myField down one
myField.scroll++;
```

See Also

maxscroll; "The scroll Property" in Chapter 18

Selection Object   control over text field selections

Availability   Flash 5

Synopsis   Selection.*methodName*()

Methods

getBeginIndex()	Retrieve the index of the first selected character.
getCaretIndex()	Retrieve the index of the insertion point.
getEndIndex()	Retrieve the index of the last selected character.
getFocus()	Identify the text field in which the insertion point currently resides.
setFocus()	Place the insertion point in a specific text field.
setSelection()	Select characters in the currently focused text field.

Description

We use the *Selection* object to control user interaction with text fields and to capture portions of text fields. In actual use, the *Selection* object methods are preceded by the keyword Selection; they always operate on the text field with focus, of which there can be only one at any given time. The methods of a *Selection* object can position the insertion point and can select or retrieve a text field's content. These abilities add subtle but important behavior to user-input systems. For example, in a user-login screen, we can prompt a user to enter his name by placing the cursor in a name-entry text field. Or we can highlight an error in a form by selecting the problematic text. We can also customize the so-called *Tab order* of a series of text fields, as shown under "Selection.setFocus( ) Method."

Positions of the characters in a text field are referred to with zero-relative indexes where the first character is index 0, the second is index 1, and so on. Character indexing is described in detail in "Character Indexing" in Chapter 4.

In Flash 5 it is not possible to cut, copy, or paste text programmatically. Further, cut, copy, and paste shortcut keys such as Ctrl-C and Ctrl-V are not functional in the Flash Player. The secondary mouse button (right-click on Windows, Ctrl-click on Macintosh) provides access to the cut, copy, and paste commands.

Usage

Clicking, a form's submit button automatically removes focus from any previously focused text field. To capture a selection before focus is lost, use the button's rollover event. For example:

```
on (rollOver) {
  focusedField = Selection.getFocus();
}
```

See Also

_focusrect, *Selection.setFocus()*; Chapter 18, *On-Screen Text Fields*

Selection.getBeginIndex( ) Method

retrieve the index of a text field's
first selected character

Availability   Flash 5

Synopsis   `Selection.getBeginIndex()`

Returns

The index of the first character in the current selection (highlighted block of text). If no text field has keyboard focus, it returns –1. If a text field has focus but no characters are selected, it returns the value of *Selection.getCaretIndex()*.

Description

The *getBeginIndex()* method identifies the beginning of a selection. To determine the span of characters currently selected, use both *getBeginIndex()* and *getEndIndex()*.

Example

The following example creates a string representing the currently selected characters and then displays that string in the Output window:

```
var firstChar = Selection.getBeginIndex();
var lastChar  = Selection.getEndIndex();
var currentSelection = eval(Selection.getFocus()).substring(firstChar, lastChar);

trace(currentSelection);
```

The following code extends the current selection by one character to the left:

```
Selection.setSelection(Selection.getBeginIndex() - 1, Selection.getEndIndex());
```

See Also

Selection.getCaretIndex(), Selection.getEndIndex()

Selection.getCaretIndex( ) Method

retrieve the index of the insertion point

Availability   Flash 5

Synopsis   `Selection.getCaretIndex()`

Returns

The index of the insertion point in the current text field. If no text field has keyboard focus, it returns –1. If the text field with focus is empty, it returns 0.

Description

The *getCaretIndex()* method indicates the insertion point (i.e., the location of the cursor) in a text field. The cursor appears as an I-beam when a text field has keyboard focus. Use *setSelection()* to set the location of the insertion point.

Example

Because *getCaretIndex()* returns –1 when no text field has focus, we may determine whether any field has focus by checking whether *getCaretIndex()* is equal to –1, as follows:

```
if (Selection.getCaretIndex() == -1) {
  trace("No field has focus");
}
```

See Also

Selection.setSelection()

Selection.getEndIndex( ) Method   retrieve the index of the last selected character

Availability   Flash 5

Synopsis   `Selection.getEndIndex()`

Returns

The index of the character after the last character in the current selection (highlighted block of text). If no text field has focus, it returns –1. If a text field has focus but no characters are selected, it returns the value of *Selection.getCaretIndex()*.

Description

The *getEndIndex()* method identifies the end of a selection. To identify the span of characters currently selected, use both *getEndIndex()* and *getBeginIndex()*.

Example

The following code extends the current selection by one character to the right:

```
Selection.setSelection(Selection.getBeginIndex(), Selection.getEndIndex()+ 1);
```

See Also

Selection.getBeginIndex(), Selection.getCaretIndex()

Selection.getFocus( ) Method   identify the text field in which
                                                        the cursor currently resides

Availability   Flash 5

Synopsis   `Selection.getFocus()`

Returns

A string indicating the full path to the text field variable that has keyboard focus (i.e., the one in which the cursor currently resides), for example, `"_level1.myTextField"`. If no text field has keyboard focus, it returns `null`.

Description

The *getFocus()* method identifies which text field currently has focus (if any) by returning its string path. To turn that string into a variable reference, we use *eval()*. For example, in the following code we identify the number of characters in the text field with focus. We retrieve the name of the field by invoking *getFocus()*, and we convert that name into a variable with *eval()*:

```
var numChars = eval(Selection.getFocus()).length;
```

Example

Because *getFocus()* returns `null` when no text field is selected, we may determine whether any field has focus by checking whether *getFocus()* is equal to `null`, as follows:

```
if (Selection.getFocus() == null) {
  trace("No field has focus");
}
```

See Also

Selection.setFocus(), eval(), Selection.getCaretIndex()

Selection.setFocus( ) Method   set keyboard focus for a specific text field

Availability   Flash 5

Synopsis   `Selection.setFocus(variableName)`

Arguments
variableName   A string representing the path (e.g., `"_root.myTextField"` or `"userName"`) to the text field variable that is to receive focus.

Returns

A Boolean indicating whether the focus attempt succeeded (`true`) or failed (`false`). A focus attempt fails only if the variable specified by *variableName* is not found or if it is not a text field variable.

Description

The *setFocus()* method sets the keyboard focus for a text field. It places the cursor in that text field, normally in order to draw attention to the field or to allow the user to enter data. The *setFocus()* method can also provide a handy means of identifying erroneous input to a user. In an online form, for example, a user may mistype an email address. To alert the user to the error, we could set the focus to the email-address text field and ask her to fix the problem. We can also use *setFocus()* to create a custom Tab key order for the fields in a form, as shown in the example that follows.

Usage

Note that setting the focus of a text field automatically selects any content in that field. To set a field's focus without selecting any characters, use the following code:

```
// First, focus myField
Selection.setFocus("myField");

// Now place the insertion point at the start of myField
Selection.setSelection(0, 0);

// Or at the end of myField
Selection.setSelection(myField.length, myField.length);
```

When a movie is viewed in a browser, a focused text field will accept text entry only if the Flash movie itself has focus (that is, the user has clicked on the movie at some point during movie play-back). Make sure a movie has focus before asking a user to type into one of its text fields. One way to do this is by including a button that says "Click Here to Start" at the beginning of your movie.

Example

This example shows how to assign a custom Tab order to the fields in a fill-in form. The corresponding sample *.fla* file may be downloaded from the online Code Depot (for more information on trapping the Tab key, see "Handling special keys" in Chapter 10, *Events and Event Handlers*):

```
// Custom Tab Order
// CODE ON THE MOVIE CLIP CONTAINING THE FORM FIELDS
onClipEvent (load) {
  // Store the path to this clip in a string. We'll use it
  // later when invoking Selection.setFocus().
  path = targetPath(this);
  // Create an array with the names of our text fields, supplied
  // in the desired Tab order. The first field listed is the default.
  tabOrder = ["field1", "field3", "field2", "field4"];
}

onClipEvent (keyUp) {
  // If the Tab key was pressed...
  if (Key.getCode() == Key.TAB) {
    // ...If no field has focus...
    if (Selection.getFocus() == null) {
      // ...then set focus to the first field in the array of fields
      Selection.setFocus(path + "." + tabOrder[0]);
    } else {
      // Otherwise, locate the currently focused field in the array of fields
      i = 0;
      focused = Selection.getFocus();
      while (i < tabOrder.length) {
        // Extract the name of the field variable from the full path
        // that's returned by Selection.getFocus()
        fieldName = focused.substring(focused.lastIndexOf(".") + 1);
        // Check each element of tabOrder for the focused field.
        if (tabOrder[i] == fieldName) {
          // Stop when we find a match
          currentFocus = i;
          break;
        }
        i++;
      }
      // Now that we know where the focused field lies in the tabOrder array,
      // set the new focus to either the next field or the previous field,
      // depending on whether the Shift key is down.
      if (Key.isDown(Key.SHIFT)) {
```

```
        // Shift key is down, so go to the previous field, unless we're already
        // at the beginning, in which case go to the last field.
        nextFocus = currentFocus-1 == -1 ? tabOrder.length-1 : currentFocus-1;
      } else {
        // Shift key is not down, so go to the next field,
        // unless we're already at the end, in which case go to the first field.
        nextFocus = currentFocus+1 == tabOrder.length ? 0 : currentFocus+1;
      }
      // Finally, assign the new focus
      Selection.setFocus(path + "." + tabOrder[nextFocus]);
    }
  }
}


// CODE ON BUTTON ON MAIN TIMELINE
on (keyPress "<Tab>") {
  // This placeholder code just traps the Tab key in Internet Explorer
  var tabCatcher = 0;
}
```

See Also

Selection.getFocus( ), Selection.setSelection( )

Selection.setSelection( ) Method

select characters in the text field with
focus, or set the insertion point

Availability   Flash 5

Synopsis   `Selection.setSelection(beginIndex, endIndex)`

Arguments
beginIndex   A non-negative integer specifying the index of the first character to be
                   included in the new selection.

endIndex   A non-negative integer specifying the index of the character *after* the last
                   character to be included in the new selection.

Description

The *setSelection( )* method selects (highlights) the characters from `beginIndex` to
`endIndex`-1 in the text field with focus. If no field has focus, *setSelection( )* has no effect. It
is commonly used to highlight problematic user input.

Usage

Though the *Selection* object does not have a *"setCaretIndex"* method, we may use the
setSelection( ) method to set the insertion point to a specific location within a text field. To
do so, we specify the same `beginIndex` and `endIndex` values, as in:

```
// Set the insertion point after the third character
Selection.setSelection(3, 3);
```

Example

```
// Select the second and third letters
// of the currently focused text field
Selection.setSelection(1, 3);
```

See Also

Selection.getBeginIndex(), Selection.getCaretIndex(), Selection.getEndIndex()

---

setProperty( ) Global Function   assign a value to a movie clip property

Availability	Flash 4 and later
Synopsis	setProperty(`movieClip`, `property`, `value`)

Arguments

movieClip	An expression that yields a string indicating the path to a movie clip. In Flash 5, this may also be a movie clip reference because movie clip references are converted to paths when used in a string context.
property	The name of the built-in property to which `value` will be assigned. Must be an identifier, not a string (e.g., _alpha, not "_alpha").
value	The new data value to be assigned to the specified `property` of `movieClip`.

Description

The *setProperty()* function assigns `value` to one of `movieClip`'s built-in properties (the built-in properties are listed under the *MovieClip* class). It cannot be used to set the value of custom (i.e., user-defined) properties. In Flash 4, *setProperty()* was the only means to assign movie clip property values; as of Flash 5, the . and [] operators are the preferred means of setting both built-in and custom movie clip properties.

Example

```
// Flash 4 syntax. Rotate the main movie by 45 degrees:
setProperty("_root", _rotation, 45);

// Flash 5 syntax. Also rotates the main movie by 45 degrees:
_root._rotation = 45;
```

See Also

getProperty(); "The "Objectness" of Movie Clips in Chapter 13; Appendix C.

Sound Class   control over sounds in a movie

Availability	Flash 5
Constructor	new Sound( ) new Sound(`target`)

Arguments

target	A string indicating the path to the movie clip or document level whose sound is to be controlled. May also be a reference to a movie clip or document level (references are converted to paths when used in a string context).

Methods

attachSound()	Associate a sound from the Library with the *Sound* object.
getPan()	Retrieve the current pan setting.
getTransform()	Determine the current distribution of the channels of a sound to the left and right speakers (i.e., balance).
getVolume()	Retrieve the current volume.
setPan()	Set the pan across a sound's left and right channels.
setTransform()	Distribute the left and right channels between the left and right speakers (i.e., balance).
setVolume()	Set the sound volume.
start()	Start playing an attached sound.
stop()	Silence all sounds or a specified attached sound.

Description

Objects of the *Sound* class are used to control the existing sounds in a movie or to control sounds added to a movie programmatically. *Sound* objects have several distinct applications. They can control:

- All the sounds in the Flash Player

- All the sounds in a particular movie clip instance or main movie (including all sounds in any nested clips)

- An individual programmatically attached sound

To create a *Sound* object that controls all the sounds in the Player (including sounds in *.swf* files on document levels), use the *Sound* constructor without any parameters. For example:

```
myGlobalSound = new Sound();
```

To create a *Sound* object that controls all the sounds in a particular clip or main movie, supply a **target** parameter indicating the clip or movie to control. Note that this also controls sounds in clips inside **target**. For example:

```
spaceshipSound = new Sound("spaceship");  // Control sounds in spaceship clip
mainSound      = new Sound("_root");      // Control sounds on main timeline
```

To make an individual sound that can be started, stopped, and looped independently, create any kind of *Sound* object and then attach a sound to it using the *attachSound()* method.

See Also

stopAllSounds(); *_soundbuftime*

Sound.attachSound( ) Method   associate a sound from the Library with a Sound object

Availability	Flash 5
Synopsis	soundObject.attachSound(*linkageIdentifier*)
Arguments	
linkageIdentifier	The name of the sound to attach, as specified in the Library under Options → Linkage.

Description

The *attachSound()* method adds a new sound to a movie at runtime and places the new sound under *soundObject*'s control. Once attached, the sound may be started and stopped individually by invoking *start()* and *stop()* on *soundObject*.

In order for a sound to be attached to *soundObject*, the sound must be exported from the movie's Library. To export a sound, follow these steps:

1. In the Library, select the sound to export.
2. Select Options → Linkage. The Symbol Linkage Properties dialog box appears.
3. Select Export This Symbol.
4. In the Identifier box, type a unique name by which to identify the sound.

Note that *all* exported sounds are loaded in the first frame of the movie that contains them (not when they are actually attached or played via ActionScript), which can cause long load delays if the sounds are large. You can gain better control over the loading of sounds by placing them in external *.swf* files and using *loadMovie()* to import them as necessary.

Usage

Only one sound may be attached to a *Sound* object at a time. Attaching a new sound to a *Sound* object replaces any sound previously attached to that object. Note that *attachSound()* will not work in movies loaded into a clip or a level via *loadMovie()* unless the attached sound is available in the Library of the document to which the Sound object is scoped. Global sound objects created without a target parameter are scoped to `_level0`.

Example

The following example adds a sound with the identifier `phaser` to the *Sound* object *phaserSound*. It then starts and stops the `phaser` sound:

```
phaserSound = new Sound();
phaserSound.attachSound("phaser");

// Start the phaser sound
phaserSound.start();

// Stop just the phaser sound
phaserSound.stop("phaser");
```

See Also

Sound.start(), Sound.stop()

Sound.getPan( ) Method

retrieve the last pan value set

Availability   Flash 5

Synopsis   *soundObject*.getPan()

Returns

A number indicating the last value set by *setPan()*. Usually in the range –100 (left channel on, right channel off) to 100 (right channel on, left channel off). Default value is 0 (both left and right channels in equal proportions).

Description

By adjusting the pan of a sound, you can create the illusion of a moving sound source. The *getPan()* method is used to determine the current distribution of the left and right channels of the sounds controlled by *soundObject*. Normally, *getPan()* is used in combination with *setPan()* to adjust the current pan of a sound.

Example

Here we alter the pan of a sound by 20:

```
mySound = new Sound();
mySound.setPan(mySound.getPan() - 20);
```

See Also

Sound.getTransform(), Sound.setPan()

Sound.getTransform( ) Method

determine the current distribution of the channels of a sound to the left and right speakers

Availability   Flash 5

Synopsis   *soundObject*.getTransform()

Returns

An anonymous object whose properties contain the channel percentage values for the sounds controlled by *soundObject*.

Description

The *getTransform()* method returns an object with properties that tell us how the channels in the sounds controlled by *soundObject* are distributed to the left and right speakers. The properties of the returned object are ll, lr, rl, and rr, as described in the entry for the *Sound.setTransform()* method.

See Also

Sound.getPan(), Sound.setTransform()

Sound.getVolume( ) Method

retrieve the current volume setting

Availability   Flash 5

Synopsis   *soundObject*.getVolume()

Returns

A number indicating the current volume as set by *setVolume()*. Usually in the range 0 (no volume) to 100 (default volume), but it can be higher.

Description

The *getVolume()* method is used to determine the current volume of the sounds controlled by *soundObject*. Normally, *getVolume()* is used in combination with *setVolume()* to adjust the current volume of a sound.

Example

Here we reduce the volume of a sound by 20:

```
mySound = new Sound();
mySound.setVolume(mySound.getVolume() - 20);
```

See Also

Sound.setVolume()

Sound.setPan( ) Method   set the balance of a sound's left and right channels

Availability   Flash 5

Synopsis   *soundObject*.setPan(*pan*)

Arguments

pan   A number between −100 (left) and 100 (right) indicating the distribution
                      between the left and right speakers for sounds controlled by
                      soundObject. If the *pan* supplied is greater than 100, the actual value
                      assigned is 200 − *pan*. If the *pan* supplied is less than −100, the actual
                      value assigned is −200 − *pan*.

Description

The *setPan()* method dictates the balance of the right and left channels of the sounds
controlled by *soundObject*. By adjusting the pan over time, we can cause a sound to move
from one speaker to the other (known as *panning*).

To play the sounds controlled by *soundObject* in the left speaker only, use a *pan* of −100.
To play the sounds controlled by *soundObject* in the right speaker only, use a *pan* of 100.
To balance the two channels evenly, use a *pan* of 0.

Note that *setPan()* affects all the sounds controlled by *soundObject*. If *soundObject* is a
global sound, *setPan()* affects all the sounds in a movie. If *soundObject* is tied to a clip or
a main timeline, *setPan()* affects all the sounds in that clip or timeline and all the clips it
contains.

The effects of *setPan()* can be changed only by another call to *setPan()*. A *setPan()* assignment affects all future sounds controlled by *soundObject*, even if *soundObject* is deleted.

Example

The following clip event handlers cause sounds in a movie clip to endlessly pan between
the left and right speakers:

```
onClipEvent (load) {
  panEffect = new Sound(this);
  panDirection = "right";
  panIncrement = 50;
}

onClipEvent(enterFrame) {
  if (panDirection == "right") {
    newPan = panEffect.getPan() + panIncrement;
    if (newPan > 100) {
```

```
      panDirection = "left";
      panEffect.setPan(panEffect.getPan() - panIncrement);
    } else {
      panEffect.setPan(newPan);
    }
  } else {
    newPan = panEffect.getPan() - panIncrement;
    if (newPan < -100) {
      panDirection = "right";
      panEffect.setPan(panEffect.getPan() + panIncrement);
    } else {
      panEffect.setPan(newPan);
    }
  }
}
```

The following clip event handlers cause sounds in a clip to react to the mouse. Assuming a
Stage width and height of 550 and 400, the sounds pan left and right with the mouse's horizontal movement and increase or decrease in volume with the mouse's vertical movement:

```
onClipEvent (load) {
  // Create a new Sound object and attach the sound bgMusic to it
  mySound = new Sound(this);
  mySound.attachSound("bgMusic");
  mySound.start(0, 999);                   // Play and loop the sound
}

onClipEvent (enterFrame) {
  // Measure the mouse's horizontal location, then set the pan accordingly
  mouseX = (_root._xmouse / 550) * 200;
  mySound.setPan(mouseX - 100);
  // Measure the mouse's vertical location, then set the volume accordingly
  mouseY = (_root._ymouse / 400) * 300;
  mySound.setVolume(300 - mouseY);
}
```

See Also

Sound.getPan()

Sound.setTransform( ) Method   distribute the left and right channels
                                                   between the left and right speakers

Availability   Flash 5

Synopsis   soundObject.setTransform(*transformObject*)

Arguments
transformObject   A user-defined object that specifies new channel settings as a series of
                     properties.

~iption

      ~ransform() method gives us precise control over how the channels in a sound are
         the left and right speakers. In principle, *setTransform()* is not unlike *setPan()*, but
      more detailed sound control over stereo sounds.

A stereo sound is a combination of two distinct sounds—the *left channel* and the *right channel*—which are normally sent separately to the left and right speakers. However, using *setTransform()*, we may dictate how much of each channel is broadcast in each speaker. We may, for example, say, "Play half of the left channel in the left speaker, none of the left channel in the right speaker, and all of the right channel in both speakers." Or we may say, "Play all of the left and right channels in the left speaker."

To use *setTransform()*, we must first create an object with a series of predefined properties. The properties express how to distribute the left and right channels of a stereo sound between the left and right speakers, as described in Table R-12.

Table R-12. Properties of a transformObject

Property Name	Property Value	Property Description
ll	0 to 100	The percentage of the left channel to play in the left speaker
lr	0 to 100	The percentage of the right channel to play in the left speaker
rl	0 to 100	The percentage of the left channel to play in the right speaker
rr	0 to 100	The percentage of the right channel to play in the right speaker

Once we have created an object with the properties described in Table R-12, we pass that object to the *setTransform()* method of our *Sound* object. The values of the properties on our `transformObject` become the new channel output percentages for the sounds controlled by `soundObject`.

To examine the current percentages of a particular *Sound* object, we use the *Sound.getTransform()* method.

Example

```
// Create a new Sound object
mySound = new Sound();

// Create a new generic object to use with setTransform()
transformer = new Object();

// Set the properties of the transform object
transformer.ll = 0;      // None of left channel in left speaker
transformer.lr = 0;      // None of right channel in left speaker
transformer.rl = 0;      // None of left channel in right speaker
transformer.rr = 100;    // All of right channel in right speaker

// Apply the new channel distribution by passing the transform
// object to the setTransform() method
mySound.setTransform(transformer);
```

See Also

Sound.getTransform(), Sound.setPan()

Sound.setVolume( ) Method   set the volume of sounds controlled by a *Sound* object

Availability   Flash 5

Synopsis   soundObject.setVolume(*volume*)

Arguments

volume   A number indicating the loudness of the sound controlled by
                    soundObject, where 0 is no volume (mute). The larger *volume*'s abso-
                    lute value (regardless of whether *volume* is positive or negative), the
                    louder the sounds controlled by *soundObject* will be. For example, −50
                    is the same *volume* as 50. The default value for *volume* is 100.

Description

The *setVolume()* method makes the sounds controlled by *soundObject* louder or softer. To
entirely mute a sound, use a *volume* of 0. To make a sound louder, increase *volume*.
Values in the range 100–200 are generally quite loud, but there is no predefined maximum.

Note that *setVolume()* affects all the sounds controlled by *soundObject*. If *soundObject* is
a global sound, *setVolume()* affects all the sounds in a movie. If *soundObject* is tied to a
clip or a main timeline, *setVolume()* affects all the sounds in that clip or timeline.

The effects of *setVolume()* remain in effect until overridden by another *setVolume()* call. A
setVolume() assignment affects all future sounds controlled by *soundObject*, even if
soundObject is deleted.

Example

The first example simply sets the volume of a movie clip:

```
var mySound = new Sound();
mySound.setVolume (65);
```

The following example shows how to make buttons that adjust a movie's volume level:

```
// CODE ON THE MAIN MOVIE TIMELINE
var globalSound = new Sound();
var maxVolume = 200;
var minVolume = 0;
var volumeIncrement = 20;

// CODE ON VOLUME-UP BUTTON ON MAIN TIMELINE
on (release) {
  globalSound.setVolume(Math.min(globalSound.getVolume() + volumeIncrement,
                        maxVolume));
}

// CODE ON VOLUME-DOWN BUTTON ON MAIN TIMELINE
on (release) {
  globalSound.setVolume(Math.max(globalSound.getVolume() - volumeIncrement,
                        minVolume));
```

`Volume()`

Sound.start( ) Method   *begin playing an attached sound*

Availability   Flash 5

Synopsis   `soundObject.start(secondOffset, loops)`

Arguments

secondOffset   A floating-point number indicating the time in seconds at which to start playing the sound attached to `soundObject` (often called an *entry point*). For example, a `secondOffset` of 1 starts playback one second after the sound's actual beginning as defined in the Library. The default is 0. There is no provision for an exit point (the time at which to stop playing the sound). The sound plays until its end unless stopped manually.

loops   A positive integer indicating how many times to play the sound attached to `soundObject`. To play the sound once, use 1 (which is the default); to play the sound twice in succession, use 2, and so on. The portion of the sound from `secondOffset` is repeated to its end the number of times specified by `loops`.

Description

The *start()* method is used to play programmatically-defined sounds that were added to `soundObject` via *attachSound()*. The *start()* method does not play all the sounds in a clip or movie; it plays only the sound most recently attached to `soundObject` via *attachSound()*.

To play only a portion of the sound attached to `soundObject`, use the `secondOffset` argument. To play the sound attached to `soundObject` repeatedly, use the `loops` argument.

Example

```
// Create a new Sound object
boink = new Sound();

// Attach a sound exported as boink to the Sound object
boink.attachSound("boink");

// Play all of boink; soundOffset defaults to 0
boink.start();

// Play only a portion of boink, starting 0.5 seconds into it; loops defaults to 1
boink.start(.5);

// Play boink three times from beginning to end
boink.start(0, 3);
```

See Also

Sound.stop()

Sound.stop( ) Method   *silences all sounds or a specified attached sound*

Availability   Flash 5

Synopsis	`soundObject.stop()`
	`soundObject.stop(linkageIdentifier)`

Arguments

linkageIdentifier The name of any sound attached to any *Sound* object with the same
target as *soundObject*. Linkage identifiers are specified in the Library
under Options → Linkage.

Description

When invoked without a `linkageIdentifier`, *stop()* silences all sounds controlled by
soundObject; if *soundObject* is a global sound, *stop()* silences all sounds in a movie; if
soundObject was created with a `target` parameter, *stop()* silences all sounds in `target`.

When invoked with a `linkageIdentifier`, *stop()* silences only the specific sound named
by `linkageIdentifier`. In that case, `linkageIdentifier` must be a sound that was
attached to a *Sound* object via *attachSound()*. However, the sound to stop need not be
attached to *soundObject* itself. It may be attached to *any Sound* object that shares the
same `target` as *soundObject*. Or, if *soundObject* was created with no `target` (i.e., is a
global *Sound* object), the sound to stop may be attached to any other global *Sound* object.

Example

```
// Create a global Sound object
mySound = new Sound();

// Attach the sound doorbell to the object
mySound.attachSound("doorbell");

// Stop all sounds in the movie
mySound.stop();

// Play doorbell
mySound.start();

// Stop just doorbell
mySound.stop("doorbell");

// Create another global Sound object
myOtherSound = new Sound();

// Attach a doorknock sound to the object
myOtherSound.attachSound("doorknock");

// Play doorknock
myOtherSound.start();

// Now stop the doorknock through mySound, not myOtherSound.
// This works because the two Sound objects have the same target.
mySound.stop("doorknock");
```

See Also

Sound.start()

_soundbuftime Global Property   length of a streaming sound, in seconds, to preload

Availability   Flash 4 and later

Synopsis   _soundbuftime

Access   Read/write

Description

The _soundbuftime property is an integer specifying the number of seconds of a streamed sound to preload before playing it. The default is 5 seconds.

Flash synchronizes movie playback with streaming sounds to ensure that, say, a cartoon character's lips match an accompanying sound track. Animations will pause until _soundbuftime seconds of streaming sound are downloaded; therefore, a long setting can cause excessive startup times on slower connections. Because network streaming may be slow or briefly interrupted, a short _soundbuftime setting can cause sound to skip (i.e., if enough sound data wasn't buffered). The ideal setting will vary from movie to movie based on the complexity of the graphics, the quality settings of the sound, and the bandwidth of the end user's Internet connection. The default setting (5 seconds) usually works well, but experimentation may be required to find the best setting for individual cases. The streaming buffer time can be changed during playback, but it is a global property and cannot be set separately for individual sounds.

Example

```
_soundbuftime = 10;  // Buffer 10 seconds of audio
```

startDrag( ) Global Function   make a movie or movie clip follow the mouse pointer

Availability   Flash 4 and later

Synopsis   startDrag(*target*)
                  startDrag(*target*, *lockCenter*)
                  startDrag(*target*, *lockCenter*, *left*, *top*, *right*, *bottom*)

Arguments

target   A string or reference indicating the path to the movie or movie clip instance that should follow the mouse pointer (references to movie clips are converted to paths when used in a string context).

lockCenter   A Boolean indicating whether the *target*'s registration point should be centered under the mouse pointer (true) or dragged relative to its original location (false).

left   A number specifying the minimum x-coordinate to the left of which *target*'s registration point may not be dragged.

top   A number specifying the minimum y-coordinate above which *target*'s registration point may not be dragged.

right   A number specifying the maximum x-coordinate to the right of which *target*'s registration point may not be dragged.

bottom   A number specifying the maximum y-coordinate below which *target*'s registration point may not be dragged.

Description

The *startDrag()* function causes `target` to visually follow the mouse pointer around in the Player (known as *dragging* the clip). The movement of a dragging clip can be constrained to a bounding box whose coordinates are provided as arguments to the *startDrag()* function. Bounding box coordinates are given relative to the canvas on which `target` resides. If that canvas is the main movie Stage, then (0, 0) is the top-left corner of the Stage. If that canvas is a movie clip, then (0, 0) is the registration point of the clip's canvas. Note that Flash's coordinate system reverses the Cartesian Y-axis; y values *increase* toward the bottom of the screen and *decrease* toward the top of the screen. Negative y values are *above* the origin (i.e., above the X-axis).

Dragging can be stopped at any time via the *stopDrag()* function. Only one movie clip or movie may be dragged at a time, so issuing a *startDrag()* function on a new `target` automatically cancels any drag operation already in progress. That said, when a movie or move clip is dragged, all the movie clips it contains are dragged along with it.

Example

```
// Drag ball, limiting its movement to the upper-left corner of the Stage
startDrag("ball", true, 0, 0, 225, 200);
```

See Also

Movieclip.startDrag(), stopDrag()

---

stop( ) Global Function   pause the movie's playback at the current frame

Availability   Flash 2 and later

Synopsis   stop()

Description

The *stop()* function is a simple but fundamental function that halts the playback of a movie or movie clip. It is the global counterpart of the *MovieClip.stop()* method. It is commonly used to wait for the user to, say, choose from a graphical menu.

See Also

MovieClip.stop(), play()

---

stopAllSounds( ) Global Function   silence a movie

Availability   Flash 3 and later

Synopsis   stopAllSounds()

Description

The *stopAllSounds()* function mutes all the sounds currently playing in a movie, no matter how deeply nested in movie clips. This applies to every sound in a movie, including programmatically generated *Sound* objects. For more precise control over stopping, starting, and setting the volume of sounds, see the *Sound* class.

Note that *stopAllSounds()* has only a temporary effect. Any sound that starts after a *stopAllSounds()* invocation will play normally. There is no way to permanently mute a movie.

See Also

Sound.setVolume(), Sound.stop()

---

stopDrag( ) Global Function   end a drag operation in progress

Availability   Flash 4 and later

Synopsis   stopDrag()

Description

The *startDrag()* function causes a movie clip to follow the mouse pointer around the Stage. A *stopDrag()* operation stops a dragging movie clip from following the mouse pointer. Because only one movie clip or movie may be dragged at a time, *stopDrag()* does not require a `target` argument; it simply cancels any drag operation in progress.

Together with *startDrag(), stopDrag()* is used to create simple drag-and-drop interfaces in Flash, as demonstrated under "Interface Widgets" in the online Code Depot.

Example

The following button code causes a movie clip to be dragged while the button is pressed and dropped when the button is released:

```
on (press) {
  startDrag("", true);
}

on (release) {
  stopDrag();
}
```

See Also

MovieClip.stopDrag(), startDrag(), String.toLowerCase(); "The toUpperCase() function" in Chapter 4

String( ) Global Function   convert a value to the *String* datatype

Availability   Flash 5

Synopsis   String(*value*)

Arguments
value   An expression containing the value to be converted to a string.

Returns

The result of converting *value* to a primitive string.

Description

The *String()* function converts its argument to a primitive string value and returns that converted value. The results of converting various types of data to a primitive string are described in Table 3-2. It's normally not necessary to use the *String()* function; ActionScript automatically converts values to the *string* type when appropriate.

Be sure not to confuse the global *String()* function with the *String* class constructor. The former converts an expression to a string, whereas the later is a class that wraps primitive string data in an object so that properties and methods may be applied to it.

Usage

Note that the *String()* function sometimes appears in Flash 4 *.fla* files that have been converted to the Flash 5 format. For information on how datatypes are handled when Flash 4 files are converted to Flash 5, see "Flash 4–to–Flash 5 Datatype Conversion" in Chapter 3.

See Also

The *String* class; "Explicit Type Conversion" in Chapter 3

String Class   wrapper class for string primitive type

Availability	Flash 5
Constructor	`new String(value)`
Arguments	
value	An expression to be resolved and, if necessary, converted to a string, then wrapped in a *String* object.

Properties

length	The number of characters in a string.

Class Methods

The following method is invoked through the *String* class itself, not through an object of the *String* class:

fromCharCode()	Generate a string from one or more Latin 1/Shift-JIS code points.

Methods

The following object methods are invoked through an instance of the *String* class:

charAt()	Retrieve a character at a specific position in the string.
charCodeAt()	Retrieve the code point of a character at a specific position in the string.
concat()	Combine one or more items into a single string.
indexOf()	Find the first occurrence of a specified substring in a string.
lastIndexOf()	Find the last occurrence of a specified substring in a string.
slice()	Extract a substring from a string based on positive or negative character positions.
split()	Convert a string to an array.

substr()	Extract a substring from a string based on a starting position and length.
substring()	Extract a substring from a string based on positive character positions only.
toLowerCase()	Return a lowercase version of a string.
toUpperCase()	Return an uppercase version of a string.

Description

The *String* class has several purposes:

- It allows us to access the `length` property of strings and perform string-related operations, such as *indexOf()* and *slice()*. *String* objects are created (and eventually deleted) automatically by the interpreter whenever a method is invoked on a primitive string value.

- It can be used to convert a datum of any type to a string.

- It is used to access the *fromCharCode()* class method to create a new string based on specified Latin 1 or Shift-JIS code points.

- It can be used to create a *String* object, which contains a primitive string value in an unnamed, internal property; however, there is little reason to do so.

Usage

In practice, the *String* class constructor is used primarily to convert other datatypes to strings. See the global *String()* function for more details.

See Also

"The String Type" in Chapter 4, *Primitive Datatypes*

String.charAt( ) Method retrieve the character from a specific position in a string

Availability	Flash 5
Synopsis	`string.charAt(index)`

Arguments

index	The integer position of the character to retrieve, which should be in the range 0 (the first character) to `string.length-1` (the last character).

Returns

The character in the position *index* within *string*.

Description

The *charAt()* method determines the character that resides at a certain position (*index*) in a string.

Example

```
trace("It is 10:34 pm".charAt(1));  // Displays: "t" (the second letter)
var country = "Canada";
trace(country.charAt(0));           // Displays: "C" (the first letter)

// This function removes all the spaces from a string and returns the result
```

```
function stripSpaces (inString) {
  var outString = "";
  for (i = 0; i < inString.length; i++) {
    if (inString.charAt(i) != " ") {
      outString += inString.charAt(i);
    }
  }
  return outString;
}
```

See Also

String.charCodeAt( ), *String.indexOf( )*, *String.slice( )*; "The charAt( ) function" in Chapter 4

String.charCodeAt( ) Method
retrieve the code point of the character at a specific position in a string

Availability   Flash 5

Synopsis   `string.charCodeAt(index)`

Arguments
index   The integer position of a character in *string*, which should be in the range 0 (the first character) to `string.length-1` (the last character).

Returns

An integer representing the Latin 1 or Shift-JIS code point, as shown in Appendix B, of the character in the position *index* within *string*.

Example

```
var msg = "A is the first letter of the Latin alphabet.";
trace(msg.charCodeAt(0));  // Displays: 65 (the code for the "A" character)
trace(msg.charCodeAt(1));  // Displays: 32 (the code for the space character)
```

See Also

String.charAt( ), *String.fromCharCode( )*; Appendix B, "The charCodeAt( ) function" in Chapter 4

String.concat( ) Method
combine one or more values into a single string

Availability   Flash 5

Synopsis   `string.concat(value1, value2,...valuen)`

Arguments
value1,...valuen   Values to be converted to strings (if necessary) and concatenated with *string*.

Returns

The result of concatenating *string* with *value1*, *value2*, ...*valuen*.

Description

The *concat()* method creates a string from a series of values. It is equivalent to using the concatenation operator (+) with strings but is sometimes preferred for clarity, as the + operator can also be used to add numbers. For details on *concat()*, see Chapter 4.

Usage

Note that *concat()* does not modify *string*; it returns a completely new string.

Example

```
var greeting = "Hello";
excitedGreeting = greeting.concat("!");
trace(greeting);                        // Displays: "Hello"
trace(excitedGreeting);                 // Displays: "Hello!"

var x = 4;                              // Initialize x as an integer
trace(x + 5);                          // Displays: 9
trace(x.concat(5));                    // Fails because x is not a string.
trace(String(x).concat(5));            // Displays: "45"

var x = "4";                           // Initialize x as a string
trace(x.concat(5));                    // Displays: "45"
trace(concat("foo", "fee"));           // Fails because concat() must be invoked
                                        // as a method of a string.
```

See Also

The + operator, in Chapter 5, "The concat() function" in Chapter 4

String.fromCharCode( ) Class Method

generate a string from one or more code points

Availability   Flash 5

Synopsis   `String.fromCharCode(code_point1, code_point2,...code_pointn)`

Arguments
code_point1,...code_pointn
          A series of one or more decimal integers corresponding to Latin 1 or Shift-JIS character code points, as shown in Appendix B, *Latin 1 Character Repertoire and Keycodes*.

Returns

A string formed by concatenating the characters represented by the specified code points.

Description

The *fromCharCode()* class method produces a character or series of characters from character code points as described in Chapter 4.

Example

```
// Makes a copyright symbol, followed by the year (2001)
copyNotice = String.fromCharCode(169) + " 2001";
```

See Also

String.charCodeAt(); Appendix B, "The fromCharCode Function" in Chapter 4

String.indexOf( ) Method   find the first occurrence of a substring in a string

Availability   Flash 5

Synopsis   `string.indexOf(substring)`
         `string.indexOf(substring, startIndex)`

Arguments

substring   A string containing the character or characters to search for.

startIndex   An optional integer position in *string* at which to start searching for *substring*. Should be in the range 0 (the first character) to *string*. `length-1` (the last character). Defaults to 0.

Returns

The position of the first occurrence of *substring* in *string* (starting at *startIndex*). Returns –1 if *substring* is not found at or after *startIndex* in *string*.

Description

The *indexOf()* method is used to search for characters in strings or to check whether a string contains a certain substring.

Example

```
// Check if an email address contains an @ sign
var email = "derekaol.com";
if (email.indexOf("@") == -1) {
  trace ("This isn't a valid email address");
}

// Check if an email address has an @ sign and is from the domain aol.com
var email = "derek@aol.com";
var atPos = email.indexOf("@");
if (atPos != -1 && email.indexOf("aol.com") == atPos + 1) {
  gotoAndStop("AOLuserOffer");
}
```

The following code shows a generic function that checks for a keyword in a string, as you might need when grading a fill-in-the-blank quiz:

```
// Generic function to search origStr for any occurrence
// of searchStr using a case-insensitive comparison
function search (origStr, searchStr) {
  var origStr = origStr.toLowerCase();
  var searchStr = searchStr.toLowerCase();
  return origStr.indexOf(searchStr) != -1;
}

var answer = "einstein";
var guess = "Dr. Albert Einstein";
```

```
// Increment score if guess contains "einstein"
if (search(guess, answer)) {
  score++;
}
```

See Also

String.charAt(), *String.lastIndexOf()*; "The indexOf() function" in Chapter 4

String.lastIndexOf( ) Method   find the last occurrence of a substring in a string

Availability   Flash 5

Synopsis   *string*.lastIndexOf(*substring*)
                    string.lastIndexOf(*substring*, *startIndex*)

Arguments

substring   A string containing the character or characters to search for.

startIndex   An optional integer position in *string* at which to start the search for
                    substring. The *string* is searched backward from *startIndex*, which
                    should be in the range 0 (the first character) to *string*.length-1 (the
                    last character). Defaults to *string*.length-1.

Returns

The position of the last occurrence of *substring* in *string* prior to *startIndex*. Returns
−1 if *substring* is not found prior to *startIndex* in *string*.

Description

The *lastIndexOf()* method is used to search for the last occurrence of a substring in a string
or to check whether a string contains a certain substring.

Example

```
URL = "http://www.moock.org/webdesign/flash/fillthewindow.html";
// Finds the last slash character
lastSlash = URL.lastIndexOf("/");
// Extracts the filename from the URL
file = URL.substring(lastSlash + 1);
trace(file);  // Displays: fillthewindow.html
```

See Also

String.charAt(), *String.indexOf()*; "The lastIndexOf() Function" in Chapter 4

String.length Property   the number of characters in a string

Availability   Flash 5

Synopsis   *string*.length

Access   Read-only

Description

The `length` property returns the number of characters in *string*. Note that a null character (ASCII 0) does not signal the end of a string, as it would in some languages, but neither is it counted in the string's `length`. For example:

```
// Create the string "A" + null + "B"
var myString = String.fromCharCode(65,0,66);
trace(myString.length);  // Displays: 2 (The null character is ignored)
```

Example

```
var myString = "hello";
trace (myString.length);  // Displays: 5
trace ("hello".length);   // Displays: 5

// Here we convert the number 1000 to a
// string in order to test its length
var age = 1000;
// Display an error message if the number has the wrong number of digits.
if (String(age).length != 2) {
   trace ("Please enter a two-digit number");
}
```

See Also

Array.length( ); "The length property" in Chapter 4

String.slice( ) Method

extract a substring from a string based on positive or negative character positions

Availability Flash 5

Synopsis `string.slice(startIndex, endIndex)`

Arguments

startIndex The integer position of the first character to extract from *string*. If *startIndex* is negative, the position is measured from the end of the string, where −1 is the last character, −2 is the second-to-last character, and so on. (i.e., a negative *startIndex* specifies the character at `string.length+startIndex`).

endIndex The integer position of the character *after* the last character to extract from *string*. If *endIndex* is negative, the position is measured from the end of the string, where −1 is the last character, −2 is the second-to-last character, and so on. (i.e., a negative *endIndex* specifies the character at `string.length+endIndex`). Defaults to `string.length` if omitted.

Returns

A substring of *string*, starting at *startIndex* and ending at *endIndex*−1, where both *startIndex* and *endIndex* are zero-relative.

Description

The *slice( )* method is one of three methods that can be used to extract a substring from a string (the others being *substring( )* and *substr( )*). The *slice( )* method offers the option of negative start and end index values, which allows us to extract a substring by measuring back from the end of a string.

Usage

Note that *slice()* does not modify *string*; it returns a completely new string.

Example

```
var fullName = "Steven Sid Mumby";
middleName = fullName.slice(7, 10);    // Assigns "Sid" to middleName
middleName = fullName.slice(-9, -6);   // Also assigns "Sid" to middleName
```

See Also

String.substr(), *String.substring()*; "The slice() function" and "Combining String Examination with Substring Extraction" in Chapter 4

String.split( ) Method   convert a string into a series of array elements

Availability	Flash 5
Synopsis	`string.split(delimiter)`

Arguments

delimiter   The character or series of characters at which to break *string* when forming elements of the new array.

Returns

An array whose elements contain the substrings formed by breaking *string* into segments demarcated by *delimiter*.

Description

The *split()* method breaks a string into substrings, assigns those substrings to the elements of an array, and returns that array. Contiguous occurrences of *delimiter* without intervening characters result in empty elements. For example, the following code:

```
owners = "terry,doug,,,jon";
ownersArray = owners.split(",");
```

assigns the following elements to **ownersArray** (elements 2 and 3 contain **undefined**):

```
0: terry
1: doug
2:
3:
4: jon
```

The *split()* method is typically used to convert a string received from a CGI script or text file into an array for further manipulation. It is also useful when parsing the parameters of an *asfunction* call from an HMTL text field <A> tag, which can pass only one string argument to a function. See "Calling ActionScript Functions from HTML Links" in Chapter 18, *On-Screen Text Fields*, for example code. Common delimiters include the comma and the Tab character.

Example

Suppose we store a list of names in a text file named *names.txt*. Each name is separated from the others by a Tab character, as implied by the whitespace shown:

```
owners=terry    doug    jon
```

On frame 1 of our movie, we load the *names.txt* file into our movie:

```
this.loadVariables("names.txt");
```

After ensuring that *names.txt* has fully loaded (see "data" in Chapter 10, *Events and Event Handlers*), we split the loaded **owners** variable into an array:

```
splitString = String.fromCharCode(9);  // Assign the Tab character to splitString
ownersArray = owners.split(splitString);

trace(ownersArray[1]);  // Displays: "doug"
```

Note that *split()* can take a long time to execute with large bodies of text. If performance is a problem, break your data into manageable portions or consider using XML instead. See the *XML* class.

Bugs

In Flash 5, using the empty string as a delimiter adds all of **string** to the first element of the array being generated. According to ECMA-262, an empty string delimiter should cause **string** to be broken at each character. Similarly, multicharacter delimiters are not recognized by Flash 5 and cause all of **string** to be assigned to the first element of the returned array.

See Also

Array.join(); "The split() function" in Chapter 4

String.substr( ) Method

extract a substring from a string based on a starting position and length

Availability	Flash 5
Synopsis	`string.substr(startIndex, length)`

Arguments

startIndex The integer position of the first character to extract from **string**. If **startIndex** is negative, the position is measured from the end of the string, where –1 is the last character, –2 is the second-to-last character, and so on. (i.e., a negative **startIndex** specifies the character at **string.length+startIndex**).

length The number of characters to extract from **string**, starting at (and including) the **startIndex**. If not specified, all the characters from **startIndex** to the end of **string** are extracted.

Returns

A substring of **string**, starting at **startIndex** and including **length** characters. If **length** is omitted, the result contains characters from **startIndex** to the end of **string**.

Description

The *substr()* method is one of three methods that can be used to extract a substring from a string (the others being *slice()* and *substring()*). The *substr()* method extracts a string based on the number of characters specified by `length`, not based on two character indexes.

Usage

Note that *substr()* does not modify `string`; it returns a completely new string.

Example

```
var fullName = "Steven Sid Mumby";

middleName = fullName.substr(7, 3);      // Assigns "Sid" to middleName
firstName  = fullName.substr(0, 6);      // Assigns "Steven" to firstName
lastName   = fullName.substr(11);        // Assigns "Mumby" to lastName

// Notice the negative starting indexes...
middleName = fullName.substr(-9, 3);     // Assigns "Sid" to middleName
firstName  = fullName.substr(-16, 6);    // Assigns "Steven" to firstName
lastName   = fullName.substr(-5);        // Assigns "Mumby" to lastName
```

See Also

String.slice(), *String.substring()*; "Combining String Examination with Substring Extraction" and "The substr() function in Chapter 4

String.substring() Method

extract a substring from a string based on positive character positions

Availability	Flash 5
Synopsis	`string.substring(startIndex, endIndex)`
Arguments	
startIndex	The positive integer position of the first character to extract from `string`. If negative, 0 is used.
endIndex	The positive integer position of the character *after* the last character to extract from `string`. Defaults to `string.length` if omitted. If negative, 0 is used.

Returns

A substring of `string`, starting at `startIndex` and ending at `endIndex`–1, where both `startIndex` and `endIndex` are zero-relative.

Description

The *substring()* method is one of three methods that can be used to extract a substring from a string (the others being *slice()* and *substr()*). The *substring()* function is identical to *slice()* except that it does not allow for negative `startIndex` and `endIndex` values, and it automatically reorders the two indexes if `endIndex` is less than `startIndex`.

Usage

Note that *substring()* does not modify `string`; it returns a completely new string.

Example

```
// Extract names from a string
var fullName = "Steven Sid Mumby";
middleName = fullName.substring(7, 10);    // Assigns "Sid" to middleName
middleName = fullName.substring(10, 7);    // Assigns "Sid" to middleName
                                           // (indexes are swapped automatically)
firstName  = fullName.substring(0, 6);     // Assigns "Steven" to firstName
lastName   = fullName.substring(11);       // Assigns "Mumby" to lastName
```

The following example is a reusable function to search for and replace all occurrences of a substring within a string:

```
// A Search-and-Replace Function
function replace (origStr, searchStr, replaceStr) {
  var tempStr = "";
  var startIndex = 0;
  if (searchStr == "") {
    return origStr;
  }

  if (origStr.indexOf(searchStr) != -1) {
    while ((searchIndex = origStr.indexOf(searchStr, startIndex)) != -1) {
      tempStr += origStr.substring(startIndex, searchIndex);
      tempStr += replaceStr;
      startIndex = searchIndex + searchStr.length;
    }
    return tempStr + origStr.substring(startIndex);
  } else {
    return origStr;
  }
}

msg = "three times three is four";
trace(replace(msg, "three", "two"));  // Displays: "two times two is four"
```

See Also

String.slice( ), *String.substr( )*; "Combining String Examination with Substring Extraction" and "The substr( ) function" in Chapter 4

String.toLowerCase( ) Method   generate a lowercase version of a string

Availability   Flash 5

Synopsis   `string.toLowerCase()`

Returns

The lowercase equivalent of *string* as a new string. Characters without a lowercase equivalent are left unchanged.

Description

The *toLowerCase( )* method creates a new, lowercase version of *string*; it can be used for formatting or to facilitate case-insensitive character comparisons. The *toLowerCase( )* method converts only characters in the range A–Z (it does not convert characters with diacritical marks such as accents and umlauts).

Usage

Note that *toLowerCase()* does not modify *string*; it returns a completely new string.

Example

```
// Set msg to "this sentence has mixed caps!"
msg = "ThiS SenTencE Has MixED CaPs!".toLowerCase();

// Perform a case-insensitive comparison of two strings
function caseInsensitiveCompare (stringA, stringB) {
  return (stringA.toLowerCase() == stringB.toLowerCase());
}

trace(caseInsensitiveCompare("Colin", "colin"));  // Displays: true
```

See Also

String.toUpperCase(); "The toLowerCase() function" in Chapter 4

String.toUpperCase( ) Method   generate an uppercase version of a string

Availability   Flash 5

Synopsis   `string.toUpperCase()`

Returns

The uppercase (a.k.a. ALL CAPS) equivalent of *string* as a new string. Characters without an uppercase equivalent are left unchanged.

Description

The *toUpperCase()* method creates a new, uppercase version of *string*; it can be used for formatting or to facilitate case-insensitive character comparisons. The *toUpperCase()* method converts only characters in the range a–z (it does not convert characters with diacritical marks such as accents and umlauts).

Usage

Note that *toUpperCase()* does not modify *string*; it returns a completely new string.

Example

```
"listen to me".toUpperCase();   // Yields the string "LISTEN TO ME"
var msg1 = "Your Final Score: 234";
var msg2 = msg1.toUpperCase();  // Set msg2 to "YOUR FINAL SCORE: 234"
```

See Also

String.toLowerCase(); "The toUpperCase() function" in Chapter 4

---

targetPath( ) Global Function   the absolute path to a movie or movie clip

Availability   Flash 5

Synopsis   `targetPath (movieClip)`

Arguments

movieClip   A reference to a movie clip object.

Returns

A string representing the path to `movieClip` in absolute terms, using dot notation (e.g., `"_level0.myMovie"`).

Description

The *targetPath()* function returns a movie clip's reference as a string that describes the absolute path to the clip (identical to the return value of *MovieClip.valueOf()*). The *targetPath()* function is sometimes used to compose placement-sensitive code that operates on a movie clip relative to the timeline upon which the clip resides.

Bugs

Note that the example code given for *targetPath()* in the Flash 5 ActionScript Dictionary does not represent the proper usage of *targetPath()*; contrary to what the example implies, it is not a synonym for *tellTarget()*.

Example

If **square** is a movie clip contained by **shapes**, which resides on the main timeline of level 0, then inside the **shapes** clip, the statement:

```
targetPath(square);
```

would return:

```
"_level0.shapes.square"
```

See Also

MovieClip._target, *MovieClip.valueOf()*; "The targetPath() function" in Chapter 13

---

tellTarget( ) Global Function   execute statements in the scope of a remote movie clip

Availability   Flash 3 and Flash 4; deprecated in Flash 5 in favor of object-oriented syntax or the *with* statement

Synopsis
```
tellTarget (target) {
        statements
}
```

Arguments

target   A string or reference indicating the path to a movie or movie clip instance (references are converted to paths when used in a string context).

statements   The statements to be executed in the scope of *target*.

Description

In Flash 3 and Flash 4, *tellTarget()* was the primary means of communicating between two movie clips (i.e., controlling one from the other). It was used to invoke functions such as *play()*, *stop()*, and *gotoAndStop()* on remote movie clips. In Flash 4, when variables were added to ActionScript, we could also use *tellTarget()* to get and set remote clip variable values. In Flash 5, these endeavors are better accomplished with the dot operator, ., and the array access operator, [ ]. Another alternative to the *tellTarget()* function is the *with* statement, described in Chapter 6, *Statements*.

Usage

The *tellTarget()* function may be better described as a statement because it requires a substatement block. The point, however, is academic, as *tellTarget()* has been deprecated.

Example

```
tellTarget ("ball") {
  gotoAndStop("redStripes");
  _x += 300;
}
```

See Also

"The *with* Statement" in Chapter 6; "Whither Tell Target?" and "The "Objectness" of Movie Clips" in Chapter 13

---

toggleHighQuality( ) Global Function   change the rendering quality of the Player

Availability   Flash 2 and later; deprecated in Flash 5 in favor of _quality

Synopsis   toggleHighQuality()

Description

Switches between High quality and Low quality rendering. When set to High, the Flash Player renders lines with antialiased (smooth) edges. When set to Low, the Flash Player renders lines with aliased (jagged) edges. The *toggleHighQuality()* function does not take any arguments; it simply switches between the two possible settings—"High" and "Low". This is problematic because it doesn't explicitly set the quality to a known setting, nor does it allow for more than two different possible quality settings.

As of Flash 5, *toggleHighQuality()* has been deprecated in favor of the global _quality property, which supports Low, Medium, High, and Best rendering settings.

See Also

_highquality, _quality

---

trace( ) Global Function   display a value in the Output window

Availability   Flash 4 and later

Synopsis   trace(value)

Arguments

value   The expression to be resolved and then displayed in the Output window. If the resolved value of *value* is not a string, it is converted to a string before being sent to the Output window, according to the rules described in Table 3-2.

Description

The *trace()* function is a debugging tool used only within the Test Movie mode of the Flash authoring environment. Though unassuming in nature, *trace()* is actually one of the fundamental components of ActionScript programming; it allows us to check the value of a variable or expression at any point during the playback of a movie.

Usage

Unfortunately *trace()* can be quite slow. Turn off tracing under File → Publish Settings → Flash using the Omit Trace Actions option.

Example

```
trace(firstName);             // Output the value of firstName
trace(myClip);                // Output the path to myClip
trace(myClip._x)              // Output the x coordinate of myClip
trace("hello" + " there");    // Resolve then output the expression
```

See Also

Chapter 19, *Debugging*

---

unescape( ) Global Function   decode an escaped string

Availability   Flash 5

Synopsis   unescape(*stringExpression*)

Arguments
stringExpression   A string (or expression that resolves to a string) that was previously encoded via *escape()*.

Returns

A new string that is a decoded version of **string**.

Description

The *unescape()* function returns a new string based on **string**. The new string contains equivalent Latin 1 characters for every occurrence of a two-digit hexadecimal escape sequence prefixed with **%** in **string**. The *escape()* and *unescape()* functions are used to encode and decode strings for safe transfer over a network. However, manual use of *unescape()* is rarely necessary as Flash automatically converts URL-encoded text when it is imported via *loadVariables()*.

Example

```
var msg = "hello!";
// Set msgCoded to "hello%21"
msgCoded = escape(msg);
// Set msgDecoded to "hello!"
var msgDecoded = unescape(msgCoded);
```

See Also

escape(); Appendix B, *Latin 1 Character Repertoire and Keycodes*

unloadMovie( ) Global Function   remove a movie or movie clip from the Player

Availability   Flash 4 and later (Flash 5's *unloadMovie()* function corresponds to Flash 4's *Unload Movie* with a target path)

Synopsis   `unloadMovie(target)`

Arguments

target   A string or reference indicating the path to the movie clip or document level to remove from the Player (references are converted to paths when used in a string context).

Description

The *unloadMovie()* function is most often used to delete movies from document levels in the Player. For example, if a movie is loaded onto level 1 in the Player, we may remove that movie from the Player as follows:

```
unloadMovie("_level1");
```

The *unloadMovie()* function can also be used on movie clip instances, in which case it removes the content of the instance but not the instance itself. The instance is left on stage as an empty shell; we may load subsequent movies into that shell. Hence, a single clip can act as a container for dynamic content that is managed through successive *loadMovie()* and *unloadMovie()* executions.

See Also

loadMovie(), *MovieClip.unloadMovie()*, *unloadMovieNum()*; "Removing Clip Instances and Main Movies" and "Method versus global function overlap issues" in Chapter 13

---

unloadMovieNum( ) Global Function   remove a movie from a document level

Availability   Flash 3 and later (Flash 5's *unloadMovieNum()* function corresponds to Flash 3's *unload Movie*, which worked only with numbered levels)

Synopsis   `unloadMovieNum(level)`

Arguments

level   A non-negative integer or an expression that yields a non-negative integer, indicating the document level to unload.

Description

The *unloadMovieNum()* function is nearly identical to *unloadMovie()* except that it requires the target *level* of the load operation to be specified as a number rather than as a string. This means that *unloadMovieNum()* can only remove movies on document levels, not movie clips. It is normally used when we wish to dynamically assign the level of a movie to unload, as in:

```
var x = 3;
unloadMovieNum(x);
```

This can also be achieved using string concatenation with the regular *unloadMovie()* function:

```
unloadMovie("_level" + x);
```

See Also

loadMovieNum(), *Movieclip.unloadMovie()*, *unloadMovie()*; "Removing Clip Instances and Main Movies" in Chapter 13

---

updateAfterEvent( ) Global Function

render the contents of the
Stage between frames

Availability   Flash 5

Synopsis   updateAfterEvent()

Description

The user-input clip event handlers (*mouseMove*, *mouseDown*, *mouseUp*, *keyDown*, and *keyUp*) often occur between frame renderings in the Flash Player. To force the screen to reflect visual changes that occur during a user-input clip event handler, we invoke *updateAfterEvent()* within any of those handlers. Note, however, that *updateAfterEvent()* is not an arbitrary screen-refreshing tool; it works only within the user-input clip events. Outside of *onClipEvent()* handlers, it has no effect.

Example

The following script attached to a movie clip causes the clip to follow the mouse pointer and refreshes the screen every time the pointer moves. Because we refresh the screen every time the pointer moves, the clip following the pointer animates very smoothly:

```
onClipEvent (mouseMove) {
  _x = _root._xmouse;
  _y = _root._ymouse;
  updateAfterEvent();
}
```

Bugs

Note that the Flash 5 ActionScript Dictionary incorrectly describes the *updateAfterEvent()* function as accepting a clip event as an argument. It does not accept any arguments.

See Also

See "Refreshing the Screen with updateAfterEvent" in Chapter 10

$version "Global" Property

the version of the Flash Player

Availability   Flash 4 Build 11 and later; deprecated in Flash 5 in favor of *get Version*

Synopsis   _root.$version

Access   Read-only

Description

The $version property contains the same string as the return value of the global *getVersion()* function (operating system, followed by Player version information). The $version property was introduced midway through the life cycle of the Flash 4 Player and has been replaced by the *getVersion()* function. It is technically not a global property, but a property of the main movie timeline; from any other movie clip timeline, it must be accessed as _root.$version.

See Also

getVersion()

XML Class
DOM-based support for XML-structured data

Availability	Flash 5
Constructor	new XML()
	new XML(*source*)

Arguments

source	An optional string containing well-formed XML (or HTML) data to be parsed into an *XML* object hierarchy.

Properties

attributes	An object whose properties store element attributes.
childNodes	An array of references to a node's children.
contentType	The MIME content type to be transmitted to servers.
docTypeDecl	The document's DOCTYPE tag.
firstChild	A reference to the first descendant of a node.
ignoreWhite	Determines whether to ignore whitespace nodes during XML parsing.
lastChild	A reference to the last descendant of a node.
loaded	Status of a *load()* or *sendAndLoad()* operation.
nextSibling	A reference to the node after this node in the current level of the object hierarchy.
nodeName	The name of the current node.
nodeType	The type of the current node.
nodeValue	The value of the current node.
parentNode	A reference to the immediate ancestor of a node.
previousSibling	A reference to the node before this node in the current level of the object hierarchy.
status	Error code describing the result of parsing XML source into an object hierarchy.
xmlDecl	The document's XML declaration tag.

Methods

appendChild()	Add a new child node to a node.
cloneNode()	Create a copy of a node.
createElement()	Create a new element node.
createTextNode()	Create a new text node.

hasChildNodes()	Check if a node has any descendants.
insertBefore()	Add a sibling node before a node.
load()	Import XML source code from an external document.
parseXML()	Parse a string of XML source code.
removeNode()	Delete a node from an object hierarchy.
send()	Send XML source code to a script.
sendAndLoad()	Send XML source code to a script and receive XML source in return.
toString()	Convert an *XML* object to a string.

Event Handlers

| *onData()* | Handler executed when external XML source finishes loading. |
| *onLoad()* | Handler executed when external XML data has been parsed into an object hierarchy. |

Description

We use objects of the *XML* class to manipulate the content of an XML (or HTML) document in an object-oriented manner and to send XML-formatted data to and from Flash. Using the methods and properties of an *XML* object, we may build an XML-structured document (or read an existing one) and efficiently access, change, or remove the information in that document.

The source code of an XML document consists primarily of a series of elements and attributes. For example, in the following XML fragment, the elements BOOK, TITLE, AUTHOR, and PUBLISHER take the same form as well-known HTML tags, and we see that the AUTHOR element supports one attribute, SALUTATION:

```
<BOOK>
   <TITLE>ActionScript: The Definitive Guide</TITLE>
   <AUTHOR SALUTATION="Mr.">Colin Moock</AUTHOR>
   <PUBLISHER>O'Reilly</PUBLISHER>
</BOOK>
```

From an object-oriented perspective, the content of an XML document can be treated as a hierarchy of objects in which each element and text block becomes an object node in a flowchart-like structure. Figure R-1 shows our simple XML <BOOK> fragment represented conceptually as an XML object hierarchy.

Let's consider the structure and semantics of this sample XML object hierarchy from left to right. We start with the main *XML* object, shown in Figure R-1 as DOCUMENT, which is created automatically by the *XML* constructor and serves as the container for our XML object hierarchy.

Moving one tier to the right in the hierarchy, we come to BOOK, which is the first element in our XML source code fragment and, in this case, also the first *object node* under DOCUMENT. The BOOK node is the *root* of our XML data structure—every well-formed XML document must have an all-encompassing root element such as BOOK that contains every other element. Branches of an XML object hierarchy are added to the tree either by parsing XML source code or invoking node-addition methods on the objects in the hierarchy.

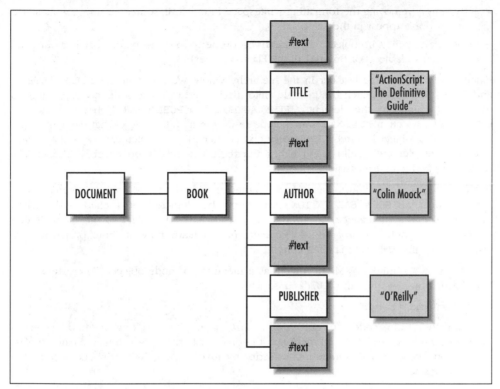

Figure R-1. A sample XML node hierarchy

When a node is contained by another node, the *contained* node is said to be a *child* of the containing node, which is known as the *parent*. In our example, BOOK is the first child of DOCUMENT, and DOCUMENT is BOOK's parent.

As we move to the right in Figure R-1, we see that BOOK has seven children, including four #text nodes that do not seem to be present in our original XML document. Each occurrence of whitespace between elements in XML source code is rendered as an object in an XML object hierarchy. If we look closely, we'll find whitespace—a carriage return and a Tab character—between BOOK and TITLE in the preceding XML fragment. This whitespace is represented by a #text node in Figure R-1, which also shows similar whitespace nodes after the TITLE, AUTHOR, and PUBLISHER nodes.

BOOK's children are *siblings* of one another (i.e., they reside on the same level in the hierarchy). For example, we say that AUTHOR's *next sibling* is #text, and AUTHOR's *previous sibling* is #text. You can see how the #text nodes get in our way when we're moving from sibling to sibling in a hierarchy. We can deal with these empty whitespace nodes in one of the following ways:

- By manually stripping them out of our object hierarchy (see the later examples for whitespace-stripping code)

- By detecting and then sidestepping them in our code (see the nextSibling and previousSibling properties for ways of moving over nodes)

- By simply removing the formatting whitespace in our XML source, ensuring whitespace nodes don't appear in the first place

- By setting our *XML* object's `ignoreWhite` property to `true` before parsing our XML source (available as of Build 41 of the Flash 5 Player)

Finally, we move to the last tier in the hierarchy where we find that the TITLE, AUTHOR, and PUBLISHER nodes each has a single child. Each child is a text node, corresponding to the text contained by the elements TITLE, AUTHOR, and PUBLISHER. Notice that the text contained by an element in XML source code resides in a child node of that element in the corresponding object hierarchy. To access text contained by an element, we must always refer to that element's child using either `firstChild.nodeValue` or `childNodes[0].nodeValue`, which we'll consider shortly.

But what of the element attributes? Where do they appear in our XML object hierarchy? You might expect AUTHOR's SALUTATION attribute to be depicted as a child node called SALUTATION. But in practice, an attribute is not considered a *child* of the element that defines it, but rather a *property* of that element. To learn how attribute properties are accessed, see the *XML*`.attributes` entry.

Let's see how to build an XML document as a hierarchy of node objects. To create a new, blank *XML* object, we use the *XML()* constructor:

```
myDocument = new XML();
```

We can then add nodes to our empty *XML* object by invoking methods such as *appendChild()*, *parseXML()*, and *load()* on the object. Alternatively, we may create an *XML* object from existing XML source in our script by invoking the XML constructor with the *source* argument:

```
myDocument = new XML(source);
```

For example:

```
myDocument = new XML('<P>hello world!</P>');
```

When a *source* argument is supplied to the *XML()* constructor, *source* is parsed and converted into a new object hierarchy, which is then stored in the object returned by the constructor. (In this case, the node P is assigned as myDocument's first child and the text node with the `nodeValue` "hello world!" is assigned as P's first child.)

Once an XML hierarchy is created and stored in an object, we may access the information in that hierarchy using the methods and properties of the *XML* class. For example, suppose we want to retrieve the text "hello world!" in myDocument. Thinking in object-oriented terms, we might assume that we could access the text of P as a property of myDocument, as follows: myDocument.P. In fact, that won't work; instead of referring to nodes by name, we use the *XML* class's built-in properties, such as `firstChild` and `childNodes`, to access nodes. For example, to access the P node, we could use:

```
myDocument.firstChild        // Accesses P
myDocument.childNodes[0]      // Also accesses P
```

Because `firstChild` returns a reference to the first child node of the specified node in the hierarchy, `myDocument.firstChild` returns a reference to node P. However, we want the text "hello world!" contained by P, not node P itself. As we learned earlier, the text of an element node is stored as a child of that node. Therefore, we can reference the text node (i.e., the first descendant of P), like this:

```
myDocument.firstChild.firstChild  // Accesses the text node under P
```

To obtain the value of a node, we use the `nodeValue` property. For example, we can display the value "hello world!" in the Output window using:

```
trace(myDocument.firstChild.firstChild.nodeValue);
```

Or, we can reassign the value of the text node under P using:

```
myDocument.firstChild.firstChild.nodeValue = "goodbye cruel world";
```

To remove the P node altogether, add a new node, or move the text "hello world!" to another node, we invoke appropriate methods of the *XML* class. For example:

```
// Delete P
myDocument.firstChild.removeNode();

// Make a new element named P
newElement = myDocument.createElement("P");

// Add the new element to our document
myDocument.appendChild(newElement);

// Make a new text node to attach to P
newText = myDocument.createTextNode("XML is fun");

// Attach the new text node to P
myDocument.firstChild.appendChild(newText);
```

As you can see, working with XML-structured data in an object hierarchy is a mediated endeavor. We build, destroy, and manipulate the data by invoking methods on, and accessing properties of, objects. To learn the various tools available for working with XML data, explore the properties and methods of the *XML* class, which are listed next.

ActionScript manipulates XML data using the Document Object Model (DOM) standard published by the World Wide Web Consortium (W3C). For thorough coverage of how the DOM represents XML-structured data as an object hierarchy, consult:

http://www.w3.org/DOM

For details on the language-independent specifications of the core DOM, see:

http://www.w3.org/TR/REC-DOM-Level-1/level-one-core.html

(pay particular attention to "Interface Node" under 1.2, *Fundamental Interfaces*). For details on how the DOM is implemented in ECMA-262, see:

http://www.w3.org/TR/REC-DOM-Level-1/ecma-script-language-binding.html

Example

We've learned that the whitespace between any two elements in XML source code is represented by a text node in the corresponding *XML* object hierarchy. Prior to Build 41 of the Flash 5 Player, undesired whitespace nodes had to be manually stripped out of an XML object hierarchy. Stripping a particular kind of node is a common task in XML handling and serves as a good example of *tree traversal* (moving through every node in a hierarchy). Let's consider two different techniques for stripping whitespace nodes from a document.

In the first example, we'll use a classic FIFO (First In First Out) stack to add all the nodes in a tree to an array for processing. The *stripWhitespaceTraverse()* function seeds an array of node elements with *theNode*, which it receives as an argument. Then it enters a loop in which it removes the first node in the array, processes that node, and adds its children (if any) to the array. When the array has no more elements, all the descendants of *theNode* have been processed. During processing, any node that has no children is considered potential whitespace (because text nodes never have children). Each of these nodes is checked to see if:

- It is a text node (as determined by its nodeType property)

- It contains any characters above ASCII 32, which are not considered whitespace

Any text nodes containing only characters below ASCII 32 (i.e., only whitespace) are removed:

```
// Strip Whitespace Using a FIFO Stack
// Strips any whitespace nodes descending from theNode by traversing the tree
function stripWhitespaceTraverse (theNode) {
  // Create a list of nodes to process
  var nodeList = new Array();
  // Seed the list with the node passed to the function
  nodeList[0] = theNode;

  // Process descendants until there are none left to process
  while (nodeList.length > 0) {
    // Remove the first node from the list and assign it to currentNode
    currentNode = nodeList.shift();

    // If this node has children...
    if (currentNode.childNodes.length > 0) {
      // ...add this node's children to the list of nodes to process
      nodeList = nodeList.concat(currentNode.childNodes);
    } else {
      // ...otherwise, this node is the end of a branch, so check if it's a
      // text node. If so, check if it contains only empty whitespace.
      // nodeType 3 indicates a text node
      if (currentNode.nodeType == 3) {
        var i = 0;
        var emptyNode = true;
        for (i = 0; i < currentNode.nodeValue.length; i++) {
          // A useful character is anything over 32 (space, tab,
          // new line, etc. are all below).
          if (currentNode.nodeValue.charCodeAt(i) > 32) {
            emptyNode = false;
            break;
          }
        }
      }

      // If no useful charaters were found, delete the node
      if (emptyNode) {
        currentNode.removeNode();
      }
    }
  }
}
```

The technique shown in the preceding example is traditionally very efficient. However, in the Flash 5 Player, the *Array.concat()* method executes quite slowly. Hence, it's quicker to strip whitespace using the technique shown in the following example. Study the comments carefully:

```
// Strip Whitespace Using Function Recursion
// Strips whitespace nodes from an XML document
// by passing twice through each level in the tree
function stripWhitespaceDoublePass(theNode) {
  // Loop through all the children of theNode
  for (var i = 0; i < theNode.childNodes.length; i++) {
    // If the current node is a text node...
    if (theNode.childNodes[i].nodeType == 3) {

      // ...check for any useful characters in the node
      var j = 0;
      var emptyNode = true;
      for (j = 0;j < theNode.childNodes[i].nodeValue.length; j++) {
        // A useful character is anything over 32 (space, tab,
        // new line, etc. are all below)
        if (theNode.childNodes[i].nodeValue.charCodeAt(j) > 32) {
          emptyNode = false;
          break;
        }
      }

      // If no useful charaters were found, delete the node
      if (emptyNode) {
        theNode.childNodes[i].removeNode();
      }
    }
  }

  // Now that all the whitespace nodes have been removed from theNode,
  // call stripWhitespaceDoublePass() recursively on its remaining children.
  for (var k = 0; k < theNode.childNodes.length; k++) {
    stripWhitespaceDoublePass(theNode.childNodes[k]);
  }
}
```

See Also

The *XMLnode* class, The *XMLSocket* class; "HTML Support" in Chapter 18

XML.appendChild( ) Method

add a new child node to a node, or move an existing node

Availability	Flash 5
Synopsis	*theNode*.appendChild(*childNode*)
Arguments	
childNode	An existing XML node object.

Description

The *appendChild()* method adds the specified *childNode* to *theNode* as *theNode*'s last child. We can use *appendChild()* to add a new node to an existing node, to move a node within a document, or to move a node between documents. In each of these cases, *childNode* must be a reference to a node object that already exists.

To add a new child node to an existing node, we must first create the new child node using *createElement()*, *createTextNode()*, or *cloneNode()* or by parsing XML source code into an *XML* object. For example, in the following code, we create a new P node and a new text node. We append the text node to the P node and then append the P node and its text node child to the top node of a document:

```
// Create a document
myDoc = new XML('<P>paragraph 1</P>');

// Create a P node and a text node
newP = myDoc.createElement("P");
newText = myDoc.createTextNode("paragraph 2");

// Append the text node to the P node
newP.appendChild(newText);

// Append the P node (including its text child) to myDoc
myDoc.appendChild(newP);

trace(myDoc);  // Displays: "<P>paragraph 1</P><P>paragraph 2</P>"
```

To move a node within a document, specify a *childNode* that is a reference to an existing node in the document. In this situation, *childNode* indicates the old location of the node, and *theNode* indicates the new parent of the node. In the process of being appended to *theNode*, *childNode* is removed from its previous parent node. For example, here we move the B node from its parent P node to the root of the document:

```
// Create a new document
myDoc = new XML('<P>paragraph 1<B>bold text</B></P>');

// Store a reference to the B node
boldText = myDoc.firstChild.childNodes[1];

// Append the B node to the root of the document, while removing it from P
myDoc.appendChild(boldText);

trace(myDoc);  // Displays: "<P>paragraph 1</P><B>bold text</B>"
```

We also could have skipped the reference-storing step and just moved the node directly:

```
myDoc.appendChild(myDoc.firstChild.childNodes[1]);
```

To move a node between documents, *childNode* should be a reference to a node in the first (source) document and *theNode* should be a reference to a node in the second (target) document. For example, here we move the B node from myDoc to myOtherDoc:

```
myDoc = new XML('<P>paragraph 1<B>bold text</B></P>');
myOtherDoc = new XML();

myOtherDoc.appendChild(myDoc.firstChild.childNodes[1]);
```

```
    trace(myDoc);        // Displays: "<P>paragraph 1</P>"
    trace(myOtherDoc);   // Displays: "<B>bold text</B>"
```

See Also

XML.createElement(), XML.createTextNode(), XML.cloneNodee(), XML.insertBefore()

XML.attributes Property   an object whose properties store element attributes

Availability   Flash 5

Synopsis   *theNode*.attributes.*attributeIdentifier*
                     theNode.attributes[*attributeNameInQuotes*]

Access   Read/write

Description

The `attributes` property stores the names and values of attributes defined by *theNode*. For example, the `ALIGN` attribute of this `P` tag:

```
    <P ALIGN="CENTER">this is a paragraph</P>
```

is accessed using *theNode*.`attributes.ALIGN` or *theNode*.`attributes["ALIGN"]`. If the `P` tag were the only tag in our XML source, we could access the `ALIGN` attribute as follows:

```
    // Create an XML object hierarchy
    myDoc = new XML('<P ALIGN="CENTER">this is a paragraph</P>');

    // Access the ALIGN attribute. Displays: "CENTER"
    trace(myDoc.firstChild.attributes.ALIGN);

    // Set the ALIGN attribute
    myDoc.firstChild.attributes.ALIGN = "LEFT";
```

The `attributes` property is itself an object. We can add new properties to the `attributes` object, thereby adding new attributes to *theNode*, as follows:

```
    // Add a CLASS attribute to the P tag
    myDoc.firstChild.attributes.CLASS = "INTRO";

    // firstChild now represents the XML source:
    // <P ALIGN="CENTER" CLASS="INTRO">this is a paragraph</P>
```

Because `attributes` is not an array, it doesn't contain a `length` property. Instead, we can access all the attributes defined on an element using a *for-in* loop:

```
    var count = 0;
    for(var prop in theNode.attributes) {
      trace("attribute " + prop + " has the value " + theNode.attributes[prop]);
      count++;
    }
    trace ("The node has " + count + " attributes.");
```

If the XML element represented by *theNode* has no attributes, `attributes` is an empty object with no properties and the preceding example would indicate zero attributes.

See Also

XML.nodeType

XML.childNodes Property   an array of references to a node's children

Availability   Flash 5

Synopsis   *theNode*.childNodes[*n*]

Access   Read-only

Description

The childNodes property is an array whose elements contain references to the immediate descendants of *theNode*. It is used to access nodes in an XML hierarchy. For example, if we create an object hierarchy as follows:

```
myDoc = new XML('<STUDENT><NAME>Tim</NAME><MAJOR>BIOLOGY</MAJOR></STUDENT>');
```

We can then access the STUDENT node using:

```
myDoc.childNodes[0];
```

We can access the NAME and MAJOR nodes (which are descendants of STUDENT) using:

```
myDoc.childNodes[0].childNodes[0];      // NAME
myDoc.childNodes[0].childNodes[1];      // MAJOR
```

If the hierarchy below *theNode* changes, childNodes is automatically updated to reflect the new structure. For example, if we deleted the MAJOR node, myDoc.childNodes[0].childNodes[1] would return undefined.

We often refer to nodes to manipulate information or rearrange a document's structure. For example, we might change a student's name or add a new student using:

```
// Check the name of the student
trace("The student's name is: "
        + myDoc.childNodes[0].childNodes[0].childNodes[0].nodeValue);

// Change the name of the student
myDoc.childNodes[0].childNodes[0].childNodes[0].nodeValue = "James";

// Copy the STUDENT node
newStudent = myDoc.childNodes[0].cloneNode(true);

// Add a new STUDENT node to the document
myDoc.appendChild(newStudent);
```

Note that as a convenience, we may also use the firstChild property to refer to childNodes[0]. The following references are identical:

```
myDoc.childNodes[0];
myDoc.firstChild;
```

To iterate through all the children of a node, we can use a *for* statement, as follows:

```
for (var i = 0; i < theNode.childNodes.length; i++) {
  trace("child " + i + " is " + theNode.childNodes[i].nodeName);
}
```

However, our example traverses only the first level of *theNode*'s hierarchy. The examples under the `XML.nextSibling` entry shows how to access all the nodes below *theNode*. If *theNode* has no children, `theNode.childNodes.length` is 0.

Usage

Remember that empty text nodes, representing the whitespace used to format XML source code, also show up in a `childNode` list. For example, in the following XML source, empty text nodes will be created by the whitespace after the BOOK start tag and the TITLE, AUTHOR, and PUBLISHER end tags:

```
<BOOK>
  <TITLE>ActionScript: The Definitive Guide</TITLE>
  <AUTHOR SALUTATION="Mr">Colin Moock</AUTHOR>
  <PUBLISHER>O'reilly</PUBLISHER>
</BOOK>
```

Hence, the first child node of BOOK is an empty text node; the second child is TITLE.

See Also

XML.`firstChild`,   *XML.hasChildNodes()*,   *XML*.`lastChild`,   *XML*.`nextSibling`,   *XML*.`previousSibling`

XML.cloneNode( ) Method   create a copy of a node

Availability   Flash 5

Synopsis   `theNode.cloneNode(deep)`

Arguments
deep   A Boolean indicating whether to recursively include *theNode*'s children in the clone operation. If `true`, clone the entire hierarchy starting at *theNode*. If `false`, clone only *theNode* itself (and its attributes, if it is an element node).

Returns

A duplicate of the *theNode* object, optionally including its subtree.

Description

The *cloneNode()* method creates and returns a copy of *theNode*, including all of *theNode*'s attributes and values if *theNode* is an element node. If *deep* is `true`, the returned copy includes the entire node hierarchy descending from *theNode*.

We often use *cloneNode()* to create a new node based on an existing template (which saves us from generating the new node structure manually). Once we've cloned a node, we normally customize it and insert it into an existing XML document using either *appendChild()* or *insertBefore()*. The following example clones the first paragraph of a document to make a sibling paragraph with the same structure:

```
// Create a new document
myDoc = new XML('<P>paragraph 1</P>');

// Make a clone of the first paragraph
newP = myDoc.firstChild.cloneNode(true);
```

```
    // Customize the clone
    newP.firstChild.nodeValue = "paragraph 2";

    // Add the clone into the document
    myDoc.appendChild(newP);

    trace(myDoc);  // Displays: "<P>paragraph 1</P><P>paragraph 2</P>"
```

Note that the text in an element is stored in a separate child node of that element, so we must set *deep* to `true` to preserve an element's text content in a clone operation. Remember that *cloneNode()* does not insert the element it returns into the node's document—we must do that ourselves using *appendChild()* or *insertBefore()*.

See Also

XML.appendChild(), XML.createElement(), XML.createTextNode(), XML.insertBefore()

XML.contentType Property

MIME content type for XML dat sent via *XML.send()* and *XML.sendAndLoad()*

Availability	Flash 5 Build 41 or later
Synopsis	*XMLdoc*.`contentType`
Access	Read/write

Description

The `contentType` property is the MIME type that is sent to a server when *XML.send()* or *XML.sendAndLoad()* is invoked. It defaults to `application/x-www-urlform-encoded`. The `contentType` property may be modified for specific XML objects, or `XML.prototype.contentType` may be modified to affect all *XML* objects.

The `contentType` property first appeared in Build 41 of the Flash 5 Player, before which it was not possible to set MIME type. Check `contentType`'s validity by comparing it to `undefined` or using the *getVersion()* function to determine the Player version and build.

Usage

See important notes on setting MIME type under the *XML.send()* entry.

See Also

XML.send(), XML.sendAndLoad()

XML.createElement( ) Method

create a new element node

Availability	Flash 5
Synopsis	*XMLdoc*.`createElement(`*tagName*`)`
Arguments	
tagName	A case-sensitive string indicating the name of the element to create. For example, in the tag, `<P ALIGN="RIGHT">`, P is the tag name.

Returns

A new element node object, with no parent and no children.

Description

The *createElement()* method is our primary means of generating new element nodes for inclusion in an *XML* document object hierarchy. Note that *createElement()* does not insert the element it returns into *XMLdoc*—we must do that ourselves using *appendChild()* or *insertBefore()*. For example, here we create and insert a new P element into a document:

```
myDoc = new XML();
newP = myDoc.createElement("P");
myDoc.appendChild(newP);
```

We can combine those steps like this:

```
myDoc.appendChild(myDoc.createElement("P"));
```

XMLdoc must be an instance of the *XML* class, not the *XMLnode* class.

The *createElement()* method cannot be used to create text nodes; use *createTextNode()* instead.

See Also

XML.appendChild(), *XML.cloneNode()*, *XML.createTextNode()*, *XML.insertBefore()*

XML.createTextNode( ) Method   create a new text node

Availability   Flash 5

Synopsis   *XMLdoc*.createTextNode(*text*)

Arguments

text   A string containing the text that is to become the nodeValue of the new node.

Returns

A new text node object, with no parent and no children.

Description

The *createTextNode()* method is our primary means of generating new text nodes for inclusion in an XML document object hierarchy. Note that *createTextNode()* does not insert the element it returns into *XMLdoc*—we must do that ourselves using *appendChild()* or *insertBefore()*. For example, here we create and insert a new P element into a document, and then we give that P element a text-node child:

```
myDoc = new XML();
newP = myDoc.createElement("P");
myDoc.appendChild(newP);

newText = myDoc.createTextNode("This is the first paragraph");
myDoc.firstChild.appendChild(newText);

trace(myDoc);   // Displays: "<P>This is the first paragraph</P>"
```

XMLdoc must be an instance of the *XML* class, not the *XMLnode* class.

Text nodes are normally stored as the children of element nodes, which are created using *createElement()*.

See Also

XML.appendChild(), XML.cloneNode(), XML.createElement(), XML.insertBefore()

XML.docTypeDecl Property   the document's DOCTYPE tag

Availability   Flash 5

Synopsis   `XMLdoc.docTypeDecl`

Access   Read/write

Description

The `docTypeDecl` string property specifies the DOCTYPE tag of *XMLdoc*, if any exists. Otherwise, `docTypeDecl` is `undefined`. *XMLdoc* must be the top-level node in an *XML* object hierarchy (i.e., an instance of the *XML* class, not the *XMLnode* class).

An XML document's DOCTYPE specifies the name and location of the DTD used to validate the document. ActionScript does not perform validation of XML documents; it merely parses them. We use the DOCTYPE tag to build XML documents that may be validated externally or to identify the type of a loaded XML document.

Example

```
var myXML = new XML('<?xml version="1.0"?><!DOCTYPE foo SYSTEM "bar.dtd">'
                + '<P>a short document</P>');

trace(myXML.docTypeDecl);  // Displays: "<!DOCTYPE foo SYSTEM "bar.dtd">"

// Set a new DOCTYPE
myXML.docTypeDecl = '<!DOCTYPE baz SYSTEM "bam.dtd">';
```

See Also

`XML.xmlDecl`

XML.firstChild Property   a reference to the first descendant of a node

Availability   Flash 5

Synopsis   `theNode.firstChild`

Access   Read-only

Description

The `firstChild` property is synonymous with `childNodes[0]`. It returns a reference to the first node object that descends from *theNode*. If *theNode* has no children, `firstChild` returns `null`.

In this XML source fragment, the `firstChild` of the `MESSAGE` node is the text node with the `nodeValue` "hey":

```
<!-- Fragment 1 -->
<MESSAGE>hey</MESSAGE>
```

Here, the `firstChild` of the `HOTEL` node is the `ROOM` node:

```
<!-- Fragment 2 -->
<HOTEL><ROOM><SIZE>Double</SIZE></ROOM></HOTEL>
```

When *theNode* is the top of the object hierarchy (i.e., refers to the *XML* document object), `firstChild` may not always be a reference to the first useful element in the document. If a document includes an XML delcaration (`<?xml version="1.0"?>`) and perhaps a `DOCTYPE` tag, there are normally whitespace nodes before the actual root element of the XML hierarchy. However, if an XML fragment has no XML declaration and no `DOCTYPE`, we can start processing it with the document's `firstChild` node, as in:

```
// Create a new XML fragment
myDoc = new XML('<MESSAGE><USER>gray</USER><CONTENT>hi</CONTENT></MESSAGE>');

// Store the XML fragment's first node in the variable msg
msg = myDoc.firstChild;

// Assign the text contained by the USER tag
// to a text field called userNameOutput
userNameOutput = msg.firstChild.firstChild.nodeValue;
```

It's good form, but not actually necessary, to use `nodeValue` to access the text contained by the `USER` tag. When we use a text-node object in a string context, the *toString()* method is automatically invoked on that node, and the text in the node is returned.

See Also

XML.`childNodes`, *XML*.`lastChild`, *XML*.`nextSibling`, *XML*.`previousSibling`

XML.hasChildNodes( ) Method   check if a node has any descendants

Availability   Flash 5

Synopsis   *theNode*.`hasChildNodes()`

Returns

A Boolean: `true` if *theNode* has any children; `false` if it does not.

Description

The *hasChildNodes()* method indicates whether any node hierarchy extends from a given node. It is synonymous with the comparison expression:

```
theNode.childNodes.length > 0
```

If *theNode* contains no subnodes, *hasChildNodes()* returns `false`.

Example

We can use *hasChildNodes()* to determine whether to operate on a node during node processing. For example, here we remove the nodes below the first child of a document until the first child has no more children:

```
while (myDoc.firstChild.hasChildNodes()) {
  myDoc.firstChild.firstChild.removeNode();
}
```

See Also

XML.childNodes

XML.ignoreWhite Property   Determines whether to ignore whitespace
                                               nodes during XML parsing

Availability   Flash 5 Build 41 or later

Synopsis   *XMLdoc*.ignoreWhite

Access   Read/write

Description

The ignoreWhite property stores a Boolean that dictates whether to discard text nodes containing only whitespace during the parsing process. The default value is **false** (don't throw away whitespace nodes). This is a global setting that applies to an entire XML document, not just a specific node. That is, instances of the *XMLnode* class do not support *ignoreWhite*.

Example

To cause a single XML document to discard whitespace nodes during parsing, use:

```
myXML.ignoreWhite = true;
```

To cause all XML documents to discard whitespace nodes, use:

```
XML.prototype.ignoreWhite = true;
```

The ignoreWhite property should be set before any attempt at parsing XML occurs (typically due to a *load()* or *sendAndLoad()* operation).

See Also

See the examples under the *XML* Class entry for manual whitespace-stripping code

---

XML.insertBefore( ) Method   give a node a new previous sibling

Availability   Flash 5

Synopsis   *theNode*.insertBefore(*newChild*, *beforeChild*)

Arguments
newChild   An existing XML node object.

beforeChild   The child of *theNode* before which *newChild* should be inserted.

Description

The *insertBefore()* method adds **newChild** to **theNode**'s child list, before **beforeChild**. The *insertBefore()* method is similar to *appendChild()* but lets us precisely position a new node in an existing XML object hierarchy.

Example

```
// Create a document
myDoc = new XML('<P>paragraph 2</P>');

// Create a P node and a text node
newP = myDoc.createElement("P");
newText = myDoc.createTextNode("paragraph 1");

// Append the text node to the P node
newP.appendChild(newText);

// Insert the new P node (including its text child) before the existing P
myDoc.insertBefore(newP, myDoc.firstChild);

trace(myDoc);  // Displays: "<P>paragraph 1</P><P>paragraph 2</P>"
```

See Also

XML.appendChild()

XML.lastChild Property   a reference to the last descendant of a node

Availability   Flash 5

Synopsis   *theNode*.lastChild

Access   Read-only

Description

The lastChild property is synonymous with childNodes[childNodes.length-1]. It returns a reference to the last node object that descends from *theNode*. If *theNode* has no children, lastChild returns null.

In the following XML source fragment, the lastChild of the MESSAGE node is the CONTENT node:

```
<MESSAGE><USER>gray</USER><CONTENT>hi</CONTENT></MESSAGE>
```

Example

```
// Create a new XML document
myDoc = new XML('<MESSAGE><USER>gray</USER><CONTENT>hi</CONTENT></MESSAGE>');

// Sets msg to "hi" because myDoc's firstChild
// is MESSAGE, MESSAGE's lastChild is CONTENT, and CONTENT's firstChild
// is the text node with the value "hi"
msg = myDoc.firstChild.lastChild.firstChild.nodeValue
```

See Also

XML.childNodes, *XML*.firstChild, *XML*.nextSibling, *XML*.previousSibling

---

XML.load( ) Method   import XML source code from an external document

Availability   Flash 5

Synopsis   *XMLdoc*.load(*URL*)

Arguments
URL   A string specifying the location of the XML document to load.

Description

The *load()* method imports an external XML document, parses it, converts it into an XML object hierarchy, and places that hierarchy into *XMLdoc*. Any previous contents of *XMLdoc* are replaced by the newly loaded XML content.

XMLdoc must be an instance of the *XML* class, not the *XMLnode* class.

Usage

Before accessing content imported with *load()*, we must be sure the load and parsing operations are complete. To do so, either check the value of the XML document's loaded property, or assign the document an *onLoad()* callback handler to respond to the load completion. See the *XML*.loaded and *XML.onLoad()* entries for details. To determine whether the loaded data was successfully parsed, check the document's status property.

XML.load() is subject to the domain-based security restrictions described in Table R-8 under the global *loadVariables()* function.

Example

```
myDoc = new XML();
myDoc.load("myData.xml");
```

See Also

XML.loaded, *XML.onLoad()*, *XML.sendAndLoad()*, *XML*.status

---

XML.loaded Property   status of a *load()* or *sendAndLoad()* operation

Availability   Flash 5

Synopsis   *XMLdoc*.loaded

Access   Read-only

Description

The loaded property returns a Boolean value indicating whether a previously invoked *load()* or *sendAndLoad()* operation on *XMLdoc* has completed. It is immediately set to false when an XML *load()* or *sendAndLoad()* operation is initiated. If the load is successful, loaded is later set to true. If no such operation has ever been executed on *XMLdoc*, loaded is undefined.

When loaded is false, the download and parsing of XML data is still in progress, and attempts to access the object hierarchy in *XMLdoc* will fail. When loaded is true, XML data has finished being downloaded, parsed, and stored in *XMLdoc* as an object hierarchy. Note, however, that the loaded XML data may not have been parsed successfully (use *XMLdoc.*status to determine whether it was).

XMLdoc must be an instance of the *XML* class, not the *XMLnode* class.

Example

The following example shows a basic XML preloader that waits for the XML data to be loaded before displaying it (XML preloaders may also be built using an *XML.onLoad()* handler):

```
// CODE ON FRAME 1
// Create a new XML document
myDoc = new XML();
// Load an external XML file into the document
myDoc.load("userProfile.xml");

// CODE ON FRAME 5
// Check if the data has loaded. If so, go to the display frame.
// If not, loop back to frame 4 and then play.
// Loop until the data is done loading...
if (myDoc.loaded) {
  if (myDoc.status == 0) {
    gotoAndStop("displayData");
  } else {
    gotoAndStop("loadingError");
  }
} else {
  gotoAndPlay(4);
}
```

See Also

XML.load(), *XML.onLoad()*, *XML.sendAndLoad()*

XML.nextSibling Property

a reference to the node after this node

Availability   Flash 5

Synopsis   *theNode*.nextSibling

Access   Read-only

Description

The nextSibling property returns the node object after *theNode* in the current level of the XML object hierarchy. If there is no node after *theNode*, nextSibling returns null. In the following XML source fragment, the CONTENT node is the nextSibling of the USER node:

```
<MESSAGE><USER>gray</USER><CONTENT>hi</CONTENT></MESSAGE>
```

Example

The `nextSibling` property is typically used to *traverse* (move through) an XML object hierarchy. For example, to view all the children of *theNode* in the order they appear, we may use:

```
for (var child = theNode.firstChild; child != null; child = child.nextSibling) {
  trace("found node: " + child.nodeName);
}
```

By extending our loop into a function, we can recursively traverse every node in an XML object hierarchy, as follows:

```
function showNodes (node) {
  trace(node.nodeName + ": " + node.nodeValue);
  for (var child = node.firstChild; child != null; child = child.nextSibling) {
    showNodes(child);
  }
}


// Invoke the function on our node or document
showNodes(myDoc);
```

Note that in both traversal examples shown, text nodes show up without a name as described under the `nodeName` entry.

See Also

`XML.childNodes`, `XML.firstChild`, `XML.lastChild`, `XML.nodeName`, `XML.nodeValue`, `XML.previousSibling`

XML.nodeName Property   the name of the current node

Availability   Flash 5

Synopsis   *theNode*.nodeName

Access   Read/write

Description

The `nodeName` string property reflects the name of *theNode*. Since only two node types are supported by ActionScript (*element* nodes and *text* nodes), `nodeName` has only two possible values:

- If *theNode* is an element node, `nodeName` is a string matching the tag name of that element. For example, if *theNode* represents the element <BOOK>, then *theNode*.`nodeName` is `"BOOK"`.

- If *theNode* is a text node, `nodeName` is `null`. Note that this diverges from the DOM specification, which stipulates that `nodeName` for a text node should be the string `"#text"`. If you prefer, you can use the DOM-compliant `nodeType` property instead.

Example

We can use `nodeName` to check whether the current node is the type of element we're seeking. For example, here we extract all the content of H1 tags on the first level of an XML document (this example checks only for tags named *H1*, not for tags named *h1* with a lower-case *h*):

```
myDoc = new XML('<H1>first heading</H1><P>content</P>' +
                '<H1>second heading</H1><P>content</P>');
for (i = 0; i < myDoc.childNodes.length; i++) {
  if (myDoc.childNodes[i].nodeName == "H1") {
    trace(myDoc.childNodes[i].firstChild.nodeValue);
  }
}
```

See Also

XML.nodeType, *XML*.nodeValue

XML.nodeType Property   the type of the current node

Availability   Flash 5

Synopsis   *theNode*.nodeType

Access   Read-only

Description

The nodeType is an integer property that returns *theNode*'s type. Since only two node types are supported by ActionScript—*element* nodes and *text* nodes—nodeName has only two possible values: 1, if the node is an element node; and 3, if the node is a text node. These values may seem arbitrary, but they are actually the appropriate values as stipulated by the DOM. For reference, the other node types in the DOM are listed in Table R-13.

Table R-13. DOM Node Types

Node Description	Node Type Code
ELEMENT_NODE*	1
ATTRIBUTE_NODE	2
TEXT_NODE*	3
CDATA_SECTION_NODE	4
ENTITY_REFERENCE_NODE	5
ENTITY_NODE	6
PROCESSING_INSTRUCTION_NODE	7
COMMENT_NODE	8
DOCUMENT_NODE	9
DOCUMENT_TYPE_NODE	10
DOCUMENT_FRAGMENT_NODE	11
NOTATION_NODE	12

*Supported by Flash. Technically, ActionScript implements so-called *attribute*, *document*, and *document_type* nodes in addition to *element* and *text* nodes, but we don't have direct access to them as objects. For example, we may manipulate the attributes of a node through the attributes property, but we do not have direct access to *attribute* nodes themselves. Similarly, we have access to the DOCTYPE tag of a document through the docTypeDecl property, but we do not have direct access to *document_type* itself.

Element nodes correspond to XML or HTML tags. For example, in the XML fragment `<P>what is your favorite color?</P>`, the P tag would be represented in an *XML* object hierarchy as an element node (`nodeType` 1). The text contained by a tag in XML source code—for example, the text "what is your favorite color?"—would be represented as a text node (`nodeType` 3).

Example

We can conditionally operate on a node based on its `nodeType`. For example, here we remove all the empty text nodes that are children of *theNode*:

```
// Loop through all children of theNode
for (i = 0; i < theNode.childNodes.length; i++) {
  // If the current node is a text node...
  if (theNode.childNodes[i].nodeType == 3) {
    // Check for any useful characters in the node
    var j = 0;
    var emptyNode = true;
    for (j = 0; j < theNode.childNodes[i].nodeValue.length; j++) {
      // Useful character codes start above ASCII 32
      if (theNode.childNodes[i].nodeValue.charCodeAt(j) > 32) {
        emptyNode = false;
        break;
      }
    }
    // No useful charaters were found, so delete the node
    theNode.childNodes[i].removeNode();
  }
}
```

See Also

The XML Class, *XML*.nodeName, *XML*.nodeValue

XML.nodeValue Property   the value of the current node

Availability   Flash 5

Synopsis   *theNode*.nodeValue

Access   Read/write

Description

The `nodeValue` property reflects the string value of *theNode*. Since only two node types (*element* nodes and *text* nodes) are supported by ActionScript, `nodeValue` has only two possible values:

- If *theNode* is an element node, `nodeValue` is `null`.
- If *theNode* is a text node, `nodeValue` is the text contained by the node.

In practice, `nodeValue` is normally used only with text nodes. To assign new text to an existing text node, we use `nodeValue` as follows:

```
// Create a new XML document
myDoc = new XML('<H1>first heading</H1><P>content</P>');
```

```
// Change the text contained by the H1 tag
myDoc.firstChild.firstChild.nodeValue = "My Life Story";
```

Although we may explicitly retrieve the value of a text node using nodeValue, the *toString()* method implicitly returns a node's value when it is used in a string context. Therefore, this code displays the text node's text in the Output window:

```
trace(myDoc.firstChild.firstChild);
```

See Also

XML.nodeName, *XML*.nodeType

XML.onData( ) Event Handler

executed when external XML source code finishes loading, but has not yet been parsed

Availability   Flash 5 (undocumented)

Synopsis   *XMLdoc*.onData(*src*);

Arguments

src   A string containing the loaded XML source code.

Description

The *onData()* handler executes automatically whenever raw XML source has finished loading into *XMLdoc* due to an earlier *load()* or *sendAndLoad()* invocation. By default, *onData()* has the following behavior:

- If the raw source received is undefined, it calls *XMLdoc.onLoad()* with the success parameter set to false.

- Otherwise, it parses the source into *XMLdoc*, sets XMLdoc.loaded to true, and calls *XMLdoc.onLoad()* with the success parameter set to true.

The *onData()* handler may be assigned a custom callback function to intercept raw XML source code before ActionScript has a chance to parse it. Under certain circumstances, manipulating raw XML source manually may offer improved performance over Action-Script's built-in parsing.

Example

The following example shows how to display raw loaded XML source while preventing it from being parsed by ActionScript:

```
myDoc = new XML();
myDoc.onData = function (src) {
  trace("Here's the source: \n" + src);
};
myDoc.load("book.xml");
```

See Also

XML.onLoad()

XML.onLoad( ) Event Handler

executed when external XML data
has been loaded and parsed

Availability   Flash 5

Synopsis   *XMLdoc*.onLoad(*success*)

Arguments

success   A Boolean value indicating whether loading was successful (true) or
                 failed (false).

Description

The *onLoad()* handler of *XMLdoc* is automatically executed whenever an external XML file
is loaded into *XMLdoc* via the *load()* or *sendAndLoad()* methods. By default, the *onLoad()*
handler of an XML document object is an empty function. To use *onLoad()*, we assign it a
callback handler (i.e., a custom-made function). For example:

```
myDoc = new XML();
myDoc.onLoad = handleLoad;
function handleLoad (success) {
  // Process XML as desired here...
}
```

We rely on *onLoad()* events to tell us when it's safe to process *XMLdoc*. If *onLoad()* is triggered, we know that the loading and parsing of external XML data have completed, so we
may safely access that loaded content. The *onLoad()* handler, hence, alleviates the need to
write preloading code to wait for data to arrive after the invocation of an XML *load()* function. For example, in the following code we load an XML document, and then we wait for
our custom *handleLoad()* function to be automatically executed when loading completes. If
loading was successful, we process our XML content with the *display()* function. Otherwise, we show an error message by executing the *display()* function. (The *displayProduct()*
and *displayError()* functions are custom functions that you've presumably written to display
information to the user, but they are not shown.)Here is the code:

```
myDoc = new XML();
myDoc.onLoad = handleLoad;
myDoc.load("productInfo.xml");

function handleLoad(success) {
  if (success) {
    output = "Product information received";
    displayProduct(); // Call custom display function
  } else {
    output = "Attempt to load XML data failed";
    displayError(); // Call custom display function
  }
}
```

Notice that the value of the success argument of *handleLoad()* is automatically set by the
interpreter to either true or false, indicating whether or not loading completed properly.
However, the success argument may appear more useful in theory than it turns out to be
in practice. Most web server error messages (e.g., "404 File Not Found") come in the form
of HTML documents. Since HTML can quite happily be parsed as XML data, the reception of
a server error page results in the parsing of that page into the target XML document object.

Because the page parses properly, the load attempt is considered "successful," and **success** is **true**, even though the actual XML file may not have been found or some other server error may have been encountered. To be positive that you have the real data you requested, test its structure or content explicitly for some identifying characteristic, such as the **nodeName** of a particular child. See also the *XML.onData( )* event handler, which can be used to perform custom parsing.

See Also

XML.load( ), XML.onData( ), XML.sendAndLoad( )

XML.parentNode Property
a reference to the immediate ancestor of a node

Availability   Flash 5

Synopsis   *theNode*.parentNode

Access   Read-only

Description

The **parentNode** property returns a reference to the node object from which *theNode* descends in the XML object hierarchy. If *theNode* is the top of the current hierarchy, **parentNode** returns **null**.

In this XML source fragment, the **MESSAGE** node is the **parentNode** of text node **"hey"**:

    <MESSAGE>hey</MESSAGE>

Here the **parentNode** of the **ROOM** node is the **HOTEL** node:

    <HOTEL><ROOM><SIZE>Double</SIZE></ROOM></HOTEL>

See Also

XML.childNodes, *XML*.firstChild, *XML*.lastChild, *XML*.previousSibling

---

XML.parseXML( ) Method
parse a string of XML source code

Availability   Flash 5

Synopsis   *XMLdoc*.parseXML(*string*)

Arguments
string   A string of XML source code.

Description

The *parseXML( )* method is akin to an internal *load( )* function; it reads and parses the XML source contained by *string*, converts that XML into an object hierarchy, and then places the resulting hierarchy into *XMLdoc*. Any previous contents of *XMLdoc* are replaced by the new hierarchy. *XMLdoc* must be an instance of the *XML* class, not the *XMLnode* class .

To include raw HTML or XML source code in a text node without parsing it, use a CDATA section as follows:

    <![CDATA[source]]>

For example, the following code creates a MESSAGE element with a single child text node containing the text "<B>Welcome</B> to my site" (the <B> tag is *not* interpreted as an XML tag and does not become part of the XML object hierarchy):

```
myDoc = new XML();
myDoc.parseXML("<MESSAGE><![CDATA[<B>Welcome</B> to my site]]></MESSAGE>");
trace(myDoc);  // Displays: "<MESSAGE><B>Welcome</B> to my site</MESSAGE>"
```

Example

We can use *parseXML()* as a means of replacing the current object hierarchy in an *XML* object with a new hierarchy based on internally composed XML source code (for example, some user input). In the following example, we create a simple XML message by combining markup with input from text fields named username and content:

```
myDoc = new XML();
myXMLsource = "<MESSAGE><USER>" + username + "</USER><CONTENT>"
    + content + "</CONTENT></MESSAGE>";
myDoc.parseXML(myXMLsource);
```

See Also

XML.load(), *XML*.status

XML.previousSibling Property   a reference to the node before this node

Availability   Flash 5

Synopsis   *theNode*.previousSibling

Access   Read-only

Description

The previousSibling property returns a reference to the node object preceding *theNode* in the current level of the XML object hierarchy. If there is no node before *theNode* in the current level of the hierarchy, it returns null.

In the following XML source fragment, the previousSibling of the CONTENT node is the USER node:

```
<MESSAGE><USER>gray</USER><CONTENT>hi</CONTENT></MESSAGE>
```

Example

The previousSibling property can be used to traverse an XML object hierarchy, although nextSibling is more commonly used for this purpose. To view all the children of *theNode* in reverse order, we may use:

```
for (var i = theNode.lastChild; i != null; i = i.previousSibling) {
  trace("found node: " + i.nodeName);
}
```

See Also

XML.childNodes, *XML*.firstChild, *XML*.lastChild, *XML*.nextSibling, *XML*.nodeName, *XML*.nodeValue, *XML*.parentNode

XML.removeNode( ) Method   delete a node from an XML object hierarchy

Availability   Flash 5

Synopsis   *theNode*.removeNode()

Description

The *removeNode()* method deletes *theNode* from an XML document. All descendants (children, grandchildren, and so on) of *theNode* are also deleted. The childNodes property of *theNode*'s parent is automatically updated to reflect the new structure of the remaining object hierarchy.

Example

Here we delete the second child node; the third child node takes its place:

```
myDoc = new XML("<P>one</P><P>two</P><P>three</P>");
myDoc.childNodes[1].removeNode();
trace(myDoc);  // Displays: "<P>one</P><P>three</P>"
```

See Also

XML.appendChild()

XML.send( ) Method   send XML source code to a script

Availability   Flash 5

Synopsis   *XMLdoc*.send(*URL*, *window*)

Arguments
URL   A string specifying the location of a script or application to which *XMLdoc* should be sent.

window   A required string, specifying the name of the browser window or frame into which to load the script's response. May be a custom name or one of the four presets: "_blank", "_parent", "_self", or "_top". For details, see the description of the window settings under the global *getURL()* function.

Description

The *send()* method converts *XMLdoc* into a string of XML source code and sends that code in an HTTP request to the script or application residing at *URL*. The script or application is expected to process the XML in some way and optionally return a response—normally a web page—to the browser, which displays it in *window*. Note that the response is not caught by Flash but by the browser; use *sendAndLoad()* to catch the response within Flash.

When *XML.send()* is invoked from the Flash Player running in a browser, *XMLdoc* is sent via the POST method. When *XML.send()* is invoked from the Flash Player running as a standalone application, *XMLdoc* is sent via the GET method. The server application receiving the posted XML string must be able to access the raw POST data of the HTTP request directly and should not attempt to parse it as normal name/value pairs. In Perl, the data in a POST request is available from STDIN, and may be extracted and stored in, say, `$buffer` as follows:

```
read(STDIN,$buffer,$ENV{'CONTENT_LENGTH'});
```

In ASP, raw POST data may be accessed via the *Request.BinaryRead* method. Some applications (e.g., Cold Fusion) may not have a direct means of accessing the data in a POST request. For these situations, it may be necessary to first convert the XML object to a string using *XML.toString()* and then pass that string to the server as a variable using *loadVariables()*.

The default MIME content type of the XML text sent to the server is `application/x-www-urlform-encoded`. This type, however, is only cosmetic—the text itself is *not* URL-encoded. In Build 41 and later of the Flash 5 Player, the MIME content type can be modified using the `XML.contentType` property. For example, to set the MIME type to `application/xml`, we use:

```
myXML = new XML();
myXML.contentType = "application/xml";
```

Nevertheless, setting the `contentType` property explicitly to `application/x-www-urlform-encoded` still does not cause the text sent to be URL-encoded.

Note that as of Build 41 of the Flash 5 Player, when XML source is parsed and the characters &, ', ", <, and > appear in a text node, they are converted to the following entities: &, ', ", >, <. This conversion is transparent in Flash because the entities are converted back to their original characters when an XML object is converted to a string; however, the entities *will* show up in XML source sent to the server.

Example

```
myDoc = new XML("<SEARCH_TERM>tutorials</SEARCH_TERM>");
myDoc.send("http://www.domain.com/cgi-bin/lookup.cgi", "remoteWin");
```

See Also

XML.sendAndLoad(), XML.load(), `XML.loaded`*, XML.onLoad(),* `XML.status`

XML.sendAndLoad( ) Method

send XML source code to a script, and receive XML source in return

Availability	Flash 5
Synopsis	`XMLdoc.sendAndLoad(`*URL, resultXML*`)`
Arguments	
URL	A string specifying the location of a script or application to which *XMLdoc* should be sent.
resultXML	A reference to an *XML* document object that will receive the returned XML source code.

Description

The *sendAndLoad()* method serializes `XMLdoc` into a string of XML source code and sends that code to a script or application that resides at *URL*. The script or application is expected to process the XML in some way and send an XML document back as a response. The response document is caught by Flash, parsed, converted into an XML object hierarchy, and placed in *resultXML*. Any previous contents of *resultXML* are replaced by the newly loaded XML content. See *XML.send()* for important information about sending XML to a server.

Usage

Before accessing content imported with *sendAndLoad()*, we must be sure that the load and parsing operations are complete. To do so, we either check the value of the *resultXML*'s `loaded` property or we assign *resultXML* an *onLoad()* event handler to respond to the load completion. See the *XML*.loaded and *XML.onLoad()* entries for details. To determine the result of parsing the loaded data, we check the document's `status` property.

XML.sendAndLoad() is subject to the domain-based security restrictions described in Table R-8 under the global *loadVariables()* function.

Example

```
// Create an XML document
myDoc = new XML("<P>hello server!</P>");

// Create an empty XML document to receive the server's response
serverResponse = new XML();

// Send myDoc to the server, and place the response in serverResponse
myDoc.sendAndLoad("http://www.domain.com/cgi-bin/readData.cgi", serverResponse);

// Add an onLoad handler to serverResponse that displays the response
// from the server in the text field output.
serverResponse.onLoad = function () {
  output = serverResponse.toString();
}
```

For a good primer on sending XML to and from a server, see Macromedia's article "Integrating XML and Flash in a Web Application," at:

http://www.macromedia.com/support/flash/interactivity/xml

See Also

XML.load(), *XML*.loaded, *XML.onLoad()*, *XML.send()*, *XML*.status

---

XML.status Property

indicates whether parsing XML source into an object hierarchy was successful

Availability   Flash 5

Synopsis   *XMLdoc*.status

Access   Read-only

Description

The `status` property returns a numeric status code indicating whether any errors were encountered when parsing XML source code. Parsing occurs when source XML is:

- Provided as an argument to the *XML()* constructor
- Explicitly parsed via the *parseXML()* method
- Loaded into a new *XML* object via the *load()* or *sendAndLoad()* methods

The `status` codes are shown in Table R-14. If no errors were encountered in parsing, success is indicated by a `status` of 0. Errors are indicated by negative numbers. Parsing terminates once the first error is encountered, so other errors may surface even after you address previously reported errors.

Table R-14. XML Parsing Status Codes

Status	Description
0	The document parsed without errors (i.e., success).
−2	A CDATA section was not properly terminated.
−3	The XML declaration was not properly terminated.
−4	The `DOCTYPE` declaration was not properly terminated.
−5	A comment was not properly terminated.
−6	An XML element was malformed.
−7	Not enough memory to parse the XML source.
−8	An attribute value was not properly terminated.
−9	A start tag had no corresponding end tag.
−10	An end tag had no corresponding start tag.

We normally use `status` to determine whether it's safe to proceed with processing an externally loaded XML file. Check the `loaded` property to ensure that a *load()* or *sendAndLoad()* command has completed before checking the `status`. Note that Action-Script's XML parser does not validate documents against DTDs, it only verifies well-formedness.

Example

```
myDoc = new XML("<BOOK>Colin Moock</AUTHOR></BOOK>");
trace(myDoc.status);  // Displays: "-10" (missing start tag)
```

See Also

XML.load(), *XML.*`loaded`, *XML.onLoad()*, *XML.parseXML()*, *XML.sendAndLoad()*

XML.toString( ) Method   the source code of the XML node, as a string

Availability   Flash 5

Synopsis   `theNode.toString()`

Returns

A string representing the source code of the XML object hierarchy starting at *theNode*.

Description

The *toString()* method converts an XML node object or an XML document object to its analogous XML source code. If *theNode* is a top-level XML document object, any DOCTYPE and XML declaration tags are included in the string. If the document's ignoreWhite property is false, whitespace is preserved and the document source code appears as it did when it was parsed.

It's not normally necessary to invoke *toString()* explicitly; *toString()* is automatically invoked any time *theNode* is used in a string context.

Example

```
var myDoc = new XML('<?xml version="1.0"?><!DOCTYPE foo SYSTEM "bar.dtd"><BOOK>
<TITLE>ActionScript: The Definitive Guide</TITLE>'
    + '<AUTHOR SALUTATION="Mr">Colin Moock  </AUTHOR>        '
    + '<PUBLISHER>O\'reilly & Associates, Inc</PUBLISHER>     </BOOK>');


trace(myDoc.toString());
// Displays:
<?xml version="1.0"?><!DOCTYPE foo SYSTEM "bar.dtd">
<BOOK>      <TITLE>ActionScript:
 The Definitive Guide</TITLE><AUTHOR SALUTATION="Mr">Colin
Moock </AUTHOR>    <PUBLISHER>O'reilly & Associates, Inc
</PUBLISHER>    </BOOK>
```

See Also

Object.toString(), *XML*.nodeValue

XML.xmlDecl Property   the document's XML declaration tag

Availability   Flash 5

Synopsis   *XMLdoc*.xmlDecl

Access   Read/write

Description

The xmlDecl string property represents the XML declaration tag of *XMLdoc*, if any exists. Otherwise, xmlDecl is undefined. *XMLdoc* must be the top-level node in an *XML* object hierarchy (that is, an instance of the *XML* class, not the *XMLnode* class.)

The XML declaration tag of an XML document is used to identify the version of XML being used in the document. We use the XML declaration tag to build well-formed XML documents that may be validated externally.

Example

```
// A well-formed document (but not validated against a DTD)
myXML = new XML('<?xml version="1.0"?><P>this is a short document</P>');
trace(myXML.xmlDecl);  // Displays: "<?xml version="1.0"?>"
// Set a new XML declaration
myXML.xmlDecl = '<?xml version="1.0" standalone="no"?>';
```

See Also

`XML.docTypeDecl`

XMLnode Class   Internal superclass of the XML class

Availability   Flash 5

Description

The *XMLnode* class defines the core properties and methods of nodes in an XML object hierarchy. Though *XMLnode* is an internal device, it may be used by programmers to extend the default functionality of XML objects.

Every XML object hierarchy technically includes two kinds of object nodes:

- One *XML* node, that serves as the main container for the hierarchy
- An arbitrary number of *XMLnode* nodes, which are the children of the main container node

The main container node is an instance of the *XML* class. For example, if we create myDoc as follows:

```
myDoc = new XML();
```

then myDoc is an instance of the *XML* class. The *XML* class inherits from the *XMLnode* class, so main container nodes have all the properties and methods defined by *XMLnode* plus those defined by *XML*. By contrast, the children of myDoc would actually be instances of the *XMLnode* class, not the *XML* class.

So, if we create myParagraph as follows:

```
myParagraph = myDoc.createElement("P");
```

then myParagraph is an instance of the *XMLnode* class. Most of the time the internal distinction between node classes does not affect our use of XML objects. However, if we wish to add an inherited property or method to all XML objects, then we must use the *XMLnode* class's `prototype`, not the *XML* class's `prototype` (see the example that follows). Any methods or properties attached to `XMLnode.prototype` are inherited by all XML nodes in a movie.

For reference, the properties, methods, and event handlers defined by *XMLnode* and *XML* are listed in Table R-15. Note that while all listed items are accessible through instances of the *XML* class, items defined by *XML* are not available through instances of *XMLnode*. For example, the *load()* method may be invoked on an instance of the *XML* class, but not on an instance of the *XMLnode* class. For a full discussion of each item, see the appropriate *XML* class entry.

Table R-15. XMLnode and XML Properties, Methods, and Event Handlers

XMLnode and XML	XML only
appendChild()	`contentType`
`attributes`	*createElement()*
`childNodes`	*createTextNode()*
cloneNode()	`docTypeDecl`

Table R-15. XMLnode and XML Properties, Methods, and Event Handlers (continued)

XMLnode and XML	XML only
`firstChild`	`ignoreWhite`
hasChildNodes()	*load()*
insertBefore()	`loaded`
`lastChild`	*onData()*
`nextSibling`	*onLoad()*
`nodeName`	*parseXML()*
`nodeType`	*send()*
`nodeValue`	*sendAndLoad()*
`parentNode`	`status`
`previousSibling`	`xmlDecl`
removeNode()	
toString()	

Example

The following code adds a custom *secondChild()* method to `XMLnode.prototype` (the *secondChild()* method is subsequently available from any XML node in our movie):

```
XMLnode.prototype.secondChild = function () {
   return this.childNodes[1];
};

myDoc = new XML("<PRODUCT>Cell Phone</PRODUCT><PRODUCT>Game Console
</PRODUCT>");

trace(myDoc.secondChild());  // Displays: "<PRODUCT>Game Console</PRODUCT>"
```

It's also perfectly legitimate to extend the *XML* class via `XML.prototype`, but such extensions apply only to main container nodes (direct instances of the *XML* class).

See Also

The *XML* Class; "Superclasses and Subclasses" in Chapter 12, *Objects and Classes.*

XMLSocket Class   support for a continuous server/client TCP/IP connection

Availability	Flash 5
Constructor	`new XMLSocket()`

Methods

close()	Terminate an open connection to a server application.
connect()	Attempt to establish a new connection to a server application.
send()	Send an XML object hierarchy to a server application as a string.

Event handlers

onClose()	Executes when the server terminates the connection.
onConnect()	Executes when a connection attempt completes.
onData()	Executes when data is received but has not yet been parsed as XML.
onXML()	Executes when data has been received and parsed into an XML object hierarchy.

Description

The majority of connections between Flash and a server have a very short life span. When Flash requests external data via the *loadMovie()*, *loadVariables()*, or *XML.load()* functions, a temporary communication channel is established. Data is sent over that channel and then the channel is terminated. This kind of short-term communication has many useful applications, but it is also limited in two important ways:

- Once the connection closes, the server has no way of contacting Flash. Flash must always initiate communication with the server.

- Each time Flash obtains information from the server, a new connection must be opened. The time and processor load involved in opening repeated connections prevents Flash from engaging in anything near real-time transactions with a server.

As of Flash 5, we can overcome these limitations with the *XMLSocket* class, which allows us to open a persistent communication link between a server application and Flash. We use *XMLSocket* to develop systems that require frequent server updates, such as a chat room or a networked multiplayer game.

In order to connect to a remote application using *XMLSocket*, we must first create and store an *XMLSocket* object, like this:

```
mySocket = new XMLSocket();
```

Then, we invoke the *connect()* method, which asks Flash to establish a communication link with the remote application. For example:

```
mySocket.connect("http://www.myserver.com", 8000);
```

Once a connection is established, the *XMLsocket* object acts as a transmitter/receiver. We send XML-formatted data to the remote application by invoking the socket's *send()* method, and we know that we've received XML-formatted data when the socket's *onXML()* event is triggered.

A server application used with an *XMLSocket* object must:

- Serve TCP/IP socket connections on a specific port greater than or equal to 1024

- Transmit XML-formatted data in segments delimited by a *zero byte* (i.e., the ASCII null character)

Server applications are typically created by server-side programmers, not Flash programmers. For an example of a simple server application that broadcasts all messages it receives to all connected clients, see the Java XMLSocket server available at the online Code Depot.

An *XMLSocket* connection stays open until one of the following occurs:

- The *close()* method of the *XMLSocket* object is called.

- No more references to the *XMLSocket* object exist.

- The server terminates the connection (this triggers an *onClose()* event).
- The movie is closed or the Flash Player exits.

Thankfully, the *XMLSocket* class also provides a way for us to monitor the status of our connection. It includes three properties—*onClose*, *onConnect*, and *onXML*—that allow us to define event handlers that will be triggered when the corresponding event occurs. Such handlers are typically known as *callback handlers* because they are triggered automatically by Flash in response to some event beyond the programmer's direct control. (In this sense they are very similar to ActionScript's built-in clip and button event handlers, except that the handler functions are programmer-defined.) For example, when a connection is closed by the server, the handler defined by the *onClose* property will be triggered.

If you fail to define callback handlers for the *onClose* and *onConnect* properties, you won't be able to perform any error checking or provide any feedback. If you fail to define a callback handler for your *onXML* property, you won't be notified when the socket receives data from a server-side application, nor will you be able to retrieve such data.

Example

The following example shows the bare-bones code needed to implement a simple chat client. The client may be seen in action running at:

   http://www.moock.org/chat

Both the server and the client are available at the online Code Depot:

```
// A Simple Chat Client
// *** General init
var incomingUpdated = false;  // Track whether or not we need to scroll
                              // to the end of incoming (the main
                              // chat text field)
var incoming = "";  // Assign the main chat text field a starting value

// Attach the scroll manager movie. It forces the chat text field to
// show the next (most recent) line each time a message is added.
// Note that we only need the scroll manager because of a
// text field scroll bug in Build r30 of the Flash 5 Player.
attachMovie("processScroll", "processScroll", 0);

// Attach sound to play when we receive a message
var click = new Sound();
click.attachSound("click");

// Attach sound to play when user joins or leaves
var welcomeSound = new Sound();
welcomeSound.attachSound("welcome");

// Turn off ugly yellow highlight on buttons
_focusrect = 0;
```

```
// *** Creates a new socket and attempts to connect to the server
function connect () {
// Create a new XMLSocket object
  mySocket = new XMLSocket();

// Assign callback functions to mySocket's handlers.
  mySocket.onConnect = handleConnect;
  mySocket.onClose = handleClose;
  mySocket.onXML = handleIncoming;

// Attempt to connect, and assign the return of mySocket.connect()
// to connectSuccess (connect() returns true if the initial stage
// of connection succeeds)
  var connectSuccess = mySocket.connect("www.myserver.com", 1025);
  if (connectSuccess) {
    trace("initial connection succeeded");
  } else {
    // connectSuccess was false, so we didn't establish a connection.
    gotoAndStop("connectionFailed");
    trace("initial connection failed");
  }
}


// *** Event handler to respond to the completion of a connection attempt
function handleConnect (succeeded) {
    // If handleConnect()'s succeeded argument is true, the connection has been
    // established and we can proceed with the chat.
    // Otherwise, show a failure message.
  if (succeeded) {
    // Set a property noting that we have an open connection available.
    mySocket.connected = true;
    gotoAndStop("chat");
    // Put the cursor in the "send message" text field
    Selection.setFocus("_level0.outgoing");
  } else {
    // Connection didn't succeed so show an error message
    gotoAndStop("connectionFailed");
    trace("connection failed");
  }
}


// *** Event handler called when server kills the connection
function handleClose () {
  // Tell the user that the connection was lost
  incoming += ("The server has terminated the connection.\n");
  // We updated the chat text field, so let the scroll manager know
  incomingUpdated = true;
  // Set a property noting that the connection was lost
  mySocket.connected = false;
  numClients = 0;
}


// *** Event handler to receive and display incoming messages
function handleIncoming (messageObj) {
```

```
    // Display the received XML data in the Output window
    trace("--------new data received----------");
    trace(">>" + messageObj.toString() + "<<");
    trace("-------- end of new data -----------");

    // We're updating the chat text field, so let the scroll manager know
    incomingUpdated = true;
    lastScrollPos = incoming.scroll;

    // Check the time
    var now = new Date();
    var hours = now.getHours();
    var minutes = now.getMinutes();
    var seconds = now.getSeconds();
    // Format time for output
    hours = (hours < 10 ? "0" : "") + hours;
    minutes = (minutes < 10 ? "0" : "") + minutes;
    seconds = (seconds < 10 ? "0" : "") + seconds;

    // The server sends NUMCLIENTS any time a client connects or disconnects
    // If we find NUMCLIENTS in the XML object...
    if (messageObj.firstChild.nodeName == "NUMCLIENTS") {
    // ...then check if the incoming messages window is empty. If it is...
      if (incoming == "") {
        // ...then the user has just joined, so add a welcome message to the chat.
        incoming += ("welcome to moock comm 1.0.0, "
            + userID + "\n"
            + "  connection time: " + hours + ":" + minutes + ":" + seconds + "\n"
            + "  server: clayton\'s javaComm generic flash xmlsocket server\n\n");
      } else {
        // Otherwise, someone has arrived or departed, so tell the user
        if (parseInt(messageObj.firstChild.firstChild.nodeValue) > numClients) {
          // Report the client arrival in the chat window
          incoming += (hours + ":" + minutes + ":"
                  + seconds + " a new user has connected.\n");
        } else {
          // Report the client departure in the chat window
          incoming += (hours + ":" + minutes + ":"
                  + seconds + " a user disconnected.\n");
        }
      }
      // Finally, keep track of the new number of clients
      // and play a welcome/departure sound
      numClients = parseInt(messageObj.firstChild.firstChild.nodeValue;)
      welcomeSound.setVolume(100);
      welcomeSound.start();
    } else {
      // No NUMCLIENTS node was found, so this is just a regular message.
      // Grab the user name and message from our XML object.
      var user = messageObj.firstChild.firstChild.nodeValue;
      var message = messageObj.childNodes[1].firstChild.nodeValue;

      // Add the message to the chat window, with a time stamp
      incoming += (hours + ":" + minutes
              + ":" + seconds + user + ">> " + message + "\n");
```

```
    // Now do the new message click.
    // If it's been more than 30 secs since the last message,
    // sound a loud click. Otherwise sound a quiet click.
    trace("time since last message: " + (now - lastIncomingMessageTime));
    if (lastIncomingMessageTime && (now - lastIncomingMessageTime) > 30000) {
      click.setVolume(200);
    } else {
      click.setVolume(30);
    }
    click.start();
  }

  // Truncate the contents of the main chat text
  // field if it's longer than 5000 characters
  if (incoming.length > 5000) {
    var nearestNewline = incoming.indexOf("\n", incoming.length - 5000);
    incoming = incoming.substring(nearestNewline, incoming.length);
  }

  // Remember when this message arrived for next time
  lastIncomingMessageTime = now;
}

// *** Sends a new XML object to the server
function sendMessage() {
  // Create the message to send as an XML source fragment.
  // Note that the spaces before the <USER> and </MESSSAGE> tags
  // are required so MESSAGE and USER always have a text child node.
  var message = '<USER> ' + userID + '</USER><MESSAGE>'
              + outgoing + ' </MESSAGE>';

  // Convert the message into an XML object hierarchy
  messageObj = new XML();
  messageObj.parseXML(message);

  // Check what we're sending
  trace("Sending: " + messageObj);

  // If a socket object has been created and is connected, send the XML message.
  // Otherwise warn the user that he needs to connect first.
  if (mySocket && mySocket.connected) {
    mySocket.send(messageObj);
    // Clear the "send message" text field
    outgoing = "";
  } else {
    // The server must have kicked us off...
    incoming += "You are no longer connected. Please reconnect.\n"
    incomingUpdated = true;
  }
}

// *** Closes the connection to the server
function quit() {
  if (mySocket.connected) {
```

```
            mySocket.close();
            mySocket.connected = false;
            numClients = 0;
            incoming = "";
            gotoAndStop("login");
        }
    }
```

See Also

oadVariables(), The XML Class

XMLSocket.close( ) Method   terminate an open connection to a server application

Availability   Flash 5

Synopsis   `socket.close()`

Description

The *close()* method severs the communication link between *socket* and a server application. Once *close()* has been executed on *socket*, subsequent attempts to invoke *send()* on *socket* fail. Likewise, the server application will no longer be able to send data to Flash through *socket*.

Note that *close()* has no effect if the *socket* is already closed or was never connected. Furthermore, *close()* does not trigger the *onClose()* handler of the socket object—*onClose()* is triggered only by a server-side connection closure.

See Also

XMLSocket.connect(), *XMLSocket.onClose()*

XMLSocket.connect( ) Method   open a connection to a server application

Availability   Flash 5

Synopsis   `socket.connect(host, port)`

Arguments

host   A string specifying a hostname such as `"www.myserver.com"` or a standard IP address (four, dot-separated, 8-bit, decimal integers such as 111.222.3.123). If `null` or an empty string is specified, it defaults to the server address from which the movie was served.

port   An integer specifying a TCP port number greater than or equal to 1024.

Returns

A Boolean indicating the initial success (`true`) or failure (`false`) of the connection attempt.

Description

The *connect()* method attempts to establish a connection from Flash to a server application running on *host* at *port*.

If *connect()* returns `true`, the initial phase of the connection completed successfully and the *socket*'s *onConnect()* handler will be invoked at a later time. From the *onConnect()* handler, we can evaluate whether the connection was fully established. Note that connection attempts can take varying amounts of time, particularly when a connection attempt fails. You should indicate to the user that a connection attempt is in progress when invoking *connect()*.

If *connect()* returns `false`, the initial connection phase did not complete successfully. In such a case, *socket*'s *onConnect()* handler will not be invoked.

It is important to check both the return value of the *connect()* method and, if *connect()* returns `true`, the value of the *success* parameter of the *onConnect()* handler.

Usage

For security reasons, *connect()* is not permitted to connect to arbitrary Internet hosts. It may connect only to hosts in the domain that the movie was downloaded from. The rules for *connect()* are the same ones applied to the *loadVariables()* function. See Table R-8 under the global *loadVariables()* function for a list of the domain matching requirements imposed by the *connect()* method. The *connect()* method returns `false` for connection attempts that violate security restrictions. Note that security restrictions do not apply to the standalone Player.

Example

```
// Create a new socket object
mySocket = new XMLSocket();
// Assign a callback handler function to onConnect
mySocket.onConnect = handleConnect;
// Attempt to connect to an application running on myserver.com at port 10000
if (mySocket.connect("myserver.com", 10000) == false) {
  // Jump to a frame showing some sort of error message
  gotoAndStop("failureDialog");
} else {
  // Jump to a frame where we'll wait until onConnect is triggered
  gotoAndPlay("connecting");
}
```

See Also

XMLSocket.close(), *XMLSocket.onConnect()*

XMLSocket.onClose( ) Event Handler   specifies the callback handler invoked when the server closes the connection

Availability   Flash 5

Synopsis   *socket*.onClose = *closeHandler*
                 socket.*closeHandler*()

Description

The *onClose* property allows you to specify a callback handler to be executed automatically whenever an open connection to *socket* is closed by the server. Server-instigated closures usually result from a server application shutting down or deliberately "kicking off" the client.

Example

To respond to an *onClose* event, we must assign our own function (i.e., our callback handler) to the *onClose* property of an *XMLSocket* object. In practice, we use this callback handler to detect an external socket disconnection. The following code assigns the function *handleClose()* to *mySocket*'s *onClose* property. The *handleClose()* function simply alerts the user that a closure has occurred by updating the value of the text field status:

```
mySocket = new XMLSocket();
mySocket.onClose = handleClose;

function handleClose () {
  status += ("\nThe server has terminated the connection.\n");
}
```

See Also

XMLSocket.close(); "Attaching Event Handlers to Other Objects" in Chapter 10

XMLSocket.onConnect( ) Event Handler defines the event handler invoked when a connection attempt is completed, successfully or otherwise

Availability   Flash 5

Synopsis   *socket.*onConnect = *connectHandler*
socket.connectHandler(success)

Arguments
success   A Boolean indicating whether the connection attempt succeeded (true) or failed (false).

Description

The *onConnect* property allows you to specify a callback handler to be executed automatically when a previously invoked *connect()* operation finishes. The execution of the callback handler specified by *onConnect* does not necessarily mean a connection has been successfully established—the callback handler is executed whenever the connection *attempt* is finished, whether or not the attempt was successful. The callback handler specified by *onConnect* is passed a *success* argument that indicates if the attempt succeeded (i.e., a connection has been established). If so, *success* is set to true. If the attempt failed (i.e., a connection timed out, was refused, or otherwise could not be established), the *success* argument is set to false. Note that ActionScript does not distinguish among network timeout, unknown host, refusal, or other common connection errors. The callback handler, therefore, may not be executed for up to a minute after the *connect()* command is issued depending on the settings of the server involved in a connection attempt, the connection speed, network traffic, and so on.

Example

We use the callback handler specified by *onConnect* to detect the success or failure of a connection attempt. In practice, we might use the callback handler to set a flag indicating that transmissions should begin if the connection was successful. We may also use the callback handler to execute fallback code when the connection fails, such as alerting the user to the problem's nature.

To respond to an *onConnect* event, we must assign our own function (i.e., our callback handler) to the *onConnect* property of an *XMLSocket* object. The following code assigns the function *handleConnect()* to *mySocket*'s *onConnect* property. By updating the value of the text field `status`, *handleConnect()* alerts the user that a connection has either succeeded or failed:

```
mySocket = new XMLSocket();
mySocket.onConnect = handleConnect;

function handleConnect (succeeded) {
  if (succeeded) {
    status += ("Successfully connected.\n");
  } else {
    status += ("Connection attempt failed.\n");
  }
}
```

For code showing the *onConnect()* handler used in a more complete system, see the example under the *XMLSocket* class.

See Also

XMLSocket.connect(); "Attaching Event Handlers to Other Objects" in Chapter 10

XMLSocket.onData( ) Event Handler

executed when external data is received, but has not yet been parsed as XML

Availability   Flash 5 (undocumented)

Synopsis   `socket.onData(src)`

Arguments
src   A string containing loaded data, which is usually XML source code.

Description

The *onData()* handler executes automatically whenever a zero byte (ASCII null character) is transmitted to Flash over **socket**. By default, *onData()* simply constructs a new XML object hierarchy from **src**, and passes that hierarchy to *socket.onXML()*. However, the *onData()* handler may be assigned a custom callback function to intercept **src** before ActionScript has a chance to parse it as XML. Under certain circumstances (such as real-time video games), manipulating the raw data in **src** manually may offer improved performance over ActionScript's built-in XML parsing.

Example

The following code shows how to assign a custom callback function to *onData()*. The callback function simply displays any data received by *mySocket* and prevents ActionScript from parsing the data as XML:

```
mySocket = new XMLSocket();

mySocket.onData = function (src) {
  trace("Received data: \n" + src);
};
```

See Also

XMLSocket.onXML()

XMLSocket.onXML( ) Event Handler
defines the callback handler invoked when data is received by an XMLSocket object and has been parsed as XML

Availability   Flash 5

Synopsis   `socket.onXML = xmlHandler`
`socket.xmlHandler(XMLobject)`

Arguments
XMLobject   The XML object that will house the incoming XML-formatted data.

Description

The `onXML` property allows you to specify a callback handler to be executed when Flash receives an incoming transmission. Whenever *socket* receives a complete block of data (i.e., a string followed by an ASCII `null` character) from the server, the callback handler specified by *socket*.`onXML` is automatically invoked. A server may send data as often as it pleases, but the callback handler is executed only when the trailing `null` character (i.e., a zero byte) is received by *socket*. In Java, a zero byte is specified as `'\0'`. When the zero byte is received, it causes ActionScript to parse any data that has been received by *socket* since the last zero byte was sent (or since the initial connection if this is the first zero byte). The parsed data is converted to an XML object hierarchy which is passed as the *XMLobject* argument to the callback handler.

If you are a Flash programmer who is responsible for the client side of a client/server application only, simply note that the callback handler specified by `onXML` receives any new XML data when it arrives. The new XML data is accessible through *XMLobject*.

To access the raw data sent over a socket, override the default behavior of the socket's *onData()* handler. See *XMLSocket.onData()*.

Example

To respond to an `onXML` event, we must assign our own function (i.e., our callback handler) to the *onXML* property of an *XMLSocket* object. The following code assigns the function *handleIncoming()* to *mySocket*'s `onXML` property. The *handleIncoming()* function accesses one of the nodes of the XML object hierarchy stored in `messageObj` and adds its value to the text field `messages`:

```
mySocket = new XMLSocket();
mySocket.onXML = handleIncoming;

function handleIncoming (messageObj) {
  trace("Got some new data!");
  // messageObj will contain the fragment: <MESSAGE>text</MESSAGE>
  var message = messageObj.firstChild.firstChild;
  messages += (message.nodeValue + "\n");
}
```

For code showing the *onXML* handler used in a more complete system, see the example under the *XMLSocket* class.

See Also

XMLSocket.send, *XMLSocket.onData( )*; "Attaching Event Handlers to Other Objects" in Chapter 10

XMLSocket.send( ) Method   transmit XML-formatted data to a server application

Availability   Flash 5

Synopsis   `socket.send(XMLobject)`

Arguments

XMLobject   An *XML* object to be converted into a string and sent to the server application or any string containing XML-formatted text.

Description

The *send( )* method transmits a message from Flash to a server application via `socket`. The message to send should be an object of the *XML* class but may also be a string. When *send( )* is invoked, `XMLobject` is converted to a string and sent to the remote application, followed by a zero byte (the first ASCII character, null). The remote application is not obliged to respond; however, any response sent will trigger `socket`'s *onXML( )* event handler.

Example

The following code sends a very simple XML-formatted message to a remote application over the socket *mySocket*, which is a valid *XMLSocket* object for which a connection has already been established (note that *message* is an *XML* object, not an *XMLSocket* object; see the example under the *XMLSocket* class entry for a full-fledged *XMLSocket* sample application):

```
var message = new XML('<MESSAGE>testing...testing...</MESSAGE>');
mySocket.send(message);
```

It is also legal to send a string containing XML-formatted text without wrapping it in an *XML* object. For simple XML messages, this is often sufficient:

```
mySocket.send('<MESSAGE>testing...testing...</MESSAGE>');
```

See Also

XMLSocket.onXML; the *XMLSocket* Class, *XML.send( )*

IV

Appendixes

Resources

The following are resources of interest. See also the URLs cited in the Preface.

ActionScript and Programming

ActionScript: The Definitive Guide Book Site
> *http://www.moock.org/asdg*

> The download center for all the samples in this book (the Code Depot), plus dozens of other common ActionScript examples. Also provides book updates, technotes, sample chapters, errata, and news. Maintained by the author.

moockmarks
> *http://www.moock.org/moockmarks*

> The author's bookmarks. Lists hundreds of sites with technical information and design inspiration for Flash and web design in general.

Macromedia's Flash Support Center
> *http://www.macromedia.com/support/flash*

> A thriving collection of information for ActionScript and Flash. Contains the entire text of Macromedia's ActionScript Dictionary and a regularly updated database of technotes for Flash developers. A trial version of the Flash authoring tool may be downloaded from: *http://www.macromedia.com/software/ flash/trial.*

Macromedia Exchange for Flash
> *http://www.macromedia.com/exchange/flash*

> A collection of professional-quality Smart Clips, *.fla* project files, and Action-Script samples. Content is hosted and endorsed by Macromedia but codevel-

oped by the Flash community. Access to samples requires use of an installation utility called the Extension Manager.

Flash Kit
http://www.flashkit.com

Internet.com's Flash Kit is the largest third-party source of Flash help. The site has everything under the Flash sun: sample files, message boards, tutorials, news, feature articles, an arcade, interviews, chat, gallery, and much more. Of special interest to Flash programmers are the ActionScript sample *.fla* files available for download at *http://www.flashkit.com/movies/Scripting*.

Ultrashock
http://www.ultrashock.com

A general portal for Flash developers, Ultrashock maintains a lively collection of ActionScript-centric *.fla* files and tutorials.

Flashcoders Mailing List
http://chattyfig.figleaf.com/mailman/listinfo/flashcoders

Hosted by Branden Hall of Fig Leaf Software, this active Flash developer's email list focuses specifically on intermediate to advanced ActionScript. It is a great place to learn practical techniques and have questions answered by peers but is *not* for general Flash questions or site checks. Archives are searchable and posted on a monthly basis. Check the archives for answers before posting questions.

Brandon Williams's and Ethan Kennedy's Flash Experiments
http://www.homepages.go.com/~ahab_flash/exper/index.htm

A large collection of advanced math-based ActionScript demos. Dozens of sample *.fla* files available for study covering 3D, fractals, and many visual physics effects. Includes in-depth articles on math-based programming in Flash.

The comp.graphics.algorithms FAQ
http://www.faqs.org/faqs/graphics/algorithms-faq

Describes mathematical solutions to a wide variety of graphics programming problems. Ranges from simpler topics such as, "How do I find the distance from a point to a line?" to advanced 3D issues, normally outside the realm of Flash programming.

Archived Macromedia Flash Players
http://www.macromedia.com/support/flash/ts/documents/oldplayers.htm

Download old versions of the Macromedia Flash Player for testing.

General Game-Programming Resources

> The following sites offer useful information for designing, planning, and programming games (these are non-ActionScript-specific sites):
>
> *http://www.gamedev.net*
>
> *http://www.flipcode.com*
>
> *http://www.chesworth.com/pv/games*
>
> *http://www.javascript-games.org*

Flash and Active Server Pages (ASP)

> The following articles from ASP 101 provide a good introduction to integrating Flash with ASP to create a simple Flash form:
>
> *http://www.asp101.com/articles/flash*
>
> *http://www.asp101.com/articles/flash2*

Macromedia Generator

> Though it is beyond the scope of this book to discuss Macromedia Generator, the following web sites offer excellent Generator development resources:
>
> *http://www.markme.com*
>
> *http://www.gendev.net*

ECMA-262 Resources

Because ActionScript and JavaScript are both based on the ECMA-262 scripting language specification, they share a common core syntax. Hence, although the following resources do not focus specifically on ActionScript, they are worthwhile reading for ActionScript programmers:

ECMA-262 Language Specification

> *http://www.ecma.ch/ecma1/STAND/ECMA-262.HTM*
>
> The official ECMA-262 language specification from ECMA, the body that maintains the language upon which ActionScript is based. Netscape's JavaScript and Microsoft's Jscript are two other implementations of ECMA-262. This is a highly technical document used to create things such as a conforming ECMA interpreter.

Netscape's Core JavaScript Guide

> *http://developer.netscape.com/docs/manuals/js/core/jsguide/contents.htm*
>
> Netscape provides very readable documentation on JavaScript in this detailed explanation of JavaScript's core language features.

Object-Oriented Programming

Netscape's Details of the Object Model
  http://developer.netscape.com/docs/manuals/js/core/jsguide/obj2.htm

A detailed article explaining the prototype-based implementation of OOP, inheritance, and classes in JavaScript. Concepts are illustrated with numerous code samples. Netscape makes a special effort to explain JavaScript's OOP in terms C and Java coders will understand.

Sun's Object-Oriented Programming Concepts (from The Java™ Tutorial)
  http://java.sun.com/docs/books/tutorial/java/concepts

Although intended as a primer for aspiring Java programmers, it covers the basics of OOP in generalized terms and makes good background reading for OOP in any language.

SWF File Format

Whereas the Flash Player is not open sourced, the *.swf* file format itself is publicly available (which is one reason it has garnered a lot of third-party support). For further information, here are some resources:

Macromedia Flash Player File Format (SWF)
  http://www.macromedia.com/software/flash/open/licensing/fileformat

Here you can obtain the SWF SDK from Macromedia, "a set of tools for developers to write Macromedia Flash 5 (SWF) files, documentation of the Macromedia Flash file format (SWF), and code to write SWF files."

OpenSWF
  http://www.openswf.org

A general information center for developers of SWF implementations. Includes tutorials, message boards, resources, and source code.

Ming
  http://www.opaque.net/ming

Ming is an open source C library for generating SWF format movies plus a set of wrappers for using the library in C++ and popular scripting languages like PHP, Python, and Ruby. See *http://www.opensource.org* for information on open source software.

Perl :: Flash
  http://www.2shortplanks.com/flash

A Perl library to allow the "dynamic, programmable generation of Flash/SWF movies." Created by Simon Wistow.

B

Latin 1 Character Repertoire and Keycodes

Table B-1 lists the characters in the Latin 1 character repertoire, the primary character set supported by Flash. The first column (labeled "Dec"), gives each character's code point in decimal (the standard ASCII value), the second column provides the Unicode escape sequence for the character, and the third column describes the character itself. See Chapter 4, *Primitive Data Types*, for more information on character encoding in Flash.

For supplementary reading on the topic of character encoding, see the following resources:

The ISO 8859 Alphabet Soup
> *http://czyborra.com/charsets/iso8859.html*

> A series of documents detailing the makeup and meaning of characters in the Latin 1 character repertoire, the primary character set supported by Flash (maintained by Roman Czyborra)

Shift-JIS Code Points
> *ftp://ftp.unicode.org/Public/MAPPINGS/EASTASIA/JIS/SHIFTJIS.TXT*

> A list of the Unicode code points for characters in the Shift-JIS character set, Flash's supported set of Japanese characters

Unicode FAQ
> *http://www.unicode.org/unicode/faq*

> A good question-and-answer format overview of Unicode, an international standard for character encoding

Table B-1. ISO 8859-1 (Latin 1) Characters and Unicode Mappings

Dec	Unicode	Description	Dec	Unicode	Description
0	\u0000	[null]	36	\u0024	$
1	\u0001	[start of heading]	37	\u0025	%
2	\u0002	[start of text]	38	\u0026	&
3	\u0003	[end of text]	39	\u0027	'
4	\u0004	[end of transmission]	40	\u0028	(
5	\u0005	[enquiry]	41	\u0029	)
6	\u0006	[acknowledge]	42	\u002a	*
7	\u0007	[bell]	43	\u002b	+
8	\u0008	[backspace]	44	\u002c	,
9	\u0009	[horizontal tabulation]	45	\u002d	-
10	\u000a	[line feed]	46	\u002e	.
11	\u000b	[vertical tabulation]	47	\u002f	/
12	\u000c	[form feed]	48	\u0030	0
13	\u000d	[carriage feed]	49	\u0031	1
14	\u000e	[shift out]	50	\u0032	2
15	\u000f	[shift in]	51	\u0033	3
16	\u0010	[data link escape]	52	\u0034	4
17	\u0011	[device control one]	53	\u0035	5
18	\u0012	[device control two]	54	\u0036	6
19	\u0013	[device control three]	55	\u0037	7
20	\u0014	[device control four]	56	\u0038	8
21	\u0015	[negative acknowledge]	57	\u0039	9
22	\u0016	[synchronous idle]	58	\u003a	:
23	\u0017	[end of transmission block]	59	\u003b	;
24	\u0018	[cancel]	60	\u003c	<
25	\u0019	[end of medium]	61	\u003d	=
26	\u001a	[substitute]	62	\u003e	>
27	\u001b	[escape]	63	\u003f	?
28	\u001c	[file separator]	64	\u0040	@
29	\u001d	[group separator]	65	\u0041	A
30	\u001e	[record separator]	66	\u0042	B
31	\u001f	[unit separator]	67	\u0043	C
32	\u0020	[space]	68	\u0044	D
33	\u0021	!	69	\u0045	E
34	\u0022	"	70	\u0046	F
35	\u0023	#	71	\u0047	G

Table B-1. ISO 8859-1 (Latin 1) Characters and Unicode Mappings (continued)

Dec	Unicode	Description	Dec	Unicode	Description
72	\u0048	H	108	\u006c	l
73	\u0049	I	109	\u006d	m
74	\u004a	J	110	\u006e	n
75	\u004b	K	111	\u006f	o
76	\u004c	L	112	\u0070	p
77	\u004d	M	113	\u0071	q
78	\u004e	N	114	\u0072	r
79	\u004f	O	115	\u0073	s
80	\u0050	P	116	\u0074	t
81	\u0051	Q	117	\u0075	u
82	\u0052	R	118	\u0076	v
83	\u0053	S	119	\u0077	w
84	\u0054	T	120	\u0078	x
85	\u0055	U	121	\u0079	y
86	\u0056	V	122	\u007a	z
87	\u0057	W	123	\u007b	{
88	\u0058	X	124	\u007c	|
89	\u0059	Y	125	\u007d	}
90	\u005a	Z	126	\u007e	~
91	\u005b	[	127	\u007f	[delete]
92	\u005c	\	128	\u0080	control chr
93	\u005d	]	129	\u0081	control chr
94	\u005e	^	130	\u0082	control chr
95	\u005f	_	131	\u0083	control chr
96	\u0060	`	132	\u0084	control chr
97	\u0061	a	133	\u0085	control chr
98	\u0062	b	134	\u0086	control chr
99	\u0063	c	135	\u0087	control chr
100	\u0064	d	136	\u0088	control chr
101	\u0065	e	137	\u0089	control chr
102	\u0066	f	138	\u008a	control chr
103	\u0067	g	139	\u008b	control chr
104	\u0068	h	140	\u008c	control chr
105	\u0069	i	141	\u008d	control chr
106	\u006a	j	142	\u008e	control chr
107	\u006b	k	143	\u008f	control chr

Table B-1. ISO 8859-1 (Latin 1) Characters and Unicode Mappings (continued)

Dec	Unicode	Description	Dec	Unicode	Description
144	\u0090	control chr	180	\u00b4	´
145	\u0091	control chr	181	\u00b5	µ
146	\u0092	control chr	182	\u00b6	¶
147	\u0093	control chr	183	\u00b7	·
148	\u0094	control chr	184	\u00b8	¸
149	\u0095	control chr	185	\u00b9	1
150	\u0096	control chr	186	\u00ba	º
151	\u0097	control chr	187	\u00bb	»
152	\u0098	control chr	188	\u00bc	¼
153	\u0099	control chr	189	\u00bd	½
154	\u009a	control chr	190	\u00be	¾
155	\u009b	control chr	191	\u00bf	¿
156	\u009c	control chr	192	\u00c0	À
157	\u009d	control chr	193	\u00c1	Á
158	\u009e	control chr	194	\u00c2	Â
159	\u009f	control chr	195	\u00c3	Ã
160	\u00a0	[no break space]	196	\u00c4	Ä
161	\u00a1	¡	197	\u00c5	Å
162	\u00a2	¢	198	\u00c6	Æ
163	\u00a3	£	199	\u00c7	Ç
164	\u00a4	¤	200	\u00c8	È
165	\u00a5	¥	201	\u00c9	É
166	\u00a6	¦	202	\u00ca	Ê
167	\u00a7	§	203	\u00cb	Ë
168	\u00a8	¨	204	\u00cc	Ì
169	\u00a9	©	205	\u00cd	Í
170	\u00aa	ª	206	\u00ce	Î
171	\u00ab	«	207	\u00cf	Ï
172	\u00ac	¬	208	\u00d0	Ð
173	\u00ad	-	209	\u00d1	Ñ
174	\u00ae	®	210	\u00d2	Ò
175	\u00af	¯	211	\u00d3	Ó
176	\u00b0	°	212	\u00d4	Ô
177	\u00b1	±	213	\u00d5	Õ
178	\u00b2	2	214	\u00d6	Ö
179	\u00b3	3	215	\u00d7	×

Table B-1. ISO 8859-1 (Latin 1) Characters and Unicode Mappings (continued)

Dec	Unicode	Description	Dec	Unicode	Description
216	\u00d8	Ø	236	\u00ec	ì
217	\u00d9	Ù	237	\u00ed	í
218	\u00da	Ú	238	\u00ee	î
219	\u00db	Û	239	\u00ef	ï
220	\u00dc	Ü	240	\u00f0	ð
221	\u00dd	Ý	241	\u00f1	ñ
222	\u00de	Þ	242	\u00f2	ò
223	\u00df	ß	243	\u00f3	ó
224	\u00e0	à	244	\u00f4	ô
225	\u00e1	á	245	\u00f5	õ
226	\u00e2	â	246	\u00f6	ö
227	\u00e3	ã	247	\u00f7	÷
228	\u00e4	ä	248	\u00f8	ø
229	\u00e5	å	249	\u00f9	ù
230	\u00e6	æ	250	\u00fa	ú
231	\u00e7	ç	251	\u00fb	û
232	\u00e8	è	252	\u00fc	ü
233	\u00e9	é	253	\u00fd	ý
234	\u00ea	ê	254	\u00fe	þ
235	\u00eb	ë	255	\u00ff	ÿ

Table B-2 lists the keycodes for selected special keys on the keyboard. These keycodes are used only with the *Key* object (see Part III, *Language Reference*).

Table B-2. Key Object Special Keycodes

Key	Keycode	Key	Keycode
;:	186	Caps Lock	20
+=	187	Control	17
-_	189	Delete	46
/?	191	Down arrow	40
`~	192	End	35
[{	219	Enter	13
\ |	220	Escape	27
]}	221	F1	112
" '	222	F2	113
Alt	18 (not trappable)	F3	114
Backspace	8	F4	115

Table B-2. Key Object Special Keycodes (continued)

Key	Keycode	Key	Keycode
F5	116	Num Pad 7	103
F6	117	Num Pad 8	104
F7	118	Num Pad 9	105
F8	119	Num Pad *	106
F9	120	Num Pad +	107
F10	121 (not trappable)	Num Pad Enter	13 (not trappable as 108)
F11	122	Num Pad -	109
F12	123	Num Pad .	110
Home	36	Num Pad /	111
Insert	45	Page Down	34
Left arrow	37	Page Up	33
Num Lock	144	Pause/Break	19
Num Pad 0	96	Print Screen	44
Num Pad 1	97	Right Arrow	39
Num Pad 2	98	Scroll Lock	145
Num Pad 3	99	Shift	16
Num Pad 4	100	Space	32
Num Pad 5	101	Tab	9
Num Pad 6	102	Up Arrow	38

Table B-3 lists the keycodes for the letter and number keys on a keyboard. These keycodes are used only with the *Key* object (see Part III).

Table B-3. Key Object Letter and Number Keycodes

Key	Keycode	Key	Keycode	Key	Keycode
A	65	M	77	Y	89
B	66	N	78	Z	90
C	67	O	79	0	48
D	68	P	80	1	49
E	69	Q	81	2	50
F	70	R	82	3	51
G	71	S	83	4	52
H	72	T	84	5	53
I	73	U	85	6	54
J	74	V	86	7	55
K	75	W	87	8	56
L	76	X	88	9	57

Backward Compatibility

Flash allows you to publish *.swf* files in a format that is compatible with previous versions of the Player. By the time you read this, the majority of users will have at least version 5 of the Flash plug-in, but you may prefer to author for the Flash 4 plug-in instead. Even if you are authoring exclusively for Flash 5, this appendix will help you avoid using deprecated ActionScript and bring you up to speed on the preferred methods in Flash 5. For statistics on the distribution of various Flash Player versions, see:

> *http://www.macromedia.com/software/flash/survey/whitepaper*

When authoring for Flash 4, use the *deprecated* techniques (i.e., those that are outdated, but supported for backward compatibility) listed in Table C-1. See also "Using Flash 5 to Create Flash 4 Content" under "Writing Scripts with ActionScript" in Macromedia's Flash ActionScript Reference Guide.

To run scripts in the Flash 4 Player you must set the Version of your *.swf* file to Flash 4 under the Flash tab under File → Publish Settings. All code is disabled if you attempt to run a Flash 5 or later *.swf* file in the Flash 4 Player.

Table C-1 summarizes key backward-compatibility issues and differences between Flash 4 ActionScript and Flash 5 ActionScript.

Table C-1. Backward-Compatibility Issues

Topic	Description
Creating variables	Flash 4's *set* function has been replaced by the *var* statement. To create dynamically named variables, use *eval()*, or (more appropriately) use arrays to manage your data. See Chapter 11, *Arrays*.
Variable and time-line references	The Flash 4–style slash-colon constructions (/square:area) have been superceded by dot notation (square.area). See Table 2-1.
String comparison operators	The Flash 4 string comparison operators—eq, ne, ge, gt, le, lt— have been superceded by the following operators in Flash 5: ==, !=, >=, >, <=, <. See Table 4-2.
String concatenation operator	When creating Flash 4 content in Flash 5 or later, use the *add* operator instead of Flash 4's & operator. When authoring for Flash 5, use the + operator for string concatenation. See Table 4-2.
String length	Flash 4's *length()* function (e.g., *length(myString)*) has been superceded by the length property (e.g., *myString*.length). See Table 4-2.
Substring extraction	Flash 4's *substring()* function (e.g., substring(myString, 1, 3)) has been superceded by the *substring()*, *substr()*, and *slice()* methods. Note that *substring()* differs in Flash 4 and Flash 5. See Table 4-2.
Character code point functions	Flash 4's *chr()* and *mbchr()* functions (used to create a character from a code point) have been superceded by *String.fromCharCode()*. Flash 4's *ord()* and *mbord()* functions (used to determine the code point of a character) have been superceded by the *String.charCodeAt()* method. See Table 4-2.
Datatype conversion	When importing Flash 4 files, Flash 5 automatically inserts the *Number()* function around any numeric data that is used as an operand of the following potentially ambiguous operators: +, ==, !=, <>, <, >, >=, <=. See Table 3-5.
The *ifFrameLoaded* statement	Flash 3's *ifFrameLoaded* statement has been deprecated. Use the _totalframes and _framesloaded *MovieClip* properties to create preloading code.
Infinite loops	Flash 4 allowed a maximum of 200,000 loop iterations. Flash 5 allows 15 seconds for loops, after which it warns users that the movie has stopped responding. See "Maximum Number of Iterations" in Chapter 8, *Loop Statements*.
Subroutines versus functions	In Flash 4, a subroutine could be created by attaching a block of code to a frame with a label and executing it using the *call()* statement. Flash 5's functions replace Flash 4's subroutines.
Clip events	Flash 4 supported only button events (i.e., functions starting with *on( )*) as shown in Table 10-1. Clip events (i.e., *onClipEvent( )*) cannot be used in the Flash 4 Player.
Capturing keystrokes	In Flash 4, *keyPress* was the only means of capturing keystrokes. Flash 5's *Key* object, in combination with the movie clip events *keyDown* and *keyUp*, offers much greater control over keyboard interaction.

Table C-1. Backward-Compatibility Issues (continued)

Topic	Description
Tell Target deprecated	Flash 4's *Tell Target* (used to control remote movie clips) has been replaced by properties and methods accessed using dot notation and the *with* statement. See Chapter 13, *Movie Clips*.
Get Property deprecated	Flash 4's *Get Property* command is no longer required for movie clip property access. Use the dot operator instead. See Chapter 13.
int deprecated	Flash 4's *int()* function (used to truncate floats to integers) has been superceded by *Math.floor()*, *Math.ceil()*, and *Math.round()*.
Random number generation	Flash 4's *random()* function (used to generate a random number) has been superceded by *Math.random()*.
toggleHighQuality deprecated	Flash 4's *toggleHighQuality* function (used to set the rendering quality of the player) has been superceded by the global `_quality` property.
_highquality deprecated	Flash 4's `_highquality` property has been superceded by the global `_quality` property.
Math object support in Flash 4	The functions and properties of the *Math* object (e.g., *Math.cos()*, `Math.PI`) are not natively supported by the Flash 4 Player. The values, however, are approximated when a movie is exported in Flash 4 format.
loadMovie versus *loadMovieNum*	Flash 3's *loadMovie()* onto a numbered level is superceded by Flash 5's *loadMovieNum()* (which accepts an integer level argument). Flash 4's *loadMovie()* into a target movie clip is still available as *loadMovie()* in Flash 5.
Printing	Flash 5 supports the native *print()* function, which was available in Flash 4 Build 20 and later as a modified *Get URL* Action only.
Objects and classes not supported	Flash 4 does not support any of Flash 5's built-in objects and classes.

Updates to the Flash 5 Player, Build 41

The following list summarizes the major changes that were made in Build 41 (Netscape) and 42 (Internet Explorer) of the Flash 5 Player (the previous public build was 30, initially released with the Flash 5 authoring tool):

- I-beams in text fields take on the color of the text.

- Movies in a table cell do not cause Internet Explorer 5.5 to crash.

- A text field's `scroll` position does not reset when field's content is modified.

- Text fields with embedded fonts do not leak outside their visual boundary when scrolled.

- The `XML.contentType` property has been added.

- The `XML.ignoreWhite` property has been added.

- When XML source is parsed and the characters &, ', ", <, and > appear in a text node, they are converted to the following entities: &, ', ", <, and >. This conversion is transparent in Flash because the entities are converted back to characters when an XML object is converted to a string; however, the entities *will* show up in XML source sent to the server.

- *Math.random()* does not return the value of 1. The maximum return value is 0.999.

- General performance is improved, especially on Windows 98.

Controlling Movie Clips

In Chapter 13, we learned how to control clips using Flash 5 techniques. Here we consider the equivalent Flash 4 techniques.

Prior to Flash 5, we would execute special *Movie Clip Actions* to control a movie clip. We would say "Tell the clip named **eyes** to play," using the following:

```
Begin Tell Target ("eyes")
    Play
End Tell Target
```

But as of Flash 5, movie clips can be controlled more directly, through built-in methods. For example:

```
eyes.play();
```

Similarly, to access the built-in properties of a movie clip prior to Flash 5, we would use explicit property-getting and property-setting commands, such as:

```
GetProperty ("ball", _width)
Set Property ("ball", X Scale) = 90
```

As of Flash 5, we can retrieve and set a movie clip's properties using the dot operator, just as we would access the properties of any object:

```
ball._width;
ball._xscale = 90;
```

Prior to Flash 5, to access variables inside a movie clip, we used a colon to separate the clip name from the variable name:

```
Set Variable: "x" = myClip:myVariable
```

As of Flash 5, a variable in a movie clip is simply a property of that clip object, so we now use the dot operator to set and retrieve variable values:

```
myClip.myVariable = 14;
x = myClip.myVariable;
```

Finally, prior to Flash 5, we would access nested levels of movie clips using a directory-tree metaphor of slashes and dots:

```
clipA/clipB/clipC
../../../clipC
```

Because movie clips are object-like data as of Flash 5, we can store one clip as a property of another clip. We, therefore, use the dot operator to access so-called *nested* clips, and we use a clip's reserved **_parent** property to refer to the clip that contains it:

```
clipA.clipB.clipC;
_parent._parent._parent.clipC;
```

D

Differences from ECMA-262 and JavaScript

Naturally this book has focused on the intricacies of ActionScript, but if you own O'Reilly's excellent *JavaScript: The Definitive Guide*, you'll notice that the reference section of the two books share many similarities.

Although ActionScript, like JavaScript, is based on the ECMA-262 standard, certain differences were necessitated by the constraints of Player size and backward compatibility. If porting code from JavaScript, Jscript, or another ECMA-262–based language, you'll find Table D-1 valuable. It summarizes the intentional differences between ECMA-262, JavaScript, and Flash 5 ActionScript. Likewise, if porting ActionScript to another language, you'll be better able to avoid the pitfalls caused by ActionScript's deviation from the ECMA-262 standard.

Table D-1 reflects the *intentional* differences between Flash 5 ActionScript and the ECMA-262 standard. It does not reflect any bugs that may exist in its attempted implementation of the standard.

Table D-1. Differences Between ECMA-262, JavaScript, and ActionScript

Topic	Description
String-to-Boolean conversion	In ECMA-262, all nonempty strings convert to `true`. In Flash 5, only the strings that can be converted to a valid nonzero number convert to `true`.
Case sensitivity	The ECMA-262 specification demands complete case sensitivity. In ActionScript, keywords are case-sensitive but identifiers are not. See Chapter 14, *Lexical Structure*, especially Table 14-1.
Function scope	When a function from one timeline is assigned to a variable in a different movie clip's timeline, the assigned function's scope chain changes to that variable's timeline. In ECMA-262, it's impossible to modify a function's scope chain through assignment; scope is determined permanently by the location of the function declaration statement.

Table D-1. Differences Between ECMA-262, JavaScript, and ActionScript (continued)

Topic	Description
Regular expressions	ActionScript does not support regular expressions.
Event handler names	Only object-based event handlers get their own named function in ActionScript (e.g., *XML*'s *onLoad( )*). Movie clip event handlers are defined using *onClipEvent (eventName)*, and button event handlers are defined using *on (eventName)*. See "Event Handler Syntax" in Chapter 10, *Events and Event Handlers*.
Global variables	ActionScript does not support true document-wide global variables. Global variables can be simulated by attaching properties to `Object.prototype`, as described under "The end of the inheritance chain" in Chapter 12, *Objects and Classes*.
The *eval( )* function	ActionScript's *eval( )* function supports a small subset of ECMA-262's intended functionality; it works only when its argument is an identifier and is used only to dynamically generate references to identifiers.
`undefined` datatype conversion	In ActionScript, the special `undefined` value converts to the empty string (`""`) when used in a string context and converts to the number 0 when used in a numeric context. In ECMA-262, `undefined` converts to the string "undefined" in string contexts and to the numeric value `NaN` in numeric contexts.
The *Function* constructor	ActionScript does not support the *Function* constructor, which is used in JavaScript to create functions with the syntax `new Function ( );`.
Date object creation	ActionScript will not accept (i.e., will not parse) a human-readable date string such as "January 9, 2001" when creating a new *Date* object.
switch statement	ActionScript does not support the *switch/case/default* statements (used to phrase complex conditionals). See "Simulating the switch Statement" in Chapter 7, *Conditionals*.
Language support	ECMA-262 requires support of the Unicode character-encoding standard, which ActionScript does not support. ActionScript uses the Latin 1 and Shift-JIS character sets and implements a subset of Unicode-style functions and conventions (such as \u escape sequences).
Object model	Naturally, JavaScript includes built-in classes and objects that relate to web browsers, whereas Flash includes those that relate to Flash movies. For JavaScript programmers who are used to working with DHTML, it may be helpful to think of the main movie of a Flash document as being analogous to an HTML document object and movie clips as being analogous to layer objects.
Timed code execution	The *setTimeout( )* and *setInterval( )* methods of the JavaScript window object are not available in ActionScript but can be simulated with timeline and clip event loops as discussed in Chapter 8, *Loop Statements*.
Object constructor	In Flash 5, the ActionScript constructor for the *Object* class does not accept any parameters. In ECMA-262, *Object* accepts a `value` parameter, which may be a Boolean, string, or number primitive.

Index

Symbols

+= add-and-reassign operator, 79
& (ampersand) concatenation operator
    (Flash 4), 65, 96
[] array-element/object-property
    operator, 126, 231
    creating references dynamically, 306
    referring to object properties, 258
&= bitwise AND assignment operator, 104
& bitwise AND operator, 340
<<= bitwise left shift assignment
    operator, 104
~ bitwise NOT operator, 343
|= bitwise OR assignment operator, 104
| bitwise OR operator, 341
>>= bitwise signed right shift assignment
    operator, 104
>> bitwise signed right shift operator, 345
>>>= bitwise unsigned right shift
    assignment operator, 104
>>> bitwise unsigned right shift
    operator, 345
^= bitwise XOR assignment operator, 104
^ bitwise XOR operator, 342
, (comma) operator, 124
    in for loops, 155
// comment markers, 330
/* */ comment markers, 331
?: conditional operator, 127, 143

{} curly braces (object initializers/statement
    block delimiters), 19, 131
-- decrement operator, 107
/= division assignment operator, 104
/ division operator, 74, 108
. dot operator, 126
    accessing movie clip properties, 282
    accessing object properties, 257
    traversing clip instance hierarchy, 301
"" double quotes in strings, 76
== equality operator (Flash 5), 81, 110–114
= (equals sign) assignment operator, 105
> greater-than operator (Flash 5), 82, 115
>= greater-than-or-equal-to operator (Flash
    5), 82, 116
++ increment operator, 106
    in do-while loops, 154
!= inequality operator (Flash 5), 81, 113
<> inequality operator (Flash 4), 113
<< left shift operator, 346
< less-than operator (Flash 5), 12, 82, 115
<= less-than-or-equal-to operator (Flash
    5), 82, 115
&& logical AND operator (Flash 5), 121
! logical NOT operator (Flash 5), 122
|| logical OR operator (Flash 5), 119
– (minus) subtraction operator, 12, 74, 107
%= modulo assignment operator, 104
% modulo operator, 109

We'd like to hear your suggestions for improving our indexes. Send email to *index@oreilly.com*.

About the Author

Colin Moock has been researching, designing, and developing for the Web since 1995. Colin served as webmaster for SoftQuad Inc. (the maker of HoTMetaL PRO) until 1997. He is currently a web evangelist for ICE Integrated Communications & Entertainment, where he divides his time between writing about the Web, speaking at conferences, and creating interactive content for companies like Sony, Levi's, Nortel, Air Canada, and Hewlett-Packard. Colin's award-winning Flash work and his renowned support site for Flash developers have made him a well-known personality in the Flash developer community. Macromedia has officially recognized his Flash expertise both on their web site and by appointing him a member of their Flash Advisory Board. Colin is a contributing author of the *The Flash 4 Bible* and *The Flash 5 Bible*.

Colophon

Our look is the result of reader comments, our own experimentation, and feedback from distribution channels. Distinctive covers complement our distinctive approach to technical topics, breathing personality and life into potentially dry subjects.

The animal on the cover of *ActionScript: The Definitive Guide* is a siren, a particular type of salamander found in North American freshwater habitats. Salamanders are amphibians with tails; they diverged from other amphibian species (including frogs) early in amphibian evolution. All salamanders have smooth skin that is kept moist by secretions from numerous glands. When their environment becomes too dry, too hot, or too cold, the cold-blooded salamanders burrow into mud and their body functions slow down. Sirens develop cocoons to shelter themselves until conditions improve.

Sirens are considered very primitive salamanders, as they are aquatic (live permanently in water), lack hind legs, have reduced front legs, gills, and other larval features into maturity, and their offspring are fertilized externally in the water. They are active at night, coming out and swimming much like eels do, using their dorsal fin in side-to-side motion to propel them forward. As they do so, they feed by gulping at insects and larvae. They expel plant matter through their gills.

Like all amphibians, sirens are an important part of a balanced ecosystem. They are small predators who in turn are preyed upon by fish and birds. Their glandular skin and fragile systems put sirens in the unfortunate position of being early pollution indicators in their freshwater habitats. *Siren intermedia*, an unusual siren subspecies that inhabits a large North American range and is known for its ability to produce vocal clicks and shrills, has nearly disappeared from Michigan, perhaps due to the presence of Rotenone, a chemical tool used to manage fisheries.

Darren Kelly was the production editor, Norma Emory was the copyeditor, and Clairemarie Fisher O'Leary was the proofreader for *ActionScript: The Definitive Guide*. Claire Cloutier, Linley Dolby, and Rachel Wheeler provided quality control. Judy Hoer wrote the index. Interior composition was done by Matthew Hutchinson, Sada Preisch, Edith Shapiro, Mary Sheehan, and Gabe Weiss.

Ellie Volckhausen designed the cover of this book, based on a series design by Edie Freedman. The cover image is a 19th-century engraving from the Dover Pictorial Archive. Emma Colby produced the cover layout with QuarkXPress 4.1 using Adobe's ITC Garamond font.

David Futato designed the interior layout based on a series design by Nancy Priest. Clifford Dyer converted the files from Microsoft Word to FrameMaker 5.5.6 using tools created by Mike Sierra. The text and heading fonts are ITC Garamond Light and Garamond Book; the code font is Constant Willison. The illustrations that appear in this book were produced by Robert Romano and Jessamyn Read using Macromedia FreeHand 9 and Adobe Photoshop 6. This colophon was written by Sarah Jane Shangraw.

Whenever possible, our books use a durable and flexible lay-flat binding. If the page count exceeds this binding's limit, perfect binding is used.